The Illustrated History of
COUNTRY MUSIC

Bradley Kincaid

The
Illustrated
History of
COUNTRY
MUSIC

from the editors of
Country Music Magazine

---

edited by
Patrick Carr

A COUNTRY MUSIC MAGAZINE PRESS BOOK

published by
RANDOM HOUSE/TIMES BOOKS

New York, New York
1995

Library of Congress Cataloging-in-Publication Data

The Illustrated History of Country Music/from the editors of *Country Music Magazine*,
edited by Patrick Carr.

p.   cm.
"A Country Music Magazine Press book."
Includes index.
ISBN 0-8129-2455-X
1. Country music—History and criticism. I. Carr, Patrick.
II. Country music (New York, N.Y.)

ML3524.I45 1995
781.642'09—dc20

95-1468

Manufactured in the United States of America on acid-free paper

98765432

Advice to the Reader

Who Was Bradley Kincaid?

Who who who? Who was Bradley Kincaid?

You sung me your folk songs with a voice like a saint
You wear your hair straight you don't powder and paint
Now you want to roam with me through sun and shade
You can go if you know who was Bradley Kincaid

Who who who? Who was Bradley Kincaid?

You sung "Michael's Rowin'" spoke of hootenanny's fame
You met Seeger and Joni told me Dylan's real name
You play the twelve-string like Leadbelly played
But I heard not a word about Bradley Kincaid

Who who who? Who was Bradley Kincaid?

I'll stay a folk singer and I'll love my guitar
I'll sleep in the grass and I'll look at the stars
Alone I'll go roaming through sun and through shade
You can't go you don't know who was Bradley Kincaid

Who who who? Who was Bradley Kincaid?

(Spoken over the music:
And you probably don't know who was Ray Duke and Dottie Brown Eyes
What about Butterball and His Red River Boys
Roy Shaffer from Blythesville, Arkansas, KLCN?)

Who who who? Who was Bradley Kincaid?

—by Vince Matthews

When *Country Music Magazine* Editor-in-Chief and Publisher Russ Barnard asked Johnny Cash to write the foreword to this edition, Cash replied, "Is Bradley Kincaid in the book?" He then sang this song, word for word, through the car phone. Cowboy Jack Clement, whose spirit has hovered over many a Pilgrim, got us a written copy of the words and put us in touch with Vince Matthews, who gave us permission to print them here. Matthews says Cash heard the song only once, in 1976.

To All Our Families from The Editors
of Country Music Magazine

RANK STRANGER

I wandered again to my home in the mountains
Where in my youth's early dawn I was happy and free
I looked for my friends but I never could find them
I found they were all a rank stanger to me....

— Albert E. Brumley
arranged by The Stanley Brothers

Acknowledgments

This book, in both its first and second editions, represents the combined talents of many individuals. Initially, there were 12 chapters, written by experts in the different eras and aspects of country music covered. In the second edition, some chapters were combined, others rewritten and still others added to cover the years since 1979. Authorship and overall editorship, therefore, breaks down as follows: Charles K. Wolfe is the author of Chapters 1 and 2 and parts of 9, 11 and 12; Douglas B. Green wrote Chapters 3, 6, and parts of 7; he collaborated with Bob Pinson on Chapter 4 and with William Ivey on parts of Chapters 9, 10 and 11; J. R. Young wrote Chapter 5; Roger Williams wrote parts of Chapter 7, other parts were added from various chapters in the original; Nick Tosches wrote Chapter 8. Patrick Carr revised and updated the entire book and wrote Chapters 13, 14, 15 and 16.

The illustrations in the second edition come from many sources. Readers familiar with the first edition will recognize some of them; the vast majority of them are newly assembled from public and private collections and from fans. *Country Music Magazine*'s own stock of photos, after more than 20 years, is quite large, and, since launching *The Journal of the American Academy for the Preservation of Old-Time Country Music* in 1991, we have learned a great deal about who has what and where in older photos. A really good photo surely is worth a thousand words, and this book now speaks volumes. The photo credits list all sources, but the editors wish to thank major contributors Charles Wolfe, Gene Bear, Les Leverett, Frank Driggs and Elvis Allen. The cover photo, taken specially in Nashville, is by Jim Herrington.

Many collaborated in our offices and elsewhere to put the book together. In addition to Patrick, who labored long and hard, I would like to single out the following: Katheryn Gray for a beautiful and inspired design; Helen Barnard and Patrick Carr for photo research; George Fletcher for both endless editing and keeping the whole project moving; Martha Trachtenberg for her discriminating reading at several levels; Dan Woog for copy-editing; and Michele Jones and Moira Allaby for proofreading (Moira also helped with photo research). Several interns helped us handle the wealth of small tasks, including Nicholas De La Mare in graphics and Bryan Sivak and John Barnard in editorial. Last but not least, Rochelle Friedman lent her understanding heart and fine-toothed eye to the project at several important stages, and cousins Jeff and Tony Loechner helped us immeasurably with various technical problems related to our computers.

The book was produced in our offices using *Aldus PageMaker* on MacIntosh computers. Scans by American Color Graphics in Denver, Colorado, and Stamford Type in Stamford, Connecticut. May it bring all who read it many hours of enjoyment.

—Russell D. Barnard, Publisher

Contents

Prince Albert Hunt

The music that we call "country" did not begin in this century, nor even in the last.

We can trace its origins back through the Middle Ages, when the wandering minstrel or troubadour literally sang for his supper, stopping overnight at any house beside the road, entertaining the family with his songs, accompanying himself (or herself) on the lute or dulcimer, or even a guitar-like instrument.

The Pilgrim often "made up" a song for the family with whom he stayed overnight, a story song of lovers, of murder, of humor, of nature, or whatever flight his fancy took.

These stories in song were later passed around, then passed down, each generation changing the lyrics or the story, until the original song might be lost to the ages. But a new song would be there in its place, which suited the contemporary question.

The Illustrated History of Country Music doesn't go back quite to the Middle Ages (thankfully), but it does begin with our recognizable roots in the last century, bringing us up through fascinating periods to the present.

The first recordings, when the fiddle was king, stringbands, the cowboys, the 30's, 40's, who was who and who was when, it is all here.

There are stories here of obscure but fascinating people, such as a man named Prince Albert Hunt, who played hillbilly and black blues with Western swing (see photo page 112 and story page 125). He died a tragic death outside the club he was playing in Dallas, 1931. No one knows whose mysterious hand that is on his shoulder in the picture opposite this page.

The eight decades starting with the 1920's are all here, so well-documented. This new edition shows the mushrooming evolution into what country music is today.

To me, *The Illustrated History of Country Music* is a valuable document. Through it I touch my roots, and in doing so, find a strong kinship with the minstrels and troubadours of old.

JOHNNY CASH

Hendersonville, Tennessee
August 1995

In 1976, when work began on the first edition of this book, the task seemed clear. It still does: to provide an account of all that has gone into the cultural phenomenon we call country music. So, unlike most other works in the field then or now, this is a history in which the social, economic, political and commercial dynamics of the music are given almost as much attention as its singers and songs. The undercurrents of America's "musical Mississippi," as our concluding chapter calls it, are if anything even more intriguing than its surface waters.

The breadth of view and depth of perspective necessary for such a work has never existed in one person, however impressive his or her credentials, so from the start *The Illustrated History* was a group endeavor. It began in 1976 with a two-day brainstorming session, held in Nashville, during which the book's philosophy and framework were established by a panel of individuals justly respected in the field of country music history: Charles K. Wolfe, Douglas B. Green, Bill Ivey, Bob Pinson, and yours truly. We agreed that Wolfe, Green, Ivey, and Pinson would share the bulk of the writing (aided by "specialists" like Nick Tosches on rockabilly, J.R. Young on the Singing Cowboys, and Roger Williams on Hank Williams), and that I would edit the work and manage the project. At the time I was the Editor of *Country Music Magazine*: the original idea for the book had been mine.

I returned to *Country Music*'s offices in New York with the skeletal plan, fleshed it out, and helped organize the Country Music Magazine Press to bring it to life in conjunction with Doubleday. Then came the usual long procession of little steps and major and minor thrills and agonies, all accumulating into publication in 1979.

The volume you hold in your hands is that same book with some major additions: 15 more years of history covered in four new chapters, plus significant expansion and revision of the middle chapters, plus a bigger and better collection of illustrations, plus a much improved design.

The new book is nearly twice as long as the first, and while it holds true to the original's framework and philosophy, it also addresses and corrects the shortcomings which for one reason or another flawed the final product in 1979, chiefly a disappointing dearth of illustration. In that respect, the opportunity to publish a new edition has been a great pleasure for its creators: a long-desired chance to bring *The Illustrated History of Country Music* fully to life.

As to the creators, some are old and some are new. The work of all the original authors remains, but the ideas, talents, and labor of the current *Country Music Magazine* staff have been added, most significantly the overall management of Editor/Publisher Russell Barnard, the photo research and editing of Senior Editor Helen Barnard, the design work of Art Director Katheryn Gray, and the editing and project management of Senior Editor George Fletcher. Russell Barnard, it bears noting, was one of the original publishers of *Country Music Magazine* in 1972 (the magazine was his idea), and he worked with me on the 1979 *Illustrated History*. My role in the current edition was to write all the new material, revise all the old, and help with the processes of editing and illustration. The book was produced at the *Country Music Magazine* offices, with the assistance and support of the whole staff.

Any history book, no matter what one's high school education might have led one to believe, is of course a highly subjective, selective enterprise, and ours is no exception. In fact, it is loaded with bias, since each of its creators has his or her particular opinions and interests; one writer's seminal genius of the music may be another's also-ran, and so on. But here of course is thoroughly *informed* bias and opinion. Messrs. Wolfe, Green, Ivey, Pinson, Tosches, Young and Williams are, after all, the world's leading authorities on their subjects, and their work in these pages has already been praised as definitive (although of course it isn't, and never can be); the 1979 *Illustrated History of Country Music* was hailed in academic, professional and popular circles as the best narrative history in the field (until its replacement by this volume).

There remains an important caveat. This volume is not the place to find a lot of data—stars' birthdates and birthplaces, recording chronologies and the like— or even to find mention of every figure significant to the course of the music. This is not to say that such an approach to the lives and times of country music is irrelevant. It certainly isn't, and in fact the Country Music Magazine Press has devoted another whole book to it—our companion volume, *The Comprehensive Country Music Encyclopedia*. This book's brief, however, is history, not chronology or biography.

A lot has been put into it. Our hope is that you will get a lot out of it.

—PATRICK CARR

Willie Nelson Picnic Program, 1973, from Patrick Carr's collection. Patrick was there. Country Music Magazine was one year old at the time.

Tennessee musicians in the 1890's.

CHAPTER 1

Across the Ocean, into the Hills

The evolution of country music—the folk music of America's white, mostly rural working class—began as soon as the first settlers set foot on American soil; the original roots, however, predate the New World, in some cases by centuries, for the oldest elements of country music are descended directly from the folk music of Elizabethan and pre-Elizabethan England, Scotland and Ireland.

After the Industrial Revolution arrived in America, with its rapid development of communications, America's folk music expanded and changed at an ever-accelerating rate. Before then, when the population was primarily rural and isolated, change was slow indeed; hence, for almost 200 years, the folk songs available to Americans were still essentially British in origin (as, for that matter, was the "high" culture of the rich and the town dwellers). The core of these songs was brought over by the first settlers, and the songs ranged in age from medieval times to the days immediately before the ships sailed for the New World. Since the Middle Ages there had been a thriving folksong culture among the English peasants and urban poor, and since these people were illiterate, the songs had been passed on orally from generation to generation. This process continued to function with little interruption once the settlers had established themselves in America; the songs were stories of love, death,

drama and infamy, and in those days of slow change they lost none of their appeal from generation to generation. They enabled the singers and listeners to see the world in very personal terms.

One way to understand the archetypal elements of these "old" songs is to understand ways in which the American pioneers modified and customized them. In many cases, we have early printed song texts from England that tell us what the songs were like before they crossed the ocean; folksong study had become stylish in England by the turn of the 19th century, and antiquarians wandered about the country collecting and later publishing these "reliques of ancient poetry." Such study did not become popular in America until the 1880's, and even then, American scholars were more interested in English folk songs than in their own. By the time serious collection of American songs had begun in the early 20th century, the American folk had had over 100 years to tinker with their borrowed songs, and some of their customizing was wondrous to behold.

An old Irish song about going to America, "Canaday-i-o," was modified into a song about lumberjacks, and, as the frontier pushed even farther west, into a song about buffalo hunters. Such well-known songs as "Sweet Betsy from Pike" and "The State of Arkansas" are British

The Cumberland Mountains of Tennessee were home to the Hicks family, known for their ballad singing, around 1900.

survivals with only minimal changes. There is also the case of the cowboy song, "The Streets of Laredo," about a cowboy dying of a gunshot wound. Though the song contains all manner of references to the Old West—spurs, six-shooters, saddles, rifles, cowboys—it also contains the refrain:

> Oh beat the drum slowly and play the fife lowly,
> Play the dead march as you carry me along,
> Take me to the green valley, and lay the sod o'er me,
> For I'm a young cowboy, and I know I've done wrong.

If the reference to fife and drum seems out of place in a song about the wild West, one can understand it better by comparing the Americanized text with the British version, which features a soldier dying of venereal disease. Though the Americans changed the setting and the circum-

stances of death—violence in the American folk imagination has always been more acceptable than sex—the reference to a British military funeral, with drum and fife, somehow remained intact. Odd, unexplained retentions like this mark many British ballads transplanted into American rural culture; mountaineers continued to sing old songs describing "milk-white steeds" and "knights" and "London town," though they knew of London only vaguely as a city "across the water."

The ways in which Americans changed these old British ballads tell a lot about the character of the American people as well. One thing the people did was to shorten the songs; a song originally called "The Lass of Loch Royal," for instance, ran to 35 stanzas in its original form, but survived in America in only three stanzas—the basis for the lovely country lyric, "Who's Gonna Shoe Your Pretty Little Foot?" Secondly, the old ballads described tragic events with a cold, detached, impersonal air; the American versions allowed the singer more involvement and reflected more sentiment toward the sad events of the song. This movement from the ballad song form (objectivity) to the lyric song form (emotional subjectivity) was to continue into the country music of today, where the majority of songs are emotional and sentimental.

British songs were also full of the supernatural, especially avenging ghosts and ominous omens. In "The Gosport Tragedy," a young man murders his pregnant girlfriend because he does not want to marry her; the murderer tries to escape on a ship, but the ship cannot get wind to sail, and the ghosts of the girl and her baby then appear on board and tear "him all in three." Singers in Kentucky renamed the song "Pretty Polly," dropped the whole section on retribution, with its supernatural overtones and reduced the song to a grim, no-nonsense description of the murder itself. The American version usually ends:

He threw a little dirt over her and started for home,
Leaving no one behind but the blue birds to mourn.

The old ballads are full of lovers' quarrels, but instead of getting a divorce, as in modern country music, the protagonists here usually settle their business with a knife or a club. Even with this level of violence, though, the American ballads were generally more genteel than their British counterparts; some of the blunt descriptions of physical love found in British originals are missing from American versions. This is understandable when we realize that most American versions were being adapted during the Victorian age, when the sight of a woman's ankle was enough to cause a man to grit his teeth.

Occasionally, when the words of an Old World

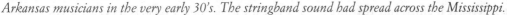

Arkansas musicians in the very early 30's. The stringband sound had spread across the Mississippi.

Bradley Kincaid made a formal study of old ballads.

song were almost totally unadaptable to American culture, they were stripped away entirely, and a completely new set of words was put to the melody. An Irish song describing a rebellion in 1798, "Hurrah for the Men of the West," was fitted with completely different words to become "The Old Settler's Song" (with its familiar refrain "surrounded by acres of clams"). From this point it was easy to take the next step and create entirely new songs, with fresh words and fresh music. Thus a native American balladry arose next to the imported British balladry, and Americans were soon singing their own songs about their favorite outlaws, cowboys, murders or disasters. The first collectors of folk songs were so interested in British songs that had survived in North America that they almost completely ignored the native ballads; but hundreds of these songs existed, and they were far more popular than the British survivals.

Naturally, the early American songs were based on the structure of the British songs, but again there were some interesting differences. American ballads were more journalistic, giving names, dates and places more readily than their British counterparts. We learn the name of the bank Jesse

James robbed, the town the murdered girl lived in, the date of the great train wreck. In many cases, American singers also tacked a moral on the end of their song. At the end of "Pearl Bryan," a Kentucky song about two medical students who murder a girl and cut off her head, we hear:

> *Young ladies, now take warning;*
> *young men are so unjust;*
> *It may be your best lover,*
> *but you know not whom to trust.*
> *Pearl died away from home and friends,*
> *out on that lonely spot;*
> *Take heed! Take heed! Believe me, girls;*
> *don't let this be your lot!*

The American Puritan ethic, after all, held that art for art's sake was frivolous, and for years American writers felt a pressure to justify their fiction by showing its morality. The folk composer felt the same pressure, and morals were tacked onto songs in ways that at times seem ludicrous. The long story of the "Wreck of the Old 97" is supposedly designed to admonish girls to "never speak harsh words to your sweetheart/ He may go and never return." Even when a natural disaster occurred and no person could possibly be blamed for it, singers drew morals about the power of God. At the end of a song about a Mississippi River flood, we are told simply: "Let us all get right with our Maker/As He doeth all things well." Such tags tended to make the songs into moralistic parables—for those who wanted moralistic parables. For most listeners, the tag was probably a formality and a way to justify enjoying a good song.

In an age before radio or phonograph records, most of these old songs were naturally transmitted via oral tradition. Much of this transmission apparently took place within the family; one modern study of folk singers in Tennessee revealed that over three quarters of the songs were learned from family members. Of course, the diffusion was horizontal as well as vertical; as vari-

The Fiddlin' Powers Family, from Virginia, one of country music's first family bands. They recorded for the Victor Company in 1924. They are: Charles, Ada, Orpha, Carrie and Cown Powers.

ous members of a family spread out around the country, especially on the frontier, they took their songs with them. Songs were carried up- and downriver by boatmen, and cross-country by railroad workers and section hands. Various itinerant minstrels roamed the land, often playing for nickels and dimes on courthouse lawns and in railroad stations. Many of the musicians were blind and had turned to this style of performing as one of the few available means for making a living.

In one sense, these anonymous minstrels were the first professional country musicians. About the only thing many of them left behind was a handful of tattered "ballet cards"—postcard-sized sheets containing the words to a favorite song they had either composed or popularized. The minstrels would often sell these cards to help pay their way, and the cards are direct descendants of the broadside ballads about current events once sold in the streets of 18th-century England. Yet the cards also show that not all folk songs were transmitted orally; many a text obviously started from these printed cards, and many of the old mountain singers had scrapbooks full of pasted-in ballet cards, or handwritten copies of such cards. Some early publishers even came out with books that were little more than bound reproductions of these early ballet cards; one such book was *The Forget-me-not Songster,* which dates from the early 1800's and which contained numerous old broadside ballets from the War of

A Sacred Harp singing school in Alabama in 1919. The Sacred Harp schools perpetuated the shaped-note method of singing. Alton and Rabon Delmore were both accomplished shaped-note singers.

1812 and the Revolutionary War. Later on in the 19th century, newspapers and magazines provided still other ways for folk songs to get printed.

But in order to understand the effect of a music on society, we have to also know something of the singer and his role in society. What do we know about the singers of these old songs?

Though the minstrels were important in song transmission, they were a rather small percentage of the overall singers, most of whom were farmers, mountaineers, and wives and husbands who sang for their own enjoyment. Cecil Sharp, who visited dozens of traditional singers in the mountains about the time of World War I, reported that very few of them seemed to have any sense of audience in their performance; most were so interested in the message of the song that they were unaware of what effect they were having. Singing was very much a natural part of life; one singer told Sharp that he couldn't re-

member the words to one particular song and then exclaimed, "Oh if only I were driving the cows home, I could sing it at once!" All kinds of people sang for Sharp: men, women, children. "In fact," he recalled, "I found myself for the first time in my life in a community in which singing was as common and almost as universal a practice as speaking."

It is noteworthy that Sharp, and later collectors as well, have found as many women singers as men; as we shall see, women seldom played instrumental music in the mountains. Perhaps the folk communities saw singing as less a specialized art than fiddling or banjo picking. The early collectors also noticed that most of the singers performed without any instrumental accompaniment; the image of the typical folk singer today, replete with guitar or dulcimer, has relatively little historical support. The old-time singers sang with the "high lonesome sound" and sang free of the rigid meters of the guitar. Nor were they self-conscious about the age of the songs; they were not consciously preserving old songs because they were old, but keeping the songs alive because the songs appealed to them. Sharp found that many of his singers did not know the history referred to in many of their old ballads, and once when he told a woman the "facts" behind the song she had just sung, the woman was delighted. "I always knew the song must be true," she said, "because it is so beautiful."

By the early 1900's people were looking on the Southern mountains as sort of a giant cultural deep freeze, where songs and music that had died out elsewhere were still preserved in their original state. As early as 1904, a writer for *Harper's* was describing a people "hidden among the mountains of Kentucky, Tennessee, and the Carolinas" whose music was "peculiarly American"; these mountaineers sang "many ballads of Old England and Scotland," and their taste in music had "no doubt been guided by these...."

Cecil Sharp, the first collector to actually prove that the mountain songs included British survivals, assumed that the isolation of the mountain folk was responsible for the preservation, and assumed that such preservation was unique to the Southern mountains. In fact, later collectors found as many "child ballads"—songs of demonstrably English origin—in New England as in the South, and such songs have also turned up in non-mountainous areas like Mississippi and Texas. The South, with its veneration of tradition and love of the old values that the folk songs represented, probably did preserve more of the music than other parts of the country, but as early as the turn of the century, the South acquired a popular image as the only source for old-time songs; it was this image that caused folk song collectors, and later record companies, to go into the South after their material.

In truth, the South was not

all that isolated from outside musical influences. The development of the railroad and logging industries brought outsiders into the mountains and gave natives a chance to travel; and the Spanish-American War and World War I allowed Southern soldiers to bring back infusions of the popular culture of the day. By 1920, Sears, Roebuck was sending over five million copies of their catalogues out into rural America, offering cheap instruments, songbooks and sheet music, and many of these catalogues were finding their way into the South.

Sheet music was by no means unknown in the mountains, and many songs once thought to be old folk melodies have been traced to published, copyrighted songs by the 19th-century version of Tin Pan Alley composers. A song from sheet music would somehow get into the mountains, it would be passed on through several generations by word of mouth, a few words would be changed or simplified, and the author and the original source eventually forgotten. The song would become just another "old song" like the more genuine folk ballads.

George D. Hay, the founder of the Grand Ole Opry, recognized this phenomenon when he said: "The line of demarcation between old popular tunes and folk tunes is indeed slight." It is thus possible to find early sheet music "originals" for many well-known folk and old-time country songs, including "The Ship That Never Returned" (1865), "Maple on the Hill" (1880), "The Letter Edged in Black" (1897), "Please Mister Conductor, Don't Put Me Off the Train (Lightning Express)" (1898), and "Kitty Wells" (1861). Even The Carter Family classic, "Wildwood Flower," has its original source in an 1860 published song. In fact, this song provides an excellent instance of how the oral transmission process can change the words to a song. The Carters, who apparently learned the song orally from someone in the

Fiddler Clayton McMichen, banjoist Fate Norris and guitarist Claude Davis in 1922.

mountains, usually sang the first line, "Oh I'll twine with my mingles/and waving black hair." This line had never made very good sense, and more than a few people puzzled over the meaning of the word "mingles." The explanation may lie in the original sheet music, in which the first line reads, "I'll twine 'mid the Ringlets." Someone probably misheard the term "ringlets," or decided the line was too hard to sing, and during the 60 years between its original publication and the time The Carters found it in the Virginia hills, the line was simplified. So is "Wildwood Flower" a folk song or a popular song? It has elements of both genres, and it shows how the two cultures could and did interact in the early history of country music.

Nineteenth-century popular culture influenced archaic country music directly as well as indirectly. Even when it was not absorbed into the folk tradition, early popular music reached into the South and into the hinterlands via the immense popularity of the minstrel shows, vaudeville, the medicine shows and songs of composers like Dan Emmett and Stephen Foster. All too often we tend to see music in 19th-century America as nothing but old ballads and fiddle tunes; in fact, from the 1820's on, America had a form of Tin Pan Alley music. A hit song during this time was defined not through record sales or radio airplay, but through sheet music sales. Many homes had pianos, and in an age before radio and television, most families made their own music, and if they wanted to hear the latest hit, they sang it themselves.

Of course, there was professional entertainment as well. The minstrel show was one of its most enduring forms. The minstrel show was a series of tunes, jokes and skits performed by white men dressed in blackface; much of the appeal of the show stemmed from this caricature of black music and black culture. The classic minstrel show consisted of three parts: a section of songs and jokes, an "olio" of skits and specialty numbers, and a longer drama or dramatic parody. In the 1830's a performer named Thomas ("Daddy") Rice dressed in blackface and rags and created a character named Jim Crow; soon Rice was popular across the country, and the idea of

C.F. Martin began building guitars in this country in 1833.

blackface entertainment was established. In 1843, four noted blackface comedians banded together to form The Virginia Minstrels, and the minstrel show itself was established. The Virginia Minstrels traveled throughout the country, including the South, where they proved exceptionally popular. Along with the crude parodies of black life and black culture, The Virginia Minstrels and those who followed them also brought a number of songs and performing styles.

Surviving accounts of these early minstrel shows suggest that much of the music they played would not seem out of place on the Grand Ole Opry today. The Virginia Minstrels featured music of the fiddle and banjo, much like the Southern folk dance music of 40 years later. The fiddler Dan Emmett is now credited with composing two songs commonly thought to be folk songs, "Old Dan Tucker" (1843) and "Blue Tail Fly" (1846). In fact, minstrel musicians either originated or popularized a number of well-known "folk" classics. Minstrel singer Cool White published the popular "Buffalo Gals, Won't You Come Out

The Martin Guitar Company plant built in 1859 in Nazareth, Pennsylvania, still houses some of the company's operations.

Tonight?" in 1844 under the title "Lubly Fan," and in 1834 a Baltimore publisher issued a song entitled "Zip Coon," which became a country-fiddle standard under its more common title, "Turkey in the Straw." The song might well have been a folk melody before it was published (there are similar tunes in both Irish and English folk music), but its publication and subsequent performance in hundreds of minstrel shows across the country certainly helped establish it as an anthem of rural America.

Instrumental tunes were also popularized by the minstrels; an 1830's folio called *Crow Quadrilles*, for instance, contained the music to several tunes, generally considered "traditional" Southern fiddle tunes, including "Zip Coon" and "Gettin' Upstairs." The folio even contains appropriate dance calls for each tune, calls that resemble modern square dance calls. We know that such folios were sold in the South and that minstrel shows toured widely in the South. Throughout the 19th century, minstrel troupes

with colorful names such as The Christy Minstrels, The Sable Harmonizers, Ordway's Aeolians and The Nightingale Serenaders provided the South with a steady diet of minstrel fare—and pop music. As late as 1925, when Vernon Dalhart was in the midst of recording a series of top-selling country music records, there were still half a dozen minstrel shows touring the country, and even in the 1930's Nashville's radio station WSM was broadcasting a Friday-night minstrel show using several members of the cast of the Saturday-night Grand Ole Opry.

Even when the large professional minstrel companies broke up, elements of them survived throughout the rural South in the form of the medicine show. The medicine show consisted of three or four people who would pull their wagon or truck into small towns, give a free "entertainment" to attract a crowd, and try to sell various medicines and elixirs of somewhat dubious quality. The shows usually contained all the elements of a larger minstrel show; songs, jokes, skits and even the burlesque drama (now called the "afterpiece"). The cast included one or two musicians, the "doctor" who hustled the medicine, and often a blackface comedian or a "Toby" clown. (The "Toby" character—who often wore a red wig—was a stereotyped rube figure who survived into modern country music as the comedy act, such as the one Spec Rhodes performed with Porter Wagoner.) Roy Acuff got some of his first professional experience traveling with such a medicine show in eastern Tennessee, and recalled that he strengthened his voice by playing all the different roles in the afterpiece and skits. Clayton McMichen, a member of the famous Skillet Lickers and a national champion fiddler, recalled even more recent experiences with such medicine shows:

"I worked in medicine shows as late as 1936. I rebuilt me a Dodge Northeast generator of 1,000 watts. Bought a little motor for lights and loudspeaker. We called the medicine shows 'the kerosene circuit' or 'the physic operas.' People had tired feet and you had to be funny.... I was raised on one password: 'Sold Out, Doc.' The medicine to fight neuralgia and rheumatism cost $10 a bottle and we really sold it. We took in $300 or $400, traveled in a Model T, carried a hammer and saw to build a platform. Before and after World War I, Tennessee was thicker with physic operas than Georgia. Georgia cracked down on 'em."

The type of medicine sold in the shows, of course, varied from doctor to doctor, from show to show. Many of today's country musicians did their stints in medicine shows, and they tell hair-raising tales of what went into the medicines.

Original instruments made by Orville Gibson.

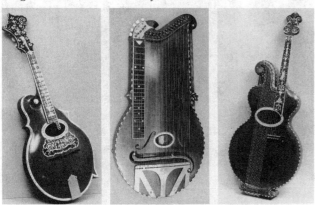

Gibson founder Orville Gibson in the 1890's.

Some were made up of just colored water, and some mountain shows actually used complex concoctions of herbs as the elixir, but Opry pioneer Kirk McGee recalled getting tangled up with a dope-sniffing doctor who used plain old gasoline as the base for his cure-all. The grass roots medicine shows lingered on into the 1950's; they may not have exposed the South to the kind of pop hits the larger minstrel shows did, but they did offer employment for musicians and they did foster commercialization of the music. After all, from one angle the purity of folk tradition is a trap; in the 19th century, rural musicians who wanted to make a living playing music full-time simply had no place to go; many were not "folk" musicians by choice. By the turn of the century, a few professional opportunities for country musicians were beginning to open up in the medicine shows and the circuses.

And then there was vaudeville, which emerged in the 1880's as the popular successor to the minstrel shows. Vaudeville apparently developed out of the "olio" section of the minstrel show, and consisted of a potpourri of unrelated acts: musicians, comics, acrobats, dancers. Unlike the minstrel and medicine shows, vaudeville acts generally followed a well-defined tour route, since most of the booking was done by companies owning theater chains. While most of these chain theaters were in the East and Midwest, a number were located in key Southern cities like Nashville. While some forms of vaudeville existed in the South from the earliest days of the 1880's, it was not until 1917 that the solid, regular routes were established. By 1910 the chiefly Southern circuit of Delmar-Keith had some 22 theaters doing healthy business, and vaudeville magnate Marcus Loew was mounting a deliberate and

expensive campaign to establish his chain in the South. This paid off, and by 1919 vaudeville performers were touring the South from Texas to Virginia.

Vaudeville singers brought even more popular music into the South, and they did so in the important decade that immediately preceded the first commercialization of country music. Yet most of the vaudeville performers of the 1917-23 era were still Northern entertainers; there were very few "hillbilly" performers on the early vaudeville stage. After some of the first-generation hillbilly performers began to record and broadcast in the mid-1920's, many of them joined vaudeville tours: Charlie Poole, Al Hopkins' Hill Billies and Uncle Dave Macon all made successful vaudeville tours. Uncle Dave Macon was an exception to the rule: Apparently he toured even before he recorded or broadcast, and did so well for Loew's theater

Kentucky fiddlers at a 1925 fiddling contest in Louisville sponsored by Henry Ford. Ford sponsored fiddling contests nationwide.

1926 regional fiddling winner Uncle Jimmy Thompson, shown here in Louisville with a Model T Ford.

chain that a rival chain tried to hire him away.

By the late 1920's vaudeville was acting as a two-way conductor of musical styles: It was bringing Tin Pan Alley music into the South, and it was taking Southern performers into the North and Midwest. For a number of years after the development of the mass media of records and radio, vaudeville and personal appearances still remained the best source of income for the would-be professional country entertainer.

Thus the commercial and the folk traditions fed countless songs into the repertory of the rural Southern singer. But many fine singers ignored both these traditions in favor of yet a third: the sacred tradition. For entire generations of rural singers, church music and gospel music provided the main outlets for singing; many singers first learned to sing sacred songs, and many others refused to sing anything but sacred songs.

Throughout the 19th century "singing conventions" were held annually or quarterly in courthouse squares and churches across the South;

people would gather to sing the old songs, visit and enjoy "dinner on the ground."

Many singers received what formal music education they had from "singing schools," where a self-styled "singing master" would come into a community and organize a singing class that would run from two to three weeks. At first these schools were run on the subscription basis: Each pupil paid a certain fee to the singing master. Later, some of them were sponsored by local churches or even gospel songbook publishers. Singing-school pupils were taught the "rudiments" of music: how to read notes, how to mark time (some masters did this by having students slap their desks with their hands, with the resounding whacks echoing throughout the countryside) and how to sing parts.

The songs taught at the singing schools were not quite commercial and not quite folk, but an odd combination of both. As Americans in the early 1800's went about settling their new country and establishing a bewildering variety of new independent religious denominations, it soon became evident that many of the sedate Old World hymns did not fit the emotions and the temperament of the New World. New hymns were written, many of them fitted to old folk melodies. Many early hymnbooks were published with words only; one compiler in the late 1700's advised of his texts, "Many of the Scots and English song tunes answer a few of them well." The Great Revival—starting about 1801 and sweeping through Virginia, Kentucky, Tennessee and much of the backwoods South—intensified this sense of grassroots religion even more; one account from Kentucky describes a particular revival meeting with over 200,000 people singing. The frontier churches liked to sing; the Methodist Church, in fact, became known as "the singing Church."

American collections of sacred songs were not slow in coming. While many originated in the North, at least 20 major collections were published in the South between 1815 and 1855. One of the most successful songbooks was William Walker's *The Southern Harmony* (1835), a collection of over 300 songs; the book was soon adopted by churches of all denominations across the South and was reprinted many times. (In fact, the book is still in print in the 90's and is still used at the annual "Big Singing" at Benton, Kentucky.) *The Southern Harmony* eventually sold over 500,000 copies, and its compiler, dubbed "Singin' Billy" by his fans, became one of the most influential figures in American church music. Walker eventually began signing his name "William Walker, A.S.H." (Author of *Southern Harmony*).

By this time the more popular hymns and "white spirituals" had attached themselves to one particular melody, and the melodies were printed in many of the songbooks with an unusual notation system consisting of shaped notes. In shaped-note singing, pitch was indicated by the shape of the note (diamond, square, triangle, etc.) in addition to its position on the staff. In many churches using these books, it was customary to sing the first chorus of a song through by singing the name of the notes ("fa," "sol," "la," etc.) instead of the words.

This system of singing, which was designed to help semiliterate congregations cope with the printed page, originated in New England in the 1700's. It soon died out there, but it was kept alive in the South, where people saw it as a cultural tradition rather than an expediency. Rural singing masters from Georgia to Virginia continued to compile books using shaped-note music; they composed some songs, "borrowed" others from earlier books, and "arranged" still others to reflect local singing patterns. Sometimes the authors got credit, sometimes not; many songs from books were committed to memory by congregations and thus entered folk tradition, as did many pop songs published in sheet music. A Georgia collection, *The Sacred Harp* (1844), was so popular that it gave its name to an entire genre of shaped-note singing; the collection was constantly revised (at one point containing over 600 songs) and is still used in the South.

As the 19th century wore on, the evangelical religions tended to become more commercialized—or at least more organized. Though it was still possible for a local preacher or song leader to issue songbooks of regional appeal, people like evangelist Dwight L. Moody and singer Ira Sankey were combining their talents to conduct revival meetings on a national scale. The idea of a "revival hymn"—a sort of Tin Pan Alley hymn—became popular with the success of the Moody-Sankey revivals and the publication (starting in 1875) of a series of songbooks under their auspices. (The songbooks had reputedly sold nearly 50 million copies by the time of Sankey's death in 1908.) These new gospel songs (the term "gospel" was used in the title of Sankey's first collection) gave more emphasis to individual salvation and the subjective religious experience than did the older songs of the Sacred Harp singers. The newer songs were considered more up-to-date and tended to describe the religious experiences in rather striking metaphors.

Life is like a mountain railroad,
  With an engineer that's brave,
  We must make the run successful,
  From the cradle to the grave.

According to authors Abby and Tillman, if you make it to the "Union Depot," with Christ as your

Sam McGee and Uncle Dave Macon in 1930.

The Milt Tolbert Tent Shows were still active in Texas and the South in the 1930's. They were like old-time medicine shows.

"conductor," you'll meet "the Superintendent, God the Father, God the Son."

Sentiment was in vogue too, and the popular gospel song books of this era also contained numbers like "The Drunkard's Home," "The Drunkard's Lone Child," "The Dying Girl's Farewell," "The Mother's Good-bye" and "Mother Always Cares for You"—songs that made no specific references to Jesus or salvation, but translated the effusive sentiments of salvation songs into secular terms.

A sort of renaissance in gospel songwriting occurred at the end of the 19th century, and the period saw a number of well-known titles that later became country music standards. These titles include "When the Roll Is Called Up Yonder," "What a Friend We Have in Jesus," "Leaning on the Everlasting Arms," "Heavenly Sunlight," "Life's Railway to Heaven" and "Amazing Grace." (This last song, with words penned by John Newton

in the 18th century, was popularized in America by "Singin' Billy" Walker; it is probably the best-known folk-country hymn today.)

Singing styles for the songs also changed during this period. Small group singing—usually done by a quartet—became popular, and music publishers began to sponsor professional quartets to tour the South. James D. Vaughan, a music publisher in Lawrenceberg, Tennessee, is thought to have been the "inventor" of the gospel quartet; as early as 1910 Vaughan hired a male quartet of highly trained professional singers to travel to churches, revivals and singing conventions, giving concerts and promoting the songs from Vaughan's songbooks.

The idea caught on so fast that by the late 1920's Vaughan had some 16 full-time quartets on his payroll. These quartets were the progenitors of what was to become a strapping cousin of country music, gospel music, and Vaughan's singers set the pace for later groups like The Chuck Wagon Gang, The Blackwood Brothers and The Statesmen.

Much of the harmony so characteristic of modern country music can be traced to early gospel quartet harmony. Many early country artists, including A. P. Carter, The Delmore Brothers and The McGee Brothers, got their first singing experience in gospel quartets and old-time singing schools, and it is quite possible that country music's characteristic use of elaborate metaphor in song lyrics stems largely from the lyrics of 19th-century sacred music.

In a sense, the gospel tradition acted as a sort of common denominator for most later professional country singers. Regardless of how far apart two singers are in their secular repertoires, they can always get together and harmonize on an "old gospel number."

Next to the human voice, the most important instrument in archaic country music was the fiddle. Fiddles were small and easy to transport, they could be repaired if damaged, and they could be constructed from scratch if necessary: They were ideal instruments for a society of pioneers moving into the wilderness. For years, the fiddle was virtually the only folk instrument found on the frontier, and white settlers in the South were probably using the instrument as early as the 17th century.

Most folklorists now agree that there once existed a flourishing tradition of black old-time country music, a tradition that went into eclipse when blues became the dominant black folk music form. In the 1941 book, *Father of the Blues*, W. C. Handy, famous author of "St. Louis Blues," recalled how this tradition touched his own life. Handy was born in 1873 into a family of freed slaves living in Florence, Alabama.

"With all their differences, most of my forebears had one thing in common: If they had any musical talent, it remained buried.... The one exception was Grandpa Brewer, who told me that before he got religion, he used to play the fiddle for dances. That had been his way of making extra money back in slavery days. His master, the kindly man that I have mentioned, allowed him to keep what he had earned from playing." Handy's account continued:

"In his day, Grandpa Brewer explained, folks knew as well as we do when it was time for the music to get hot. They had their own way of bearing down. A boy would stand behind the fiddler with a pair of knitting needles in his hands. From this position the youngster would reach around the fiddler's left shoulder and beat on the strings in a manner of snare drummer. Grandpa Brewer could describe vividly this old method of making rhythm, but for his own part he had forsaken such sinful doing, and I had to wait for Uncle Whit Walker, another old-timer, to show me just how it was done. Uncle Whit, lively and unregenerate at 80, selected his favorite breakdown, 'Little Lady Goin' to the Country,' and would let me help him give the old tune the kind of treatment it needed. Uncle Whit fiddled and sang while I handled the knitting needles." The words to the song went:

Fiddlin' John Carson with daughter Rosa Lee in the 20's. His fiddle, made in Ireland in the 1700's, came over in a flour sack.

Sally got a meat skin laid away
Sally got a meat skin laid away
Sally got a meat skin laid away
To grease her wooden leg every day.

"Uncle Whit stomped his feet while singing. A less expert fiddler, I learned, would have stomped both heels simultaneously, but a fancy performer like Uncle Whit could stomp the left heel and right forefoot and alternate this with the right heel and left forefoot, making four beats to the bar. That was real stomping. Country gals and their mirthful suitors got as much enjoyment out of a fiddle at a breakdown or square dance as jitterbugs or rug-cutters get nowadays from a swing band."

Many settlers brought fiddle tunes and traditions from Scotland and Ireland to the New World. Many jigs and reels, like their vocal counterparts, made their way across the water to find new homes and often new names. "Moneymusk," "Soldier's Joy" and "Fisher's Hornpipe" are 18th-century British tunes that entered American pioneer tradition and remained relatively unchanged throughout the years. Many titles were Americanized: "Miss MacLeod's Reel" was rechristened "Did You Ever See a Devil, Uncle Joe?," while a distinguished title like "Lord McDonald's Reel" was redubbed "Leather Breeches." Old tunes were preserved, new ones were created in similar molds, and frontier fiddlers added personal touches and new strains.

In a rural and semiliterate culture, instrumental tunes were more difficult to preserve than song lyrics; one had to write and read music, and few fiddlers had that skill. Thus nobody really knows how many different tunes might have existed; a

Charlie Poole, center, and The North Carolina Ramblers, Posey Rorer and Roy Harvey, in the 1920's. As a musician, Poole was ahead of his time.

conservative guess by experts places the number at well over 1,000. Many of these tunes had dozens of different names in different parts of the country.

As the country grew, distinct regional fiddling styles developed in areas like New England, southern Appalachia, the Ozarks, northern Georgia and the Southwest. These playing styles are similar to speech dialects, and modern fiddling devotees can still to some extent play the same game as *My Fair Lady*'s Professor Higgins, placing a man by listening to his fiddling style rather than his accent.

Like American folk songs that retained Old World phrases, some fiddling styles retained Old World sounds. Many versions of "Sally Goodin" that feature the use of a drone string echo the Celtic bagpipe music that spawned so many old fiddle tunes. Even the pioneer fiddler's habit of holding his instrument against his chest instead of under the chin (as would a "violinist") seems to be a survival from early European fiddlers.

Fiddling had a number of important social functions in the frontier and farming communities of the 19th century. While the individual often played to entertain only himself or his family, to while away long lonely nights, fiddlers were in demand for all types of rural social gatherings. People would often meet for "work gatherings" to do an especially big or arduous job, and then celebrate afterward with a meal and perhaps a dance. Fiddling has been reported at log-rollings, log-raisings for barns and cabins, hog killings, "lassy makin'" (molasses making), husking bees, bean stringings and even quilting bees. In addition to playing at such work parties, the fiddler might also be expected to show up at weddings, shivarees, wakes, the end of cattle drives or roundups, and "moonlights" (community pie-and-ice-cream suppers). Though it wasn't usually possible for a man to make a living playing his fiddle in those days, he could win a great deal of prestige and considerable local fame as an accomplished fiddler. The attitude of a frontier community toward its fiddler is reflected in this description of a local fiddler in Sumner County, Tennessee, in 1793:

"He and his fiddle (and they were inseparable) were always welcome, and everywhere. He had a sack of doeskin, in which he placed his 'fiddle and his bow,' when not in use or when traveling.... He could make his fiddle laugh and talk. There was such potency in its music that he often charmed away the pains of the body and silenced the groans of the sick.... Whenever there was to be much of an entertainment or considerable dance, the girls would say, 'O

get Gamble! Do get Gamble! We know he will come.' And Gamble was, indeed, always willing to come."

It was the country dance, or square dance, where the old-time country fiddler really shone. In the South, such dances customarily lasted through the night; in Texas and the Southwest, where people were more scattered and gathering was more difficult, dances sometimes lasted for three days. Often a house was selected, the furniture moved out, a fiddler found, and the dance was on. Sometimes the fiddler was paid— one old custom was "ten cents on the corner," a complicated system relating to the number of sets the fiddler played. Sugar or meal was often spread on the rough wood floor to help the dancers, and prodigious quantities of food were cooked up ahead of time for a midnight supper. The fiddler was usually the whole band; he played by himself, did the dance calls and led the singing (if any). If the fiddler's endurance waned as the night wore on, and if his technique slipped into little more than choppy sawing, the audience seldom complained. Ubiquitous stone jugs, pungent and stoppered with corn cobs, helped fuel the festivities, and many an old-time fiddler echoed the sentiments of Grand Ole Opry pioneer Uncle Jimmy Thompson: "I just naturally need a little of the white lightning to grease my arm."

Nobody is sure how the country square dance originated; it might have been derived from the French quadrille (some old fiddlers occasionally still call their faster pieces "quadrilles"), or it might have derived from English country dances. Whatever its origin, the country square dance soon developed a distinctly American quality; it lost much of its Old World dignity, courtesy and formal movements, and became an energetic, foot-stomping "frolic." The fiddle music that accompanied these dances reflected the good-times feeling; even the titles of the tunes reflect the wild, surrealistic humor of the American frontier: "Tramp the Devil's Eyes Out," "Shoot the Turkey Buzzard," "Jay Bird Died With the Whooping Cough," "Throw the Old Cow Over the Fence," "How Many Biscuits Can You Eat?" and "There Ain't No Bugs on Me." Often the fiddler would sing a stanza or two as he gave the "calls" for the dance:

Come along boys, don't be so lazy.
Dip that hunk in a whole lot of gravy.
Rope the bell, bell the calf,
Swing your corner once and a half.
Treat 'em all alike.

There were other stanzas that were interchangeable and that floated back and forth between fiddle tunes, depending on the mood and memory of the fiddler.

Fly around my pretty little miss,
Fly around, my daisy,
Fly around, my pretty little miss,
You almost drive me crazy.
My wife died Friday night,
Saturday she was buried,
Sunday was my courtin' day,
Monday I got married.

Some of the titles and stanzas were pretty earthy, full of double-entendre for those familiar with folk speech; titles like "Forky Deer" or "Clabber Cod" are suggestive enough, but some· fiddle-tune stanzas are even more explicit:

Sally in the garden sifting, sifting,
Sally in the garden, sifting sand,
Sally in the garden sifting, sifting,
Sally upstairs with a hog-eyed man.

Old-timers today won't tell a stranger what "hog-eyed" means, but they grin when somebody asks them.

It was partly because of such frolics and tunes that many righteous folk considered the fiddle "the devil's box." When settlers and mountaineers embraced religion, they did so with a zest that nourished intolerance, and fiddling—long associated even in the Old World with frivolity and indolence (e.g., the fable of the grasshopper and the ant, or the legends of Nero fiddling while Rome burned)—soon had a very negative image in some quarters. "The man who 'fiddled' was hardly worth the damning," asserts a Southern mountain man in the 1887 local-color novel, *Behind the Blue Ridge*, and a folklorist writing at the turn of the century noted: "Particularly does the devil ride upon a fiddlestick. People who think it a little thing to take a human life will shudder at the thought of dancing."

Some fiddlers got converted and gave up fiddling, but, unable to bring themselves to destroy their beloved fiddles, concealed them in the walls of their cabins. Others turned to church music; As a Kentucky fiddler recalled, "Once I got the Spirit here, I gave up frolic tunes and played only religious music."

In spite of all this, the fiddler endeared himself to the American folk, and fiddling has traditionally been associated with the classic American heroes. George Washington had his favorite tune ("Jaybird Sittin' on a Hickory Limb"), as did Thomas Jefferson ("Grey Eagle"). Davy Crockett was a fiddler, and Andrew Jackson's victory over the British in the War of 1812 is forever immortalized in the fiddle standard, "The Eighth of January." Bob Taylor, one of the most popular politicians to be elected governor of Tennessee, played the fiddle on the campaign trail in the 1880's and asserted of the old fiddle tunes, "Every one of them breathes the spirit of liberty; every jig is an echo from flintlock rifles and shrill fifes of Bunker Hill...." Henry Ford, one of the most popular folk heroes of the early 20th century, sponsored fiddling contests across the country and argued that old-time fiddling helped preserve American values. Politicians soon found that fiddling helped them win elections and helped mark them as true men of the people.

In truth, fiddling was a genuine folk art. While tunes were transmitted—and transmuted—a healthy folklore grew up about the fiddle itself. There was a lore about the proper way to make a fiddle, since many mountaineers and settlers had no other source; curly maple, poplar and apple woods were popular in fiddle building, and horsehair—then as now—was often strung for the bow. Many musicians also made it a point to know the history of their own fiddle, and this lore became part of the fiddle culture. Rattlesnake rattles were said to improve the tone of the fiddle—especially if you had killed the snake yourself. There was a lore about fiddle tunes, about where they were learned and what they meant, and even a lore about the great fiddlers: fiddlers who could play a thousand tunes, or who could play "triple stops" (sound three strings at once). A common tale even today tells of a "mys-

Clayton McMichen

tery fiddler" who shows up at a small local contest, speaks to no one, plays brilliantly, and vanishes into the night.

While dancing was the most common social event that featured fiddling, there soon developed another tradition that was to be of even more importance to the development of the music: the fiddling contest. Here groups of local fiddlers would meet together and compete with each other to determine who was the "best" fiddler. Often a prize was awarded, but many old-time fiddlers saw that as less important than the prestige attached to a contest. Fiddling was considered not so much a fine art as a manly skill, like shooting, boxing, or wrestling; many of the early fiddling contests were held in conjunction with shooting or wrestling contests at local fairs and celebrations. Well-known area "champion" fiddlers wore their reputations with the nervous aplomb of Western gunfighters; there was always a brash youngster wanting to go up against the champion, and there was always the danger of the champion's age catching up with him. Some of the older contests were trials of endurance: One Texas contest at the turn of the century ran eight days. And both fiddlers and audience took the contests seriously; it was a matter of great local pride for a county to have a champion fiddler (even though the sobriquet "state champion" meant only that some promoter had decided to dignify his contest with the title).

Researcher Dick Hulan has recently found that

The guitar became more popular in the late 1890's. Spanish American War soldiers brought it back to the Southern hills.

the first documented fiddling contest dates from November 30, 1736, and was held in Hanover County, Virginia. The Virginia *Gazette* of the time reported that "some merry-dispos'd Gentlemen" had decided to celebrate St. Andrew's Day by staging a horse race and by offering a "fine *Cremona* Fiddle to be plaid for, by any Number of Country Fiddlers." Other events of the celebration included "Dancing, Singing, Football-play, Jumping, Wrestling &c." and the awarding of "a fine Pair of Silk-Stockings to be given to the *handsomest Maid* upon the Green, to be judg'd of by the Company." The winner of this contest is unknown, but the "merry-dispos'd Gentlemen" must have had a good time, for they were back the next year (1737) with an even bigger contest. This contest promised a horse race, wrestling, and a dancing contest, and the promoters announced "that a violin be played for by 20 Fiddlers, and to be given to him that shall be adjudged the best; No Person to have the Liberty of playing, unless he brings a Fiddle with him. After the Prize is won, they are all to play together, and each a different Tune; and to be treated by the Company." Singing got into the act that year with the announcement that "a Quire of Ballads" would be "sung for, by a Number of Songsters; the best Songster to have the Prize, and all of them to have Liquor sufficient to clear their Wind-Pipes." After the contest, the *Gazette* was able to report that "the whole was managed with as good Order, and gave as great Satisfaction, in general, as cou'd possible be expected."

Fiddling contests of various sorts continued

Kirk and Sam
McGee in 1936.

Fiddlin' John Carson in the 30's. He first recorded in Atlanta in 1923.

cause the fiddle was the most common folk instrument of the 19th century and because many of the standard fiddle tunes were well known to audiences and musicians alike. A fiddler might learn an occasional new tune at a contest, but by and large the music he heard was as familiar and as comfortable as an old shoe, and it served to reaffirm both his aesthetic and his social values.

In the smaller, local contests at the grass-roots level, the prizes did not always include much cash; it was common for local merchants to contribute goods as well. As late as 1931, a local Tennessee contest announced that prizes included "such handy and useful articles as fountain pens, flour, shirts, pocket knives, inner tubes, rocking chairs, rubber heels, cigars, gasoline, shotgun shells, cigarettes, coffee...talking machine records, candy, cow feed, neckties, half soles, cakes, hair tonic, flashlights, pencils and water glasses."

An important element of the fiddling contests—then as now—was nostalgia. Many Americans somehow associated fiddling with "the good old days," patriotism and old-fashioned American values. A newspaper account of an 1891 contest mentioned that each fiddler "played the sweet old tunes of bygone time with charmed bow string." A 1909 account quotes a fiddler in a contest as bragging that he is playing his "great-grandfather's pieces." It was partially this element of nostalgia that was responsible for the growth and commercialization of these fiddling contests.

By the end of the 19th century, cities like Knoxville, Tennessee, and Atlanta, Georgia, were holding regular fiddling conventions that attracted scores of talented musicians from a radius of a hundred miles. The

throughout the 19th century, but did not become widely popular until after 1865 or so. Often they were held at one-room mountain schoolhouses or at the county seat when people came into town for the circuit-court meetings. The judges were often local prominent citizens, though on occasion other fiddlers judged. Most of the time a fiddler was expected to "whup it out by hisself," standing alone on the stage and playing solo, with no guitar or banjo backup man. In some early contests, every fiddler had to play the same tune, often a common one known by all, such as "Arkansas Traveler" or "Sally Goodin." In today's contests, fiddlers are expected to be creative as well as technically proficient, but in older contests, the prize often went to the person who played in the most authentic style. If a fiddler was suspected of having any formal training, he was disqualified.

Fiddling contests worked be-

Atlanta Fiddlers' Convention—which was to play an important role in the development of the early country music recording industry in Atlanta—dates from 1913, while the country's most famous annual contest, that at Union Grove, North Carolina, dates from 1924. Though the contests often included other categories of musical competition such as singing, string band playing, banjo picking and "clog" or "buck" dancing, the fiddling remained at the center of the event: It always offered the most prize money, attracted the most contestants, and was regarded the most seriously.

As fiddling developed throughout the 19th century, it was exposed to influences other than the Scots-Irish English fiddling styles. In Texas and the Southwest, Spanish and Mexican styles were much in evidence, and in Louisiana Cajun fiddlers developed a distinctive use of high droning sounds. American Indian fiddlers brought a new sense of timing and harmonics to fiddling; Cherokee and Choctaw Indians living in the mountainous Southeast exchanged songs and ideas with white settlers in the area. Slave fiddling was rather common in some parts of the South, and there are numerous accounts of slaves fiddling for their masters' dancing parties. On their own time, black fiddlers experimented with sliding notes and unorthodox tunings, and devised their own instrumental styles, which were not exactly hillbilly and not exactly blues.

Fiddle music came out of the 19th century as the dominant instrumental music in the Southern mountains and in rural America generally. Though it was gradually replaced by the guitar as the major symbol of country music, for decades it carried the instrumental burden of American folk music. There is something archetypal about the fiddle, something that suggests not only the music it made but also the

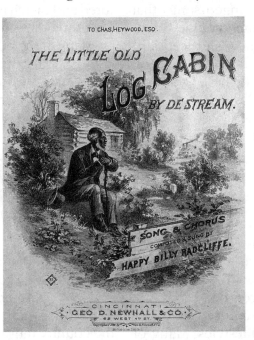

values of those who listened to the music.

The assault on the fiddler's supremacy in folk music actually began with the growing popularity of other stringed instruments in the late 19th century. The first such instrument was the banjo, which has been called "the outstanding American contribution to the music of folklore." In reality, the banjo was of African origin and was almost certainly brought to the New World by slaves; throughout the first half of the 19th century the banjo, or *banza*, was associated almost exclusively with black musicians. Slave banjos were usually made from gourds and were reported in Maryland as early as 1774. Thomas Jefferson, writing in 1781 about the blacks on his own plantation, remarked that "the instrument proper to them is the Banjar, which they brought hither from Africa." Another writer about the same time listened to a black singer accompany himself on the banjo, and a novel published in 1832 described a banjo player who could improvise songs on the spot or sing requested numbers, and who was as much at home playing for slave dancing as serenading the young ladies of his master's household. By 1847 we have accounts of an African-American dance that featured the music of banjos and fiddles being played together. In fact, the stereotype of the happy, fun-loving African-American playing the banjo was so established by mid-century that a foreign visitor would report, in all seriousness, that runaway slaves could be lured from their hiding place in a forest by the sound of banjo music.

From the black folk tradition the banjo gradually moved into white folk tradition, especially in the southern Appalachians, where musicians made banjos out of groundhog skins and adapted their songs to the limitations of the instrument's harmonics, but at this time a parallel commercial tradition of banjo music that was to have even more effect on modern country music was also developing. This commercial tradition began with a "whitening" of black banjo songs. In the 1790's a Boston musician named Graupner heard a group of blacks in Charleston playing the banjo and singing to its accompaniment. He bought a banjo, learned to play it, wrote down some of the tunes, and in 1799 wrote the first "minstrel" song, "The Gay Negro Boy." The minstrel show developed as a major form of entertainment in the 1840's and established its basic format of white professional performers dressing as blacks and singing arranged songs that were supposedly derived from genuine "plantation melodies." The banjo became a central symbol of the minstrel show and of its stereotyped image of the black. The popular songs of Stephen Foster, songs like "Ring, Ring the Banjo," helped feed this stereotype. As the minstrel show gave way to vaudeville, the popularity of the banjo with white entertainers grew even more; but the racial connotations of the instrument were passed down also, and the 1880's saw a boom in lively banjo-thumping singers doing "coon" songs—songs composed in deliberate parody of black lifestyles. Many of these songs survived into the early commercial era of country music.

The person who perhaps best typifies the commercial banjo tradition was a Virginia man named Joe Sweeney, who supposedly "invented" the five-string banjo about 1830. This fifth string, a drone or thumb string higher in pitch than any of the others and fastened by a peg halfway up the neck, is what distinguished the country banjo from its city cousin. The latter has only four strings, and is used primarily as a rhythm instrument in jazz bands and dance bands; the five-string can be picked, and is often used as a solo instrument.

While Sweeney may have added the fifth string, the idea of a thumb string probably originated with black folk musicians, who sometimes

used three strings with a fourth thumb string. Sweeney, however, did a lot to popularize the banjo and its music. He wrote many songs based on genuine black folk melodies he heard on his plantation. Billed as "The Banjo King," he toured through the South and made a hit on the New York stage (he even got to give a command performance for Queen Victoria in England). During all these performances he impressed many musicians both in the North and the South with the potential of the banjo as a serious instrument, and by the 1850's, banjos were being manufactured and merchandised, a sure sign that the white lower-middle class was accepting the instrument.

Many of the performing styles of the 19th-century stage—from minstrel shows to vaudeville—were picked up by amateur musicians across the South and fed back into the folk tradition. Soon the solo fiddler at country dances was joined by a banjo player, and two-thirds of the classic country string band was established. The last third of the string band, the guitar, actually has a longer pedigree than the banjo, but it was accepted as an American folk instrument much later.

It is perhaps fitting that the guitar, like the country music it has come to symbolize, was the product of two traditions: the popular commercial one and the folk-transmission process. Given the lack of informants to describe the folk processes of the 19th century, the commercial tradition is, naturally, better documented.

While the banjo was being played almost exclusively by blacks in the South, the guitar was recognized as a "proper" parlor instrument for the cultured upper classes of the North. An import from London drawing rooms, the guitar was seen as a link with Old World culture, and its early players included notables like Ben Franklin and Francis Hopkinson, one of the signers of the Declaration of Independence. Instruction books like *The American Guitarist* were appearing by the 1830's, and a number of American "classical" guitarists made names for themselves on the concert stage.

By 1833, C.F. Martin had started making the guitars that would eventually have a legendary reputation among country pickers, but for much of the 19th century, the guitar tradition was confined to the cultured classes; it was only in the 1880's and 1890's that the parlor tradition began to filter down to the lower middle classes. By this time the light classical and semi-classical numbers of the earlier repertoire had given way to more popular compositions for guitar—numbers with titles like "Siege of Sebastopol," "Wild Rose Melody" and "Midnight Fire Alarm." These specific compositions for guitar had a pronounced influence on playing technique (such as thumb picking) and tuning patterns. Guitar historian Robert Fleder has pointed out, for instance, that the open D tuning of a piece like "Siege of Sebastopol" (1880) soon became popular even in folk tradition. Even today, black guitarists across the country call the D tuning "Vastopol."

By the turn of the century, the class diffusion of the guitar was well under way. In 1902, the Gibson Company—a name soon to be as revered as that of Martin by country pickers—began manufacturing mandolins and guitars, and shortly thereafter embarked on an orchestrated campaign to get its instruments, "The Musical Pals of the Nation," into every town. Gibson sponsored various mandolin and string orchestras everywhere, and printed pictures of them in their catalogues, proclaiming "Every one a 'Gibsonite.'" The mandolin and guitar societies, however, were still the provinces of the middle class; it took Sears, Roebuck to change that. As early as 1894 Sears was offering as many as seven guitar models in its annual catalogue, along with instruction books and even books of popular vocal songs arranged for guitar accompaniment. By 1909 Sears' guitar line had grown to 12 models, indicating the success it was having with its cheap mass-market guitars. And cheap they were: The lowest-priced ("The Serenata") sold for about two dollars, while the cheapest Gibson cost well over a hundred. The guitar, unlike the banjo, was not easily homemade, and so a readily available source like Sears was important in making the guitar a folk instrument. The popular vogue for

Hawaiian music in the era between 1890 and 1910 fueled interest in the guitar, and especially in the use of the "steel" guitar.

Soon amateur string bands began to crop up in all sorts of rural settings, both North and South. Old photos show mandolin and guitar bands from Minnesota, Ohio, Indiana, North Dakota and even upstate New York. Fiddlers, of course, were as ubiquitous as ever. The bands played rags, waltzes, polkas, schottisches and even jazz, and for a time were a staple of rural lower middle class life. Sears catalogues went everywhere into rural America, and people who couldn't afford even a Sears model soon figured out how to build their own.

It was in the South, though, that this rural string tradition sank its deepest roots, and it was in the South where it was subjected to the commercial impetus that was to forge it into a popular art form called country music. The popular commercial guitar tradition especially had a substantial impact on the music of the South. After all, the first guitar manual in the country was printed in South Carolina in 1820, and though the various mandolin and guitar societies have been traditionally associated with large Northern cities, the Gibson catalogues reveal that such orchestras existed across the South in cities like Knoxville and Memphis, Tennessee; Macon and Atlanta, Georgia; Houston, Texas; and Jackson, Mississippi. During the Spanish-American War and World War I, Southern soldiers were exposed even more to the guitar. This double movement of the guitar into the working classes and into rural America reinforced the existing folk traditions and soon made the guitar immensely popular.

The folk (as opposed to classical) traditions of guitar music stemmed from two sources: the Mexican music of the Southwest and the black blues and ragtime music of the South. In Spanish America and Mexico the guitar was as ubiquitous as it was in Spain itself, and as Anglo-Saxon settlers moved into Texas, New Mexico and California, they found the Mexican settlers living there playing guitars. American cowboys learned from their Spanish and Mexican counterparts that the guitar was good company on the lonely prairies and long cattle drives, and

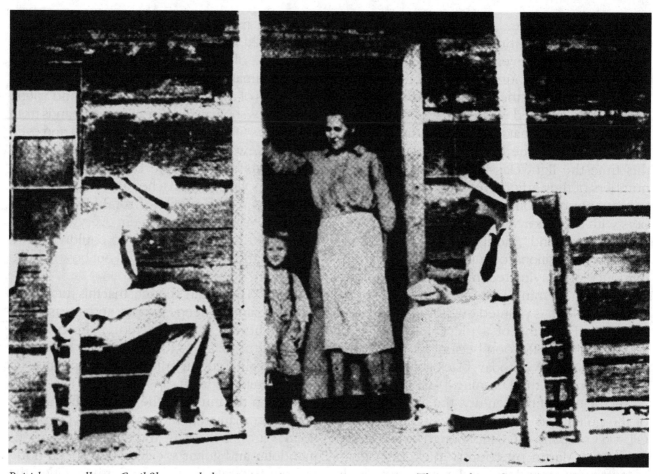

British song collector Cecil Sharp took down mountain songs on paper in 1917. The age of sound recording was coming soon.

by 1900 the guitar had established itself in the Southwest as an appropriate partner for the fiddle at local dances.

Though guitars were almost certainly known in rural areas of the South before World War I, many old-time musicians insist that they never saw a guitar before this time; furthermore, many of them recall that when they saw their first guitar, it was in the hands of a black musician. Folklorist Alan Lomax, one of the first trained scholars to pay attention to folk instrumental styles, recalled in the 1950's: "Negroes introduced the guitar and the blues into the hills sometime after the turn of the century, so recently in fact that the most complex of hillbilly guitar styles is still called 'nigger pickin'."

There are few written records to indicate how the guitar got into black folk tradition, but it did, and black singers soon adapted it to their blues style. While at first the white country guitarists played little more than rhythm behind their sing-

ing, the black country blues singers had devised ways to punctuate their singing with melodies too. They used the index and middle fingers to pick on the high strings, while the thumb kept up a steady rhythm on the bass strings. It wasn't long before white country guitarists adopted this same style, and the guitar became the third instrument of the basic country band.

By the end of World War I, all the diverse ingredients of modern country music were securely established in rural Southern life. The old ballad singers had Americanized their British models and developed a thriving native ballad tradition; semi-professional musicians in vaudeville shows, circuses and medicine shows were exposing rural and Southern audiences to popular music of the day, from sticky sentimental laments to rough-hewn minstrel parodies; gospel publishing houses were encouraging the performance and the writing of new gospel songs, while singing schools and conventions kept the older church music alive; country fiddlers were moving out of the exhausting drudgery of night-long mountain dances and into the limelight of the fiddling contest where audiences were listening with a new attentiveness; the classic string band of fiddle, banjo and guitar was becoming the standard instrumental combination, and amateur pickers across the South were busy exploring the limitations and possibilities of the string band format.

These elements had already shown a healthy tendency to overlap when a song called "The Little Old Log Cabin in the Lane" came upon the scene. It had been written and published back in 1871 by Will Hays, a Kentucky riverman who had a long and successful career grinding out songs for the vaudeville stage. It was one of his biggest hits, and was sung widely throughout the country as a pop song. The tune and idea, however, had appealed to the folk imagination, for soon settlers in the West were singing a version called "My Little Old Sod Shanty on the Plains," and railroad men were singing another version called "The Little Red Caboose Behind the Train." To complicate matters more, a Salvation Army hymn-writer named Charles W. Fry had grafted a gospel lyric to the tune in 1881; this new hymn was popularized widely in an 1887 edition of Ira Sankey's *Gospel Hymns Number 5*

under the now-famous title, "Lily of the Valley." Thus Hays' song had started in the pop tradition, moved into folk tradition, and even into gospel tradition.

And, perhaps symbolically, it became the first country song to be recorded. In 1923 the Okeh Phonograph Corporation, as a favor to a client, recorded a 55-year-old fiddler from Fannin County, Georgia, named Fiddlin' John Carson. On his record, Carson combined two of the most important 19th-century performing traditions: the solo fiddle and the vocal. He sang in a rough, untutored voice, and played the fiddle simultaneously. And his two selections reflected two song traditions: "The Little Old Log Cabin in the Lane" was of course from the pop-vaudeville tradition, while the song on the other side, "The Old Hen Cackled and the Rooster's Going to Crow," was probably an old minstrel song that had gone into folk tradition. The record, in short, was a perfect symbol of the diverse strains of 19th-century music merging under the pressure of the new mass media. But the executives of the Okeh Phonograph Corporation didn't see all this at the time; they thought Carson's singing was "pluperfect awful." They were sure that the record wouldn't amount to anything.

Jimmie Rodgers

CHAPTER 2

The Birth of an Industry

To the men from New York, Bristol in the summer of 1927 must have seemed quaint, provincial and remote. Located high in the Appalachians between the Cumberland Plateau and the Blue Ridge Mountains of Virginia, Bristol straddled the Tennessee-Virginia border; State Street, the town's main street, was literally the state line.

For years musicians from the nearby hills used the town as an informal gathering place. They would come down in wagons, on horseback, in Model T Fords, even on foot; they would attend fiddling contests, have dances, gossip and listen to the latest records played on the Victrolas local merchants would wheel out on the sidewalk in front of their stores. Not that there was much to interest the hill people on early Victrola records: Most of the sides were dance band music, the likes of Paul Whiteman's "Love Nest" or Zez Confrey's "Kitten on the Keys," or the Scots songs of Harry Lauder, or the vaudeville fare of Al Jolson. Some of the newfangled "blues" songs by Bessie Smith weren't so bad, but most of the hill people listened to the demonstration records out of simple fascination with the gimmickry of the thing; few of them toted any of the Paul Whitemans or Al Jolsons home with them.

Bristol had already enjoyed a reputation as a center for old-time folk music. Ten years earlier, in 1917, noted English folk song collector Cecil

Sharp had visited the region and had found that the mountains in the area were full of singers who knew old English folk ballads dating from the 17th and 18th centuries. Now, in late July of 1927, another folk song collector of a slightly different type was arriving from New York. Where Sharp went about his work with notepad and good faith, this new collector was using a new electric recording machine and a file of contracts.

The "collector" was a young, moonfaced man named Ralph Peer, and his plan was not to collect material for some distinguished university archive but to make commercial phonograph records for the Victor Company. When he drove into Bristol, he had with him his wife, two engineers and half a carload of portable recording equipment. Peer rented an empty building on State Street—it was an old hat factory—and his engineers set out to fix it up as a temporary studio. Blankets were hung around the walls for sound baffles, and a six-foot platform was erected to hold the recording turntable. The crew worked for a couple of days getting the temporary studio in shape and then took a break for the weekend to look over the town. They found a pleasant city of over 8,000 people, in a strange mixture of rural and urban culture. Some aspects of the city were right out of the recent best sellers by Sinclair Lewis: two newspapers full of wire service reports, a super-active Kiwanis Club, a YMCA,

Ralph Peer came to Bristol, Tennessee, or Bristol, Virginia—the state line runs down the main street—in the late 1920's to record local talent. Among his finds were The Carter Family and Jimmie Rodgers.

an emerging upper-middle class that dabbled in the bullish 1927 stock market, and a fancy new hotel—with a hot jazz band. Peer saw at once that his musicians would have to come out of the nearby hills, not out of the town. He also saw he had to justify his interest in "hill country" tunes to the newly sophisticated townsmen. Thus in the Sunday morning paper, Peer planted a news story that explained his mission:

"Mountain singers and entertainers will be the talent used for record making in Bristol. Several well-known native record makers will come to Bristol this week to record. Mr. Peer has spent some time selecting the best native talent. The mountain or 'hillbilly' records of this type have become more popular and are in great demand all over the country at this time. They are practically all made in the South. In no section of the South have the prewar melodies and old

mountaineer songs been better preserved than in the mountains of East Tennessee and Southwest Virginia, experts declare, and it was primarily for this reason that the Victor Company chose Bristol as its operating base."

Peer had been through Bristol in the spring of 1927 and had auditioned several possible groups for recording; he lined these up to record during his first few days in town, and hoped that the publicity would attract other musicians from the surrounding hills. On Monday Peer began recording Ernest "Pop" Stoneman and his family, one of the "well-known native record makers" (and a family that was to endure into the present country music era), and he deliberately let the word get out that Stoneman was not only making records, but also was getting paid for it—to the tune of $100 a day. The citizens of the town were astounded that people would pay to hear hillbilly music—but the aspiring musicians in the area were even more astounded. They swarmed into Bristol looking for "the record man."

"I was deluged with long-distance telephone calls from the surrounding mountain region," Peer recalled. "Groups of singers who had not visited Bristol during their entire lifetime arrived by bus, horse and buggy, trains or on foot." Relatives of informants who had sung freely and innocently for Cecil Sharp ten years earlier now had a burning desire to see their names on a Victrola disc. The commercialization of mountain folk music had come, and it had come with a bewildering suddenness.

At the center of the new hillbilly boom he had described for the local paper was Ralph Peer himself, and behind this watershed Bristol field trip was a fascinating four-year struggle to get early country music inserted into the channels of burgeoning mass media. In a very real sense, Ralph Peer had grown up with the commercial recording industry. He was born in 1892 in Kansas City, where he spent his youth helping his father manage a store that sold sewing machines, pianos and the then-new home phonograph machines. Before World War I Peer had gone to work for Columbia Records, working in a variety of positions and learning the ins and outs of the new record business. One early artist he worked with was W.C. Handy, famous composer of "St. Louis Blues." By the end of the war, Peer had joined the General Phonograph Corporation, a fairly new company that had just decided to start a record label called Okeh.

During this time the record industry was booming; major companies like Victor were reporting record sales of over 100 million records

in 1921. Most of these records, of course, were vaudeville songs, band music, light classics and samples of a strange new instrumental cacophony called jazz. Compared to the major companies like Victor, Columbia and Edison, Okeh was insignificant, with sales of only three million to four million records a year. Naturally, the company was looking for ways to increase sales. To make matters worse, a depression in 1921 crippled much of the entertainment industry; and worse still, by 1922 radio was becoming popular. Radio could offer sound reproduction comparable to that of many of the primitive acoustic records as played on windup Victrolas, and radio was much less expensive. Columbia's sales dropped over 50 per cent just between 1921 and 1922; other companies had similar losses. The record market seemed to be drying up, and any new ideas were welcomed.

One of these ideas was to create records that would appeal to a specialized audience. For some time the record companies had produced ethnic records in various "foreign" series for sale overseas and to various ethnic immigrant groups in large Northern U.S. cities. Peer was aware of this type of marketing, and so he was interested when he noticed that a recording he had helped supervise in 1920, Mamie Smith's "Crazy Blues," was having fantastic sales in the black sections of Northern cities. Mamie Smith was one of the first black blues singers to record, and Peer sensed that such records could be marketed to the vast black population. By mid-1921 the Okeh Company had initiated a special "race" series of records, a series designed to appeal to a black audience. Other companies soon followed, and blues became a lucrative part of the record business.

Peer decided to try a further appeal to spe-

Ralph Peer

cialized markets: In an attempt to appeal to regional audiences, he would do a series of recordings "on location." With that plan in mind, he set out using some newly designed portable recording equipment and working with recording pioneer Charles Hibbard, a onetime associate of Thomas Edison himself. Peer asked his regional distributors to help round up local talent—jazz bands, church singers, amateur violinists, anybody popular on the local scene. June 1923 found him in Atlanta, where his local distributor, a furniture dealer named Polk C. Brockman, paraded his finds before the microphones. Peer later recalled:

"See, everything I recorded he agreed to buy, I don't know, 2,000 records or something, just to make it worthwhile. Finally there was this deal where he wanted me to record a singer from a local church.... This fellow had quite a good reputation and occasionally worked on the radio. So, we set a date with this fellow...and he just couldn't make the date. So to take up that time, my distributor brought in Fiddlin' John Carson. He said, 'Fiddlin' John had been on the radio station and he's got quite a following, he's not really a good singer, but let's see what it is....' I can't claim there was any genius connected with it...not on my part, not on his part."

Arthur Satherley

Because Brockman had placed an advance order for the Carson records, Peer went ahead and pressed them, though he thought John's archaic, folk-styled singing was "pluperfect awful." Peer saw the job as a custom pressing, and didn't even give the record a catalogue number. Brockman received the records in Atlanta a month later, and took them with him to a local fiddling contest; there Fiddlin' John himself came onstage and played "Little Old Log Cabin in the Lane" and "The Old Hen Cackled and the Rooster's Going to Crow." Then Brockman put a windup phonograph machine onstage and played the same tunes as John had put them on record a month before.

Brockman recalled, "We sold them just like hotcakes—right there in the hall.... That was the daddy of them. That was it." Brockman reordered records from Peer in New York—and then reordered again. Finally the record was given a catalogue number, and Peer quickly made arrangements to record more of Carson. He sensed the presence of yet another vast, untapped record audience: the white, middle-class South. And, taking his cue from his experience with the "race" series, he set out to find the specialized music that appealed to this new audience.

Thus Fiddlin' John Carson's "Little Old Log Cabin in the Lane" became the first real "country" record and the first real "country" hit. To be sure, there had been occasional earlier attempts to record rural music. There had been occasional cylinder recordings of comedy-fiddle pieces like "Arkansas Traveler" and a few fiddle records such as John Taylor's "Devil's Dream Reel" for Victor as early as 1909. Charles Ross Taggart's "The Old Country Fiddler" pieces had been popular in the teens, and in 1922 Victor had recorded a couple of fiddlers named A.C. "Eck" Robertson and Henry Gilliland. But the companies had seen these as novelty pieces and had not tried to market them to any specific audience. They certainly started no trend, and, indeed, Victor didn't even release the 1922 Robertson sides until after the success of Carson's record. Carson's recording was the first conscious, deliberate attempt to program a mu-

In the 1920's, Atlanta's Peachtree Street drew musicians from all over the region to record in makeshift and ever-changing groups. Polk Brockman, a descendant of President James K. Polk, was one of the leaders on the burgeoning recording scene.

sic toward the traditional country music audience. Like many pioneer country recording artists, Fiddlin' John had actually been performing for years at local fairs, carnivals and political rallies, and he simply transferred this performing style to the new mass media of records and radio.

In Carson's case, his reputation as a colorful entertainer had won him an invitation to broadcast on Atlanta radio in 1922, and his success on radio had a lot to do with his getting a chance to record. Much of the time, though, he used radio merely to publicize his personal appearances, and he looked on records in the same way: His touring car proudly bore the words, "Recording Artist." In this respect he was like many of the early hillbilly performers who used mass media as a tool, a means to an end.

Carson himself went on to have a long and successful career in music, recording dozens of times with his band, The Virginia Reelers, and with his daughter, an insouciant comedienne named Moonshine Kate. John's songs were as colorful as his life: "If You Can't Get the Stopper Out, Break the Neck," "You Can't Get Milk from a Cow Named Ben," "Who Bit the Wart Off Grandma's Nose?," "It's a Shame to Whip Your Wife on Sunday" and "What You Gonna Do When Your Licker Runs Out?" On a more serious side, John sang a number of very popular sentimental songs, like "You'll Never Miss Your Mother Till She's Gone," and even a few topical political songs such as "The Farmer Is the Man That Feeds Them All" and "Georgia's Three-Dollar Tag" (about a license-tag controversy). Carson stopped recording in 1934, and spent his later years as the elevator operator at the Georgia State Capitol, a job given him by Governor Herman Talmadge, for whom he had campaigned. Carson died in 1949, a patriarch who had received at least some recognition for his role in transforming American popular music.

Carson's success inspired not only Peer but the other major record companies as well. Within a year several semi-professional Southern musicians gained status as recording stars. A millhand from Fries, Virginia, named Henry Whitter had the second country best seller in "The Wreck of the Old 97" and "Lonesome Road Blues." Whitter, who sang and accompanied himself with guitar and harmonica (using a wire rack), had actually recorded his songs before Carson's discovery, but the company had refused to release them. Another millworker who worked with Whitter, Ernest Stoneman, heard Whitter's records, decided he could sing better, and soon found himself with a successful recording of a classic country ballad, "The Sinking of the Titanic." Also from Virginia came The Fiddlin' Powers Family to record fiddle tunes for Victor, while the northern Georgia team of Gid Tanner and Riley Puckett did the same for Columbia. Peer returned to Atlanta to find The Jenkins Family, the archetype of hundreds of modern country gospel groups, who were immensely successful on records and radio and as songwriters. The first woman soloist to record country music was Reba Stanley, a superb singer from Georgia who recorded "Single Life" in 1924. Other female pioneers were Samantha Bumgartner and Eva Davis, North Carolinians who recorded with fiddle and banjo; Vocalion Records brought them to New York from Tennessee with three veteran minstrels—George Reneau, Charlie Oaks and banjo-thumping Uncle Dave Macon—to record mountain ballads and old vaudeville songs. Though most of this first generation of country entertainers were from the Southeast, Okeh recorded a group called Chenoweth's Cornfield Symphony Orchestra from Dallas—the first Texas country band to be recorded—in 1924. By the end of 1924 the first country record catalogue had been issued by Columbia records: *Familiar Tunes on Fiddle, Guitar, Banjo, Harmonica and Accordion*, designed to list the records of musicians whose "names are best known where the square dance had not been supplanted by the fox-trot."

Thus by early 1925—barely 18 months after Carson's pioneering recording—most of the major record companies were so successful with this new type of record that they were establishing a separate series of "hillbilly" recordings designed to feature rural Southern artists and to be distributed and sold primarily in the South. Nobody, however, knew exactly what to call this music:

Reba Stanley

Some of it was genuine folk music, but a lot of it was composed of old sentimental songs, old popular songs, and old vaudeville tunes. The different companies came up with an interesting variety of names. The Okeh Company called their product "Old-Time Tunes"; Columbia chose "Familiar Tunes—Old and New"; other companies chose names like "Songs from Dixie," "Old Southern Tunes" and "Old Familiar Tunes and Novelties." When Sears, Roebuck got into the business and began to sell this music through their catalogues, they listed it as "Southern Fiddling and Song Records," "Mountain Ballads" and "Old-Time Southern Songs."

In this early period, the term "country music" was never used, though Peer himself used the term "hill country music" as early as 1925, and Montgomery Ward's catalogue listed the music as "Hill Country Melodies." Many Northerners persisted in using the term "hillbilly" to describe the music, though the term had very negative connotations for most rural Southerners. A 1926 writer for *Variety*, the show business newspaper, discussed "hill-billy music" and explained that "the 'hill-billy' is a North Carolina or Tennessee and adjacent mountaineer type of illiterate white whose creed and allegiance are to the Bible, the chautauqua and the phonograph." They had, according to *Variety*, "the intelligence of morons" and delighted in "sing-song, nasal-twanging vocalizing." However, partly because of the success of an early stringband led by Al Hopkins that appealed to vaudeville audiences by playing up their hayseed image and calling themselves The Hill-Billies, the adjective "hillbilly" gradually became attached to the music in the early 1930's. Today the term "hillbilly" is seldom used (and when it is, it's used with pride). Its frequent use by Northern recording executives in the early days reflects the fact that they looked down on the music and endured it only because it made money for them.

Many of this first generation of country performers were amateur or semi-professional Southern musicians, and many of them had been brought North to record in New York studios. Peer's occasional forays into the field were not emulated much by other companies; it was easier for them to record in permanent studios. But to do this, the companies had to locate genuine Southern musicians, talk them into coming North, and take care of them as they wandered about the big city. Many of these musicians had rather limited repertoires, and some found it hard to learn new tunes. Ernest "Pop" Stoneman was very popular with the companies, for instance, because he could learn new songs easily and thus could produce "cover" versions of hit records.

An ideal solution to this problem was for the companies to find a way to combine the authentic elements of Southern music with the professionalism of Northern studio musicians. In one case, at least, these qualities were brought together

in the person of country music's first superstar, Vernon Dalhart.

Dalhart—his real name was Marion Try Slaughter—was an East Texas native who had come to New York in 1912 to try to make it as a popular stage singer. He enjoyed moderate success at this, and was recording non-country songs as early as 1916, often specializing in "coon" songs in which he imitated black dialect. Because his pop career was on the decline, Dalhart decided to try to aim a record at the newly defined country market: He thus became the first pop singer to undergo the "Nashville treatment," whereby an artist tries to shore up a sagging pop career by "going country."

Dalhart chose to cover Henry Whitter's 1924 hit, "Wreck of the Old 97," and finally persuaded Victor to let him record it. For the B side, he chose a lonesome dirge called "The Prisoner's Song"; this tune, with its now-famous line, "Oh if I had the wings of an angel," based on an old poem, was written by Dalhart's cousin, Guy Massey, and arranged by Victor's sophisticated musical director, Nat Shilkret. It was hardly a folk song, but it sounded like one, and it soon went into folk tradition. And no wonder: The 1924 Victor pairing became country music's first million-selling record, and was so successful that it was rerecorded on as many as 50 different labels over the next two decades. Dalhart had succeeded in shoring up his career in spectacular fashion.

During the rest of the 1920's, Dalhart produced an amazing string of hits: There were old sentimental songs from the 19th century like "The Letter Edged in Black" and "Little Rosewood Casket"; there were genuine folk songs like "Golden Slippers" and "Barbara Allen"; there were new Tin Pan Alley rustic-flavored songs like "My Blue Ridge Mountain Home" and "The Convict and the Rose." But best of all, there were the event songs, topical songs about a tragedy, a murder case or a famous criminal. Frank Walker, who supervised Dalhart's recording of dozens of such songs for Columbia Records, recalled:

"An event song is something that had happened, not today, maybe years ago, but hadn't permeated through the South because of a lack of newspapers and no radio and no television in those days, but they had heard of it. For instance, some of the biggest sellers we were ever able to bring out was things like 'The Sinking of the Titanic.' Bring out a record after it happened and tell a story with a moral. 'The Sinking of the Titanic' was a big seller, but there was a little bit of a moral that people shouldn't believe that they could build a ship that couldn't be sunk. That's the way they talked about it; of thinking God took it upon himself to show them that they couldn't build anything greater than He could. Everything had a moral in the event songs."

Henry Whitter recorded "Wreck of the Old 97" late in 1923.

Dalhart sang event songs about everything from the Scopes "monkey" trial to Lindbergh's flight across the Atlantic, from the death of cave explorer Floyd Collins to the sinking of the submarine S-5, and from the exploits of Tennessee badman Kinnie Wagner to the California murder of Little Marian Parker. Though these event songs were all of contemporary composition, they were part of a long and noble folk ballad tradition dating back to 17th-century England, when "broadsides" of recent events were sold in the streets. Oddly enough, some of the record companies sensed this connection and used it to add a certain dignity to their "hillbilly" event songs. A 1925 Victor catalogue supplement, describing Dalhart's "Death of Floyd Collins" disc, read:

"Popular songs of recent American tragedies. They belong with the old fashioned penny-ballad, hobo-song or 'come-all-ye.' The curious will note that they are even in the traditional 'ballad' metre, the 'common metre' of hymnodists. They are not productions of, or for, the cabaret or the vaudeville stage, but for the roundhouse, the watertank, the caboose, or the village fire-station. Both have splendid simple tunes in which the guitar accompanies the voice, the violin occasionally adding pathos. These songs are more than things for passing amusement; they are chronicles of the time, by unlettered and never self-conscious chroniclers."

Perhaps the "unlettered and never self-conscious chroniclers" were not all that folksy: Most of them had enough sense to copyright their event songs. There were some genuine folk composers in the lot—men like Peer's discovery, the Reverend Andrew Jenkins of Atlanta, a blind evangelist who wrote dozens of event songs, including "The Death of Floyd Collins," to order. Jenkins (or "Blind Andy," as he was billed on his own records) was able to synthesize older folk material with his own creative impulses to produce simple, moving songs that were often indistinguishable from American folk songs. Blind Andy was never much of a singer himself, but he found in Dalhart a superb interpreter of his work. This was yet another way in which Dalhart's music represented the ideal compromise between Southern authenticity and New

York professionalism.

In one sense, Jenkins was the first successful country songwriter, but he was soon emulated by other writers who copied his style and technique, especially with event songs. Kansas-born Carson J. Robison worked closely with Dalhart in producing songs like "My Blue Ridge Mountain Home," and Robison had a number of his own records become popular; Memphis-born Bob Miller was an early A&R (artists and repertoire) man for Columbia in the 1920's and wrote scores of popular songs, including "Eleven-Cent Cotton and Forty-Cent Meat" and "Twenty-One Years." Though both men became skilled Tin Pan Alley songwriters, both saw their early products popularized by country singers. The fact that all three of these men could make their living primarily by songwriting shows how quickly the music was becoming professionalized.

Both the Vocalion and Columbia record labels tried to capitalize on the 1920's interest in Southern music.

There were few singers as skilled as Dalhart in interpreting old-time songs, and though he recorded under dozens of pseudonyms, the companies soon realized they would have to find other ways to secure "authentic" material. The means for this came in 1925 when Western Electric engineers invented the new electrical recording process; this new "orthophonic" process yielded much sharper and louder sound reproduction and made it possible for a singer to be heard without bellowing his lungs out. More subtle singing and instrumental styles were possible, and for a music dominated by stringed instruments, like country music, the effect was considerable. Even more interesting, however, was the fact that the new electrical process meant that portable recording units were much more easily made, and once made, they got much better sound in the field. Rather than have Dalhart try to imitate country singers, or try to transport authentic

native singers to New York, it now became possible for the company to go to the singer and record him in his native South. By 1926, talent scouts were touring the South, driving across the dusty back roads in search of hill country talent. Temporary recording studios were set up in towns and cities across the South, and the race was on.

Columbia and Victor soon emerged as the two dominant companies in the era of field recordings, probably due to their superb technology. Columbia had as its chief talent scout a man named Frank Walker. Walker's role in the development of early country music is almost as important as Peer's; Walker pioneered recording techniques, invented ways to attract new talent and found new ways to merchandise his product. He remained active in the recording industry until his death in the 1960's; he even played a key role in the recording career of Hank Williams. In the 1920's it was Walker who was scouring the backwoods South looking for music. "I rode horses into the woods to find people who were individualistic in their singing and who could project the true country flavor," he recalled.

Walker, and the men who followed in his footsteps—men like Art Satherley, Dick Yoynow, W.R. Calloway, and Eli Oberstein—seldom went wandering aimlessly. They established a network of local contacts, usually men who were record dealers or radio station operators, and these people referred likely prospects to them. Then a field unit would set up for a week or two in a nearby city, and all the prospects from that area would be recorded. In an area especially rich in musicians, such as eastern Tennessee, advertisements for musicians to record were occasionally placed in local papers. Working in this way, record companies held field sessions at various

Southern cities, all the way from Ashland, Kentucky, to Richmond, Virginia, to Birmingham, Atlanta and Memphis, from 1926 to 1933. One of these field sessions was held in Nashville in 1928 by Victor, thus becoming the first recording session in Nashville. Though several Opry artists were recorded, the expedition in general was a failure; nearly half the sides were never even released.

A by-product of these early field sessions was the preservation of many rare folk songs and fiddle tunes, but few of the recording companies were conscious of this noble aspect of their work: They recorded the songs for one reason and one reason only—to sell records and to make money.

Walker made Atlanta his base of operations and began to visit the city twice a year. It wasn't long before his visits proved to him that one of the most popular and most authentic forms of old-time music was stringband music. When Fiddlin' John Carson played the fiddle, he played it solo. The classic stringband form, on the other hand, combined all modes of old-time music: fiddle, banjo, guitar and singing. A group called Henry Whitter's Virginia Breakdowners was probably the first stringband to record in the classic style, but the records were hardly successful. Far more successful was an offshoot of The Virginia Breakdowners, a four-piece band from North

Ralph Peer dubbed Al Hopkins' band "The Hill-Billies" after he recorded them in 1925. The term stuck and soon became a label for the music as well. Here's Charlie Bowman, Tony Alderman and Al Hopkins, rear, and Al's brother John, front right.

Ernest Stoneman around 1918.

and these early sides hardly captured the hard-driving excitement of a mountain stringband. But by 1926, when Walker and his crew descended on Atlanta, the recording technology could meet the challenge of this type of music.

Atlanta had been an important center for old-time music since 1913, when the Georgia Old Time Fiddlers' Association organized and began sponsoring an annual fiddling contest. These contests quickly grew in prestige. In 1915 the *Atlanta Journal* editorialized:

"In these russet festivals, the melodies of the Old South are awakened, and the spirit of folklore comes back to flesh and blood. The life of mountain and meadow, of world-forgotten hamlets, of cabin firesides aglow with hickory logs, the life of a thousand elemental things grows vivid and tuneful. From every part of the State come the fiddlers, graybeards and striplings, some accompanied by their faithful houn' dogs, others bearing a week's rations strapped to their shoulders, and all asweat with ambition to play their best and win the championship. Unique in all things, Atlanta has nothing more distinctive than this."

A few years later poet Stephen Vincent Benét would immortalize one of these contests in the poem, "The Mountain Whippoorwill." For many of the musicians in the area, these contests provided the first real forum for their music, the first hint that people would pay to hear such music, and the first vestiges of respectability for the music. Fiddlin' John Carson had acquired his reputation at such contests prior to his radio and record work. In fact, when WSB radio started in Atlanta in 1922, it found an established pool of old-time music talent it could draw on. The climate established by the annual fiddling contest (which, incidentally, also included banjo picking, singing, flat-foot dancing and stringband categories), and the willingness of WSB to program old-time music, created a ready-made opportunity for the recording industry.

Two of the more popular musicians in town were a fiddling chicken farmer named Gid Tanner and a blind guitarist-singer named Riley Puckett. Tanner and Puckett had long been fixtures at the annual fiddling contest; they had first

Carolina and Virginia led by Al Hopkins, which recorded for Ralph Peer in 1925. The band had no name, so Peer dubbed them "The Hill-Billies." The name stuck, both to the band and to the music, and the group was soon recording widely, touring and broadcasting over radio stations in Washington, D.C. The band was a highly commercial outfit, much given to gimmicks and vaudeville routines, yet it was home for a number of genuine folk musicians of considerable talent, including Civil War fiddler Uncle Am Stuart, early slide guitarist Frank Wilson, and mountain fiddler Charlie Bowman. The early stringband recordings, however, were marred somewhat by the limitations of the acoustic recording technique,

teamed up at the 1916 contest, when they brought down the house with a version of "It's a Long Way to Tipperary." Tanner was a big, red-faced man who was famous as a clown as well as a fiddler. "He could turn his head around like an owl," a friend recalled. (It is noteworthy that Tanner and Carson, as well as Uncle Dave Macon, perhaps the three most famous country performers of their day, were regarded by their contemporaries as musicians and comedians, with equal weighting to the two professions.) In 1924, just after Fiddlin' John Carson's first record became a hit, Tanner and Puckett had gone north to record some of their old-time and vaudeville tunes.

Walker noticed that these two performers were immensely popular with Atlanta audiences, and he knew that their early records had been moderately successful. He also noticed that another local act, a band led by an automobile mechanic turned fiddler, Clayton McMichen, was a big hit on WSB. McMichen had recorded for Ralph Peer in 1925, but without much success. Though McMichen was a superb fiddler who could play the traditional fiddle tunes with ease and style, he was more interested in modern, jazz-tinged music. In this he was at odds with rough, rustic Gid Tanner, but Walker put his idea across anyway: He would combine Puckett, Tanner and McMichen into a new sort of super stringband, an outfit that would bring together Tanner's comedy and authentic folk music, Puckett's singing skill and McMichen's fiddling virtuosity. One of the old groups that regularly played at the fiddling conventions during World War I had been called The Lickskillet Orchestra, and this name suggested the name for the new group: The Skillet

One lineup of The Skillet Lickers Band included Bill Helms, Riley Puckett and Gid Tanner. The roster changed frequently.

Gid Tanner in the 1930's.

Lickers. It was to become the most famous name in stringband history, and it was to sell more records than any other similar group of the time.

In a sense, The Skillet Lickers was a pick-up group, originally formed just for recording purposes. Its success marked one of the relatively few instances where the mass media of the day actually affected the performing style and repertory of older folk musicians; usually traditional performers were able to make the transition from pre-commercial to post-commercial music with minimum changes in their style.

The Skillet Lickers made their first recordings in early 1926, mostly of old traditional tunes like "Watermelon on the Vine," "Alabama Jubilee" and "Turkey in the Straw." Their biggest hit of that year, "Bully of the Town," backed with "Pass Around the Bottle and We'll All Take a Drink," ran up sales of over 200,000 copies. Soon the basic band (Tanner, McMichen, Puckett and banjoist Fate Norris) was augmented with other musicians who dropped in and out of sessions with a confusing casualness.

Polk Brockman's furniture store, home of Okeh Records.

Frank Walker encouraged the use of as many as three fiddles on many sessions, an important innovation which anticipated by some years the multi-fiddle harmonies later popularized by Western swing pioneer Bob Wills. Wills featured the harmonies on slower tunes, whereas The Skillet Lickers often had two fiddles playing fast breakdowns in near unison.

The Skillet Lickers' greatest success on records dawned when Walker came up with the idea of mixing rustic comedy with the music. He wrote, with help from the boys, a skit called "A Corn Licker Still in Georgia," a playlet about a group of Georgia moonshiners who also happened to be musicians; between running off a batch of "sugar licker" (white lightning flavored with

brown sugar) and getting in scrapes with the sheriff, the boys were always willing to "have a little tune." The original "Corn Licker Still" (1927) sold over 250,000 copies—an astounding figure for a regional audience—and inspired a series of sequels, which finally ended during the Depression with "A Corn Licker Still in Georgia—Part 14."

The free-wheeling, hard-drinking lifestyle of the northern Georgia musicians as portrayed on these skits was not too far from the private lives of The Skillet Lickers themselves; one of the band members had his fiddle hand shot off in a brawl in northern Georgia, and Atlanta bootleggers made regular stops at the Columbia studios down on Peachtree Street. A Skillet Lickers session was a party, and all kinds of bystanders got roped in; one old fiddler recalls recording on several Skillet Lickers sessions and "never getting anything but $25 and drunk." Other old-timers remember a bathtub of moonshine, complete with a well water dipper. The 1929 Columbia catalogue reflected this high humor of the band: "Here's a team indeed! It's a dance combination, and no high-stepping affair down their way draws the crowd like Gid and these pals of his, an all-star group."

The Skillet Lickers as a band made over 80 sides during the five years they stayed together, and individuals from the band made a good many more records under their own names; in fact, some of the members became regular studio musicians for Columbia's Atlanta studio. Yet the men of the band still made most of their money from personal appearances, not from records. Gid Tanner recalled those days: "Got to playing, making big hit records, and then we got on the road and made some money. Got tuxedo suits, y'know...they'd shine like silver. Said, 'We'll have to play a while for these, got to get up some money...."'" The Skillet Lickers did indeed make money for Columbia: They were responsible for making fiddle band music the dominant form of country music in the late 1920's, and for making Atlanta the Nashville of the 1920's. One of The Skillet Lickers' records, "Down Yonder," was still in print as late as the 1950's.

It was no wonder that Frank Walker bent over backward to keep the group together, but it was a hard job. The band was an unstable compound of brilliant, creative egos: Gid was too old-timey, McMichen was too pop-oriented, and Puckett was too experimental in his guitar runs. They bickered constantly and often toured separately, yet like the latter day Beatles, they were less impressive as individuals than as a band. By coincidence, the Depression intervened and knocked the bottom out of the record business just as they were ready to dissolve anyway. Gid went back to chicken farming, while McMichen and Puckett tried to make it as professionals in the new musical world of the 1930's.

If one discounts "citybilly" singers like Vernon Dalhart, Riley Puckett was the first genuine country singing star. Puckett, born in 1894 in Alpharetta, Georgia, was blinded shortly after birth, and as a teenager he was playing and singing for dance parties and on street corners. He began broadcasting over Atlanta's station WSB in 1922, and had soon established a national reputation. He made numerous records with just himself and his guitar, and many approached hit status; he and Vernon Dalhart dominated Columbia's early country music charts.

After he left The Skillet Lickers, he began to record for Victor, but, unlike Jimmie Rodgers, he was never really able to attract a national audience. He tried to expand his repertoire, adding more traditional items like "Ragged but Right" and "Chain Gang Blues," and even going to straight pop material like "When I Grow Too Old to Dream." But he never really broke out; perhaps he lacked proper management, perhaps he lacked the kind of original material Rodgers had. Whatever the problem was, he ended his career playing radio stations across the South, appearing at fiddling contests, and traveling with his own tent show. His 200-plus recorded songs remain as examples of fine, early, straightforward country (as opposed to folk) singing, and his guitar backup style, featuring single-note bass runs, is still admired by guitar pickers today.

Following the success of The Skillet Lickers, dozens of stringbands with bizarre, surrealistic names paraded through the recording studios. There were Bird's Kentucky Corn Crackers, Dr. Smith's Champion Hoss Hair Pullers, Wilmer Watts and The Lonely Eagles, The West Virginia Snake Hunters, Fisher Hendley and His Aristocratic Pigs, Gunboat Billy and The Sparrow, Seven Foot Dilly and His Dill Pickles, Joe Foss and His Hungry Sand-Lappers, Mumford Bean and His Itawambians (from Itawamba County, Mississippi), and Ephriam Woodie and His Henpecked Husbands. Many of them were family groups, and many were semi-professionals who played mainly for local dances. They would do a handful of recordings and then disappear back into the countryside; today researchers and fans of this vibrant and exciting stringband music are not even sure what part of the country some of the early recording artists came from. When such groups recorded at a field session, there was no discussion of royalties; they were usually paid a flat rate of $50 per record, and that was the end of it. If the record did well, the band might expect another session the next time the field crew was in the area, but that was all. The musicians would resume their full-time jobs as mill hands, railroad men, farmers, sign painters or whatever, unaware of where their records might have gone or whom they might have influenced.

A few country stringbands did, however, make it big on records. A group from Mississippi called The Leake County Revelers sold nearly 200,000 copies of their "Wednesday Night Waltz" and helped win elections for Huey Long. A rural Texas dance band called The East Texas Serenaders made a string of successful recordings for Columbia; they featured a fiddle, guitar, banjo—and a cello, played both bowed and plucked style—and their music helped pave the way for Western swing. There are numerous reports of early rural stringbands using the cello, though relatively few of them recorded with such combinations.

In the eastern mountains, The Carolina Tar

*Guitarist Riley Puckett in 1925
with his Model T touring car.*

Atlanta's Hometown Boys: This lineup includes Clayton McMichen, Robert "Punk" Stephens, Bob Stephens and Lowe Stokes.

Heels were popular; they used a harmonica instead of a fiddle, and featured the strong mountain singing of Clarence Tom Ashley and the whistling antics of a man who billed himself as "the human bird." (Ashley was later rediscovered and made a mainstay of the folk revival of the 1960's.) Charlie Poole, a very influential singer whose career was cut short, and Kelly Harrell both pioneered the techniques of singing to stringband accompaniment, and functioned as transitional figures between the stringband style and the emergence of vocal stars in the early 1930's.

The main catalyst in this transition, however, was to be Ralph Peer, and the major event was to be his trip to Bristol in the summer of 1927. That trip has been called the starting point for modern commercial music, but Peer was hardly aware of that during his first week in Bristol. In one sense, he was trying to prove himself. After pioneering the recording of old-time music and the use of field recording sessions to collect authentic material, Peer had seen his ideas grow into the "hillbilly" boom of the late 1920's, but in 1926 he quit his job with Okeh and for a time decided to get out of the record business; he had an idea that he could get rich mass-producing apple pies in bakeries. It was an idea whose time had not quite come, and he eventually went to work for Victor. Victor was certainly one of the leading companies of the time, but, partly because of their prestigious "Red Seal" image, they had not really gone after the "hillbilly" market.

After a while, though, they could no longer resist the sales potential of this market, and so they hired Peer to go out into the hills after talent for them. They gave him $60,000, two engineers, and a portable recording setup, and told him to head South.

Peer, for his part, wanted certain conditions. While working for Okeh (General Phonograph Corporation), Peer had sensed that the day would come when copyrighting these old-time Southern songs would prove valuable. In 1925-26 he had seen a complex series of copyright lawsuits follow in the wake of the success of "The Wreck of the Old 97," and even earlier had suggested that the Okeh Company take over copyrights to the songs of their exclusive artists. So when he was negotiating with Victor, he brought this matter up. As he recalled later in life, "I sat down and wrote a three-paragraph letter and said that I had considered the matter very carefully and that essentially this was a business of recording new copyrights and I would be willing to go to work for them for nothing with the understanding that there would be no objection if I controlled these copyrights."

Not thinking there was much of a future in "hillbilly" copyrights, Victor had no objections, and in July 1927, shortly before he left for his field trip, Peer organized the United Publishing Company. Later it became The Southern Publishing Company, and Peer recalls once looking at a three-month royalty check for a quarter of a million dollars.

Peer couldn't expect to make much money from actual sheet music publication of the songs he recorded, but as publisher of the songs, he stood to make a good deal off record sales. (He later admitted that he made as much as 75 per cent of the royalties from record sales.) Thus it was to his advantage to find material in the field that was either original or traditional enough not to be in copyright, so that he could act as publisher

for the songs. This had both good and bad effects. From a folklorist's point of view, it was good because it forced Peer to hunt out authentic folk performers of traditional material and to urge his musicians to emphasize original or traditional songs instead of pop material. (In this way, for instance, Peer recorded the first version of "Tom Dooley," in 1929, by blind Tennessee fiddler G.B. Grayson and singer Henry Whitter.) On the other hand, the method caused him to reject some fine musicians who didn't have original material. "That was the test," he recalled, and if artists didn't have original material, he threw them out. Later Peer became convinced that no country artist could really succeed unless he had original material, either written by himself or secured by his manager. He would also sign many of his field discoveries to personal management contracts if he thought they had potential.

He was testing these new methods of his for the first time in Bristol, and as he started his second week in the town, he found dozens of people eager to sign up and record. One of these new groups was a vocal trio from nearby Maces Springs, Virginia, consisting of farmer-carpenter-fruit tree salesman A.P. Carter; his wife Sara, and his sister-in-law, Maybelle Carter. Sara and A.P. Carter had been singing together for informal mountain gatherings for over ten years, and for the last year they had been joined by Maybelle. Sara played the autoharp (a zither-like instrument fitted with a series of chording dampers, well known in the rural South) and usually sang lead, while Maybelle played guitar and sang harmony. A.P. seldom played an instrument and confined his singing to, in his own words, "basin' in" every once in a while. A.P.'s father had been a mountain banjo player who had gotten religion and turned to old ballads and religious songs for his music; A.P.'s mother sang a number of old ballads like "The Wife of Usher's Well," "Sailor Boy" and "Brown Girl," and A.P.

*The Carter Family:
Maybelle, A.P. and Sara.*

learned to appreciate them. The fondness for old ballads and religious songs was to mark The Carter Family repertoire throughout their career.

After reading the newspaper story about Peer's recording session, A.P. got his crew together, loaded them in his old Ford, and headed for Bristol. Peer was somewhat disarmed by the group that appeared at his recording studio: There were A.P. and Sara, their three children, and Maybelle, who was expecting a child in a couple of months. Peer recalled: "They wander in—they're a little ahead of time and they come about 25 miles and they've come through a lot of mud...and he's dressed in overalls and the women are country women from way back there—calico clothes on—the children are very poorly dressed."

Mrs. Peer took two of the children outside to feed them ice cream and keep them quiet, while The Carters began singing "Bury Me Under the Weeping Willow," "Little Old Log Cabin by the Sea," "Storms Are on the Ocean," "Single Girl, Married Girl." "As soon as I heard Sara's voice...that was it, you see," recalled Peer. "I began to build around it.... I knew that was going to be wonderful. And they had plenty of repertoire.... A.P. had been apparently quite a traveler—he'd gone around quite a bit—collecting songs." The Carters made six sides at this first session, with Sara singing lead on five of them.

When the first Carter Family record came out, A.P. Carter didn't even have a record player. He heard their first record on a floor-model Victrola at a store in Bristol; he didn't even know the record had been released. The local Victor dealer reported that he had sold 200 copies of the disc in a few days and that Ralph Peer had reported that the release was doing well all over the South, having sold over 2,000 copies within a month in Atlanta alone. The Carters soon got their first royalty check, which A.P. dutifully split up three ways; it was probably only a quarter of a per-

cent of retail sales income, but it was enough to keep the family interested in making records.

Seven months later Peer called the group to Camden, New Jersey, for their second session: 12 sides that were to include the family's most enduring songs. Recorded here were "Keep on the Sunny Side," an old 1906 pop song that became the group's theme song; "Anchored in Love," an old gospel hymn that became a Carter Family standard; "Little Darling Pal of Mine," later to become a folk-bluegrass warhorse; and "Wildwood Flower," an old pop song that The Carter Family had learned orally.

With the latter record, it became obvious that the family had another valuable asset in Maybelle's guitar style; she liked to pick the melody with her thumb and kept the rhythm with her fingers. Her rhythm style and use of melodic lines, which served to sketch the tune in a deceptively simple outline, influenced generations of Southern guitar players, all the way from blues singer Leadbelly to folk singer Woody Guthrie. "Wildwood Flower" became the test of accomplishment for all kinds of amateur guitar players. Maybelle's picking style, along with The Carters' full, low-pitched, mountain church harmonies and their easy, flowing tempo, made them unique among early country artists. They were the first successful country group vocal act; before them group singing had been pretty much a function of church or gospel music, and secular country music had been the province of solo singers or stringbands. The Carters combined these two worlds in a beautiful and striking way.

But The Carters, in spite of their influence via records, would not become real professionals for a number of years. For instance, in 1929 A.P. had to leave Virginia to go to Detroit to find work as a carpenter—and this was during the height of the group's Victor recording career. In fact, the need to keep regular non-musical jobs of-

Jimmie Rodgers and Maybelle, A.P. and Sara Carter in Louisville in 1931. Rodgers became nationally known early on.

ten kept the members of the family apart during the Depression years. Peer was publishing their songs on a 50-50 basis, and they were receiving Victor royalties, but this was not enough to allow them to make ends meet.

Peer was acting as unofficial manager for the band but felt that their appeal wasn't broad enough to get them booked into the big theater and vaudeville circuits, where the big money was. So while his other big country act, Jimmie Rodgers, was touring these circuits to the tune of $600 a week, A.P. Carter was nailing Carter Family posters to trees in backwater mountain communities: "Admission 15 and 25 cents. The Program is Morally Good." Most of The Carter Family "personals" were the result of their own advertising and A.P.'s informal promotion; letters would come from people asking about concerts, and A.P. would casually arrange them—no formal booking, no contracts, no agents. They appeared throughout the mid-South, and as far

north as Maryland and Indiana. The personnel of the concert shows would depend on which members of the family happened to be in the area, and this in turn depended on their full-time jobs and private lives.

Carter Family researcher Ed Kahn has sketched what a typical stage show in these days was like. Often The Carters would arrive at the hall or schoolhouse early, mingle with the crowds until show time, and sell tickets themselves. Shows would run from 7:30 to 9:00 or 9:30, and were usually opened by a little jingle that began, "How do you do, everybody? How do you do?" A.P. would act as emcee for the show, introducing the members of the group, and perhaps telling stories about the songs—where they learned them, when they recorded them. The family never sold records from the stage, though they did sell little songbooks. Sara and Maybelle usually sat, while A.P. wandered around the stage; he was by nature very nervous, and this often gave his singing voice its distinctive quality. The group often took requests from the audience; if a request meant re-tuning the instruments, the audience waited; there was no comedy to cover it up. After the show, The Carters often stayed with a family in the neighborhood, and often they took these occasions to gather new material. A.P. was always interested in seeing old song books, handwritten ballets (the old "ballet" cards) or old sheet music. Once the group was recording regularly, A.P. made regular song-hunting trips back into the hills, sometimes traveling with Leslie Riddles, a black guitar player, a friend of the family; while A.P. would copy the words of songs, Leslie acted as a sort of human tape recorder, remembering the melody line.

The Carter Family continued to record until the eve of World War II, spreading some 270 sides over the labels of every major American record company. Their records were popular not only in America; they were released in Australia, Canada, England, India, Ireland and South Africa as well. Yet The Carters never really enriched themselves as much as they enriched the record companies, the publishing companies, and the radio stations. By the late 1930's, they were at least able to play full time professionally, and were broadcasting nationally over Mexican border station XERA. Beset by personality differences (Sara and A.P. had separated in the early 1930's) and changing musical tastes, the act broke up for good in 1943.

Various members of The Carter Family continued to make a mark in later country music. Mother Maybelle continued to perform with her daughters up until the 1960's, and A.P. Carter performed with his children until his death in 1960. June Carter, one of Maybelle's three daughters, became a regular on the Grand Ole Opry and, after a marriage of a few years' duration to singer Carl

Smith, eventually married Johnny Cash. She and her sisters, Helen and Anita, continued to perform together after the death of Mother Maybelle in 1978, sometimes adding June and Carl Smith's daughter, Carlene Carter (a popular recording artist in her own right) into the act.

The Carter music has become a hallowed canon in both country and folk music. It was The Carters who arranged and popularized "Wabash Cannonball" in 1929, not dreaming that the song would become an anthem for Roy Acuff. "Worried Man Blues" ("It takes a worried man/ To sing a worried song") and "Engine 143," old folk songs codified by The Carters, enriched the repertoires of city-bred coffeehouse folk singers of the 1960's. "I Am Thinking Tonight of My Blue Eyes," "Foggy Mountain Top," "East Virginia Blues" and "Jimmie Brown the Newsboy," all performed by The Carters, became the bluegrass standards of Mac Wiseman, Flatt and Scruggs, and others. "Will the Circle Be Unbroken" and "Gospel Ship" became gospel standards, and the former gained new symbolic significance as the title of the 1971 album by The Nitty Gritty Dirt Band. Not all Carter songs were original compositions—many were re-composed or rearranged

Maybelle and husband Ezra Carter's Clinch Mountain home in the early 1940's.

Jimmie Rodgers, Anita and Ralph Peer, Carrie Rodgers and Rodgers' daughter
Carrie Anita in 1931. Dad corresponded with daughter Anita.

versions of older songs that Peer quickly stamped with a copyright—but no other early country music group preserved so many genuine folk items and injected them into commercial channels.

Peer, of course, could foresee little of this during that hot afternoon in Bristol. After The Carters left, he continued to audition other acts: a gospel group, a family stringband, a husband-and-wife vocal team. But then, on August 4th, another singer with commercial potential showed up. His name was Jimmie Rodgers, and he had phoned Peer the week before from Asheville to say that he thought he had the kind of music Peer wanted, and asked for an audition. Peer granted it.

Rodgers arrived in Bristol the night before the session with a stringband in tow, The Jimmie Rodgers Entertainers. They planned to audition together, but Rodgers and the band got into an argument over how they would bill themselves, and Rodgers went over to audition for himself. It was

an historic audition, but few realized it at the time.

For Rodgers, it was another chance in his continuing scramble to make it as a professional entertainer. The annals of early country music are full of men who turned to music because of handicaps that prevented them from doing a "normal day's work"—many were blind, and a few (like DeFord Bailey, the first black star of the Grand Ole Opry) were physically handicapped. In these early days, there was little that was attractive about the life of a professional musician, and many turned to it only as a last resort. Jimmie Rodgers was probably one of these, at least at first. He was often in poor health, and by the time he was in his mid-20's, he had contracted tuberculosis. Before then he had spent half his life working on railroads as a callboy, baggagemaster, flagman and brakeman. This was nothing out of the ordinary, since he was the son of a section hand and since the time and place of his birth—1897 in Meridian, Mississippi—gave him few other opportunities for a living.

Rodgers often carried a little banjo with him in his railroading days, and when he got sick in 1924, it was natural that he should join a medicine show and sing songs in blackface to rural audiences in Tennessee and Kentucky. He went through a series of such jobs, trying to make enough to support his family; for a time he even played in a dance band with his sister Elsie McWilliams, later to become co-author of many of his famous songs. Eventually he landed in Asheville, North Carolina, right in the middle of the southern Appalachians, and decided to form his own band. He told his wife that he wanted to get "boys who'll be willing to work whatever date I can get—schoolhouse, barn dance, roadhouse, beer joint, anything.... Folks everywhere are gettin' tired of all this Black Bottom—Charleston—jazz music junk. They tell me the radio stations keep gettin' more and more calls for old-fashioned songs: 'Yearning,' 'Forgotten,'

things like that, and even the old plantation melodies. Well, I'm ready with 'em." The band landed one job on Asheville radio, and it lasted barely a month; they were back to playing the sticks when they read the account of Peer's recording in Bristol.

When Peer first auditioned Rodgers, Peer had mixed feelings. He described them later for *Billboard*:

"...I was elated when I heard him perform. It seemed to me that he had his own personal and peculiar style, and I thought that his yodel alone might spell success. Very definitely he was worth a trial. We ran into a snag almost immediately because, in order to earn a living in Asheville, he was singing mostly songs originated by New York publishers—the current hits. Actually, he had only one song of his own—'Soldier's Sweetheart'—written several years before.... In spite of his lack of repertoire, I considered Rodgers to be one of my best bets. Accordingly, I asked

Rodgers was quite successful on the vaudeville circuit and had amassed considerable wealth by mid-career.

The Atlanta Biltmore Hotel, home to radio station WSB. The station was started by The Atlanta Journal.

him to sign a managerial contract, explained to him the necessity to find new material, and talked to him about his future plans."

Rodgers' first record was "The Soldier's Sweetheart," his rewrite of an older folk song, and a yodeling song, "Sleep, Baby, Sleep." Peer felt the choice was an accurate sample of Rodgers' skills. Rodgers wanted to record a song he had done on the radio with a lot of success, "T for Texas, T for Tennessee," but Peer felt he had enough for the time being. He paid Rodgers a token sum, and they parted.

Peer spent one more day recording in Bristol and then packed up his gear and headed for his next stop, Charlotte, North Carolina. In his two weeks in Bristol he had recorded over 70 tunes by 20 different groups; only a few of these groups would ever record again. Rodgers, for his part, moved his family to Washington, D.C., to play local

clubs and theaters and await word from Peer.

Rodgers' first record sold well enough (though not as well as The Carters'); it brought in a modest royalty check of $27—but no call from Peer. Rodgers finally took it upon himself to go up to New York to ask for another session; Peer let him record four more numbers in the New Jersey studio, one of which was "Blue Yodel," more commonly called "T for Texas." This song was an instant hit, and within a month after its release Peer was hustling Rodgers back into the studios to record legendary songs like "In the Jailhouse Now," "Treasures Untold" and "Brakeman Blues." Within six months Rodgers' royalties jumped to over $2,000 a month. Peer took over as his manager, encouraged him to come up with more and more original material, and used it to establish his own Southern Music Publishing Company as a viable firm.

It is still unclear exactly what made Rodgers so immensely popular so fast. It might have been his singing style, it might have been his repertoire, or it might have been something nobody today can really understand. Rodgers was by no means the first successful country singer (as opposed to instrumentalist or stringband); both Vernon Dalhart and Riley Puckett had preceded him by several years. Rodgers' stylistic innovation was to combine the imagery and stanza pattern of black country blues with the white tradition of yodeling. Rodgers' high falsetto wordless passages may have had more roots in old-time mountain "hollerin'" than in formal yodeling, but whatever the case there had been nothing like them in country music— or in pop music, for that matter. Unlike The Carters, Rodgers had few genuine folk songs in his repertoire; however, many of his "Blue Yodels" (there were eventually to be 13 of them) contained stanzas borrowed from earlier blues singers.

Some argue, in fact, that much of Rodgers' success lay in his ability to popularize and "whiten" traditional black music, to make the ever-popular blues acceptable to a white audience. Carrie Rodgers, in her biography of her husband, describes how Rodgers as a boy would carry water to black section hands in Mississippi: "During the noon dinner-rests, they taught him to plunk melody from banjo and guitar. They taught him darkey songs; moaning chants and crooning lullabies.... Perhaps that is where he learned that peculiar caressing slurring of such simple words as 'snow'—'go.'..." In any case, songs like "In the Jailhouse Now" (recorded by blues singer Blind Blake before Rodgers recorded his version) gave Rodgers a black element in his repertoire. He recorded with a number of black sidemen, including, on one auspicious occasion, jazz great Louis Armstrong.

The gulf that separates modern country music from black music was not all that great in the 1920's, when white and black singers often shared stanzas and tunes. Rodgers simply took advantage of this musical commonality.

Rodgers was undoubtedly the first country singing star to attract a national, as opposed to a regional, audience. He was also the first country singer to get rich from his music, and the techniques Peer used to build his success became lessons for later country singers striving for professional status. Peer coordinated incomes from record sales, publishing royalties and personal appearances, and made Rodgers enough money so that in 1929, not quite two years after the first Bristol session, the singer could build his $50,000 "Blue Yodeler's Paradise" in his adopted hometown of Kerrville, Texas.

Peer did all this not by emphasizing Rodgers' country origins, as had Walker with The Skillet Lickers, but by minimizing them. Rodgers was always billed as "America's Blue Yodeler" and nothing more—nothing about old-time singing or hill country roots. His publicity pictures showed him in a railroad brakeman's outfit, or in a white suit with a broad-brimmed straw hat, or with a suit and a white Stetson hat, or even with a jaunty little beret and tie—but never in anything resembling hillbilly garb. Rodgers was able to get bookings on theater circuits and on tours that other country performers couldn't get, and his typical stage show was a Dutch mixture of different sorts of entertainment. In a 1929 stage show in Chattanooga, for instance, Rodgers used Clayton McMichen, the virtuoso fiddler who was trying to break out of his Skillet Lickers mold; Texas Tom, a blackface comedian; Billy Burke, of Fort Worth, "The Crooning Guitarist of WBAP"; Howard Campbell, a magician; and a backup

Atlanta Journal coverage of its WSB fiddlers.

band that included a clarinet player and a bass violinist. Such an assortment could indeed appeal to a Southern audience—his Chattanooga concert filled the Municipal Auditorium and caused a mammoth traffic jam—but it could also appeal to a Western or a Midwestern audience.

Rodgers' wide appeal can also be measured by the fact that in 1929 he made a short ten-minute film called *The Singing Brakeman* and that the next year he did a screen test for a possible film with comedian Will Rogers. (Later, he also did a series of concerts with Will Rogers for the benefit of victims of the Dust Bowl in 1931.)

In his recordings, Rodgers soon abandoned his simple guitar accompaniment for backup units of various studio musicians: jazz bands, dance bands, Hawaiian music, trumpets, clarinets, jug bands, and even, on one occasion, a musical saw. These may be seen as concessions to commercialism, as Rodgers selling out his country roots, but they helped him attract the kind of "crossover" audience he needed at the time. People who say that modern country music started with Jimmie Rodgers often stress his folk music background; it would, however, be more accurate to stress his (or Peer's) ability to package and merchandise the music.

Many of Rodgers' finest songs were co-authored by his sister-in-law, Elsie McWilliams, in 1928 and 1929; these included many of his sentimental favorites like "My Old Pal," "Daddy and Home," "The Sailor's Plea," "I'm Lonely and Blue" and "Mississippi Moon." Many of them were in the sentimental tradition of the 19th century, but others departed drastically from this genteel tradition.

WLS program director George Biggar with his family in 1933.

Such were the famous blues-based songs, like "T for Texas," "Blue Yodel Number Four (California Blues)," "Blue Yodel Number Eight (Muleskinner Blues)" and "Blue Yodel Number Nine (Standin' on the Corner)," and the "rough and rowdy" songs like "Pistol Packin' Papa," "Waiting for a Train" and "In the Jailhouse Now." The persona—the speaker—of the heart songs of the 1890's was a prim, gushy, sentimental gentleman; the persona of these Jimmie Rodgers songs was a tough, gritty, realistic and self-mocking working man. That was, in short, the speaker we still recognize in modern country song. This is one of the reasons why Rodgers' songs have endured in the country repertoire more than those of any of his contemporaries.

Jimmie Rodgers died on May 26, 1933, not even two days after his last recording session; he was 35, and his career had spanned only six years. How commercially successful was that career? Rodgers became such a legend so soon that it's difficult to get an accurate, meaningful picture. Sales of his records have been wildly exaggerated; by no means did he have a string of million sellers. The most recent evidence suggests that Rodgers, during his career, had only one genuine million-seller, the coupling of "Blue Yodel Number One" ("T for Texas") with "Away Out on the Mountain." Only four of his releases reportedly sold more than 250,000 copies during his career, and his total sales on the Victor label (78 rpm only) were probably between three and four million; his last release, in the depths of the Depression in 1933, sold barely a thousand copies. Of course, in the 1920's a record sale of 100,000 was a giant hit, and Rodgers' records continued to remain in print throughout the years; sales today might well total over 20,000,000 copies.

His influence was far greater than his sales would indicate. Singers like Gene Autry, Bill Cox, Cliff Carlisle, Daddy John Love, Ernest Tubb and Hank Snow began by imitating Rodgers; probably three-fourths of the country singers starting in the 1930's were in some way influenced by him. Rodgers himself became a culture hero, and a half dozen good songs (and a dozen bad ones) were written about his life and untimely death. The restless, rambling, driven, sentimental, family-loving Horatio Alger figure who dies before his time has become the archetypal country singer hero; Rodgers' tragic fate has been re-enacted by later singers with almost ritualistic compulsion.

The tragedy of Jimmie Rodgers was not meaningless, for his music formed a new popular mass art form that became an integral part of the lives of millions of Americans suffering through the trauma of the Great Depression. He refined the music of these people, but more importantly, he devised ways to effectively communicate it in a world of mass media where the old channels of person-to-person folk transmission were being disrupted and the old values displaced. He made Ralph Peer and his publishing empire rich, to be sure, but he also made countless other people rich in another way. Roy Horton, later to be a key execu-

tive at Peer-Southern, was raised in the 1930's in a grim mining town in the Alleghenies, and he recalled an anecdote that illustrates this richness: "I recall that many times we went to the 'company store' to buy a loaf of bread, a pound of butter, and the latest Jimmie Rodgers record—he was that much a part of so many people's lives."

The development of the country recording industry was the first real step toward the commercialization of the music. Many old-time musicians first thought of going professional—making money with their music, developing their music from a part-time hobby to a full-time vocation—when they had successful records. This pay, as we have seen, was meager enough—a $50 lump sum, or, for the lucky ones, royalties amounting to a fifteenth of a cent per record on a release that retailed for 75 cents—but the business worked, and the companies never went lacking for singers and pickers to record.

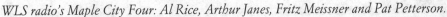

WLS radio's Maple City Four: Al Rice, Arthur Janes, Fritz Meissner and Pat Petterson.

WSM first broadcast country music when George D. Hay and Uncle Jimmy Thompson went on the air on November 28, 1925.

In the 1920's the business was dominated by seven major companies, three of them located in Chicago. By 1926 Sears, Roebuck was selling country records, leasing masters from other companies, and issuing them on their own label; Montgomery Ward soon got into the business, too, and a number of Southern department store chains followed suit. Thus while a wide variety of labels seemed to exist, many of the actual masters were drawn from common company archives. Furthermore, as Rodgers' case shows, record sales in the 1920's were often not commensurate with the musical influence of the records. The average old-time release in the 1920's sold around 5,000 to 10,000 copies, and during the Depression 1,000 copies was a good sale. Frank Walker's important Columbia 15000 series, so much prized today by historians and folklor-

ists, averaged sales of 15,000 to 20,000 copies per release in the pre-Depression years. In many years, just four or five big hit records would account for a third or even half of a company's total old-time music sales. The total number of old-time titles issued by the seven major companies prior to 1930 was about 3,700. Yet it is unsettling to note how comparatively few recordings the major artists of this time made as compared to modern artists. Jimmie Rodgers' 110 recorded songs are equivalent to only nine modern albums—and a modern singer like George Jones, who in the mid-1990's was still going strong, could claim at least 100 albums and over 1,000 songs to his credit.

Early country records also had to get distributed without the most utilized tool of modern promotion, radio airplay. Ninety-five percent of early Southern radio was "live." Some record companies did start sponsoring shows to plug their latest records, but few of the companies felt that old-time music records were important enough to plug in this way.

There remains the matter of the authenticity of these early pioneer recordings: How accurately do they represent the voice of the people, and the music of the people? Some of the records were genuine folk music; some were mass-produced pop product. Only about five percent of the pre-Depression old-time releases by major companies were old folk ballads in the strictest sense, but many older pop songs had gone into oral tradition and had been recorded by people who had little knowledge of the song's original publication and author. Many of the field recordings by men like Walker are probably fairly authentic reflections of rural folk culture, but there were many instances of the companies interfering with the musicians' repertoires, telling them to use some songs and forbidding them to use others (the Columbia field office in Atlanta had a well-stocked library of popular sheet music even during the heyday of The Skillet Lickers in the late 1920's). The first generation of country music recordings were not quite the simple, natural, folksy artifacts they are sometimes made out to be, but they were still a long way from the slick, rootless products of Tin Pan Alley.

If records were the music's prime medium in the 1920's, radio was to be the prime medium of the 1930's. Throughout the first decade of the music's development, radio was developing along with it. It is harder to understand the exact impact radio made on the country music fan of the 1920's, however, because none of the actual radio shows were preserved. They were all done live, of course, and there was no way to preserve them. We can go back today and actually listen to the first big country hits of Fiddlin' John Carson, but there is no way we can ever hear the actual sound of the early Grand Ole Opry or the *National Barn Dance*. We can only rely on the memories of those who were there and measure the effect the shows had.

That effect was considerable. Unlike the recording industry, which flourished for over 20

years before it discovered old-time music, the radio industry was interested in the music almost from the start. It is generally acknowledged that commercial radio began officially in 1920 when station KDKA in Pittsburgh broadcast the Harding-Cox election results to an audience of some 2,000. Sixteen months later, in March 1922, old-time music was on the air, courtesy of Atlanta station WSB, the South's first commercial broadcasting station. WSB had begun as a public-service station owned and operated (as were many early stations) by the local newspaper; finally the paper hired a station director, Lambdin Kay. Kay brought all kinds of rural talent into his broadcasting studios, including Fiddlin' John Carson, The Jenkins Family and a group of Sacred Harp singers. He later explained his rationale by arguing that "hillbilly or country music talent appeared on the station, since this was a folk music of the region and was both popular and was available at little or no cost."

Most of the early artists were paid absolutely nothing for broadcasting, though they were allowed to announce where they were appearing, what fiddling contest they were a part of, or whatever. This sort of trade-off continued on many rural stations well into the time of World War II. Early radio hardly encouraged country musicians to think they could make a living with their music, and it's noteworthy that the two biggest names of the time—The Carter Family and Jimmie Rodgers—seldom appeared on radio in the 1920's.

Radio grew with breathtaking speed. By the end of 1922, there were some 510 active stations broadcasting, and 89 of these were in the South. Some were tiny local stations with a radius of a few miles and a power of 10-20 watts; others were powerhouses like the 500-watt WSB, which easily commanded a nationwide audience. The formats of many smaller stations were extremely flexible, and anyone who wandered in with an instrument could probably get on the air.

Small-town newspapers seldom printed detailed broadcasting schedules, so today there is no way to determine the exact extent of local country programming, but researchers have determined that one of the first country "barn dance" type programs originated at WBAP, Fort Worth, in January 1923. The barn dance format was to become one of the most common in country music broadcasting. It was usually an anthology program that featured a sort of repertory company of different types of musicians; it was informal and unstructured, and the company of musicians was presented as one big happy family. Audience feedback was important, and requests were often answered on the air. All sorts of old-time music was presented, from barbershop quartets to Hawaiian bands to comedians to singers of sentimental songs, but the key image of the barn dance show was the fiddle band, and the fiddle band music was often accompanied with square dance calls so that those listening at home could dance along. (Nobody knows if anyone ever really danced to the music of these shows.) It was a warm, folksy format, and it served to personalize the new-fangled piece of technology, the radio, and to offer rural Americans an oasis of normalcy in a desert of strange accents and stodgy announcers. The widespread popularity of Fort Worth's informal and irregular old-time show—it was heard as far away as New York, Canada and Hawaii—attracted the attention of other program directors, who began to realize that there was a vast rural audience that was being ignored by the constant programming of semi-classical music, dance bands and noodling piano players. During the early 1920's most Americans were living in towns of 8,000 or less population.

The two major barn dance programs were soon born: the *National Barn Dance* of WLS, Chicago, and the Grand Ole Opry of WSM, Nashville. The *National Barn Dance* began in 1924 and was broadcast regularly until 1960; the Opry began in late 1925 and is still heard weekly in the 1990's. The shows had a good deal in common: Both were started by companies that wanted to sell products to rural America, and both saw the music, first valued as a marketing tool, turn into a product in its own right. The Opry tended to be a shade more authentic, a little bit funkier, perhaps because it drew from the vast pool of native Southern talent in and around Nashville. There were few mountains around Chicago, though there

were many Southerners attracted north by factory work, and a supply of vaudeville performers skilled at appealing to rural tastes.

WLS (the initials stood for "World's Largest Store," in deference to the station's owners, Sears, Roebuck & Company) began the *National Barn Dance* on April 19, 1924, just a week after the station went on the air. They announced it as a program "planned to remind you folks of the good fun and fellowship of the barn warmings, the husking bees and the square dances in our farm communities of yesteryear and even today."

The fiddle band of Tommy Dandurand (banjo, fiddle, guitar—and drums!) helped spark early shows. George C. Biggar, the director of the show, recalled other early successful acts: "When Chubby Parker picked his little old banjo and sang 'I'm a Stern Old Bachelor,' he struck responsive chords in countless hearts." Also identified with earlier days of the *National Barn Dance* were Walter Peterson and his "Double-Barreled Shotgun" (Peterson played guitar, sang and played harmonica on a neck rack); Cecil and Esther Ward; the good old Maple City Four; and Bradley Kincaid, the "Kentucky Mountain Boy." Through his performances, Kincaid popularized dozens of unpublished mountain ballads.

Nearly all the early *National Barn Dance* stars established their reputations solely by radio; few recorded very much, and what they did record was on Sears' own label and was sold because of their radio popularity (many of these record labels identified the performer as a WLS star). Bradley Kincaid, a rather self-conscious singer and collector of folk songs, reached a vast audience through his radio broadcasts and through his sale of songbooks over the air; his case proves that the history of country music is by no means the history of country music records.

The leading announcer for the *National Barn Dance* during its first year was former Memphis newspaper writer George D. Hay, who billed himself as "The Solemn Old Judge" and started each show off with an imitation steamboat whistle. Hay was an Indiana native who had gotten into radio when the newspaper he worked on in Memphis started station WMC. Hay found himself appointed radio editor, which meant that

*DeFord Bailey holding a photo of
the Pan American Express train.*

Dr. Humphrey Bate and His Possum Hunters: Bate, Oscar Stone, Walter Ligget, Staley Walton, Paris Pond and Oscar Albright.

he was also announcer on the station. WLS hired him away from WMC in 1924, and later that year he won the *Radio Digest* award as the country's most popular announcer. Hay was not at this time associated especially with the *Barn Dance*: He was the leading announcer for all types of shows on WLS, so when the National Life and Accident Insurance Company of Nashville decided, in 1925, to build the fanciest radio station in the South, they went after the best talent. They asked Hay to come back to the South and become station director for WSM, "The Air Castle of the South."

Hay arrived in Nashville in November 1925 and began to cast about for ways to improve the anemic fare then being offered to the good citizens of Nashville: story ladies, brass bands, women's-club culture. He noted that some old-

time musicians, including a lively stringband led by a local physician named Dr. Humphrey Bate, had already appeared informally on Nashville radio and had drawn a surprising audience response. He decided to experiment further, and on November 28, 1925, he invited a 77-year-old fiddler, the uncle of a staff musician, to play the fiddle on the air. The fiddler, a Tennessee native named Uncle Jimmy Thompson, had a repertoire that stretched back to the Civil War, and he was anxious, in his own words, "to throw my music out across Amerikey."

Later, Hay himself described Thompson's first appearance:

"Uncle Jimmy told us he had a thousand tunes...he was given a comfortable chair in front of an old carbon microphone. While his niece,

Mrs. Eva Thompson Jones, played the piano accompaniment, your reporter presented Uncle Jimmy and announced that he would be glad to answer requests for old-time tunes. Immediately telegrams started to pour into WSM. One hour later at nine o'clock we asked Uncle Jimmy if he hadn't done enough fiddling to which he replied, 'Why shucks a man don't get warmed up in an hour. I just won an eight-day fiddling contest down in Dallas, Texas, and here's my blue ribbon to prove it.'"

Other WSM executives were astounded at the response to Uncle Jimmy, but Hay was not really surprised; he had seen the same thing in Chicago when the *National Barn Dance* had begun to broadcast old-time music. Hay began to make plans; he told a friend that he planned to start a new show, "something like the *National Barn Dance* in Chicago, and expected to do better because the people were real and genuine and the people really were playing what they were raised on." Thus on December 26, 1925, about a month after Uncle Jimmy first appeared on the air, the Nashville *Tennessean* announced: "Because of this recent revival in the popularity of old familiar tunes, WSM has arranged to have an hour or two every Saturday night...." Thus a regularly scheduled barn dance show was born, and within a few months Hay had assembled about 25 regular acts for the show.

The people of Nashville were not too happy at the idea of having a hillbilly show originating from their city, which they liked to call "the Athens of the South." Some protested, but National Life was reaching a vast rural audience beyond the city of Nashville itself, and it was an audience to which they wanted to sell insurance. The show grew; soon it was running to over three hours on Saturday nights. WSM increased its power until it had the strongest clear-channel signal in the South, and soon, letters about the Saturday night *Barn Dance* were coming in from all over.

The NBC radio network was formed in 1927, and WSM signed on as an affiliate. Most nights the station carried slick, well-produced network shows originating out of New York, but on Saturday night, WSM refused the network fare and

stuck to the Opry—except for one 15-minute segment when the Opry was interrupted by *Amos 'n' Andy*. By this time other Nashville stations were trying to copy the WSM success by starting their own barn dances, using the same local musicians who had made the *Barn Dance* a hit. Partly because of this, WSM started paying its performers. Usually it was only a token payment of something like one dollar a minute, and most performers seldom performed more than 15 minutes.

Hay knew his audience, and he would often admonish his musicians, "Keep it down to earth, boys." He rejected innovations and new tunes. He wrote press releases that emphasized the rustic backgrounds of his performers; in 1929 he was arguing that "every one of the 'talent' is from the back country" and that the music represented "the unique entertainment that only Tennessee mountaineers can afford." He posed his musicians in overalls, in corn fields with coon dogs, even in pigpens; he gave the bands colorful names like The Gully Jumpers, The Possum Hunters and The Fruit Jar Drinkers. This upset some of the musicians; many of them were not rustic at all, but were Nashville citizens working at occupations like garage mechanics, watch repairmen and cigar makers. For instance, Dr. Humphrey Bate, whose band Hay dubbed The Possum Hunters, was a well-educated physician who enjoyed classical music and wintered in Florida. Yet Hay, sensing the popularity of the hillbilly image that was enriching groups like The Skillet Lickers, continued to impose this image on his new show. The final touch came in December 1927 when Hay, in an off-the-cuff remark, dubbed the show "Grand Ole Opry." The name was a deliberate parody of "grand opera," the term used to describe a series of programs that had been coming to WSM over NBC. It stuck, and Hay used it to enhance the hayseed image of the show.

In spite of the fabricated nature of the hayseed image, the show was not lacking in colorful characters and authentic folk music. Uncle Jimmy Thompson, for instance, was wont to complain vociferously when his niece had his trousers pressed prior to his performance. "Hey thar," he would say, "who ironed them damned wrinkles in these britches? I like my britches smooth and round. Fit my kneecaps." Obed Pickard, the first vocal star of the show (much of the pre-1930 music was stringband fare), played for Henry Ford himself and parlayed his Opry success into a national network radio show of his own with The Pickard Family.

Dr. Humphrey Bate, whom Judge Hay called "the Dean of the Opry," was probably the first country musician to broadcast over Nashville radio. He was basically a harmonica player, and he led a large band that often included as many as six or seven pieces; all the band members lived in a little hamlet northeast of Nashville and had played together for years. In fact, Dr. Bate had led stringbands in the area since the turn of the century, playing on riverboat excursions, picnics, and even for silent movies. Dr. Bate's band was the mainstay of the early Opry shows, and he appeared more than any other stringband; for years, his band opened the Opry with "There'll Be a Hot Time in the Old Town Tonight." Dr. Bate learned a lot of his instrumental tunes from an old ex-slave he knew as a boy; his repertoire was full of rare and unique folk melodies, as well as ragtime, pop music and even John Philip Sousa marches. When Dr. Bate died in 1936, his band was taken over by his fiddler Oscar Stone, and it continued to be a part of the Opry cast up until the 1950's. Dr. Bate's daughter, Alcyone Bate Beasley, started playing with the band at the tender age of 13 and had a successful career in pop music at WSM; she appeared on the Opry until shortly before her death in the 1980's. The band with which she played, The Crook Brothers, was another early band from the first years of the Opry. Leader Herman Crook learned a lot from Dr. Bate and carried on his harmonica tradition.

DeFord Bailey was the Opry's sole black performer, a tiny, fiercely proud harmonica player and blues singer. DeFord joined the Opry during its first year, and, though condescendingly labeled the show's "mascot," he was immensely popular; in 1928, for instance, he appeared on the show twice as often as anyone else. DeFord always worked alone, and specialized in har-

monica virtuoso pieces like "Pan American Blues," "Fox Chase" and "John Henry"; in the days before amplification systems he used a large megaphone attached to his harmonica to make himself heard. DeFord was almost certainly the only black man of his generation—or several generations to come—to have a regular role in a major country radio show. Exactly what his presence on the early Opry implied for black-white music interchange is still being debated by historians.

DeFord apparently never really saw himself as a blues musician in a hillbilly setting. He grew up in rural Tennessee, not far from Nashville, in the early 1900's, and most of the music to which he was exposed during his formative years was what DeFord himself called "black hillbilly music." As a boy DeFord knew many black men who played old-time music; his father played the fiddle, and his uncle was the best black banjo player he knew. DeFord's own picking had a delightful ragtime touch to it, and there were relatively few links between his music and that of other country blues artists of the time. He might well have been one of the last exemplars of the tradition of "black hillbilly music." It is a tradition hardly documented in the field recordings of the 1920's, since the commercial companies pigeonholed blues into special "race" series and country into the special "hillbilly" series. Black hillbilly music didn't really fit into either, and when the field scouts ran into it, they usually ignored it. It is interesting that DeFord's own records were released in the "hillbilly" series by one company, and in the "race" series by another.

DeFord continued to play regularly on the Opry throughout the 1930's, traveling and touring with people like Uncle Dave Macon, Roy Acuff and Bill Monroe. He left the Opry in 1941 amid a good deal of bitterness, though still widely respected at the time by thousands of white listeners as "The Harmonica Wizard," and opened a shoeshine stand in downtown Nashville. That wasn't the end of his musical career, however. He played at various events around Nashville in the folk revival years (even being invited to appear at the Newport Folk Festival, though he

*The Binkley Brothers' Dixie Clodhoppers
Band played the Opry in the 1920's.*

Uncle Dave Macon in the 1930's.

declined), and during the 70's he made appearances on Opry Old-Timers' Nights. Before his death in 1982 he was the subject of several home recordings and a biography, and was even offered a part in the Burt Reynolds movie, *W.W. and the Dixie Dance Kings* (which he also turned down).

The McGee Brothers, from Franklin, Tennessee, both served apprenticeships with early Opry giant Uncle Dave Macon and then went on to become mainstays of Opry stringband music. The elder brother, Sam McGee, was one of the major purveyors of old-time mountain solo guitar style. Sam was one of the first country musicians to start playing the guitar in middle Tennessee; he soon developed a unique "flat top" style wherein he played the rhythm and melody simultaneously. By 1926 he was recording solo numbers like his famous "Buck Dancer's Choice," one of the most difficult of old-time guitar standards. Sam utilized a lot of blues and ragtime in his guitar stylings and came up with a creative mixture of folk and pop influences. Though he was not as well-known as the other major old-time guitar stylist, Maybelle Carter, and though he spent much of his early career as a sideman, Sam's early records like "Franklin Blues," "Knoxville Blues" and "Railroad Blues" show that he was the first country musician to really exploit the guitar as a solo instrument. Up until his death in 1975, at age 81, he continued to play regularly on the Opry. Discovered by the young Northern musicians in the folk revival of the 1960's and given his due as the pioneer instrumentalist he was, Sam died with at least some idea of the influence his music had had on the world. He was luckier than many old-time pioneers who died quietly in obscurity, never having any idea of the influence their old records had had on other people.

Sam's younger brother, Kirk McGee, was a

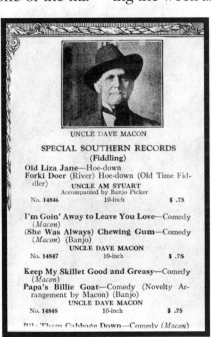

UNCLE DAVE MACON

SPECIAL SOUTHERN RECORDS
(Fiddling)

Old Liza Jane—Hoe-down
Forki Doer (River) Hoe-down (Old Time Fiddler)
    UNCLE AM STUART
    Accompanied by Banjo Picker
No. 14846   10-inch $ .75

I'm Goin' Away to Leave You Love—Comedy (*Macon*)
(She Was Always) Chewing Gum—Comedy (*Macon*) (Banjo)
    UNCLE DAVE MACON
No. 14847   10-inch $ .75

Keep My Skillet Good and Greasy—Comedy (*Macon*)
Papa's Billie Goat—Comedy (Novelty Arrangement by Macon) (Banjo)
    UNCLE DAVE MACON
No. 14848   10-inch $ .75

Pile Them Cabbage Down—Comedy (*Macon*)

banjoist, fiddler and singer who brought to The McGee Brothers act a repertoire of old fiddle tunes and a love of sentimental songs and even church songs. Kirk played with Sam most of the time and was the entrepreneur of the team—"I went out and got the business," he said later. In the 1930's The McGees teamed with a Dickson, Tennessee, fiddler named Arthur Smith to form one of the most influential stringbands of the decade, The Dixieliners. Touring out of the WSM Opry bureau, the band traveled during the week and broadcast on Saturday nights; it was a no-nonsense, old-time stringband that emphasized technical ability over showmanship, but the audiences ate it up. Kirk recalls, "Arthur was a very solemn fellow. But his fiddling impressed them. He just whipped it out and played, and they sat up and listened." Smith popularized a long string of original fiddle numbers, many of which have gone into folk tradition and have become bluegrass standards. They include "Pig in the Pen," "Dickson County Blues," "More Pretty Girls Than One" and "Beautiful Brown Eyes." The Dixieliners never recorded in their prime, and they are another instance of how radio performers could and did influence the music without the benefit of hit recordings.

The mainstay of the Grand Ole Opry in its first decade was a man who has come to symbolize the spirit of old-time music, Uncle Dave Macon. Born in 1870, Uncle Dave lived to the ripe old age of 81. Along with The Carter Family and Jimmie Rodgers, Macon was a prime mover in the music of the 1920's, and a major link between the folk and commercial traditions. However, unlike The Carters and Rodgers, who worked primarily on phonograph records, Macon was very active in both records and radio. A.P. Carter was 36 when he made his first record and launched his career, and Jimmie Rodgers was 30, but Uncle Dave was 54, and his musical

The Opry's Fruit Jar Drinkers: George Wilkerson, Claude Lampley, Tom Leffew and Howard Ragsdale.

heritage went a good deal further back into the 19th century. In fact, Uncle Dave had a career that began with singing and playing the banjo on the vaudeville stage and at rural, lantern-lit schoolhouses, and extended all the way up to his appearance on television in the early 1950's. During this time he became one of the most beloved entertainers in the music's history. Folklorists have called Uncle Dave a cultural catalyst and a preserver of countless traditional songs; radio historians called him "the first featured star of the Grand Ole Opry"; the popular press of the time referred to him as "the king of the hillbillies" or "the Dixie Dewdrop." Uncle Dave was more modest; he described himself merely as "banjoist and songster, liking religion and meetings, farming, and thanking God for all his bountiful gifts in this

beautiful world he has bestowed upon us."

Uncle Dave (born David Harrison Macon) came from the Cumberland plateau in middle Tennessee, near McMinnville. As a teenager he lived in Nashville, where his father, a former Confederate Army officer, operated an old hotel. This hotel catered to the many vaudeville and circus performers who came through Nashville in those days, and the young Macon learned to love their songs and music. By the time he was 15, he had his first banjo; in his own words, it was Joel Davidson, "a noted comedian and banjoist...that inspired Uncle Dave to make his wishes known to his dear aged mother and she gave him the money to purchase his first banjo." Soon he was learning many of the popular vaudeville songs of the day, and he began to play informally for friends and relatives. When he married, he moved back to the country and there continued to sing and learn old folk songs from people in the community, playing and singing for his friends. He formed a freight hauling company, the Macon Midway Mule and Transportation Company, and hauled freight with mule teams; as late as the 1980's, old-timers in the area could recall him singing as he drove along, or stopping to rest under a shade tree and taking out his banjo.

In 1920 Uncle Dave became a victim of technological unemployment: A truck line started in competition with Macon Midway, and he chose not to compete. At the age of 50, he began thinking seriously about a new career—one in music. His first public performance (about 1921) was a charity event in Morrison, Tennessee; as he recalled later: "The Methodist church there needed a new door. I gave a show, then passed the hat and collected the money, $17." Soon a talent scout for the Loew's vaudeville theaters heard him and offered him a contract, and suddenly Uncle Dave found himself a stage star, playing his banjo and telling his jokes at Loew's theaters around the country. He was so popular that other theater chains tried to buy his contract. In 1923 he hired a young partner, a skinny Nashville fiddler and singer named Sid Harkreader. A little later he added a "buck dancer" to his cast. By 1924 Uncle Dave's name was famous across the South.

In the summer of 1924, a local furniture company sent Uncle Dave and Sid Harkreader to New York to make their first and most famous records: "Keep My Skillet Good and Greasy," "Hill Billie Blues" and his imitation of an old-time hunt, "Fox Chase." Uncle Dave also got his first look at the big city of New York, and took it in style. Once, after he had visited a barber shop and ordered "the works," he was presented a bill for $7.50 and was barely able to conceal a gasp. Finally recovering his poise, he muttered, "I thought it would be $10." Afterward he wrote in his expense book: "Robbed in barber shop...$7.50."

Uncle Dave's records were so successful that he was called back into the studios repeatedly in the 1920's; for a time he made regular trips to New York, twice a year. The songs he recorded came from many sources. He learned some from oral tradition, many from the old vaudeville circuits, and a number from old sheet music via an aunt who played parlor piano. He owed— and acknowledged—a debt to black musicians; he was exposed to black music as a child on the farm and later as he listened to roustabouts working on the Cumberland River. Many of his songs were moralistic, such as "You Can't Do Wrong and Get By," an old gospel hymn; others had a rowdy, good-time flavor, such as "Bully of the Town" and "Keep My Skillet Good and Greasy." Some, like "Them Two Gals of Mine," can hardly be played on the radio even today. Apparently he saw no hypocrisy in singing a church song one minute and a gamy song the next. Once he took a stringband into a recording studio and recorded one day as "The Fruit Jar Drinkers" and the next day as "The Dixie Sacred Singers." This sort of schizophrenia apparently took its toll: Uncle Dave suffered from acute or chronic depression, and more than once was hospitalized for it.

Uncle Dave was also a skilled banjo player, and his style influenced generations of pickers. His "rapping" style was a three-finger style probably derived from the minstrel techniques of the 19th century; his combination of thumb, index and middle fingers yielded a bewildering variety of rolls and runs. He was also a trick banjoist; one of his early posters announced, "Uncle Dave Macon is the only man in captivity who plays and sings on two banjos at the same time." He would twirl the banjo, toss it in the air, and dance around it, never missing a beat. His *tour de force* was called "Uncle Dave Handles a Banjo the Way a Monkey Handles a Peanut."

Uncle Dave also pioneered country comedy. On many of his records he would introduce his songs with a story or a joke, or even a bit of doggerel poetry. On "Tennessee Jubilee" he starts by saying:

"Well, well folks, I'm a-feeling fine, just ate a hearty dinner, and now I'm going to play you something that's round here, an old Tennessee Jubilee. But before I sing you the piece, I have a cousin lives down in Rutherford County, Tennessee. She's a woman, and her brother was a-telling me about her swappin' a dry cow for an old Ford car last summer. And she learned to run it pretty well in the wheat fields after they got done thrashing. And she decided to go into the city on Saturday. But she went out to the highway, and the traffic was so thick that she backed out, and started to go in at night. First thing she done, she drove over the signal line and the traffic officer stopped her and there she was; she stuck her head out the window and says, 'What's the matter?' The traffic gentleman says, 'Why, you haven't got your dimmers on.' She says, 'Lord, Lord, I reckon I have—I put on everything Mam laid out for me to wear before I left home.' And she says, 'Who is you anyhow?' He says, 'I'm the traffic-jam man, ma'am.' 'Well, I'm mighty glad you told me. Mam told me to fetch her a quart—have it ready for me when I go out, will you, please?'"

Uncle Dave wanted to make each record sound more personal, to get across with each song some of his own high spirits and good humor. He wanted each record to be a miniature performance, just like he was used to giving onstage. Whereas the barn dance format functioned to personalize the machine of the radio, Uncle Dave's format tended to personalize the machine of the phonograph.

Though Uncle Dave recorded more than most other musicians of his day, he derived most of his income from personal appearances on tour. His sometime partner Sam McGee recalled traveling hundreds of miles in an old touring car with side curtains on the windows. When Uncle Dave was not booked on the vaudeville circuit, he

WSM's signal was heard across the South and the Midwest.

booked his own shows through voluminous personal correspondence. He was his own agent, booker and advertising agency. He felt, however, that the best advertising was word of mouth. When he drove into a town where he wanted to do a show, he usually headed for the school. There he would offer to do a free show for the children. After the show, he would be sure to mention where he would perform that night (it was often the same schoolhouse) and let the kids carry the word home to their parents. The grapevine would do the rest, and the evening show would be well-attended—at 25 cents a head.

When Hay's *Barn Dance* started in 1925, Uncle Dave was one of the first performers; in fact, for some time he was about the only real professional on the show. He was not on every show—he could still make more money from touring than from Hay's one dollar a minute—but when he did appear, his audience was waiting for him. One local Tennessee resident recalls that his family had one of the first radios in the community, and when they learned that Uncle Dave would be on the *Barn Dance*, they kept the news quiet; they were afraid the neighbors would find out and "swarm into the house to hear Uncle Dave and trample us." Since Uncle Dave was the Opry's first really big star, it was natural that in 1931 he headlined the first touring company sent out by the Opry: Uncle Dave Macon and His Moonshiners.

By the early 1930's Uncle Dave was a regular fixture on the Opry, and in 1939 he went to Hollywood to star with Roy Acuff in the film titled *Grand Ole Opry*. He also toured with such legendary figures as The Delmore Brothers, Roy Acuff and Bill Monroe. Until just a few months before his death, Uncle Dave was playing regularly on the Opry; by then he had become one of the Opry's most cherished links with its folk heritage, for his colorful personality and stubborn individuality made him a legend. Long after his death, veteran musicians would sit around in Opry dressing rooms swapping Uncle Dave stories; one can argue that Uncle Dave has become one of the music's few occupational heroes.

Some people like to call the 1920's the "golden age" of country music, but for the musicians, it was far from that. Few enjoyed the success of a Rodgers or a Dalhart. Most struggled constantly to improve their lots and to try to make a decent living—or part of one—with their music.

The period was a bewildering transition era that saw the music attempting to define itself and to adapt itself to the new forces of mass media, yet it is not quite accurate to speak of the age in terms of crass commercialism finally winning out over a noble folk tradition. Since the late 19th century, commercialization had been an ever-present part of the folk tradition; the term "old-time music" embraced all forms of older music, folk and pop alike. The impulse to professionalize was present throughout the 1920's, from the earliest recordings of Fiddlin' John Carson and Henry Whitter. However, it was only toward the end of the era, when Peer and others had established country music as a distinct genre of pop music, that this impulse bore real fruit.

For his part, Peer only realized the effect he was having on the music after the fact. He later recalled that he had intended to use the profits of his hillbilly business to establish himself as a publisher of mainstream popular songs—but before long, it was clear that his means were overshadowing his end.

Waiting for the National Barn Dance to begin outside the Eighth Street Theatre in Chicago.

CHAPTER 3

Depression and Boom

The popular image of country music in the 1930's—the Depression years—is romantic. It features Southern families filing into grocery stores, ordering up what meager supplies they could afford "and the latest Jimmie Rodgers record"; it is a Norman Rockwell portrait of a frail and feeble, threadbare but proud, slowly growing musical outcast isolated on Walton's Mountain. The facts of the matter are another story.

Country music in the 1930's was far from just a regional Southeastern phenomenon; it was a genuine daily event all across rural America. More than that, though, it was also an era of experimentation and creativity that has yet to be matched in country music's history. It seemed that the whole country was bursting with excitement over the music. Radio had discovered a dedicated market, the American farmer, who warmly accepted country music into his home and listened to it with clockwork regularity, and no one group was more excited than the talented singers and musicians who suddenly found that by playing music (whether creating it or re-creating it) they could make a living. Young musicians from literally every part of the country began forging unique and individual sounds and styles, combining the music from whatever their ethnic background might be with the diverse new sounds brought to them by record, by radio, and, as time went by, by personal appearances. The

era was tremendously creative and exciting musically. The panorama of musical styles developed was extremely diverse, and the entire decade, despite the hardships wrought by the Depression at one end and the threat of world war at the other, was for country music one of stretching and flexing young muscles, striving to grow and develop in innumerable ways all at once.

At the beginning of the decade, country music was made up of four basic styles: the fiddle bands, the solo singers, followers of The Carter Family, and followers of Jimmie Rodgers. Despite the grinding effects of the Depression, there were imitators and practitioners of all these styles trying to earn a living in music, most of them through the medium of radio.

Although radio had been around since the early 1920's, its popularity skyrocketed during the Depression for the simple reason that while a phonograph and a radio might have roughly the same initial price (which was rather high for the era), the continuing cost of buying new records (at 75 cents each) made the phonograph a luxury fewer and fewer could afford. Roland Gellatt, in his *The Fabulous Phonograph*, first pointed out the astonishing statistic that record sales reached a peak of 104 million in 1927, but by 1932 the total sales for the year were but six million, an astonishing 5.8 percent of the entire

The Cumberland Ridge Runners, stars of WLS. Rear, Carl Davis, Red Foley, John Lair (who would soon found the Renfro Valley Barn Dance), Hartford Connecticut Taylor; front, Slim Miller, Linda Parker and Hugh Cross.

total of only five years earlier.

Records continued to sell, of course, but into this astounding sales gap stepped radio, with its one-time purchase price and free programming. Its boosters were quick to respond to rural America's desire for country music, filling the early morning and noontime hours with live local broadcasts, alternating homespun country music with ads for farm products or tools. It was a forum in which most of the country stars of the next decade got their start.

The Saturday nights were something else again. The music that caught the interest of the farmer in the early morning and noontime hours seemed a natural for a full-fledged barn dance on Saturday night, a nostalgic harkening back to the real dances in barns and the apple peelings and corn shuckings that were a staple—romanticized with the passage of time—of life before World War I, "The War to End All Wars."

No other single factor explodes the myth of country music-as-Southeastern-phenomenon in the 1930's as much as the quick and widespread proliferation of these Saturday night radio barn dances on a nationwide basis throughout the decade.

One of the earliest was the *National Barn Dance*, heard over WLS in Chicago. Contrary to the commonly held assumption that the Opry reigned supreme from its inception, the *National Barn Dance* was in fact far more popular in this era, serving an immense amount of Midwestern, Great Plains and Southern territory with its homespun acts, many of whom—like big-voiced sentimental singer Henry Burr and organist Grace Wilson—were not really "country," but had a definite romantic and nostalgic appeal to a segment of rural listeners.

Among those we would call real country entertainers, longtime staples of the show were the immensely popular Lulu Belle and Scotty, The Hoosier Hot Shots, Arkie the Woodchopper, Mac and Bob, The Cumberland Ridge Runners and Karl and Harty. A list of cast members who came and went on to other things is even more impressive: Gene Autry, Rex Allen, Eddie Dean, Patsy Montana, George Gobel, Louise Massey and The Westerners, Homer and Jethro and Red Foley.

The importance of the WLS *National Barn Dance* is nearly impossible to underestimate, and is even more dramatic when some statistics are brought to bear on the subject: In 1930, 40.3 percent of American homes had a radio, and more than three-quarters of those were in the Northeastern and North-Central United States. In the South (including Texas and Oklahoma) only 16.2 percent of families had radios at all; taken together, they amounted to a mere 11.9 per cent of the total number of radio owners in the nation. Thus the audience to which the Chicago-based WLS was beaming at 50,000 clear-channel watts was much larger than that of Nashville's WSM or any of the South's other radio barn dances. Also, the *National Barn Dance* from WLS went on the NBC Blue Network (sponsored by Alka-Seltzer) in 1933, a full six years before the Grand Ole Opry's famous *Prince Albert Show* was carried by a national network.

How the *National Barn Dance* lost such an overwhelming advan-

tage—so that by 1950 it was completely overshadowed by the Opry, and by 1960 had disappeared from WLS—is an interesting and intricate story, and is inextricably entwined in the narrative of this history. For the moment, however, it is important to see it as the reigning barn dance of this era, influencing and catering to the tastes of millions of rural Americans on a nationwide basis.

The *National Barn Dance* was the first of the barn dances to form its own Artist Service Bureau, which booked touring casts and further whetted public appetite for country music. Their tours rarely took them too far South (although Tennessee and Kentucky were not at all out of reach), but they blanketed the Midwest and not infrequently reached the mining towns of northern Minnesota and the isolated Upper Peninsula of Michigan.

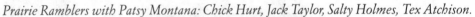

Prairie Ramblers with Patsy Montana: Chick Hurt, Jack Taylor, Salty Holmes, Tex Atchison.

Gene Autry in his WLS days.

Although the show had decided pop elements and even pop leanings, it was the country singers—particularly Gene Autry, whose success on the station in the early 1930's was phenomenal—who were the stars, the focal points of the show.

Autry's full career will be described in Chapter Five, but his few years (1931-34) on WLS are of singular importance. His early professional career was spent in direct imitation of Jimmie Rodgers, a style with which Autry was moderately successful. After a short stint at KVOO in Tulsa, he came to WLS with an entirely new image: "Oklahoma's Yodeling Cowboy," replete with rope tricks (at which he was adept, having grown up on a ranch) and flashy outfits. No longer restricted to Rodgers-like blues, he scored with plain country songs like 1932's "Silver Haired Daddy of Mine" (the first of his many mega-hits), and Western numbers like "Yellow Rose of Texas" (1933) and "The Last Roundup" (1934). His popularity rose explosively, and before long

Lulu Belle and Scotty, two of WLS' most-loved stars.

Sears was selling thousands of Gene Autry Roundup guitars at $9.95 through its catalogue. As Sears owned WLS—World's Largest Store—for its first few years, such tie-ins were only logical. It was Autry's WLS-developed popularity that led him to be considered as a candidate for Mascot Films' singing cowboy experiment, which in turn led to his becoming the first truly national country music star.

The WLS *National Barn Dance* dominated both its era and its area, but there were other important shows of a similar nature, even in WLS' home territory, the great Midwest. The WHO *Iowa Barn Dance Frolic*, for example, began in 1932, and by 1936 had boosted its signal to the legal

maximum of 50,000 watts. The WHO show was reminiscent of WLS, featuring heavy doses of barbershop quartets, organists and novelty acts. On the other hand, like WLS it had an Artist Service Bureau to book tours of its cast members, and featured as headliners a host of country entertainers, most of whom (with the exception of Zeke Clements and Texas Ruby) have drifted into obscurity. Like the *National Barn Dance* and unlike the slowly changing Grand Ole Opry, the *Iowa Barn Dance Frolic* laid heavy emphasis on singers and singing, featuring very little instrumental stringband music. The *Iowa Barn Dance Frolic* was never able to attract the major performers necessary to make it as important as WLS, but its central Midwestern location and the clear-channel power of its signal spread country music over a broad segment of the Midwest.

Another big barn dance, launched when longtime fixture David Stone left the Grand Ole Opry to create and develop a barn dance in Minnesota's twin cities of Minneapolis and St. Paul, was the KSTP *Sunset Valley Barn Dance*. The emphasis was on the solo singers and the cowboy—the show's stars were Billy Folger; Cactus Slim, the Lonesome Serenader; Trapper Nash; Six-Gun Mel; Chuck Mulkern, the Flash of Rice Street; and Frank and Esther, the Sweethearts of Radio—but the big 50,000-watt station had goals typical of nearly every radio barn dance. As their 1943 song folio states: "Hundreds of thousands of people from all parts of the country have attended these shows and listened to the broadcasts and enjoyed to the fullest the songs of hearth and home, the breakdowns and fiddle tunes, ringing banjo melodies, harmonica blues, together

This 1933 WLS tour included Gene Autry, Bill McCluskey, Millie Good, Alma Taylor, an unidentified performer, Paul Rose, Christine Holmes, J.L. Frank, Clina Taylor, Dolly Good, Jack Taylor, Patsy Montana, Tex Atchison and Robert Gardner and Lester McFarland of Mac and Bob. Seated are Jimmie Long, Max Terhune, Smiley Burnette, Salty Holmes and Chick Hurt.

with the fun and comedy of the big Saturday night jamboree."

Two other 50,000-watt stations in America's heartland developed barn dances. KVOO in Tulsa, famous as the longtime home of Bob Wills and His Texas Playboys, developed a show under the direction of Herald Goodman (who had been a member of The Vagabonds on the Grand Ole Opry) called *Saddle Mountain Roundup, the Southwest's Greatest Barn Dance*, in 1938. The stars were Goodman, singing cowboy Ray Whitley, and the fiddle team of Georgia Slim (Rutland) and Big Howdy (Forrester). Similarly, Pappy Cheshire led a gang called his Hill-Billy Champions over a CBS network barn

dance out of KMOX in St. Louis. Again, the show was short on the major names that seemed ultimately to make or break a barn dance, but it did feature Decca artist Sally Foster and one of the finest yodelers to come out of the era, Skeets Yaney.

Country music and the radio barn dance, however, were not restricted to just the Southeast and the Midwest in the 1930's, for by the end of the decade there were barn dances on both the East and West Coasts of the nation. In New York (where country music had been active since the days of Vernon Dalhart), Crazy Water Crystals—a company that sponsored country music nationwide all through the 1930's—had sponsored a series of shows on WMCA, starring Zeke Manners and Elton Britt, who had recently returned from California, having split with The Original Beverly Hillbillies. By 1935 the sponsor and the artists had moved to WHN, and two singing cowboys who had come to the Big Apple to seek their fortune were named co-hosts: Tex Ritter and Ray Whitley, both of whom soon left for Hollywood to pursue film careers. The WHN *Barn Dance* lasted several years, and Manners followed it in 1938 with the *Village Barn Dance* broadcast live from Greenwich Village. On the West Coast there was the *Hollywood Barn Dance* hosted by Peter Potter. Gene Autry had made Western music (and musical westerns) quite a fad, and so the emphasis here was heavily on sagebrush symphonies: The show's stars were The Sons of the Pioneers, Ray Whitley and Smiley Burnette. This cast formed the first all-star radio cast to tour the West Coast.

There were other, smaller non-Southern barn dances that seemed to threaten to glut the era: the WOWO *Hoosier Hop* from Fort Wayne, Indiana; the KMBC *Brush Creek Follies* from Kansas City, Missouri; the WFIL *Sleepy Hollow Ranch* from Philadelphia, and even the CKNX *Barn Dance*, which originated in Wingham, Ontario. The existence of all these institutions goes to prove that country music and the barn dance were not at all exclusively Southeastern or even Midwestern phenomena, but constituted a form of entertainment that appealed to rural North America as a whole.

Still, the barn dances that lasted longest are those that began in the Southeast; it was these (with the exception of the once-mighty *National Barn Dance*) that supplied the nation with its country stars. Yet they too have mostly faded; today, the *Wheeling Jamboree* over WWVA and the Grand Ole Opry in its new home at Opryland are the sole survivors of a once strong tradition.

The whole barn dance concept actually be-

gan in the Southwest in 1923, when WBAP in Fort Worth began its short-lived barn dance. Perhaps the scarcity of radios in the region made for the demise of the program, but it was obviously an idea whose time had come. WSB in Atlanta began its barn dance the next year, featuring the area's newfound recording star, Fiddlin' John Carson, and this show was to survive well into the 1940's. Within a couple more years WLS and WSM had started their barn dances. It is interesting that the first recording, the first million-selling record, and the formation of the three major barn dances in country music history all happened in the years between 1922 and 1925.

WSB's *Barn Dance* originally featured Fiddlin' John Carson, The Skillet Lickers, and others, but later on shifted to more modern entertainment such as James and Martha Carson, and Cotton Carrier. This kind of shift in emphasis was undertaken by all major barn dances, and the idea that it was the Opry that began the shift from stringbands to singing stars with the coming of Roy Acuff is actually erroneous: The Opry in fact, was rather recalcitrant in moving to singing stars, and proved somewhat inept until the coming of Acuff, when it did make the effort.

For some time the general impression (not denied by Acuff himself) seems to have been that when Acuff joined the Opry in 1938, he brought the art of vocalizing with him, and his tremendous success marked an abrupt shift in country music tastes away from stringbands toward singing stars. It is evident from a quick glance at the makeup of most of the other barn dances that by 1938 all of them were devoted to the singing-star format and that Acuff came extremely late to be considered a trendsetter. In fact, historians like Charles K. Wolfe and Richard Peterson have, with a minimum of research, discovered that the Opry was well into the process of becoming a singing star-oriented program when Acuff arrived. Acuff's role was that of the singing star with enough talent and charisma to bring it off.

The move actually began in the early 1930's, when groups like The Vagabonds, The Delmore Brothers, and Asher and Little Jimmy Sizemore—with not a fiddle among them—were hired. The Vagabonds (composed of Dean Upson, Curt Poulton and Herald Goodman) were a smooth-singing, semi-pop trio who specialized in sentimental songs and who wrote one of the Opry's early hits, "Lamplighting Time in the Valley." Sentimental songs (with the age-old appeal of a talented child singing them) were the stock-in-trade of Asher and Little Jimmy Sizemore, and The Delmore Brothers' careful, intricate harmony, guitar lead, and strong blues influence were far from the stringband sound. They too had an early Opry hit, "Brown's Ferry Blues," in 1933. Zeke Clements and his Bronco Busters featuring Texas Ruby—hardly a mountain stringband—joined the Opry in 1933, and then there were Ford Rush, a WLS alumnus, and Jack Shook and The Missouri Mountaineers, both acts joining before Acuff and featuring heavy reliance upon vocals. Following their incorporation into the Opry came the arrival of Pee Wee King and His Golden

Zeke Manners

West Cowboys—a big, slick band featuring a cowboy image and a penchant for Western songs, and, soon after joining the Opry, a spectacularly voiced young man called Eddy Arnold—in 1937.

Acuff, in this light, is obviously far more a part of a trend than a trendsetter. He was simply the most successful of Opry vocalists, his "Great Speckled Bird," "Wreck on the Highway" and "Wabash Cannonball" becoming some of the biggest hits of the era. He was followed—again as a part of this trend—by Zeke Clements ("The Alabama Cowboy") and Bill Monroe (who, despite the strong

Elton Britt went from West Coast to East to continue in radio.

instrumental tradition of bluegrass, was best known on the Opry for his rafter-reaching tenor voice and crackling yodels) in 1939. They in turn were followed by a parade of vocalists who marched into the 1940's: The Williams Sisters, Clyde Moody, Ernest Tubb, Wally Fowler, Eddy Arnold, Paul Howard, Red Foley, and many more.

If the Opry was late in finding the singing star of national stature they sought, they were still very much in the mainstream of barn dance practice in attempting such a move. This is not to denigrate Acuff's importance—he literally put the Opry on the map nationally, and it is a tribute to his tremendous popularity that after just two years on the program (a period that qualified him only as a relative rookie) he was chosen to host the Opry's first radio network tie-in, the *Prince Albert Grand Ole Opry* in 1939, and to star in the first movie about the show, *Grand Ole Opry*, in 1940. It was not until the end of the 1940's, when Ralston Purina picked up an Opry show starring Eddy Arnold and featuring Bill Monroe, Curly Fox and Texas Ruby, Uncle Dave Macon, and Rod Brasfield for network broadcast, that the Opry began to challenge the *National Barn Dance* for the number one national slot.

Other Southeastern barn dances sprang up in the 1930's, and their histories are pretty much a repetition of the same formula: WWVA in Wheeling, West Virginia, for instance, began its well-known *Wheeling Jamboree* in 1933 as a stringband program, but quickly expanded in popularity with the addition of its first star vocalists, Cowboy Loye and Just Plain John, the following year; they were joined by longtime favorite Doc Williams and The Border Riders in 1937.

The barn dances that began toward the end of the decade followed the then-standard formula: They featured singing stars hosting the shows, with little mention of stringbands or "authentic" old-time music. WHAS in Louisville began broadcasting the *Renfro Valley Barn Dance* in 1937 with Red Foley and later Ernie Lee as hosts. (Cincinnati's *Boone County Jamboree* on WLW also had Foley as its headliner for a while, the star obviously being as important as the format as the decade rolled along.) WRVA in Richmond, Virginia, began its *Old Dominion Barn Dance* at the close of the decade, with its longtime star Sunshine Sue at the helm. The only anachronism seemed to be the *Crazy Water Crystals Barn Dance* over WBT in Charlotte, North Carolina, which emphasized a fine stringband, Mainer's Mountaineers—but even they proved most successful with Wade Mainer's vocalizing on songs like "Maple on the Hill" and "Sparkling Blue Eyes."

The 1930's, then, were marked by a tremendous proliferation of barn dances, particularly in the early part of the decade when the Depression laid low much of the record industry. In a way, the move to singing stars over stringbands can be seen as a function of this very process: nostalgia-oriented stringband-heavy barn dances were valuable alternatives for the fans when recordings by Dalhart, Rogers, The Carter Family and others were still affordable. When the records became difficult to afford, it was more than logical that radio should step in to try to fill both needs. Barn dance shows, still carefully maintaining that nostalgic image and flavor, yet stocked with singing stars who sang the latest hits (and their own if they had them), became the order of the day.

While the barn dance is a handy reference factor, there was plenty of other national country music activity in the 1930's. In fact, the landscape of country music reflected in great measure the vast panorama that was the working America of the decade: farmers, Dust Bowl refugees, factory workers, the elderly, the young, those entranced by show business or the magic of Hollywood or radio or record, the small businessmen, the thousands who made up rural and small-town America, who heard in the country music of the time a nostalgic return to pioneer (or at least pre-jazz) America—either that or their own

The Original Beverly Hillbillies were West Coast radio favorites in the 1930's.

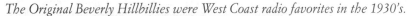

Roy Acuff in the late 30's.

feelings and emotions expressed for them with an eloquence they could not achieve themselves.

Take California, for instance. When The Sons of the Pioneers formed in 1933, with their sole emphasis on songs of the range, the plains, and the cowboy, they were commonly assumed to be Texans. In fact, their makeup was extremely diverse, demonstrating the already wide spread of country music: Bob Nolan was a Canadian; Len Slye (Roy Rogers) was from Duck Run, Ohio; and Tim Spencer was a native of Missouri. Only the Farr brothers (Hugh and Karl) were Texans, who had migrated to California to find work in the 1920's—and even they were hardly Texas cowboys, a major portion of their ancestry being American Indian.

The early 1930's in California found The Beverly Hillbillies, who had formed in the 1920's, still going strong, and Texan Stuart Hamblen, who had formed his Lucky Stars in California, scoring big hits with "Texas Plains" and "My Mary"— and Gene Autry's success on the screen as a singing cowboy proved so monumental that an entire chapter of this history is devoted to the subject. Suffice it to

Little Jimmie Sizemore and dad Asher in the 30's.

say here that, never slow to pick up on a money-making idea, Hollywood began cranking out hordes of these "horse operas," and a stampede of singing cowboys rushed to Hollywood from all over the country to fill the demand: Tex Ritter and Ray Whitley from New York City, Bob Baker from Colorado, Art Davis and Bill Boyd from Texas, Johnny Bond and Jimmy Wakely from Oklahoma, and Eddie Dean from Chicago. Although occasionally caught in the Hollywood glitter, these men at one time or another made some exceptionally fine country music of the era on record, on transcription, on film or in person.

Texas, too, has made such a mark on coun-

try music that it has been assigned an entire chapter of this history. We should note here, however, that the single most impressive characteristic of Texas music in the 1930's was its diversity. Within the era, the music of Bob Wills, The Light Crust Doughboys and Milton Brown had come to be called Western swing, one of the most popular sounds in the country. Texas, moreover, had sent its share of singing cowboys to Hollywood, and yet it was also the home of two of the most popular of the gospel singing groups, the old-fashioned Stamps Quartet and the more modern Chuck Wagon Gang, who pioneered the bridging of the gap between country and gospel music.

In this era Texas produced Cajun music in the far eastern part of the state and fostered the unusual combination of Western swing and Bohemian dance music in the person of San Antonio's Adolph Hofner. Honky tonk got its start with Crisp's Ernest Tubb and Denton's Al Dexter. Big (but not necessarily swing) bands reigned in Texas as well, Bill Boyd's Cowboy Ramblers providing two big instrumental hits ("Under the Double Eagle" and "Lone Star Rag"), while Ted Daffan's Texans became known nationwide for Daffan compositions like "Worried Mind," "No Letter Today," "Heading Down the Wrong Highway" and the country music classic, "Born to Lose." Yet solo singers like Tex Owens ("Cattle Call") and old-fashioned duets like The Shelton Brothers ("Just Because") also thrived in this region and decade.

Texas' neighboring state, Louisiana, was also active musically. Famous for the Cajun music that continues to hallmark the state's sound, it was also the home of Jimmie Davis, who started his career as a Jimmie Rodgers imitator in 1929 but who had a stream of hits on Decca Records, including "Nobody's Darling," "Sweethearts or Strangers," "It Makes No Difference Now" and, of course, the ubiquitous "You Are My Sunshine," in the 1930's.

Texas' neighboring nation, Mexico, managed to provide some of the most interesting, bizarre and influential music of the decade, thanks to the so-called X stations (Mexico's radio stations were assigned the initial letter X, like the United States' W and K and Canada's C), which boomed tremendous amounts of country music over North America during the decade.

The Mexican border station era was introduced by a shady and fascinating entrepreneur named Dr. J.R. Brinkley, who lost his radio license in Milford, Kansas, because of his more-than-questionable goat-gland operation designed to restore sexual potency to men. Brinkley moved to Mexico in 1930, setting up station XER at Villa Acuna, located right across the border from Del Rio, Texas. The main features of XER and the many other X stations that followed were country music and innumerable ads for patent medicines, geegaws, baby chicks and the like. Bill Malone, in *Country Music U.S.A.*, quotes one of the owners of such a station as saying "[this] programming...was giving listeners the unsophisticated material that the big networks neglected."

Whatever the reason, a number of important country entertainers were prominent on these border stations, either live or (more frequently) on transcriptions: The original Carter Family ended up their careers on XERA (1935-41); also featured on such stations at one time or another

Jack Shook's Missouri Mountaineers stringband brought emphasis on vocals to WSM's Opry broadcasts even before Roy Acuff joined in 1939. Here they are: Jack Shook, Dee Simmons, Bobby Castleman, fiddle virtuoso Arthur Smith and Nap Bastian.

Pee Wee King, at far left, and His Golden West Cowboys brought a new look and style to WSM in the late 30's.

were The Delmore Brothers, The Pickard Family, The Callahan Brothers, Mainer's Mountaineers, J.R. Hall ("The Utah Cowboy"), Roy Faulkner ("The Lonesome Cowboy"), who moved with Brinkley from Milford to Del Rio; and the king of the border stations, Cowboy Slim Rinehart.

The reason the border stations were so influential was their tremendous range. It seems that in the early days of radio, the governments of the United States and Canada divided up the long-range broadcast band between them, leaving neither Mexico nor Cuba with any clear channels at all. Understandably miffed, the Mexican Government did not apply the 50,000-watt upper limit to a station's broadcast power stipulated by the United States and Canada, so even when WSM and WLS were at their peak, broadcasting at 50,000 watts on a clear channel, they were no match for border stations blasting across the entire West at two, three, and as much as ten times their power. The old story that you could

tune in one of the Mexican stations simply by sticking your head up against the nearest barbed-wire fence sounds too good to be true, but it does illustrate the immense power generated from across the border. The stations came in as clear as locals well into Canada, and for those who cared to listen (and put up with the relentless advertising), they provided a fine source of often excellent (and sadly under-recorded) country music.

Another rather unlikely locale for country music was Miami, where a handsome San Antonio cowboy named Red River Dave McEnery, who kept bouncing in and out of New York City all through the decade, was the chief radio attraction. Best known in the 1930's for his "Amelia Earhart's Last Flight," he achieved notoriety in the 1970's for "The Ballad of Patty Hearst." Other local favorites of the Miami area were The Rouse Brothers, best known for their instrumental classic, "Orange Blossom Special."

Just as Miami seemed foreign to country music, so did Milwaukee. Although heavily influenced by the *National Barn Dance* sound, the area retained its own ethnic flavor and in the 1930's gave country music one of its best-liked characters and best songwriters: an accordionist of Polish descent who became known as Pee Wee King. He began his career in Milwaukee dance bands (his father was a polka band leader), but, always enamored of the Western image, he formed his Golden West Cowboys after apprenticing with Frankie More's Log Cabin Boys in Louisville. Similarly, Red Blanchard, longtime fixture of the last gasps of the *National Barn Dance*, got his start on several Wisconsin radio stations.

Just Plain John and Cowboy Loye, early stars of WWVA.

The Great Lakes provided starts for a few more entertainers: Skeets MacDonald got his start on WEXL in Royal Oak, Michigan, and WFDF in Flint, the same place from which Little Jimmy Dickens was to launch his career a few years later. In fact, the Detroit area was to be a fruitful one for country music during the war years—Ernie Lee, Jerry Byrd and others appeared there—but only after the influx of Southerners into the war plants. Rural Michigan listened to a good deal of WLS talent, but actually produced rather little of its own.

Yet another Northern industrial city had a surprising amount of country music in the 1930's: Pittsburgh's KDKA (the station famous for pioneering radio by broadcasting returns of the 1920 presidential election) featured, at one time or another in the decade, ex-Skillet Lickers Clayton McMichen and Slim Bryant, Mac and Bob, and Bradley Kincaid.

Bradley Kincaid, a Kentuckian who pioneered country music on WLS while in college in 1922, deserves a great deal of credit for opening up the Northeast to country music, for although he was with barn dances on WLS, WLW and WSM at different times in his long career, he spent the bulk of the 1930's on WBZ in Boston; WGY in Schenectady, New York; WTIC in Hartford, Connecticut, and WHAM in Rochester, New York. His taste ran to pure mountain folk music, and may well explain the Northeast's historic preference for that particular facet of country music, as opposed to more "modern" types. Other country music stars spent time in New England and New York during this time as well: Grandpa Jones in Hartford, Otto Gray in Schenectady, and Yodelin' Slim Clarke in Maine.

Proceeding farther north, Canada was in those days—as it still is—a thriving country music area, although in the 1930's attention centered pretty much around three individuals: Wilf Carter, a yodeling cowboy who found fame in the United States after moving to New York City and billing himself as Montana Slim; Hank Snow, a young Nova Scotian who first began recording in the 1930's as The Yodeling Ranger (in imitation of his idol Jimmie Rodgers, The Yodeling Brakeman), and Don Messer, a fiddler who led a large semi-pop dance band he called his Islanders, because of their association with CFCY on Prince Edward Island.

Perhaps the most surprising of all, however, was the activity in New York City, where a considerable amount of country music was heard locally, on network and local radio and on records, during the 1930's. Those who were there at the time say it was definitely an uphill battle for acceptance, but there appeared to be at least enough interest for a country music "scene" to thrive throughout the decade. For one thing, New York City was left with the legacy of Vernon Dalhart and Carson J. Robison, both of whom were still quite influential as the decade opened. Early in the period, Frank Luther and Zora Layman, Zeke Manners, Ray Whitley, Tex Ritter and Elton Britt came to the Big Apple, many of them appearing on WMCA, which had a six-city hookup ranging as far north as Boston and as far south as Washington, D.C. Rex Cole's Mountaineers had a long-running show on a rival station, and when WHN began their *Barn Dance*, they dipped

deeply into this pool of talent, hiring as co-host the young Texan who was aspiring toward a career on the Broadway stage, Tex Ritter.

Wilf Carter (as Montana Slim) proved a success on network radio, and Denver Darling became a longtime fixture of the scene, introducing super yodeler Rosalie Allen (herself from Old Forge, Pennsylvania) late in the decade. Perhaps the most interesting of the New York City musicians, though, was a young Okie who apprenticed on radio in California, where he became increasingly sympathetic to the plight of his fellow migrants, drifting through the Depression as described in *The Grapes of Wrath*. Becoming increasingly political, Woody Guthrie left behind his country-singer aspirations (which his cousin Jack did not, becoming a popular country singer

Doc Williams, at far right, and The Border Riders, longtime stars of Wheeling's WWVA, shown here in the 1930's.

of the 1940's) and moved to New York, where he became the darling of the socially conscious set and the founder of a whole movement of American music quite on his own. More than any of the self-conscious folk singers to come out of the 1940's, Woody Guthrie's roots as a 1930's country singer were quite evident, nowhere more than in the many melodies taken directly from Carter Family songs to which he wrote his own words, for example, "Wildwood Flower" becoming "Reuben James," and "Little Darling Pal of Mine" becoming "This Land Is Your Land."

The other area where country music was surprisingly strong—as surprising, in a way, as New York City—was the Great Plains. Eddie and Jimmie Dean, for instance, played stints in Yankton, South Dakota (WNAX), and Topeka, Kansas (WIBW), before going to Hollywood, and Bill and Charlie Monroe worked Shenandoah, Iowa, and Grand Island, Nebraska, before heading to the area of their greatest fame, Charlotte, North Carolina. The Willis Brothers played in such far-flung outposts as Shawnee, Oklahoma, and Gallup, New Mexico, while Dr. Brinkley, as noted, pioneered country music in Milford, Kansas, using the talents of Fiddlin' Bob Larkin and Roy Faulkner ("The Lonesome Cowboy") between pitches for his goat-gland operation. The reason why there wasn't more local country music was actually twofold: the 50,000-watt power of WLS beaming in from the Midwest, and the fantastic coverage of the 100,000-watt-plus border stations to the South. Given the small and widely scattered population and a half-dozen radio stations that could be picked up as well or better than local 500 or 5,000 watters, there was little need for the local stations at all, and in fact they were scarce in the Great Plains in the 1930's.

Wilf Carter on CBS in New York City in 1935.

Finally, regarding regional diversity in country music, it is interesting to look at the rise of country music parks—now a widespread phenomenon, and in a sense the precursor of the outdoor bluegrass festivals. Probably the first outdoor park was opened by Buck and Tex Ann Nation, a couple of New York City country music personalities, in 1934. This was the C-Bar-C Ranch in Pennsylvania, a state that has always been among the most active in its support of country music. Four other parks—Sleepy Hollow Ranch, Sunset Park, Himmelreich's Grove and Ravine Park—opened up in the area shortly thereafter and, significantly enough, when the Nations decided to relocate the C-Bar-C Ranch in 1941, their move was not to the South, but north to Maine. It was not until 1948, in fact, that such parks began opening in the Southeast, perhaps the most famous being Roy Acuff's Dunbar Cave near Clarksville, Tennessee, and Bill Monroe's Bean Blossom near Nashville, Indiana.

In short, the point is that country music was a nationwide phenomenon in the Depression-to-World War II era, not something introduced to Northerners by Southern soldiers or defense workers, as has been commonly assumed (although, of course, this kind of interaction took place as well).

Regional diversity, however, was not the most impressive or even the most important characteristic of the decade. Rather, it was the surge of creativity in all regions, seemingly all at once, that made for the staggering musical diversity of the period. It is little wonder, considering that this widespread diversity allowed for nearly every taste, from crude to slick, from blues to pop, from Anglo-American ballad to big-band instrumental, from fiddle breakdowns to modern love songs, that the music spread so widely.

*Cincinnati's WLW
launched its barn dance
show in 1939.*

*Joe Troyan, Bradley Kincaid
and Grandpa Jones in
the mid-30's.*

The decade began with the four major strains discussed earlier; they soon evolved and branched into a dozen or more. In the overview, the influence of Jimmie Rodgers was perhaps the most powerful of all; it must be remembered that the Mississippi Blue Yodeler spent a full half of his short six-year professional career in the 1930's, a major portion of his most influential records coming after 1930 (although the effects of the Depression curtailed his total sales, as they did those of every other artist).

Of his songs, it has to be said that some are so rooted in their own time as to be hopelessly dated, while others are American classics. Probably his greatest legacy was his influence on young up-and-coming singers, who adopted his blues style before developing their own. His black-derived twelve-bar blue yodels were tremendously influential and frequently heard in the early part of the decade—far more, in fact, than his sentimental songs.

Gene Autry, for example, perfected the Rodgers style to the degree that their voices are virtually indistinguishable on record, and in fact the first hit record of many in Autry's long career was "Blue Yodel No. 5." Jimmie Davis was also a blue yodeler at first, recording such racy items as "Tom Cat and Pussy Blues" for Victor long before his association with Decca. Bill Carlisle's first popular record was a blues tune called "Rattlesnake Daddy," and it is well known that both Ernest Tubb and Hank Snow were first influenced by Rodgers' yodeling blues. That so many of the following decades' most influential performers began as blues yodelers is a testimony to the massive popularity of Jimmie Rodgers and his popularization of the blues; the fact that in every instance each of these Rodgers devotees went on to develop his own highly individual-

In 1934 Frankie More's Log Cabin Boys included both Pee Wee King and The Callahan Brothers.

ized styles is further testimony to the creativity of this most creative of decades.

The legacy of Ralph Peer's other August 1927 discovery, The Carter Family, also remained strong throughout the 1930's, although the Carters themselves, because they did not devote themselves to touring or the other necessities of show business, remained merely popular, not spectacularly so. Their main contribution to the music of the 1930's was their songs, which were obligatory in the repertoire of nearly every country act or singer of the era, particularly in the Southeast. Also, the remarkable and innovative guitar style of Maybelle Carter, who above any other single performer encouraged the use of the guitar as a lead instrument among aspiring musicians, was a powerful factor.

There was, in addition, a solo-singer tradition held over from the 1920's that was quite apart from the Jimmie Rodgers style and that is too often forgotten when the credit for turning commercial country music from an instrumental into a vocal form is meted out. Rodgers tends to get all the credit for this rapid reversal of trends, and while the magnitude of his popularity cannot be underplayed, there was a long and influential tradition of solo singers before he ever recorded, from Henry Whitter to Kelly Harrell to Carl T. Sprague to Bradley Kincaid. The king of them all, of course, was Vernon Dalhart, who sold millions of records and recorded thousands of sides under more than 100 different pseudonyms. The importance of these men (with the exception of Kincaid) diminished in the 1930's, but the tradition they popularized and helped found continued with great vitality. During the 1930's, singers like Wilf Carter, Stuart Hamblen, Zeke Clements, Red Foley, Bob Miller,

*The Sons of the Pioneers:
Bob Nolan, Tim Spencer,
Leonard Slye and Hugh
and Karl Farr. Slye
became Roy Rogers.*

Tex Ritter and many others emerged out of a solo-singing tradition (or traditions) quite removed from that of the Mississippi Blue Yodeler.

The fourth musical form at its peak when the decade began was the stringband, a sound and a style that were to diminish alarmingly as the decade advanced. The most popular sounds of the 1920's—provided by The Skillet Lickers, The Leake County Revelers, Charlie Poole and The North Carolina Ramblers and others—receded very quickly in the face of the onslaught of singers and "stars." In the Southwest, fiddle-band music was quickly transformed by its rapid exposure (largely, again, due to radio) to pop, jazz, and blues into Western swing; in the Northeast (with the exception of some hold-outs in Canada) it disappeared entirely. Only in the musically conservative Southeast did the tradition survive, but we've already seen how rapidly the Opry moved away from the fiddle-band format by as early as 1933. A couple of these Southeastern fiddle bands, Arthur Smith and The Dixieliners and Mainer's Mountaineers, were able to achieve record-selling popularity in the 1930's (although many others, including the Skillet Lickers, were to remain local radio favorites).

Smith's sound was bluesy and unique, and he left a very important legacy to country music in his soulful fiddle style. He was assisted—at least in his years on the Opry—by two of the ablest old-time musicians in the business, Sam and Kirk McGee. A more versatile (and ambitious) man than his early Bluebird records and Opry appearances may have made him appear, Smith later went on to lead the backup band in several of Jimmy Wakely's singing cowboy films, playing surprisingly hot fiddle and even singing a tune or two.

Mainer's Mountaineers came out of North Carolina and were headed by the two Mainer

brothers, a fiddler who went by his initials, J.E., and his banjo-playing younger brother, Wade, whose sprightly two-finger banjo style presaged the bluegrass music of a decade later. Although they were a fine breakdown fiddle band of the old school, Wade's banjo playing gave them a distinctive sound, and his clear, strong, evocative mountain voice was the factor that really accounted for the popularity of the band (at least on record). As Mainer's Mountaineers they had several popular records, among them "Wreck of

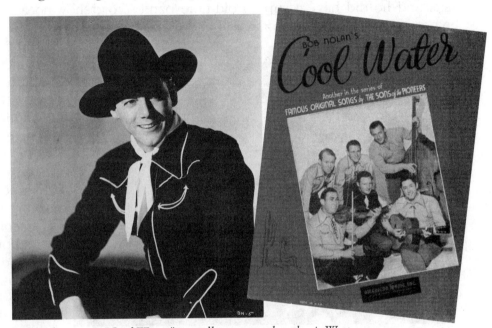

Bob Nolan wrote "Cool Water," as well as many other classic Western songs.

Number Nine" and an old Carter Family gem, "Maple on the Hill." As brother acts often will, they eventually split, and Wade Mainer's new band, called The Sons of the Mountaineers, was one of the last of the stringbands to have a major hit record in the 1930's: "Sparkling Blue Eyes" in 1939. It is a fine performance of a fine song, and its success in that year is even more remarkable considering that it competed against a host of much more modern and slick records: Bob Wills' "San Antonio Rose," Autry's "Back in the Saddle Again" and Jimmie Davis' "It Makes No Difference Now."

The only stringband to stay strong in the 1930's and outlast Wade Mainer into the 40's (although Mainer was active in that period, recording a host of fine sides for King) was one that achieved popularity late in the decade: Roy Acuff's Smoky Mountain Boys. But like Mainer's band, the emphasis was heavily on the singing. That Acuff, a tremendously popular singing star by 1940, should have chosen an old-fashioned stringband for backup says more about him than it does about his success—his voice and his material were right for the times, and would probably have been a success on record with any unobtrusive backing. In all fairness, however, he had long been a champion of traditional mountain music, and he did have a superb old-time band whose powerful in-person musical and come-

The Carters on XERA: A.P., Janette (A.P. and Sara's daughter), announcer Bill Rinehart, Sara, Maybelle, and Helen, Anita and June (Maybelle's girls).

dic effects were great aids to his stage shows.

While Acuff and the various stringband-style artists continued the pre-1930's traditions, others were at work developing the music in new ways. This, in fact, was the main thrust of the 30's.

There was, for example, the development of the mandolin-guitar duet style in old-timey music. Before 1930 there was very little of this tradition, the only significant activity being that of two blind musicians named Lester MacFarland and Robert Gardner, known professionally over WLS as Mac and Bob. Their simple, homey (though slightly stiff) sound—old or old-sounding songs, sung in harmony, accompanied by rhythm guitar, with the mandolin playing brief turnarounds between verses—was, however, tremendously in-

fluential, and they were quickly followed at WLS by Karl and Harty (whose full names were Karl Davis and Hartford Connecticut Taylor), who played basically the same style, but composed some of the best and most successful traditionally oriented songs of the decade: "I'm Just Here to Get My Baby Out of Jail," "The Prisoner's Dream" and "Kentucky."

The effects of this music were not lost on two Kentucky youngsters working in Chicago-area refineries, who eventually went with the WLS road show not as musicians but as square dancers in the early 1930's. They were Charlie and Bill Monroe, who created some of the most innovative, exciting, and certainly most popular duet music of the middle 1930's. Bill's mandolin work, in fact, revolutionized the use of the instrument entirely—after his powerful, energy-charged and lightning-fast solos were spread around on record, the instrument graduated from simple turnaround work to being a virtuoso instrument in and of itself.

Although Monroe himself continued to develop so rapidly as a musician that to this day, nobody has really been able to compete with his mastery of the instrument, he was challenged in the 1930's. The challenger was Jethro Burns of Homer and Jethro, whose popular cornball humor sometimes effectively disguised his brilliant and sophisticated musicianship. Burns' mandolin style—syncopated, rhythmic, heavily influenced by jazz, and spacing notes in short, trumpet-like bursts—differed radically from Bill's approach, which was smooth, fluid, and above all played at a breakneck pace that left other musicians in awe.

The Monroe Brothers were popular for more reasons than Bill's revolutionary use of the mandolin, however. Their singing was high and forceful, and they played a great many of their tunes at racing tempos, a stirring contrast to the deliberate pace that characterized most contemporary duets. Their voices did not express as much feeling—in the sense that the country singer uses that word—as musical excitement, an excitement

Cowboy Slim Rinehart

Red River Dave McEnery

in the music they were creating and an implicit challenge to others to try to top them (nobody ever accused either brother of being short of ego). Much of this same feeling pervades bluegrass (which Bill was to create after The Monroe Brothers split up in 1938) today. Although The Monroe Brothers recorded for only two short years (1936-38), much of their material influenced old-time and bluegrass bands of the future profoundly. They had one considerable hit record, "What Would You Give in Exchange for Your Soul?," in 1936.

The Blue Sky Boys (Bill and Earl Bolick) were influenced by The Monroe Brothers very directly—Bill Bolick was forced to take up the mandolin simply because of the many listener requests to feature the instrument, so greatly had Bill Monroe popularized it—but their approach to the same form and type of music was radically different from that of the Monroes. Concentrating on religious songs, sentimental songs and some exceedingly lovely Anglo-American ballads, their tempos were slow and their voices were mournful, and they produced some of the most haunting music of the era. In fact, Bill Bolick made some revealing comments about the audience they played to in the Depression-wracked South of the time: "People ask, 'Why did you sing so many sad songs?' Well, people weren't in the mood to hear a bunch of crazy junk all the time. There wasn't a heck of a lot of happiness then." The Blue Sky Boys were one of the few duets to remain popular throughout the 1940's (they officially retired in 1951), although World War II disrupted their career for five full years.

Another duet that first achieved popularity in the 1930's and managed to maintain it well into the next decade was The Callahan Brothers. Like The Blue Sky Boys, Homer and Walter Callahan were from North Carolina, but unlike the Bolicks, who never compromised their material, The Callahans adapted with the times. Moving steadily westward (Asheville, Knoxville, Cincinnati, Louisville, Tulsa), they settled in Texas, changed their names to Bill and Joe, and made a career play-

ing the more swingy music of that region well into the 1950's. It is fascinating that the two duet teams that lasted the longest were those that used entirely different means to accomplish it: one, The Blue Sky Boys, holding a loyal following by refusing to change; the other, The Callahan Brothers, by adapting skillfully to changing tastes and regions.

Although there were several other fine duet teams—The Morris Brothers, The Shelton Brothers, The Allen Brothers—two youngsters from Elkmont, Alabama, named Alton and Rabon Delmore formed the only 1930's duet team to gain contemporary parity with The Monroe Brothers, The Blue Sky Boys and The Callahan Broth-

Carson Robison with Pearl, John and Bill Mitchell on New York radio.

ers. Among the first of the transition groups on the Grand Ole Opry who attempted to make a living at their music, they created an eclectic style with elements of blues, boogie, hymns and old-time country. The opposite of the rural stringbands, their music (played on rhythm and lead tenor guitar) was intricate, precise, smooth and polished. They were among the first of the soft singers, and as Charles K. Wolfe points out in his *The Grand Ole Opry: The Early Years*, their acceptance as soft singers was made possible by technological improvements in microphones. They were extremely popular both on the Opry and after they left it, and their controlled, careful approach to performance set high musical

Also on the New York radio scene: Woody Guthrie in 1940.

standards that other duets and bands attempted to emulate. They were also prolific songwriters; "Brown's Ferry Blues," "Freight Train Boogie," "Blues Stay Away from Me" and many other classics came from their pens.

More than most of the other musical forms of the decade, the mandolin-guitar (or, in the case of the Delmores, the guitar-guitar) duet was based, in sound and repertoire, on traditional forms. Most of the other new music of the 1930's was more innovative, but even so, all of it relied heavily on the country music with which the nation entered the decade. For instance, Western swing music—the history of which is detailed in Chapter Four—was a merging of the fiddle-band tradition with the jazz feel and repertoire of Jimmie Rodgers, with the addition of drums, brass and reeds from pop music. It included the newly developed electric and steel guitars, and filled the psychological need for Depression-era rural America to get up and dance.

Similarly, the cowboy songs that originally came out of Texas were the very real bases for the traditionally oriented cowboy hits of the early 1930's: "Texas Plains," "The Strawberry Roan" and others. To this was added a suddenly booming film industry which, caught in the tremendous demand for singing-cowboy films, needed original cowboy songs badly. Into this void stepped many talented songwriters who, taking traditional cowboy songs as bases, wrote many of the classics of the era: Johnny Bond ("Cimarron"), Ray Whitley ("Back in the Saddle Again"), Eddie Dean ("Banks of the Sunny San Juan"), Tim Spencer ("Rainbow Over the Range"), Jimmy Wakely ("Song of the Sierras"), Foy Willing ("Sing Me a Song of the Prairie"), Johnny Marvin ("Rainbow on the Rio Colorado") and even Fred Rose, who before his celebrated move to Nashville wrote dozens of songs for Gene Autry movies, one of which— "Be Honest With Me"—was nominated for an Oscar. Another Tin Pan Alley songwriter, Billy Hill, deserves a good bit of the credit for getting the whole Western song boom rolling, for his pop-oriented Western songs quickly became cowboy classics: "Wagon Wheels," "The Last Roundup" and the like.

No mention of Western songwriters would be half complete without the name Bob Nolan, one of the handful of the truly great country songwriters. It is a shame, in a way, that a songwriter's greatness is too often tied to number of records sold, for Bob Nolan's greatness has been partially hidden because Western songs, despite their popularity on the screen, have traditionally been unexceptional sellers on record. And Bob Nolan's songs have, in overwhelming proportions, been Western in theme. Still, no other country songwriter, outside of Hank Williams and Fred Rose (together and apart), has come up with so many songs of such exquisite lyric and melody. Among the most memorable of his hundreds of compositions are "Cool Water," "Tumbling Tumbleweeds," "A Cowboy Has to Sing," "Way Out There," "I Still Do," "Love Song of the Waterfall," "Blue Prairie," "Song of the Bandit," "Chant of the Wanderer" and "When Payday Rolls Around." Without question, Nolan is one of the underrated geniuses of country music.

Honky tonk music was another form that developed in the 1930's. Like Western swing, its creation and development are inextricably entwined with the state of Texas, and are dealt with in detail in the following chapter. Although the music achieved its greatest popularity in the 1940's and the 1950's, its roots are firmly planted in the late 1930's, when Al Dexter ("Honky Tonk Blues") and Ted Daffan ("Headin' Down the Wrong Highway" and "Born to Lose") began to explore the problems that would so obsess postwar America. It was also in the Texas of the 30's that Ernest Tubb developed the honky tonk style he would bring to the Grand Ole Opry in 1942, popularizing it in the Southeast as well as in the Southwest.

Cajun music also took its first steps toward national prominence in the 1930's, although it too had roots going back to the 1920's and long before. In one sense it was being influenced—modernizing, in a way—with the mixing in of instruments associated with Western swing and other musical forms outside Cajun culture during the 1930's, but at the same time it was influencing the musical styles in areas that surrounded it. The band that best symbolized this emergence was The Hackberry Ramblers, which was probably the first and certainly the most popular Cajun band to mix other musical styles and repertoires with their traditional folk music. Recording Western swing, pop, jazz and straight-ahead

Comedy and music: Jack Shelton, J.E. Mainer, Curly Shelton and Wade Mainer with blackface comedian.

country in a unique mixture of stringband and traditional Cajun sound, they sang both in English and in Cajun French. Their popularity was regional, but at the same time their music was both influenced by and influential to the broader scope of country music and of American music in general.

Another style of ethnic music that played a role in the country music in the 1930's—albeit smaller and even more localized than Cajun—was the music of Mexico. Just as record companies formed budget-priced sub-labels for blues and country (or, as they called these genres, "race" and "hillbilly"), they also had sub-labels for Mexican recordings. For instance, Bluebird, a sub-label for Victor, had a sub-sub-label for their Mexican series, the lovely and familiar buff-and-blue Bluebird label remaining the same in design but changing colors to buff and light green. The influence of the Mexican recordings was far from overwhelming, but they were very popular along the Texas border. They had a definite influence on Western swing musicians who grew up in southern Texas, and made a distinct addition to the Western swing repertoire, the standards "Cielito Lindo" and "La Golondrina" being the most famous of the Mexican tunes.

At the other end of the scale from these ethnic music forms was the increasingly important self-conscious folk music beginning to appear among intellectuals and activists in New York City. These people were the first urbanites to succumb to the spell of what might have been called the John Denver

Charlie and Bill Monroe in the 30's.

syndrome among city dwellers by the late 1970's: a romantic and unrealistic longing for country life and its supposed simplicity. Spurred on by the arrival of Woody Guthrie in 1938, urban folk music flourished, with singers like Burl Ives, Cisco Houston and, later, Pete Seeger joining the fray. Although heavily political in overtone, this self-conscious folk music genuinely introduced thousands to folk, country and country-like music, although the strength of this introduction was not to be felt until some 20 years later, when the legacy left by these people erupted in the "folk song revival" of the late 1950's. This revival—the intellectuals' reaction to rock 'n' roll—had a tremendous revitalizing effect on traditionally oriented country music, and the effects are still very much in evidence.

While urban folk music was in its early stages an entirely different musical form was being born, and it too began to flourish in and outside the Southeast. This was country-oriented gospel music, music based on and taken from the hymns of the old Vaughan or Stamps-Baxter singing schools, then modified and blended with traditional country music styles. It was a trend that was to accelerate rapidly in the 1940's, but its original boom began in the 1930's with a group called The Chuck Wagon Gang. Although their first couple of sessions featured non-religious songs ("Take Me Back to Renfro Valley," "Oklahoma Blues"), their repertoire from then to the present has been exclusively religious in nature. Their music, however, has always featured guitar, mandolin and other instruments not at all associated with the traditional quartet-and-piano sound of gospel music. In this The Chuck Wagon Gang was unique, and this can be seen as a direct result of Southwestern influences. While the repertoire of most Southeastern bands was heavily dominated by religious material, the Southwestern bands were different; 28 of The Monroe Brothers' 60 recorded songs were sacred in nature, but Bob Wills recorded only one sacred song in his entire career, and the rare sacred songs of the singing cowboys were not traditional hymns but new compositions that reflected the outlook of the synthetic screen characters and/or a romanticized west. The Chuck Wagon Gang, operating mostly in the Southwest, was musically in tune with the country music of the Southwest, but lyrically sacred in the Southeastern tradition.

A final innovative byway taken by country music in the 1930's was one we tend to think of as a strictly modern phenomenon (which goes hand in hand with the other common misconceptions about the regionality and supposed purity of country music in the era): the singer-songwriter. As country music became a real business in the 1920's, with more and more bands and singers recording, the limited reservoir of traditional material simply ran out. Also, as the nostalgia-oriented barn dances became more and more a showcase for the emerging stars, the public demand for new individualized material from these stars increased.

Jimmie Rodgers had enlisted the songwriting help of his sister-in-law Elsie McWilliams in the 1920's, and Carson J. Robison had migrated to New York City from Kansas mainly to become a songwriter, beginning a long and fruitful association with Vernon Dalhart upon his arrival. Dalhart's 1925 recording "The Death of Floyd Collins" had sparked a (still thriving) tradition

More close harmony singing: The Blue Sky Boys with Curly Parker in the late 40's, and their precursors, Mac and Bob of WLS, in the early 30's.

of "event songs," and this too was part of the impetus toward more and more new original material. In fact, many of the biggest stars of the 1930's wrote, co-wrote or bought the material that made them famous; Gene Autry's "That Silver Haired Daddy of Mine" and Jimmie Davis' "Nobody's Darling" and "You Are My Sunshine" were examples of this phenomenon. Other popular bands and singers featured a high percentage of new material written by themselves; Bob Wills and Roy Acuff are good examples. Also, singer/songwriters like Rex Griffin ("The Last Letter") began to come to the fore; it was in this area that Bob Nolan forged an entire country music genre almost single-handedly, and Red River Dave began his career of "event songs" with "Amelia Earhart's Last Flight."

Country music in the 1930's, then, was nothing if not diverse—diverse in region, diverse in sound, diverse in personality. It was indeed the most creative single decade in the music's history. Yet for all this remarkable creativity, there were a great number of things that tremendously influenced and changed the music that were not in any way related to the genius of individual musicians or the greatness of certain bands. There were a host of interrelated technological innovations and business decisions that abruptly changed and altered the course of country music many times in many ways. An examination of country music in the 1930's would not be complete without at least a cursory look at technology and economics.

The influence of radio in the Depression has already been seen as a factor of primary importance in spreading the sound of country music, as much in the Midwest as in the South. In fact, the technological innovations of radio and record may well in themselves account for the tremendous surge of creativity that characterized the 1930's, for suddenly, aspiring musicians were able to hear varieties of music vaster and broader than they had ever imagined. As an example, Bob Wills' Texas Playboys recall that, in their barnstorming days in the 1930's, when they played the radio it was not to listen to country songs—those they knew well enough—but to tune in fresh and inspiring big bands and blues singers. Radio and records suddenly disseminated an enormous quantity and variety of music an open-minded musician was quick to use as building blocks for his development as a musician, and eventually synthesize into his own style.

The increasing sensitivity of microphones during the 1930's was also a factor in changing the style of both radio and records. Combined with improvements in home receivers and speakers, this development made it possible for relatively low-volume, subtle singing to be recorded successfully and reproduced as adequately as louder, more dramatic singing. Thus during the 30's, the big-voiced exhortative singers of the 1920's (The Carters and Dalhart, for example) gave way to the gentler singers like Autry and The Blue Sky Boys. The shift in style was as much a result of improving technology as it was a product of musical creativity or changing public taste.

Nowhere is the implication of technology more evident than in the development of electric string instruments, which by the end of the decade radically changed the sound of country music. Although the technology needed to produce electric instruments was advanced enough by 1925 that an ex-Gibson engineer named Lloyd Loar marketed electric violins, mandolins and basses, electric pickups on guitars weren't really used in pop, jazz or country music until the middle 1930's. It is generally held that Bob Dunn, the innovative, jazz-oriented steel guitarist for Milton Brown's Musical Brownies, first attached a crude pickup to his Martin Hawaiian guitar, thus bringing the electric steel guitar to Western swing and eventually to all of country music. Leon McAuliffe of The Texas Playboys was not slow to follow Dunn's lead, and soon the sound of the electric steel was as indigenous to country music as that of the fiddle.

It was in the late 1930's that the electric guitar—played upright, as opposed to the steel—got hooked up as well, and soon Western swing bands were all featuring electric rhythm and lead (which, like the steel, was not pioneered but popularized by another Texas Playboy, in this case Elton Shamblin). Again, this sound spread

*Rabon and Alton
Delmore in the 1930's.*

rapidly to country music at large.

The spread of country music can be attributed to yet another set of technological advances: the increasingly well-built automobiles and the improved roads on which to drive them. For both band and fan, the simple existence of well-made cars and good roads made extensive touring both practical and profitable: The performer could better reach his public and, as importantly, his public could reach him as well.

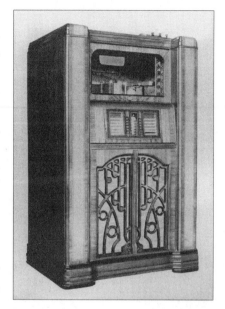

The greatest economic/technological factors in country music's rapid spread during the 30's, however, were the new media: radio and records. Radio's sudden boom period was in large part due to the inability of a large segment of the population to purchase luxuries like records, which at the time sold for 75 cents each, with some artists commanding as high as $1.25 per disc. Before the Depression, certain sub-labels sold for as low as 25 cents, but not until 1934 did a brand-new company called Decca settle on a price of 35 cents per disc, seriously undercutting the other labels since they featured their first-line artists (Bing Crosby, for example) at this price. This was a major breakthrough, which had an immediate effect on the rapid, healthy growth of the Decca company and put considerable pressure on the other labels to also cut their prices (Victor's Bluebird line, originally a reissue label, suddenly became the haven for their country, blues and dance bands, and came out with a purchase price of, you guessed it, 35 cents). Decca had a healthy country catalogue throughout the 1930's (Jimmie Davis, Tex Ritter, Rex Griffin,

Tennessee Ernie Ford playing records over Bristol's WOPI in the late 1930's: another trend is born.

Milton Brown, The Carter Family, The Shelton Brothers, Eddie Dean, The Sons of the Pioneers), but their main contribution was in driving the price of popular records down, making them affordable to the segment of the public that had given them up as an unnecessary luxury. Decca's move revitalized a sagging industry, and once again the important singers and groups of the era were recorded extensively on wax.

A second major reason for the revitalization of the once nearly moribund record industry (and one that gave a strong boost to Western swing, and virtually gave birth to honky tonk) was the development and promotion of the jukebox, which shortly after its introduction around 1935 became a national institution in taverns, truck stops and restaurants. Jukebox operators bought thousands of records, mainly Western swing, for the big beat was easily heard on the contraption—and it did not take long before songs aimed at the jukebox's listeners appeared: Al Dexter's "Honky Tonk Blues" (1937) and Ted Daffan's "Truck Driver's Blues" (1939). The jukeboxes not only bolstered the record industry, but also did a lot to shape, change and inspire an increasingly large part of country music style, taste and form for years to come.

A third reason for the revitalization of the record business has to do with the playing of records over the radio, a phenomenon taken totally for granted today but one that met with intense resistance in its day. In fact, for years radio and records considered themselves rivals for the public's entertainment dollar, and often bitter rivals at that. Each side was resistant and competitive, their last thought that of cooperation. Radio saw its advantages lying in its spontaneity, having no need for anything so mechanical as records, while the record industry saw airplay of their records simply as lost sales: Why would anyone buy a product they could hear for free? Hence the small print found on numerous records of the 1930's: "Not Licensed For Radio Broadcast."

In the late 1930's, somewhere around 1937-38, this began to change. Radio men discovered the obvious economic advantages of paying one man to spin records rather than paying half a dozen to sing the same hit songs, and record men found, quite to their surprise, that far from damaging sales, airplay boosted sales tremendously. Suddenly the record and radio industries, adversaries since 1920, found themselves scratching each other's back. The result was greater profit for radio stations, and greater profits and sales for the record companies. The proliferation of labels in the years that followed was a direct result of this Johnny-come-lately cooperation. The only people who lost out were the poor live musicians, who increasingly had to become recording artists to succeed.

With all these creative and technological changes conspiring together, the 1930's was truly a hotbed decade for country music. It was a decade that demanded, and received, escapist entertainment and dreamy musical romanticism, and the sources for the music were scattered all across the nation. The road to Nashville was embarked upon during this decade, but it was a road that came out of a thousand different paths. It was not until the *Prince Albert Show*, featuring Roy Acuff and The Smoky Mountain Boys, went on network radio in 1939 that the Grand Ole Opry and the city of Nashville began to indicate their future dominance of the country music field.

Ernest Tubb

CHAPTER 4

Music from the Lone Star State

Now, Texas is a big state: big in area, big in population. Still, its contributions to country music over almost 80 years of recording history are far greater than even its size might explain.

In the 1970's, at the height of the Outlaw movement in country music, there was a lot of talk about Texas music as if it were something new: a trend; a phenomenon arising from a scene like the San Francisco sound of the psychedelic 60's. That was understandable, for the scene in Austin at the time really was a vital, fascinating musical environment, but such talk obscured a larger fact. Texas had been influencing country music very heavily since the very beginning. The list of country musical accomplishments by sons and daughters of the Lone Star State is impressive indeed, and includes not just major stardom, but the creation of major musical movements. Singing cowboy music, Western swing, honky tonk—all were begun by Texans.

Why the Lone Star State has produced such a magnificent lineup of major country stars, from Eck Robertson all the way down the years to Clint Black, is open to conjecture. Ethnic diversity in and of itself doesn't make for a thriving country music heritage, for if it did, New York, Detroit, and Chicago would be active country music centers. But there is, on the other hand, little

doubt that many musical cultures were influential in the development of Texas music. The state is a melting pot of various ethnic strains, many of which were incorporated into Texas music, particularly in the variety called Western swing.

The most obvious of these ethnic strains and influences, the one that is the foundation for all of country music, is the Appalachian musical tradition of Anglo-American folk song and minstrelsy, a tradition brought over from the mountains of the Southeast to the plains of Texas by its first settlers. These musical ancestors of both Bob Wills and Bill Boyd were, like Davy Crockett and Sam Houston before them, transplanted Tennesseans. These settlers brought with them their fiddles, songs, hymns and love of square dancing, and given this background—although time has altered the style—it is little wonder that the fiddle tradition was (and is) so strong in Texas. Bob Wills, for all his audible and visual antics, was a prize-winning old-time fiddler: his first-rate old-time fiddling was merely upstaged by the hot jazz of the super fiddlers he loved to employ.

This influence from the Southeast was not only a pre-1900 phenomenon, either: Homer and Walter Callahan, a popular mountain duo along the lines of The Monroe Brothers or The Blue Sky Boys, were North Carolinians by birth and upbringing, but like many others of their era

The Cajun strain of Texas music: The Hackberry Ramblers in 1937.

Prince Albert Hunt, in blackface at right, mixed old-time fiddle and blues.

Cowboy gospel: The Chuck Wagon Gang—Dad, Anna, Rose and Jim Carter.

they became enchanted with Western music. In their early years they played in groups like The Cliff Dwellers and Frankie More's Log Cabin Boys; later they toured with singing cowboys Ray Whitley and Jimmy Wakely, and ended up their career in the late 1940's and early 1950's in Texas, among the stars of the *Big D Jamboree* in Dallas, where by then, for some peculiar reason, they had changed their names to Bill and Joe.

Of course, Southeastern mountain-style fiddling and singing were far from the only influences. Texas has long had a heavy settlement of German, Bohemian and other central European peoples, who brought their love of polkas, schottisches and waltzes with them, forever to become associated with Texas music. In fact, it is they who left the squeezebox accordion, a small affair capable of but one key and two chords, with the Cajuns on their way through Louisiana to Texas in the 19th century, contributing to the rich, distinctive sound of that musical style. At any rate, the German and Slavic influence has been especially strong in south-central Texas, where waltzes and polkas have been perennially popular among country bands and country fans.

The classic case is Adolph Hofner of San Antonio, still a busy entertainer in the 1990's, playing several days a week, never venturing across the state line. Hofner's career goes back to the 1930's and is thoroughly Western swing in outline, but throughout he has recorded and performed in Bohemian as well as English, and one of his biggest records, "Green Meadow Waltz," was sung in Bohemian. Today his band includes trumpets, fiddles and accordions, and he blithely says, "If they want mariachi, we give them that; if they want the Slavic, we give them that;

and if they want plain country, we give them that too." He shrugs off his role as a living example of the mixing of three rich musical cultures in the music of Texas. The mixed tradition continues to this day.

The Cajun sound of Louisiana, which owes at least the accordion to the German immigrants, has been another strong influence on the music of Texas, especially in the areas along the state's southeastern border. Cajun music was and is extremely popular in southeastern Texas, as popular as in the bayou country, and in fact the legendary Cajun fiddler Harry Choates spent most of his time in Texas. He did the majority of his recording in Houston, and died in the Austin jail in 1951. A Hank Williams-like figure, Choates died at the age of 28, after a short, wild life, a regional celebrity, especially after his 1946 hit, "Jole Blon."

Harry Choates in 1945.

Several figures moved interchangeably between the worlds of Texas and Cajun music: Moon Mullican was a country star, a swing pianist, a blues singer, and one of his hits was "Jole Blon," which was also a hit for Red Foley and Roy Acuff and a bigger one yet for Choates. And the music itself was mixed and mingled as well, for while Opry singers sang "Jole Blon" in traditional Nashville style, Harry Choates borrowed instruments and styles from Western swing, and one extraordinarily popular Cajun band of the 1930's, The Hackberry Ramblers, used instrumentation similar to Southeastern string bands of the same era, with, of course, the exception that they sang in that curious patois known as Cajun French. And they were unafraid to venture outside familiar musical genres: One of their more popular records was "Fais Pas Ca," simply a Cajun version of the old blues classic "Trouble in Mind."

So Cajun gave to and took from country music in general and Texas music in particular, adding yet another ingredient to the rich ethnic stew that composes its sound.

Another such ingredient was the Norteño music of northern Mexico, which lent its distinctive sound to a region obviously eager to accept and adapt different types of music. Aspiring musicians growing up in southern Texas were bound to be affected by this music, if not for its own compelling musical merits, then simply by having been so surrounded by it.

Different from the mariachi brass sound, which also had a profound effect on Texas music, the Norteño market was treated by the major labels much like "race" and "hillbilly" music were in their infancy, with specialty sub-labels manufactured specifically for the Tex-Mex audience. Victor's lovely buff-and-blue Bluebird label, for example, was a familiar sight to most country record buyers, who picked up The Monroe Brothers, The Delmore Brothers, The Blue Sky Boys, The Prairie Ramblers and Bill Boyd; similarly, the buff-and-green Bluebird label was as popular in many parts of Texas, only here the stars were Lydia Mendoza and Narciso Martinez.

The sound was close harmony, twelve-string guitar, bass and accordion, once again introduced by the German and Slavic settlers. And so close was the relation between Anglo and Norteño music at times that, for example, The Tune Wranglers, a country swing group of the 1930's, had several songs co-released on Bluebird's Mexican series as Tono Hombres, "Ye Old Rye Waltz" becoming "Centenos Vals" and "Rainbow" becoming "Arco Iris." Conversely, Mexican artists like El Ciego Melquiades (The Blind Fiddler) and Bruno Real had occasional records released in the standard U.S. series.

So the Tex-Mex music of late is really nothing new to native Texans, and while the coming of

Moon Mullican

My best wishes
Moon Mullican

Johnny Rodriguez and Freddy Fender in the 60's and 70's may have seemed to many country fans like the breaking of old taboos, it was old hat to the creators of Texas music, who assimilated long ago this Norteño music as well as mariachi, German, Appalachian, Slavic, the blues and many other strains to form the many thriving energetic forms of the music of the Lone Star State.

Yet another field to which Texas has contributed significantly has been gospel music, especially in the persons of The Chuck Wagon Gang, consisting of D.P. (Dad) Carter and three of his children, Rose, Anna and Jim, whose odd combination of cowboy (or at least frontier) image and gospel material made them popular for decades. They were first formed in Lubbock around 1933, but made their greatest impact in the Fort Worth area. In fact, their radio show—sponsored by Bewley Mills—went on the air over WBAP just before The Light Crust Doughboys' program, sponsored by Burrus Mill. Although their first recording sessions consisted of both secular and sacred material, they soon switched to an all-gospel format, for which they became best known.

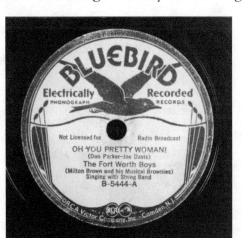

A trio called The Herrington Sisters (Winnie, Ida Nell and Olga) had a similar approach, doing about half gospel and half country, folk and sentimental material. Based in Wichita Falls, they boomed out over the entire central United States on the Mexican border stations.

One of the most famous names in gospel music, The Stamps Quartet, originated in the Lone Star State as well. They became popular over KRLD in Dallas, and, interestingly, some of their early (about 1929) Columbia recordings featured guitar, although they soon settled into the piano/vocal quartet formation that was to become the hallmark of gospel quartets for years to come.

Yet all of these influences are but part of the story, for while they are important ingredients indeed, they are still added ingredients, spices for the two basics of Texas music: the songs of the singing cowboy and the music of the square-dance fiddle band, which formed the foundation for the music of the Lone Star State.

Cowboy music and song began as early as the arrival of the first settlers in the Alamo days of the 1830's, although the occupational songs of cowboy life with which we are familiar today did not really come into being until after the Civil War, when the West began to develop rapidly. What the settlers brought with them were the popular songs of the East and the folk songs and tunes of their particular ethnic cultures, particularly England and Ireland from where, in fact, many of the original cowboys had emigrated.

The lonely, if romantic, image of the cowhand and his guitar crooning his cattle to sleep is largely a figment of the imagination of writers of Western novels, films and songs. In actuality, the guitar was a relative latecomer to the West, and it was certainly an impractical instrument to carry around on horseback—too large and too fragile. The cowboy did indeed sing, both to his cattle and to occupy his time, but except in rare instances the songs were, much like his work, monotonous and dreary, his voice rough (a turn-of-the-century writer said, no doubt with accuracy, "whatever voice he had to begin with he lost bawling at cattle"), and his vocalizing unaccompanied by any instrument.

Well before the turn of the century it became the practice of newspapers in the West to publish the poems of would-be bards of the West (among whom were some genuine cowboys), and some of these verses caught on with the public. Usually put to an old tune, they were quickly assimilated into folk repertoire. It was here that the classic ballads of the West were born, these poems set to one of the handful of tunes that made up the bedrock of the cowboy repertoire. And many were to become classics: "Little Joe the Wrangler," "Utah Carroll," "The Zebra Dun," "The Strawberry Roan" and many others.

Although cowboy song was a thriving tradi-

Tex Ritter's career began in New York: H. Bailey, Ritter, Hank Worden and Judd Carvell in the play, Green Grow the Lilacs.

tion in Texas, no authentic versions were actually recorded until 1925, when, following the mammoth success of Vernon Dalhart's 1924 recording of "The Prisoner's Song," a Texan named Carl T. Sprague ventured to the Victor Company in New York to see if he couldn't do as well at this new business of recording. His "When the Work's All Done This Fall" sold some 900,000 records beginning the following year, and from that point on cowboy songs were here to stay.

The 1920's saw a rash of cowboy songs sung by Texans: Dalhart himself, although hardly a cowboy singer, had a significant number of Western songs in his repertoire, "The Dying Cowboy" and "Home on the Range" among many others. Others, like Sprague, stuck almost strictly to cowboy songs: Jules Verne Allen and The Cartwright Brothers, for example. And, in his early

period, even Stuart Hamblen's first recording nickname was "Cowboy Joe." Hamblen was to become famous in the 1930's with songs like "Texas Plains" and "My Mary," and, after his celebrated conversion at a Billy Graham crusade, for sacred and semi-sacred songs like "This Ol' House" and "It Is No Secret (What God Can Do)." So dramatic was the conversion, in fact, that the former hell-raiser ran for president on the Prohibition ticket in 1952.

The cowboy image proved a popular one on record, and even The Mississippi Blue Yodeler, Jimmie Rodgers, recorded several cowboy songs such as "When the Cactus Is in Bloom," "Cowhand's Last Ride" and "Yodeling Cowboy," and had at least one publicity photo made of himself in full cowboy regalia—ten-gallon hat, chaps and all. His glamorization of the cowboy and cowboy life certainly helped move cowboy music farther into the realm of mainstream country music, and his widely heralded move to Kerrville increased his identification with the state of Texas throughout the years, despite his Deep South roots and raising.

Texas cowboys moved right into the 1930's as well, as Tex Owens became a major country music star with his version of "Cattle Call," and Cowboy Slim Rinehart became the king of the border stations, that peculiar, even bizarre, segment in radio's history. Yet by far the greatest glorification of Texas music and cowboy music came not via record but via film, and it was Texas singers who were more influential in the creation and propagation of the popularity of that colorful bit of Americana known as filmdom's singing cowboy.

Easily the most authentic of these heroes of the silver screen was Woodward Maurice Ritter, who learned to love authentic cowboy songs and ballads from noted scholar J. Frank Dobie while attending the University of Texas in Austin. Ritter spent a year at Northwestern University Law School near Chicago before heading for New York and a career on the stage. He appeared in *Green Grow the Lilacs* and other productions (acquiring the nickname Tex in the process). He also starred in an extremely popular radio series called *Cowboy Tom's Roundup* and hosted a country-music barn dance called the WHN *Barn Dance* before going West to pursue a career in films.

Tex's first recordings—for ARC (the American Record Company) in 1932—are probably as close to authentic cowboy performances as were ever commercially recorded: Sung with deliberate

Ken Maynard, center, first sang on screen in 1930. Here he is in a 1937 Hollywood film called Trailing Trouble.

More singing cowboys: Bill Boyd and Art Davis, left and center, in a Hollywood western.

grew up in that era, and his Academy Award-winning rendition of the theme song for the 1953 film, *High Noon*. A great lover of authentic cowboy and country music, Ritter was one of the guiding forces behind the Country Music Hall of Fame and was throughout his long career one of the most visible, accessible and knowledgeable proponents of Texas music the Lone Star State ever had.

But Ritter was not the first film singing cowboy by any means. He was preceded on the screen in that role as early as 1930 by

lack of sophistication (Ritter later proved himself to be a far better singer), with little attention paid to time or meter, and only a rudimentary guitar accompaniment, it is easy to see why these records ("Good-bye, Old Paint," "A-Riding Old Paint," "Every Day in the Saddle" and "Rye Whiskey") didn't sell. But they are a fascinating look into an authentic re-creation of a sound.

Ritter was to become one of America's most popular film stars of the 1930's, and in the 1940's he decreased his recording of cowboy songs and recorded a barrage of hit country love songs: "There's a New Moon Over My Shoulder," "You Two-Timed Me One Time Too Often" and "Jealous Heart" (written by Jenny Lou Carson) among them.

Although his screen career pretty much ended in 1945, he remained visible throughout the 50's through his hosting of *Town Hall Party* in Los Angeles, his recording a set of children's records of cowboy songs popular with those who

Ken Maynard in *Song of the Saddle*. Not actually a Texan (he was born in Vevay, Indiana), Maynard projected a Western image and was an accomplished rider. He sang and played, providing musical interludes between the action sequences in his films. He even did a bit of recording in 1930, the old black Columbia label reading "Ken Maynard (The American Boy's Favorite Cowboy)."

The Cass County Boys, Gene Autry's backup band and one of Hollywood's many Western harmony trios, also had roots in Texas: They met in Los Angeles, but took their name from lead singer Fred Martin's home county of Cass in, of course, Texas.

Although Maynard was technically the first cowboy to sing, the first singing cowboy brought into film specifically in that role—whose action sequences were simply interludes between songs, as opposed to the other way round—was a true Texan named Gene Autry. Born on a ranch near Tioga, Autry ac-

Stuart Hamblen left Texas for Hollywood.

tually spent his teenage years in Sapulpa, Oklahoma, but in both locations he became a good rider and developed his talents as a singer and entertainer as well. Although for quite some time he had no serious plans of a career in music, he had at least flirted with the idea: He ran away from home while still in high school to join The Fields Brothers' Marvelous Medicine Show.

Autry searched for a style for a time; rumor had it that he even auditioned with Al Jolson's "Sonny Boy" on his first round of record-company tryouts, and was told to go back to Oklahoma (where he was employed as a telegrapher) and practice his guitar and try to learn some tunes like this hot new sensation named Jimmie Rodgers. Autry returned the following year (1929) apparently having taken this advice to heart: His early records for Grey Gull, Okeh, Gennett and Victor are virtually indistinguishable from Rodgers'. However, around 1930 Autry began to develop his own style and to exploit his authentic Western background by surrounding

himself with the trappings of cowboy regalia. He obtained a spot on WLS in Chicago as "Oklahoma's Singing Cowboy," and there he had the first of his many megahits, "That Silver Haired Daddy of Mine." By 1933 he was firmly in the cowboy mold, and he introduced such songs as "The Last Roundup" (1933) and "Tumbling Tumbleweeds" (1934) to country audiences via record, and they responded warmly (Chapter Five describes Autry's career in detail).

Meanwhile, in Hollywood, studio head Herbert J. Yates and producer Nat Levine had come up with the concept of a singing cowboy in a film series, and the popular young singer with the cowboy image, the blond hair and the flashing smile was chosen. It is said that while casting that they found actors who could sing but couldn't ride, and actors who could ride but

couldn't sing, before settling on Autry, the singer who could ride but couldn't act.

If anything, however, his naiveté and ingenuousness before the camera made him somehow more appealing, and he was not just a hit, he was a sensation. The success of his first few films not only delineated a new country music genre in and of itself, but also opened the floodgates for the horde of singing cowboys who poured in from all over the nation in the next decade: Ritter from Texas via New York, Ray Whitley from Alabama also by way of New York, Roy Rogers from Ohio, Bob Baker from Colorado, Eddie

Vernon Dalhart left Texas for a career in popular music and never looked back. A 78 rpm disc of his "The Wreck of Number Nine" is a collector's item.

Dean from Texas by way of Chicago, Jimmy Wakely and Johnny Bond from Oklahoma, Monte Hale from Texas, bandleaders Bill Boyd and Art Davis from Texas, Rex Allen from Arizona by way of Chicago, and on and on.

Two place names keep cropping up here: Chicago and Texas, for WLS and the *National Barn Dance* were the training grounds not only for Autry, but for Dean and Allen as well; and Texas, in the vanguard of this movement, provided a host of musicians and actors for both the film and recording industries.

Eddie Dean had teamed with his brother, Jimmie (no relation to fellow Texan Jimmy Dean of "Big Bad John" and pork sausage fame; these Dean Brothers were born with the surname Glosup in Posey, Texas), and apprenticed on the *National Barn Dance* before heading West. Eddie appeared in many Tex Ritter films before starring in his own series for PRC in 1946-49, while Jimmie never got the breaks as an actor but was an essential part of several groups as a singer and musician, notable among them the popular band led by yet another Texan, Foy Willing and The Riders of the Purple Sage. Eddie achieved his greatest fame as a songwriter, however, not an actor, his "One Has My Name, The Other Has My Heart" and "Hillbilly Heaven" the best known among his many songs.

Foy Willing's Riders of the Purple Sage were similar (although far from identical) to a group whose close harmony singing defined the style for all Western groups to come: The Sons of the Pioneers. Often associated with Texas, none of the co-founders were from anywhere near the state (Bob Nolan from Canada, Len Slye—later known as Roy Rogers—from Ohio, and Tim Spencer from Missouri), but two extremely important later members were indeed Texans, Hugh and Karl Farr, the fiddle-and-guitar brother team whose sound was integral to that of The Pioneers.

Texan Eck Robertson first recorded in 1922.

Bill Boyd and Art Davis approached Hollywood from a different angle but were nonetheless from the Lone Star State. Boyd was the guitar-playing leader of a band called his Cowboy Ramblers (best known for "Under the Double Eagle" and "Lone Star Rag"), while Davis, himself an ex-Cowboy Rambler, first joined Gene Autry as his fiddle player before going into films himself and, in the early 1940's, fronting his own Western swing band, The Rhythm Riders.

On the other hand, a Texas singing cowboy who was mostly an actor was Monte Hale. Although he sang in many movies (he was hired as a backup to Roy Rogers, should Rogers defect from the studio or make difficult contract demands, much as Rogers had himself been hired during a disagreement between Republic Studios and Gene Autry) and recorded for MGM and other labels, he never really caught on with the record-buying country music audience. Nevertheless, he enjoyed a brief heyday in films. Like many talented singing cowboys, he entered the field as its popularity was waning. Although he might have been a major star had he been born a decade before, today most film histories simply treat him as an also-ran. The genre had few years left when he, Rex Allen, and even Jimmy Wakely to an extent made their bids for screen stardom.

One of Texas' most colorful singing cowboys was Red River Dave McEnery of San Antonio, who became a popular singer of cowboy songs in New York, recorded for Decca and Continental, and also appeared in Miami, Florida, and throughout Texas on various radio stations, based for the most part in San Antonio. After a retirement of nearly two decades, McEnery—bedecked with gold boots and leonine silver hair and goatee—made a comeback as one of Nashville's prominent characters in the 1970's.

McEnery made a few movies, but his base in New York City introduced him via network radio to thousands of listeners nationwide. And on a more local level, it introduced him to one of the most important figures in the history of country music, a sturdy, deep-chested fellow Texan named Vernon Dalhart. Although past his prime when he recorded McEnery's composition, "Johnnie Darlin'," at his last recording session in 1939, Dalhart had been country music's first recording star, and the man who sang

Curly Fox and Texas Ruby. Texas Ruby was Tex Owens' sister.

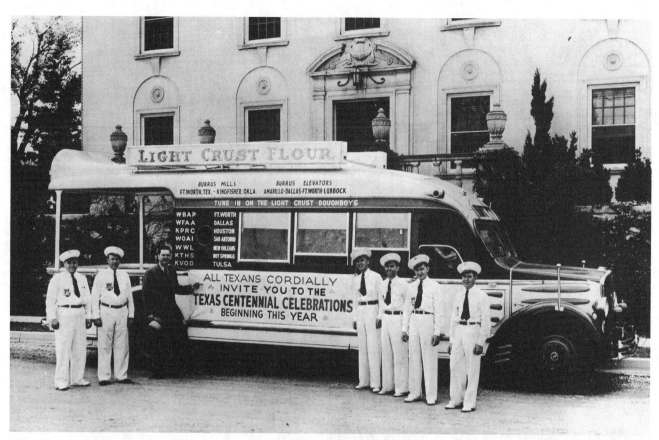

The Light Crust Doughboys, first of the Western swing precursors. Milton Brown and Bob Wills were two of many great alumni.

country music's first million-seller.

Vernon Dalhart was born Marion Try Slaughter in Jefferson, Texas, and aspired to an operatic career. In pursuit of that dream he moved to New York around 1915. By 1916 he had already made his first recording, and was to have quite a successful career on Broadway and in light opera for several years. Among his specialties—especially on record—were the Southern "darky" songs that were extremely popular for some time around and after the turn of the century. Dalhart's biggest early hit had been such a number: "Can't Yo' Heah Me Callin', Caroline?"

Dalhart apparently felt that country tunes could be as popular, especially given the success of Henry Whitter's "The Wreck of the Old 97" in early 1924, but few of the

record companies with which he dealt agreed with his judgment. (The practice of signing artists to exclusive contracts, taken for granted today, was rare in Dalhart's day, and he was free to record for any number of companies on per-record contracts.) Eventually he persuaded Edison to try "The Wreck of the Old 97" in May of 1924, then recorded it again in August for Victor, backed with a tune he and his cousin composed, "The Prisoner's Song." The accompaniment had a country flavor—guitar, harmonica and voice—and what happened is the stuff of which legend is made: "The Prisoner's Song" took off like no record before and few since, and estimates on its total sales on the multitude of labels on which Dalhart recorded it run from three million to nine million to

27 million! Thus did Vernon Dalhart become country music's first recording star.

As mentioned, because Dalhart did not have a long-term recording contract with Victor, he recorded for nearly every label then in existence, ultimately using well over a hundred pseudonyms by the time his career was over in the late 1930's; some of them still have scholars guessing.

Dalhart was certainly country music's first star, and his 1916 recordings for Thomas Edison make Dalhart the first country singer to record, but these recordings were basically not country in sound, style or intent. The honor of the first genuinely country recordings to be made go to—you guessed it—a fellow Texan, named Eck Robertson, in 1922.

Alexander Campbell Robertson, although actually born in Arkansas, moved to Texas at the age of three and became one of the Lone Star State's champion fiddlers, the winner of numerous contests, and a figure of great local popularity. It was he who took the train to New York, having teamed up at a Confederate veterans' reunion in Richmond, Virginia, with 74-year-old Henry Gilliland, marched into the Victor Records offices in a full Confederate Army uniform (although he was, in fact, born over two decades after the end of the Civil War), and demanded to make a record. That they did, and their June 30-July 1, 1922, sessions mark the first in country music's history, consisting of six tried-and-true fiddle tunes. From here sprung the long fiddle band recording tradition in Texas music, captured on wax as it had been practiced live for years.

Robertson, in addition to his fearsome reputation in fiddling contests, was active as well in the old frontier tradition of playing house parties—that is, Saturday night gatherings at one home or another at which the rugs were rolled back and dancing lasted well into the morning. The gradual shift from dancing at house parties

Milton Brown, left, and His Musical Brownies laid more groundwork for Western swing. Brown died in 1936.

Bob Wills and friend in the 1930's.

to dancing at night clubs coincided with the growth of Western swing.

A crusty old contemporary of Robertson's was M.J. Bonner, an authentic Civil War veteran (could this be where Robertson got the inspiration for his costume?) who recorded but one session for Victor in March of 1925 as Captain M.J. Bonner (The Texas Fiddler). Like Robertson's, his repertoire was basically composed of Southeastern hoedowns. Bonner's little niche in history is well-deserved, however, because it was he who hosted the initial broadcast of the WBAP *Barn Dance*, the first such program in the nation, on January 4, 1923. Backed by, of all the unlikely groups, Fred Wagner's Hilo Five Orchestra, Captain Bonner played a rousing hour-and-a-half of old-time fiddling, interspersed with Hawaiian music, and listener response was so great that the nation's first radio barn dance became a fixture at WBAP for several years thereafter.

Other bands in the early days of recording reflect this hoary Texas fiddle-band tradition as well: Solomon and Hughes, and Steeley and Graham, both from the Dallas-Fort Worth area, made pioneer recordings in the late 1920's, and both duos were exclusively stringband in sound. Ervin Solomon on fiddle and Joe Hughes on second fiddle were later joined by a guitar-playing younger brother, Jim Solomon; their only recording consisted of two old stringband classics, "Ragtime Annie" and "Sally Johnson." They continued to play house parties with an increasingly larger band (which even included a steel guitar) well into the mid-1930's. A.L. Steeley and J.W. Graham relied very much on the same kind of material (they too recorded "Ragtime Annie" on Brunswick at the same time Solomon and Hughes were recording theirs for Victor), but were extremely atypical of Texas tradition in that Graham played the five-string banjo. Clearly, at this point at least, the fiddle-band traditions of the Southeast and the Southwest were not far different at all. The division of styles was yet to come.

Another example of this same tradition was the short-lived Prince Albert Hunt, who was one of the first to bridge the gap between breakdown fiddle and what was to become Western swing. A fiddler in the old-time tradition, he was also a showman, and not only enlarged his band, but also went from playing house parties to playing for dances in dancehalls and the small bars that became known as honky tonks.

His association with blacks and with blues was an interesting and revealing part of his music and his life. Hunt lived "across the tracks" in the black section of Terrell, Texas; he was frequently found on the front porch of his shanty jamming with black musicians, and he recorded several rather strange blues, such as "Blues in a Bottle," with a rough, bluesy fiddle style. His close association with black musicians is more than reminiscent of Bob Wills' famous learning experiences in the cotton fields with black co-workers in his youth.

At any rate, Prince Albert Hunt's move from house parties to dancehalls was both historic and symbolic, and was, in Hunt's particular case, the cause of his bizarre demise at an early age in March 1931. While strolling out of a Dallas dancehall at the conclusion of one of his dances, his fiddle under one arm and a good-looking, overly affectionate lady on the other, he was shot to death in his tracks by the jealous husband of his companion. Dallas was still a frontier town in many ways.

A couple long associated with Hunt were the uncle-and-nephew team of Oscar and Doc Harper, who recorded for Okeh the same day as Hunt and apparently backed him on his session. Oscar, a better fiddler than Hunt, stayed around long enough to make several recordings for the Library of Congress on John Lomax's celebrated field trip of 1942.

The band that bridged the gap between old-time mountain stringband music and Western swing more than any other was an outfit called The East Texas Serenaders. Both the size and

The King of Western Swing: Bob Wills and His Texas Playboys in the mid-to-late 40's. In the band are Herb Remington, The McKinney Sisters, Louis Tierney, Ocie Stockard, Willard Kelso, Tiny Moore, Eldon Shamblin and Tommy Duncan.

the musical scope of the group presaged the development of the Western swing that grew out of the Texas swing band. They were led by a left-handed fiddler named D.H. Williams, whose parents, like so many Texans, had migrated from Tennessee, and his repertoire was full of mountain square dance tunes like "Sally Goodin" and "Old Joe Clark." In the late 1920's he teamed up with guitarist Claude Hammonds, tenor banjo player John Munnerlin, and a fellow named Henry Bogan, who played a three-string cello like a string bass, and they called this motley aggregation The East Texas Serenaders.

Their recording career (for Brunswick, Columbia and Decca) lasted from 1927 to 1934, and probably could have gone on longer, but they were never full-time musicians and did not care to travel. In addition, they grew up playing at house parties, and were quite uncomfortable in the honky tonk/ballroom atmosphere in which dances increasingly took place as the 1930's progressed. However, their four-piece group and their selection of "rag" material ("Mineola Rag," "Combination Rag") were definite steps away from the standard fiddle band tradition, and steps toward the swing-string music to come. In addition, in later years Williams was to tutor one of the great jazz/swing fiddlers of all time: ex-Texas Playboy and long-time Willie Nelson associate Johnny Gimble.

The repertoire of The East Texas Serenaders eloquently demonstrates the shift many fiddle bands were making toward swing, largely because of the awesome influences of both radio and record. Williams recalls that in between the square-dance tunes and the jazzier rags, they frequently sang hits of the day, learned from radio or record, such as "Five Foot, Two" in the early days, and "Rosetta" and "Stardust" later on. The fiddle music of the Western frontier, not far different from that of the Southeast for many years, was suddenly exposed to a wide variety of other influences over the airwaves: nearby Cajun and Norteño music, the more distant strains of New Orleans and Chicago jazz, and the increasingly swinging sounds of mainstream popular music. Creative and adaptable musicians were quick to make elements of all these styles their own, and thus was born Texas music's most distinctive offspring: Western swing.

Tommy Duncan

It all got under way with a group called The Light Crust Doughboys, who were not all that different from The East Texas Serenaders. Not that this was a swing band—it really wasn't at all—but it was heading that way, and among its graduates are all the early greats of the genre: Milton Brown, Johnnie Lee Wills, Tommy

Duncan, Leon McAuliffe, Herman Arnspiger and, of course, Bob Wills.

The Doughboys were led— maybe directed is more like it— by an ambitious flour executive for Burrus Mill named Wilbert Lee O'Daniel, who although not a musician served as their announcer, boss and agent. He even wrote some of their more memorable songs as well, "Beautiful Texas" and "Put Me in Your Pocket" among them. He heard a group called Aladdin's Laddies on the radio one day, and decided this might just be one heck of a way to sell flour, so he took this band—composed of Bob Wills, Milton and Derwood Brown and Herman Arnspiger—and renamed them The Light Crust Doughboys (the name was decided their first time on the air in Fort Worth) after

The Texas Troubadour, Ernest Tubb, center, took his music to Nashville in the early 1940's. At far right is Harold Bradley.

E.T. and His Texas Troubadours:
Leon Short, Kemo Head, Johnny Sapp,
Jack Drake and Jimmie Short.

the brand of flour he wanted to promote.

W. Lee O'Daniel was inspired by the tremendous popularity of The Doughboys (a band that, in various permutations, has lasted to the present) to propel his career as a politician with a band of the same sort, The Hillbilly Boys. O'Daniel eventually rose to governor of the state of Texas, and later United States senator, but he was an autocratic and high-handed bandleader, and there was considerable disaffection within The Doughboys band.

The first to break away was vocalist Milton Brown; his high-pitched, sweet, pop-tinged vocals sparked the band's sound, and he went on to form the first "real" Western swing band, which he called his Musical Brownies. Building on what he'd learned as a Doughboy, he and his innovative musicians (primarily Cecil Brower, Cliff Bruner, Papa Calhoun, Wanna Coffman, Ocie Stockard, brother Durwood Brown and legendary pioneer steel guitar player Bob Dunn) combined the musical styles of their region with the swing and pop styles

E.T., Clayton McMichen and Jimmie Rodgers' guitar.

of the day to become one of the most exciting and influential bands of the era. Milton Brown's influence was every bit as great as was Bob Wills' in his era, but the promise of a legendary career was cut short by a fatal 1936 automobile accident, and all that remains are some great recordings on Decca and Bluebird, which only hint at the greatness possible.

When Milton Brown left The Light Crust Doughboys, he was replaced by a deeper-voiced singer with a real feel for the blues named Tommy Duncan, and although his sound was rather different, it was just as popular. Still, fiddler and more or less de facto leader Bob Wills chafed at the bit, and in the late summer of 1933 he finally left The Doughboys, taking with him his banjo-playing brother Johnnie Lee and vocalist Tommy Duncan. Adding the Whalin brothers, Kermit and June, this fledgling swing band moved to Waco, where they called themselves Bob Wills and his Playboys—the "Texas" was added to the band name only after they moved to Tulsa, Oklahoma, the following year.

Although always firmly associated with the Lone Star State, Wills and his Texas Playboys found their greatest success—artistically and financially—during the nine years they headquartered at KVOO in Tulsa. Subsequent moves to California and Texas were never able to rekindle the greatness of that era.

The hot dance music Bob Wills and His Texas Playboys provided from their very first recording session caused them to become a local sensation, then a regional one, and eventually a national one, with the 1941 million-seller "New San Antonio Rose." Propelled by a swing beat, the band never lost its country feel, with Bob's exuberant hollering a trademark both on record and in person, and with the ever-present steel guitar of Leon McAuliffe as well. It was a music that saw its popularity decline in the 1950's, but that in the 1970's and 1980's came back stronger than ever.

At about the time The Light Crust Doughboys were still going strong, and Bob Wills was beginning to become a star in Tulsa, and Milton Brown was meeting his untimely death, a host of other swing bands began to crop up all over the state of Texas. It would be easy to brand them as imitators—most were indeed inspired by both the sound and the success of Brown and Wills—but on the other hand, most were exactly like the Brown and Wills outfits: Texas fiddle bands

Hank Thompson

experimenting with the new sounds they heard over the radio and on record, and striving to adapt those strains to their own music. Although none approached the popularity of Wills, a host of such Texas swing bands made their indelible mark on the music of the Lone Star State.

A band that maintained a Western swing feel but never went to brass instruments was Bill Boyd's Cowboy Ramblers. While its mainstays over the years were Bill and his brother Jim, The Cowboy Ramblers saw a host of illustrious sidemen pass through their ranks, including Jesse Ashlock and Art Davis. Davis had the unusual distinction of cutting Boyd's first hit, "Under the Double Eagle," in 1935, and his last, "Lone Star Rag," in 1950, although he spent the intervening years touring with Autry, appearing in films on his own, and leading his own Western swing band as well.

Extremely close to the traditional fiddle-band sound, Boyd nevertheless adopted the fancy Hollywood cowboy image (he, in fact, made several films in the late 1930's, and has ever since been confused with William Boyd—Hopalong Cassidy) and sported a host of swingy songs. Still his staples were the fiddle tunes and waltzes that have characterized Texas music from the beginning.

There were other groups: for example, The Hi-Flyers, a Fort Worth group who, according to leader/banjoist Elmer Scarborough, predate The Light Crust Doughboys. Their progress, too, parallels that of many other pioneer swing bands in that they started small, then grew larger and added electrified instruments along the way, their repertoire going from fiddle tunes and reworked pop hits to an increasing number of original songs as time went on. Perhaps the band's most interesting accomplishment was the pairing of Lefty Perkins and Bob Dunn on twin steel guitars on border station XEPN, a sound that unfortunately was never preserved on record.

An interesting and peculiar band of the period was The Tune Wranglers of San Antonio. Despite two full-fledged hit records (for Bluebird) of the era—"Texas Sand" in 1937 and the novelty "Hawaiian Honeymoon" in 1939—little was heard of them thereafter. They apparently disbanded in 1940 and never reformed. Led by Buster Coward, they claimed to be authentic ranch hands, and their sound was a mixture of stringband, swing and heavy doses of cowboy, although they played down the stringband aspect perhaps more than most, while on the other hand featuring more original material than the majority of their contemporaries. As far as best-selling records go, their moment in the sun was impressive, but it was at the same time surprisingly brief.

A band that delved more deeply into jazz than most was Roy Newman and His Boys, who worked mainly out of Dallas. Recording as early as 1934, their specialties were numbers like "Tin Roof Blues," "Sadie Green, The Vamp of New Orleans" and "Tiger Rag," which shows, if nothing else, the widespread influence of jazz material (spread rapidly by radio and record) on Texas bands. Since Bill Boyd and His Cowboy Ramblers were also playing at WRR in Dallas at the same time, they freely exchanged and shared band members, Art Davis among them. One of Roy Newman's Boys who went on to glory on his own was vocalist Gene Sullivan, later to join with Wiley Walker in Oklahoma to become an extremely popular singing and songwriting ("Live and Let Live," "When My Blue Moon Turns to Gold") duet of the late 1930's.

A couple of other bands made contributions to (or at least were reflections of) elements of the burgeoning Texas swing sound, but relatively little is known about them. The Nite Owls, led by Jack True, were extremely typical of these bands, going from fiddle tunes to blues, rehashed pop, jazz, and even Mexican ("Cielito Lindo,"

"Rancho Grande") and some original material, none of it unusual enough to make them household words. Their home base of Austin was a bit out of the ordinary, predating the music scene there by some 40 years. Rather the opposite approach came from a West Texas group formed by Bob Kendrick, but dubbed Bob Skyles' Skyrockets by record producer Eli Oberstein, which was both the brassiest and the corniest of all country swing bands. Working out of Pecos, their sound was sort of a brass version of The Hoosier Hot Shots, and novelty numbers like "Arkansas Bazooka Swing" and "Bazooka Stomp" were their stock in trade.

The far-flung locations of The Nite Owls and Bob Skyles' Skyrockets do, however, point out one interesting aspect of Texas swing. While the bulk of the action took place in the Dallas-Fort Worth area, it was a genuinely widespread phenomenon throughout the Lone Star State. Other Texas swing bands include: Adolph Hofner and the Tune Wranglers in San Antonio, Doug Bine (as well as Bob Wills in his early years) in Waco, Cliff Bruner in Beaumont, Ted Daffan in Houston, and more and more as the 1930's ended and the 1940's progressed.

Another very interesting minor swing band was The Crystal Springs Ramblers, not so much for their own good but unexceptional music as for the band members who came out of the troupe. Link Davis ("Big Mamou"), Bob Wills' longtime left-handed fiddler Joe Holley, and fid-

Hank Thompson and His Brazos Valley Boys updated Western swing for the 50's. Monte Hale, center, joined them in Dallas.

dler Leon Selph all were alumni of the outfit, named after the Crystal Springs dance pavilion northwest of Fort Worth, where they were the staff band for years under the direction of Papa Sam Cunningham. Although they had only two recording sessions (both in June of 1937), they were an extremely popular band in person for years.

Though fiddler Leon Selph did not record with The Crystal Springs Ramblers, he was an important member, and he left the band to form an extremely influential group called The Blue Ridge Playboys—a rather odd name for a swing band—in 1935. Two original members later went on to develop the offshoot of Western swing known as honky tonk in the following decade: lead singer and guitarist Floyd Tillman, and steel guitarist Ted Daffan. Both were to write songs that sold into the many millions in years to come, and a couple of them (Tillman's "Slippin' Around" and Daffan's "Born to Lose") were to become country music landmarks in addition to racking up big sales.

The importance of The Blue Ridge Playboys is further underscored by three other members who went on in a honky tonk rather than in a swing vein: their pianist Moon Mullican, a sometimes vocalist and guitarist named Chuck Keeshan (who was to spend some years with Ted Daffan), and guitarist Dickie McBride, a long-time fixture of the Houston area well into the television age. If the seeds of honky tonk as a musical style can be said to have been sown somewhere, then it surely must have been with The Blue Ridge Playboys in the 1930's. It was a style created not so much by men as by economics; it was a music for jukeboxes and small bands in roadside dance taverns. With the exception of Ernest Tubb and Al Dexter, every major early figure in the style came out of but one band, The Blue Ridge Playboys.

Still, while honky tonk was developing in a setting governed by the rise of the jukebox and the tavern, there was considerable activity in the field of swing, activity that was to span three decades and that, despite a period of dormancy, is very much a part of Texas music even into the 90's.

Leon McAuliffe left The Playboys and founded his own band.

Another swing band that bridged the gap between the swing and the honky tonk styles was Cliff Bruner's Texas Wanderers, which has among its many accomplishments the honor of recording and releasing country music's first truck-driving song, a Ted Daffan composition called "Truck Driver's Blues," in 1939. Bruner began his career as a fiddler with Milton Brown's Musical Brownies, participating in Brown's last recording session, and he is still an active performer. Although based in Beaumont, the Texas Wanderers seemed to borrow band members (Tillman, Mullican, McBride) freely from The Blue Ridge Playboys, which may well explain their propensity for honky tonk.

Western swing reached an awkward point in the era after World War II: While for some bands, like Wills and Spade Cooley, it was an extremely successful time in their career financially, on the other hand, a good bit of the music at the local level was dying on the vine. It was a symptom that accurately paralleled the national disaffection with the smooth, dreamy, danceable big band sound and its concurrent turn to the lonely honky tonk sound, to songs like "Slippin' Around," and, ultimately, to the simple, direct, Southeastern sounds of Hank Williams and Kitty Wells. It was a rough period for Texas in general, and Western swing specifically, one from which this particular genre of Texas music was not to recover until the early 1970's.

That swing was fading in Texas after the war is dramatically demonstrable: Most swing bands

Honky tonker Al Dexter's "Pistol Packin' Mama" was a 1940's smash hit.

disbanded during the war, and few reorganized after V-J Day. Those that did (with the exception of Hofner) were unable to get major label affiliation any longer. The exceptions, Wills and Cooley (who was actually from Oklahoma, not Texas), were enjoying considerable success, but not in Texas; both were based in California, and after about 1950 even their big record-selling days were over as well. Bob's younger brother, Johnnie Lee Wills, also enjoyed considerable success in postwar Tulsa, but despite two hit records—"Rag

Mop" and "Peter Cottontail"—his success was regional. Tastes and fashions inevitably changed, and Western swing went quickly out of favor, not to return for two decades.

Still, some new faces appeared in the 1940's, although they had to be extreme diehards or extremely adaptable to survive. An example of the former was an unabashed Bob Wills imitator and admirer named Hoyle Nix, who led his West Texas Cowboys in Big Spring ever since the late 1940's, faithfully preserving the Bob Wills sound. He was rewarded by a guest appearance on Wills' 1974 album, *For the Last Time*. Similarly, a group called The Miller Brothers (real name: Gibbs; Sam Gibbs was later to become Bob Wills' manager) struggled along in Wichita Falls with a devoted local following—their sound good, traditional Western swing.

The other approach was taken by Waco's Hank Thompson, who returned from the Navy to build an extremely successful career with a swing band. He was able to get away with it in the 1950's (while Wills struggled and most of the rest gave up) by a combination of a music much smoother than any of the other swing bands had been able to get, with the occasional exception of Cooley, and also by the use of contemporary material, much of it self-written. He achieved his greatest success in Oklahoma, making the Trianon Ballroom in Oklahoma City his home base. The smooth sound of The Brazos Valley Boys led to their being named the top Western swing band for 13 straight years by trade publications like *Billboard, Downbeat* and *Cashbox*. In the 1990's Thompson was still booking out as a solo artist.

So while Wills endured (his bands dwindling in size until, in the late 1960's, just he and a vocalist were appearing), Hoyle Nix dug in and holed up inside a pocket of loyalty, and Hank Thompson adapted swing to meet the demands of the day, an approach also followed with less success by Leon McAuliffe, who had founded his Cimarron Boys after the war. McAuliffe went so far as to record "Sh-boom" in smooth Western swing style. Even Ray Price had a fling with Western swing, starting out with a small Hank Williams-type band (in fact, he used The Drifting Cowboys for a couple of years after Hank's death), then going on to form a big, beautiful swing band in the mid-1950's before settling down to the smaller honky tonk shuffle band with which he achieved his greatest success.

But for all this, Western swing was for most purposes dead by the late 1950's, kayoed by the triple punches of the negative impact of television, the Southeastern sound revival of the early 1950's, and the explosion of rock in mid-decade. Still, tastes and fads vary and shift, and music has always been prone to cyclical swings of popularity. What was once discarded is now discovered to be precious, and so Western swing rose once again, riding the pendulum back into popularity in the 1970's. Reunions of The Texas Playboys became big events, and a revamped group of ex-Playboys was signed to do new recordings for Capitol Records. But time had taken its toll, for during the period of the surging revival of Western swing, former Playboys Jesse Ashlock, Noel Boggs, Keith Coleman, Sleepy Johnson and the grand old man himself, Bob Wills, died as the music they created was being reborn.

Much of the impetus

Floyd Tillman in the 1940's.

for this rebirth came from country-rock bands like Commander Cody and His Lost Planet Airmen, and a group of Austinites (via San Francisco and their native Pennsylvania/ West Virginia area) called Asleep at the Wheel, who delved deeply into the Bob Wills sound; they helped introduce this sound to a whole new and enthusiastic generation and kept on keeping on, in one form or another, into the 1990's. An adopted Texan (actually born in Oklahoma) in this same tradition was Alvin Crow, the fiddling leader of his Pleasant Valley Boys, who pursued a half-original, half-revivalist approach to Western swing.

As has been seen, the history of Western swing is closely entwined with that of honky tonk. The basic thrust of both musical styles is the same—dance-a-billy—but as time went on they both took on quite distinct and unique characteristics. For

Floyd Tillman in the early 1980's—a rare New York appearance at the Lone Star Cafe.

Lefty Frizzell

one thing, honky tonk was usually performed by a small band, with electric guitar and steel lead (to cut through the din of crowded roadside taverns), while the trend in swing was, of course, to bigger bands, full rhythm sections, and often horn sections as well. Thematically the songs differed as well: Western swing songs were for the large part beautiful, danceable melodies, with dreamy lyrics generalizing on the subject of love lost or found. Honky tonk, however, was directed at the patrons of these roadside taverns and the realities of their lives, and as the years went by they became increasingly honest, even harsh, in dealing with the problems that beset honky tonkers directly: excessive drinking, slipping around, frustration in life and in love. It is a style that has never died: For every Ray Price who changes stylistic horses in midstream there is a Johnny Bush, Moe Bandy or Randy Travis to take up the honky tonk banner. The music appeals to something in a rather large percentage of country music's populace.

The rise of honky tonk as a musical style parallels the rise of the honky tonk as a social gathering place. With the advent of the jukebox, dancing in small taverns became possible, and dancing, it must be remembered, was a national pastime of major proportions in the era; certainly it was the basis for Western swing and for honky tonk first and foremost. But the crowd who did the two-step to the jukebox or the three-piece band was a different one from those who paid to dance at Cain's Academy or the Crystal Springs Pavilion. Hard drinkin' and easy lovin' increasingly became the themes of honky tonk songs.

As noted before, most of the early honky tonk greats came out of The Blue Ridge Playboys: Ted Daffan, Floyd Tillman and Moon Mullican. And that this is one of the purest forms of Texas music is self-evident. All were Texans by adoption if

not by birth as, indeed, were the two honky tonk greats who were not ex-Blue Ridge Playboys, Ernest Tubb and Al Dexter.

Daffan came out of Houston (although actually born in Louisiana), a Hawaiian guitar player who joined The Blue Ridge Playboys on country steel. Even if he didn't start with country, he had what it took, and he was to write more than one country music classic: His first session with his own band contained the jukebox instrumental favorite "Blue Steel Blues" as well as the perennial "Worried Mind."

Honky tonk stylist Lefty Frizzell and his recording band in the early 50's.

Daffan went in for big bands, usually recording with six to eight musicians, sometimes as many as 12; in fact, *Billboard* reported in the late 1940's that he was planning to build a 22-piece orchestra on the West Coast, but there is no evidence that his plans ever materialized. However, even with large bands Daffan's approach was far more honky tonk than swing. The band rarely swung, but instead concentrated on the lyrics of his songs, many of them—"Headin' Down the Wrong Highway" the classic in this case—speaking directly to the honky tonk patron.

Ted Daffan's Texans reached their peak at their February 1942 session for Okeh Records: Here the extremely popular "No Letter Today" was cut, as was the anthem of country music's dispossessed, "Born to Lose." It was a song that on its

Ray Price

face dealt with hard luck and lost love but that took on a pervasive meaning to those who floundered and struggled in the perplexing World War II years, thrust into a faster-paced world for which they were ill prepared.

Daffan's career, like that of most big-band leaders, slid sharply after the war. After a fling in California he returned to Houston, where he lives today. His songwriting powers stayed strong, however: "I've Got Five Dollars and It's Saturday Night," "Tangled Mind" and "I'm a Fool to Care" became postwar hits for Faron Young, Hank Snow, and Les Paul and Mary Ford, respectively.

Daffan's old bandmate with The Blue Ridge Playboys, Floyd Tillman, also distinguished himself largely as a songwriter, although he was a singer of great popularity, his strange, looping voice one of the most distinctive in country music. Although actually born in Oklahoma, he moved to Post, Texas, as a child, and has been closely associated with Texas music ever since. Tillman remained active into the 90's, a popular denizen of Austin, known affectionately as "the original cosmic cowboy."

"I Love You So Much It Hurts," "Each Night at Nine" and "It Makes No Difference Now" are Tillman's best-known compositions, along with another of country music's true landmark songs, "Slippin' Around." One of the first songs to face the issue of infidelity head-on, without apology or moralizing, it was daring in its day and has proved to be a landmark in country music's history, although the way had been paved by Eddie Dean's "One Has My Name, The Other Has My Heart." Jimmy Wakely and Margaret Whiting's version of "Slippin' Around" was a quick million-seller in 1949-50 and was symptomatic of the postwar mood, speaking to millions not only in honky tonks but outside them as well.

Aubrey "Moon" Mullican was at once both more and less honky tonk than his two fellow Blue Ridge Playboys. His bluesy, bawdy-house piano style was in and of itself closely entwined with the honky tonk sound, and because of it his association with honky tonk was natural and inevitable. On the other hand, he was a performer who was a master of a great many styles—blues, Cajun, straight country, pop, honky tonk,

Dixieland, ragtime and many more—and who, like Daffan and Tillman (although to a lesser degree), was well known for his songwriting, including "Pipeliner's Blues" and "Cherokee Boogie." Still, this East Texan's greatest contribution was his dynamic, exciting piano style, which had a profound effect on Jerry Lee Lewis and many other rockabillies, who forged from Moon's style their own hybrid creations.

It should, however, be pointed out that the roots of honky tonk are not solely with The Blue Ridge Playboys among early Texas musicians.

Billy Walker made the move from Texas to Nashville.

For example, The Shelton Brothers were an extremely popular and influential pre-honky tonk band, recording as early as 1933 with Leon Chappelear as The Lone Star Cowboys. They grew to stringband proportions, then wholeheartedly adopted the honky tonk sound in the late 1930's, with songs like "Rompin' and Stompin' Around." Their two most popular songs—"Deep Elem Blues" and the ubiquitous "Just Because"—helped pave the way for the honky tonk sound.

But the two real kings of honky tonk, as the form became more and more popular in the 1940's, were Troup's Al Dexter and Crisp's Ernest Tubb, who brought the sound to the

Jim Reeves, right, began his career as an announcer on Texas radio. Here he is at station KGRI with Cole Knight and Al Courtney. The live show went on daily at noon.

tonk band, and the term "honky tonk" shows up early in his work: "Honky Tonk Blues" in 1936 (which may well be the first use of the term in a song title), "Honky Tonk Baby" in 1937, and "When We Go A-Honky Tonkin'" and "Poor Little Honky Tonk Girl" in 1940. He wrote and recorded the wartime smash, "Pistol Packin' Mama," a humorous and unabashed description of the perils of honky tonk life. Dexter was capable of writing other fine country material ("Guitar Polka," "Rosalita," "Too Late to Worry, Too Blue to Cry"), but his brief, glorious moment in the sun revolved around the honky tonk sound that had made him famous and that he, in turn, helped popularize on a national level to a far greater degree than ever before.

Less explosively popular but with a career of far greater durability was Ernest Tubb, who began as a Jimmie Rodgers imitator on Bluebird records. (Rodgers' rare old Martin 000-45 guitar was given to him by Jimmie's widow, Carrie.) Tubb later developed his own very distinctive style, becoming well-known in Texas while being sponsored by a flour company, as The Gold Chain Troubadour. He began recording for Decca in

Southeast when he joined the Opry in 1942.

Al Dexter (born Albert Poindexter) began recording in 1936, and late in that decade began what turned out to be an extremely successful flirtation with the honky tonk style. Al Dexter and His Troopers were basically a small honky

1940, and had his first big hit with "Walking the Floor Over You" in 1941, which brought him to the Opry. His sound was always (with the exception of his very early Jimmie Rodgers period) pure honky tonk. Perhaps the Opry was groping for a successful, up-to-date sound when they hired him;

at any rate, he was an immediate success, and he helped spread the sound into the roadhouses and jukeboxes of the Southeast.

Tubb was not the first to bring an electric guitar onto the hallowed stage of the Grand Ole Opry (Sam McGee, Pee Wee King and Paul Howard all claim the honor), but he was the first to make it a major part of his sound, especially after Jimmie Short made that little four-note guitar lick an integral part of the Ernest Tubb sound. Often working with just the electric lead guitar, a steel, and bass, Tubb's approach was pure honky tonk: straightforward, loud, direct, unsubtle, with the lyrics focusing on drinking, dancing and the honky tonk life. The man didn't know the meaning of the word rest: Although he nominally lived in Nashville, he rarely saw the town, touring over 100,000 miles a year of grueling one-nighters.

Ray Noble Price, of Perryville, fell right into this mold as well: Up until his celebrated image change in 1967, he had been known as The Cherokee Cowboy, and his band's sound—with the exception of his all too brief fling with Western swing—was hard-nosed Texas honky tonk. In fact, more than anyone he defined the honky tonk sound of the 1950's: walking bass, heavy-handed drumming, and song after song in the two-step shuffle: "City Lights," "Crazy Arms," "Release Me," "My Shoes Keep Walking Back to You," "Heartaches by the Number" and many more. With Willie Nelson's bluesy composition "Night Life" in 1963, Ray Price at once got as deep into honky tonk as anyone ever had, and yet hinted strongly at the mellow-voiced, resonant, country-pop Price of "For the Good Times" and beyond. It was a turning point for him, but he left behind him a host of imitators to fill the void (Johnny Bush was among the most conspicuous), and the legacy of the greatest honky tonk music of the 1950's.

Although his peak years came later, George Jones of Beaumont was also into the honky tonk/

Hank Williams mold pioneered by Price in the 1950's. In fact, while stationed in Northern California while in the Marine Corps (about 1952) Jones appeared on a local basis. Frequently his repertoire consisted exclusively of Hank Williams' songs. Born in Saratoga, Texas, Jones first hit on the Starday label in 1955 with "Why, Baby Why?" and had a long string of hard-core honky tonk hits. But George Jones has always been extremely intimate with a song, and has drifted away from the raucous honky tonk sound into something very personal and unique of his own. If anything, this explains the remarkable phenomenon of his popularity, even after four decades in country music.

Honky tonk was a style that wouldn't die. The Southeastern sound revival of the early 1950's helped knock off cowboy music and Western swing, but it couldn't knock off honky tonk, nor could the rock 'n' roll phenomenon later in the decade, nor could the ultra-slick Nashville Sound of the 1960's, nor could the Urban Cowboy fad of the 1980's. And, true to form, it was Texas that carried the honky tonk banner through it all, good times and bad.

A pair who helped it weather the rock years were Charlie Walker, of Collin County, and Johnny Horton, of Tyler. Walker went the time-honored route of disc jockey to singer, and scored biggest in 1958 with "Pick Me Up on Your Way Down." Horton, on the other hand, gave up a promising career in music, having been a high school singing star, to become a professional fisherman, but drifted back into performing on the West Coast. He returned to the area of his native East Texas around 1952, joining the cast of the *Louisiana Hayride* (Shreveport is just over the Texas/Louisiana border). Horton was firmly in the honky tonk tradition—in fact, "I'm a Honky Tonk Man" was an early hit for him—but drifted into the historical-song vein, of which he quickly became king with "Johnny Reb," "Springtime in

Alaska," "North to Alaska," and the two super hits "Sink the Bismarck" and "The Battle of New Orleans." His career was spectacular but all too short: He was killed in an automobile accident on November 5, 1960.

It is a peculiar historical quirk that many of the greats of Texas music are from the eastern part of the state, from Vernon Dalhart to Willie Nelson. It's hard to account for the unusual musical fertility of this area, other than the relatively sparse population of the more desolate middle and west of the state. The southeastern part of Texas has always had the seaports and good farmland (as well as oil later on) to support a large population. Then, too, in a musical sense, it was a location where the mixture of various cultures—hillbilly, black, Cajun, Mexican, Ger-

Singer and governor Jimmie Davis and Johnny Horton.

man and others—were able to mix and intermingle very freely.

It is a debatable point, of course, and purely a subjective one, but perhaps the greatest of them all was an ex-boxer and oil-field worker from Corsicana named William Orville Frizzell. From romping paeans to the honky tonk life ("If You've Got the Money, I've Got the Time") to gushy sentimentality ("Mom & Dad's Waltz") to straight country love songs ("I Love You a Thousand Ways"), Lefty had a spine-tingling sincerity to his voice: It was a voice capable of spectacular yet emotive vocal effects, a voice of tremendous warmth and intimacy, a voice that has had a remarkable effect on all who have followed. It was a sound so new (although instrumentally and thematically it was pure honky tonk, through and through) that Lefty exploded with four songs in the country Top Ten at one time, a feat never since duplicated. But after the novelty wore off, Lefty couldn't seem to sustain this success, his personal life marred by bouts with the bottle, his records all too often wasting his magnificent voice on nondescript material, although when he found the right song later on ("Long Black Veil," "Saginaw, Michigan"), public response was there. It's a shame he didn't live up to his awesome potential, but even as it is, he ranks in the pantheon of the all-time greats of Texas music.

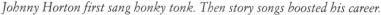

Johnny Horton first sang honky tonk. Then story songs boosted his career.

Although Lefty died all too young, at 47 in 1975, the honky tonk tradition lives on in the likes of Willie Nelson, Moe Bandy, and the host of young singers working in the style after Randy Travis revived it in the mid-1980's.

Ernest Tubb's move to Nashville in 1943 signaled the beginning of another movement that was, in the 1950's, to accelerate rapidly. That was the migration of many Texan entertainers to Tennessee (reversing the steps of many of their ancestors), where the Grand Ole Opry and the Nashville Sound predominated. If there is a decade in which the importance of Texas music can be said to have been minimal, then, that was it: the decade between the late 1950's and the late 60's. In those years, the combined forces of rock 'n' roll and the Nashville Sound overwhelmed everything.

The term "Texas in Nashville" describes the decade as well as any other, for many of the era's biggest Nashville stars were in fact transplanted Texans. After Tubb came Ray Price in 1950, then George Jones, Goldie Hill and Billy Walker, who took the time-honored route of moving from the *Louisiana Hayride* to the Opry after serving time in what might be called the high minors.

Goldie Hill was of course not the first female singer (or songwriter) produced by Texas. Others included the noted singer-songwriter Cindy Walker, songwriter Mae Boren Axton, Texas Ruby Owens (Tex Owens' sister) and Laura Lee McBride, who was Owens' daughter, Dickie McBride's wife and Bob Wills' first "girl singer." Jeannie C. Riley, Barbara Mandrell, Billy Jo Spears, La Costa and Tanya Tucker were among the next generation of women Texas sent up to Nashville.

Easily the most important influence in the Texas-in-Nashville movement was Jim Reeves

Rex Allen and Jack Jones with Jimmy Dean on The Jimmy Dean Show on TV in 1964.

who, despite many years in the Lone Star State (he was born in the same county as Tex Ritter), came out of it without a touch of Texas in his smooth, romantic, appealing voice. An ex-disc jockey and aspiring baseball player, Reeves turned his attention to singing while working on the *Louisiana Hayride* as an announcer, and with the success of "Mexican Joe" and "Bimbo" moved to the Opry and to a full-time career as a singer.

But if there was any performer ready to shuck the good-old-country-boy image it was Reeves, who was quite eager to go along with the emerging Nashville music, the slick "countrypolitan" sound that developed when rock all but killed the hard Southeastern sound of the early 1950's. Although Reeves never lost his country image to many country fans—including the English who revere him today as much as ever—he clearly made a conscious effort at invading the country-pop territory mined so successfully by Eddy Arnold, who pretty much had the field to himself. Unafraid to tackle smooth, popular material, Reeves and the burgeoning Nashville Sound helped pull the town and the music through the lean rock years.

The Texas-in-Nashville phase continued in the

Johnny Cash, Texas songwriter Mae Axton and George Jones in 1957.

early and mid-1960's with the arrival of Willie and Waylon, although by then the character of the movement was beginning to change, and the seeds of a Texas revival were being sown. But in the meantime there was precious little to say for Texas during the late 1950's and early 1960's, for other than Reeves, whose sound was not remotely a reflection of Texas, and already established stars like Tubb and Price, few landmark performers or sounds emanated from the Lone Star State. One exception was Plainview's Jimmy Dean (born Seth Ward), who began recording as early as 1953, with "Bumming Around" on 4-Star. Solidly in the Texas-in-Nashville mold, Dean didn't actually move to Music City, but instead was based out of the Washington, D.C., area for his local television show, and then New York for his CBS daytime network television show and his ABC network show in the evening in the early 1960's.

Country music seemed to take a dramatic shift toward the Southeastern sound in the 1950's. It had begun in the late 1940's with Hank Williams, and continued with Kitty Wells, Webb Pierce, Ray Price and Hank Thompson, the last two Texans who tried to fuse

Early Starday publicity shot of George Jones.

the styles of the Southeast and the Southwest. Gone was interest in the jazzy complexity of Western swing and the dreamy romanticism of the singing cowboys; here was hard, harsh, direct, simple, gutbucket hillbilly. The Southeastern sound revival lasted only a few years, and country music's shift to the Southeast rebounded westward after a few years, settling instead in the Memphis-northern-Mississippi-Arkansas area, with the powerful phenomenon known as rockabilly, a fusion of the hillbilly soul of the Southeastern-revival and the energetic, dynamic, powerful music of the blacks, which had fascinated and inspired Western swing musicians for so long.

One of Texas' major rockabilly figures was Roy Orbison, born in Vernon in 1936. His first real band was formed in Wink, Texas, and was known as The Wink Westerners, a band that became prominent through a radio show. Although he was one of the early Sun Records rockabillies, Orbison's high, strained, liquid, totally unique voice and style drew little from country music or Texas music, and gave little to it in return, although partly because of its very uniqueness it made him extraordinarily popular—particularly overseas—for years.

Texas' contribution to rockabilly was impressive, but not on the magnitude of Memphis. There was a pretty popular band called Sid King and The Five Strings, and Bob Loman who, after his "Let's Think About Living" rockabilly days, became a died-in-the-wool Texan-in-Nashville. Fort Worth native Charles Erwin "Mac" Curtis was successful, as was the Big Bopper, a huge, crewcut bear of an ex-disc jockey named J.P. Richardson, who scored with "Chantilly Lace" before a famous plane crash ended his career and his life. And there was that other passenger on that small plane: Buddy Holly.

Born Charles Hardin Holly in Lubbock in 1936, Buddy Holly showed an early interest in performing, singing tenor in a country duo in high school, which became his first professional job after graduation. Known as Buddy and Bob, their style was a blend typical of the emerging rockabilly style: Western and bop—that somehow seems to sum it up. When they were scouted by Decca Records, however, it was Buddy who was signed, not Bob, and Holly did his first recordings—unsuccessful recordings, as it turns out—in Nashville, backed by Nashville studio men. When he caught on, however, it was explosive, creating a legend in less than two years. "That'll Be the Day" was released in June 1957, and Holly died

*Another Texan,
Waylon Jennings.*

(along with singer Richie Valens and the Big Bopper) in February of 1959. Holly's music was alive and innocent and bursting with energy and sounds which, for all his hiccuping mannerisms, are not so terribly dated today.

Two of his sidemen were to join him on that plane that night as well, but gave up their seats to the headliners. Both fellow Texans, they have each gone on to make large impressions on country music themselves. The lead guitarist was Oklahoma-born Tommy Allsup, whose roots were so deep into Western swing that he played with Art Davis' Rhythm Riders as well as Holly, and cut several "country-politan" guitar albums as well. An occasional session musician in Nashville, Allsup became a well-known producer who recorded Hank Thompson, neo-swing stars Asleep at the Wheel, and the master himself, Bob Wills, late in his career.

The bass player was a youngster from Littlefield named Waylon Jennings, who put together a lot of the elements of Texas music to become one of the leaders of the Texas revival and one of the most influential performers of our day. With a touch of cowboy and a dollop of rockabilly and a great large helping of pure, old-fashioned honky tonk, Jennings, after an uncomfortable Texas-in-Nashville period of country/folk in the mid-1960's, blossomed into a leader of the highly publicized Outlaw faction—singer-songwriters who went their own way, doing their own music, successfully flouting the established Nashville way.

The de facto leader of the Outlaw movement (although it can be said, in some ways, to have begun with a sometime Texan, Kris Kristofferson) was Willie Nelson, who stepped out of the honky tonk genre into the Nashville scene in the early 1960's and astonished the professional world with his awesome songwriting abilities: "Night Life," "Crazy," "Hello Walls," "Funny How Time Slips

Away" and many, many others. Although he tried extremely hard to fit into the up-and-comer's role (especially as the Nehru-jacketed featured vocalist on Ernest Tubb's syndicated television show), his singing was just too odd, too different, too jazzy and strangely toned and phrased, and his successes as a singer were rather limited, despite the continued successes of his songs.

Fed up with being a Texan-in-Nashville, tired of limited success, feeling he was going nowhere, Willie moved back to Texas around 1970, and the results were explosive. Somehow the Texas counterculture was ready for his musical

Buddy Holly and Roy Orbison smoothed off the rough edges of rockabilly.

adventurousness; somehow he was able to appeal with remarkable strength to long-hair and redneck alike, and in bringing together those cultures he brought about the energetic and vital musical interplay loosely called the Austin sound.

Not that what Willie was doing was all that new: The three biggest hits of his Outlaw period were songs 25 years old: "Blue Eyes Crying in the Rain," "Remember Me" and "If You've Got the Money, I've Got the Time," which was even done in the same key and in the same tempo as Lefty Frizzell's original. As always seems to happen, whenever the music gets too complicated, too sophisticated, too formulaic, somebody—be it Jimmie Rodgers or Hank Williams or Elvis Presley or Willie Nelson—comes up with

Johnny
Rodriguez

Texas Playboys Reunion

The many strains of music from the Lone Star State.

Jeannie C.
Riley

Barbara
Mandrell

Freddy
Fender

Asleep at the Wheel

Moe Bandy

music of urgency, of intensity, and most of all, of simplicity.

Popular music goes in cycles; in the 1970's, it was Willie Nelson who brought it around to simplicity again.

The Austin scene to which he was so central, and to which he brought such attention, had its time in the limelight, and then the light moved on. Austin, however, remained a fascinating musical melting pot and playground, and continued to provide a home and/or a stage for a wonderful variety of hyphenated-country, pickers, poets and pioneers. Between the late 1970's and the mid-1990's, Austin's cast of creative characters either resident or visiting frequently included Jerry Jeff Walker, Doug Sahm, Delbert McClinton, Steve Forbert, T-Bone Burnett, Steve Young, Robert Earl Keen, Kelly Willis, Tish Hinojosa, Lyle Lovett, Lucinda Williams, Nanci Griffith, Townes Van Zandt, and, of course, the three outstanding writer/performers who had once been The Flatlanders: Joe Ely, Butch Hancock, and Jimmie Dale Gilmore. And that's not counting all the other roots-ori-

ented musicians, like blues singers Lou Ann Barton and Marcia Ball and former cow-punker Alejandro Escovedo, who were integral components of the scene but couldn't be shoehorned into an acceptable definition of country with any kind of hyphen.

In terms of pure creative power, then, an acre of Austin continued to be just as productive as an acre of Nashville in the 1980's and 90's, if not more so. And, naturally, the Nashville turf continued to be thick with Texans: Steve Earle, considered by many of his peers to be the most promising songwriter of his generation; George Strait, the man who brought both swing and honky tonk music back into the Nashville mainstream; Clint Black, one of the biggest stars of the late 1980's and early 90's; lesser but still substantial lights like Lee Roy Parnell and Mark Chesnutt, and songwriters as enduringly great as Guy Clark and the inimitable Billy Joe Shaver.

Texas, in short, has been very good for country music.

Gene Autry

CHAPTER 5

The Singing Cowboys

The legend of the cowboy is unique in the annals of American history, the one purely American tradition. Thus, to look at the legend of the cowboy in his travails through the "dime novels" of the late 1800's and the movie Westerns from their beginning to the present is to look not simply at the cowboy as he really was but at the cowboy as a series of narrow reflections of the country's most basic (and changing) wants and needs embodied in one continuing character.

There are certain basic qualities in the legend of the cowboy that have become universal despite the changes wrought upon him through the passing of time. In the simplest possible terms, the legend of the cowboy created a man of destiny. He was a free man, unencumbered by the encroachment of pending civilization, although each act he performed brought that same civilization one step closer to its final result: the cowboy's total demise and the full domestication of the Old West. That is the one inescapable fact. In the legend of the cowboy, settlers involved in the civilizing process needed the cowboy much more than the cowboy needed civilization. He was a loner, independent, self-reliant, existing in a violent, untamed world. He was deadly when crossed. His struggle with the elements, whether they were man-made or products of nature at her most awesome, was not a civilized one, but rather an archetypal struggle of sheer survival in the terrifying midst of the unknown, and it was not a struggle to be easily shirked. If there was a challenge, the challenge must be met with all that was available to him, and those tools, too, were largely elemental: courage, skills of survival, an understanding of the land and its untold dangers, and a dogged determination. There was little else at his beck and call, and if he failed, the one reality was his death. It was that reality that lent him a certain awareness of his own mortality and insignificance, but at the same time managed to elevate his struggle for survival to a position of greater importance than the mere meaninglessness of his life. The struggle was everything, because there was no reward but his own survival. The tools of survival that he mastered were rendered obsolete as the homesteaders and the barbed wire localized him and drew him further and further into the world of domestication.

The cowboy provided a terrific legend that lent itself perfectly to the dreams and fantasies of a people finding the restraints of growing modernity binding and claustrophobic. The cowboy, with his sense of freedom and simplicity of action, offered not only the hope of escape, but also the realization that if the cowboy got his job done, we would all have warm beds to come home to each night. You couldn't ask more of any legend.

But who was the real cowboy, and what was on his mind? As one scholar noted: "The cowboy needed no particular ability except to sit on a horse and pay attention." If we are to believe authentic accounts of the life of a cowboy, his was a lot that was more tiresome than heroic and more boring than romantic—or as a cowboy himself said: "There are more cows and less butter, more rivers and less water, and you can see farther and see less than any place in the world."

Following the Civil War, with the South in ruins and overrun with carpetbaggers, and the North attempting to restructure a total society, there were thousands upon thousands of young men who had nothing to return to. Houses, farms and cities were gone. Families had been torn apart, if not destroyed, and the broken pieces were simply too scattered to put back together. So many men—soldiers, freed slaves, the displaced, the restless, the adventurers and more than a few renegades—went West. With them went the rivalry of the Blue and the Gray, complete with the legacy of violence and chaos, as they all began carving out a new life west of the Mississippi.

That life was based on the longhorn cattle that were descendants of animals brought to Mexico by the Spanish in the 1600's. By 1800, these hardy beasts numbered in the hundreds of thousands as they roamed at large over the southern plains. The use of the animal for its tallow, hide, bones for fertilizer, and meat constituted the wealth of the land, but the cattle trade was disorganized and monopolized by shippers on the Gulf Coast.

It was not a major industry by any means, and the Civil War put a further crimp in its development by drawing off the manpower and closing many markets. The situation changed abruptly when the war ended; the men returned to civilian life, and a peacetime economy opened markets back up again.

In 1867, Abilene opened up as the first stockyard to which cattle from all over Texas were driven, then shipped North by rail to the slaughter- and packinghouses of Chicago. The use of the train was a revolutionary idea, both in its efficiency and its introduction of beef to the diet of Easterners. The man who put it all together was Joseph McCoy, a young Chicago livestock trader who knew that cattle on the hoof on their own range were worth but four bucks a head. McCoy offered 40 dollars a head for all cattle delivered to Abilene, while promising Chicago that he would deliver 200,000 head within a decade. Within the first four years of operation, however, he shipped two million cattle North, exceeding even his wildest dreams, and thus gave rise to the term "the real McCoy."

It was the cowboy's role to cover the entire range where the cattle roamed, to brand new calves, to drive the cattle into herds, and then to herd the cattle to the railroad. Suffice it to say that it was rough out there. The cowboy's life was hard and lonely, the elements unrelenting whether it was winter or summer, the food awful, and his only real companion was the wretched (but perfectly suited) little pony he rode. The dangers were real enough, ranging from irate settlers fearful of their plowed land being trampled, to irate Indians, to being thrown from a horse and mangled in one of the frequent stampedes. For the most part, however, his life was one of simple and constant drudgery, except for the infrequent stops at the end of a drive in one of the famous cowtowns. There the cowboy indulged himself in all the luxuries of civilization: gambling, loose women, poison whiskey, and fast guns. Given that the days in such towns were few in comparison to the days in the saddle, the hell-raising was a release valve for the endless solitude of the range. And they really blew it off.

East of the Mississippi, those who stayed behind to reshape the broken remnants looked West with keen interest. With the completion of the transcontinental railroad in 1869, the Western expansion of the telegraph, and the growing number of roving correspondents for the Eastern papers, the people were kept more than simply abreast of Western developments. They were force-fed the details of the Indian wars, the shootouts, the cattle drives, and life out West in general. And the Easterners loved it. Simple interest quickly grew into rapture, and the legend of the cowboy was born.

To nurture that rapture, the "dime novel" was

William S. Hart

created to glorify the West, and the "details" that whetted the Easterner's interest soon turned to heroics fraught with gross exaggeration and misinformation. It was, however, just the tonic that the East needed to revive the spirit of a nation staggering through a postwar depression, revealing as it did (and in the most romantic of terms) a united nation turning the combined energies of the Blue and Gray into a glorious decimation of a common enemy: the redskin. The conquering of the West was to be our salvation, and to conquer an enemy in print, heroes were necessary.

William "Buffalo Bill" Cody was the initial focus of the Eastern adulation (although interviews with and stories of Wild Bill Hickok were also quite popular). Cody had established his credentials as a genuine Western hero early. He was left the man of his family at 11, and worked on a number of wagon trains that took him as far as Fort Laramie. There he met the great trapper Jim Bridger and the great pathfinder Kit Carson, from whom he learned sign language as well as the language of the Sioux. Before Bill was 15 he had trapped, panned gold and ridden for the Pony Express. He returned to Kansas and worked as a general roustabout, fought with the Jayhawkers conducting a guerrilla war against Quantrill's Raiders, served as an Indian scout for the cavalry, and woke up one morning to find that he'd enlisted in the Union forces while under the influence of a terrific drunk. In 15 months he rose from recruit to full private, and was discharged honorably as a hospital orderly. Following the war, Bill returned to scouting and then, in 1868, was hired to kill buffalo to feed the workers laying track on the

Tom Mix

Kansas Pacific Railroad. In 18 months, at $500 per month, he killed 4,280 of the dumb beasts, carving off only the hump and the hindquarters and leaving the rest to rot in the sun. This feat garnered Bill Cody his first public notice.

When Ned Buntline (real name E.Z.C. Judson), the leading "dime novelist" of his time, went West in 1869 to find a new hero, Cody was ready and waiting. The legends of Daniel Boone and Davy Crockett had long since ceased to interest the East. All eyes had turned toward Western expansion—the *new* West—and Cody fit the bill perfectly. Within a year he was a national hero by virtue of a few meager facts, an assortment of tall tales, the racial arrogance of an Anglo-Saxon nation that truly believed in "Manifest Destiny" and, last but not least, the mass production and distribution of the "dime novel" following the widespread use of the continuous roll printing press introduced in the mid-1860's. It's said that in the meeting between Buntline and Cody, Buntline gave Cody his famous name, Buffalo Bill. In any case he took a snippet of conversation here, a callous boast there, and turned them into a whole series of rugged, stirring adventures with such titles as *Buffalo Bill: The King of the Border Men, Buffalo Bill's Best Shot* and *Buffalo Bill's Last Victory.* His first Buffalo Bill epic was actually a play called *The Scouts of the Plains* (1873) in which Buffalo Bill himself sometimes appeared.

In 1894, Cody cashed in on another brand-new entertainment sensation: Thomas Edison's Kinetoscope, the hand-cranked peep show machine that gave each viewer five different

John Wayne in the 1930's.

Gene Autry, wife Ina Mae and Champion.

but short examples of the magic of the moving picture for a quarter. Edison himself took Bill, Annie Oakley, Lost Horse and Short Bull (the latter one of the few Indians who had both seen the Indian Messiah and learned the Ghost dance from Him) into his studio in West Orange, New Jersey, and made the first Western Kinetoscopes: Bill and Short Bull "talking" in sign language; Annie's sharpshooting skills; Lost Horse performing the Buffalo Dance. Eventually, Edison also filmed *The Parade of Buffalo Bill's Wild West Show, The Procession of Mounted Indians, The Buck Dance, The Ghost Dance* and other staged mini-documentaries. These little flash films played coast to coast as penny arcades sprung up in city after city. In a not-so-prophetic aside to Bill during one shooting, Edison confided, however, "The development of the big screen will spoil everything. We're making these peep shows and selling a lot of them at a profit. If we put out a screen machine, there will be use for maybe about ten of them in the whole country."

Nonetheless, the silver screen full of moving images bigger than life did develop (and with Edison at the forefront, naturally, whistling a different tune), and its unveiling in New York in 1896 created a sensation; people could sit in a chair and watch Fatima dancing at the World's Columbian Exposition at Chicago, or Sarah Bernhardt perform the dueling scene from Hamlet, or the *Pennsylvania Limited* roaring straight at them at 60 miles an hour (which sent men, women and children screaming for the nearest door the first time they saw it). It was an unprecedented and godlike experience, and by 1906 *Billboard* reported: "Store shows and five-cent picture theaters might properly be called the jackrabbits of the business of public entertaining because they multiply so rapidly."

The year 1903 was a turning point for movies in general and the western in particular when

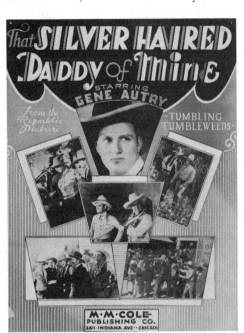

Edison released *The Great Train Robbery*, a film often regarded as the first feature (a grueling ten minutes long) and the first western (a disputed claim). It was a true narrative film, and established once and for all the basic western formula of crime, pursuit, showdown and justice, in addition to highlighting the western movie staples of fist fights, saloons, horse chases, gunplay and plenty of action. It was a well-paced film, and the fact that it was filmed in New Jersey with men who rode horses as if the beasts had been invented yesterday didn't bother theater patrons one bit (as if they really knew). *The Great Train Robbery* was a giant success, and is credited as being the reason why theaters were established in many towns and cities. For a high percentage of Americans, it was the first moving picture they had ever seen, and they were in awe. The movie industry had a major bankable commodity. Imitations of *The Great Train Robbery* proliferated, and sometimes those imitations were a scene-by-scene ripoff with nothing changed except perhaps the calendar date hanging on the wall of the station master's office. Edison even produced a tongue-in-cheek version called *The Little Train Robbery*, featuring a cast of children on ponies.

The one essential missing ingredient, however, was the star, the hero, the source of audience identification. Buffalo Bill was dead (he died broken and practically penniless, a casualty of modern times and technology, in 1917). It was time for the cowboy legend to be transferred from print to celluloid, and the man who embodied the transition came, strangely enough, from the cast of *The Great Train Robbery*. He became not only the first cowboy movie star, but also the first movie star of any kind.

G.M. Anderson (born Arson), a big, beefy former model who had once posed in dude cowboy gear for the cover of *The Saturday*

Evening Post in the midst of a singularly unsuccessful vaudeville career, was cast in *The Great Train Robbery*, but when he revealed he couldn't even get on a horse, much less stay on one, he was pushed into the background. Anderson, however, didn't really care, because he was only interested in making a few bucks. A few months later, however, when he wandered into a theater to see the movie, he was amazed at the tumultuous reception the film received, and from that night on the possibilities of the film medium excited him. He wasn't interested simply in performing in front of the cameras, but rather wanted to produce and direct. He moved to Chicago and got into the business, producing and directing rather undistinguished one- and two-reel westerns and early Ben Turin comedies. Then, in a strange and unplanned twist, Anderson packed up and moved West to Nile, California, 20 miles south of San Francisco, to launch a West Coast studio. It wasn't exactly Hollywood, but it was the first production unit in the Golden State.

Once again, Anderson set out to make westerns, taking advantage of the rolling hillsides and the frost-free weather. He also had something else in mind, something brand new: a cowboy hero with a distinct personality. Stars, however, were difficult to come by in Nile, and finally he chose to play the hero himself. It would be nice to say that it was a wise and calculated move, but as it turns out, it was merely a matter of circumstance. There was just no one else.

Anderson was still big, still beefy, not terribly handsome (but then there was no Robert Redford or Roy Rogers to compare himself with), but he did have a certain sincerity, and that, in

Autry with producer Brad Brown and his family on a Hollywood movie set in 1941. The singing cowboy was here to stay.

addition to a fumbling but ingratiating awkwardness when it came to dealing with the ladies (on the screen, of course) and the ability to throw his brawn around effectively in a fight, made him an instant hit. The first film was *Broncho Bill and the Baby,* a sentimental tale in the "dime novel" tradition in which Broncho Billy, a "good-bad man," gives up his chance for freedom to save a child who finally reforms him. Anderson had no idea just how successful the film was to be, but three months later he realized that he would forever be a Broncho Billy in the minds of moviegoers. He capitalized on that new identity, and by the time he called it quits seven years later he had "starred" as Broncho Billy in 375 one-reelers, close to 100 two-reelers, and even a few features toward the end. The final result was cinematic history, for he had created the first western hero, the first western series, and had opened the West Coast as the new Mecca for film production.

"Broncho Billy" Anderson solidified the notion of the hero in his peppy, adolescent action films, but the sharp edge of a carefully defined hero was left to be honed by a resolute former stage actor, William S. Hart. Hart knew the West from his childhood, and his films tried to capture the sordid and dismal realism

Fay McKenzie, Gene Autry and Smiley Burnette in Republic Pictures' Sierra Sue. Smiley, just visible at left, also joined Gene for Gaucho Serenade.

that he remembered, while also including a strain of idealism that complemented an evangelical mood growing within the country as it embarked on its first sacred quest: freeing the world from the Hun.

Hart's films have been called the first "adult" westerns, and rightfully so. They were brilliantly done, and they raised provocative questions

regarding the growing complexities of a rural nation suddenly beset by urban challenges. His hero's ultimate question was always whether to follow the Law of the Gun (the one rule in the Old West) or to follow the Laws of Civilization (the new rules that the Easterners had brought with them to tame the Old West). The films were very heady affairs, and extremely popular, until the Great War in Europe proved to be anything but a spiritually uplifting experience. In fact, it was damned bloody, and no fun at all. The warriors came home weary and wanting only to forget, and they forgot Bill Hart rather quickly. He was much too serious, especially when there were so many other things to think about and do, like have fun. And there were now so many ways to implement that idea. In 1915, there were only two million cars in the United States and no radios. By 1929, that figure would mushroom

Roy Rogers with songwriter and performer Jenny Lou Carson.

to over 25 million cars and 12 million radios. In those 14 years, the country loosened up. Modern young women in once-forbidden silk stockings and rising hemlines were getting into Model T's everywhere along with smooth and experienced young men just back from *over there*. Together, armed with a hip flask of bathtub gin, they drove their older parents crazy as they raced wildly into the Roaring 20's, stripping away all remnants of the Victorian Age. It was all devilish good fun and high-spirited action, and it was an attitude that spawned Tom Mix movies.

Tom Mix had all the credentials of a celluloid hero, including a real past that was a publicist's dream. He saw action in the Philippine Insurrection, the Boxer Rebellion, the Spanish-American War and the Boer War, and served as a cowboy, a rodeo performer, a Texas Ranger

and a U.S. marshal (not to mention his experience guiding Theodore Roosevelt through darkest Africa). His movies were just as action-packed as his life, and featured a western landscape where anything went as long as it went *fast*. In his lavish "streamlined" westerns, Mix combined the best of the Old West with modern niceties like racing cars, sleek stallions, airplanes, ocean liners, trains, tanks, pretty girls; snappy direction and camera work; beautiful locations (he was fond of using national parks), and crisp, tailored cowboy outfits—in short, anything that would make a good, fast show. Mix quickly became the biggest cowboy star of all. By 1925 he was earning $17,000 a week at Fox, and had given rise to a whole host of self-styled imitators like Hoot Gibson, Tim McCoy, Buck Jones, Ken Maynard and many other lesser stars. Every major studio had its own cowboy stars, and westerns were being churned out by the hundreds. The more they made, the cheaper and more formularized they got. But in the world of silent films, they were still paying bills.

Sound wiped all that out. By 1929, all the major studios (with the exception of Universal) had axed their cowboys. The formula western didn't seem to justify the production expenses that sound required. Thus a lot of cowboys were out of work. That's when the independents of "Poverty Row" took over.

"Poverty Row" was a stretch along Gower Street in Hollywood between Sunset and Santa Monica Boulevard where most of the independents—Puritan, Resolute, Beacon, Majestic, Crescent, Victory, Mascot, Monogram and more—worked out of bungalows. They were all run by guileless hustlers who had no capital, no equipment and no sound stages, but who assumed the task of delivering the specialized films that the majors abandoned with the onset of sound: serials, action adventures and cheap westerns. They rented cameras, sound equipment, costumes and stage properties, and hired whoever was cheap, available and willing to work long, hard hours.

Roy Rogers

Roy Rogers and Gabby Hayes in the Republic Pictures film, In Old Caliente.
Bob Nolan and Roy were together in Apache Rose in 1947.

humiliating times and pictures before spitefully dropping him. In a matter of three years, Duke had gone from being a promising actor at Warner's to walking up and down "Poverty Row" in search of any job that would pay the bills.

In those days, "Poverty Row" was an ever-changing parade of fading stars, fading beauties, lovely young starlets fresh from the Midwest, rangy stunt men, midgets, assorted freaks and, of course, cowboys. The cowboys, in full Western regalia, all hung out at Gower Gulch (the center of which was the Columbia Drugstore at Sunset and Gower—and thus the term "drugstore cowboys"), so named because everything a cowboy needed could be found within easy walking distance. Sometimes they even found work. John Wayne did.

In the late summer of 1933, Wayne signed with Monogram Pictures' Lone Star Productions to do a series of eight westerns ($2,500 per picture, a very good deal considering that Lone Star turned out a movie in *five* days). In September the first five-reel feature hit the screen: *Riders of Destiny.* John Wayne starred as Singin' Sandy, the singing secret agent of the U.S. Secret Service. Wayne wasn't the first singing cowboy. That honor went to Ken Maynard in 1930 in the Universal film, *The Wagon Master*, in which Maynard sang "The Lone-Star Trail" and "Cowboy's Lament" (both of which he recorded for Columbia Records). Wayne's role as Singin' Sandy, however, was the initial attempt by a studio to create a singing cowboy from scratch, even though John Wayne was already a known figure at the Saturday matinees.

At first, Wayne put up with the singing as a gag, figuring that anyone who sounded like he did wouldn't be singing too long (some Western buffs insist that it wasn't Wayne singing at all, but a real cowboy singer named

Following 1929, that meant a lot of people. John Wayne was one of them.

By 1933, Duke Wayne had already starred in Warner's first major western effort, *The Big Trail*, but it bombed at the box office and Warner's dropped him. He signed next with Columbia, but boss Harry Cohn heard a rumor on the grapevine that Wayne was "foolin' around" with the young starlets (specifically one in whom Cohn himself was interested). Although the accusation proved false, Cohn still put Wayne through some

Smith Ballew). Much to Wayne's chagrin, however, the singing formula stirred audiences, especially in the South, and before he knew it the singing had become a staple in his films. He didn't like it.

"They finally got up to four songs in one picture," Wayne recalled, "and before you know it, they had me going on public appearances, and over the top of my horse crappin' on the stage, everybody's screamin': Sing! Sing! Sing!"

By the time Wayne's contract with Lone Star was up in 1935, many of the best of the "Poverty Row" enterprises had merged under the leadership of a former Wall Street executive, Herbert J. Yates, and formed Republic Studios, the studio that would soon bring the B western to full fruition. Yates himself was a shrewd moneyman (intent primarily on tripling his money each year) and didn't know the first thing about movie production. He did know, however, that there was money to be made if westerns could be made cheaply enough, because there were still 5,000 theaters across the country showing them. He seldom if ever read scripts, rarely saw movies and cared little about his actors. He only knew what sold. He was out to make money, not art.

In late 1935, Republic released its first film, *Westward Ho*, starring John Wayne. It was a non-singing John Wayne, though, because when Duke signed his new contract, he was most explicit about that issue when he faced Yates. "I've had it," Duke said. "I'm a goddamned action star, you son-of-a-bitch. I'm not a singer. Go get yourself another cowboy singer."

The question that eventually must be asked is: Did the real-life cowboy really sing? In a manner of speaking, the answer is yes, the cowboy did sing. Out on the endless rangeland, herding and tending the wild, long-horned beasts that were his charge, the cowboy learned early that the sound of the human voice, no matter how rude, had a soothing and reassuring effect on the skittish herd. The animals tended to stampede at the howl of a wild animal, a bolt of lightning or absolutely nothing at all, and a stampeding herd meant both lost time and weight. So the cowboys sang to the cows as they kept their long, solitary vigil through the night. The

Cowgirl queen Dale Evans. Roy's wife, too.

songs they sang were usually traditional hymns and camp-meeting songs they remembered from childhood or from poems printed in newspapers. As time passed, both the tunes and the lyrics became more vague, and the cowboys resorted to mixing and matching different tunes and lyrics, and then creating their own lyrics. Most cowboys, in fact, based their whole repertoire on two or three melodies, and developed an endless number of verses. One of the favorites was "The Old Chisholm Trail," and in the 30-plus years that the cowboy worked the range from Texas to Montana, literally thousands of verses were passed orally from cow camp to cow camp. "Sam Bass" was another favorite, recounting in homespun verses the legend of the famous outlaw. Instruments on the trail were virtually unheard of, but if there was an instrument, it was something as simple as a Jew's harp, or a rude fiddle carried in the chuck wagon. The guitar as an instrument of accompaniment did not become popular until the 1900's, and even then the picture of a cowboy with a guitar strapped to his horse is pure hokum. For the most part, it

Gene Autry's Melody Ranch radio cast in the CBS Hollywood studio in 1940: Among them were Gene, Mary Lee, Jimmy Wakely, Dick Reinhart and Johnny Bond. The show, with its theme song, "Back in the Saddle Again," ran for 17 years.

was simply the voice of the cowboy singing or humming low as he moved slowly through the long, black night on his wiry little pony.

With the disappearance of the real cowboy in a domesticated West, his songs were incorporated into a larger body of folk and traditional songs performed by folk and hillbilly singers. There was a group who called themselves "cowboy balladeers" in the 1920's, capitalizing on both the romance of the West and the phonograph boom before the Depression hit. These artists included "Mac" McClintock, Jules Allen and Carl T. Sprague, but by the time these men recorded their "authentic" cowboy ballads, there was relatively little market for such sparse stylings, and for the most part they were regarded as cultural oddities. After all, it was the Jazz Age. Thus the Western music that the American public was to hear throughout the next decade had almost nothing to do with the music that the real cowboys had made. In fact, it is safe to say that except for an occasional song, the real cowboy had virtually no influence either vocally or instrumentally upon the development of popular or country music.

With John Wayne out as a singing cowboy, Herbert J. Yates' right-hand man at Republic, Nat Levine, went looking for someone to replace him. By 1935, singing and dancing had become a staple of the Hollywood film, and Busby Berkeley had developed the big production number to a high and lavish art. People all across the nation flocked to their local theaters to see the "all-singing, all-dancing, all-talking" extravaganzas as a simple way to escape the realities of the Depression as it settled in for a long stay. Levine meant to cash in on all that.

Levine had received many letters requesting auditions, but one young singer from the WLS *Barn Dance* in Chicago was most persistent. He claimed he had sold millions of records and was America's most popular cowboy singer. Levine finally consented to the audition and brought him West. The cowboy's name was Gene Autry.

Gene Autry seemed like an unlikely candidate for a new type of singing cowboy, and executives at Republic tried to talk Levine out of even considering him. As they saw it, Autry was pleasant-enough looking but hardly handsome, and the only way he looked halfway slim was when he stood next to his rotund sidekick, Smiley Burnette. Also, he had never acted before, and besides that, he had a definite aversion to horses. What, then, other than a slightly nasal voice that kept in tune, did he have to offer? It was a question that was to be asked many times, but five years later the question proved to be purely academic as Autry's popularity and money-making capacity ranked him in Hollywood with Clark Gable, Gary Cooper and Bing Crosby.

Gene Autry was born in Tioga, Texas, in 1907, and his early upbringing indicated little interest in the Texas tradition that would later make him famous. His earliest dream, in fact, was to be a major-league baseball player. It wasn't until his early teens that he became interested in music. By the time he was 15, he was making $.50 a night singing popular ballads at a Tioga nightspot, followed shortly by a three-month stint with The Field Brothers' Medicine Show.

Gene's father bought a cattle ranch in Achilles, Oklahoma, a short time later, and one of Gene's duties was to drive the cattle a short distance to the railroad yard. The bustling railroad station interested Gene far more than the business of moving cattle, and at the urging of one of the station hands he learned how to operate the telegraph machine and soon became the regular operator for the graveyard shift. To while away the long, slow hours of the night, Gene began playing a guitar he had picked up

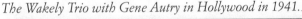

The Wakely Trio with Gene Autry in Hollywood in 1941.

in trade for his old saxophone (at one time he wanted to be a singing saxophone player), and he sang popular and traditional songs. He became so good that he drew an official rebuke from the Frisco Railroad because the operators up and down the line were listening in while Gene sang into the company telephone.

One night a stranger walked into the office with a telegram he wanted to send. He saw the guitar and asked Gene if he was a singer. Gene nodded and the man requested "They Plowed the Old Trail Under." Gene obliged, and then the stranger himself sang "Casey Jones." For the next hour, the two men traded songs until finally the caller had to go—but not before he offered Gene some final words of encouragement: "You've got something, boy. Work hard, and you may go somewhere." The man was Will Rogers.

Three years later, Autry headed off to New York with his guitar in hand. His first stop in the Big Apple was at the Victor offices, the company that recorded Jimmie Rodgers. Autry had fallen under the Rodgers spell and had developed a soft tenor much like that of his idol, plus the very popular and distinctive blues yodel. By the time Autry hit New York in 1929, Rodgers was already the most popular hillbilly singer in rural and small-town America, especially below the Mason-Dixon line. Autry's repertoire included many of Rodgers' songs, and Victor, therefore, seemed to be the right label for him.

Autry sat politely in the anteroom for several hours waiting to sing for anyone who would listen, but to no avail. Finally, he pulled his guitar from the case and began to sing for the secretary. A Victor official passed by and liked what he heard, and gave Autry his first official audition. It was short and bittersweet. "You've got a voice," he told Autry, "but you haven't had enough experience with a microphone. Go home, get a job on the radio, and work hard. Come back in about a year."

Autry traveled home to Tulsa and got work on KVOO (sans pay) doing his own show, but within a year he had moved on to the WLS *National Barn Dance*, which originated from Chicago. The *National Barn Dance* was different from most of the radio barn dances because it included many pop tunes and sentimental "old favorites" in addition to the basic hillbilly music. It thus allowed Autry to branch out into different musical categories. He returned to New York in 1929 and, under the tutelage of Art Satherley, recorded his first records for the American Record Company, which leased the masters to many smaller companies. One label to carry Autry's records, naturally, was the Sears label, which sold its records through the Sears catalogue. Of course, Autry sang all his releases on the Sears-owned WLS *National Barn Dance*, whose powerful beam reached almost the entire nation. Few of the songs that Autry sang were of a Western nature; his repertoire was drawn from the Southern rural tradition in both selection and performance. He had also taken to writing songs, and one of his first compositions (written with friend Jimmy Long) was "That Silver Haired Daddy of Mine," which sold 30,000 copies during the first three months of its release (it would eventually sell far more than a million

Johnny Bond

copies) and established "Oklahoma's Yodeling Cowboy" as the nation's best-known cowboy singer. His records were prominently displayed in the Sears catalogue, followed shortly by a number of Gene Autry songbooks and guitar instruction manuals and, finally, a Gene Autry "Roundup" guitar, along with a reminder that Autry had become a star by simply "learning how to play the guitar while on the ranch."

Roundup? Ranch? Oklahoma's Yodeling Cowboy? In a master stroke of image building, Autry had taken on the guise of a cowboy (B western variety, very streamlined), because it was in rural America that the legend of the cowboy loomed largest, and it was in rural America that the Sears, Roebuck catalogue was second in importance only to the family Bible. By 1934, Autry's popularity in small-town America was unparalleled, whereas in New York and the other sophisticated metropolitan areas (even as late as 1940, by the way), the name Gene Autry meant very little. That in itself might explain why Hollywood was somewhat dubious about a singer who almost invited himself to the big audition. "After all," you can almost hear the film moguls saying, "if we don't know him, how can anyone else?"

In Nat Levine's mind, however, Autry was the man, and he signed him for $100 a week, along with his sidekick, Smiley Burnette, for $75 a week. Levine figured that since Autry had already sold a few million records and had been appearing on one of the nation's biggest barn dances, he must have a built-in audience out there in the hinterlands, and that was exactly where the B westerns were going. Half the battle for acceptance seemed to have already been won.

Autry was first cast in a Ken Maynard vehicle, *In Old Santa Fe*, and appeared somewhere in the middle of the movie for a ten-minute musical interlude between fist fights and horse chases. Maynard even sang a song, but it was clear from the mail response that there were indeed Gene Autry fans out there, and they wanted more.

Autry was next seen in the Maynard serial *Mystery Mountain*, but only in passing, because behind the scenes at Republic the studio was working diligently with Gene to make some sort of an actor of him. The big test came with *Phantom Empire*, Autry's first solo vehicle. It was a 12-chapter serial that immediately guaranteed

him at least a 12-week stay at all the local Saturday matinees across the country and, in Levine's shrewd mind, a sure way to get the Gene Autry message across. The most unique feature of the film, however, was that it not only starred Gene Autry but also represented Gene playing *himself*, an unprecedented but quite calculated move. Levine was hoping to capitalize on his star's established popularity, and if that wasn't enough, he portrayed Gene as a singing-cowboy *radio personality*. The movie was a strange science fiction epic about the subterranean civilization of Murania, which was located directly underneath Gene's Radio Ranch. The Muranians, led by Queen Tika (who had a hankering for Gene's body), feared that the people above ground would find the secret en-

Johnny Bond and Ray Whitley with The Cass County Boys, Gene Autry's touring band: seated in front are Freddy Martin, Frankie Marvin and Jerry Scoggins. Carl Cotner and Bert Dodson are next to Ray Whitley.

trance and destroy the sunken city. Therefore they wanted Autry out of the way so that they wouldn't be disturbed. As if that weren't enough, Gene also had to contend with above-ground criminals who wanted to get rid of him and take over the ranch because they had discovered deposits of radium. Gene's one real mission, however, seemed only to escape in each episode in order to get back to the ranch and make his broadcast. And if the kids still didn't get the message about just who this guy Gene Autry was, Gene sang "That Silver Haired Daddy of Mine" in eight of the 12 chapters. The serial was a great success.

Jimmy Wakely, center, and His Rough Riders: Wayne Benson, Scotty Harrell, Johnny Bond and Noel Boggs in 1939. For them, Hollywood was still a dream.

Autry's fourth film and first starring feature, *Tumbling Tumbleweeds*, established him as the most important newcomer in western films, in addition to providing him with yet another giant hit record, the title tune "Tumbling Tumbleweeds." Republic was ecstatic, and quickly put more money (within Yates' limits, of course) and energy into the Autry films. Within two years, Autry was the kingpin of the studio and of B westerns in general. In short, he was a giant, and he was changing the shape of the industry. Republic made a few Autry films with historical settings, but that mode proved too cumbersome to show-

case Autry's talents, so the studio quickly reverted not only to "streamlined" westerns, but also to "ultra-streamlined" *musical* westerns. Action, which had always been the staple of the B western, gave way to a certain extent to a new emphasis on musical numbers, and to a new world in which those numbers were performed.

The Depression turned the world upside down and created a modern villainy—the city, seat of evil incarnate, breeding ground for sedan-loads of sharp-eyed smoothies wearing pencil-thin mustaches whose only goal was to separate the trusting rural rubes from their just dues. That was the prevailing attitude toward the city in rural America.

Autry plugged into that attitude in virtually all his movies, and always found himself at the end of the final reel as the vanquisher of the evil and the savior of the populace. Somehow it was always the result of his songs or his singing, and given the bizarre problems he had to face, it's little wonder that the world in which this character lived came off as a little beyond the pale. *Mexicali Rose* is a good example (and is also another film with a title tune that became the most popular "hillbilly" record of 1936, but which, like most B western film titles, had absolutely nothing to do with the movie itself). In the movie the city slickers had once again hit town. This time they were selling phony oil stock to the good honest local folk, including an orphanage in deep financial distress. They hired Gene to promote the stock by singing its praises on the radio. He did so, and everybody in town invested everything but their milk money. Gene, however, soon suspected some chicanery, and did a little detective work (with the help of a darling pair of orphans, of course). He discovered the ruse and *sang* a sensational exposé. In a neat twist, however, it turned out that there really was oil on

Jimmy Wakely

The Spade Cooley Band in the mid-40's. Spade is center, front, in light suit, flanked by Tex Williams, Ella Mae and Smokey Rogers. The band drew huge dance crowds.

(glamour gals in cute-as-a-button cowgirl miniskirts parading down the town streets carrying placards reading "Autry for Sheriff," racing cars and music, music, music) combined into one slick, entertaining piece of film fare that disarmed the critics and put the Autry films into an enchanting ozone of their own. If one doubted that, the final proof was the word from the box offices, and the word was SRO.

In the never-never land that Autry created, a new type of song was needed, one that evoked images different from those offered by the Southeastern hillbilly songs then dominating country music. Autry's own songs prior to his movies were basically within the hillbilly genre, but with his growing cinematic success they began to change. Traditional song sources were forsaken in exchange for Tin Pan Alley tunesmiths and a growing body of writers influenced by both the movies and the newer country sounds coming out of the Southwest. Mountains and green valleys soon gave way to blue prairies and purple canyons and whatever else could be mustered from the scenic myth of the New West, and these new songs jibed perfectly with the picture of Autry dressed in his form-fitted and neatly trimmed cowboy suits. The music and instrumentation changed little, however, but with Autry's success, the term "hillbilly music" was soon supplanted by the term "Western music" in the mind of the nation. "Hillbilly" had long been a pejorative term, not only to those who played and listened to it, but to an even larger audience of those who sneered at it. Autry's success, however, opened

the land, and the good people not only held onto their money, but also apparently got rich.

In addition to phony oil stocks, similarly fraudulent schemes were hatched: Various films featured helium wells, super dams, a fake Sun Valley, dude ranches, a threat of hoof and mouth disease, dairy farming, sleazy politics and so on. When World War II began, Gene also fought Nazis, spies and submarines, and always with a song at his lips. The mind-boggling incongruities of the traditional western motifs (horse chases, fast gunplay, knock-down, drag-'em-out fist fights) and the thoroughly modern motifs

up a brand-new audience and proved that it wasn't so much the music as the hillbilly style usually *surrounding* the music that turned off a greater audience. Thus the hillbilly music-makers followed Autry's lead simply by changing their dress code. Straw hats and patched overalls were quickly replaced in many quarters with white Stetsons and starched and spangled cowboy outfits. It's been that way ever since, although there have been some staunch holdouts (Roy Acuff always maintained that his Smoky Mountain Boys were "a country band, and do country music, and thus dress like country people...not cowboys!").

For the first five years of his movie career, Autry had it all his way in Hollywood western circles, although most studios tried to capitalize on his success by producing their own singing cowboy. It was rare, in fact, that any cowboy of any renown didn't take at least one shot at warbling, but those who actually stayed with it in a continuing series of westerns were few. Dick Foran was Warner's entry, and he was a lusty baritone who was often backed by The Sons of the Pioneers, but even that wasn't enough. The high point of Foran's career was when he introduced the pop standard "I'll Remember April" in Abbott and Costello's *Ride 'Em Cowboy*, years after he'd washed out of the singing-cowboy competition. Fred Scott had a nice husky voice, but it was apparent he wasn't a cowboy. Jack Randell, on the other hand, was a fine action actor, but his voice was so bad that often when the film distributors got their Randell films back from theaters, all the vocalizing had been neatly excised. Bob Baker was a tall, baby-faced kid, who, like Autry, had come from the WLS *National Barn Dance*, but his films were under-budgeted and he never had a chance. Tex Ritter's films suffered from the same budgetary problems, and it wasn't until he gave up the film industry that he went on to become the coun-

try music legend he is now.

The first real threat to Autry's popularity occurred in 1937 when he decided that he wasn't sharing in enough of the financial rewards his pictures were providing for Republic. Studio head Yates, however, was still a tough man with a buck at the bargaining table, and he remained unswayed by Gene's astute and businesslike arguments at contract time. So, in 1938, Gene simply took a walk when his option came up again. Yates' reaction was typical: "*To hell with Autry! We'll just get another singing cowboy!*" It was an odd statement considering the number of existing singing cowboys who were barely

Spade Cooley, Tex Williams and Smokey Rogers. Spade's personnel was topnotch.

getting by. Autry's strength was based not simply on his movies, but also on his continuing succession of hit records. No other singing cowboy could claim to have that advantage. Yates, however, would not relent, and the search for a new singing cowboy was on. Strangely enough, Yates didn't even have to leave the Republic lot to find his next star. He was there begging to be discovered. His name was Leonard Slye. Two weeks later it had been changed to Dick Weston, and then again a few months later to Roy Rogers. It never changed again.

Roy Rogers was born in Cincinnati in 1911,

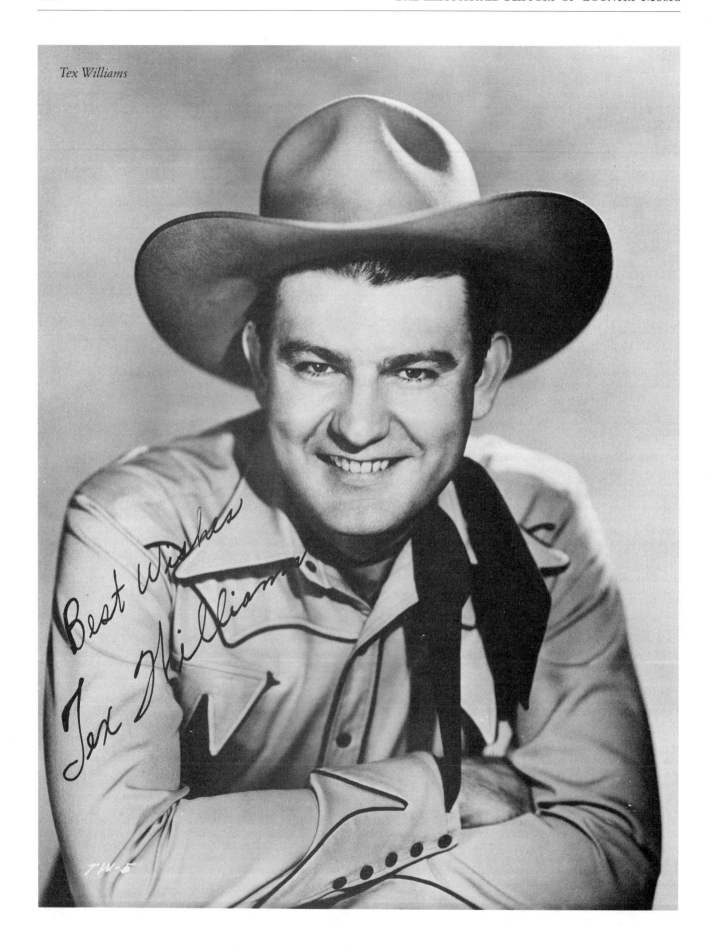

Tex Williams

the son of a shoe factory worker, but from age seven on through his teens, he lived on a small farm in Duck Run, Ohio, raising vegetables and farm yard animals and "developing the bottoms of my feet like elephant's hide." Roy's family was musically inclined, and by the time he was ten, he was the best square-dance caller in the county. A few years later he added a little guitar-playing to his act, plus the yodeling techniques he, like Autry, had heard on Jimmie Rodgers records. When the Depression hit big, Roy's dad found himself out of work, so he took the $200 the family had saved, packed up everybody in the '23 Dodge truck, and drove to California to visit one of Roy's married sisters. She was living in Lawndale, then a small agricultural town just south of Los Angeles. It seemed like heaven on earth compared to the bitter cold of Ohio. The days were warm and clear and breezy, but after four months the family returned to Ohio, much to Roy's disappointment. Two months later, however, he hitchhiked back and moved in with his sister. He worked around Los Angeles at a series of odd jobs, including moving sand from the ocean beaches to the sand traps at the golf course by the Hollywood race track, picking fruit, and boxing in the back room of a bar for a couple of dollars a round. At night he would sit on the back porch and sing to the sound of the crickets while his sister tried to convince him that he should try singing on the radio. Roy finally gave in to her gentle but persistent demands and joined a hillbilly group called The Rocky Mountaineers. They were older musicians, and Roy was the only vocalist, so he ran an ad in a local paper: "Singer wanted." He got two replies, one from a young Santa Monica lifeguard by the name of Bob Nolan, and the other, by coincidence, from a friend of Nolan's, Bill Nichols. They both joined Roy in The Rocky Mountaineers, and soon found their har-

monies quite acceptable, but since playing dates were rare for the group, Nolan quit to become a caddy at the exclusive Bel-Aire Country Club.

Undaunted, Roy ran another ad, and this time Tim Spencer answered it. Again Roy had a trio, but following a short and unsuccessful barnstorming tour of the Southwest, the band broke up altogether. Connections, however, had been made.

Roy then joined Jack and His Texas Outlaws on Los Angeles radio station KFWB and, again displeased with the vocal quality of the group, he called on his old partners Spencer and Nolan and offered to share his meager $15-a-week sal-

Tex Williams formed his own band, The Western Caravan, in the mid-40's.

ary if they'd join him. They both accepted, and soon were ensconced in a Hollywood boarding house practicing their precise harmonies day and night. Their arrangements became quite tight, especially on "The Last Roundup" (a big Gene Autry hit), and one morning in the *Los Angeles Herald Examiner*, noted columnist Bernie Mulligan wrote in his "Best Bets" column, "If you want to hear the best arrangement of 'The Last Roundup,' tune in 8-9 on KFWB and listen to The Pioneer Trio." That impressed the KFWB brass, and soon the trio had their own show and a new name: The Sons of the Pioneers.

Tex Ritter: a top singing cowboy and Capitol Records' first country signee.

The Sons of the Pioneers' popularity grew quickly, and in short order they were appearing in western movies with Dick Foran, Charles Starrett and Gene Autry, and playing such venues as the Texas centennial. The group moved from KFWB to KNX and Peter Potter's *Hollywood Barn Dance.* Soon they were recording for Decca and had expanded the group to six men. By 1937 they were the pre-eminent "Western" group in the nation.

Roy, however, had other plans. He was in Glendale one afternoon having his Stetson cleaned when an actor rushed in looking for a new hat to wear to try out for the singing cowboy audition at Republic. It was the first Roy had heard about it, and his ears perked up: a new singing cowboy? The next day, in his full cowboy regalia, Roy too was at the Republic gate, but without a pass, and the guard wouldn't let him in. He finally sneaked in with a group of carpenters, and wasn't more than 50 feet inside the gate when someone tapped him on the shoulder.

"What are you doing?"

Roy turned to find himself looking at Sol Seigel, the very man conducting the auditions. "Looking for you," he answered. Within the day he was auditioned, within the week he was screen tested, and within two weeks he was signed.

From the beginning (discounting the Dick Weston days), Rogers had all the earmarks of success, and prexy Yates, in an obvious slap at the delinquent Autry, lavished all the care usually accorded the original singing cowboy, including Republic's best writers, directors and the usual bevy of beauties, on the Rogers films. Roy proved to be an instant hit from his very first starring role, *Under Western Skies,* and by the end of 1938 he was a proven star and the equal of Gene Autry. Rogers' films were more action-oriented than the Autry vehicles (*Variety* noted in a scurrilous review of Autry's *Gaucho Serenade,* a 66-minute film, that the first horse wasn't mounted until the 44-minute mark, the first fist was not heaved faceward until the 50-minute mark, and the first gunshot was not heard until the 56-minute mark!), but the musical interludes by Rogers and his pals, usually coming within the last ten minutes of the film, were basically the same "western" stylings. Autry himself, somewhat taken aback by the newcomer's meteoric rise, soon returned to the Republic fold, and as the country headed into World War II Republic could lay claim to the two biggest cowboy stars in the business.

The sheer visibility of Autry and Rogers in the public's eyes commanded the attention of country music performers all across the nation. Not only had the acceptance of Roy and Gene changed the clothing style of country music performers (in addition to influencing the musical styles), but also many established country artists saw Hollywood and the movies as a means of extending their own popularity. Thus, throughout the 1940's, many made the almost obligatory trek West to the sound stages and rolling hills surrounding the San Fernando Valley to appear in the proliferating B westerns. Roy Acuff, Ernest Tubb, Hank Snow, Bob Wills and His Texas Playboys, Lulu Belle and Scotty, Jimmie Davis, Red Foley and His Hoosier Hotshots, Dale Evans (the "Queen of the Cowgirls," who had established a musical career in Chicago before moving west, acting in these films, and teaming with Roy Rogers, both on-screen and in real life) and many others made the trip. For some of the established country recording artists,

Tex Ritter

the lure of Hollywood was a passing fancy, but for the unknown artists Hollywood seemed like the new mecca, and in the minds of many aspiring young country artists, the notion of making it in Hollywood became the ultimate dream. They didn't, however, come to California alone.

Just as the United States was the melting pot of the world at the turn of the century, California had become the melting pot of the nation by the late 1930's and on through the 1940's. During the Depression, thousands upon thousands of dispossessed laborers and farm people from

course, the enlisted men simply passing through by the tens of thousands on their way to the Pacific zone, but staying on permanently once they had returned and were discharged. The state had opened its arms to all, and nowhere was that more true than in Southern California, with its developing industrial and technological facilities. The incredible growth of the Southland generated a whole new musical audience whose roots were steeped in country music of every possible variation, and the crosscurrents of those musical stylings flowing into each other dispelled hardline traditional attitudes. If there is one thing that can be said of the country music that developed in Southern California, it is that it was indefinable, a product of the traditional country singers, Western singers, Western swing, honky tonk, novelty and a heavy dose of pure popular music. Musical divisions blurred as it became the first country music sound created in a somewhat sophisticated and growing urban environment for both pop and country audiences. California, it might be said, spearheaded the first commercial movement in modern country music.

KFWB radio stars: Herman the Hermit (Cliffie Stone's dad), Darol Rice, Georgia Brown, Cliffie Stone, Tex Atchison and Joe Strand. Kneeling are Eddie Cletro and Merle Travis.

the Midwest, South, and Southwest had migrated to California looking for a brand new start and a new direction in life as hope gave out elsewhere. That constant westward flow of people continued through the war years as soldiers, sailors and war workers found themselves leaving from, stationed at, or working on the sunny southern shores of the Golden State. There were the migrant workers of the blossoming San Joaquin Valley, the shipyard workers of San Pedro and Oakland, plus the supporting cast working in industries that maintained the war effort, and, of

Gene Autry and Roy Rogers were undoubtedly the most prominent singing cowboy stars, but their success created the opportunity—and the fashion—for others. By 1940, The Wakely Trio had arrived in Hollywood with the promise of Gene Autry still ringing in their ears: "If you boys ever get to California, look me up." Gene had first heard The Wakely Trio on their own local radio show on WKY in Oklahoma, and had been quite impressed. The boys—Jimmy Wakely, Johnny Bond and Scotty Harrell—had been equally impressed with Gene's promise.

Cliffie Stone

Johnny Mercer

one of the major stops for touring country music stars. Wakely soon became so popular that he formed a backing trio, The Saddle Pals, was featured in more than 30 B westerns, and was eventually signed with Monogram Pictures to star in his own western series. He turned his band-leading chores over to a rising young Western swing bandleader from the Northwest, Spade Cooley.

In California the Spade Cooley Band, featuring Tex Williams on lead vocals, soon became as popular—if not more so—as the Bob Wills congregation, and Spade took to calling himself "The King of Western Swing." In the late 1940's he moved from the Venice Pier into his own ballroom in Santa Monica, and was regularly drawing crowds of 6,000 on Saturday nights in addition to the SRO crowds he drew when he took his band on the road. His band backed up both Roy Rogers and The Sons of the Pioneers on many of their recordings and was featured in many western movies as both the posse and the purveyors of that good ol' Western music. Bob Wills moved his base of operations from Tulsa to California in

They almost beat Autry back to California, and within months had joined him on his new Sunday afternoon national CBS radio broadcast, *The Melody Ranch Show*. It was a fortuitous move for Wakely, Bond and the development of a country music scene in California.

The Wakely Trio was an immediate hit on the national airwaves, and within two years the two principals, Bond and Wakely, had broken up the trio and moved on to broader horizons.

Johnny Bond signed with Columbia Records in 1941 and became a mainstay for that label for the next 14 years, also appearing in B westerns with Autry (both singing and accompanying Gene on guitar), Charles Starrett and others. He also became popular in the lively Los Angeles country ballroom scene that was developing, and was usually backed by The Cass County Boys, Gene Autry's own touring band. He wrote over 400 songs, and in 1953 joined the cast of the popular country music television show on Los Angeles' KTTV, *Town Hall Party*.

Jimmy Wakely, a smooth and handsome fellow who patterned himself after Autry, formed his own band after leaving *The Melody Ranch Show* and moved into promoter Foreman Phillips' popular *Los Angeles Country Barn Dance* on the Venice Pier,

The Sons of the Pioneers with Bing Crosby and Leo Spencer in 1936, on location for Rhythm on the Range. *Johnny Mercer wrote "I'm an Old Cowhand" for the film.*

Merle Travis

1944 (even Wills was lured West by the movies, appearing first with Tex Ritter in 1940, and later in a series that starred ex-Hopalong Cassidy sidekick Russell Hayden in *Wyoming Hurricane*, Wills actually engaging in a rough-and-tumble barroom brawl), but even with Wills in the area, Cooley's popularity remained undiminished through the early 1950's. In 1949, Cooley even starred in a mediocre western, *The Silver Bullet*. He also recorded many successful sides for Columbia Records.

Tex Williams had achieved celebrity status by 1946 as Cooley's vocalist, and in that year, Tex formed his own 12-piece band, The Western Caravan, and not only played to giant local crowds in such places as the American Legion Hall in Placentia, the Foster Park Ballroom in Ventura, and the Harmony Park Ballroom in Anaheim (ballrooms at that time dotted the entire state), but also traveled as far away as the Aragon Ballroom in Chicago. In the late 1940's he also appeared with his band in 15 Universal Western-musical shorts, as well as being featured in films starring Charles Starrett, Buster Crabbe and Judy Canova.

In 1942, two local giants of the Southern California record business decided that it was high time there was a major label on the West Coast. Decca, Columbia and Victor had offices in Los Angeles, but there was little action coming out of them, considering how fast the West Coast music scene was growing. Glenn Wallichs, owner of Los Angeles' largest retail music store, Wallichs' Music City, and Johnny Mercer, one of America's

Merle Travis, Hank Penny and Joe Maphis in WLW days.

foremost popular tunesmiths, combined forces and started Capitol Records in offices located above Wallichs' Music City at the corner of Sunset and Vine, just three blocks away from the original Gower Gulch. (Mercer had gained fame in 1936, when he wrote the tongue-in-cheek standard, "I'm an Old Cowhand," for the Bing Crosby film, *Rhythm on the Range*, in which virtually the entire cast, including Bing, Martha Raye, Louis Prima and The Sons of the Pioneers, then still led by Roy Rogers, took turns at the song.)

Capitol Records' first country music signee, Tex Ritter, was a blockbuster. Tex had recorded for both Decca and Columbia, but it wasn't until he recorded with Capitol that he established himself as a country legend, beginning with his very first release, "Jingle, Jangle, Jingle." His success opened the doors of Capitol Records to other country singers, which in turn led Capitol to sign Cliffie Stone as their country-Western musical consultant. Stone was a man who was to figure prominently in California music circles for the next 20-plus years.

Cliffie Stone was a local product (born and raised in Burbank) who first became interested in country music in 1935 under the tutelage of Stuart Hamblen, a longtime country performer and disc jockey in Los Angeles. Cliffie was only 17 when he became a local DJ and country bumpkin comedian on KFVD's *Covered Wagon Jubilee*. Within ten years, however, he had become a top-rated country DJ (in the mid-1940's he emceed 28 Western radio shows a week!) and was both a respected country musician and one of the most knowledgeable authorities on the burgeoning California country scene—he had played with virtually all the new country singers making names for themselves, in addition to fronting his own band. By the time he joined Capitol Records, he was known as a man who could make careers. He proved that at Capitol almost immediately by signing Jimmy Wakely, Tex Williams, Merle Travis, Tennessee Ernie Ford (another local Los Angeles DJ and country comedian) and Hank Thompson to the label.

Nudie, called "The Tailor to the Stars," outfitted almost everyone. Here he's with Rex Allen, Gene Autry, Eddie Dean, Roy Rogers and Smokey Rogers.

With Cliffie's help, the head of Capitol's country division, Lee Gillette, soon established Capitol as a major country label, although theirs was not an exclusively country audience. From the beginning, Capitol was willing to take a few chances as it sought out the largest audience possible for its country artists. One result was a style of music that could easily be called "pop-Western," which featured modern musical arrangements, including string backgrounds; it predated the lush modern Nashville Sound of the early 1960's by more than ten years. It was a sound that generated as much interest in pop as in country circles.

Jimmy Wakely scored one of the big pop-country hits of the 1940's when he was teamed with popular singer Margaret Whiting on "Slippin' Around" and then later with "I'll Never Slip Around Again," "Till the End of the World" and more, while also establishing the pop-Western duo genre later repeated by George Morgan and Dinah Shore, Tennessee Ernie Ford and Kay Starr, and even Ernest Tubb and The Andrews Sisters. As a solo artist, Wakely hit big with "One Has My Name, The Other Has My Heart," "I Love You So Much It Hurts" and many more.

Tex Williams exploded on the pop and the country charts in 1947 with his third Capitol release, "Smoke! Smoke! Smoke! (That Cigarette)," and it became the label's first million seller. Williams had other similar hits during the late 40's.

"Smoke! Smoke! Smoke!" was written by Merle Travis. The legendary singer-songwriter, known for his unique guitar style, left Cincinnati's WLW for California in 1944. There he recorded for small labels, produced singles for King Records and worked extensively as a sideman on shows and records. Capitol signed him in 1946, and honky tonk hits like "Cincinnati Lou," "No Vacancy," "Divorce Me C.O.D." and "So Round, So Firm, So Fully Packed"—the latter two both Number One hits for 14 weeks in 1946 and '47, respectively—made him a national star. Travis worked on West Coast television shows such as Cliffie Stone's *Hometown Jamboree,* and wrote "Sixteen Tons," which was one of the best-selling hits of all time when recorded by Tennessee Ernie Ford in 1955. Meanwhile, the thumb and finger guitar style Travis had learned in his native Kentucky influenced Chet Atkins and countless other musicians.

Other successful ventures in the developing pop-Western vein at Capitol Records were the

Rex Allen and Nudie in Nudie's shop.

Riders in the Sky: Too Slim, Ranger Doug, Woody Paul, with Grand Ole Opry manager Hal Durham and Ernest Tubb in 1982.

tongue-in-cheek efforts of Red Ingle and His Natural Seven featuring Cinderella G. Stump (in reality Jo Stafford) on rousing pseudo-hillbilly versions of "Temptation" and "Them Durn Fool Things." Both records became pop hits, and also created a country music backlash when country DJ's refused to play them on the grounds that they sullied the name of country music. Popular songstress Helen O'Connell also had a big hit with her fun-filled pop-country version of "Slow Poke." It was the success of these records that paved the way for other labels (notably Columbia, under the leadership of Mitch Miller) to provide the first commercial "covers" of country material to the pop market in the early 1950's. In those years, Tony Bennett recorded Hank Williams' "Cold, Cold Heart" and sold one and a half million copies; Jo Stafford had a big hit with "Jambalaya"; Rosemary Clooney scored with "Shotgun Boogie" and "This

Ol' House"; Frankie Laine hit with "Kaw-Liga"; Guy Mitchell succeeded with "The Yellow Rose of Texas"; and Joni James hit with "Your Cheatin' Heart." It was country music's big entree into pop music—or vice versa. Whatever the case, it was definitely a product of the rise of country music in California.

By the end of the 1940's the B westerns had long since seen their best days and were nearing a much-needed retirement. They had become rather shoddy as the budgeting in the studios become more and more restrictive, and production costs rose. Rogers had succeeded Autry as the new "King of the Cowboys" during Gene's three-year stint overseas in the Army Air Force during World War II, but upon his return the title didn't really mean much, anyway. However, Autry's recording career at Columbia resumed, and soon he was selling more records than at any time in his career—usually around Christmas, when he had a series of pop-novelty-pseudo-country hits including "Here Comes Santa Claus," "Rudolph, the Red-Nosed Reindeer," "Frosty, the Snowman" and (let's throw in Easter) "Peter Cottontail." Roy Rogers also scored with a few minor hits at that time, including "Don't Fence Me In" and "Blue Shadows on the Trail," featuring The Sons of the Pioneers from Walt Disney's *Melody Time*. Roy, however, didn't sell nearly the number of records Gene did, but then he never had. In 1951, Roy made his last feature film, *Pals of the Golden West*, and called the movies quits (other than for a long cameo in Bob Hope's *Son of Paleface* and a quick flash in another Hope comedy, *Alias Jesse James*). In 1953, following *The Last of the Pony Riders*, Autry called it quits with the movies, too. Both, however, moved quickly into television. Roy (and Dale) did the popular *Roy Rogers Show* ("Happy trails to you....") for a few seasons, and Autry had his own *Gene Autry Show*. Autry's company, Flying A Productions, also produced early-TV favorites *Annie Oakley*, *Buffalo Bill Jr.*, *The Range Rider* and *Champion* (starring, of course, Champion), but it was never the same. Television was, in fact, *the* prime mover in the destruction of the B western, and by the time Rex Allen was making the very last B western at Republic in 1954, the early films of Gibson, Maynard, Jones, McCoy and even Gene Autry were already appearing on Saturday-morning television.

There were some instances of singing cowboy revivalism down the years. In the 1980's the Nashville-based group Riders in the Sky began roaming their range with cowboy music old and new and a gentle, often hilarious parody of the Saturday-morning entertainment on which they'd grown up. They never made any hit records, but in other ways they were quite successful. They and their weekly radio show, *Riders Radio Theater*, won a considerable number of loyal fans, and they were still performing in the mid-90's. In the real West, meanwhile, there was a revival of cowboy music orchestrated by singer-songwriter Michael Martin Murphey and featuring rancher/cowboy/poets like Waddie Mitchell and Don Edwards. Its focus, though, was the life of the working cowboy present and past, not the guy in the B movies. To all intents and purposes, that guy, very much a man of his time, has vanished.

His legacy, however, is immeasurable. It goes far beyond the oversimplified stale popcorn/Saturday afternoon matinee at the local Bijou stuff by which most people fondly remember him today. In the 20-plus years that he sang and galloped cross the silver screen, the wildly popular singing cowboy changed the shape and scope of country music. He made country music at least palatable to a "sophisticated" audience that had previously jeered at it, and thus he laid the groundwork for the greater popularity to follow. "Hillbilly" was out; "Country and Western" was in.

The singing cowboy injected a certain mythic quality into the music by changing the stylistic elements of the songs; he also changed the appearance of the musicians so that a developing nation weaned on the legend of the cowboy (the one true American legend) became more comfortable with the sights and sounds of a music that in reality had little to do with the Old West. The singing cowboy also gave established stars a new form of exposure in his films, and he gave rising stars a new venue in which to achieve stardom. And, perhaps as important as any one other thing, he opened up the West Coast as a new and creative focal point for both playing and recording that was far more important than Nashville in the 1940's. The singing cowboy represented the first popular commercialization of country music on a grand and sweeping scale.

Eddy Arnold

CHAPTER 6

The Road to Nashville

If the 1930's were a decade of explosive creativity and expansion in country music, the 1940's were a period of problems and confusion. The decade was characterized overall by a shifting pattern of power and influence within the industry, culminating in a lessening of influence from Chicago and Hollywood and a rush to Nashville as the new country music center; additionally, there were problems with the unions and, of course, the complex of troubles brought on by the second World War.

As the decade began, Nashville was relatively insignificant as a production center for country music. The Opry was still lagging behind Chicago's *National Barn Dance* in the race for the top radio show spot, and there was practically no recording or music publishing coming out of Nashville. Chicago, on the other hand, seemed well set up; it was the home of the nation's leading country radio show and had both recording studios and publishing companies. Even so, it seemed in 1940 that if any single city was going to emerge as a center for country music it would be Hollywood. All the ingredients that were eventually to make Nashville the home of the country music industry were present in Hollywood at this time: the stars, the studios, the presence of major labels, the songwriters, the radio programs, the musicians, the demand for music by a large populace, and a major barn

dance. It never happened, however, and the reason is a matter for conjecture. Perhaps the relative success of country music seemed pale in the glamorous shadow (and Hollywood in this era prized glamour above all else) of success in films. Perhaps the "Tinseltown" image repelled the average country music record-buyer. Perhaps there was not the kind of in-studio creativity and flexibility that was to draw musicians and producers to Nashville late in the decade. Whatever the reason, it just never happened, and it took only some impressive public relations by the Nashville-based Country Music Association to steal Hollywood's thunder entirely and create the impression that Nashville had always been at the center stage of country music.

The country music boom on the West Coast had begun in the 1930's, when the migration to the supposed land of milk and honey began in earnest, thousands of Dust Bowl farmers straggling across the country in barely running old Fords, a picture straight out of *The Grapes of Wrath*. Some found a home in the West; some did not. Most—like the parents of Merle Haggard—brought with them a love for country music and the desire to hear more of it. And more than anything, it was Western swing they wanted to hear. Popular bands that normally played just jazz and swing found themselves having to include country tunes in their repertoire or lose

WLS National Barn Dance Cast, October, 1944

WLS National Barn Dance cast in 1944. The Grand Ole Opry was about to take over as the nation's premier barn dance show.

their audiences. The second great influx of country-rooted people, brought on by the wartime demand for labor in the California defense plants, pushed the California music scene farther in the direction of country and Western swing music, and it wasn't long before a well-known California promoter by the name of Foreman Phillips had built a string of some half-dozen country-swing ballrooms to cater to public demand. Foreman's most famous venue was the Venice Pier ballroom. Foreman did not have the market to himself, however; the leader of one big country dance band that played in Phillips' ballrooms went out on his own and opened a ballroom in Santa Monica. The place was soon drawing 5,000 people every weekend, and the name Spade Cooley rose to prominence. In 1945, Cooley had the Number One record of the year,

"Shame on You." He went on to assemble the biggest Western swing band of all time—25 musicians, including a large string section and even a harp player.

As the ballroom phenomenon continued to grow—even after the war—bandleaders from Texas were imported in droves, and existing bands broke up into multiple aggregations as successful band members formed their own bands. One such graduate was Tex Williams, the vocalist for Spade Cooley's band who left to form his own Western Caravan in 1946. The Caravan toured the nation from its home base at the popular Riverside Rancho nightclub in L.A.

Ray Whitley and Jimmy Wakely fronted big bands of the era, Whitley's Rhythm Wranglers and Wakely's Cowboy Band. Whitley's band featured Merle Travis and fiddler Jesse Ashlock, while

Wakely's band produced the lovely Colleen Summers (who can be heard harmonizing on "One Has My Name, The Other Has My Heart"), later known as Mary Ford of Les Paul and Mary Ford fame. Merle Travis led his own band for a while, as did Wesley Tuttle and Wade Ray, a transplanted Chicagoan who had been The Prairie Ramblers' fiddler on the *National Barn Dance*.

The California scene drew musicians from all over the country—Foy Willing and Art Davis from Texas; Spade Cooley, Jimmy Wakely and Johnny Bond from Oklahoma; Hank Snow from Canada; Merle Travis from Kentucky by way of Cincinnati; Joe Maphis from Virginia; and Jenny Lou Carson, born Lucille Overstake, from WLS in Chicago. The Opry even lost a member to the lure of Hollywood—Zeke Clements, "The Alabama Cowboy," who headed West to be the voice of Bashful in Walt Disney's *Snow White and the Seven Dwarfs.*

Besides the dance halls, the film industry was an inducement for many, for while the singing cowboy films ensured places for certain stars, there was also a constant need for backup groups who could provide musical interludes. The Sons of the Pioneers were followed by similar harmony groups like Foy Willing and The Riders of the Purple Sage, The Cass County Boys, Andy Parker and The Plainsmen and others. There was also room for singing sidekicks like Ray Whitley, who was featured in a series of westerns with Tim Holt and George O'Brien, and Bob Wills (with an abbreviated band of Texas Playboys), who co-starred in eight films with Russell Hayden. Wills doubled as a semi- comic sidekick, usually in the role of top hand of a bunch of cowpokes (who of course seemed to have steel guitars and fiddles packed away in their saddlebags). In one case, 1943's *Riders of the Northwest Mounted*, Wills played a sergeant in the Mounties.

Radio—much of it network—was also a factor on the West Coast in the golden age of that medium. Gene Autry's *Melody Ranch,* sponsored by Wrigley's Gum, began in 1940, and was to run into the late 1950's, an American Sunday afternoon tradition. *All-Star Western Theater* was another popular show of the time, featuring many guest stars (Ritter, Wakely, Dean, even Eddy Arnold) as well as Foy Willing and The Riders of the Purple Sage, the staff band. *The Hollywood Barn Dance* was not a network show, but was a popular local program, and television programs like *Town Hall Party* in Compton began in the 1950's as that medium began to gain popularity.

With all this activity it is not surprising that recording studios were relatively commonplace. Columbia did a great deal of cutting in their Hollywood studio. Capitol, whose tower was to

Spade Cooley and his all-star band packed 'em in for Foreman Phillips on the West Coast.

Wesley Tuttle, Ernie Ford and Eddie Kirk in 1946.

dominate the West Coast music scene for so long, had the bulk of their recording roster on the West Coast in the 1940's: Tex Ritter, Jimmy Wakely (with or without big band singer Margaret Whiting), Tennessee Ernie Ford, Tex Williams and Merle Travis.

In 1942 California was going strong, Chicago was waning, and the Opry had yet to begin the talent hunt that would eventually launch it toward a position of absolute prominence in the field. It was in 1942, however, that a serious problem hit the entire country music industry. The recording ban or the Petrillo ban began when James C. Petrillo, president of the American Federation of Musicians, called a general strike on August 1, 1942. The main issue was that the proliferation of jukeboxes and radio stations (all playing prerecorded material) was, according to Petrillo, forcing musicians out of "live" work. Petrillo demanded the creation of a fund, supported by the record companies, for unemployed musicians. The demand was not met, so the union called the strike, thereby ending all recording.

The negative effects were immediate: Without recording income, it became hard for bandleaders to keep their big bands together. But the effects on posterity were worse: Many of the best and biggest versions of the big bands went completely unrecorded with star soloists entering and leaving the bands while the ban was in effect. Bob Wills' largest version of The Texas Playboys, for instance—22 pieces—was never recorded at all. The effects on country music were serious indeed. The available backlog of recordings was quickly used up, and performers found it difficult to sustain their popularity and their income without the help of new records.

Decca became the first company to give in to the demands of the musicians' union, signing the desired agreement in September of 1943. When, in November of that year, Victor and Columbia caved in, the strike was for all intents and purposes over. Petrillo called yet another strike in 1948, and its main effects were the same: More benefits went to musicians, but much important music was left unrecorded. Bob Wills, for example, did not record from November 12,

1947, until May 5, 1949, and many others had similar stories: Bill Monroe was not recorded from October 28, 1947, through October 22, 1949; Johnny Bond from December 29, 1947, until March 18, 1949; and Al Dexter from December 15, 1947, until September 27, 1949.

Another purely business decision, completely out of the hands of the musicians, was the creation of BMI as a rival to ASCAP in 1940, and the subsequent war of sorts between the two that

Foy Willing and The Andrews Sisters in the 1940's.

added to the confusion of the era, although it was ultimately of enormous benefit to country music, musicians and songwriters.

The beginnings of the rift go all the way back to 1914, when the American Society of Composers, Authors and Publishers—ASCAP—was formed to protect songwriters from unlawful use of their material. Called a licensing agency, it registered the compositions of songwriters and collected the fees due to them and their publishing companies for the use of their songs. At the time of ASCAP's formation, sheet music publication and performance royalties were the

Bob Wills in the 40's.

main sources of income. ASCAP's territory was extended to cover sound recordings when that medium came along; then, later, to the playing of material over radio.

Formed mainly by and for Broadway composers for their own protection, ASCAP as an organization tended to think of minor music forms—like "race" and "hillbilly"—as both musically and financially unworthy, and so many fine country songs, unless in the hands of an honest publisher big enough to ensure collection, went unprotected, earning their authors little or nothing. The problem came to a head in 1940 when ASCAP announced that they were raising their rates for radio play. Broadcasters, having foreseen the problem on the horizon, had begun their own licensing organization, Broadcast Music Incorporated—BMI— in October of 1939. The contract with ASCAP expired on December 31, 1940, and as of January 1, 1941, radio stations no longer played any ASCAP material, and the resulting confusion was immense. Big bands, for example, had to play either public domain material (hence the astonishing surge in Stephen Foster material at the time), or the work of young, often unknown writers not affiliated with ASCAP, and even had to change their well-known theme songs as well.

BMI's catalogue was pretty scanty at the time, but they had two things going for them. First, they were open and eager to have a minority catalogue, including country and blues; second, they began to add some very important songwriters to their list of supporters. Pop publisher Edward B. Marks was the first to switch over to BMI, followed by two of the giants in country music, Peer International and M.M. Cole of Chicago, which published hundreds of songbooks in the 1930's and 1940's. Perhaps the most important individual to switch was an old Tin Pan Alley songwriter named Fred Rose, who had written pop hits like "'Deed I Do" and Sophie Tucker's "Red-Hot Mama."

ASCAP and the broadcasters patched things up in October 1941, but by that time BMI had a firm foothold in the publishing world, and soon most popular country music writers were publishing through BMI-affiliated companies. BMI gave country songwriters a chance, and it gave them the opportunity to be fairly and adequately compensated for their work. But more than this, it gave them—and country music in general—a respectability long denied it by serious musicians and popular composers. On a more mundane level, it was an acknowledgment of the growing financial stature of the music.

This rising financial power led to another con-

Former President Harry Truman and James C. Petrillo in 1957. In the 1940's, Petrillo called two strikes that changed the music industry.

fusing business development that marked this decade of confusion: the proliferation of record labels. As with many other industries, the Depression had pretty much wiped out most of the old companies, with only the biggest surviving. As the 1940's began there were a few small labels, but the vast majority of country music performers recorded for Victor (usually on their subsidiary Bluebird), Columbia (usually on their subsidiary Okeh), or on the relative latecomer (1933) Decca. There was, however, big money in country music, and as the last strains of the Depression faded away, more and more people wanted some of it. Easily the most successful new label of the decade was Capitol, founded in 1942 by Johnny Mercer and Glenn Wallichs, which became a "major" almost immediately. Their first country signee was Tex Ritter, an indifferent seller

The Maddox Brothers and Rose were stars of the postwar era. Like T. Texas Tyler, they recorded for a West Coast label.

on Decca who suddenly supplied Capitol with a long string of Number One records in the 1940's: "Jingle, Jangle, Jingle," "There's a New Moon Over My Shoulder," "Jealous Heart" and "You Two-Timed Me One Time Too Often." He was followed by Merle Travis, who did the same with "Divorce Me C.O.D." and "So Round, So Firm, So Fully Packed." Later in the decade came super sellers like "Smoke! Smoke! Smoke! (That Cigarette)" by Tex Williams, and "One Has My Name, The Other Has My Heart" and "Slippin' Around" by Jimmy Wakely. Capitol got on its feet early and has remained strong in popular and country music ever since.

Another company to join the fray was MGM, which organized in 1947 and immediately went after the best, signing Hank Williams and Bob Wills right off the bat. In fact, they had the honor of having the last hit of Carson J. Robison's long and illustrious career. A songwriting pioneer who began with Vernon Dalhart in the 1920's, Robison had a big seller in 1948 called "Life Gits Tee-jus Don't It." Mercury had entered the field a year earlier, with Rex Allen heading up a stable that included Lulu Belle and Scotty and The Prairie Ramblers, among others.

There were many other labels as well. Some of them went on to prominence while others faded away to become prized items for collectors only. Majestic, in New York City, came into the field as a pop label, yet important country acts like Eddie Dean, Foy Willing and The Riders of the Purple Sage and Pete Cassell graced the label, while Rich-R-Tone in East Tennessee first recorded such staunch and important non-traditional groups as The Stanley Brothers and

Wilma Lee and Stoney Cooper. Regional location didn't mean much to new labels, either. Detroit's Fortune Records had Skeets MacDonald, The York Brothers and Skeeter Davis (with Betty Jack Davis as The Davis Sisters), while Texas was the home base of several small labels including Macy's, which released early records by Jim Reeves; Bluebonnet, which at one time had both Hank Thompson and Sheb Wooley, and Globe, on which Hank Thompson's first records were released.

Back in the Motor City, some of the most unusual records ever produced were first released in the 1940's—Vogue's picture records. Implanting a photo image in wax was not new: Victor put out a Jimmie Rodgers memorial record shortly after his death with a photo of the late Blue Yodeler in all his glory. But Vogue went a step farther, using full-color depictions of the events in the song, done in maudlin *True Confessions* style, full of bold motion and bright colors. The process, as might be expected, was prohibitively expensive, and the Vogue picture record did not last terribly long, although they had at least one substantial hit in Lulu Belle and Scotty's "Have I Told You Lately That I Love You?"

One of the most important of the new labels was King,

a Cincinnati-based outfit that at one time had the largest country catalogue of any record label. As one who was present at the creation, Grandpa Jones (then a star of the *Boone County Jamboree*) described how King got its start: "The last part of 1943 there was a man by the name of Sydney Nathan, who had a record shop close to WLW, and he came over one day and said he was going to start a record company and he wanted some of us to record for him. We were all eager to record; at least the ones like me who hadn't recorded before. So one day Sydney took Merle Travis and I up to Dayton. He said there was a studio up there he could use as he didn't have one yet and knew there was none in Cincinnati. I remember we recorded upstairs over the Wurlitzer Piano Company. We cut a few sides and coming back Sydney said, 'What will we call the company?' We decided on King Records: 'King of them all,' Syd said."

Besides Travis and Jones (whose first record

Wesley Tuttle, Jimmie Dean and Merle Travis in 1944. Jimmie was Eddie Dean's brother.

was released under the pseudonym The Sheppard Brothers), Syd Nathan quickly signed up a host of country music stars, many of whom were to have big hits on the label: Cowboy Copas, The Delmore Brothers, Moon Mullican, Paul Howard, Mainer's Mountaineers and others, including the superb gospel singing of The Brown's Ferry Four, which consisted of Jones, Travis and The Delmore Brothers. But no one record put King Records on the map as much as Clyde Moody's "Shenandoah Waltz," King's only Gold record. King remained a factor in country music into the 1970's, but actually much

Art Satherley and Gene Autry and one of Autry's hits of the era.

of its vitality had disappeared with the death of Syd Nathan years before. Still, of all the labels that started as shoestring operations, King was the most successful. With no outside backing, and removed from recording and publishing centers, Syd Nathan built a label that often rivaled the true majors in sales and popularity.

Two West Coast labels also came to prominence in the 1940's. Although based in the West, Imperial did a great deal of recording (both blues and country) in the Texas-Louisiana area, one of their first country artists being the remarkably adaptable Adolph Hofner, who recorded for them both in English and in Bohemian, a great deal of his popularity being with the large middle-European community scattered throughout Texas.

Hofner's "Green Meadow Waltz" was one of Imperial's first records. In the 1950's Imperial was to have big hits in three fields, with Slim Whitman in country, Fats Domino in rhythm and blues and Ricky Nelson in pop.

Another thriving label was the California-based 4-Star. It got its start as a specialty label, recording only Mexican material, but was taken over shortly after its formation by a country music sharpie named Bill McCall, who turned it, for the most part, into a country label (although some blues and Mexican music were still recorded). Their line-up of talent in the 1940's included Smokey Rogers, Buddy Starcher, The Maddox Brothers and Rose, and the first recordings of Hank Locklin. But their big gun was T. Texas Tyler, "the man with a million friends," who had a nationwide hit with Scotty Wiseman's "Remember Me" (it became his theme song) and who scored again in the early 1950's with "Deck of Cards." McCall hired a young apprentice named Don Pierce, who went on to bring a small Texas-based label called Starday to Nashville, and to prominence in the 1950's by presenting the vitality of supposed old-timers like Cowboy Copas and Johnny Bond, proving they still had muscle when it came to record sales. (Starday was also the label on which George Jones had his first hit, "Why Baby Why," in 1955.)

The final small label to make its mark in this era was based, interestingly, in Nashville. Bullet Records—owned by ex-Opry announcer Jim Bulleit—began in the mid-1940's, and his December 1945 recording of Sheb Wooley was the first Nashville studio recording produced neither on portable equipment nor in WSM's studio.

Bullet Records flourished for a while, and their roster—on and off—included some important people indeed: Ray Price (who did his first recordings there), Clyde Moody, Leon Payne and Wally Fowler, among others. Their big country sellers, however, were both by a non-Opry act: Bob Wills' younger brother, Johnnie Lee Wills, who scored twice with "Rag Mop" and "Peter

Cottontail." Their best seller of all, however, was a purely pop record: "Near You," by Francis Craig, a Nashville hotel bandleader. Jim Bulleit also recorded a lot of fine blues artists, B.B. King among them. As the 1950's progressed, Bullet Records lost most of its vigor, and is now defunct.

Bullet was as much a sign of the times as anything: It showed that by 1945 there was enough first-rate talent in Nashville to make recording feasible, and it showed the desire to improve upon and expand the extremely limited recording facilities that existed at the time in what was to become Music City. Bullet Records was hardly a threat to Capitol, but it was one of the first of many harbingers that accurately fore-

told the decline of the West Coast and the ascendance of Nashville as country music's home.

Still, as disruptive as any one of these sources of confusion might have been, all were cast deep in the overwhelming shadow of World War II, which disrupted musical life every bit as much as it did the lives of every American. The effects of the war were numerous, varied and complex, and were felt for decades. Some were major, some minor; some helped country music grow, some retarded its progress. One thing is for sure: Country music was never the same.

One (maybe the least) of the deep effects of war can be summed up in one word: shortage. Restrictions on gasoline and rubber made travel

Opry tour in the 40's with Uncle Dave Macon, Dave's son Dorris Macon, Roy Acuff, Bashful Brother Oswald and George D. Hay. In front are Lonnie Wilson, Jess Easterday and Cousin Rachel. Roy was enormously popular during the war.

increasingly difficult for both entertainers and fans, who might have driven miles to hear a favorite singer or group before the war. The vinyl shortage was even more severe. Columbia A&R man Art Satherley recalled that during the worst years of the war he was not only forbidden to sign new artists (thereby missing Eddy Arnold, a loss he regretted ever thereafter), but also he was allowed to record only the "Big Three" of his huge Columbia stable: Gene Autry, Roy Acuff and Bob Wills. In addition, Satherley turned over his entire enormous collection of records (many of which dated back to his days with Edison) to the war effort as scrap vinyl, a priceless collection lost forever. The hardships of shortage were obvious. A performer who can do only limited traveling, plays before smaller audiences and has no records released or available, is a performer with prob-

Ernest Tubb and other Nashville stars kept the home fires burning during the war years. Among the performers are The Duke of Paducah, Jimmie Short, E.T., Johnny Sapp, Bill Westbrook, Bill Monroe, Leon Short, "Butterball" Paige and Eddy Arnold.

lems. During the war, such artists' only consolation must have been that they were not alone.

A far more serious hardship was the draft. Musicians in general were young and often single, prime prospects as soldiers, and the spirit of patriotism ran high, causing a great many to volunteer. A classic case was Bob Wills' famous vocalist, Tommy Duncan, who strode into the studio of KVOO in Tulsa for The Playboys' regular noon broadcast on December 8, 1941, and announced to the band: "I don't know about you guys, but I'm going to join 'this man's Army' and fight those sons-of-bitches!" He and several other Playboys were gone by Christmas, followed shortly by Leon McAuliffe, the steel player whose sound was so much a part of Western swing; he became an Army Air Force pilot. Wills himself was drafted at the age of 37 in 1943, totally dismantling the Texas Playboys until late the following year.

No career was more visibly affected than Gene Autry's: He enlisted in the Air Force as a pilot and spent much of the war ferrying supplies in Burma. Autry left as America's most popular country singer and one of its favorite actors, and returned to find Roy Rogers as "The King of the Cowboys." Another seriously damaged career was that of The Blue Sky Boys, who split up in 1941, separating for a full five of their best years and reuniting in 1946 to play before a new and changed public. In fact, the draft so decimated the ranks of musicians that several bandleaders, faced with this and the difficulty of travel, simply closed up shop for the duration.

There is a case to be made, however, for some positive effects of wartime on country music, especially the long-held theory that in bringing Southern soldiers in contact with Northern, a taste

West Coast DJ George Wilhelm and Elton Britt.

for country music was spread and new fans made where none would have existed otherwise. Defense workers in the North and the West were also exposed to the music by the Southern and Southwestern migrants working alongside them. While it has been adequately demonstrated that country music was a nationwide phenomenon long before World War II, there is no doubt that the music was spread by such contacts. An illustrative and well-documented case in point occurred in occupied Germany, where GI's were polled as to their favorite singer, and Frank Sinatra was nosed out by Roy Acuff. A country music radio program was begun immediately.

Country music was quick to respond to the exigencies of wartime with appropriate music, and hardly had the war begun when records such as Johnny Bond's "Draftee Blues," Cliff Bruner's "Draft Board Blues" and The Sons of the Pioneers' ironically prophetic "They Drew My Number" were available in record stores. Patriotic feeling was also strong, as Denver Darling's "Cowards Over Pearl Harbor" attests, and the war provided material for a legion of songs, many immediately forgettable, some country music classics. The theme of patriotism rang out in "Smoke on the Water," a hit for both Red Foley and Bob Wills, and in Carson J. Robison's "1942 Turkey in the Straw" and The Sons of the Pioneers' "Stars and Stripes on Iwo Jima." Sometimes patriotism was a theme expressed in comic vein, as with Johnny Bond's "Der Fuhrer's Face." Most common among the wartime themes, however, was loneliness; the love of a girl for her faraway soldier, or the concern of a GI in a far-off land over the faithfulness (or lack of it) of the girl he left behind. From the female side, Judy Canova used Patsy

Ernie Ford, George Wilhelm, songwriter Cindy Walker, Redd Harper and Jimmy Wakely.

Montana's "Goodnight, Soldier" at the end of every wartime broadcast, and Bob Wills expressed the sentiment definitively in his "Silver Dew on the Bluegrass":

Soldier boy so far from me
How I wish that you could see
Silver dew on the bluegrass tonight.

From the male viewpoint, Ernest Tubb wondered plaintively (in one of his greatest songs) "Are You Waiting Just for Me, My Darling?" while Gene Autry received the bad news by letter in one of the last of his big hits, "At Mail Call Today." And, of course, there was the recurrent theme of the son who did not return, as in Ernest Tubb's "Soldier's Last Letter," revived by Merle Haggard during the Vietnam War. Even the after-effects of war were examined in country songs, from Roy Acuff's story of a young lady "Searching for a Soldier's Grave," to two looks at the fearsome technology of the atom age that was born at Hiroshima and Nagasaki, The Buchanan Brothers' "Atomic Power" and The Louvin Broth-

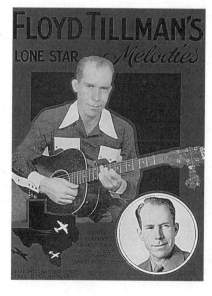

ers' "Great Atomic Power."

The ultimate World War II song was, of course, Elton Britt's "There's a Star-Spangled Banner Waving Somewhere," a corny but moving tale of a crippled mountain boy trying somehow, in some way, to help the war effort. "Let me show my Uncle Sam what I can do, sir/Let me help to take the Axis down a peg," he begged his draft agent. Britt's multi-million seller was in fact awarded country music's first Gold record. Although there had been million-sellers in country music going all the way back to Dalhart's "The Prisoner's Song" in 1924, the practice of awarding a Gold record for sales in excess of a million did not arise until Columbia gave one to Glenn Miller for "Chattanooga Choo Choo." The award was given fitfully for a few years; its first recipient in the country field was Britt's 1942 hit.

Country music's songwriters, singers and A&R men have always demonstrated a remarkable flexibility when it comes to reacting to a national mood. The patriotic and "lonely soldier" songs were one example of this phenomenon; the sudden and wholesale change in the nature of the music after the war was another. Where pre-war America was dreamy, romantic, impulsive and escapist, post-war America was just the opposite: Hardened by the grim reality of war, the soldiers who returned wanted music that honestly reflected life's realities regardless of how unpleasant they might be. In truth, reality was often unpleasant: Consumption of alcohol rose rapidly during the post-war period, and many men returned to wives and sweethearts as changed by the effects of war as they were themselves. The result was often divorce, loneliness and anomie, frequently assuaged by the bottle. Post-war America confronted a time of alienation, confusion and an increasingly "wild side of life," a time of adjustment and adaptation that was not always easy or successful, and just as country music had been quick to respond to the feelings of Americans at war, it also was quick to express the difficulties of the war's aftermath. The story of one song in particular, "One Has My Name, The Other Has My Heart," exemplifies the rapidity with which these changes took place.

The song was written by singing cowboy Eddie Dean with his wife, Lorene ("Dearest"), and Hal Blair. Dean shopped both it and himself around to the major record labels but none would touch it, infidelity being quite taboo as a subject for records, especially infidelity as explicit and unrepentant as in Dean's song: "So I'll go on living my life just the same/While one has my heart, the other has my name." Dean recorded it himself on a small label called Crystal (over the heated objections of the morally offended owner), but even with the finished product in hand he found he couldn't get disc jockeys to play it: "It's a great record, Eddie, but you know we can't play that kind of song over the air!" The climate had changed so much by 1947, however, that Capitol Records, remembering the song, got one of their own singing cowboys, Jimmy Wakely, to cut it, and it became one of the following year's biggest hits. "One Has My Name" became the song that got the whole "cheatin' song" genre under way.

Wakely followed this release with a Floyd Tillman song that has proved to be the classic of the style, a pure country duet with big-band singer Margaret Whiting called "Slippin' Around." It was an immediate million seller. It set a tone of resignation, not regret—"Oh you're tied up with someone else/And I'm all tied up too"—and placed the problem right out in the open.

The changes in taste were evident in all forms of music—the big bands, for example, at their

Blue grass took the Opry by storm in the 1940's. Bill Monroe, center, and His Blue Grass Boys with the "Blue Grass Special" touring limousine around 1946. This lineup includes Birch Monroe, Chubby Wise, Lester Flatt and Earl Scruggs.

The Louisiana Hayride: faces in the crowd include Slim Whitman and Johnny Horton, Goldie Hill, Jim Reeves and Floyd Cramer. M

peak a few years earlier, were all but extinct by 1950. Gone was the blithe optimism of the 1930's ("You Are My Sunshine") and the willingness to drift into the dreamy escapism of cowboy songs and danceable ditties like "San Antonio Rose." Here to stay was a certain cynicism, a certain hardness, and an implicit demand for songs that were straightforward about the very real, very pervasive, very painful events which were an

increasingly large part of life in post-war America.

Another historically significant record also appeared in 1948, and it too spotlighted the new morality (or at least the new honesty about the old morality). It was one of Bob Wills' first releases on the MGM label, "Bubbles in My Beer," and it treated the old "born to lose" theme with frankness, dealing with drunkenness without apology or moralism: a radical departure from

...was launched on the Shreveport barn dance show.

In point of historical fact, the honky tonk genre had begun before the war, with songs like Al Dexter's "When We Go a-Honky Tonkin'" and "Honky Tonk Blues." Ernest Tubb championed the sound throughout the 1940's, more or less introducing it to the Southeast via his position on the Opry, but Dexter was the unquestionable leader of the pack. Although capable of beautiful love songs like "Too Late to Worry, Too Blue to Cry," he had one of the top songs of the entire decade with "Pistol Packin' Mama." Yet any song beginning with "Drinkin' beer in a cabaret/Was I havin' fun..." is a song with strong comic overtones, and "Pistol Packin' Mama," like most early honky tonk songs, was basically comic. Therein lies the difference between them and "Bubbles in My Beer"; that song, anything but lighthearted, was a landmark because of its willingness to treat drinking as a problem and face it in a manner both serious and straightforward. America had changed forever, and country music changed with it.

It is indicative of the complexity and variety of country music that a third major movement was developed in the 1940's alongside the cheatin' and honky tonk genres. This was bluegrass, a music both traditional and innovative, which in one sense was a late manifestation of a line of development that began in the 1930's, yet also presaged the Southeastern Sound revival of the early 1950's. Bill Monroe clearly stamped the music as his own as early as 1939, when he and his Blue Grass Boys (hence the name of the music) joined the Grand Ole Opry and let loose with their wild new blend of galloping tempos, unique rhythms and "high, lonesome sound." The creative music of one man—Monroe—became a whole new style with the arrival of Earl Scruggs, who joined The Blue Grass Boys in December 1944. Scruggs' unique and dramatic approach to banjo playing, with Monroe's already established sound, electrified Opry audiences.

After the war, country music on the West Coast was probably stronger than it had ever been, and for some, like Bob Wills, it proved to be the financial peak of their career. In retrospect, however, the writing was on the wall for big bands such as The Texas Playboys (and indeed the

past country music. Like all Wills tunes, "Bubbles in My Beer" was above all danceable, featuring twin fiddles, steel and Tommy Duncan's mellow vocalizing, but Cindy Walker's pointed and poignant lyrics ("I know that my life's been a failure") opened the door to the deluge of frank honky tonkin' songs that followed, epitomized by the Webb Pierce classic of the 1950's, "There Stands the Glass."

Shreveport stars before they joined the Opry: Ray Adkins, Jack Anglin, Kitty Wells, Paul Warren and Johnnie Wright.

whole West Coast scene), for national interest turned away from singing cowboys at about this time. The focus of West Coast country music seems to have been too narrowly based on film stardom and dance bands, and when public interest turned from those two forms, the West Coast was, in a way, left high and dry. That trend was not obvious at the time, however. In fact, the country charts were dominated by West Coasters from 1945 to 1949—that is, until the coming of Hank Williams, who accelerated the shift to Nashville. In that pre-Hank period the big stars were Merle Travis, Gene Autry, Spade Cooley, Johnny Bond, Tex Williams and especially Jimmy Wakely, whose two big hits of the era had, as we have seen, implications far wider than their sales alone.

Still, Wakely's two great cheatin' songs were his last big hits, and he wasn't alone in that respect. Even the pre-war king of the West Coast,

Gene Autry, didn't have a huge hit after his 1945 war song, "At Mail Call Today," although he did have a few lesser hits in the later 1940's (and, of course, "Here Comes Santa Claus" and "Rudolph," which were country in neither sound nor intent). Much the same is true of Bob Wills, who was extremely successful for a time in the fading ballroom scene on the West Coast, but who didn't have a hit after his 1950 Top Ten, "Faded Love," until his "Heart-to-Heart Talk" in 1960. By the early 50's, the charts were all Hank Williams, Hank Snow and Red Foley, with an occasional Texan like Lefty Frizzell or Hank Thompson thrown in; except for a few hits by Tommy Collins, and Tennessee Ernie Ford's "Sixteen Tons" in 1955, the West Coast scene was pretty much out of the charts until Buck Owens began the California comeback in 1959.

The West Coast was of tremendous importance throughout the decade, and no trumping up of Nashville or the Grand Ole Opry can deny it. But despite the dominance of California in this era, the slippage of influence eastward to Nashville is apparent with the convenient hindsight time gives, and the foundations of the West Coast dominance had been so fragile (or

Jim Denny and Jack Stapp "modernized" the Grand Ole Opry.

the reasons seem obvious: While the Opry went out and signed a host of singing stars, moving right along with the trend toward solo singers and away from the big-band sound, the *National Barn Dance* stuck with its tried-and-true format and lineup of stars. But as popular as Lulu Belle

so narrowly based) that it took only the power of one Southeastern Opry singer, Hank Williams, to tip the balance forever.

Chicago was another story altogether. The nation's leading barn dance throughout the 1930's, the *National Barn Dance* lost ground so rapidly in the 1940's that it had become nearly insignificant in the 1950's. Rock 'n' roll was a hard storm to weather, but Nashville and the Opry did just that, while WLS eventually dropped the *National Barn Dance* altogether in 1960, the entire station switching to a rock format that year (although the show hung on, just an echo of its former self, over WGN until 1970). In retrospect,

and Scotty, Arkie the Woodchopper, Doc Hopkins, Karl and Harty, The Hoosier Hotshots and The Prairie Ramblers were—and they were extremely popular—without an influx of the "hot" new talent, the lovable old *National Barn Dance* grew stale. In the 1940's the show added only two major stars to its roster: Bob Atcher, who, although a major artist, had long been a Chicago fixture; and Rex Allen, whose stay was relatively short, for he fled to Hollywood to become the last of the singing cowboys when film roles were offered.

While the Opry was busy overtaking the *National Barn Dance*, the *Louisiana Hayride* down in Shreveport, relying on the star system alone, appeared late in the decade to move quickly into second place behind the Opry. The acts that began on the *Louisiana Hayride* are impressive indeed: Webb Pierce, Johnny and Jack, Faron Young, Red Sovine, Goldie Hill and, of course, the greatest of them all, Hank Williams. The only reason the *Hayride* didn't come to dominate the more traditional Opry, in fact, was that the Opry had so quickly and so firmly developed the image as the Number One country show that in every case performers jumped the *Hayride* to join the Opry at the first opportunity. Ultimately the *Hayride* became known as the "cradle of the stars," a sort of farm club where talented entertainers

The Opry Old Guard in 1945 included Uncle Dave Macon, Staley Walton, George D. Hay, Alcyone Bate Beasley (daughter of Humphrey Bate) and Oscar Albright.

Red Foley

matured before joining the big leagues at the Grand Ole Opry.

By 1950 the Opry was at the top of the heap, and it is fascinating to see how they did it. A study of the Opry in the 1930's quickly reveals that Roy Acuff was not the first singing star of the show, but simply the first to hit with powerful national impact. His success on the *Prince Albert Show* (the Opry program carried nationwide on the NBC Blue Network in the 1940's) not only assured his continuing stardom and fired the Opry's rise to the Number One position among barn dance programs, but also sent the venerable institution on a massive talent hunt for new singing stars. Many were successful, some have been forgotten, and magic on the Roy Acuff scale didn't happen again until Hank Williams joined in 1949, but the immediate result was that the Opry became stuffed with singing stars in the 1940's.

Most of the credit can be given to Jack Stapp and Jim Denny, the men who wrested control of the Opry away from George D. Hay, "The Solemn Old Judge," in the

Cowboy Copas made a splash with his suits and his songs.

early 1940's, determined to "modernize" the Opry. In a way this was not an easy period for performers, but Stapp and Denny's efforts turned the Opry from a popular barn dance into a star-studded super-show, packed not with high-spirited fiddle bands but with singing stars. The cast grew enormously, and most of the major recording stars of the period became Opry members, turning the show into every performer's ultimate goal. The Opry became a showcase of stars, but lost its barn-dance flavor and, after not too long, lost the Solemn Old Judge, too. Hay, confined to a figurehead role, left the show in

1953, 15 years before his death, as new star after new star—all featuring those hated electric guitars and increasingly gaudy outfits—was added to the show: Hank Williams, Webb Pierce, Ray Price, Carl Smith, Faron Young and others.

Ernest Tubb, The Texas Troubadour, was among the first new cast members to join the Opry in the early 40's, arriving in late 1942 with his electric guitars and honky tonk sound—two innovations with powerful ramifications for the future. Drums made their first appearance on the Opry in 1944 during a guest shot by Bob Wills and His Texas Playboys, although they wouldn't become steady Opry fare for well over a decade (in fact, Wills' drummer was forced to play behind a curtain, so the offensive instruments wouldn't be seen by the audience).

Predating Tubb were Paul Howard, who joined the Opry as a solo singer in 1940 and ended up building the Opry's only Western swing-type band during the mid-40's, and Pete Pyle, a graduate of Bill Monroe's Blue Grass Boys, who brought a gentle country sound to the Opry for a few years. Before them came two major stars who joined in 1939: Bill Monroe, popular then and now, and Zeke Clements. It was after the coming of Tubb, however, that the floodgates seemed to open, beginning in 1944 with the brightest new star of country music, Eddy Arnold, whose plaintive, evocative voice was a marvel of heartbreaking ingenuousness, its achingly beautiful tones never really captured on record. At the same time, one of country music's true pioneers was added to the cast: Bradley Kincaid, a tremendously influential entertainer who has never received the historical attention he has deserved.

In 1946 the Opry scored a major coup by hiring Red Foley to host the *Prince Albert Show*, replacing Roy Acuff, who had left the segment in a contract dispute. Foley was a big name, having starred on the *National Barn Dance*, the *Renfro Valley Barn Dance* and the *Boone County Jamboree*, although he had not had much success on record except for "Old Shep." The boost the *Prince Albert Show* gave his career, and the contributions of Nashville's increasingly skilled studio musicians and technicians, changed his fortunes. After years of recording, he suddenly seemed to get the Midas touch, and sold millions upon millions of records in the 1940's and 50's.

Clyde Moody stepped out of Bill Monroe's Blue Grass Boys into a solo spot with Roy Acuff before joining the Opry on his own in 1945, and the Midas touch worked for him for a while, too:

His "Shenandoah Waltz" was to sell well over a million records in the decade.

In 1946 one of the Opry's long-time favorites, a solo singer with a Western flavor named Cowboy Copas, joined the cast on the strength of his big hit, "Filipino Baby." Copas was almost universally liked by his fellow Opry members, and he brought with him a Western image which, they seemed to feel, would add some of the glamour of the singing cowboy to the show, particularly since Zeke Clements, The Alabama Cowboy and the only Opry performer other than Tubb who affected Western dress at the time, had recently departed from the ranks. The flashy Western duds of another Alabama cowboy named Hank Williams, and the even gaudier outfits of his protégé, Ray Price, just a few years later, show that the Opry not only

Pee Wee King, left of mike, gave Eddy Arnold his big break. They remained friends after Eddy, second from right, left the band.

went along with a trend toward Western clothing and songs, but did a lot to keep it going. The names of the bands—from The Smoky Mountain Boys and The Blue Grass Boys in 1940 to The Drifting Cowboys, The Cherokee Cowboys and The Rainbow Ranch Boys in the early 50's—reflected this change.

Eddy Arnold, the show's most popular star during the second half of the decade, left in 1947. Clearly a solo singer, he had first played the Opry as a member of Pee Wee King's Golden West Cowboys, then struck out on his own in 1943. (Interestingly, Cowboy Copas was his replacement). By 1947, he and his group, The Tennessee Plowboys, were outgrowing even star billing on the Opry, and working hand in hand with his manager, Colonel Tom Parker (of Elvis fame), he left WSM and the Opry for the Mutual Radio Network and his own show. He began pursuing a pop market (as he was to do with such great success in the 50's), and consciously changed his style; the Eddy Arnold with the high, plaintive voice was superseded by a more mellow-voiced version with slick pop phrasing, and the sound of Roy Wiggins' steel replaced with a smoother background, even at times the ultra-smooth Hugo Winterhalter Orchestra.

The search for an Arnold replacement, given a high priority by Opry management, yielded a young George Morgan, who was brought in on the heels of his 1948 hit, "Candy Kisses." His style—high, with a touch of yodel and a restrained vibrato—was reminiscent of Arnold's but was clearly his own, and although Morgan never had another hit as big as his first record, he was, like Copas, one of the best-loved of the Opry cast, and continued as an integral and important part of the show until his death in 1975.

The same year also saw the signing of Little Jimmy Dickens, a fine singer of throbbing heart songs who was best known for his comic ditties like "Sleeping at the Foot of the Bed" and "Take an Old Cold Tater and Wait." It was June Carter who described him, upon seeing one of his outlandish outfits on his 4'11" frame, as "Mighty Mouse in pajamas."

As 1950 dawned, the star-gathering process was still very much in evidence. Both Hank Snow

Hank Snow and Nudie the Tailor. Snow was another customer.

and Carl Smith joined that year, and both were to be constant hitmakers throughout the 50's, very much in tune with the increasingly fashionable melding of cowboy look and country sound. Snow, a Canadian, Smith, from East Tennessee, and the West Virginian Dickens paraded a succession of dazzling Western outfits—all tailored by the famous Nudie of Hollywood.

The Opry's biggest catch, though, was Hank Williams, who moved to the Opry from the *Louisiana Hayride* in 1949. His career and its enormous influence on country music past and present are explored fully in Chapter Seven, but for the moment it is important to see that his appearance on the Opry was part of a logical progression that had begun about 15 years earlier. Just as Roy Acuff, in the late 1930's and early 40's, was the one great charismatic singer the Opry had been seeking since 1933, Hank Williams became by far the greatest star of the late 1940's and early 50's. And it was his enormous success that was the deciding factor in the Opry's long campaign to make Nashville the nation's country music capital. With his Western image

Minnie Pearl

and hillbilly songs—already, as the Opry had demonstrated, a winning combination—Hank was the performer and songwriter who put it all together, and put Nashville on top to stay.

It's interesting in this regard to note that the Opry, in addition to adding a host of solo singers to its roster, also went heavily into comedy during this period, far more than before 1940. Minnie Pearl joined that year; Rod Brasfield and the Duke of Paducah joined in 1942; Lonzo and Oscar entered the picture in 1944; and the following year Stringbean left his job as Bill Monroe's banjo player to team with Lew Childre. Clearly the Opry's push for dominance didn't rely on singing stars alone.

The changing of the order at the Opry was a difficult thing, but momentous in its time and increasingly so later, for it not only made the Opry the major country music show, but also made it easier for major record labels to justify setting up studios in the Opry's home city. Increasingly it was where the stars were and the musicians were, and rather than sending field men out to Chicago, Charlotte, Atlanta, Knoxville and Dallas, setting up and tearing down equipment at each stop, they simply set up shop in Nashville, where all the hot talent seemed to be anyhow.

There were, however, other factors involved in the centralization of the country music industry in Nashville. First and most obviously, there was the decline of both Hollywood and Chicago. The waning of national interest in the singing cowboys, ballroom dancing and the big bands was a severe blow to the mainstays of West Coast music; Hollywood's narrowly based concerns were unable to support a full range of country music, while Nashville's broader base could. Then too, Hollywood's noted disdain for "losers" (what Johnny Bond called the "Yeah, but what have you done lately?" syndrome), compared to the traditional ultra-loyalty of Grand Ole Opry fans in the Southeast, had a lot to do with it; Nashville was (and is still) very much in the center of the heartland, and in many ways it was a much more friendly, easy-going place in which to begin a career. None of this meant that California became moribund as a musical center—far from it; Hollywood stayed active as a country music

scene—but by 1950 it was clearly secondary to Nashville.

Another reason for Nashville's growing prominence was the rise of publishing companies in that city. In 1940 there was not a single music publisher in Nashville; by 1950 song publishing was a big business there. The man chiefly responsible was Fred Rose, one of the

Little Jimmy Dickens came to the Opry from West Virginia.

greatest country songwriters of all time. Rose had written hits for Sophie Tucker on Tin Pan Alley ("'Deed I Do," "Honestly and Truly") before drifting into drink and despair. His career foundering, he spent some time in Nashville as a pop pianist in the 1930's before singing cowboy Ray Whitley took him under his wing to Hollywood, and soon the two of them began cranking out movie scores for Gene Autry, as well as many hit records: "Ages and Ages Ago," "Lonely River," "I Hang My Head and Cry" and others, as well as many the reformed Fred Rose wrote by himself (often on Whitley's piano), such as Autry's "Be Honest With Me," which was nominated for an Academy Award.

Roy Acuff and Fred Rose, founders of Acuff-Rose, about 1949.

Having developed a feel for country music, Rose returned to Nashville in the early 40's, and after quitting ASCAP to join BMI, decided to set up his own company, the first country music publisher in the Southeast. With financial backing from Roy Acuff (for whom Rose had already written hits like "Fireball Mail" and "Low and Lonely"), Acuff-Rose Publishers opened its doors in 1943. The company went on to become an international giant, due largely to Fred Rose's productive genius; his output was so voluminous and of such high quality that virtually every major country artist of his day, and many of later years, can thank him for at least one hit. Another of his talents was almost as important, though— his ability to recognize talent in others. Hank Williams is the most obvious example of writers he "found," but there were many others: Felice and Boudleaux Bryant, Marty Robbins, Jenny Lou Carson, The Bailes Brothers, The Louvin Brothers and hundreds more. Rose's major coup of the 40's was obtaining the songs of Pee Wee King and Redd Stewart, which included the million seller "Slow Poke," standards like "Bonaparte's

Retreat" and "You Belong to Me," and the all-time, most-recorded, most-sold country song, "Tennessee Waltz." Rose died of a heart attack in 1954. His son Wesley, who had been running Acuff-Rose since 1945, continued expanding the company (he is credited with having "discovered" Roy Orbison and The Everly Brothers, among others) until his own death in 1990.

Acuff-Rose flourished under Wesley Rose's stewardship, always seeming to sign the right writer at the right time: Marty Robbins, Don Gibson and Doug Kershaw all published their early works through Acuff-Rose, and the outfit seemed to pull the best work from several fine writers like Leon Payne ("I Love You Because," "Lost Highway"), Jimmy Work ("Making Believe," "Tennessee Border") and Melvin Endsley ("Singing the Blues"). In fact, a young couple named Felice and Boudleaux Bryant helped Acuff-Rose weather the rock boom as much as any other single factor. Their "Wake Up Little Susie" and "All I Have to Do Is Dream," written for The Everly Brothers, were among the best-selling songs of the late 50's.

Huge sales like the ones Acuff-Rose began having in the mid-40's don't go unnoticed, and although other companies didn't have Rose's genius to fall back on, Acuff-Rose soon found themselves far from alone in the country music publishing field. In the late 1940's two Swiss-born brothers named Aberbach formed Hill and Range Music, using large cash advances to lure some of country music's biggest stars, including Bob Wills, Bill Monroe and Hank Snow, to sign with them. Although the Aberbachs—and Hill and Range—were headquartered in New York, they continued to maintain a strong Nashville presence until they were absorbed into the vast Chappell Music empire in the mid-1970's.

When Opry manager Jim Denny and country music's then biggest star, Webb Pierce, formed Cedarwood Music in the mid-1950's (opening day was June 26, 1954, to be exact), they added further impetus to Nashville's continuing growth as the center of the industry and set the stage for a group of publishers to open shop in what was becoming known as Music City, U.S.A.: Tree Music, Pamper Music, Combine Music, Central Songs and many others became associated with

On Cedarwood Music's opening day: Frankie Moore, Teddy Wilburn, Doyle Wilburn, Johnny Wright, Ernest Tubb, Minnie Pearl, Carl Smith, June Carter, Kitty Wells, Bill Carlisle, Jack Anglin, Jim Denny; in front, Hank Snow, Webb Pierce and Ray Price.

Music Row and built million-dollar catalogues from the pens of country songwriters. Within a decade of the founding of Acuff-Rose, country music publishing was a major business concern; within two decades it was a multinational, multi-million-dollar industry

Another main factor in Nashville's rise is perhaps the most obvious: the growth of the recording industry. Nashville's centralized location and the presence of the Opry would seem to have made it a logical recording center long before, yet it was not. It may be indicative that when Bluebird recording artist Pete Pyle joined the Opry in the early 1940's, he, Bill Monroe and Roy Acuff were the only members of the entire cast who

had recording contracts at all. Recording took place most often in New York, Chicago or Los Angeles, with a few regional field trip recordings made in Dallas, Atlanta and Charlotte a couple of times a year.

The Nashville recording scene began developing rather slowly after the war, when WSM engineers George Reynolds, Carl Jenkins and Aaron Shelton took it upon themselves to set up a crude but workable studio in WSM's smallest and least-used radio studio. It was there that Jim Bulleit recorded Sheb Wooley in December of 1945, which may well give Bulleit the honor of producing the first recording ever done in Nashville by a Nashville company. (To Victor goes

*Eddy Arnold,
Minnie Pearl,
Tex Ritter and
Roy Acuff: fun
in the late 40's.*

the honor of having produced the first Nashville recordings of any sort—a result of their 1927 field trip during which DeFord Bailey, The Crook Brothers, The Brinkley Brothers and others were recorded. Victor may also claim the first Nashville studio recording, Eddy Arnold's sessions in the makeshift WSM studio in December 1944.)

The position of the enterprising WSM engineers soon became somewhat uncomfortable—they were, after all, using their employer's premises—so they moved their base of operations to a suite in the old Tulane Hotel in downtown Nashville and called their outfit Castle Studios. The name is now legendary. Castle Studios opened in 1947, and the very first recording done in the Tulane Hotel location was a jingle for Shyer's Jewelers, sung by Snooky Lanson (later of *Your Hit Parade* fame on television) and backed by Owen Bradley on piano, Harold Bradley on guitar and the ex-head of the Nashville local of the American Federation of Musicians, George Cooper, on bass. It wasn't long before most of the major record labels, including the West Coast-based Capitol and the new Cincinnati-based King, began to use the Castle Studios facility frequently.

The impetus toward expansion in the number and quality of recording studios came when Castle Studios began to lose popularity due to the engineers' unwillingness to change, modernize, or invest in their business (they had proved reluctant to purchase an echo chamber, for example, when that sound came into vogue). Into this obvious gap stepped a popular local society band leader and his guitar-playing brother—Owen and Harold Bradley, respectively—who decided to build a new studio for producing not only records, but also films for that hot new medium, television. They built their first studio not on what is called Music Row today, but on the second floor of the Teamsters' Union office at Second and Lindsley. The year was 1952, but the location didn't last long. The Teamsters, knowing a good thing when they saw it, tripled the rent on the Bradleys the following year, so they moved to a small building on 21st Avenue South behind Hillsboro Village, just south of the Vanderbilt University campus. In its heyday the

place was host to numerous sessions for Mercury, Dot and Decca. Still, the ceilings were too low, the space too limited and the sound not really first-rate. Finally Decca A&R man Paul Cohen considered moving the bulk of his company's country recording to the Beck studio in Dallas. Once again, in 1955, the Bradleys went into action, moving the Bradley recording complex to 16th Avenue South to an old home on a quiet residential street; the first recording studio was actually in the house's basement. A Quonset hut was put up in the back yard, intended as a film studio. The Quonset hut was sold to Columbia Records in 1961, and although a large modern building has been constructed around it, Columbia's Studio B, as it is now known, is still very obviously the old Quonset hut with the addition only of updated equipment.

The Quonset hut was typical, in some ways, of the Nashville studios to follow. By and large they were (and remain) far more intimate than those in other recording centers, and they tend toward wood, earth tones and other "natural" decor more often than not. Many of the studios themselves have become legendary. The Quonset hut certainly has; in the 1970's it remained the single most popular studio in Nashville, and its interior, considered one of the most perfect acoustic environments in the world, was taken to be magical, with everyone fearing to remodel it in case that special sound might be lost. Back when Columbia Records first bought the hut from the Bradleys, the CBS president, Frank Stanton, made his first visit to Nashville and naturally examined Columbia's new acquisition, the Quonset hut. It had a tattered interior—old drapes covering part of the ceiling and burlap covering the rest. Stanton looked around with cold efficiency and allowed that "the studio is fine, but we must remodel immediately, of course. Tear down all these old curtains." Stanton's Nashville staff blanched, gulped, and quietly ushered their leader from the hallowed room. The old studio was already a star, and deserved protection. It was finally closed down in 1982, the last record made there John Anderson's *Wild and Blue* album; now, preserved exactly as it was on the last day of recording, it is open to the public.

The men who built the Quonset hut, Owen and Harold Bradley, are of course legendary figures. Harold went on to become the dean of Nashville session musicians for at least two decades, and Owen produced most of Decca's country acts in the 1950's and 1960's, discovering Patsy Cline, Loretta Lynn and others. And of course, back in the early days of the Quonset hut, it was their work which kept Decca recording in Nashville. From that point on, the recording boom became an avalanche, and Nashville became the undisputed center of country music.

Although the process came to fruition in the 1950's and especially in the 60's, all the groundwork was laid in the late 40's. It was pretty obvious by the end of that decade that recording was quickly becoming Nashville's domain, for the Nashville studios had already produced a giant pop hit—Bullet's "Near You" by the Francis Craig Orchestra—as well as a giant country hit— "Chattanoogie Shoe Shine Boy" recorded by Red Foley in the Castle Studios—and a host of lesser but still substantial sellers. It was a trend that was to mushroom and eventually develop into a giant industry, certainly the most visible and glamorous of all Nashville's businesses, and it was an enterprise that helped itself grow: More recording meant more money for the studios, which went into better equipment, hence better recording, hence more recording, and the cycle began again. And as the tempo of recording picked up, musicians were drawn to Nashville in ever-increasing numbers, creating the nucleus of talent that was to make possible the Nashville Sound of the 50's.

RCA was also a pioneer major label in Nashville, largely due to the insistence of Steve Sholes. Sholes, who recorded all over the country, used a third early studio, the Brown Brothers Transcription Service, when he came to Nashville. After the Browns sold their business to Cliff Thomas, RCA recorded for a time at the Methodist Publishing Company, then eventually built their own studio about 1957. During this time, Sholes made an appointment of extraordinary wisdom when he hired as his assistant and Nashville coordinator a fine guitarist who helped him line up musicians and lead the sessions themselves as early as the field trips at Brown Brothers. His name was Chet Atkins, and his lesser known contributions to the music industry changed, affected, and influenced the course of country music every bit as much as, if not a great deal more than, his contributions as a musician.

Redd Stewart and Pee Wee King wrote "Tennessee Waltz" and many more.

Columbia did most of its recording at the state-of-the-art Jim Beck Studio in Dallas, but following Beck's untimely death in 1956, when he was accidentally poisoned by chemicals used to clean the recording equipment, it too came to Nashville. Under the leadership of Don Law, the label had some of the top acts of this period: Lefty Frizzell and Marty Robbins (both denizens of the Beck studio in Dallas), Little Jimmy Dickens, Johnny Cash, Johnny Horton, Flatt and Scruggs, Carl Smith and others. Likewise Capitol, although they didn't have their own studio there, began increasingly to focus on Nashville as a country music center, a process that culminated in the mid-70's when the country division of the label moved from Los Angeles' Capitol Tower to what was by then most definitely Music City, U.S.A.

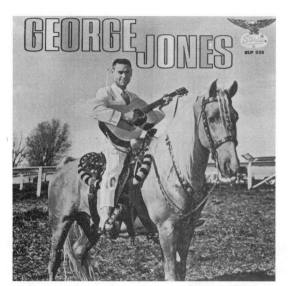

The role of Starday Records (which originated in Texas but came to Nashville) was also considerable. While continually acting in the role of underdog, Starday had a great deal of success with records by established artists who were no longer on major labels, banking on both the loyalty of their fans and on their inherent talent. The formula resulted in Number One records like Cowboy Copas' "Alabam'" and Johnny Bond's "Ten Little Bottles." The label also had the first hits of George Jones, who sounded frighteningly like Hank Williams in those days, but who went on to become one of the most influential singers in country music.

The later contribution of the Country Music Association to the tremendous growth of country music—and, for a time, its survival—was enormous. Although the formation of the organization came late in the 1950's, 1958 to be exact—beyond the scope of this chapter—the constant and effective public relations promotion of country music and of Nashville as the Country Music capital by the CMA has strongly affected our vision of that era and its importance.

That the persistent boosting by the CMA has benefited the commercial and even the creative health of the country music industry ever since the organization was founded by a group of Nashville music industry types and artists is beyond question, but it is also a fact that despite the efforts of the occasional West Coast-oriented board member like Tex Ritter or Gene Autry or Johnny Bond, the CMA encouraged a decidedly pro-Nashville outlook from its inception. This boosterish attitude gave a Nashville bias to the histories that began to pour out of the organization in the early 1960's. To read those documents, one would think that Nashville had been the center of country music from the word "go." This is not, in fact, the case: Nashville began its real-life struggle to the top of the heap in the late 1940's and the 1950's, not before.

The 1940's were a period of confusion, conflict and catharsis for country music as well as the nation at large—but while the music of the period pales in comparison with that of the preceding and following decades, the 40's did see the establishment of Nashville as a major creative center, ready for the boom to come.

Hank Williams

CHAPTER 7

Hank and the
Heartbreak Revival

Raw-boned and semi-literate, Hank Williams hit country music like a cyclone in 1949. What he did, quite simply, was rise to the top of the business faster than anyone ever had, and become in the process the finest songwriter, one of the finest performers, and the most influential figure country music has ever produced. That he then fell as fast as he had risen has detracted not a bit from the love popular music enthusiasts feel for him. Indeed, his flameout at the age of 29 served to frame the greatness of his work in a solid-gold legend.

"Hank Williams," Johnny Cash once said, "is like a Cadillac. He'll always be the standard for comparison." Cash noted the "beautiful simplicity" of Williams' lyrics, a simplicity that "effectively communicates heart-to-heart ideas." The esteemed jack of all pop music trades, Mitch Miller, expressed a similar idea, calling Williams "an absolute original" and classing him with Stephen Foster as the best American songwriter. "So indelible, so timeless" are Williams' songs, Miller added, that "they can take any kind of musical treatment." And take it they have, including much that should be called abuse, from crooners and wailers and orchestras and choruses and rock bands and God knows what else. His own recordings, meanwhile, have been issued, reissued, repackaged, restyled, renovated, restored, and reissued again in every format ever since his

death, and they have always sold well. As the first edition of this book was being prepared in 1976, for instance, there was a Hank Williams *single* on the American charts—the bouncy "Why Don't You Love Me?," a cut from the just-released album *Hank Williams Live on the Opry Stage*—while that album, *Hank Williams' 24 Greatest Hits,* and a *Me and Hank* album by Hank's onetime protégé Ray Price were earning places on *Billboard*'s album charts, and the original recording of "Jambalaya" was rising to the top of the singles charts in several European countries. All in all, quite a remarkable showing for an artist dead nearly a quarter century at that point.

Born in 1923 in south-central Alabama, Williams grew up in an era of country music giants whose influence spread across the United States: Jimmie Rodgers, The Carter Family and the young Roy Acuff. Rodgers, the "Blue Yodeler" and "Singing Brakeman," was the rage during the years when young Hank was trying to break in as a professional musician, but neither Jimmie Rodgers nor The Carter Family had a perceptible impact on his style. He didn't yodel or imitate the very imitable Rodgers, and neither (except, perhaps, in a few of his sacred songs) did he pattern himself at all on the Carters. Williams himself said years later that his style was something of a cross between Roy Acuff and Ernest Tubb—the wailing sound of Acuff, and the phrasing of The Texas

Audrey gets her wish to sing with Hank—in an Alabama store in 1946.

today are almost as well known by pop fans as they are by country fans, and the permanent place so many of them have found in the enduring repertoire of American popular music. No other country writer can boast a comparable list: "I'm So Lonesome I Could Cry," "Cold, Cold Heart," "Hey, Good Lookin'," "Jambalaya" and "Your Cheatin' Heart," to name only the most obvious examples.

Hiram Hank Williams was born the son of Lilly and Lonnie Williams. Lonnie, a logging camp railroad worker and shell-shocked World War I veteran, ended up in a Veteran's Administration hospital; Hank was then raised by his mother, a re-

Troubadour. According to Hank's mother, the singer who influenced him most was unknown outside of south-central Alabama: a black street singer whom everyone called Tee-Tot. Tee-Tot supposedly played on the sidewalks of Georgiana and Greenville, the towns in which Hank lived, and taught the white boy for a few dollars or a good meal. Was it from him that Williams learned all he needed to know about basic country guitar, blues rhythms, and how to put across a song? Current research has yet to confirm the details of this story.

sourceful, overbearing woman. Hank steadfastly resisted formal education, daydreaming through some classes and—after playing a show date the night before—dozing through others. Eventually he dropped out of high school to go for broke on a country music career.

Except for an interlude as a shipyard laborer,

Williams the songwriter owed nothing to anyone. Although his songs are wholly in the country genre, they are indelibly, uniquely his own. One indicator of Williams' songwriting talent is the fact that he sang very few compositions by other writers. Better indicators are the adaptability of his songs, which

Drifting Cowboys with Hank: Don Helms, Bob McNett, Jerry Rivers and Hillous Butrum.

Williams never worked at anything but country music. His lack of education and marketable skills would have made any other kind of good job hard to find. He consistently mangled the English language, and he didn't possess even a rudimentary knowledge of business affairs or social niceties. He suffered from poor health as well: hookworm as a child, a bad back as a young man and again in his later life, and a variety of ailments either induced or aggravated by alcohol and drugs.

By his late teens, Williams was a scarred survivor of southern Alabama's rowdy, blood-bucket honky tonks. He broke his hands fighting on a couple of occasions, broke guitars over antagonists' heads on a couple of others and, in a honky tonk brawl, lost "a plug outta my eyebrow, hair and all" to a man who sank his teeth into it. From age 13 on, he had his own band, a sometimes shifting collection of musicians who always played under the name he first gave them, The Drifting Cowboys. Without exception, they were country boys, and as instrumentalists they

Hank slouched when he sang. Chet Atkins backed him here in 1951.

were all more talented than he. (Williams never attained proficiency on the guitar, and his only other instrument was the fiddle, which he played poorly and hardly at all after he reached the big time.) But as with all "backup" men, in country music and elsewhere, they did not have the leader's inventiveness and charisma.

The Drifting Cowboys were: Jerry Rivers, fiddle; Don Helms, steel guitar; Bob McNett and then Sammy Pruett, lead guitar; and Hillous Butrum and then Cedric Rainwater, bass. Helms was the key to the band's instrumental sound—Williams valued his ability on the steel guitar and gave him unusual latitude to improvise in the midst of otherwise set arrangements. As Butrum notes, "The lonesome sound of Don's steel playing fit right in with the lonesome sound of Hank's singing." In the tradition of country band bass

players, Butrum and Rainwater filled the roles of comics, complete with baggy pants. When Rainwater joined the group in 1950 it marked the last change in The Drifting Cowboys' ranks until Williams left Nashville.

During the band's early years, Lilly Williams served as treasurer and paymaster—and, at times, as first aid administrator and booster of fragile teenage spirits. Later that job fell to Audrey Mae Sheppard, a country-pretty, southern Alabama blonde who became Hank's wife. Although she was a better bookkeeper than singer, she never lost her desire to be a star, and the couple recorded a number of mostly forgettable duets. As almost every Hank Williams fan knows, Audrey played a critical and often dramatic role in his life. Their turbulent relationship and her goading, status-seeking personality provided the flint

Hank and son

against which Williams struck his creative genius. The sparks eventually consumed the marriage, but they also led directly to many of his best songs.

Williams reached Nashville in the fall of 1946, a bony, almost gaunt 24-year-old with an open manner, a winning smile, and a look that melted some women. Comedienne Minnie Pearl, who first saw him at about this time, vividly remembers his "haunted and haunting eyes...deep-set, very brown, and very tragic." Williams came to Nashville not to play the Opry—he was far too green for that—but to get a start as a commercial songwriter. He'd been turning out songs, especially what he called hymns, for ten years. None of them, however, had been published; what country music publishing existed in those days was to be found in Nashville. Williams went straight to a firm that had earned a reputation for honest dealings with songwriters: Acuff-Rose.

Legend has it that Williams wowed Rose and his son Wesley by writing, in their studio and on demand, the hit "Mansion on the Hill." In fact, Williams sang a half-dozen songs he had written already, and the Roses promptly signed him to a contract. He then recorded, at WSM's primitive studio, four sides for Sterling Records: "My Love for You," "Never Again," "Wealth Won't Save Your Soul" and "When God Comes and Gathers His Jewels." Armed with these recordings, Fred Rose secured a contract for Hank with MGM Records; Williams then gained a spot on the *Louisiana Hayride*. After a decade of grinding anonymity, Hank Williams was on his way to country music immortality.

A couple of years on the *Hayride*—and off it, when his worsening drinking problem got out of hand—earned Williams a shot at the Grand Ole Opry. On June 11, 1949, he sauntered up to the microphone in Nashville's Ryman Audi-

torium and made Opry history with a performance of "Lovesick Blues." Since Williams had made a well-received recording of the song, he was expecting some response to it, but nobody was prepared for the response he got: a standing ovation when he began singing and a commotion when he tried to stop that obliged him to take a half-dozen encores and to sing the closing lines—*"I'm lo-o-onesome, I got the lovesick blues"*—over and over. Jerry Rivers recalls that the applause and cheers lasted at least five minutes after Hank and the band finally returned to the dressing room. (Ironically, "Lovesick Blues" was not Williams' own song but a 40-

Rod Brasfield, Red Foley, Jimmy Dickens, Minnie Pearl and Hank Williams were among the Grand Ole Opry stars to tour U.S. military bases in Europe.

year-old Broadway-type tune recorded by numerous other country singers without notable results.)

Although they were worried about Hank's drinking and tendency to miss show dates, the Opry managers couldn't keep him from becoming an Opry regular after that sensational debut. For the next three years, except when bouts with alcohol sidelined him, he was an Opry headliner, playing there for peanuts on Friday and Saturday nights in order to build a demand for his recordings and appearances. In less than a year his price for a show date went from $250 to $1,000, a modest sum today, but top dollar for a country performer at that time.

Meanwhile, Fred Rose concentrated on making him a hit songwriter. Rose started with a daring premise: that Williams' songs, sung by pop artists, could be as successful in the pop field as in the country field. Rose took a handful of the best songs to New York pop music executives, who turned him down flat, but when he got to Mitch Miller, then director of popular music at Columbia Records, his luck changed instantly and permanently. Miller snapped up "Cold, Cold Heart" and placed it with an up-and-coming singer named Tony Bennett. That turned out to be one of the most fateful moves in the course of American popular music. Bennett's recording of "Cold, Cold Heart" sold over a million copies and became Number One on the pop charts. In the process, it broke the artificial barrier that for so long had separated the pop and the country forms, and as often happens with seemingly impregnable barriers, once broken it proceeded to dissolve. "Hank," said Wesley Rose, president of Acuff-Rose, "was the first writer on a regular basis to make country music, national music."

Molly O'Day

What made Hank Williams' songs such a powerful cross-cultural force? One cannot readily distinguish them from other good country songs because the difference is a matter of degree. The best country music is simple, sincere, lyrical and catchy, if not pretty. The best of Williams, rated on a scale of one to ten, would score at least nine in each of those categories, with a ten-plus for lyricism. In one of the wondrous transformations that art brings about, the man who was crude and inarticulate in conversation became, with a pencil in his hand and a song on his mind, a folk poet. His oft-quoted opening lines to "I'm So Lonesome I Could Cry" are worth quoting

again: "Did you ever see a robin weep/when leaves began to die?/That means he's lost the will to live/I'm so lonesome I could cry." One could ponder the meaning of these lines indefinitely, but nobody could deny their lyrical beauty. (Typically, Williams was so unsure of their worth that he asked a fellow songwriter, after reading the verse aloud, "D'you think people will understand what I'm tryin' to say?") Country music fails if it does not pluck familiar, personal chords deep within the breasts of its listeners; Hank's songs did that with a consistency unmatched by other writers.

"Hank Williams had a way of reaching your guts and head at the same time," Mitch Miller has said. "No matter who you were, a country person or a sophisticate, the language hit home." That was probably Williams' single most important talent: the ability to elevate basic English—the only kind he knew—to folk poetry. Vic McAlpin, a Nashville songwriter who used to swap songs with him, says that Williams concentrated on lyrics and "didn't worry about melody.... Three or four of Hank's songs were taken from the same melody. The meter and tempo and the lyrics, of course, are different."

Hank carried the country songwriter's practice of creating songs directly out of his own experience to new lengths; if it seems facile to say that his finest songs—the ballads of love and loneliness—were musical vignettes taken from his life, that is nonetheless the case. His eight-year marriage to Audrey, with its endless series of emotional highs and lows, yielded an unknown number of songs and song themes—unknown because he seldom talked about his marital difficulties. Some songs were obviously spawned

Webb Pierce

by spats with Audrey: "I Can't Help It (If I'm Still in Love with You)"; "Cold, Cold Heart"; "My Love for You"; "Your Cheatin' Heart"; and, perhaps the most direct product, "Mind Your Own Business," a pointed rebuff to Nashville gossips who liked to talk about the latest Williams family battle. Not directly connected with Audrey, but premonitory as well as autobiographical, was "I'll Never Get Out of This World Alive," composed not long before his death. And it must be added that not all of the Audrey-based songs were anguished or doleful; Hank had good years and good times with Audrey, and some of his early, exuberant songs reflected them.

Williams liked to make fanciful comments

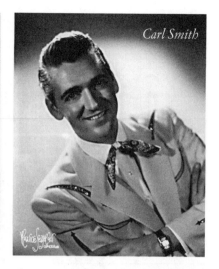

Faron Young

Carl Smith

about writing in bursts of inspiration. He once said of his hymns, "I just sit down for a few minutes, do a little thinking, and God writes the songs for me." Inspiration did play a part in his writing, but it was inspiration of a very earthly sort. "I Saw the Light" owes its title and basic idea to a chance remark made by his mother when she and the band were returning from a show date in the small hours of morning. Weary from the night's work, she spotted the lights of the Montgomery airport, only a few miles from home, and exclaimed, "Thank God, I saw the lights." Williams awoke with a start, asked her to repeat what she'd said, and settled back in his seat. By the time everybody was climbing into bed, he had worked out the structure and many of the words of his best hymn. He was a resourceful songwriter. Struck by an event or a remark or a chance acquaintance, he would scribble a note to himself on a piece of paper and tuck it away for future use. He stored these scraps, ranging from titles to complete verses in old shoeboxes. Years afterward they would be resurrected and carefully evaluated by Acuff-Rose then turned over to Hank Williams Jr., for expansion into full-fledged and highly salable songs.

When Hank Jr. was still in diapers, Fred Rose was doing a more complex but less publicized kind of song enhancement for Williams. Rose was a master

Teddy Wilburn, Webb Pierce and Jack Kay. Kneeling are Ike Inman and Jack Lowe. Webb called his group The Wondering Boys.

Grand Ole Opry meets grand opera: Marty Robbins, Minnie Pearl, Carl Smith, Marguerite Piazza, Rod Brasfield and Grandpa Jones on a 1955 Opry TV show. Marguerite Piazza, from Memphis, was a star of The Sid Caesar Show.

craftsman of popular songwriting. He worked with many of Williams' songs, reconstructing, polishing, adding a twist here or a different word there. The most notable example is "Kaw-Liga," which Rose turned from a banal tune about love between a couple of Indians into a memorable number about unrequited love between *wooden* Indians. It is doubtful that any other country star of the first rank has had such an important accomplice. Rose personally supervised all of Williams' recording sessions as a kind of super A&R man. Rose alone decided when and how the records would be released. "My father never came back to the market with the same kind of song," Wesley Rose says. "He went from a blues to a ballad to something else." The Country Music Hall of Fame elected Williams and Fred Rose to

membership together in 1961, although the citations on both of their plaques diplomatically avoid mentioning Rose's singular contributions to Hank's success.

Rose also influenced what seem to be the most personal of Hank's songs, the "Luke the Drifter" recitations that he recorded now and again. Although Hank's name was not publicly associated with the recitations, everyone in the business knew they were his. For the most part they were small sermons on homespun virtues set against a mournful, three-quarter-time musical backdrop. A couple of the recitations carried a muffled social message; for example, one called "The Funeral," based on a black funeral procession he once happened upon, cites "the wisdom and ignorance of a crushed, undying race." That line is so for-

Cherokee Cowboy Darrell McCall with boss Ray Price.

eign to his old-Southern attitude toward blacks, and to his choice of words, that one automatically suspects the hand of Fred Rose.

All of Hank's attitudes came out of a time and place that now, in the era of the New South, seem terribly remote. Williams was pure country in dress, speech, humor, even food (he doused everything with ketchup). A celebrated maker of malapropisms, he once told a disc jockey inquiring about the abundance of sad situations in his songs: "Yes, I guess I am kind of a sadist." Williams was a generous man and, in his high-riding days, an easy touch for down-and-out members of the country music fraternity. Money was less important to him than the cheers of audiences and the acceptance of his songs; he did, however, love being rich. In one uncharacteristic display of childlike greed, he drew some $4,000 in one-dollar bills from the bank and stacked them in piles in his den. Scooping up handfuls of bills and scattering them onto the floor, he told Vic McAlpin, "I was so poor most of my life, I've always dreamed about being able to do this."

Even as a star, Hank was less vain than might be expected. Bob McNett, lead guitarist with The Drifting Cowboys, recalls how the boss would goad his band members into playing their solos so well that the audience applauded in the middle of them. "Hank really wanted us all to shine, not just himself," McNett says. Also, beneath his easy-going manner he bore a fierce pride, a legacy of his years of anonymity and hard work. Jack Cardwell recalls that when Hank came to Mobile as an Opry headliner, he took a room at the best hotel in town and went straight over to the leading radio station with a sizable crowd on his heels. "He walked into the boss's office and told him, right in front of all of us, 'When I was in Mobile before, I tried to get on this station. I wasn't good enough then. I reckon I still ain't good enough.' He turned on his heel and went over to the other station and went on the air there."

The dominant components of Hank's personality, however, were an instinctive openness and a naive delight in things around him. They helped make him a great stage performer. In today's hyped-up world of country music, one is never certain whether the Johnny Nashville at the microphone is the real Johnny or someone milking the now-bountiful country market. With Hank Williams, there was never a doubt. What you saw and heard was the genuine article. It was not just that Hank didn't know any other style; he wouldn't have used it anyway. Country musicians who have seen scores of Nashville stars invariably cite sincerity and an ability to "make people feel he was one of them" as the hallmarks of a Williams performance. "You could hear a pin drop when Hank was working," says Little Jimmy Dickens, who shared many stages with him. "He seemed to hypnotize those people. You couldn't put your finger on the reason. Simplicity, I guess. He brought the people with him, put himself on their level."

Don Gibson in the 1950's.

Beyond sincerity was what Minnie Pearl has described as "a real animal magnetism." Says Pearl: "I was so proud to be onstage with Hank. He destroyed the women in the audience. They just had to have his autograph and get close enough to touch him. It wasn't sex per se, like with some artists. He appealed to their maternal instincts a lot." Hank would doubtless have been embarrassed by the suggestion that he appealed to maternal instincts, but after he'd blushed he would savor the notion of his having animal magnetism. Throughout his adult life he was a persistent—and by most accounts frustrated—woman chaser. Well before Elvis Presley came along, Hank used swaying, suggestive, Presley-like body movements onstage. To get really into a song, Hank hunched over the mike, buckling his legs and turning his hips, fixing the first few rows of the audience with the dark, haunted eyes that so impressed Minnie Pearl. The effect was often spellbinding. "Now and again," recalled

Don Helms, the steel guitar player, "he'd close his eyes and swing one of those big long legs, and the place would go wild."

Hank's voice was a large part of his appeal as a performer. It must rank as one of the most memorable country music voices, and like the man himself, it was genuine. He used no vocal tricks and no studio gimmicks. Also like the man, the voice was rough and unpolished. It was capable of sustaining notes across a broad range, and it was ideally suited to the material he performed. His successes with such songs as "I Saw the Light," "Lovesick Blues" and "Your Cheatin' Heart" stemmed largely from his stunning vocals. He adopted a distinctly country characteristic in his singing—the "tear," or quick sobbing warble, that Nashville singers inject into their songs. His sloppy speech patterns did not hurt his singing any more than they inhibited his writing; he enunciated cleanly and with a professional's sensitivity to the material. "Lovesick

Hank Thompson and The Brazos Valley Boys kept Western swing and honky tonk alive in the mountain sound era.

Kitty Wells' singing style was typical of the era. George D. Hay hands her one of many awards on the Opry stage in 1952.

Blues," a vocally demanding piece, is an excellent illustration of his singing talents.

Williams fell from country music's heights as quickly as he had ascended them, ruined by inner torment and the abuses of his body to which it led. He had been a drinker since his early teenage days around Alabama lumber camps, and what began as a boyish game became an incurable habit. He went to extreme and sometimes comical lengths to conceal the bottles and the effects their contents had on him. People who might have been expected to help him were disarmed by his lovableness as a drunk and, more important, by his insistence on keeping a certain distance from everyone. Hank had no close friends, no one who could pierce his shell of lonely discontent. Audrey tried, if only in her own interest, but failed. The pill popping began later, apparently as a legitimate palliative for his bad

back and other physical discomforts, but it quickly got out of hand, and toward the end of his life he used pills, as well as alcohol, indiscriminately. Gradually, both the country music promoters and their audiences became fed up with Hank's offenses: appearing onstage too drunk to perform decently, often not appearing at all. Nashville promoter Oscar Davis remembers an ugly incident in Peterborough, Ontario, that should have shaken some sense into Hank but didn't. Hank had gotten drunk in his hotel room and had told Davis he wasn't going to play the date. Davis put his star under a shower, then pushed him onto the stage, and immediately wished he hadn't bothered. "Hank stumbled on the steps, crawled up to the mike, and began singing. He repeated the lines to songs a dozen times. Finally he fell down, and we had to drag him off the stage. The crowd was furious. They really wanted to get him. We called the Mounties, and they escorted us all out of town."

In August 1952, the Grand Ole Opry had had enough. It tossed Hank off the show. Six weeks earlier, Audrey had been granted a divorce, getting not only a hefty share of their assets but also one half of all his future royalties from songwriting and recording—a provision that was to make Audrey, who died in 1976, a wealthy woman. Hank went back to the *Louisiana Hayride*, supposedly to shape up for a return to the Opry, but he was a broken man. His last few months were a wild kaleidoscope of scenes and characters: Billie Jean Jones Eshlimar, a stunning young woman from Shreveport who traveled with Williams and eventually married him in two "performances" at the New Orleans Municipal Auditorium (the validity of the marriage has been contested ever since); Toby Marshall, a medical charlatan, who, in the guise of treating Hank's alcoholism, gave him all the "bennies" and Seconal he wanted; Hank's mystic sister, Irene, who says that just after midnight on New Year's Eve 1953, she clutched her throat and cried out, "Hank just died!"; and Charles Carr, a Montgomery teenager who was driving Williams to an Ohio show date when his famous passenger died quietly in the back seat, the victim of alcohol-induced heart failure.

The funeral was the biggest seen in the South until the one accorded Martin Luther King Jr. 15 years later, and the lawsuits that followed have been among the most complex and prolonged in the annals of the entertainment industry. Literally millions of dollars have been at stake in suits involving the renewal of publishing rights to Hank's songs and the guardianship of Hank Jr. (who came of age in 1967 and—after a serious and disfiguring accident in 1975—rebuilt his own country music career). With the man's songs constantly on the charts and his legend appreciating in value with every passing year, the commercial future of the long-dead Hank Williams

and his music have no foreseeable limits. There are many millions of Hank Williams fans, and the number has grown rather than diminished in the years since his death, even though at this point the majority of his fans are too young to have seen him perform or even to have listened to his records during his lifetime. As with any great artist, however, Hank Williams will live not just in sales receipts and commercial promotions, but also in the esteem of his audiences.

Hank Williams has never been simply a cult figure. His appeal has been more enduring and more broadly based—more so, it appears, than that of any other long-deceased figure in the history of American popular culture. "The thing with Hank gets bigger and bigger," said Wesley Rose

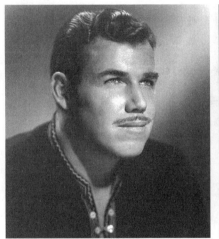 

Slim Whitman's and Hank Locklin's high tenors fit the taste of the times.

of Acuff-Rose Publishing in late 1976. "It could go on forever."

Hank's effect on country music during and immediately after his time at the top was profound. Basically, he changed everything.

When he first arrived on the Opry, country music was a pretty smooth affair. Although Roy Acuff and his high mountain sound were still immensely popular, and artists like Molly O'Day, Bill Monroe, The Bailes Brothers and The Bailey Brothers continued with varieties of the true old-timey Southeastern sound, the big records came, for the large part, from anywhere but the Southeast. California-based Gene Autry and Jimmy Wakely (with and without his duet partner, Margaret Whiting) were big sellers. From the

Johnnie and Jack, center, kept the duo tradition alive. With them in 1957: Ernest Tubb, Kitty Wells, Forrest White and Billy Byrd. In front are Fender Instrument founder Leo Fender and Shot Jackson. The pedal-steel is Shot's Sho-Bud design.

Southwest came the honky tonk hits of Al Dexter and Ernest Tubb, and the smooth-yet-hot sounds of Bob Wills and His Texas Playboys (recently transplanted to the West Coast). New York-based Elton Britt, maybe the sweetest-voiced of all, was also in his prime after the wartime hit "There's a Star-Spangled Banner Waving Somewhere," and even in Nashville, on the Grand Ole Opry, that bastion of country music conservatism, the stars of the show were smooth-singing Red Foley and the rising young star fresh out of Pee Wee King's band, Eddy Arnold, who was scoring hit after easygoing hit. The flirtation with pop music was intense; the mountain style of country music seemed doomed to obscurity. But of course, Hank changed all that. His simple, eloquent, intensely

moving music brought the mountain sound back with a vengeance.

Hank wasn't really a mountain singer, and he was modern enough to use electric instruments and even a hint of percussion, but compared to Wakely, Arnold, Wills, George Morgan *et al*, he was hard, hard country: no fancy frills, just raw repressed emotion, classic Southern country soul.

His impact was tremendous. He spawned a host of imitators—most bad parodies, some who grew to prominence after developing in their own styles—and even more importantly, he opened the ears of the record companies and the public to the reborn mountain sound. It was a fantastic rebirth, for the updated "hillbilly" singers almost literally blew the sweet singers off the map.

Perhaps the most important of them, and certainly the most popular for a time, was a native of West Monroe, Louisiana, named Webb Pierce. Although his sound seems dated today (as Hank's, for example, does not), Webb racked up a mind-boggling row of 21 Number One records in the early and middle 1950's, and was, with Hank Snow, the most distinctive country stylist of the era: Webb's tight vibrato and throat-busting, always-at-the-very-top-of-his-range vocal style gave his voice instant recognizability. The 1950's were studded with his hits like "Wondering," "Backstreet Affair," "In the Jailhouse Now," "More and More," "I Ain't Never" and the honky tonker's anthem, "There Stands the Glass."

Pierce's hit "Slowly" was a landmark for more reasons than simply being his second biggest hit. It sent scores of steel guitarists drilling holes and attaching coat hangers to their instruments trying to hook up jury-rig methods of duplicating the mind-blowing sound of the pedal steel guitar as introduced on record by Webb's steel player Bud Isaacs. Although Isaacs didn't invent the pedal steel by any means, his was the first prominent use of the instrument's note-bending possibilities. Its sliding, tearful, evocative sound was an instant ear-catcher for not only the steel guitarists, but also the record-buying public in general.

Like so many of that period—including Hank Williams—Pierce came up through the ranks at the *Louisiana Hayride* in Shreveport, where he began performing for free while selling shoes at the local Sears, Roebuck store. Three Number One singles in a row—culminating with "There Stands the Glass"—brought him to the Opry and superstardom, at least until rock 'n' roll took the wind out of country music for several years. Despite a big crossover hit of the era—"I Ain't Never"—Webb's glory days were over by the early 1960's. He is best remembered for his hits of the 1950's and his symbols of success: the guitar-shaped swimming pool, and the silver-dollar and leather-encrusted Pontiac.

A protégé of Pierce's was a cocky youngster named Faron Young, who came to Nashville and the Opry at around the same time as his mentor. If Hank Williams opened the door for a singer like Webb Pierce, who had already fashioned his own unique style, then he made a direct impression on Faron Young. It's hard to imagine, but the mellow, crooning Faron Young we know today started out sounding as nearly identical to Hank Williams as imaginable. Fortunately, a string of good material—especially "I've Got Five Dollars and It's Saturday Night"—established his identity despite his derivative style. Through the 1960's and into the 70's he was one of the few country stars able to flirt with the pop market and pop sound while retaining a firm identity in country music.

The Williams influence goes on: George Jones' early Starday records display a remarkable stylistic similarity to Hank's work; Jones didn't develop the choked, close-mouthed vocal style for which he's revered today until later in his career. Carl Smith, from Roy Acuff's hometown of Maynardsville, Tennessee, was yet another singer who was strongly influenced by Hank's style. Like Faron Young, he was careful enough to come out with unique material that became associated with him, from old-timey sounding songs like

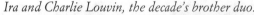

Ira and Charlie Louvin, the decade's brother duo.

Hank Snow

"Are You Teasing Me" to the pre-rockabilly "Hey Joe!" to Western swing like "Deep Water." Yet the stylistic derivation from Hank Williams is clearly marked on songs like "Orchids Mean Goodbye" and "If Teardrops Were Pennies."

Carl Smith is retired today, but he racked up some 31 Top Ten records on Columbia in the 1950's, and even hosted his own show on Canadian television. Like many of the post-Hank Williams hard-country singers, though, his career was hobbled when rock 'n' roll eroded country music's audience in the mid- and late 50's.

While on Canadian television, Smith switched to a much bigger band than was common at the time in country music, a move also made by Little Jimmy Dickens; *his* band, the loudest in the business, featured twin guitars, steel, and heavy, heavy drumming. Although we remember Dickens for his comedy songs like "A-Sleeping at the Foot of the Bed," "Take an Old Cold 'Tater (And Wait)," and "May the Bird of Paradise Fly Up Your Nose," he was actually an emotionally moving singer in the best country tradition, with a catch in his intense, throbbing voice best displayed on "We Could" and other weepy love songs.

The man who fused the styles of the Southeast and Southwest most successfully was, oddly enough, a close friend and confidant of Hank Williams, Ray Price. A college graduate out of Texas, Price brought to Nashville a love for the Bob Wills music he'd grown up on, and the result—exemplified by performances like "I'll Be There"—was a curious and extremely exciting amalgamation of Eastern and Western country music styles: unpolished, broken-voiced, Williams-style vocals backed by three fiddles and The Texas Playboys' heavy beat.

As the years went by, Price developed a tense vibrato, and his music became characterized by a Texas shuffle, a Southwestern-style fiddle, and classic honky tonk songs, a combination that made for hit after hit in the late 1950's and early

1960's: "City Lights," "Heartaches by the Number," "The Other Woman," "Invitation to the Blues" and "Crazy Arms." The formula was so successful that he was reluctant to abandon it. Still, as the 1960's progressed, the rhinestone-bedecked Cherokee Cowboy transformed himself through a series of records—"Night Life," "Danny Boy" and "For the Good Times"—into the tuxedo-clad countrypolitan crooner we know today.

Another who followed this course, although quite independently, was Texan Hank Thompson, who began his career just as the mountain-sound revival began. For years Thompson never

Jimmie Rodgers' widow Carrie with Ernest Tubb and Hank Snow at an early Jimmie Rodgers Memorial Festival. Tubb and Snow both idolized Rodgers.

compromised on his big Western swing band, providing, by the late 1950's and early 60's, almost the only taste of that music still available nationally. His singing owed nothing to Hank Williams; it was full, rich and strongly reminiscent of Merle Travis. What Hank Thompson did have that allowed him to walk the thin line between East and West with such agility was good material. Beginning with "Humpty Dumpty Heart" and then the classic weeper "The Wild Side of Life" (often best known by the first line of its chorus, "I didn't know God made honky tonk angels"), he showed a gift for writing or choosing great lyrics in the straight-forward Southeastern-sound mold. And he added a strong honky tonk flavor, which served him well through the years.

Quite apart from singers like Thompson, Price, Pierce and the others he influenced in one way or another, Hank Williams had the more general effect of attuning the ears of record producers and artists to songs that weren't so smooth, jazzy, and/or dance-oriented as the material that had been in style before his rise. Words—lyrics—were back, and back in a big way, and a plaintive catch or a throaty throb, not mellow ease, were once again vocal characteristics of value in a country singer. The sound and content of Nashville music changed radically, then, and many of the resultant records had great power; it's probably still true that most people over 30, when they hear the term "country music," think of that particular gut-wrenching sound.

One of the greatest singers in the newly revived mountain sound tradition was Muriel Deason, known professionally as Kitty Wells. After several years of alternating between the roles of housewife and featured singer with her husband's band, Johnnie and Jack, she took the country music world by storm with her answer to Hank Thompson's "The Wild Side of Life" called "It Wasn't God Who Made Honky Tonk Angels," a lonesome, plaintive, yet angry look at the rarely glimpsed woman's side of the cheatin' coin. Kitty Wells' high, quavering, catchingly different Appalachian-homespun voice, which spoke of pain and woe and hardship, was a voice America seemed most eager to hear in the early 1950's. It made her a string of hits including "Poison in Your Heart," "Whose Shoulder Will You Cry On?" and "Makin' Believe," and those made her the

Don Law and Lefty Frizzell in the Jim Beck studio in Dallas.

reigning Queen of Country Music. (She never lost her title, and didn't lose her supremacy until Loretta Lynn arrived almost 15 years later.)

Kitty Wells represents, in a way, the very best of the mountain sound revival. Unashamedly sincere and deeply emotive in the bitten-back deep-country manner, she moved men and women alike. Not the least of elements in her appeal was the way she expressed sentiments that would later be regarded as women's liberationist, while retaining a kind of shy dignity befitting her royal stature.

Wells' music was based on an approach to the listener—an intimate, direct communication of mostly sad stories and mostly troubled feelings—which ran directly counter to the dreamily impersonal lyrics of most big band and country crooner music, and in that respect she was typical of her time. In fact, as long as that basic (Hank-inspired) approach was used, a performer had considerable room to maneuver in matters of style.

The rise of two singers with a strong Irish influence, Hank Locklin and Slim Whitman, is a good example. Their sky-high tenors and rich vibratos wrung tears across the heartland of country music, and if their voices were unusual for the period it didn't prevent their successes. In fact, Whitman's biggest hit was probably the most surprising of the decade: an arcane pop tune, popularized by Jeanette MacDonald and Nelson Eddy, called "Indian Love Call." As late as the 1970's both Locklin and Whitman were, despite a lack of recording success in the United States, very big stars in England and Ireland. (Whitman's American comeback as a hugely successful mail-order item in the 80's was somewhat less logical.) It's doubtful that many Americans

Lefty Frizzell

*Johnny Horton, Johnny Cash
and Faron Young, with attendant
at left, on a publicity tour for
Faron's film, Daniel Boone.*

recognized it as such, but the Irish tradition behind the music of Locklin and Whitman was by no means new to country music; it had been there in many of the songs and song forms at the roots of American music in the first days of the colonies.

The birth of bluegrass as a modern form in which the most traditional mountain music could continue was another milestone of the 1940's. Bill Monroe, father of the movement, remained popular in the 50's, when he produced some of the best music of his long career. Meanwhile, other bluegrass stars enjoyed tremendous popularity. Mac Wiseman was Dot's biggest seller until Pat Boone came along, and Lester Flatt and Earl Scruggs became popular enough to join Columbia Records, eventually moving to the Grand Ole Opry in 1956.

Speaking of bluegrass, it's interesting that one of Don Gibson's early 78's with RCA was backed by a bluegrass tune of his own composition, "Carolina Breakdown," featuring the banjo and mandolin work of The Brewster Brothers, long a staple of the Knoxville bluegrass community. Gibson's

Roy Acuff, Ernest Tubb and Tex Ritter: giants of the day.

early sound was strictly mountain—although, with the exception of "Carolina Breakdown," not bluegrass—and that factor and his brilliant songwriting gift brought him hit after hit in the late 1950's and early 1960's, including "Sweet Dreams," "I'd Be a Legend in My Time," "Blue Blue Day," "Oh Lonesome Me," "I Can't Stop Lovin' You" and one that he did not write, "Sea of Heartbreak." After a decade-long dry period, Gibson again showed chart muscle with a Number One song in 1973, "Woman (Sensuous Woman)."

Yet another traditional form, the male duet, was enjoying its last years in the late 40's, perhaps given a short extended lease on life by the mountain sound revival. Having begun with Mac and Bob in the early years of recording, risen to glory with The Monroe Brothers and The Blue

Sky Boys in the 1930's, continued with The Bailes Brothers and Bailey Brothers in the 1950's, and more or less ended with The Wilburn Brothers in the 1960's and early 70's, the male duet reached surprising heights in the era between the rise of Hank Williams and the explosion of rockabilly.

One of the last male duet acts was Johnnie and Jack—Johnny Wright (Kitty Wells' husband) and Jack Anglin. Popular Opry members until Jack's death in 1963, they scored big with Caribbean-flavored numbers like "Poison Love" and "Ashes of Love," as well as with straight country heart songs like "I Can't Tell My Heart That."

Like Johnnie and Jack, The Louvin Brothers had a sound and repertoire steeped in tradition. What set them apart was their powerful songwriting and intense, emotional harmonies. Considering their brilliant singing, there is much justification for those who have called The Louvins the greatest of the brother duets. Charlie Louvin was a fine singer with a powerful yet supple voice, but Ira must be considered one of the greatest country singers of all time. Sky-high, filled with repressed pain so intense it was almost palpable, Ira Louvin's voice embodied Appalachian soul, and the pure mountain sound has perhaps never been captured on record as well as on such Louvin Brothers' cuts as "Too Late," "My Baby's Gone," and especially "When I Stop Dreaming."

The mountain sound revival, and the galvanizing success of Hank Williams that had begun it, brought on a tremendous migration of traditional-minded musicians to Nashville. Nobody came farther than Hank Snow, a native of Nova Scotia, who had been hacking his way across Canada for nearly 15 years and recording a string of moderately successful records for Canada's RCA subsidiary. Snow, a Jimmie Rodgers devotee, was persuaded by Ernest Tubb to try to make

Marty Robbins

it in the States, and went broke trying in Texas and in Hollywood before moving to Nashville in 1950. He joined the Grand Ole Opry, and, almost as if by magic, the hits rolled in: "I'm Moving On," "Rhumba Boogie," "A Fool Such as I," "Bluebird Island" and "I Don't Hurt Anymore." In fact, he, Hank Williams and Lefty Frizzell just about dominated the country music charts in the very early 1950's.

Unquestionably, Hank Snow was a traditional singer, although his Canadian accent, back-of-the-palate tone and precise diction made him perhaps the most easily recognized—and imitated—country singer of his day. Still, with his backup of fiddle, non-pedal steel and his own acoustic guitar picking, there was little "uptown" about him. He was one of the first to benefit from the trend toward traditional music in the early 1950's and, due to his relatively early success in the ten years between 1947 and 1957, he did a great deal to further strengthen and solidify that trend.

The honky tonk tradition from the Lone Star State that had spawned Al Dexter and Ernest Tubb was also important in this period. The two major newcomers with this style to emerge in the 1950's—Lefty Frizzell and Johnny Horton—used the four-piece bands, forsaking the Bob Wills big band sound entirely and, just as importantly, were careful to sing the kind of straightforward one-on-one lyrics the temper of the times demanded. Whether they were leading or following their public in that regard is a moot point. Before the rockabillies came along, they did very well.

Horton struggled for years on the *Louisiana Hayride*, his unusually high, emotional voice (with a touch of a growl borrowed from T. Texas Tyler) eloquent on love ballads like "All for the Love of a Girl," and raunchy on pre-rockabilly songs like "Honky Tonk Man." He really hit his stride around 1960, cashing in on the brief if powerful vogue for historical songs, with "Battle of New Orleans," "Sink the Bismarck" and "North to Alaska."

Lefty Frizzell burst on the scene in the early 1950's, racking up the hits and pulling off a feat yet to be duplicated: four records simultaneously in *Billboard*'s Top Ten. The string of Frizzell classics includes "Always Late," "I Love You a

Thousand Ways," "If You've Got the Money, I've Got the Time," "Long Black Veil," "Saginaw, Michigan," "Mom & Dad's Waltz" and "I Want to Be with You Always." As they were for Hank Williams, sudden wealth and fame were difficult for Lefty to deal with, and this Texan from an impoverished family spent the next 20-odd years in a battle with the bottle, the enormous talent with which he was born flashing through from time to time. He seemed to be getting himself together (one more time) in the mid-70's, and had written or co-written a score of chart

Marty Robbins goes Hawaiian at the Grand Ole Opry.

records within a period of a few months, when he was felled by a stroke in 1975. He was only 47 years old.

As the years went by, Lefty Frizzell, whose genius was so obvious during his lifetime, emerged as a very powerful influence on other country writers and singers, to the point that by the 1990's, the phrase "Hank and Lefty" had become a kind of shorthand for "the great masters of honky tonk country." His sliding, drawling phrases and rich vibrato can be heard in the singing of everyone from Merle Haggard through Johnny Rodriguez to Randy Travis and Alan Jack-

Typical package tour of the mid-50's: Joe Zinkan, Ray Crisp, Shot Jackson, Johnnie and Jack, Kitty Wells, Ernest Tubb and The Texas Troubadours and Doyle and Teddy Wilburn. Stonewall Jackson is just visible in the Ernest Tubb Record Shop window.

son. The way country singers have of saying "wie" for "way" (listen to Buck Owens, for example) traces back to the strange, unique phrasing and pronunciation of Lefty Frizzell. More than that, though, Lefty Frizzell was a singer who could truly be intimate with a song. He wasn't a smooth singer in the cowboy or Western swing tradition, and he wasn't a singer with a big, emotive voice like Roy Acuff or Hank Williams. There was an immediacy, warmth and depth of subtle feeling to Frizzell's voice that was spellbinding. It could literally send shivers up your spine.

A very different character, and singer, was Marty Robbins, an Arizonan whose style wasn't derived from any particular tradition or artist (though he did sound somewhat like Eddy Arnold and two other country crooners of the 40's, the underrated Pete Cassell and Zeke Clements). Robbins had a voice so superbly expressive and flexible—strong, caressing, capable of everything

from high, clear yodels to the smoothest of croons—that the country music establishment welcomed him with open arms; he joined the Opry in 1953. His first nickname was "Mr. Teardrop," and he played the role to the hilt with magnificent songs like "Time Goes By," "At the End of a Long Lonely Day" and "Sing Me Something Sentimental."

Robbins was probably the most versatile country singer of his day, and he began to expand his repertoire widely in the early years of rock, scoring the first of his Number One hits with "A White Sport Coat (And a Pink Carnation)," and recording several other rockabilly sides like "Mean Mama Blues" and even Chuck Berry's "Maybelline." And rockabilly was but one of the many styles he flirted with. He recorded two Hawaiian albums (highlighted by Jerry Byrd's tender touch on the steel) that are among the best of that genre, and chalked up a big hit in the voguish calypso sound with "Devil Woman" in 1962. And of course he is noted as one of the few ever to have hit records with cowboy songs: his back-to-back successes with "Big Iron" and "El Paso," both of which were included on *Gunfighter Ballads and Trail Songs,* one of the earliest country albums to be awarded Gold-record status. He eventually recorded three albums in the cowboy style, all of them testaments to the power of his rich, versatile voice. On most of the cuts he was backed only by a bass, a rhythm guitar, the brilliant gut-string lead guitar work of Grady Martin, and sometimes the powerful harmonies of the Glaser Brothers.

Such forays into fields other than straight country music didn't keep Robbins from staying squarely in the mainstream with pure country love songs like "Don't Worry 'Bout Me" and "Singing the Blues." Somehow he always kept his identity with the country fans, who never deserted him despite his wide-ranging musical explorations. He did well commercially all the way into the 80's; at the time of his fatal heart attack in 1982, one of his records had just fallen out of the country Top Ten.

The Hank Williams-inspired mountain sound revival that began his rise was, like all musical movements, a complicated meshing of gears, a bewildering combination of energy, drive, vision and blind luck on the part of a host of businessmen, boosters, and entertainers who worked together (often without any common goal at all) to make the Southeastern style dominant in country music. The music of the period was very strong and very memorable—memorable enough to inspire a major revival in the 80's and 90's, and quite conceivably strong enough to become the permanent standard by which other country music is measured. At the time, though, it became instant history with the coming of rock.

Johnny Cash and Luther Perkins

CHAPTER 8

Rockabilly!

The decade following World War II was a period of great growth within the recording industry. In 1940 there were but three major record companies in America: Columbia (founded in 1889), Victor (founded in 1901), and Decca (formed in 1933 as the American subsidiary of British Decca). In the 40's, new majors began to appear. Capitol Records began in Los Angeles in 1942. MGM Records was formed by its parent film company in Los Angeles in 1945. Mercury was founded in Chicago that same year.

More important than the new majors, however, were the many smaller, independent companies that blossomed during this period. In 1942, Ike and Bess Berman started Apollo Records in New York City, and Herman Lubinsky formed Savoy Records in Newark, New Jersey. In 1943, Sydney Nathan opened King Records in Cincinnati. In 1945, Jim Bulleit founded Bullet Records in Nashville. That same year came Al Green's National Records in New York City, and three Los Angeles labels: Art Rupe's Specialty Records, Jules and Saul Bihari's Modern Records, and Eddie and Leo Mesner's Philo Records (which became Aladdin Records the following year). In 1947, Leonard and Phil Chess started Chess Records in Chicago, and Lew Chudd started Imperial Records in Los Angeles. In 1948 came Jerry Blaine's Jubilee Records, and Herb Abramson's and Ahmet and Nesuhi Ertegun's Atlantic Records,

both in New York City. In 1949, Don Robey formed Duke/Peacock Records in Houston. In 1950, Randy Wood started Dot Records in Gallatin, Tennessee. The following year, Al Silver formed Herald/Ember Records in New York City, Lester Bihari started Meteor Records in Memphis, Lillian McMurry and Johnny Vincent began Trumpet Records in Jackson, Mississippi, and Sam Phillips started Sun Records in Memphis in 1952. In 1953, Ernie Young formed Excello Records in Nashville as a branch of the Nashboro gospel label, George Goldner founded Rama Records in New York City as a subsidiary of Tico Records (a company that specialized in Latin music), Archie Bleyer started Cadence Records in New York City, and Vivian Carter and James Bracken began Vee-Jay Records in Chicago. These and many others were in operation in 1953, the year of Hank Williams' death.

The independents—or "indies," as they were called in the music business—often issued products that the major companies would have no part of. Theirs was, and is yet, an avant-garde of economic necessity. It was no major company that released the first Hank Williams records in 1946, but Sterling Records, a New York City indie so ill-secured that it changed its telephone number at least five times in three years. (Nor, later, was it a major label that issued the first Beatles records in America, but Vee-Jay, a Chicago indie

Wynonie Harris cut "Good Rockin' Tonight." Fats Domino cut "The Fat Man," and the rock 'n' roll era was born. Harris recorded for the King label. Fats Domino recorded for Imperial.

that dealt primarily in rhythm-and-blues.)

Although many of the independents, such as Aladdin and Vee-Jay and Chess, employed mostly black artists, and others, such as Dot and Cadence, employed mostly white artists, the indies discovered that artistic miscegenation often led to profit. Thus Savoy released not only jazz records but also ersatz hillbilly records, and its artist roster included both Charlie Parker and The Texas Top Hands. King issued some of the finest jump blues records ever made, and also some of the finest country records. Jubilee Records put out anything available, from Jewish *schtick* records to street-corner doo-wop. Bullet Records issued B. B. King's first record, and also Owen Bradley's.

Every major American record company today makes most of its money from rock 'n' roll sales. In the beginning, however, they wouldn't touch the stuff. Columbia had Benny Goodman, Victor had Perry Como, Decca had Bing Crosby, Capitol had Frank Sinatra. What need had they for this reprehensible new "nigger music"? It was the indies that gave rise to rock 'n' roll.

It is impossible to discern the first rock record,

just as it is impossible to discern where red becomes yellow in the color spectrum. The phrase itself was nothing new to music. In a 1934 film called *Transatlantic Merry-Go-Round,* The Boswell Sisters sang a song called "Rock and Roll," written by Sidney Clare and Richard A. Whiting, both of whom were born in the 1890's. There are quite a few records from the 1940's that can be comfortably described as early rock 'n' roll. In 1947, Roy Brown cut his song "Good Rockin' Tonight" for Deluxe Records, and in the summer of the following year, Wynonie Harris had a hit version of the same song on King. Harris' version of "Good Rockin' Tonight" was, like Brown's original, a jump blues, the most popular type of music among urban blacks of the 1940's. But it was markedly rawer, less mellow than the usual jump-blues records. It rocked. The following year, Imperial issued Fats Domino's first record, "The Fat Man," and it sold well. Black music began rocking strong, and in 1951 there were several pure and unmistakable rock 'n' roll records: "Sixty Minute Man" by The Dominoes on Federal (the biggest rhythm-and-blues hit of the year), "It Ain't the Meat" by The Swallows on King, "Rocket 88" and especially its sequel, "My Real Gone Rocket," by Jackie Brenston and His Delta Cats on Chess.

There were also more than a few hard-rocking country records in this period, records that must be separated from the bulk of hillbilly boogie records due to their extremism. The Delmore Brothers, like Moon Mullican and Arthur Smith, pioneered hillbilly boogie, but in such King releases as "Freight Train Boogie" (1946) and "Whatcha Gonna Gimme?" (1952), they went beyond boogie into an effervescent sort of country-rock. Freddie Slack and Ella Mae Morse's hip country recording of "House of Blue Lights," released by Capitol in 1946, was such a fine primitive rocker that Chuck Berry covered it 12 years later. Red Foley's "Tennessee Saturday Night" on Decca was one of the biggest country hits of 1948, and it rocked. "Rootie Tootie," Hank Williams' third MGM record, cut in 1948, is a jivey rocker, full of nonsense lyrics, funky call-and-response, and hot instrumental licks. A handful of Tennessee Ernie Ford's early records on Capitol, such as "Smokey Mountain Boogie" (1949), "Shotgun Boogie" (1950), "Blackberry Boogie" (1952) and "I Don't Know" (1953), are among the best, and strongest, examples of country music's gropings toward rock 'n' roll.

While these rumblings from country music circles pointed to new directions, the full-scale rush toward rock 'n' roll was begun by three individuals: disc jockey Alan Freed, singer Bill Haley and recording entrepreneur Sam Phillips.

In 1952, 29-year-old Alan Freed was hosting his *Moondog Rock 'n' Roll Party*, a nightly show broadcast from WJW in Cleveland. Freed's programming of black music for white kids, one of the most revolutionary media moves in the 20th century, was actually the idea of Leo Mintz, an acquaintance of Freed who operated the biggest record store in Cleveland. In March 1952 Freed promoted his first concert, which he called a Moondog Ball, at the Cleveland Arena. The Arena had a capacity of 10,000. There were 9,000 tickets sold in advance. On the night of the show,

Moon Mullican, at the piano, with other Opry artists in 1951. Moon's hillbilly boogie helped pave the way for rock 'n' roll.

Alan Freed was an early promoter of rock 'n' roll: here in a 1956 movie titled Rock, Rock, Rock.

in sound to the work of Texas saxophonist Bob Herrick, who played in the band of Texas Playboys alumnus Leon McAuliffe, and was featured on such McAuliffe records as "Plain-Talkin' Man from the West," released by Majestic in 1947.

Curiously, the debut recording of Haley's group was a version of Jackie Brenston's recent "Rocket 88." On his new Essex label, Dave Miller continued to issue Haley's records under the new group name of Bill Haley and His Comets: "Rock the Joint," "Real Rock Drive" and then, in 1953, "Crazy, Man, Crazy." There had been rock 'n' roll records on the rhythm-and-blues charts, some records that could be called rock 'n' roll on the country charts, but "Crazy, Man, Crazy" was the first rock record to become a national pop hit. Those weird glimpses of something new in the music of such men as Wynonie Harris and The Delmore Brothers, the outright fiery newness of Jackie Brenston's rock 'n' roll rocket, were smuggled into the backyards of America by Bill Haley. Some called it a fad, a passing silliness, but it was an irreversible and uncontrollable energy that would rule and haunt for decades.

Bill Haley, the first white rock 'n' roll singer, was the man who brought rock to the top of the pop charts, but Haley was more an entertainer than a rock 'n' roll madman. Vernon Dalhart's 1924 Victor record of "The Prisoner's Song" was the first million-selling hillbilly record, but there

between 20,000 and 30,000 kids showed up. They bashed the doors open, stomped the outnumbered police and screamed. "Everybody had such a grand time breaking into the Arena," said Freed, "that they didn't ask for their money back."

William John Clifton Haley was born in the Detroit suburb of Highland Park in 1927. When he was seven, Haley's family moved to Booth's Corner, a small town in southeastern Pennsylvania. During his high school years Haley started playing country music, and in 1951 he and his band, Bill Haley and The Saddlemen, had their first record issued by Holiday Records, a Chester, Pennsylvania, label operated by Dave Miller. Bill Haley's country roots were deep and strong. In the late 1940's he had billed his group as Bill Haley and The Four Aces of Western Swing. His 1952 recording of "Icy Heart" on Essex was obviously derived from Hank Williams. The saxophone work of Rudy Pompilii, which Haley added to his later records, is very similar

is no way Dalhart himself can be termed a hill-billy singer. He was a pop singer, and his inter-pretations of hillbilly music betrayed this with his schmaltzy affectations of folkiness. Haley was something similar: he was a country singer, a pop singer when he wished to be, but not a rock 'n' roll singer. His singing was clean, manicured. It is significant that his biggest and most remem-bered hit, his 1955 Decca record of "Rock Around the Clock," was written by Freedman and Jimmy DeKnight. Freedman, the Tin Pan Alley author of "Sioux City Sue" and "Blue Danube Waltz," was born in Philadelphia in 1895. Jimmy DeKnight was really Jimmy Myers of Myers Music Inc., who published the song.

Like Alan Freed, Haley spread interest in modern black music so that by the close of 1954, every hip kid in America was into rock 'n' roll. Freed was doing in the biggest city in the nation what he had done in Cleveland. His first New York *Moondog Rock 'n' Roll Party* (later simply "Rock 'n' Roll Party") was broadcast over WINS on the night of September 8, 1954. In the November 6, 1954, issue of *Billboard,* in an article titled "R&B Music Success Sends Major Diskers Back to Field," it was noted that black music was increasingly showing up in white-area jukeboxes.

Monday, July 5, 1954. The most popular al-bums in America are Jackie Gleason's *Tawny* on Capitol; Frank Sinatra's *Songs for Young Lovers,* also on Capitol; the film soundtrack of *The Glenn Miller Story,* and the television soundtrack of *Victory at Sea,* both on RCA/Victor. The Number One song on *Your Hit Parade* is "Three Coins in the Foun-tain." The biggest-selling rhythm-and-blues art-ists are The Midnighters, and the biggest-selling country artist is Webb Pierce. Although rock 'n' roll is a widespread phenomenon, only one white rock singer has yet achieved any success: Bill Haley. On this summer day, something is hap-pening down in Memphis that will eventually change the course of American music. Within the Sun Record Company at 706 Union Avenue, Sam Phillips is cutting a first session on a local kid named Elvis Presley.

Sam Phillips got into the record business by way of radio. Born in Florence, Alabama, in 1925, he began working as a radio announcer after drop-ping out of high school in 1941. At night he studied engineering, podiatry and embalming. In 1942,

Bill Haley and His Comets at the New York Coliseum in 1958 with guitarist Gene Beecher.

The King

he became a disc jockey at WLAY in Muscle Shoals, and the next year at WHSL in Decatur. In 1945, he worked at WLAC in Nashville, and from 1946 to 1949 at WREC in Memphis. In Memphis, he also promoted shows at the Hotel Peabody. With the money he had saved as a disc jockey and promoter, Sam Phillips opened a recording studio at 706 Union Avenue in 1950. There he made recordings of Southern blacks and leased them to the independent record companies: Chess, Modern, Meteor, Trumpet and others. He also recorded weddings and club meetings, and transcribed them onto single-faced LP's, charging nine dollars a shot.

One of the earliest records Phillips cut and leased was Jackie Brenston's "Rocket 88," recorded in March 1951. Some of the record's success as a rocker should be attributed to Phillips. He added extra amplification to Willie Kizart's guitar work, and in doing so added a brash dimension to the final product. Other bluesmen recorded by Phillips were Bobby Bland, Little Milton, James Cotton, Sleepy John Estes, Earl Hooker, Walter Horton, Howlin' Wolf, B. B. King and Joe Hill Louis.

In 1952, Sam Phillips decided to start his own record company. He took his brother Judd on as partner and paid a commercial artist on Beale Street to design a label for his company, which he called Sun. The early months of Sun Records are unclear. The first known Sun record, "Blues in My Condition" (B-side, "Selling My Whiskey"), by Jackie Boy and Little Walter, is Sun 174, recorded on February 25, 1952. It is not known, however, when this record was released, if indeed it ever was. Still focused on blues, Phillips and Sun kept Joe Hill Louis and also recorded Walter Horton, Rufus Thomas, Memphis Ma Rainey, The Prisonaires and Junior Parker.

The first country record issued by Sun was "Silver Bells" by a quartet from Ripley, Tennes-

see, called The Ripley Cotton Choppers. The record was released in October 1953, with HILL-BILLY stamped in red upon its yellow label. With subsequent releases, it became obvious that Sam Phillips was trying to coax a new sound from his country sessions. "Boogie Blues" by Earl Peterson, a country singer from Michigan who had known Sam since his disc-jockey days, was issued in March 1954. This record, a wry, up-tempo cut featuring a yodel-trimmed vocal, also bore the HILLBILLY stamp. Peterson was basi-

Bill Black, Elvis and Scotty Moore. On Monday, July 5, 1954, they made history.

cally an old-line country singer (there were traces not only of Hank Williams, but also of Jimmie Rodgers in his style), but "Boogie Blues" possessed a lively, youthful edge.

Sidney "Hardrock" Gunter's "Gonna Dance All Night" was released in May of the same year. Gunter had been recording since the 1940's, and was best known for his 1948 "Birmingham Bounce" on the Bama label. He continued to record for small labels right on into the 1960's, when he worked for a time as a disc jockey at WWVA in Wheeling, West Virginia, before retiring to Golden, Colorado. When he recorded for Sun, Gunter was a member of the WWVA *Jamboree*. "Gonna Dance All Night" and its flip, "Fallen Angel," were indeed a new sort of country

Elvis, The Jordanaires and producer Steve Sholes recording "Hound Dog" in New York in 1956.

music. "Gonna Dance All Night" was not merely an up-tempo country song, it also bordered on rock. Sam Phillips added a saxophone to Gunter's sound, obviously influenced by the work of Rudy Pompilii in Bill Haley's recent records, and the combination of country honky tonk, rolling saxophone, and lyrics such as "We're gonna rock 'n' roll while we dance all night" wrought a strong effect.

A side recorded the same day as "Gonna Dance All Night," and released in June of 1954, came closer to country rock than anything Phillips had previously produced: "My Kind of Carryin' On" by Doug Poindexter and The Starlite Wranglers. This was a country record, but barely traditional. It fluttered and jarred like a creature flirting with madness. It was a great record, but it was Poindexter's only Sun single.

Johnny Cash and Elvis at the Opry.

In 1955, Arkansas-born Poindexter retired from the music business following the breakup of his band. His lead guitarist, Scotty Moore, and his bassist, Bill Black, had joined a new singer named Presley. Later, Doug Poindexter worked in the insurance business in Memphis.

Monday, July 5, 1954, Sam Phillips, Elvis Presley, Scotty Moore and Bill Black are in Sun's pokey, 30-by-20-foot studio messing with "Blue Moon of Kentucky," a song Bill Monroe and His Blue Grass Boys had recorded for Columbia in 1945. It isn't a country song they're trying to set down on tape, nor a rhythm-and-blues song in the Haley mode, but a weird bastard sound that Phillips has been carrying in the dampness of his brain. Finally the sound is in the air, its configurations caught on magnetic tape. Sam Phillips grins. "Hell, that's different," he says. "That's a pop song now, Little Vi. That's *good.*" These are perhaps the most apocalyptic words in the history of American music.

Born in Tupelo, Mississippi, on January 8, 1935, Elvis Aron Presley was 19 that July day in Memphis. Six years earlier, in 1948, his family had moved to that western Tennessee city, and in the spring of 1953, Elvis graduated from Humes High School there. His photograph in *The Herald,* the Humes High School yearbook, shows a boy with sideburns, Corinthian pompadour and a hint of acne. He had participated, his yearbook caption says, in ROTC, Biology Club, English Club, History Club and Speech Club. The summer after graduation, Presley went to work for the Precision Tool Company. He left that job after a short while and began work at the Crown Electric Company, where he was paid $42 a week to drive a truck.

On a Saturday afternoon in late 1953, Elvis made his first visit to the Sun studio. As a sideline operation to Sun, Phillips still maintained his Memphis Recording Service, administered by Marion Keisker, the former Miss Radio of Memphis. It was to the Memphis Recording Service, and not Sun Records, that Elvis came that afternoon. He paid Keisker the four dollar charge, entered the studio with his acoustic guitar, and recorded two songs directly onto a double-sided ten-inch acetate disk. On the one side Elvis cut "My Happiness," with which The Ink Spots had hit on Decca in 1948. On the other side he did "That's When Your Heartaches Begin," a mawkish ballad written by Zeb Turner and recorded by Bob Lamb on Dot in 1951.

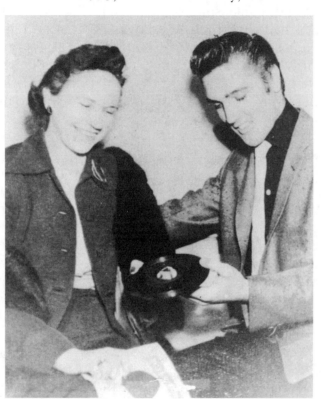

Songwriter Mae Axton and Elvis with "Heartbreak Hotel."

Struck by Presley's voice and raw acoustic guitar work, Marion Keisker recorded the end of "My Happiness" and the whole of "That's When Your Heartaches Begin" on a length of used tape. Seventeen years later, she told Elvis biographer Jerry Hopkins, "The reason I taped Elvis was this: Over and over I remember Sam saying, 'If I could find a white man who had the Negro feel, I could make a billion dollars.' This is what I heard in Elvis, this...what I guess they now call 'soul,' this Negro sound. So I taped it. I wanted Sam to know."

Marion also took note of Presley's address, 462 Alabama Street, and when she next saw Phillips she played the tape of Elvis' performance. Sam seemed mildly impressed, but did not pursue the matter. Several months later, on January 4, 1954, Elvis visited the Memphis Recording Service again. Marion Keisker was not in, but Sam Phillips was. They spoke, Sam calmly and plainly and easily, Elvis nervously. Elvis gave Sam four dollars and cut another acetate: "I'll Never Stand in Your Way," a 1941 country song written by Clint Horner, and "Casual Love Affair," a song of unknown origin that may have been learned quickly from a demo Phillips played for Elvis.

In the early summer of 1954, about eight months after Elvis had first visited the Sun studio, Sam's mail yielded a demonstration record of a composition called "Without You," recorded in Nashville by an unknown black singer. Sam was so impressed by the demo that he wanted to release it on Sun. He called Nashville in search of the singer, so that he might obtain permission to issue the record. He was told that nobody knew who the kid was, that he had just happened to be hanging around the studio when the song arrived. Phillips decided he must find someone else to cut the song in a hurry. "What about the kid with the sideburns?" suggested Marion Keisker.

Elvis was contacted that same Saturday afternoon, and he rushed to the studio. Phillips played the demo for him. Elvis sang it. By all accounts, it was horrible. He tried again, then again, and still it was bad. Phillips forsook "Without You," suggesting that Elvis try "Rag Mop," a song written by Johnnie Lee Wills and Deacon Anderson. In 1950, Johnnie Lee Wills (Bob Wills' brother) had a Top Ten country hit with his recording of the song on the independent Nashville label Bullet; that same year, The Ames Brothers had a million-selling pop version on Coral. It seemed a fairly easy song, but again Elvis failed.

During a break, Sam, a bit disturbed, asked Elvis just what it was he could sing. "Oh anything," Elvis replied. Do it, Sam said. And then it poured forth, a crazy rush of disparate sounds: gospel (earlier in 1954, Elvis had almost joined The Blackwood Brothers, a gospel quartet who performed regularly on the WMPS program, *High Noon Roundup*), hard-core country, rhythm-and-blues, middle-of-the-road pop. For hours it went on, no cool Apollonian eclecticism, but fevered glossolalia. In the end, Elvis remarked he was looking for a band.

Sam contacted Winfield Scott Moore, better known as Scotty, the 22-year-old guitarist who had recorded with Doug Poindexter several weeks before. That Sunday, Independence Day, Elvis and Scotty got together at Scotty's home, where they fooled with several recent country hits such as Eddy Arnold's "I Really Don't Want to Know" and Hank Snow's "I Don't Hurt Anymore," both on RCA/Victor, and a few of jazz singer Billy Eckstine's MGM sides. After a few hours, bass player Bill Black, Scotty's neighbor who had also played at Doug Poindexter's session, dropped by for a few minutes. Black was not impressed with the goings-on. Nonetheless, the next evening, July 5, Black found himself in the Sun studio with Phillips, Presley and Moore. It was Sam's idea for Scotty and Bill not to bring the rest of The Starlite Wranglers with them. No fiddle, no steel guitar. It was obvious that Sam had a different kind of country session in mind.

That first recording of "Blue Moon of Kentucky" was never released legally. "Blue Moon of Kentucky," as released on Elvis' first record,

Sun 209, is surer, tougher than the earlier take. Like a young boxer after his first professional knockout, Presley is dizzy with the confirmation of his prowess. "Blue Moon of Kentucky" is daring to the point of insanity. It is Elvis walking on iron blades, through fire, invincible with the knowledge he sees in Sam's eyes, hears in his own voice, and feels in his own flushed body; the knowledge that right now, this instant, he, Elvis Aron Presley, is the greatest singer in Memphis and the universe.

After "Blue Moon of Kentucky," Elvis and the boys cut "That's All Right," a song originally recorded by Mississippi-born bluesman Arthur Crudup (better known as Big Boy Crudup) for Victor in 1946. As Elvis performed it, it was no more a blues song, and no less a country song, than "Blue Moon of Kentucky." Where Bill Haley's versions of rhythm-and-blues songs were playfully mimetic, Elvis' were frighteningly creative.

The first Elvis Presley record, "That's All Right" (with "Blue Moon of Kentucky" as the B-side), was released on July 19, 1954, a Monday. Sam Phillips took a copy of the record to Dewey Phillips, the disc jockey who hosted the *Red Hot and Blue* show on WHBQ, and he broadcast "That's All Right." Listeners called in their enthusiastic reactions. On station WHHM, disc jockey Sleepy Eye John began playing "Blue Moon of Kentucky." The record took off, and as the weeks passed, "That's All Right" became the Number One country record in Memphis.

That is when rockabilly became fact, and Elvis became its god. On September 25, Elvis' second record was issued, a coupling of "Good Rockin' Tonight" and "I Don't Care if the Sun Don't Shine," written by Mack David, author of "Bibbidi Bobbidi Boo" and "La Vie en Rose." Elvis made his debut on the Grand Ole Opry, a guest on Hank Snow's segment, where he sang both sides of his first single. On October 16, Presley played

Elvis at work

Carl Perkins with his brothers, Clayton and Jay B.

the *Louisiana Hayride*, where he went over so well that he was brought back the following week to become a regular member. The third Elvis record, released on January 8, 1955, was "Milkcow Blues Boogie," originally cut by Kokomo Arnold on Decca in 1935 (and done in a country swing version by Johnnie Lee Wills in 1941, also on Decca), and "You're a Heartbreaker," a strong country weeper, closer to a honky tonk performance than any of Elvis' other Sun sides. "I'm Left, You're Right, She's Gone," written by a Sun session man, steel-guitarist Stan Kesler, and "Baby Let's Play House," which had been a minor rhythm-and-blues hit for Arthur Gunter on Excello earlier in the year, comprised Elvis' fourth single, issued on April 1, 1955. For the first time, one of Presley's records hit the national country charts; "Baby Let's Play House" rose to the Number One position. As "Baby Let's Play House" was high on the charts, Elvis' last Sun disk was issued: "Mystery Train," a rhythm-and-blues song Junior Parker had cut for Sun in 1953, and "I Forgot to Remember to Forget," another Stan Kesler song. The record became a double-sided hit, and rose to the Number One position on the country charts. Elvis Presley, rock 'n' roll madman, had the best-selling country record in the nation.

Late in 1955, Elvis signed with RCA Victor. On January 5, 1956, in Nashville, Elvis cut his first sides for his new label. Now, in addition to Scotty and Bill and drummer D.J. Fontana (who had joined the group early in 1955), there were Nashville cats involved: guitarist Chet Atkins, pianist Floyd Cramer and the vocal group, The Jordanaires. Elvis' first RCA Victor recording, "Heartbreak Hotel," was released in February 1956. It became the Number One song on the country and the pop charts. Written by Texas songwriter Mae Boren Axton, "Heartbreak Hotel" was a superlative rockabilly song, full of austerity, sex and stone-hard rhythm. For the next two years, Elvis continued to cut rockabilly material on RCA Victor: "Don't Be Cruel," in 1956, "Jailhouse Rock," in 1957, "Hardheaded Woman," in 1958. But with each new session, Elvis grew farther from rockabilly. By the time he was drafted into the Army in 1958, the golden days of rockabilly had passed.

All things that contain more creativity than formula, more emotion than intellect, cannot be precisely defined, and this is true of rockabilly music. As the word implies, rockabilly is hillbilly rock 'n' roll. It was not a usurpation of black music by whites, as Haley's rock 'n' roll might justifiably be termed, because its soul was white, full of the redneck ethos.

Country music and the blues are two tributaries of a common source.

Carl Perkins

Nothing in traditional American music is as white as it might seem, or as black. Waylon Jennings' album, *Dreaming My Dreams*, released in June 1975, has a song on it called "Waymore's Blues," credited to Waylon and Curtis Buck. The song ends with this couplet:

I got my name printed on my shirt;
I ain't no ordinary dude, I don't have to work.

Now go back a bit, to 1951, when Harmonica Frank Floyd, the first white singer to record for Sun, cut a song called "Rockin'-Chair Daddy," in which you can hear:

Rock to Memphis, dance on Main,
Up stepped a lady and asked my name.
Rockin'-chair daddy don't have to work,
I told her my name was on the tail of my shirt.

Search back another couple of decades, to Jimmie Rodgers' 1930 recording of "Blue Yodel No. 9":

It was down in Memphis, corner of Beale and Main
He says, "Big boy, you'll have to tell me your name."
I said, "You'll find my name on the tail of my shirt,
I'm a Tennessee hustler, I don't have to work."

To stop here in the genealogy of this perennial country lyric would be misleading. In 1928, blues singer Furry Lewis cut his two-part "Kassie Jones":

Had it written on the back of my shirt:
Natural-born eastman, don't have to work.

Two decades earlier, when there were neither blues records nor country records, folklorist Howard Odum collected a song in the field and later published it in his 1925 book, *The Negro and His Songs*:

I got it writ on de tail o' my shirt:
I'm a natu'el-bohn eastman, don't have to work.

Going back farther, you enter the lyric's prehistory. Was it ultimately invented in 1901 or 1855? Was it a black man or a white man who invented it?

The first blues, of course, was sung in a white man's language, played on a white man's instrument. Both Leon McAuliffe's steel guitar and Elmore James' slide guitar are descended from the music of vaudeville's Hawaiian guitarists. The searcher of ethnic purity in popular American music finds little.

Black versions of country songs are not uncommon. Darrell Glenn cut the first version of "Crying in the Chapel" (which his father wrote) for Valley Records in the summer of 1953. Rex Allen covered it on Decca and had a Top Ten country hit on it. The most widely known version of the song, however, is that of the rhythm-

Jerry Lee Lewis had the two biggest hits in Sun Records' history: "Whole Lot of Shakin' Goin' On" was the first in 1957.

and-blues group, The Orioles, who cut it for Jubilee. The Pearls, another black group, covered Hank Williams' "Your Cheatin' Heart" for Onyx Records. Eddy Arnold's 1947 hit, "It's a Sin," was cut in 1961 by Tarheel Slim and Little Ann on Fire Records. "Jealous Heart," the Al Morgan country hit of 1949, was covered that same year by King artist Ivory Joe Hunter (who returned to country music in his records shortly before his death in 1975). Solomon Burke's first successful recording, on Atlantic in 1961, was "Just Out of Reach," a country song. Bobby Comstock cut both "Tennessee Waltz" and "Jambalaya," the first on Blaze in 1959, the second on Atlantic in 1960. Wynonie Harris' big 1951 rhythm-and-blues hit, "Bloodshot Eyes," on King, was a cover of the Western swing original cut the year before by Hank Penny on the same label. Bullmoose Jackson, another black King artist, covered both Wayne Raney's 1949 "Why Don't You Haul Off and Love Me" and Moon Mullican's 1951 "Cherokee Boogie." Blues guitarist Earl Hooker, at a 1953 session in Memphis, cut not only Leon McAuliffe's "Steel Guitar Rag" but also the perennial "Red River Valley."

Johnny Cash and Jerry Lee in their Sun Records era. Again, Sam Phillips had struck gold.

When Elvis cut Big Boy Crudup's "That's All Right," he was no more usurping black culture than Wynonie Harris was usurping white culture when he cut Hank Penny's "Bloodshot Eyes" three years before. Presley's version of "That's All Right" is better than the original, just as Harris' version of "Bloodshot Eyes" is better than its original.

There was an affinity between rockabilly and black music of the 1940's and 1950's, as there had been an affinity between Western swing and black music of the 1920's and 1930's, but it was not, really, more than an affinity. Of the 16 known titles Elvis recorded as a Sun artist, five were de-

rived from rhythm-and-blues records: "That's All Right," "Good Rockin' Tonight," "Milkcow Blues Boogie," "Baby Let's Play House" and "Mystery Train." (Two of these, in turn, were derived from country records: Arthur Gunter's "Baby Let's Play House" from Eddy Arnold's 1951 hit, "I Want to Play House with You," and Junior Parker's "Mystery Train" from the Carter Family's 1930 "Worried Man Blues.") During his Sun years, as during the decades after, Elvis derived the bulk of his music from country and pop sources.

What blackness there was in rockabilly in no way constituted an innovation in country music. The black enculturation in the music of old-timers such as Jimmie Rodgers and Bob Wills was far greater, far deeper. Nor was there much of a technical nature in rockabilly that country music had not known before. The slap-bass technique, one of the watermarks of classic rockabilly, can be heard in country records of the prewar era: Listen to bassist Ramon DeArmon in The Light Crust Doughboys' 1938 Vocalion record, "Pussy, Pussy, Pussy." The echo effect heard in many rockabilly recordings had been used by Wilf Carter in such sides as his 1935 "Sundown Blues," and later by Eddy Arnold in his 1944 "Cattle Call."

What made rockabilly such a drastically new music was its spirit, which bordered on mania.

Sam Phillips and Johnny Cash in 1962 with Cash's Gold record for "I Walk the Line."

ers. His early years were spent on a plantation in Lake County, Tennessee, where his family were the sole white sharecroppers. In 1945, the Perkins family relocated in Bemis, where Carl began working as a laborer in a battery plant, then at a bakery in nearby Jackson.

Musically, Carl was reared on a mix of country via Nashville's WSM, and rhythm-and-blues via sharecropper neighbors and black radio broadcasts. In 1945, Carl won a talent show in Bemis. He taught his brothers, Jay B. and Clayton, to play guitars, and together the three began performing locally as The Perkins Brothers Band.

Late in 1953, after Carl and his Mississippi-born wife, Valda Crider, moved to Parkview Courts, a government-subsidized housing project in Jackson, Carl began sending demo tapes to various record companies in Nashville and New York. In December 1954, after several unsuccessful attempts, he had an audience with Sam Phillips at Sun. Several weeks later, in February of 1955, Sam issued Carl's first record on the Flip label (a Sun affiliate): "Movie Magg," which Carl had authored in 1945, and "Turn Around," a straight country piece. In "Movie Magg," it became immediately apparent that Perkins was a consummate rock guitarist, given to rapid-fire high-note runs on his Les Paul Gibson. The Flip record got decent disc jockey response in Memphis, as had Elvis' first records during the previous seven months, and Sam signed Carl on as a regular Sun artist.

Over the next three years, until Carl left Sun

Elvis' version of "Good Rockin' Tonight" was not a party song, but an invitation to a holocaust. Junior Parker's "Mystery Train" was an eerie shuffle; Elvis' "Mystery Train" was a demonic incantation. Country music had never known such vehement emotion, and neither had black music. It was the face of Dionysus, full of febrile sexuality and senselessness; it flushed the skin of new housewives, and made teenage boys reinvent themselves as flaming creatures.

Although Elvis was the god, the unforgettable boy-daddy of rockabilly, there were others. In Memphis, and across the South, burning ever North, they drove country music berserk.

Carl Lee Perkins was born on a welfare-supported tenant farm near Tiptonville, Tennessee, on April 9, 1932, the second of three broth-

in 1958, there were only seven of his singles released. This is odd, considering the fact that four of these records were country hits, and three of these four crossed to the pop charts. (One of Carl's records, the giant "Blue Suede Shoes," was a Top Ten hit on the country, pop and even rhythm-and-blues charts in 1956.)

Like Elvis, Carl Perkins sometimes used black material, as in his 1957 record of "Matchbox," a hard-edged version of Blind Lemon Jefferson's 1927 "Matchbox Blues" (which was covered previously by several country acts: Larry Hensely in 1934, Joe Shelton in 1935, Roy Shaffer in 1939, and Roy Newman and His Boys also in 1939). Unlike Elvis, however, Perkins was a consummate songwriter who was at his best in songs such as the 1956 "Dixie Fried," a raving whorl of whiskey and violence, and the 1957 "Put Your Cat Clothes On"

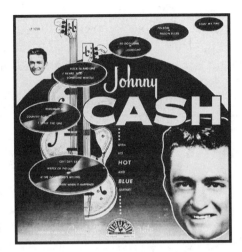

(unreleased until 1971), an anthem of redneck rock.

From Sun, Perkins went to Columbia; then, in 1963 he went to Decca. After Decca, he signed with Dollie, and in 1968 he returned to Columbia, where he remained until 1973, when he joined Mercury, with whom he released only one album and a handful of singles.

Born in Ferriday, Louisiana, on September 29, 1935, Jerry Lee Lewis signed with Sun late in 1956. Of all rockabilly artists, Jerry Lee projected the most hellish persona. To some he was a redneck prince, the spirit of Southern rock 'n' roll; to others he was sin itself, the most despised and feared of the 1950's pop heroes.

Jerry Lee's debut record was a coupling of "Crazy Arms," the Ray Price hit that was still on the charts when Jerry Lee cut it in the fall of 1956, and "End of the Road," an original piece. Although

Jerry Lee Lewis, Carl Perkins, Elvis and Johnny Cash at Sun Records: The Million Dollar Quartet.

he did not pursue the writing aspect of music in subsequent years (of the several hundred titles he has cut in the past four decades, only five bear his signature: "End of the Road," "High School Confidential" and "Lewis Boogie" on Sun, "Lincoln Limousine" and "He Took It Like a Man" on Smash), in "End of the Road," Jerry Lee proved himself a masterful evoker of lurid mood and dark thirsts, and it is precious, and poetically just, to consider the song a statement of purpose, an existential anthem of the career to follow:

> Well, the way is dark,
> Night is long,
> I don't care if I never
>   get home:
> I'm waitin' at the end of
>   the road!

Jerry Lee had the two biggest hits in Sun's history: 1957's "Whole Lot of Shakin' Goin' On," which had originally been cut by The Commodores on Dot in 1955, and the 1957-58 giant "Great Balls of Fire," written by Otis Blackwell, the rhythm-and-blues singer and author of "Don't Be Cruel," "All Shook Up" and others. "Whole Lotta Shakin' Goin' On" rose to Number One on the country charts, Number One on the rhythm-and-blues

Waylon Jennings and bossman Buddy Holly.

charts and Number Three on the pop charts. "Great Balls of Fire" hit Number One on the country charts, Number Three on the rhythm-and-blues charts and Number Two on the pop charts. In 1958, Lewis' "Breathless" again went to the Top Ten in the country, rhythm-and-blues and pop charts. In the spring of that year, however, something bad happened to Jerry Lee.

In England on a promotional tour in May, Jerry Lee became the victim of a sensationalistic press that smarmed and tsk-wailed the fact that Lewis' wife, Myra, was his 13-year-old cousin. With his customary élan, Jerry Lee re-

sponded to the British press: "Myra and I are legally married. It was my second marriage that wasn't legal. I was a bigamist when I was 16. I was 14 when I was first married. That lasted a year, then I met June. One day she said she was goin' to have my baby. I was real worried. Her father threatened me, and her brothers were hunting me with hide whips. So I married her just a week before my divorce from Dorothy. It was a shotgun wedding."

Jerry Lee's British tour was canceled after three shows, and he returned home to Memphis (though not before dropping in for a few nights at the Star Club in Hamburg, there to be recorded in an amazing performance released a quarter century later by Rhino Records). The publicity did not wane. In the June 9 issue of *Billboard* appeared a full-page advertisement titled "An Open Letter to the Industry from Jerry Lee Lewis." It began, bluntly: "Dear Friends: I have in recent weeks been the apparent center of a fantastic amount of publicity and of which none has been good...."

Jerry Lee's next record, "High School Confidential," from the film of the same name, reached Number Nine on the country charts, Number 16 on the rhythm-and-blues charts and Number 21 on the pop charts. It was Jerry Lee's last appearance in the Top Ten of the country charts until 1968 and his last appearance, period, in the Top 20 of either the rhythm-and-blues or the pop charts. But Jerry Lee kept pumping away. In 1968, he rose anew with a series of country hits that began with "Another Place, Another Time" on Smash.

Jerry Lee recorded for Sun from 1956 to 1963. When he left the label, the days of Sun were already numbered. After "Carry Me Back to Old

Buddy Holly

*The Everly Brothers—
Phil and Don*

Virginny," Lewis' 23rd and last Sun record, Phillips issued only 11 more records; then, after a decade, it was over. In 1952, the world's first Holiday Inn had opened, in Memphis. By the end of the 1950's, Holiday Inn was one of the fastest-growing, wealthiest operations in the nation, and Sam Phillips, who as a small-time Memphis businessman had invested in Holiday Inn, emerged as one of its major stockholders.

Sun began to dissolve in 1958. The previous year, Johnny Cash, Bill Justis and Jerry Lee Lewis had given Phillips great crossover hits (Justis' hit "Raunchy" was on the Phillips International label). By the fall of 1958, Justis and Lewis had ceased to have hits, and Johnny Cash had signed with Columbia. During the same period, Judd Phillips, Sam's brother and partner at Sun, faced payola allegations for his promotional activities, and the brothers broke their relationship. (It was then that Judd founded his own Judd label.) Early in 1959, producer Jack Clement, who had been at Sun since 1955, and had been responsible for much of Sun's most imaginative work in the late 50's, suddenly left the company.

Early in 1961 Phillips opened a studio on 17th Avenue in Nashville and started using many of that city's pop-country musicians at his sessions: Floyd Cramer, Hank Garland, Buddy Harmon, Bob Moore, Pig Robbins, Billy Sherrill and others. But Phillips did not succeed in making Sun a part of the ever more lucrative Nashville Sound, and the company languished. In 1966, Sam closed his company, Phillips International. From 1964 to 1968, Sun released only 20 singles, most of them bad. In 1968 Sun Records ended. On July 1, 1969, Nashville entrepreneur Shelby Singleton Jr. acquired from Phillips an 80 percent interest in the Sun catalogue and became the major stockholder in a newly formed Sun International Corporation. Beginning in 1969, Singleton released a steady flow of budget-line Sun reissues.

Presley, Perkins and Lewis were the three most famous, most successful rockabilly artists. Others, less enduring, less famed, made music often as good, sometimes better.

Vincent Gene Craddock, more widely known as Gene Vincent, was born in Norfolk, Virginia, on February 11, 1935. Gene served in the Navy

Felice and Boudleaux Bryant: million-seller songwriters.

during the Korean War. He was severely injured in combat, and it was thought that his leg would have to be amputated. Vincent did not permit the amputation, and instead wore a leg brace through the rest of his life. Thin, wan, crippled, Vincent was an unlikely pop star, but a pop star he nonetheless became.

After performing on radio station WCMS, Vincent and his band, The Blue Caps, went to Capitol Records, and in the spring of 1956 his first disc was released: "Be-Bop-a-Lula," written by Vincent and Sheriff Tex Davis (and inspired by a "Little Lulu" comic book), and "Woman Love." On the country charts, "Be-Bop-a-Lula" hit Number Five, and on the pop charts Number Nine. It was a strong song, and a unique one. Vincent delivered its basically light, cute lyric with a febrile psychopathy. It was a perverse, gothic performance and one of the perfect rockabilly records. "Woman Love" was an obvious emulation of Elvis, but it possessed that powerful sense of the macabre that came to be Vincent's trademark. It is one of the most overtly sexual recordings of its time, roiled full with Vincent's unceasing flow of orgasmic pantings.

"Be-Bop-a-Lula" was Vincent's only country hit, and his only Top Ten pop hit. Capitol issued 19 singles by Vincent before he left the label in 1961. During the next ten years, Vincent recorded for Challenge, Forever, Dandelion and Kama Sutra, all without commercial success. On October 12, 1971, Gene Vincent died in California from internal hemorrhaging. He was 36.

Of the major rockabilly artists, Buddy Holly alone never had a hit record on the country charts. Born Charles Hardin Holly in Lubbock, Texas, on September 7, 1936, Buddy's musical heritage was hard-core country, but by the mid-1950's he had developed an interest in black music.

After several years of playing in clubs and on radio in the Lubbock area, Holly was signed to

Decca early in 1956, and on January 26, in Nashville, Owen Bradley produced Holly's first session. In April a single was released: "Blue Days, Black Nights" and "Love Me." Four more discs followed, including the classic "That'll Be the Day," but little happened. In March 1957, Buddy Holly and The Crickets were signed to Brunswick/Coral, and late that year "Peggy Sue" became Holly's first hit, eventually rising to Number Three on the pop charts. Within the next two years, Holly had five more pop hits, but none entered the Top Ten.

On February 3, 1959, near Fargo, North Dakota, an airplane carrying Holly, Richie Valens and The Big Bopper (J. P. Richardson) crashed, killing all aboard. Waylon Jennings, who was in Holly's band at the time, had given his seat to

Rock 'n' roll fever: Joe E. Lewis, Harold Jenkins, Blackie Preston, Jack Nance in 1958. Jenkins became Conway Twitty.

The Big Bopper at the last minute.

Although Holly was a rockabilly artist, he was very different from the rockabilly mainstream. His was a softer music. His records sounded less neurotic, effervescent instead of turbulent. Buddy Holly was the gentleman of rockabilly, the first soft rocker. In Holly's records, rockabilly can be heard deflecting from country music toward a more refined, Apollonian form, perhaps best exemplified by the music of The Everly Brothers.

Johnny Cash joins Columbia Records, and a new era begins. Shown here, the cover art for his 1958 album, The Fabulous Johnny Cash, which cracked the Top 20 on the pop album charts.

Don Everly was born in Brownie, Kentucky, in 1937; his brother Phil followed in 1939. The duo cut their first sides for Cadence in early 1957, and they were received immediately and enthusiastically by both pop and country audiences, thanks partly to the talents of the incomparable songwriting team of Felice and Boudleaux Bryant, who wrote hits for everyone from Little Jimmy Dickens to Eddy Arnold to The Osbornes. "Bye Bye Love," "Wake Up Little Susie," "All I Have to Do Is Dream," "Bird Dog" (all by the Bryants) and "('Til) I Kissed You" were Top Ten records in the late 1950's on both the pop and country charts. In 1960, The Everly Brothers left Cadence for Warner Brothers, and their first release on that label rose to Number One on the pop charts:

"Cathy's Clown." Although the duo disappeared from the country charts after 1961, they continued to have moderate success on the pop charts through the late 1960's. In 1972, The Everly Brothers left Warner Brothers for RCA, and in the summer of the following year, they announced their breakup; they wouldn't sing together again until their reunion in the mid-80's.

The historical importance of The Everly Brothers is not to be overlooked. With their harmonious sound and rosy-romantic material, they were the pivotal rockabilly act, rooted more deeply in pop than in country. It was the final, inevitable step, the homogenization. With Buddy Holly, the mania had ebbed. Now it was merely an echo in the blood.

The Jordanaires

CHAPTER 9

The Nashville Sound

For journalists in the 1960's, nothing seemed to capture their feeling of excitement in the discovery of country music as much as in the elusive, heady phrase, "The Nashville Sound." It became a shorthand means of explaining the rise of country music from the ruins left by rock, and the increasing dominance of the form all through the 1960's.

On the surface the concept of the Nashville Sound is simple. Nearly everyone has heard the phrase—it conjures images of Chet Atkins, late-night recording sessions in dim studios and creative camaraderie. The term is actually quite complex, however, for it has multiple meanings; it refers to a specific style of recording, to an era in the development of Nashville as a recording center, and finally to a mystique that grew up around the city in the years when the marriage of pop and country music was consummated.

Something about the Nashville Sound—the actual sound itself, not yet burdened by historical or mystical overtones—made singers want to record in Nashville, made people want to buy records produced there, and brought country music to the mid-American public for the first time since the days of Gene Autry and Bob Wills. Because even musicians found it hard to define with any precision, those who discovered Nashville and its sound called it "loose," "jazzy," "swinging," "subtle" and a host of other vague

adjectives. Growing out of the jamming of sophisticated musicians (this in itself was a great surprise to many who "discovered" country music around this time), it was all this and more, and like any sound or combination of sounds, it had its magnificent moments and its excesses, ranging from the sublime to the ridiculous—but at a time when "hard," traditional country music was stone-cold dead, the Nashville Sound pulled country music (and the city that came to be called Music City, U.S.A., as a direct result) out of terrible doldrums. Whether the resulting music helped improve the quality of country music or helped destroy it—there are persuasive spokesmen presenting both extremes—it saved the industry when things looked bleakest, and that is the dominant legacy of the Nashville Sound.

The Nashville Sound was the result—as many things seem to be in retrospect—of a succession of fortunate accidents, a whole series of the right people being in the right places at the right time. Historically speaking, the growth in number and quality of recording studios in Nashville gave as much impetus to the development of the Nashville Sound as anything else, for it was this proliferation that gave rise to a group of studio musicians who played so often and so smoothly together that they made recording in Nashville easy, relaxed and incredibly efficient. They were disciplined and creative at the same time, musically sophisticated and cooperative; they knew each other's music by feel, and were able to work out stunning arrangements in a matter of minutes. In the 1970's a lot of criticism was leveled at the mechanical, businesslike, sound-alike approach this technique produced, but when the approach was new it was a thrill for both the artist, who found a superb, solid, creative band behind him (so different from many road bands), and for the producer, who could enter the studio and cut four or five musically

in New York and Los Angeles, where sidemen were frequently connected with the work of a single company-owned studio. Second, Nashville sidemen did not usually read music on recording sessions. They were all sophisticated musicians, and many could and did read music when it was necessary, but most played instruments that were frequently learned "by ear" and thus found an "aural" approach to arrangements more comfortable than reproducing sounds indicated on a written chart. Because it was derived from folk song, country music has always placed its greatest emphasis on the message of the song—the text. The basic musical structure was frequently simple: A 1-4-5 chord progression or perhaps a 1-4-2-5 progression would handle many country songs. These chord sequences were repeated verse after verse, so detailed charts for an entire song were rarely needed; similarly, time signatures were unnecessary because country songs rarely changed tempo once begun. It was, then, the simplicity of much of the music, combined with the "by ear" orientation of

Jim Reeves and Chet Atkins, two reasons RCA was a leader in the Nashville Sound era.

strong sides in just three hours. It created substantial savings, too, in both time and money, and there existed always the assurance of high quality. The Nashville musicians had built a better mousetrap, and in that light it is easy to see why singers, studios and record labels began falling over themselves to get to Nashville, particularly when they couldn't seem to make a hit recording in New York or Los Angeles.

Certain informal rules came into being in the Nashville recordings of the early years. First, a single group of talented sidemen moved from studio to studio and worked on the sessions of many singers on many different record labels. This approach stood in contrast to that practiced

many Nashville musicians, that kept the strict classical notation pretty much out of Nashville studios.

Instead, a musical shorthand was substituted for "notes," and for most sessions today the system remains in use. In "Nashville notation" the musician simply records the chord progression of a song when he first hears it (usually when it is played for him on tape at the beginning of a session). He writes down a number for each measure in which a particular chord is played and makes his lines of numbers conform to the phrasing of a song. It looks like this:

1 1 4 4   5 5 1 1

If the numbers were translated into chord names in, for example, the key of C, the same

Chet Atkins

diagram would look like this:

C C F F G G C C

If the musician played one measure of these chords in 4/4 time, this pattern could serve, for example, as accompaniment for Ernest Tubb's "Walking the Floor Over You," or, for that matter, "The Great Speckled Bird," or "There's a Star-Spangled Banner Waving Somewhere," or country music's first hit, "The Prisoner's Song," or one that came later: John Denver's "Back Home Again."

This type of notation merely provides a framework—the barest skeleton—for a musical performance. The individual sidemen improvise parts that fit this skeleton, either playing chords or appropriate melody lines. The frame is, in fact, so open to invention that the specific background arrangement evolves as the sidemen rehearse in the recording studio, and when musicians are familiar with the system and comfortable with each other, a complete arrangement will emerge after four or five runthroughs of the song. And if the musicians are creative, and if they're not tired or bored, their individual ideas will equal or surpass an arrangement written out in advance; each musician contributes something very individual to what ultimately becomes a well-structured and homogenized unit. The payoff is that musicians who are friends as well as co-workers, playing in an environment in which their ideas can find a place on every record and in which every arrangement is considered to be evolving, should be able to produce relaxed, creative, fresh-sounding recordings.

A unique instrumentation was also a part of the Nashville Sound, and Music City was (and is) strongly oriented toward the sounds of the rhythm section and particularly toward the sound of the guitar in each of its many incarnations. The "standard" Nashville recording team in the 1960's consisted of bass, drums, piano, sometimes a fiddle, and guitar (or, more properly, guitars); one and sometimes two acoustic guitars were strummed for rhythm. If two were used, one usually had a special set of high-pitched strings to produce a brilliant ringing of the chord toward the high end of the audio spectrum. Usually one electric guitar played "lead" lines—either single notes or simple intervals—while the ubiquitous pedal steel guitar fulfilled a number of functions, sometimes playing single string solos like an electric lead guitar and at other times playing background chord fills. Often a six-string bass guitar—an electric instrument tuned one octave below a guitar and one above a string bass—was used in conjunction with an upright string bass to double the bass line and contribute the crisp bass "punch" associated with Nashville recording. (This was the famous "tic-tac" technique used by Harold Bradley and others). The four-string electric bass was in widespread use by the mid to late 60's, eventually supplanting the older acoustic bass.

The way the various instruments were combined was also unique to the Nashville Sound. Restraint is a large part of Nashville musicianship.

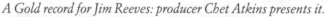

A Gold record for Jim Reeves: producer Chet Atkins presents it.

Jim Reeves

Country pickers know when not to play, which is most of the time, for their function is to support, to showcase, and to frame the work of a featured vocalist effectively. The New York style—a big-band, wall-of-sound approach to recording in which there is *always* something complicated going on in the orchestra—never worked in Nashville. Nashville players divide playing into three activities: "backing," "filling" and "soloing." Most of the playing is just back-

Owen Bradley with The Anita Kerr Singers: Louis Nunally, Winifred Breast, Anita Kerr and Karl Garvin. Background voices were a key ingredient of the Nashville Sound.

ing—playing the proper chord in the proper meter in the proper voicing. Filling brings a single instrument out front, usually to "fill" a musical hole left by the singer's phrasing. Soloing is, of course, an instrumental break featuring a lead line on one instrument. Even solos are kept intentionally simple, however, so as not to detract from the lyrics of the song. Playing is simple, only one instrument is out front at a given moment, and all of the instrumental work is subordinated to that of the vocalist. The creativity comes in on the "licks," those little one or two-beat ideas

that knock us out, grab our attention, and fix it firmly on the song. Just as countless great songs have survived mediocre performances, so too many mediocre songs have been saved by catchy instrumental devices. When both are present, the results can be special. Think of how much that descending dobro line added to "Harper Valley PTA" in 1968, or going further back, how that unbelievably simple little steel-guitar lick on Webb Pierce's "Slowly" in 1954 not only made the recording a sensation (it was the top song of the year), but also excited and inspired so many steel guitarists that the use of pedals on steel guitars became mandatory almost overnight. The Nashville approach to recording provided maximum opportunity for these lucky accidents. Drummer Ferris Coursey's thigh-slapping occurred in-studio as a whimsical bit of humor while recording Red Foley's "Chattanoogie Shoe Shine Boy" in 1950. By the time the song was rehearsed that way, so the legend goes, Coursey's thigh had grown so tender he switched hands and recorded the song with left hand slapping left thigh. Similarly, the now-commonplace but then-striking fuzztone guitar on Marty Robbins' "Don't Worry" (1961) was the result of guitarist Grady Martin plugging into a studio amp with a blown speaker. Instead of putting the amp in the corner and using one in good shape, he began experimenting with the strange, rasping sound, and a hit record was born. The presence of these "accidents" on country records did much to spread the word about Nashville sidemen to singers in other fields.

Over the years, there has been remarkable

continuity in this approach to recording in Nashville. The sidemen may have had a rougher, more energetic, more experimental sound in the middle-to-late 1950's when the Nashville Sound approach was being formed than they did in later years. In general, however, the Nashville approach to rhythm-section recording remained the city's hottest commodity for almost 20 years. Some of the musicians who backed Jim Reeves in the late 1950's played for Bob Dylan a decade later as the Nashville Sound came to symbolize relaxed creativity in recording, and by the mid-90's at least two generations of studio greats had followed in the footsteps of the originals.

If the Nashville Sound is a style, it is also an era. In the late 1950's, Nashville was still the provincial capital of a small country music scene; ten years later it was recognized internationally as a recording center co-equal with New York and Los Angeles. In the late 1950's Nashville had two studios; by the late 1960's it was home to dozens. The decade of the Nashville Sound made reality of the dreams of the 1950's. Major record labels opened huge offices, and local executives emerged to lead the Nashville music community. Nashville's musicians placed a distinctive stamp on the city's recordings, and their success eased Nashville into a decade of unprecedented growth.

Very significant in that growth were certain key individuals. It is genuinely surprising to find that a movement of this magnitude was the creation of a mere handful of men and women—probably fewer than a dozen, all told, really got it rolling—and this in itself is a telling indication of the lack of direction in the country music community at the time. That so few talented people could take control of the sound of a major segment of American popular music is remarkable, to say the very

Don Law with Columbia artist Marty Robbins in the late 50's.

least. It also shows just how small, in relative terms, the country music industry of the late 1950's and early 1960's really was.

Of these dozen or so prime movers, three stand out as particularly influential, going beyond musicianship and helping to produce, publicize, and sell the sound they created. First among them was Chet Atkins, whose name is as synonymous with the Nashville Sound as it is with the sound of modern country guitar playing. Born in an isolated Appalachian hollow near Luttrell, Tennessee, and reared there and in rural Georgia, Chet followed in the footsteps of his elder half brother, Jim, a superb musician who was best known as the singer and rhythm guitarist in The Les Paul Trio during the 30's when the group worked on band leader Fred Waring's NBC radio show.

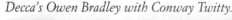

Decca's Owen Bradley with Conway Twitty.

Floyd Cramer, like other Nashville Sound instrumentalists, remained active well into the 70's.

Chet worked as a staff guitarist on many radio stations, but in those early years he did not achieve recognition as a soloist. That came later, after he was signed by RCA Victor in the late 1940's as competition to Capitol Records' star songwriter/guitarist Merle Travis. Those early RCA 78's (on which he both played and sang) were not successful, and he continued to work in radio as an instrumentalist. He hooked up with The Carter Sisters and Mother Maybelle, moving to the Grand Ole Opry in 1950, and performing a solo instrumental spot on the network segment of the Opry, sponsored by Prince Albert Tobacco.

Though Atkins had been disappointed in the results of his first RCA recordings, that early work had brought him into contact with Steve Sholes, the RCA A&R man who signed him to the label. Sholes cut country records in studios all over the country as well as in Nashville. When he was faced with the difficulties of assembling musicians and booking a studio, he fell back on the many talents of Chet Atkins, whose versatility, taste and faultless execution quickly made him a fixture of the then-budding studio scene, still very much in its infancy. Sholes came to Nashville every few months to produce recordings by everyone on RCA's country roster (although, like most of the early A&R men, he recorded rhythm & blues, gospel, children's records and anything else in the grab bag left over from mainstream pop). His Nashville roster varied from The Blue Sky Boys—who recorded their final RCA session at the Brown Brothers' studio in March of 1950—to Elvis Presley, who recorded his first RCA session on January 5, 1956, at the Methodist Publishing Company location RCA used for a time.

Sholes came to rely heavily on Atkins, and Chet began to spend a good deal of his time setting up sessions, arranging for musicians and studios and the like in preparation for a Sholes appearance in Nashville. The inevitable result, in Chet's own words (from his 1973 autobiography, *Country Gentleman*) was: "Steve came to me one day to ask: 'Chet, how would you like to take over the new RCA studio we're building?' 'You mean me run it for you?'" Chet asked him. "'Sure, you know the business and the people and the songs. It would be a perfect deal for both of us,' Sholes replied." Although he made it appear simple, Atkins admitted candidly, "My biggest problem was fear." He quickly overcame that problem. Among his first successes were hits with Jim Reeves in 1956. On his 1957 recording session producing "Oh Lonesome Me" and "I

Celebrated Nashville Sound sidemen: Hank Garland and Boots Randolph.

Can't Stop Loving You" with Don Gibson, Atkins knew he'd hit a groove: "When we released the recording a few days later—varoom! Both sides were smashes and I was an A&R man."

In his role as head of operations for RCA's Nashville office, Chet produced many of country music's biggest stars for RCA. Traditional country singers like Hank Snow, rockabilly's superstar Elvis Presley, and country-pop singer Jim Reeves all came under his production control in the late 1950's. His ability to succeed with the diverse styles of these singers indicates that Atkins himself was never bound by the stylistic limits of country music. Chet was influenced by—and recorded at one time or another—jazz, pop and classical material; he was as much at home with violins as with fiddles, and was, in the late 1950's and early 1960's, the right man to ease country music away from its traditional regional and cultural audience, and toward greater impact on the popular music scene.

Ferlin Husky and Ken Nelson's recording of "Gone," recorded November 7, 1956 in Nashville, had all the characteristics of the Nashville Sound. There were no fiddles, there were no steel guitars, there was a male vocal chorus in the background and very prominent vibraphones. In many ways this record, though produced by Capitol's West Coast-based A&R man, strongly hinted at the direction Atkins, Owen Bradley and Don Law would continue. Working independently, yet part of an era, all three set out to broaden the audience of country music, adding a fuller, lusher sound to country recordings in the hope of making them appealing to listeners who were not fans of the rawer country sounds of the early 50's. Atkins' method, like that of the other two, had a twofold purpose and result. He altered the production values of country music—mainly through the use of strings, horns and background voices—thereby broadening the audience, and, as Bill Ivey wrote in 1976 in *Stars of Country Music* : "His work with pop entertainers"—artists like Perry Como and Al Hirt— "convinced New York and Los Angeles record men that Nashville musicianship had something of value to offer non-country performers."

In 1976, hindsight led Atkins to reflect on his role in developing the Nashville Sound, and his reflections were clearly filled with mixed emotions: "I hate to see country going uptown because it's the wrong uptown. We're about to lose our identity and get all mixed up with other music. We were always a little half-assed anyway, but a music dies when it becomes a parody of itself, which has happened to some extent with rock. Of course, I had a lot to do with changing country, and I apologize. We did it to broaden the appeal, and to keep making records differ-

ent, to surprise the public."

The second major figure in the creation of the Nashville Sound was Owen Bradley. Born in rural Westmoreland, Tennessee, he moved to Nashville at age ten, where he eventually became a popular pianist and orchestra leader. He led WSM's radio orchestra from 1946 to 1956, as well as playing the usual run of society dances. Like Chet Atkins a few years later, Bradley was asked by a country A&R man to take some of the load of Nashville recording off his shoulders. The man in this case was Paul Cohen, the record company was Decca, and the year was 1947. Although producing records was far from his only (or even major) source of income, Bradley built his first studio above the Teamsters' Union in 1952 with the help of his younger brother, Harold (who by the 1970's was the dean of Nashville's studio guitarists). Comparing those days to the 1970's, Owen once said: "When I started, there were just three of us fishing from the same hole; now you can hardly find a place to drop your line!"

With his pop music background, it was no surprise when Decca's Bradley-produced records began to exhibit what was coming to be called the Nashville Sound. Although he was able to produce traditional country records by Bill Monroe, Ernest Tubb and Kitty Wells, Bradley was also responsible for the lusher sound of Brenda Lee and Patsy Cline (just as Atkins used Jim Reeves as his main Nashville Sound breakthrough artist). In fact, it is an old rumor that the country division was the only thing that pulled Decca through the lean rock years, for unlike other labels, Decca seemed unable to develop a rock or rockabilly artist like Elvis Presley or Chuck Berry or Carl Perkins. The closest they came was Buddy Holly; Bradley in fact produced Holly's first session in early 1956 (it was one of the early Quonset hut records), but the mixture of the burgeoning Nashville Sound and raw Texas rockabilly were about as compatible as STP and water, and the early

Patsy Cline

records went nowhere. Holly was dropped, only to be signed by a Decca subsidiary, Coral, where he made his brief but brilliant mark. When Cohen left Decca Records in 1958, Bradley took over all country A&R duties, eventually becoming a Decca vice president; he retired in 1975.

Where Atkins' approach was, generally speaking, characterized by fuller instrumentation—strings and horns—Bradley's tended more toward background voices, as a cursory examination of early Decca Nashville Sound hits (Jimmy Newman's "A Fallen Star" or Bobby Helms' "Jingle Bell Rock" are good examples) will show. The voices were usually provided by either The Jordanaires, the long-lived, Nashville-based quartet, or (more frequently) The Anita Kerr Singers. The Anita Kerr Singers, contracted to Decca for their own recordings, were led by Anita Kerr, herself a key contributor in the larger group of Nashville Sound creators.

Originally from Memphis, Anita's talent as a jazz pianist won her a staff job on a local radio station at the age of 14. She moved to Nashville in the late 1940's, and by 1951 had put together her acclaimed group and begun recording with Decca. Although mildly popular on record and a frequent guest on television—notably on Arthur Godfrey's show—the group made its mark in the recording studio behind other singers, where they provided the "ooooohs" and "aaaaahs" that enhanced many records of the era (and buried many others). There are few sounds as characteristically Nashville Sound as that of smooth voices set to country tunes; the close-harmony chorus is the quintessence of the "country-politan" sound. Its effects were often overused in the dawning days, the genuinely experimental early period of the Nashville Sound, but there can be no question that the use of background voices helped broaden country music's base in an era when it desperately needed all the help it could get.

The final member of this extremely important threesome—and the only non-musician among them—was Don Law, who was Columbia's distributor in the 1930's in Dallas when he met and eventually joined Art Satherley, Columbia's longtime A&R man. Satherley and Law shared both a love of traditional music and British birth. They each produced half of Columbia's country recording in 1945, Satherley cutting everything west of El Paso, Law doing all recording to the east. Upon Satherley's retirement in 1953, Law took over all country recording for Columbia until his own retirement in the middle 1960's.

Law's importance lies not only in the number of important artists he discovered and produced for Columbia—Marty Robbins and Lefty Frizzell (whom he inherited from Art Satherley), Carl Smith, Flatt and Scruggs and Johnny Cash were just a few among many—but also in the fact that he was one of the first to begin using Owen Bradley's famous studio complex (including the Quonset hut, known as "Studio B"). He found in it such an amenable atmosphere that he persuaded Columbia to purchase it when they set up a full-fledged Nashville operation in 1962. He was always more than eager to use and develop and promote the Nashville Sound—despite the wide variety of styles among his artists—and was the single most important factor in persuading Columbia to open up an office in Nashville.

The presence of these and other individuals in Nashville in the decade from 1955 to 1965 not only created the Nashville Sound, but also helped to make Nashville's music a bigger and bigger part of the pop-music whole. Certainly there was much musical activity in Nashville in 1957, but the scene didn't rival New York or Los Angeles, and showed signs of blossoming importance only to prophets. But then, through industry leaders like Chet Atkins, Owen Bradley and Don Law, Nashville developed divisional offices for major record companies, and with those offices the musical community developed national visibility and clout for what had once been a regional recording center producing records for a minority audience. It must be remembered that before the late 1950's, virtually all recording was done either in New York City or Los Angeles, or on location by traveling A&R men who returned to New York as soon as a session or series of sessions was completed. Nashville A&R men like Atkins and Bradley, who developed as assistants to traveling producers, gradually convinced New York that it didn't really understand Nashville and country music; the best technique for the large record

The Nashville Sound meets old-time picking: Patsy Cline and Jim Reeves with Grandpa Jones in the early 60's.

companies, they argued, was simply to leave the Nashville offices alone. Atkins, Bradley and Law kept cutting hits, and year by year they carved out greater independence for their respective country divisions. Nashville's profits frequently ended up in New York, but with the exception of total fiscal control, Nashville divisions possessed virtual autonomy by the middle 1960's.

It was within this business environment that country music's third generation of stars came along. If the 1920's and 1930's produced artists like Jimmie Rodgers, The Carter Family, Gene Autry and Bob Wills, then the 1940's and early 1950's can claim Eddy Arnold, Ernest Tubb, Red Foley, Hank Williams, Lefty Frizzell and Kitty Wells. From the late 1950's to the late 1960's the list would include many artists who are considered legends in the 90's. As Atkins and Law and Bradley solidified Nashville's control over its pro-

fessional destiny, they asserted their control by producing hits by Johnny Cash, Loretta Lynn, Marty Robbins, Patsy Cline, Jim Reeves, Brenda Lee and even newcomer Waylon Jennings. Other Nashville producers cut Tammy Wynette, Roger Miller, David Houston and Faron Young during those same years. The interaction of personality, business independence and artistic excellence produced an era in which Nashville gained its reputation as the place to record, and Chet Atkins, Owen Bradley and Don Law had the largest definable roles in that drama.

There were many others, of course, who contributed to the growth and development of the Nashville Sound and remained active for years: musicians like bassist Bob Moore and legendary guitarist Hank Garland; Boots Randolph, who introduced the saxophone as a solo instrument in country music; and Floyd Cramer, whose "slip note" piano style brought about a great wave of interest in country music and an appeal to what is called today the "easy listening" market. All had a share in creating the Nashville Sound.

Just as there were certain producers who effected this change, there were certain performers who symbolized it. Probably the best example was James Travis Reeves who, blessed with a rich full voice with a lulling vibrato, was the most natural artist to make the switch from hard country to the Nashville Sound. His early records like "Mexican Joe" (1953) and "Bimbo" (1954) were solid country, and songs like Jimmie Rodgers' "Waiting for a Train" were staples of his repertoire. But his 1957 hit, "Four Walls," marked the change dramatically, for it was total Nashville Sound: muted accompaniment (no wailing fiddles or crying steel guitars); cushy backup singing; soft and easy through and through. Reeves joined the cast of the network radio show *Sunday Down South* late in 1957, performing purely as a pop singer, partially out of economic necessity—the rock explosion hurt him as much as any other country singer, and both the price and the frequency of his appearances had dropped rapidly—and partly to expand both his singing style and his audience. He weathered the

Don Gibson took off with "Oh Lonesome Me."

inevitable criticisms of having "gone pop," and went on to build a new career filled with crossover hits and epitomizing the Nashville Sound.

Although her background, like Reeves', was thoroughly country, Patsy Cline's entire recording career, from "Walking After Midnight" in 1957 onward, was predicated on the Nashville Sound, and while she continued to appear on country shows as she became popular, she quickly shed her cowgirl outfits for soft sweaters. Her singing, always reminiscent (although gentler in tone) of Kay Starr's, was, like Reeves', a natural for the laid-back Nashville Sound approach. It was

smooth, full, distinctive and supple, and many of her hits exemplify the sound and style to perfection, particularly "I Fall to Pieces" (1961) and "Crazy" (1962)—the latter, incidentally, written by Willie Nelson.

Three others of the same era were also major forces in the spread of the Nashville Sound: Don Gibson, Faron Young and Hank Locklin. Gibson's early career was filled with frustration, as he was able to achieve success as a writer but made no waves as a singer. As Chet Atkins recounted earlier in this chapter, however, when Gibson cut "Oh Lonesome Me" and "I Can't Stop Loving You" for RCA in 1958, his career as a singer was assured. His unusual voice and sophisticated sense of phrasing no doubt accounted for much of his appeal, but the background over which he sang was once again the subtle instruments and full voices that typify—some might say stereotype—the Nashville Sound.

Faron Young came to the style quite another way: A hard-core honky tonk singer with a voice reminiscent of Hank Williams at the time he scored his first hits—"Goin' Steady" in 1953 and "I've Got Five Dollars and It's Saturday Night" in 1956—he metamorphosed into a smooth Nashville Sound singer (after a brief and abortive attempt at becoming a teenage heartthrob) with his classic version of "Hello Walls" (again, a Willie Nelson song), outstanding among many successful Nashville Sound records.

Although his sky-high Irish tenor didn't fit into the standard Nashville Sound mold, the musical background used on Hank Locklin's recordings did, and the combination proved an effective one in the late 1950's as he scored big with "Send Me the Pillow That You Dream On" in 1958 and "Please Help Me, I'm Falling" in 1960. Another tenor whose records were steeped in the Nashville Sound was Jimmy Newman, whose "A Fallen

Hank Locklin with The Jordanaires—Hoyt Hawkins, Neil Matthews, Locklin, Gordon Stoker and Ray Walker—in 1963.

Star" was, in 1957, one of the earliest of the heavy-handed Nashville Sound hits.

An interesting historical anomaly of the period was the rash of "epic" or "saga" songs, which appeared first in 1959 with Johnny Horton's "The Battle of New Orleans," Marty Robbins' "El Paso," Eddy Arnold's "Tennessee Stud" and The Browns' "The Three Bells" (although these were all antedated by the Kingston Trio's "Tom Dooley," which won the Grammy award as Best Country Song of the Year in 1958, the first year such a category was listed). A rash of such material—apparently country music's answer to the folk-song boom—followed. Horton, an ex-honky tonk singer, led the movement with "When It's Spring-time in Alaska" in 1959, "Sink the Bismarck" in 1960 and "North to Alaska" in 1961, before his untimely death at the height of his career in a 1960 automobile accident ("Alaska" was released

after his death). Marty Robbins' foray into the genre (with "El Paso" in 1959 and "Big Iron" in 1960, plus an album called *Gunfighter Ballads and Trail Songs*, which earned Gold record status) can now be seen as a stopping point in a remarkably diverse career that has touched upon pure hard country, rockabilly, Western, Caribbean, Hawaiian, pop and other musical styles. Other landmarks of this genre include Lefty Frizzell's "The Long Black Veil" (of which co-author Danny Dill said, "I got on a kick with Burl Ives songs—those old songs —but I didn't know any, and I had no way to find any at the time, or was too lazy to look. So I said 'I'll write me a folk song'—an instant folk song, if you will") in 1959, and Jimmy Dean's "Big Bad John" and Jim Reeves' "The Blizzard," both in 1961. Lefty's "Saginaw, Michigan" ended this cycle of saga songs, in 1964.

The saga song anomaly (and the occasional rockabilly foray like "Bye Bye Love" in 1957 and "Guess Things Happen That Way" in 1958) aside, however, the period between Elvis and Roger Miller was dominated by the Nashville Sound, and its main exponents were Jim Reeves, Patsy Cline, Don Gibson and, to a lesser extent, Faron Young and Hank Locklin. It was these artists who took the sound out of the hands of the in-studio creators and presented it to an American public obviously quite ready to receive it.

Chet Atkins, as we have seen, has apologized for his influential role in bringing the Nashville Sound's blandness to country music, but in perspective—as much, anyway, as the limited distance will allow—it is clear that country music had to do something desperate and radical to survive. For better or for worse it was the Nashville Sound that stepped in, took the lead, and brought success and prosperity where there had been confusion and failure. There were, however, distinctly negative effects of the coming of rock from which many careers would never recover, even with the help of the Nashville Sound. As Charlie Louvin said so succinctly when recalling the

Sun-era Charlie Rich: pre-"Sherrillization."

times, "We [The Louvin Brothers] had made about the first 120 dates with Elvis that he worked, but when he came along, the music changed. The people like Webb Pierce, who had 25 Number Ones, went down the drain, and there was a terrible slump in our kind of music right then, and so it did get lean. It was a living, I'll put it that way, but that's about all it was."

Similar things were happening to traditional country singers and acts throughout the business with the coming of rock. Some, like The Louvin Brothers, toughed it out; others retired. A few tried to jump on the bandwagon with results that were in a few cases fine, but were generally embarrassing. It was a terribly hard time and, for the traditional act, the advent of the Nashville

Sound was scarcely more a friend than rock; these acts appeared as antiquated and outmoded by one trend as by the other. Still, although the Nashville Sound has fallen into critical disfavor today, there is ample evidence to show that it pulled country music up by its bootstraps—although they were now patent leather and velvet pumps—during these tempestuous times.

Rock 'n' roll hurt country music in two ways. First of all, it drained country music's talent and audience as artists like Elvis, Conway Twitty, Carl Perkins, Jerry Lee Lewis and Buddy Holly—artists who in another era would have found careers in country music—abandoned country roots for rock and the lure of pop superstardom. The rock era also dragged American popular music toward the black, Afro-American tradition of city blues. For the period between 1957 and 1967, it is fair to argue that mainstream pop music did little more than rework and extend the city blues developed in the late 1940's. With the appearance of Elvis Presley, popular music moved into a flirtation with the black musical tradition unlike that of any other period since the 1930's, when the popularity of jazz linked Harlem and South Chicago with the popular music scene. Meanwhile, Nashville and country music groped for an antidote to the deadly poison that rock 'n' roll was to them. Some industry leaders argued that country music should retreat into a minority role, serving fans in the South and in a few urban centers, that its performers should play one-night stands for a few hundred dollars and call any record that sold more than 5,000 copies a hit. Another route away from oblivion found greater impact: Take the talent of Nashville's soloists and sidemen, bring in large doses of pop music style (pop music of the Perry Como/Jo Stafford variety, that is), and compete head-to-head with rock for a portion of the popular market; try to sell country records to individuals who

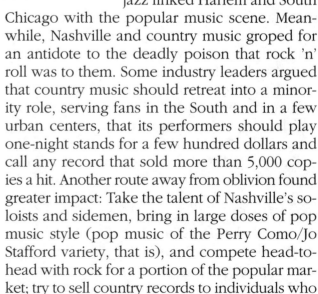

*A much later
Charlie Rich.*

Tammy Wynette

longed for the bland approach to recording taken by popular music in the early and middle 1950's. This survival tactic was pioneered by the leaders of the Nashville music scene in the Nashville Sound era.

As the 1960's dawned, the effects were taking hold. Where country music had occasionally reached into the pop market, now the term "crossover" was being invented to describe the success in the pop field of a country record such as Jim Reeves' "He'll Have to Go" in 1960, or the concomitant phenomenon of a pop record selling strongly in the country market, as with Connie Francis' "Everybody's Somebody's Fool" (of the same year), a Number One pop record recorded in Nashville (by Danny Davis, long before his Nashville Brass days) with country musicians, with a country feel, and with the Nashville Sound.

There occurred a palpable quickening of the pulse of this once-moribund city with the rapid success of the Nashville Sound and the acceptance of country music by the outside world. The Nashville Sound quickly became the sound of country music—not exclusively, of course, but in the public eye—for everybody is eager to jump on a winner's bandwagon, particularly in an era of heavy losers. Nashville Sound-alike records began to pour out of Music City, and the league of session musicians expanded to two, then three, then four teams as studios proliferated like rabbits, and every label large or small grabbed a piece of the Nashville Sound action.

In addition to the forces already explored, there were a number of other, independent factors that played a part in the success of the Nashville Sound. All of them seem to point to the ironic fact that at the very time when it looked like there was to be almost no future at all, country music's day was dawning.

As we've seen, the Nashville Sound broadened the audience for country music by making it acceptable to new ears. In addition, the term itself gave journalists and critics something tangible with which to explain the strange and rapid growth throughout the course of the 1960's of what had so recently been called "hillbilly music." The term was short, catchy, and gave

the impression of saying so much about country music, while actually being quite adaptable to any meaning the writer cared to give it. Phrases like this have a snowballing effect: The more they are used, the more they tend to be used, and it didn't take long before country music and the Nashville Sound became synonymous terms to much of the American public. It was not because country music had become a monochrome music—it clearly had not, for the California sound and the rebirth of bluegrass both occurred at about this time—but simply because the phrase had become so handy, so convenient, so popular. With the phrase so apparently meaningful

The couple of the decade: George Jones and Tammy Wynette.

and so readily at hand, it can be no surprise that Paul Hemphill's interpretive look at Nashville—the book which stood alone for over five years—was entitled simply *The Nashville Sound*. In addition, the term gave direction to an industry plagued by vagueness and indirection and generated excitement, enthusiasm and even pride, a sense of creativity and willingness to help each other, and a bit of the joy of victory and the smell of success: intangible but important assets in the propagation of a sound and an image.

As to the sound itself, the slicker it got, the more it filled a gap. The rock onslaught had left a vacuum in the easy-listening middle of American pop music—Elvis hit New York and Los Angeles just as hard as he hit Nashville—and it was into this space that Nashville ventured. Certain segments of the public wanted

Tammy Wynette and Billy Sherrill: He discovered her, produced her and was her principal songwriting partner.

a smooth, bland, easily listenable and most of all soothing type of music, and Nashville supplied just that. The tunes were catchy, the pace was slowed to an unthreatening crawl, the rough edges were knocked off and polished to a high gloss, and the music offered enough mildly interesting elements to please without placing any demands on the listener. If this was not exactly an artistic breakthrough—it has been compared to the innovation brought about by $20 original oil paintings in the 1970's—it was certainly a broadening of the market. In commercial terms, it did not hurt the country music that broke out of it—the Outlaws, Western swing revivalists, rockabillies and honky tonk singers of the 1970's—at all, for by the time they revolted against the Nashville Sound's excesses, the Nashville Sound had built an impressive distribution machine that awaited their use. It is interesting to

note, in fact, that the Nashville music business turned to the Outlaws in the 1970's for the same kind of reason it turned to Chet Atkins and his methods in the 1950's: a larger market for the music and a bigger share of the bucks.

As an approach to recording, the Nashville Sound remains strong despite the effects of its excesses and the howls of its detractors. Pound for pound, Nashville sidemen tend to create more quickly, more easily and with less emotional strain on one another than sidemen in any other recording environment, and so Nashville remains the place to record those musical styles and forms that don't require complex written charts. Today that includes almost everything but symphonies, Broadway musicals and grand opera. Nashville became a national recording center because its musicians were flexible, and it remains so today for the same reason. During the peak years of the Nashville Sound, the marketing motives of Nashville's music business executives created a situation in which the pickers' talents were sorely underutilized, but the commercial success of their records did at least provide work where before there was none and made the existence of a recording community possible. Thus when more "gutsy" music proved to be more commercial yet than the Nashville Sound style, the pickers were already assembled—as were the studios, publishing houses, and record company setups. Today many forms of work are available in Nashville—the opportunity to pursue one's own art exists, but there is also more on-demand, commercial-type work than a flexible professional musician can handle, and the method of recording that generated the Nashville Sound is still alive and kicking; Nashville produces more cheap, easy, country-flavored pop and commercial music than ever.

The Nashville Sound came in for a lot of criticism during the 1970's, when the pendulum of musical style swung away from suburban "sophistication," and even today a lot of critics frown upon it from a distance. It's easy to see why: its excesses often came close to ruining otherwise fine, energetic, moving performances, and made a mockery of more than one usually distinctive, emotive singer.

Cover art for Tammy's Stand By Your Man album.

Chet Atkins may have felt that he had to apologize in this context, but the fact remains that he and Owen Bradley and Anita Kerr and the rest of the Nashville Sound's architects saved country music (all of it) from obscurity and maybe even oblivion. They kept Nashville working, thereby ensuring that when the time for greater expansion arrived, Nashville's artists, pickers and businessmen would still be there to take advantage of it.

Something like the same could be said for another important figure who has received his fair share of abuse down the years (but has never felt the need to apologize): Billy Sherrill, the hugely successful producer whose style, if it weren't already called "The Billy Sherrill Sound" would have to be called "Son of Nashville Sound." For while Sherrill's techniques and values were far different from those of Atkins or Bradley, he had very much the same aim in mind: to pull Nashville music into the middle of the road and sell it to pop fans.

Sherrill arrived in Nashville in the early 1960's, coming from an Alabama background of gospel music (his parents were evangelists, and the young Billy played piano for their meetings) and honky tonk dance bands. He got his apprenticeship with Sam Phillips, the founder of Sun Records and developer of rockabilly and one of the pioneer crossover producers, and learned a lot from him, attitudes as well as techniques. Moving to Epic Records, Sherrill produced a wide variety of music from the bluegrass of Jim and Jesse to the black gospel of The Staples Singers, and in 1966 he scored his first major success: David Houston's recording of "Almost Persuaded," a song Sherrill had written with Glen Sutton, which went to the top of the country charts and won a Grammy as Best Country & Western Recording. After that came an enviable string of hit singles and albums, and within a year Sherrill was recognized as one of the most successful and innovative producers in Nashville. Soon he was producing artists like Tammy Wynette, Charlie Rich, Tanya Tucker, Johnny Paycheck and Barbara Fairchild, and winning wide exposure to a pop audience for many of them.

It's difficult, though, to really identify any formula for Sherrill's middle-of-the-road music. He himself admitted that his approach was in part to buck the traditional Nashville Sound formula: "The Nashville Sound in my opinion is what you get when you turn the session over to the musicians. In order to really sell," he insisted, "a record has to be different rather than pretty." Some characteristics, however, mark Sherrill as different from the Nashville producers around him. He was, for instance, oriented toward the hit single rather than the album. He tried to make a hit single every time he turned the tape on: "That's the baby," he said. "That's it. Hit singles are the best concept for albums in the world."

Therefore, he saw the song as quite often more important than the singer— "Finding the right song is the rough part of the record business. Recording is just the gravy." He'd even hold off on recording a hot young prospect until he'd found him, or her, precisely the right song, and he felt that original material was an integral part of any major success. When an artist came into his office, he said, "the first thing that comes into my mind is, 'Do you have a source of material? Are you a writer? Do you have a friend that writes?'"

Original material had at one time been a vital element in country stardom, but in the late 1960's it wasn't regarded as a crucial

Billy Sherrill and the harvest of Gold.

factor. According to the philosophy then current, an established singer would sell a limited but steady number of albums solely on the basis of his personality and fan appeal. Sherrill realized the shortcomings of that approach in the more fickle but much more lucrative pop market, and acted accordingly.

He was pragmatic about what it took to break into the pop market. He had no idealism about maintaining the purity of the country tradition. "Nobody can ever put down Hank Williams and Hank Snow and Ernest Tubb. But to say we can't broaden the appeal is ludicrous,

ridiculous," he once said. "I think people [can] learn how to write better country songs.... I don't think we'll lose our identity. I think our identity will grow with people that can do something with a wider range of lyrics, melodies and instruments. It doesn't necessarily have to be two guitars and a banjo. I don't think you're losing anything, I think you're gaining something."

The "wider range" embraced in Sherrill's recordings included, on occasion, elaborate orchestrations, overdubbing of vocal effects and background harmonies, and the use of horns and piano stylings. With those kind of arrangements he created a distinctive aural image for his artists—bland, easygoing, easy-listening music— but at the same time, the songs he chose (and often wrote or co-wrote) dealt with the powerful, traditional country themes of lost love, loneliness, cheatin', and found love. A closer look at the way Sherrill developed his three major artists—Charlie Rich, Tammy Wynette and Tanya Tucker—reveals more of his philosophy, and more of the nature of his "new" Nashville Sound.

Perhaps the most spectacular of Sherrill's successes was the elevation to stardom of a middle-aged, silver-haired Arkansas singer named Charlie Rich. In the mid-1970's Rich absolutely dominated the country recording field, producing an astonishing string of "crossover" hits, among them "Behind Closed Doors," selling over three million; "The Most Beautiful Girl," with sales over two million, and "A Very Special Love Song," selling nearly one million. In October of 1974, when Rich was voted Entertainer of the Year by the Country Music Association, his album containing "Behind Closed Doors" had been on the charts

Tanya Tucker

Part of Decca's all-star lineup in 1970: Doyle Wilburn, Loretta Lynn, Conway Twitty, Jan Howard, Bill Anderson, Peggy Sue (Loretta's sister) and her husband, Sonny Wright. The duets between Loretta and Conway lay just ahead.

for 79 weeks—far longer than any other country album of its day. In fact, according to the 1974 *Billboard* survey, Rich led all country artists in sales, with five singles and six albums on the charts, a feat accomplished in spite of the fact that Rich's new recordings with Sherrill were meeting competition from six other labels reissuing old Rich material. The year 1975 saw Rich's hit album, *Every Time You Touch Me (I Get High)*, and his winning a string of *Billboard* awards for Best Male Vocalist, Best Male Singles Artist, Best Album Artist and others. These awards were, of course, in the "country" category, but his songs were also appearing routinely on pop charts. And significantly, Rich himself was still reluctant to describe himself as a country singer.

His reluctance was probably due to the fact that he was selling records to a popular, easy-listening audience, while he himself came from a rich and eclectic musical background. Before he met Sherrill, he had spent some 20 years managing to survive as a pianist, singer and songwriter. Much of that time was spent in northwestern Arkansas, where he'd grown up listening to the blues played by black sharecroppers on his father's plantation; the blues and jazz in his piano playing and singing had deep roots. In the 1950's he was involved in the Sun Records scene with Sam Phillips in Memphis, and always seemed on the verge of great success; everyone from Sam Phillips himself to Bob Dylan predicted it for him. But major success didn't come. He moved to Nashville and became known as a fine piano player, a blues-styled singer, and a writer of songs like "Lonely Weekends," "Sittin' and Thinkin'" and "Who Will the Next Fool Be?"

Sherrill produced Rich's hit, "Behind Closed Doors," in 1973, and the crossover sales began. The Sherrill treatment for Rich was typical of his method: a basic, simple country lament cushioned on elaborate orchestral arrangements, overdubbing and background vocals. It had worked earlier for singers like Jim Reeves, and it worked for Rich: He became "The Silver Fox," a packaged, middle-of-the road commodity. That upset some of Rich's earlier fans, including his wife, who had enjoyed his funky gospel-jazz-blues-swing-rockabilly style, and it also upset some country purists when the CMA named him Entertainer of the Year in 1974—he was now too slick, too commercial. The same people were upset with him the next year when he set fire to the winner's envelope as he was announcing that year's CMA Awards winner—then he was too gauche, not slick enough, a rebel.

Rich seemed upset with the blandness of the Sherrill sound, and yet a prisoner of it: It made him the leading Nashville-based singer of the mid-1970's. He became a fixture at the Las Vegas Hilton and was one of the few country singers able to command as much in performance fees as the leading pop acts.

Sherrill had already perfected the middle-of-the-road formula he used with Rich some five or six years earlier when he began marketing the sound of Mississippi-born Tammy Wynette. Unlike Rich, who had already established a musical identity on which Sherrill had to impose a new image, Tammy Wynette was a product (some would say a victim) of Sherrill's packaging technique almost from the beginning of her career. She had been turned down by four labels before Sherrill found her, but as soon as he did, her career took off, beginning with "Apartment #9" in August of 1966, and her records began crossing over into the pop charts. In 1967 she had one of country music's Top Five hits in "I Don't Wanna Play House," and the next year she had two of the Top Five in "D-I-V-O-R-C-E" and "Stand By Your Man" (which sold over two mil-

lion copies, and might well be the largest-selling single by any woman country singer).

The image Sherrill imposed on Tammy Wynette was one of a slightly masochistic *hausfrau*, a woman content with being a suffering, dominated, middle-class housewife. Such an image is nothing new to country music; at that point it had been a given for 20 years. The songs that sold millions for Tammy showed little or no consciousness of the sexual revolution; divorce was something to be dreaded and avoided at all costs—for the children's sake. You stood by your man, even if you had to endure the archaic Southern double standard of morality, and having a good man was much more important than any vague notion of self-fulfillment. Tammy accentuated this image of passivity by recording successful romantic duets with David Houston ("My Elusive Dreams") and later with George Jones, one of the "purest" male country singers. She married Jones in 1968, and Sherrill produced a series of George-and-Tammy duet albums that rank among the best country duet recordings ever. Even after the marriage broke up, Tammy continued to try to work with him

In spite of the fact that her image ran counter to prevailing trends in feminism (or maybe because of it), Tammy continued to be successful. It's doubtful, though, that a common perception of the day—that her success was based on her championship of a female "silent majority"—really held water. Tammy was after all a very intelligent, adaptable singer who worked well with Sherrill's elaborate approach to recording ("I can sing Tammy Wynette a song, and she'll sing it right back to me," said Sherrill admiringly), so her finished material was usually a cut above the rest; she and Sherrill made some pretty hot records together, regardless of their sociopolitical content. Then too, Tammy simply had a wonderful voice, with a sound and a power all its own—one critic's assessment, that she sounded like a cross between Doris Day and Patti Page, conveyed her appeal as a pop singer quite well, though it fell short of doing her justice. She would have had considerable appeal singing (as the old quip goes) the Nashville phone book.

Image was a crucial factor in the career of

Hotbed of songwriters—and, soon, rebellion—Tootsie's Orchid Lounge. Performers from the Ryman dropped in between sets.

one of Sherrill's later successes, Tanya Tucker. Where Charlie Rich and Tammy Wynette were both mature performers when they worked with Sherrill, Tanya Tucker began her career with him as a 13-year-old prodigy in 1972. Born in Texas, Tanya spent her early life moving around to various Western towns while her father, Beau Tucker, tried to get both her and her sister, LaCosta, started on singing careers. After a couple of years struggling along trying to get auditions, doing demos, singing for amateur talent shows and doing a brief stint on Judy Lynn's show, Beau and Tanya finally got some home tapes to Sherrill. Sherrill was impressed with Tanya's voice and flew to Las Vegas, where he signed her on the spot, planning to record her as soon as the right song was found.

He soon found it: Alex Harvey's "Delta Dawn." Within a month after signing Sherrill's contract, Tanya was recording the song for Columbia, backed by the full Sherrill studio

treatment. The song was an immense hit, as usual on both country and pop charts, and by 1973 Tanya found herself on the Opry, touring widely (sometimes with another successful young singer, Johnny Rodriguez), and being a nominee for two Grammy Awards, one for "Delta Dawn" and one for Female Country Singer of the Year. Tanya turned 15 in 1973.

If Tanya was "packaged" by Sherrill, it wasn't exactly clear which audience she was aimed at. Her youth obviously gave her a certain appeal to the teenaged market, and *Rolling Stone* lavished a cover story on her, yet there is also evidence that she appealed in a Lolita-like way to older male country fans, especially in the West, where her tours were so successful. On tours she often dressed in skin-tight pants suits and used stage movements that owed more to Mick Jagger than to country tradition. Songs like "Would You Lay With Me (In a Field of Stone)" had lyrics more suggestive than many sung by artists like Tammy Wynette.

Tanya herself seemed oblivious to that particular aspect of her success. "When Billy Sherrill heard my demo tapes, he heard my *sound*," she once said. "Everybody says I sound older and look older than I really am, but I think being 14 was really an advantage. People hear my records and then see me. It's hard for them to believe."

Sherrill emphasized another facet of the Tucker image: the quality of the songs: "You find a basic country station somewhere, and it'll put you to sleep.... That's why Tanya Tucker exploded. She had a unique voice and we did some blood-curdling songs. Somebody got killed in every record we did. I don't think anybody got killed in 'Would You Lay with Me,' but there was blood somewhere."

Possibly because of this confusion about what Tanya's most appealing (and most marketable) quality was, Sherrill and she parted ways in 1974, before he had been able to establish her securely in either the pop or the country field. At the time, the notion that Tanya's future success would lie in that very fact—that she wasn't typecast into one category or another—seemed entirely credible. As it happened, she went on to try hard, but unsuccessfully, for a career in rock before settling in as a mainstream, but never dull, country singer in the late 1980's.

Sherrill and the producers who emulated him showed that country hits could become cross-over hits. Earlier in the game, Nashville had seen country hits become pop hits when rerecorded by pop artists, but Sherrill's recording style was able to embrace both markets with the same original record, and that implied a change in the economic philosophy that had governed the Nashville studios for years.

One of the reasons behind the birth of the original Nashville Sound was the holding down of studio costs; a large company, looking at the limited sales potential of a strictly country record, was reluctant to invest a lot of time, effort, and money in albums. Thus a technique was born whereby an artist went into a studio with five or six good musicians and hacked out an album. But Sherrill and his followers realized that to reach a pop audience, more care and expense would have to be given to production; he did that, and he showed that sales of artists like Rich in the larger pop market fully justified the added expense. For Nashville, that was a very long, significant step.

After his prime in the late 1960's and early 70's, Sherrill was relatively inactive in the boom times of the 80's and 90's. The influence of his work was everywhere, though, as were the precepts of the Nashville Sound recording method. In fact, those two approaches had fused into a winning combination: a pool of expert, intuitive musicians able to create and adapt arrangements in the studio, plus all the high-tech, big-budget tricks with which to reach the pop market. So the story of the Nashville Sound ends in a happy irony—what had begun as a hard-times survival tactic ended up making Nashville the busiest recording center in the world.

Buck Owens

CHAPTER 10

The Slumbering Giant

During the 1960's, a decade which saw popular music dominated by Englishmen, country music was a slumbering giant. The studios of Nashville stayed busy with the Nashville Sound and its refinements, and the city's producers, engineers and session musicians honed skills that would become highly prized. And if the explosion of rock 'n' roll in the 50's had made instant anachronisms of Webb Pierce, Kitty Wells and Gene Autry, it hadn't killed country music completely; it had simply forced the forging of new paths, the development of new sounds and the creation of a new generation of stars.

Billy Sherrill's stable of winners, beginning in 1966 with David Houston ("Almost Persuaded") and continuing into the 1970's with Tammy Wynette, George Jones, Charlie Rich, Tanya Tucker and others, was one major source of new directions, but there were others just as productive.

One was Bakersfield, California. The end of the line for thousands of country people displaced during the Dust Bowl and Depression years—*Grapes of Wrath* folks—it was the reality they'd found in place of California's Garden of Eden image: a land where the only gold at the end of the rainbow was the fertile earth of the San Joaquin Valley, and the only way to turn it into food, shelter and clothing was backbreaking work. Conditions for the migrants, who went to work (when they could get it) alongside blacks and Mexicans as stoop labor for the established farmers who owned the land, were as hard as it gets this side of widespread starvation, and the music which is actually about their lives, from Woody Guthrie's songs of class struggle to Merle Haggard's unflinchingly bleak memoirs of his own family's deprivation—his mother's "Hungry Eyes," for instance—still rings today with pain and strife. This is not nostalgic music; no yearnings for the good old days in *these* songs.

The music in the fields and bars of Bakersfield, however, was designed to provide relief, not reflection. As Buck Owens put it, "I think we made music so much to avoid dealing with the reality of how hard we worked, and how little we got paid for it." The music began in the voices of workers in the fields (Owens remembers picking cotton in a shifting weave of his own folks' gospel, the blacks' blues and "those beautiful Mexican harmonies"); was added to by whatever styles came over the radio, from Bob Wills to Hank Williams to Bing Crosby to Chuck Berry; and ended up in the bars, where what worked was developed further and what died a death got dropped.

Generally, Bakersfield music had an energy lacking in much Nashville product of the era; it was, after all, born of trial and error in live performance for working people, not conceived as

In the 60's, Bakersfield held country music's future. In the 90's, its signature arch still spanned one of the old main drags.

competition for middle-class pop music. Owens described his version of what worked in the clubs: "It was a plain old drivin' country sound with a hell of a beat and a bunch of twangy guitars and a couple of old boys like Don Rich and me singin'—no pretenses, no bullshit, just plain music. It begins with a four-beat bass, a heavy shuffle with a heavy afterbeat, kinda reminds me of a runaway locomotive."

He said his biggest influence was Bob Wills. "Then I go back to 'Skinny Minnie,' 'Bony Maronie,' 'Jenny Jenny' and 'Good Golly, Miss Molly'—all those Little Richard songs—'Tutti Frutti' and Fats Domino, Elvis Presley and Chuck Berry...Eddie Cochran. Eddie Cochran, in fact, used to come into the Black Board when he came through town, and I even played a couple of dates with Gene Vincent. I used to do a lot of rock at the Black Board, anyway, so the rhythm came natural to me. I felt it."

The Black Board, one of Bakersfield's many night spots, was Buck's main training ground. He got a job there playing guitar with Bill Woods' Orange Blossom Playboys, and that's what turned him into a singer; he didn't want to step out front,

but one night he had to, or lose his spot in the band altogether, when the regular vocalist didn't show up. Folks liked his singing a lot, and that was that. A recording contract with Capitol resulted from his work playing guitar on other artists' sessions (notably those of Tommy Collins, for whom he also worked club dates). Nothing much in the way of success ensued at Capitol, however, and Buck took a job as a DJ in Tacoma, Washington. But in the fall of 1959 his recording of "Under Your Spell Again" hit big, and he moved back to Bakersfield, playing the clubs and traveling to Hollywood to record.

"Under Your Spell Again" was a significant record, putting a real kick into the country scene of the early 60's. "I'd always been criticized because I used too many drums on my records," Buck recalled in later years, "but when this one broke it changed a lot of people's minds. I think I always felt more beat than the country music people who grew up in the East. I mean, I was influenced by all the greats, but I never played the schools and the churches and those type of affairs where people sit down. From Arizona to Bakersfield, I played dances in VFW halls, and barrooms and clubs."

That first hit was the beginning of a fabulous string of successes, from "Love's Gonna Live Here" and "Together Again" in the early 60's to "Roll in My Sweet Baby's Arms" and "Made in Japan" in the early 70's. In the 60's he had no fewer than 26 straight Number One country hits.

He continued to live in Bakersfield all that time, resisting early suggestions that he join the gang in Nashville and being quite frank that such a move was anathema to him; as he said later, he had no desire whatsoever to "play their silly games." Something of a rift developed between him and the Nashville establishment. "They'd told me at the start that I'd never amount to anything if I didn't live in Nashville, and here I was the biggest thing in country music. For years I owned the country charts, and I lived in Bakersfield. I never missed a chance to hold that up to them, and they didn't like it one bit."

Owens was a shrewd businessman, and also one of those sons of the Depression motivated by a deep desire to never, ever experience poverty again. By the late 60's he had built himself quite a business empire: a recording studio, a TV production company, real estate and radio stations, and a booking agency and management company through which he soon controlled most of the music business in Bakersfield. He was a very rich man, and largely due to his efforts, the town began to acquire the status of a "Nashville West." Journalists in search of an angle began suggesting that therein might lie the future of country music.

It was not to be. In 1968 he embarked on his career as co-host, with Roy Clark, of *Hee Haw*, an institution he once characterized as "a show of fat old men and young pretty girls," and he suffered the consequences. As he put it, "TV did the same for me that it did for other people who were on it weekly, starting with Perry Como. When he got on weekly television, his record sales went away. Television is the quintessential bare bones of what you are. All mystery is removed." His last Number One (until Dwight Yoakam and he took "Streets of Bakersfield" to the top in 1988) was "Made in Japan" in 1972.

What really sank Buck's musical career, though, was the death of Don Rich, his lead guitarist, harmony singer and longtime friend, in a motorcycle accident. Buck told *Country Music* that "Don worked with me when he was a sophomore in high school, and 16 years later he was still with me. When he was killed in 1974, all the heart went out of me. I just never got it together after that.... I used to think a nervous breakdown was where a guy goes whacko and

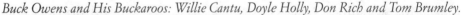

Buck Owens and His Buckaroos: Willie Cantu, Doyle Holly, Don Rich and Tom Brumley.

In the studio with Buck Owens, Jelly Sanders, Lewis Talley and Tommy Collins.

energy of swing and rockabilly music into mainstream country, *and* he had an enormous influence on the course of pop and rock music in his time. His songs ("Crying Time," for instance) were recorded by dozens of pop, rock, R&B and middle-of-the-road singers, and he figured, along with Chuck Berry and Carl Perkins, as a primary influence on The Beatles. And until the Outlaws successfully challenged Nashville's "country-politan" imperative in the 70's, it was Buck's California stronghold (and to a lesser extent, Cash's fortress of integrity in Tennessee) that kept country music more or less honest—even though he did record songs like "Bridge Over Troubled Water" and crossed over into the pop charts with some regularity.

When Owens was coming up in the bars of Bakersfield, there were already some indigenous recording stars. Missourian Wynn Stewart, whose career began in 1950 on Hollywood's Intro label, was one. He ended up on Capitol in 1954 with his first hit, "Waltz of the Angels," and, after a move to Las Vegas and a string of duets with Jan Howard, got into the national Top Ten with "Wishful Thinking" in 1960. He kept on keeping on through the 60's and 70's, scoring a Number One country hit in 1967 with "It's Such a Pretty World To-

they have to come and drag him off in a straitjacket, but that ain't necessarily it. I was just confused for a long, long time...looking in a lot of places for something that I'd lost."

Buck quit recording in 1979 and touring in 1980, and retreated into retirement. That is where young Dwight Yoakam confronted him in 1987 and somehow inspired him to take to the stage and even the recording studio again—and so in the late 80's and early 90's, Buck Owens was making albums just as vital (though nowhere near as commercially successful) as his 60's work.

It's difficult to overstate the importance of Buck Owens. His influence, though routinely under-credited by writers on country music—a clear case of Nashville boosterism at work—was enormous. He was after all the biggest country star of the 60's (with the possible exception of Johnny Cash), and he was the musician who finally and forever wove the

Wynn Stewart

day." Although he was never a star of Buck Owens' magnitude (nobody was), Stewart was a strong presence on the California country scene for three decades.

Tommy Collins was a hot item, too, one of the hardest-driving performers and most talented writers on the scene; Merle Haggard has always credited him as his songwriting mentor. His recording of "You Better Not Do That" (on which young Buck

Owens played guitar, replacing Ferlin Husky in producer Ken Nelson's session band) sold half a million copies in 1954, and was followed by several more national hits. But in 1956 Collins, born Leonard Sipes in Oklahoma, scuppered his career in the big time by entering the Golden Gate Theological Seminary in Oakland, from which he graduated in due course and worked in the ministry, as well as continuing to record a mixture of sacred and secular material for Capitol (and selling shoes and driving an oil delivery truck) until seeing a different kind of light. He tried to get a recording career going again in the early 60's, but never matched the commercial success he'd had a decade earlier, and blew it all with alcohol and pills. (He sobered up eventually, inspiring Merle Haggard to write "Leonard" about him in 1980.)

Collins was one of a core of California pickers, writers and singers who shared friendships, band jobs, session work, songs and stages at various points through the 50's, 60's and 70's. Collins, Owens, Haggard and Ferlin Husky all played on each others' records at one time or another, and all manner of musical relationships connected them with stars-in-their-own-right like

guitarists Roy Nichols and Lewis Talley, steel virtuoso Ralph Mooney, fiddler Tommy Williams, songwriter Dallas Frazier, picker/label owner Fuzzy Owen, and of course Buckaroos Don Rich (gui-

Bonnie Owens

tar), Tom Brumley (steel) and Doyle Holly (bass). Rose Maddox, who, as well as her own recordings, made a series of hot duets with Buck Owens in the early 60's, was another regular on the scene. So, in the early 50's anyway, was singer/ bass player Jean Shepard, whose family lived near Bakersfield, and whose early career featured successful duets with Ferlin Husky. Shepard joined the Opry in 1956, though, and based her long career in Nashville; she married Hawkshaw Hawkins and was widowed by the plane crash that killed him, Cowboy Copas and Patsy Cline in 1963. Both Shepard, who remains an Opry member today, and Maddox continue to perform into the 90's. Freddie Hart became a fixture on the California country scene in the mid-50's after a time in Nashville during which he played in Lefty Frizzell's band, and he recorded consistently, though without any great commercial success, until his cut of "Easy Loving" established him as a crooner of super-sentimental chart-toppers. His string of hits continued into the mid-70's.

Bonnie Owens, born Bonnie Campbell in Oklahoma, was a longer-term fixture on the Bakersfield scene. First married to Buck Owens (they'd met in a band called Mac's Skillet Lickers and tied the knot in 1948), she started her own professional singing career on the *Cousin Herb*

Members of the Bakersfield music community: clockwise, Jean Shepard, Bill Woods, Johnny Cuviello, Fuzzy Owen, Jelly Sanders, Lewis Talley and Gene Breeden.

Hensen's Trading Post TV show, and by the early 60's had won a recording contract with Marvel Records. Divorced from Owens, she fell in with Merle Haggard, whom she married in 1965, and with whom she worked as both a featured singer on his road show and a duet recording partner. The pair were voted Best Vocal Duo of 1965, '66, and '67 by the West Coast-based Academy of Country & Western (now just Country) Music, Owens herself being chosen as Top Female Vocalist in '65. She went on working with Merle, even after their divorce in the 70's.

Susan Raye, from Oregon, was another singer to find her way into country recording via Bakersfield. She first toured with Buck Owens in 1965, then returned to the Owens fold in '68 after a hiatus in Oregon, and went on to a featured spot on *Hee Haw*, duet recordings with Buck, and her own solo career in the country charts during the early and mid-70's.

The name that keeps cropping up, Merle Haggard, was of course the second great star to come out of Bakersfield—in his case literally, for unlike the Texan Owens, Haggard was actually born there (in a converted railroad refrigerator car alongside the Southern Pacific tracks in nearby Oildale).

Haggard's father, who after a long, hard struggle had finally found a steady job with the Santa Fe Railroad, died when Merle was just nine, and the familiar saga of Merle's troubled youth began: running away from home and school, committing petty and not-so-petty crimes, and winding up in San Quentin, "turning 21 in prison."

Merle as a teenager and, later, after he taught himself to play fiddle for his 1970 tribute album to Bob Wills.

He stayed there for two years and nine months, until 1960, but he learned a trade: music. When he got out he headed straight back to Bakersfield, and soon he was earning his keep as a sideman in a variety of bands, among them Wynn Stewart's. His break into recording came after he'd met Bonnie Owens, and the two had signed with the Tally label. Then Capitol bought Tally, and Merle was on a national label. His first hit was a Liz Anderson song, "(My Friends Are Gonna Be) Strangers," in 1965; his first country chart-topper was his own "I'm a Lonesome Fugitive" in 1967.

Haggard and Owens were two very different characters and artists: Owens the extroverted, high-energy, crowd-oriented entertainer, Haggard the introvert and country blues man; once he developed his own style, his work was intensely personal, at that time the most autobiographically inspired body of songs in country music. Like Owens, though, he put together a great band with whom he recorded as well as took on the road (by no means the norm in country music then or now), and he kept his home and most of his business out West. The early version of his band, The Strangers (named after Liz Anderson's song), featured Roy Nichols and James Burton alternating on lead guitar, Glen Campbell on rhythm and harmony vocals, Glen D. Hardin on piano, and Ralph Mooney on steel—as fine a country band as was ever assembled. Their sound was subtle, almost folkish; Merle was moving away from the Bakersfield norm of hard-driving rhythms, screaming steels and Leo Fender's Tele-

Merle Haggard

*Johnny Cash outside
Folsom Prison, 1968.*

casters turned up and tuned high.

The style he developed owed a great deal to Lefty Frizzell, and the influence of his other musical masters, mostly Jimmie Rodgers, Bob Wills and Bing Crosby, was readily apparent; Merle, however, had such charisma that from the start he seemed like a master in his own right. His authority was enhanced, and his identity established far beyond the world of country fans, by "Okie from Muskogee," the infamous hippie-baiting song he claimed to have written as a joke; from that point on he was, if not the musical spokesman for Spiro Agnew's "Silent Majority" (a role he never embraced), at least America's primary poet of the working man. *That* was a job he could sink his teeth into, and he did; he could usually be counted on to deliver tough little doses of blue-collar reality all the way through the 70's and most of the 80's, even if he could never be relied upon to keep his messages simple. For instance, right after he followed "Okie" with the similarly belligerent "Fightin' Side of Me," he wrote and recorded "Irma Jackson," a sympathetic song about an interracial love affair. (Naturally, Capitol refused to release it. People might have gotten confused.) As John Morthland, with his usual astuteness, once observed of Merle, "He thrives on disorganization, and much of what's been interpreted as his 'politics' is really his simple refusal to be pinned down. Try to pin him and he'll slip away faster than a steel player and a guitarist can trade eight bars."

The role of sociopolitical lightning rod occupied just part of Haggard's range as a writer, however, and down the years he was responsible for some of country's greatest drinking, cheating, heartbroken, lonely, wistful, regretful and nostalgic songs; often complex and surprising works, but immediately recognizable as examples of classic country form, and always emotionally accurate.

Stylistically, his music took a twist in 1970 when he recorded *A Tribute to the Best Damn Fiddle Player in the World*, his Bob Wills album,

and started playing a lot of Western swing in concert (he'd taught himself fiddle especially for the album, and he added two former Texas Playboys, guitarist Eldon Shamblin and electric mandolinist Tiny Moore, to The Strangers). As his range expanded, and he and the band got the hang of the new style, his shows edged further toward something very close to country perfection. The legend of Merle and The Strangers, a unit able to kick into virtually any song in Merle's repertoire at a second's notice and play it through flawlessly, including improvised solos, got started.

Cash, Luther Perkins, W.S. "Fluke" Holland and Carl Perkins inside Folsom.

However, his records through most of the 70's weren't nearly as inspiring as his earlier work, though all that changed in 1979 with *Serving 190 Proof*, as bleakly beautiful a treatment of middle-aged alienation as has ever been created.

Right after that, in 1980, he made *Rainbow Stew/Live at Anaheim Stadium*, certainly the best of his concert performances on record and arguably the best of anyone's. But then his work faltered again. While his concerts remained first rate, his recordings tailed off, with only occasional tracks, like "Out Among the Stars," as strong as his best. Perhaps he was in a creative doldrum; perhaps the business, changing around him, was too constricting; whatever the reason, the turn of the decade from the 80's to the 90's found

Country on TV: Bob Dylan and Johnny Cash on The Johnny Cash Show in 1969. Cash, June Carter and Roy Clark on Cash's Christmas Special in 1977.

Sun I would be limited in what I could do, where with a major company I could do all that and reach more people with my music. I think I was right, too. Sam Phillips couldn't understand it back then, we had a little misunderstanding at the time, he couldn't see me wanting to go to another record company—but I could." Any doubts lingering in his mind were dispelled immediately: His first Columbia single, "Don't Take Your Guns to Town," was an instant hit, and his first album, *The Fabulous Johnny Cash*, sold over 400,000 copies.

Cash's career with Columbia, 28 years of it, went all over the musical map, for Cash was an artist of exceptional restlessness, creative ambition and curiosity. He loved the broad sweep, the grand vision, and time after time he harnessed his prodigious energies to some great concept, studying and shaping his subject matter—Native American social reality, the lore of the railroad, the mystique of the Western outlaw, the stories of Jesus and John the Baptist—and, more often than not, producing a unified, coherent work, be it an album, film or book. At the same time, of course, he managed to score hit after hit through the 60's: "Ring of Fire," "It Ain't Me, Babe," "The Ballad of Ira Hayes," "Orange Blossom Special," "Jackson," "If I Were a Carpenter" and all the others. It was a success story all the more remarkable for its background, the personal crises of drug addiction, recovery and redemption through which he traveled, with his new wife June Carter's help, in the mid- and late 60's. Once firmly established in the public eye as a lost soul now saved, he went on to even greater successes, both as a TV star and a maker of hits—"A Boy Named Sue," "Sunday Mornin' Comin' Down," "Man in Black," "If I Had a Hammer," "Any Old Wind That Blows," "Ragged Old Flag," "One Piece at a Time," "After the Ball" and many more. It's fair to say that

him silenced, without an active major label recording contract, prior to signing with Curb. But at least he was in good company. By that time, Cash too was out in the cold.

Cash, who had joined the Opry in 1956, moved from Sun Records to Columbia in 1958, thus (in a way, anyway) beginning his "official" country career. "There were so many things I wanted to do," he explained to Peter Guralnick. "I had all these ideas about special projects, different album ventures like *Ride This Train, From Sea to Shining Sea*, the Indian album, but I felt like at

in the late 60's and early 70's, he was easily the best-known country star among the American public, and indeed around the world. Johnny Cash meant country music, and vice versa. His popularity reached a crescendo in 1969, when the 1968 release of his electrifying *Live at Folsom Prison* album had so galvanized sales of all his work, including 1969's *Live at San Quentin,* that according to CBS market research figures, he was accounting for fully five percent of all record sales in the U.S.—and this in the time of Bob Dylan, Janis Joplin, Simon & Garfunkel and The Beatles.

Cash, however, was a person far more complex and even more contradictory than the fixed, familiar, Mt. Rushmore-like image encouraged by Nashville boosters and the producers of TV specials. As one writer put it in the 90's, "in Cash the person and the artist, you have everything from a loving Christian witness to a feral junkie dog." As the songs he sang, causes he espoused, and people he chose as friends attested, he de-

fied stereotyping with even more vigor than Merle Haggard.

There was, however, a strong theme running through all his choices and stances, and that was the theme of integrity. Cash was a man with a very strong conscience, seeming to attempt honesty in all his affairs, so he always had moral authority. He used it, and the power that came with his stardom, well, particularly in helping newcomers and outsiders through Nashville's often impenetrable social and professional barriers. The Statler Brothers' entree was through Cash, as was Kris Kristofferson's, and Larry Gatlin's, and writers like John Prine, Steve Goodman and Rodney Crowell can also thank him for his sponsorship. And of course his duets with Bob Dylan on Dylan's *Nashville Skyline* album, and Dylan's guest spot on his TV show in 1969, were acts of enormous symbolic importance (even more progressive, noted one wag, than when he used those trumpets on "Ring of Fire"). Not that such

More TV: Buck Owens and Roy Clark had a hit on their hands with the country-bumpkin antics of Hee Haw.

gestures were in any way unpredictable; Cash had always straddled the social fence between folk and country music, doing his best to keep the barrier from becoming too forbidding.

In the late 70's and 80's, his penchant for musical adventurism, and/or his record company's desire for some sort of new formula to revive his failing track record as a hitmaker, led him to try all kinds of approaches, from orchestral-extravaganza productions to reprises of the good old *boom-chucka-boom* sound. Though studded with some truly memorable moments—spine-tingling versions of John Prine's "Unwed Fathers" and Bruce Springsteen's "Highway Patrolman"; virtually every track on *Rockabilly Blues*; and perhaps another two dozen truly great songs of all shades—the approach was very uneven as a whole, and was not commercially successful on any consistent basis. CBS dumped him in 1987, and he signed with Mercury, but although his music was much more satisfying than it had been for a while (he was working with Jack Clement, the former Sun Records producer who'd always been able to coax the best from him), no commercial bonanza resulted. The politics and economics of the business were stacked high

Loretta Lynn's husband Mooney took this first publicity shot of her in front of a bedspread.

against him at that point; radio had other, younger fish to fry, and Nashville had plenty of them ready for the pan. Cash had the last laugh, though. In 1994, he took his business to Rick Rubin, a young producer/independent label owner who'd never operated in the country field before (though he'd had major successes in "alternative" pop), and made a devastating album of typical Cash songs—a range from "Tennessee Stud" and "A Cowboy's Prayer" to Leonard Cohen and Nick Lowe numbers—all sung with just his own guitar accompaniment. It was a huge success, especially in the world outside the country mainstream, and

Cash was off and running on another career in the big leagues. As he wrote in a letter to *Country Music* publisher Russ Barnard, "I couldn't be happier. A *third* time around?! How did I get so blessed? I wish every country artist could experience this: Let the band play on, but just once take that guitar and sit down and show the folks what you got." Cash, of course, had plenty, as the grandchildren of his original fans were finding out.

One of Cash's companions in the ranks of Nashville-based 60's country music stars was a young lady from Butcher's Hollow, Kentucky, Loretta Lynn. A singer and songwriter who'd worked clubs in Washington State in the 1950's (and appeared on a local TV show hosted by Buck Owens), she broke into the recording scene via a connection with steel guitarist Speedy West. He and other first-rate L.A. session musicians worked on her first single, "Honky Tonk Girl," and thanks to their professionalism and her own talent she had something substantial in hand when she and her husband, Oliver "Mooney" Lynn, embarked on a grueling cross-country road trip to promote the record personally to local DJ's. The song got onto the country charts, and soon Loretta was invited to sing on the Opry. Once in Nashville, she was signed as a writer by The Wilburn Brothers' publishing company, Sure-Fire Music, and joined the cast of their syndicated TV show. A recording contract with Decca followed in 1962, and her hits, produced by Owen Bradley, began that same year with "Success." Her real impact, though, was made by songs with an attitude: "Don't Come Home A-Drinkin' With Lovin' on Your Mind," "You Ain't Woman Enough" and "Fist City"—all in the distinguished tradition of Kitty Wells' "It Wasn't God Who Made Honky Tonk Angels," and wildly popular with female fans.

Loretta herself, a warm, outspoken, totally

Loretta Lynn

unaffected hillbilly girl, was wildly popular with just about everyone. Pretty soon she was far ahead of any other woman singer of her day, and remained unchallenged until the emergence of Tammy Wynette in 1966. The duet work she began doing with Conway Twitty in the early 70's was just as successful as her solo recordings, becoming the standard by which all other country duets were judged—a status challenged, once again, only by Wynette's work with her sometime husband, George Jones.

In the 70's Loretta transcended all that, moving up the scale of celebrity into the consciousness of the public at large with a couple of items: her song "The Pill," which did for her what "Stand By Your Man" had done for Tammy Wynette (but in the opposite ideological direction), and the autobiography she wrote with George Vecsey, *Coal Miner's Daughter*. It hit the best-seller list in very short or-

der, and in 1980 was turned into a movie, also a hot ticket, starring Sissy Spacek. Such complete exposure, however, might have been bad for her recording career, just as it had been for Perry Como and Buck Owens. Her break with The Wilburn Brothers certainly was: With a court battle ongoing over the ownership of her song copyrights, she quit writing her own material and lost her identity as a recording artist—an identity so strong that nothing else could match it, especially not her attempts at a "country-politan" sound. Her last album with MCA was in 1988: a very disappointing outcome indeed. She continues performing on the Opry and elsewhere, however, and in 1993 teamed with Dolly Parton and Tammy Wynette for the *Honky Tonk Angels* album.

As Loretta Lynn's star was rising in the early 60's, Connie Smith's was also beginning to shine. Discovered by Bill Anderson and signed to RCA

Loretta Lynn's career broke down many industry taboos. In 1972, she became the first woman ever to win the CMA Entertainer of the Year Award. Here she wins it again in 1973, with Merle Haggard and Glen Campbell looking on.

by Chet Atkins in 1964, she sent her very first single, "Once a Day," to the top of the country charts, and saw it stay there for a full ten weeks. Her success continued for the next few years — *Billboard* named her the third best female country singer in 1968—but she wasn't happy trying to balance motherhood, the role of the traveling troubadour, and the ghosts of her childhood (she'd grown up with an alcoholic father). "I got to where I never opened my mouth till I got on stage, and then I never opened it again till the next show," she told *Country Music* in 1974, admitting also that she considered suicide. She experienced a religious awakening, however, and went on to greater happiness and a string of hits with RCA which continued into the 70's, as well as some of the most powerful country gospel albums of the era. By the 90's, after recording on both the Columbia and Monument labels with less commercial success than in her RCA days, she was still an active member of the Opry, and still regarded by many of her peers as one of the best pure singers Nashville had ever produced.

The woman who edged her out of *Billboard's* number two spot in 1968, Lynn Anderson, was the daughter of Liz Anderson, who wrote "The Fugitive" and "(My Friends Are Gonna Be) Strangers" for Merle Haggard and scored several country chart hits of her own in the 60's. The younger Ms. Anderson exceeded her mother's achievements late in 1970 when her recording of Joe South's "Rose Garden" hit the top of the charts. It was one of those songs—instantly memorable, and a standard almost from the day of its release—and it set her up as one of the prime performers of early 70's country-pop. ("Rose Garden" was an international pop hit, a Grammy winner, and a platinum record in the U.S.) She had neither Connie Smith's depth nor Loretta Lynn's charisma, though, and her impact was relatively shallow. Although she proved her worth as a stylist with a couple of independent label albums in the early 90's, her front-line career was over by the late 70's.

Roger Miller, on the other hand, was an artist whose work continued to influence country music long after his peak as a chart-topping singer in the mid-60's. One of Nashville's most inventive and idiosyncratic minds, notorious in coun-

Loretta with Sissy Spacek, who starred in Coal Miner's Daughter.

try music circles for his manic genius, he conquered the world in 1964 and '65 with loony hits like "Dang Me," "Chug-a-Lug," "England Swings" and, of course, "King of the Road"—all preceded by a career as one of Nashville's better semi-anonymous songwriters ("Invitation to the Blues" for Ray Price, "Half a Mind" for Ernest Tubb, "Billy Bayou" for Jim Reeves), and jobs in Faron Young's and Minnie Pearl's bands.

Miller's brilliant, foolish, catchy hits, which shattered long-held songwriting conventions and provoked both admiration and imitation from his fellow performers and songwriters, opened the floodgates for a whole new wave of country songwriters who were not only challenged and inspired by his inventiveness and unconventionality, but were also made aware of the level of sophistication country audiences could and would accept and enjoy. It all resulted in Miller's astounding sweep of six Grammy Awards in 1965, an achievement that among other things prompted NARAS to limit crossover voting in following years.

Obviously, country music was breaking out

Glen Campbell

of its cultural and geographic shell. The era of crossover was upon it, and after Miller's success the country-pop hits came in a dizzying rush: "Gentle on My Mind," "Honey," "Harper Valley P.T.A.," "Folsom Prison Blues," "A Boy Named Sue," "Daddy Sang Bass," "Okie from Muskogee," "Sunday Morning Coming Down," "Rose Garden," "Help Me Make It Through the Night," "Me and Bobby McGee," "For the Good Times" and more than a few more.

The growing commercial vitality of the music was of course directly attributable to the strength of its new generation of stars: Roger Miller, Johnny Cash, Buck Owens, Merle Haggard, Glen Campbell, George Jones, Loretta Lynn, Tammy Wynette, Conway Twitty and, a little later, Dolly Parton and Charley Pride. There were, though, other forces working simultaneously.

The growing attraction of folk and pop musicians was one, but so was what drew them: the vitality of Nashville's and Bakersfield's best, and the well-organized existence of expert studio sidemen and industry executives ready to push country music beyond its traditional regional and ethnic boundaries. The vacuum left by the demise of British rock, which peaked creatively and commercially in the late 60's, provided opportunity, and the national media suddenly provided mass exposure of country music. The result was that just as the middle 1950's witnessed the beginning of a decade in which American popular music, through rock 'n' roll, copied and reworked the black urban musical tradition, the late 1960's witnessed the beginning of an era in which country music became pop's touchstone.

Songwriter Jimmy "Wichita Lineman" Webb and Glen Campbell. Webb also wrote "By the Time I Get to Phoenix."

An indicator of the existence of this explosion in country music's popularity every bit as graphic as the *Billboard* and *Cashbox* charts was the appearance of country music on what had become America's great mass medium: television. Syndicated shows (Porter Wagoner's and Flatt and Scruggs' the most memorable) had been part of country music for a long time, and Jimmy Dean, the *Ozark Jubilee* and the Opry itself had made brief network appearances in the 50's and early 60's. Toward the end of the 60's, however, country entertainers began appearing on shows like *Today, The Mike Douglas Show* and others, and prime-time network shows became devoted to country music (or at least the network executives' conception thereof). *The Johnny Cash Show* was first, in 1969, followed by *The Glen Campbell Goodtime Hour* and *Hee Haw*, all on CBS. Each offered a different view of what CBS brass thought country music was all about: Cash's show a romantic view of country as the music of the common man, its story told by the hobo/historian with a heart of gold; Campbell's an hour full of mild amusement and vapid good cheer, with a little hot picking thrown in for good measure and the occasional flash of something real; and Buck 'n' Roy's *Hee Haw* a madly schizophrenic mixture of cornpone *schtick* and genuine country tradition—not just Owens' and Clark's music, but that of their guests and authentic old-time regulars like Stringbean and Grandpa Jones. Cash's show was canceled in 1971 amid speculation that network interference with his purist approach had been a problem (which it had). Campbell's *Goodtime Hour* and *Hee Haw* were canceled at the same time, even though both shows had high ratings; CBS feared it had developed "too rural" an image and acted accordingly, simultaneously canceling *Green Acres* and *The Beverly Hillbillies,* its two rubes-meet-sophisticates sitcoms. *Hee Haw* went into Saturday night syndication, where it was seen on more stations than when CBS had it (and it perhaps played the *Grand Ole Opry* radio show's old role), subsequently developing a half-life seemingly equivalent to that of plutonium. Though CBS didn't think it relevant to its financial health, grassroots support for country music on TV was evidently strong, to say the least.

Another factor of signal importance in the rise of country during the 60's was the empowerment of the country songwriter (which paralleled the rise of singer-songwriters like James Taylor and Joni Mitchell in the pop music field). Although Roger Miller, Kris Kristofferson and Willie Nelson stand out as particularly influential in this era, the process had begun a good bit earlier. Actually, for years Nashville had but one real professional songwriter, Fred Rose. Singers either sang their

Lynn Anderson, the "Rose Garden" girl.

own songs or standards, covered new hits made popular by other singers on other labels, or did a tune or two or more of Rose's. That situation began to change in the mid-50's, however, when Opry manager Jim Denny left WSM to form his own booking agency and team up with Webb Pierce in a new music publishing company, Cedarwood Music. There he assembled a staff of writers, among them Mel Tillis, Danny Dill, Marijohn Wilkin and Wayne Walker, and the list of songs they created was awesome: "Detroit City," "Burning Memories," "The Long Black Veil," "Waterloo" and "Slowly," to name just a few. The staff-writing concept pioneered by Acuff-Rose and given a strong boost by Cedarwood's success was quick to catch on, and Tree (Roger Miller's publisher), Combine (Kristofferson's pub-

lisher) and Pamper Music quickly became multimillion-dollar operations, producing songs and songwriters to fill the needs of the pop industry as well as the booming country field.

With the overwhelming success enjoyed by Kristofferson, a whole new wave of singer-songwriters hit Nashville. The old stereotype of the feckless, fancy-free but chronically broke musician hanging out in Tootsie's Orchid Lounge waiting for a band job was replaced within a few years by a new model: the feckless, fancy-free but chronically broke songwriter hanging out in Tootsie's Orchid Lounge waiting to get his songs recorded. The result, of course, was better songs; simple mathematics dictated that more writers meant more dross, but also more gold. So rapidly did the trend advance that these new characters came to be in demand as performers as well. The era of the singer/ song- interpreter seemed to be over, and the singer-songwriter's day dawned.

Many of the most important songwriters of the period are covered in some detail in Chapter Twelve (*The Outlaws*), but one, Tom T. Hall, seems to fit better here. For one thing, he was never really identified with the Outlaw movement. He belongs with Roger Miller more than Lee Clayton, Billy Joe Shaver or Steve Young.

A preacher's son and former DJ from Olive Hill, Kentucky, Hall hit Nashville in 1964 and scored his first (very) major coup with "Harper Valley P.T.A." for Jeannie C. Riley in 1968. He was a master of the deceptively simple, utterly compelling story song, taking his subject matter, the South and its ways and people (himself included), and composing tight, telling little character sketches: "The Year That Clayton Delaney Died," "(Old Dogs, Children And) Watermelon Wine." Naturally, the songs also dwelt on the great themes: love, death, prejudice, loss, loneliness, tragedy. His songs were recorded by

Roger Miller

Tom T. Hall

dozens of singers and, though noted as a "reluctant star," he sent seven of his own singles to the top of the country charts in the 70's.

Hall was in some ways a transitional, or perhaps more appropriately, a connective, figure in country's 60's and 70's. Possessed of a sophisticated, literary intelligence, he was one of the first Nashville writers to expand his creative domain beyond popular music into "serious" literature; his memoir, *The Storyteller's Nashville,* was a warm-up act for a novel, and even before the publication of that work he counted literary giants like Kurt Vonnegut and William Styron as friends (and fans). He also wrote short stories, songs and children's books, and was a persistently progressive influence in the internal politics of country music.

So was Bobby Bare, a singer from Ohio who was signed to RCA by Chet Atkins in 1962, achieving stardom the following year with Mel Tillis' "Detroit City." Bare was drawn towards songs, like those of Tom T. Hall (and Bob Dylan), which went beyond the confines of what was understood to be "straight country" at the time, and was an important force in popularizing wider visions and unfamiliar styles. His second hit was "500 Miles Away from Home," which he followed with numbers like Ian Tyson's "Four Strong Winds," Jack Clement's "Miller's Cave," and "The Streets of Baltimore," the latter dealing with the subject of prostitution. He was also responsible for connecting Waylon Jennings with Chet Atkins, which resulted in Waylon's RCA recording contract; he gave Billy Joe Shaver his break, signing him to his publishing company, and he was one of the first artists to record the songs of Shel Silverstein, the *Playboy* cartoonist who, unlikely as it seemed, became one of the best songwriters in Nashville during the 70's (he wrote "A Boy Named Sue," as well as much less humorous material). Bare, whose biggest hit was Silverstein's "Marie Laveau" in 1974 and whose recording career continued well into the 80's, hosted a wonderfully relaxed, intelligent music-and-interview TV show on The Nashville Network in the 80's; it didn't last long but, like most of Bare's projects, it was great fun while it did.

Bare was one of the key figures in Nashville's

shift from interpretive singers to singer/songwriters as the dominant presence on scene—a shift that had begun its evolution in the late 1950's and early 1960's with the Nashville Sound.

In the early days of Nashville's success, the music business consisted of a chain of individuals linking songs with records. Writers brought their material to a publisher; publishers made demonstration records and hired a song plugger to pitch songs to A&R (Artists and Repertoire) men around town. The A&R men picked material for their artists, helped the singers learn and interpret each new song, and helped hire musicians for a recording session. So by the time a country singer actually put a selection down on tape, four or five different links in the chain had been

Tom T. Hall was a disc jockey in Morehead, Kentucky in 1954.

activated, and each had taken (or would take) some kind of fee for its contribution to the overall success of the song.

It was inevitable that some of these functions would be combined, because the more activities that could be concentrated in one individual or corporation, the greater the share of the profits that would stay in one place. Quickly, A&R men were also songwriters, or A&R men owned their own publishing companies, or singers not only wrote but also published their own material, or record companies themselves owned publishing companies. The list of possible combinations seemed endless, but the results were nearly always the same: The creative process was undermined or circumvented. If a singer is also a songwriter, it follows as night follows day that he or she will tend to record his or her own material. If an A&R man is also a writer, then he too is more than likely to encourage his artists to sing his songs. And if a record company owns a publishing firm, it may require, or at least strongly suggest, that an artist sing material from that company's catalogue, or may force or encourage new singer/ songwriters signed to the label to place their songs in the company-owned publishing house. The pressures and combinations were, again, virtually endless.

Influential singer, songwriter and music publisher: Bobby Bare.

self to the company as a package: "If you want him as a performer, you have to take his songs as well." Thus the increasing concentration of power in the hands of producers and record companies helped reinforce the importance of the singer/songwriter to Nashville. The result was that by the late 1960's the doors of Nashville were simply not open to a singer who didn't have access to a fund of new

In the late 1960's, with record companies in increasing control of the publishing side of the music business, it became more and more difficult for independent publishers—the real heart of the Nashville music business—to place songs with singers. The publishers, then, turned to the singer/songwriter as a solution to the problem of getting material on record. Rather than try to pitch songs to an A&R man or producer, publishers could bring the singer/songwriter him-

songs, because the industry had learned that the really big money in commercial music was not so much in records but in publishing.

The struggle to control the copyright to a successful song remains one of the greatest areas of conflict in Music City; in the late 1960's it combined with the charisma of new singer/songwriters to make people like Kristofferson fixtures on the Nashville scene.

Connie Smith, a favorite singers' singer, in the early 1970's.

Another major change in the complexion of the Nashville music business came from the institution that had been at the very heart of country music for almost 30 years: the Grand Ole Opry. The Opry's 1974 relocation from its home in the Ryman Auditorium in downtown Nashville to Opryland, a brand-new theme park built on the banks of the Cumberland River far out on the fringe of the city's suburbs, was a change far more significant than the 20 minutes it added to the drive from Music Row.

The story of Opryland is, in a sense, the story of the National Life and Accident Insurance Company's attempt to merchandise their most curious product, the Grand Ole

*The Statler Brothers—
Harold Reid, Phil Balsley,
Don Reid and Lew DeWitt.*

The Ryman Auditorium in downtown Nashville. Completed in 1892 as The Union Gospel Tabernacle by a reformed riverboat captain, it was home to the Grand Ole Opry from 1943 until the spring of 1974.

Opry. By the early 1960's the Opry had created a rather embarrassing image problem for the prestigious life insurance company. The rockabilly stars of the 1950's, including Jerry Lee Lewis, Elvis Presley, Johnny Cash and The Everly Brothers, had brought to the music (and to the Opry) unorthodox lifestyles and freewheeling behavior, and in the late 1950's mainstream Opry stars like Red Foley and Ernest Tubb were involved in brushes with the law. Also, the area of Nashville around the Ryman Auditorium had been degenerating into a neighborhood full of massage parlors, tacky souvenir shops, pawn shops, adult movie houses and funky old bars. To be sure, many of the traditional patrons of the Opry rather liked that atmosphere, and Opry performers enjoyed the convenience of being able to slip across the alley from the Ryman into the back door of Tootsie's Orchid Lounge for a beer or two between shows. But the WSM officials were bothered by "image," and Edwin Craig, the National Life executive who had overseen the found-

ing of the show in 1925, was also bothered by the direction in which things were going. He had seen the show start out as an informal, genial collection of Tennessee natives playing old-time music; now he saw an unstable coalition of highly professional entertainers specializing in honky tonk music and songs about lost love. Given his innate conservatism, it was inevitable that sooner or later, Craig would do something about it all.

Early in 1962, WSM officials went to California to inspect Disneyland and brought back some ideas for improving the Opry's appearance. One of the real problems was the Ryman Auditorium itself. Completed in 1892 as a religious tabernacle, by 1960 it was restricting the Opry's attendance (it held only about 3,500) and making those who did come uncomfortable. The old hall was hot in the summer (there was no air conditioning) and cold in the winter, and the seats were the hard wooden pews of the old church; the floor of the balcony was covered with a sort of tar paper that allowed soft drinks spilled in the balcony to drip down on the audience below. The building was only a few blocks from the heart of downtown Nashville, and parking was a nightmare. Over and over again, audience polls showed that most of the complaints were about the building itself.

As a result of the Disneyland tour, some attempts to renovate the old Ryman were made. The off-duty policemen who had been serving as ushers were replaced by pretty young girls in hostess uniforms. In 1963 National Life went ahead and bought the old building for about $200,000, and a few further reno-

Jeanne Pruett on the last night at the Ryman.

vations were made. Yet the shortcomings of the structure were becoming even more apparent. The Opry was essentially a radio show, and attempts to produce anything beyond radio in the Ryman met with nightmarish complexity; television broadcasting, as Johnny Cash found out when he tried to originate his network show from the Ryman, caused problems at which even network technicians balked. National Life looked at numerous plans to remodel the Ryman, but all would have cost more than the purchase price of the building, and none would have solved the problem of the environment of Lower Broadway.

Meanwhile, a new generation of executives was emerging at National Life; in contrast to the older generation, which felt that the company should restrict itself to the life insurance business, this newer generation felt that the company should branch out into non-insurance areas. One of these areas was the exploitation of the Opry name and image. Thus in October 1968 it was announced that the company had hired the California firm that had planned Disneyland to study the feasibil-

ity of building a new Grand Ole Opry house and creating a tourist attraction around it. The new complex would be called "Opryland U.S.A." The old National Life people saw that meaning just a new home for the Opry, but the new generation saw it as a chance to use the Opry appeal to generate even more television and tourism and to begin attracting a wider audience.

In fact, the report from the California group argued that such a park could not succeed if it focused only on country music, and recommended that it was worth only a modest investment. Opry manager Bud Wendell argued that the Californians didn't understand the appeal of the Opry name. (He recalled that they admitted that "there is no other park in the country other than Disneyland that has the built-in image acceptance that the Grand Ole Opry represents. It is synonymous with purity, patriotism, the flag, motherhood and apple pie.") Besides that, though, was the fact that WSM, the radio/television arm of National Life, was not thinking of a park featuring only country music. From

Marty Robbins in the deserted pews after the last show—March 9, 1974.

The Ryman's replacement, the Opry House in suburban Opryland. Opening night, March 16, 1974, featured Roy Acuff giving then-President Richard Nixon a yo-yo lesson.

audience, and that it was threatening to break out from its traditional geographical and class appeal.

Thus in 1969 work was begun on Opryland, and the park opened in 1972, two years before the new Opry House itself was ready. It quickly exceeded its owners' expectations in both attendance and income, generating over $6 million in its first two years. Visitors coming to the park saw a number of country music motifs—a roller coaster called "The Wabash Cannonball," various characters dressed up as guitars and bass fiddles, Roy Acuff's country music museum—but they were by no means exposed to a steady diet of country music. In addition to taking rides and playing games, they could attend any number of free shows throughout the park; one of these was a mountain music show featuring bluegrass and "folk" music and one was a country show, but others were rock shows, Broadway-like musicals and Dixieland jazz bands. Few "name" stars appeared at any of the shows; the musicians comprised a sort of repertory company of young artists chosen from auditions held around the country, from New York to Dallas. Only a few of these singers had any ambitions of becoming country stars—most of them wanted to break into Broadway, the movies or television. The country shows at Opryland were generally rather trite rehashes of old country hits

the beginning of the project, WSM president Irving Waugh had had the idea, in the words of Opry historian Jack Hurst, "to illustrate country music's role as a musical melting pot by surrounding the Opry with live performances of the other kinds of music to which the American people have given rise—blues, jazz, Western, folk and the rest." Also, the California group did not sense what some of the Nashville men did: that country music was appealing to an increasingly wider

performed in an imitative style; they were a very watered-down version of real country music, and at times they seemed almost to parody the music. Opryland management, however, felt that these were the best methods by which the increasing numbers of non-country fans at Opryland could be attracted to the music.

The new Opry House was opened on March 16, 1974, and among the guests was the President of the United States. For many fans of country music, the spectacle of seeing the president appear alongside Roy Acuff, and of hearing "Hail to the Chief" played by a fiddle, banjo and steel guitar, seemed the final proof that the music's long struggle to gain respectability was won. Acuff himself, who had barely 20 years earlier heard a Tennessee governor complain that the Opry and the hillbilly image were embarrassing to the state, later admitted that he felt that in spite of the Watergate scandal, Nixon's visit to the Opry stage was the greatest thing that had ever happened to country music. To the older musicians like Acuff and Hank Snow and The McGee Brothers, who could remember the years they spent trying to establish their music as a legitimate profession, the president's visit was especially meaningful.

Many of the younger Opry members who had always seen their profession as relatively respectable were impressed with the physical aspects of the new Opry House. These were signs that the music was being taken seriously; the house had an elaborate lighting system, plush seats, superb acoustics and expensive television facilities. "It's more like a real opera house," one young Opry member commented. The convenience of running across the alley to Tootsie's was gone, but the dressing rooms were larger and more comfortable than the cramped, confining quarters at the old Ryman. The entire place intimidated audiences so much that at first Grant Turner had to encourage people to cheer and whoop it up like they did in the old Ryman. The singers, who had thrived on the close audience contact, now complained that they couldn't hear the audience very well. Respectability did have its price.

Opryland can be seen as a symbol of the new type of country music originating from Nashville in the early 1970's, for both Opryland and the music being turned out by producers like Billy Sherrill were lush and artificial. Artificiality was in fact a central quality of Opryland. One of the rationales for building the park, according to WSM president Irving Waugh, was to "go outside the city to a place where we could control our own environment." Opryland can thus be seen, in one sense, as an attempt to create an "other world" environment for the Opry that would have none of the real-life problems of the Lower Broadway neighborhood surrounding the Ryman. The new park itself was totally fabricated, taking as its natural base only the Cumberland River; the design was so cunning that once in the park, the visitor could detect relatively little of the original natural terrain, and even lost his sense of direction. The music and shows in the park were likewise orchestrated, and often choreographed and staged by sophisticated arrangers.

The Nashville music of the early 1970's achieved its artificiality by different methods—string arrangements, overdubbing, studio enhancement and orchestration as opposed to concrete and landscaping—but the end product was just as pleasant, easy to assimilate, and sterile. Such qualities were, of course, very appealing in some sectors of society. In others, people were looking for something very different indeed.

Emmylou Harris

Hyphenated Country

It's about three in the morning at Columbia's Studio A, the big, symphony-sized studio buried in Columbia's office complex in the middle of Nashville's Music Row. A bass player and guitar player sit improvising idly—the atmosphere is stoned—and two drummers sit in opposite corners of the high-ceilinged room. Both play constantly, and now and then they drift weirdly out of phase and then back in again. The star sits in the center of the room on a high stool and reads movie magazines. Every now and then he looks up and makes some remark, and several of the musicians laugh reflexively.

The drumming goes on. The star's manager stands in the studio control room. Periodically he takes a quarter from his pocket and flips it, hard, against the acoustical tile ceiling. The quarters stick. The drummers keep drumming, sometimes in, sometimes out of phase. This is the building, the very building, in which Tammy Wynette, George Jones, Sonny James, Marty Robbins and Johnny Cash record. But this is not a typical Nashville session. This is Bob Dylan, king of the folkies, an experimenter with rock music, recording in the capital of country music in 1966; the most important musical figure of the decade at work in the hometown of a music known only to (at best) a third of America's population. Here is America's folk poet, the conscience of a generation, recording in a style long associated with a Neanderthal social outlook and a sometimes ignorant, sometimes devious, sometimes violent culture.

Out of context, these *Blonde on Blonde* sessions were improbable, isolated occurrences. In hindsight, though, they stand out quite clearly as the point where some major trends in American popular music came together—trends that would bring country music into pop music's realm, and would eventually elevate it to undreamed-of heights of nationwide and even worldwide popularity.

Although the threads that came together in Dylan's Nashville adventure can be traced back to the beginning of commercial recording, they first became truly apparent in the mid-1950's when the youth of white America, weary with the monochromatic landscape of popular music, discovered the rich variety of their nation's ethnic music, both black and white. Contemporary black music found its way into the mainstream through rock 'n' roll (courtesy of Sam Phillips *et al.*), while older, more rural music entered via the folk revival; discovering and embracing both the primitive blues of the Mississippi Delta and the old-time country of Appalachia, middle-class youth deserted the pop wasteland en masse for the music of Robert Johnson, Lightnin' Hopkins, The Carter Family and Bill Monroe.

The music, that is: not the musicians. Although significant minorities of folkies did indeed seek out "Crossroads" and "Wildwood Flower" in the original and thus become active fans of performers from Maybelle Carter, Doc Watson and Bill Monroe to Sonny Terry and Brownie McGee, the great majority were more comfortable with shorter cultural distances and performers more like themselves than not: The Kingston Trio; Peter, Paul and Mary; The Limelighters; The Chad Mitchell Trio. By 1960, two years after their groundbreaking release of "Tom Dooley"—the first major smash of the folk-revivalist movement—The Kingston Trio and their co-horts were among the hottest acts in the nation, selling noncommerciality very professionally and mass-popularizing blues, calypso, mountain ballads and any other material that seemed to possess cultural authenticity. Some authentic country performers also found occasional success on a national level with records of folk-tinged material: Johnny Horton with "The Battle of New Orleans,"

The late 60's saw Bob Dylan recording in Nashville.

Marty Robbins with "El Paso" and "Big Iron," Lefty Frizzell with "Long Black Veil" and "Saginaw, Michigan," and Tennessee Ernie Ford with "Sixteen Tons."

The revival itself—the spirit of revival—was heady stuff. It took a generation of American musicians and listeners and carried them into ethnic cultures and lifestyles, and it was the moving force behind pop music's late 60's/early 70's swing away from hard rock towards various forms of hyphenated country. The prime movers of that cultural shift—John Denver, Judy Collins, Gordon Lightfoot, Joan Baez, Joni Mitchell, Paul Simon and of course Bob Dylan— all came of musical age during the folk revival days. A group of second-generation folkies like Linda Ronstadt, Emmylou Harris, James Taylor,

Stephen Stills, Jim Croce and Gram Parsons followed closely on their heels. Others who achieved recognition as soloists, and whose influence was equally profound, also learned to perform in the revival days: Jerry Garcia of The Grateful Dead, Mike Bloomfield of The Paul Butterfield Blues Band, Neil Young of Buffalo Springfield, Jesse Colin Young of The Youngbloods.

All these artists and more had grown to love country and folk material on the coffeehouse circuit, and they also learned that imitation—often crossing cultural and racial boundaries —was the key to producing vigorous pop performances. And so the folk revival, coming on the heels of the birth of rock 'n' roll, completed the ethnicization of American popular music, and in fact changed our definition of what qualified as popular music. Before 1955, romantic, synthetic ballads and Broadway tunes dominated the record industry in the decade; since then it's been rare indeed to find hit records of any given period that have not been derived from some form of American folk music. Only very strong mainstream material—the work of writers like Henry Mancini or Burt Bacharach—has been able, on occasion, to crack the solid front of ethnic-based music.

Even though rock and folk songs brought new energy to the American pop scene, both fell victim to the same undermining forces that crippled jazz in an earlier era. One of the few "givens" within popular music seems to be the tension between minority music and popularity. Folk music—any folk music—is visceral, minority value-oriented and disinclined to change, while music that is broadly popular tends towards the bland, majority-oriented and trendy. Thus, as soon as rock and folk music captured the imagination of a few, the material and its performance began to deteriorate. In the early 1960's rock had lost much of its early virility and been replaced in the popular arena by more effete, less visceral forms, such as surf music and the black-controlled but white-aspiring Motown sound.

The folk boom, in some ways healthier than rock, also showed a lack of energy in the early 1960's, for overly slick groups like The Limelighters and The Chad Mitchell Trio had turned off much of the early folk music audience, and television exploitation of the folk movement (on shows like *Hootenanny*) drove home the final coffin nails. By 1964 the folk song revival had lost its grip on the popular music audience, having become an almost embarrassing parody of itself, and both the most committed fans and the strongest performers of the folk revival—Bob Dylan and Phil Ochs—had moved on into new forms of expression. The earnest innocence of "Puff The Magic Dragon" made way for heavy drugs, psychedelic rock and violent political action. It was a radical change, and the fate of Puff himself says it all: He ended up lending his name to a spectacularly lethal military aircraft used to deliver saturation fire against ground targets in Vietnam.

Fifties rock 'n' roll did not fare much better than 60's folk, although with far different manifestations, for the rock 'n' rollers became the agents of a rebellion so dramatically successful that they were left with no place to go. Nobody, by God, was stepping on their blue suede shoes now, and to all intents and purposes, it was they who were running the popular music show. So what was there left to rebel against? How, for example, could the rock movement express a sneer-

Peter, Paul and Mary kept folk music alive in the 1960's.

The Mamas and The Papas had a distinctively American sound.

The Lovin' Spoonful drew on the American jug band tradition.

Bands that changed the course of country included The Band: Levon Helm, Garth Hudson, Robbie Robertson, Rick Danko and Richard Manuel.

The Eagles: Don Henley, Joe Walsh, Randy Meisner, Glen Frey and Don Felder.

The Byrds: Chris Hillman, Roger McGuinn, Kevin Kelley and Gram Parsons.

ing view of the establishment when Bobby Darin and Bobby Rydell were playing Vegas, and Frankie Avalon and Fabian were making fools of themselves on-screen? And speaking of films, what about Elvis? The tough street punk with the surly voice was now crooning love ballads with a big orchestra and a bigger vibrato in beach movies! What was next? Chuck Berry as Gidget? Jerry Lee Lewis as Mary Poppins? The John Milner character in *American Graffiti* summed it up quite concisely when he said, "Aw, rock 'n' roll's been going downhill ever since Buddy Holly died."

It has always been difficult for any essentially faddish art to sustain passion and commitment. Because changes in taste have always been cyclical, the era of commitment to the music's message—implied or explicit, rock or folk—was simply coming to an end. There appeared an awkward void in popular music (although the music industry kept churning out these increasingly lifeless songs), for there was really nothing in American music to replace it. Into this void, then, stepped The Beatles, who borrowed from rockabilly, country, English dance hall, middle of the road, blues and just about every other musical form—later including modern electronic invention—to develop an always melodically enchanting music containing a little something for everyone. In a sense, The Beatles (and other British groups like The Rolling Stones) were the master revivalists, dipping into a worldwide variety of ethnic and popular forms in order to produce a new pop amalgam. Much of their early work was a mere imitation of blues or rock or country performances, and not a terribly distinguished imitation at that. But what The Beatles lacked at first in musical talent they made up for in presence, in style. They presented an image of boyish rebellion and good-natured defiance that touched the collective heart of American (and European) youth.

Over and above their musical substance and repertoire, The Beatles' influence on American music was powerful indeed. Where less than a decade before the American sound had come to dominate the world, now the English sound—and look—came to dominate America, driving American music into either slavishly imitative or wildly divergent forms. It produced, on one hand, groups like that headed by current Texas country-blues-rocker Doug Sahm, The Sir Douglas Quintet, who were packaged, produced and marketed as though they were an English band. It also produced the psychedelic excesses of many American West Coast groups, a music "full of sound and fury," but so introverted, contrived, pretentious, heartless and drug-dependent as to lose all meaning.

For about four years, the domination of the American pop scene by the English was nearly complete. The Beatles, Manfred Mann, The Rolling Stones, Freddie and The Dreamers, Petula Clark, The Dave Clark Five, Donovan—all of these and more had hit after hit on American radio. The English

Seminal albums of country-rock included The Grateful Dead's Workingman's Dead...

...Gram Parsons' hugely influential Sweetheart of the Rodeo, made with The Byrds...

...and the first album from the Parsons-era Flying Burrito Brothers. Gram is second from right.

look, sound and style were dominant for what, in retrospect, was only a short time—1964 through 1967—but the extent of that domination was so widespread and total that American music was for a time virtually submerged beneath it. Old-fashioned pop had died, a victim of rock; old-fashioned rock was passé; folk music went underground; American rock splintered. Country, meanwhile, went quietly on its own way, a slumbering giant, calmly and methodically (if unknowingly) developing and refining the Nashville Sound and studio techniques which would blow the whole town wide open within just a few short years.

As Nashville grew, virtually unnoticed, English rock and the largely imitative American rock scene themselves became slavishly imitative. One group copied The Beatles, the next copied the copiers, the next copied the copiers' copies, and so on. The Beatles' own later work in electronic experimentation created in imitation a flood of introspective, overblown, album-length studio extravaganzas. English rock quickly began to wither on the vine—a decline hastened by the breakup of The Beatles—setting the stage for the death of rock and the rise of country music.

Just as the impact of the British sound is explainable,

so is its rather short life understandable. The English scene was removed—quite literally—from the cultural sources of the music its musicians played. Black American music was still at the headwaters of the rock movement, and the best that can be said of the British rockers is that, most of the time anyway, they imitated their sources well. It's interesting to note that, of the surviving British bands from that era, those that remained closest to imitation and took part in less experimentation maintained greater commercial viability. In 1965 few would have seen The Rolling Stones as the band that would long outlive The Beatles, and fewer still would have guessed that The Stones might one day be seen as having greater artistic impact. Perspectives shift with the times.

It's a marvelous bit of irony that it was right at this time, when Nashville was really learning big city ways, aiming for ever lusher arrangements, and learning about the rich rewards of the crossover, that city kids all over the Western world began to idolize the supposed freedom and purity of rural life in general and country-style music in particular. In England, outfits like The Incredible String Band and Fairport Convention moved to the fore of the hippie music scene; in the United States, Gram Parsons formed his International Submarine Band (which may claim the honor of being the first "city" country music band to record), and The Lovin' Spoonful broadcast far and wide the joys of life in Music City, U.S.A., in "Nashville Cats."

The irony lies in the ossification that was at that very time becoming a part of the Nashville music scene, a gradual evaporation of the vitality and energy of the original Nashville Sound as it was developed in the late 1950's as an antidote to rock 'n' roll. That hardening of the creative arteries was, within the space of just a couple more years, to cause Willie Nelson to make his celebrated hejira to Austin, disenchanted with the formulaic, close-minded approach he felt was ingrained in Nashville. So for those like Willie who were aware of what had been and, even more, what potentially could be, Nashville in the late 1960's was a disillusioning place.

For the musicians discovering country music

and visiting Nashville, however, it was a town of tremendous excitement. They flocked there to record, to play, to write songs, to drink Blue Ribbon at Tootsie's, to eat grits at Linebaugh's and to snack on Goo-Goos and moon pies, all the while glorifying the Nashville studios and musicians, many of whom—Pete Drake, Harold Bradley, Charlie McCoy—became instant cult heroes through their identification as sidemen on the backs of albums by Bob Dylan, Joan Baez, George Harrison, Ringo Starr, Neil Young and Buffy Ste. Marie.

Many a city musician fell under the Nashville spell, and if the bulk of the music they created in Music City was not great, at least it was interesting. Moreover, it introduced a whole new set of fans and musicians to the sincerity and simplicity of country music, country songs and country life. There was a genuine charm to the countrification of the psychedelic generation, a laid-back feeling and flavor that evoked a more straightforward, far less complicated age. If the rebellious turn to rock 'n' roll had been a bang in the 1950's, this was more of a gentle murmur—but it was rebellious nonetheless, rejecting technological complexity (while still, of course, enjoying its benefits) for the age-old serenity of the farm and the country.

But somewhere along the line the relationship between country music and its traditional audience began to change. On the one hand, country singers and producers were embracing the values of pop—elaborate production, big promotion, crossover potential—while on the other hand, poppers and rockers were going crazy for the world of the Opry, a love affair that peaked around 1970, when one of the hippest places a celebrity could be seen on any given Saturday night was backstage at the funky, tumbledown old Ryman Auditorium.

Countrification happened on many levels, of course, but in popular music the overall effect was of a movement away from blues and English rock as sources of inspiration, and toward Anglo-American "hillbilly" for that inspiration. City—even foreign—rockers started to dig country music, incorporating it into their performance style. This tended not only to help legitimize

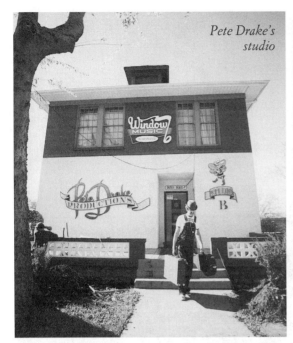

Pete Drake's studio

Pete Drake

Rock and pop performers came to Nashville to record in the city's studios with Music City musicians.

Buddy Spicher

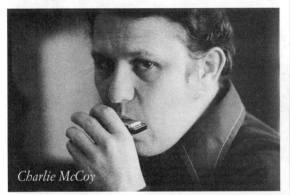

Charlie McCoy

Henry Strzelecki

Hargus "Pig" Robbins

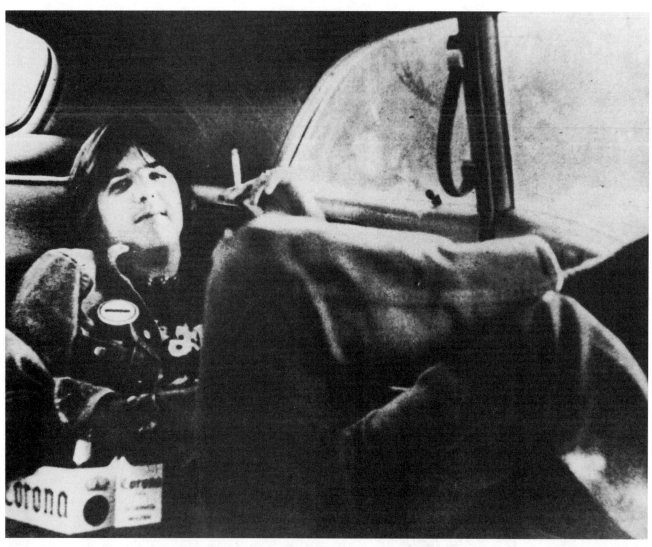

Georgia-born, Harvard-educated Gram Parsons, 1946-1973: the Hank Williams of country-rock.

country music (a process that had begun in traditional pop music with Perry Como and Al Hirt's treks to Nashville to record, as well as Dean Martin and Ray Charles' dabblings in the genre), but also in fact to lend it a measure of hipness.

By the time British rock wound down in psychedelic splendor in the late 60's, an American alternative had developed in the popular music marketplace. For some years American pop acts had drawn inspiration entirely from the British scene, but two groups came along who possessed a distinctively American sound: The Lovin' Spoonful and The Mamas and The Papas. The Spoonful, with John Sebastian and guitarist Zal Yanovsky, and The Mamas and The Papas, led by John Phillips (who had been the lead singer of a late folk-song revival group,

The Journeymen), had their origins in the folk-song revival. The Mamas and The Papas were essentially a vocal band, with instrumental invention secondary, even incidental, to their complex vocal arrangements. They were, in an obvious and refreshing way, unlike British pop groups. The Lovin' Spoonful had a different, jug-band-based sound that was just as distinctively non-British. They drew heavily upon black pop music and country styles, and presented interesting material written by John Sebastian. Their anthem to country music, "Nashville Cats," was an early statement of the growing interest and involvement of pop musicians in the country scene.

On the West Coast, The Byrds were among the first to exploit country style in a pop context effectively. Their *Sweetheart of the Rodeo* album stood as a significant landmark, for as well as giving new life to their fading career as folk-rockers, it converted many ears previously closed to the country sound. It was not, most country purists thought, great music—The Byrds' renditions of older country songs sounded somewhat weak in comparison to the originals—but it was interesting, provocative music, and it gave birth to several West Coast groups like The Flying Burrito Brothers and others who traveled farther along the path of pseudo-country, tongue-in-cheek country and country-rock.

It was inevitable, of course, that the best of pseudo-country would become as good as the authentic country it sought to emulate. This is not to say, of course, that country music or its musicians are inherently superior to folk, rock, or indeed to city musicians. But because country music does, to many ears, sound deceptively simple, and because it has often been parodied through third-rate imitation or played for a campy joke, country musicians have been viewed as inferior to those in other fields. In fact, country music demands control, taste and lifelong familiarity with the Southern white culture from which country style and song spring, and few urban musicians have been able to render it convincingly. But the late Gram Parsons, who led The Byrds into *Sweetheart of the Rodeo* (and preceded and followed them with his International Submarine Band and Flying Burrito Brothers) sang country with authority and authenticity. So did his protégée/harmony singer, Emmylou Harris, who unlike him was accepted among country musicians, singers and fans as one of their own. She was the first urban revival performer to be so accepted.

Despite Harris' background in the country music-rich Washington, D.C., suburbs, the pseudo-country movement was by and large a product of the West Coast. It was in California, for

example, that Commander Cody and His Lost Planet Airmen (transplanted from Ann Arbor, Michigan) and Asleep at The Wheel (hailing from Ohio and Pennsylvania) first grew to prominence, and of course the main country rock initiative, that of Parsons, was entirely Californian (though Parsons was a Georgian). By the early 70's the whine of the pedal steel, which for years had cued pop fans to tune the radio to the next station, was showing up in all kinds of seemingly unlikely places. The Grateful Dead, those notorious voyagers of the outer acid-rock limits, built a whole offshoot band, The New Riders of The Purple Sage, around Jerry Garcia's new pedal steel guitar—which impressed the heck out of many thousands of Deadheads, creating whole new generations of country fans, but didn't move the country mainstream one bit. The Dead's country initiative, like that of Parsons, remained alien to hard country fans.

Two solo artists, however—both women—won through: the previously mentioned Emmylou Harris, and Linda Ronstadt. Of the two, Ronstadt's road to country was the more roundabout. She

The Grievous Angels tour with Gram Parsons and Emmylou Harris in 1973.

Linda Ronstadt

came to California from a well-to-do German-Mexican family in Arizona, and by 1967 had joined a pop-folk group called The Stone Poneys, recording for Capitol and scoring one big hit with "Different Drum." The group broke up almost as soon as the record hit, and Ronstadt found herself trying to work as a solo singer in the maelstrom of Los Angeles musical styles. She began to do solo albums for Capitol, albums that were full of dressed-up folk songs and toned-down country songs. For her first four albums in the early 1970's she was regarded, in the words of *Rolling Stone*, as "no more than a barefoot, bra-less, pleasant-sounding country singer."

But the country influence on her at this time had filtered through the California folk-rock bands; she had had little direct connection with hard-core country, and few of her own records had reached the traditional country audience. That changed with her 1974 album, *Heart Like a Wheel*, which reached the top of the pop charts at the time of the first big pop-to-country crossover surge, and almost overnight she found herself with a substantial country audience, as well as growing numbers of pop fans. Some of her biggest single hits in the next three years were accomplished reworkings of older country standards: "When Will I Be Loved" (formerly a hit for The Everly Brothers), "I Can't Help It (If I'm Still in Love with You)" (Hank Williams *et al.*) and "Crazy" (Patsy Cline), and her influence on the country community grew accordingly. Her success with "When Will I Be Loved" helped make it the most performed BMI country song for 1975.

Linda Ronstadt's music resists categorization, in part because she was one of the young performers who had grown up in a musical world in which crossover and cross-pollination were the rule rather than the exception. She never hesitated to appropriate material from any genre, be it country, rock, reggae, Tex-Mex, folk, jazz or soul, and in fact the whole key to her success was her skill as an interpreter. She could sing virtually any kind of material and make it convincingly her own.

As a performer she was remarkably open and even vulnerable. Her style was intensely lyrical and personal, what *Time* called in 1977 "torchy rock," and there was virtually no distance between her and her songs, very little of the pop singer's customary detachment. She looked on her choice of songs as an expression of her personality, not as some sort of product, and therefore sought out suitable material with singular intensity. "I'd take three giant steps toward an early death if I could find one good song," she once said.

This symbiosis between song and personality was rather unusual in 70's rock and pop, but common in country music. Traditionally, though, it was the domain of male singers: Hank Williams, Kris Kristofferson, Willie Nelson. The great women country singers had always sung realistically about life, but the older singers had been products of a Southern morality that frustrated their identifying too closely with the lyrics of the songs. No woman singer had really committed herself to a performance as did, for example, the great blues singers like Bessie Smith and Billie Holiday. Linda Ronstadt was able to make such a commitment, and to make it at precisely the right moment in the development of the music.

Some of Ronstadt's most successful records contained fine harmony singing by Emmylou Harris. Unlike Ronstadt, Harris had developed clear affinities with classic country music early in her musical life. In 1971 she met Gram Parsons, then embarking on the post-Byrds, post-Burritos phase of his short but brilliant career, and went west with him to help him produce his two hugely influential solo albums, *GP* and *Grievous Angel*. "Gram introduced me to a vein of music I call the High Lonesome," she recalled years later, "the beautiful heartbreak harmony duets you hear in songs by the young Everly Brothers, Charlie and Ira Louvin, Felice and Boudleaux Bryant."

The music to which Harris and Parsons were responding—virtually extinct in regular country music circles since the late 1950's, though it survived in some bluegrass bands—had grown out of the melancholy purity of the great brother acts of the 1930's (notably The Blue Sky Boys and The Delmore Brothers), and it represented one of the music's most unique and valuable resources. Harris and Parsons were beginning to

Emmylou Harris, the keeper of the Parsons flame, in 1975, and below in working mother guise in the early 80's.

explore and popularize this music in refreshing new ways when Parsons died suddenly of a drug overdose in 1973.

Shattered by his death, Harris eventually forced herself to carry on the tradition by herself, and that same year she used some of Parsons' former sidemen to help her make a solo album, *Pieces of the Sky.* It was as poised, delicate and personal as any by Linda Ronstadt. Emmylou had the same kind of clear, pure vocal quality as Ronstadt did, quite distinctive from the husky alto range employed by most country women singers, and she also had another advantage: She was herself an accomplished composer. Her autobiographical "Boulder to Birmingham" was one of the highlights of *Pieces of the Sky;* it was nestled there among the other songs by Billy Sherrill, The Louvin

Brothers, Dolly Parton and Merle Haggard. Her Louvin Brothers song, "If I Could Only Win Your Love," became a hit single, and soon Emmylou was working with Bob Dylan and James Taylor.

The fact that both Linda Ronstadt and Emmylou Harris came, in a sense, out of the California scene was probably less important than another quality they shared: Both were young, articulate, independent, highly talented women who were being accepted on their own terms by a huge popular audience. This is not surprising in view of the way the creative impetus in 70's pop music had been carried by singers like Carole King, Carly Simon and Helen Reddy, but the success of Ronstadt and Harris with a country audience suggested that the heavy *machismo* that had dominated both the music and its fans for years was finally giving way. Loretta Lynn, for instance, without making any pop concessions in her music, became a national heroine for millions of women who were finding that it was possible to take a new pride and a new strength from their roles and their lives.

Emmylou Harris committed herself fully to country music, moving her home from California to Tennessee in the mid-80's, ending her marriage to California producer Brian Ahern, and entrenching herself deeply within the Nashville music business community, as well as continuing to explore varieties of deeply rooted country music. By the early 90's, in fact, she was working with an all-acoustic band and had come to be regarded almost as a guardian angel of country tradition—a considerable achievement, given that her work during the few years after Gram Parsons' death, when her Hot Band featured players such as Ricky Skaggs, Rodney Crowell, Vince Gill, Tony Brown and Albert Lee, also confirmed her as the patron saint of country-rock, or at least that genre's most ardent and accomplished practitioner.

Linda Ronstadt, on the other hand, abandoned her country career, moving on into a succession of interesting, if commercially and perhaps also creatively less successful, new fields. However, she too remained enormously influential. Virtually all the women country singers of the 90's grew up listening to her, and credit her as one of the greatest influences on their musical development.

The other stellar practitioners of country rock also moved on or fell away from commercial and/ or creative vitality. The Band, who worked behind rockabilly Ronnie Hawkins before hiring on with Bob Dylan and making their own first album, *Music from Big Pink*, under his wing in Woodstock, proceeded through a triumphant few years and albums, redesigning the interfaces between rock, folk, country and the blues, and weaving a whole new fabric of imaginative Americana until they broke up (spectacularly, under the movie cameras of director Martin Scorsese) with a final concert, *The Last Waltz*, on Thanksgiving Day 1976. The Grateful Dead, in one of American popular music's most intriguing sagas, were still on the road and in the studio until Jerry

Garcia's death in mid-1995, delivering country-folk-tinged music as part of their fare all along, even though the cultural distance between their 90's audience and Nashville's could be measured in light years. The Eagles, who worked as Linda Ronstadt's band before securing their own recording deal in 1971, moved progressively farther from the pleasantly mellow, country-folkish rock of their debut album ("Peaceful, Easy Feeling," etc.) towards denser, harder music ("Hotel California") until their breakup in 1979, but were perhaps more influential than any other single group or a solo artist on the "Young Country" performers of the 90's. Poco, formed from one component of Buffalo Springfield (Richie Furay

Glyn Johns, Emmylou Harris and Levon Helm at work on The Legend of Jesse James in 1981. Cash was on the project too.

and Jim Messina), soldiered on into the 1980's, but not in their original form and not with any great success or influence after their first hot flush. Crosby, Stills, Nash & Young (refugees from The Byrds, Buffalo Springfield and The Hollies) maintained their individual country-folk-rock paths and even came back together again in various combinations under various names after they first disbanded, adding and shedding players like Richie Furay, former Byrd Chris Hillman, songwriter J.D. Souther, ex-Eagle Randy Meisner and various other California-based country rockers.

Of all of these characters, the one who came

closest to the country mainstream after his country-rock youth was Chris Hillman, whose trail led from The Byrds and The Flying Burrito Brothers with Gram Parsons in the late 1960's, to the founding of The Desert Rose Band in the late 80's. Others dove straight into the middle of Nashville with their versions of straight country music, then jumped right out again: Leon Russell with his *Hank Wilson's Back* album, John Fogerty of Creedence Clearwater Revival with an album called *The Blue Ridge Rangers,* and the brilliantly anachronistic Neil Young.

California country-rock was at its commercial peak in the mid-70's, and that was also the prime

Bluegrass heroes for a new generation: The Flatt & Scruggs Band—Earl and Lester at the door of the bus—and "Daddy Bluegrass" Bill Monroe, opposite.

time for other new forms of hybrid country. Most significant were the genres that came to be called Southern rock, the "Atlanta sound," and the new, expanded bluegrass music. These trends overlapped to some extent, and by no stretch of the imagination could either Southern rock or the Atlanta Sound be considered "pure" country music. But country music was a part of all three developments, and all three movements caused repercussions that were felt in Nashville and throughout pop music.

By the 1970's bluegrass had emerged as a flourishing branch of country music. Yet there were a number of striking differences between it and mainstream country music. In contrast to the increasing professionalization of the country music world, the bluegrass scene included many

semi-professionals who worked at the music part-time. While bluegrass shared much of the same audience with country music, increasing numbers of bluegrass fans were scornful of the "commercialized" Nashville Sound. For many of these fans, bluegrass was becoming a participatory experience, almost a lifestyle, that embraced outdoor festivals, a veneration of old instruments, and a love of amateur picking. Country music, on the other hand, was becoming more and more of a passive spectator sport. Furthermore, bluegrass found its audience without going through the normal Nashville channels of records and radio airplay. There were a few big bluegrass hits coming out of Nashville (such as The Osborne Brothers' "Rocky Top" in 1971), and the Opry maintained a short but illustrious roster of bluegrass acts, such as Bill Monroe, Lester Flatt, Jim and Jesse and The Osbornes. But Nashville was really not all that sympathetic to bluegrass, and mostly contented itself by staging a token "early bird" bluegrass concert at the annual Fan Fair.

Yet the end of the 1970's saw more bluegrass bands than at any time in the 30-year history of the style. Many recorded on small independent labels and heard their records occasionally played on local stations that set aside three to four hours a week for special bluegrass shows. But the main medium for bluegrass was a phenomenon known as the "bluegrass festival" or "bluegrass convention," and nearly everybody who played bluegrass spent at least some summer months playing them. The first of these was staged near Roanoke, Virginia, in 1965 by a man named Carlton Haney. He had been a manager and promoter for the team of Reno and Smiley, and he sensed that there was a vast, if disparate, audience for bluegrass that would drive hundreds of miles to see their favorite bluegrass stars in one series of concerts. The festival was held outdoors in an informal, simple, back-to nature setting. People arrived in campers and vans, set up tents, unfolded alu-

Bill Monroe

Hippies and rednecks found common ground in bluegrass music.

minum lawn chairs and unpacked their own instruments. In between formal concerts, stars like Bill Monroe, The Stanley Brothers and Mac Wiseman mingled easily with the fans and conducted informal workshops on picking techniques. The area was dotted with impromptu jam sessions and picking sessions, so much so that some scheduled performers missed their sets onstage. Bright-eyed fans were walking around saying, "I just played back of Ralph Stanley" or "Bill Monroe let me hold his mandolin." Sunday morning brought an old-fashioned hymn-singing, and on Sunday afternoon there was a nostalgic "history of bluegrass" program. Everyone left with a good, satisfied feeling, full of praise for Haney's bright idea.

The idea of the festival spread and soon bluegrass, which had gained most of its commercial exposure in the smoky bars of Detroit or Cincinnati or Baltimore, found a new home on makeshift stages set up in reformed cow pastures. Festivals were set up throughout the United States and Canada, and within a few years Bill Monroe, who established one of the major festivals at Bean Blossom, Indiana, was able to announce from his stage that the festival included people from every state in the union, including Hawaii and Alaska. Not all the festivals attracted the immense crowds that flocked to rock festivals like Woodstock, but the bluegrass festivals made up in frequency what they lacked in individual size. By the mid-1970's every summer weekend brought news of five or six major festivals in different parts of the country, and bluegrass fans could, with a little hard driving, spend most summer weekends camped out under a portable PA system blaring forth the sounds of a five-string banjo. The endless string of festivals also provided steady work for the many new bands that emerged as bluegrass sought to expand its audience.

The bluegrass audience, which had formerly been virtually identical with the traditional country music audience, now attracted many people who had little or only passing interest in other forms of country music. Bluegrass was attracting a broad, ecumenical band of listeners as early as 1959, when the Newport Folk Festival invited Earl Scruggs and The Stanley Brothers to appear. Soon other bands, such as The Osborne Brothers, were playing concerts at colleges in the North and Midwest, and bluegrass found itself caught up in the intense fervor of the "folk revival." The music of Flatt and Scruggs reached vast popular audiences when it was used for the theme music to the hit television show, *The Beverly Hillbillies,* in the early 1960's, and later as the background music for the award-winning 1967 movie *Bonnie and Clyde* when the soundtrack was released in 1968. Another major film success of the mid-70's, *Deliverance,* made a national pop hit out of an old bluegrass standard, "Dueling Banjos." The simple, unamplified, downhome sound of bluegrass also formed a musical counterpart to the ecologically-oriented, back-to-basics lifestyle of the 70's, and the music began showing up in all sorts of films and commercials.

The music soon attracted an intellectual audience, an audience who found the dazzling, complex instrumental techniques of bluegrass more satisfying than the predictable sameness of most country music; not a few echoed the critic who openly compared Flatt and Scruggs' album,

Carlton Haney held the first bluegrass festival in 1965.

Foggy Mountain Banjo, to jazz. A number of young musicians, some from quite sophisticated backgrounds, began to form new bluegrass bands and to develop new styles. In the mid-1960's one such new musician, Amherst graduate Bill Keith, joined Bill Monroe's venerable band and proceeded to revolutionize banjo styles with his "chromatic" melodic style. Some old-timers scoffed at this and developments like it—they called Keith's style "Yankee picking"—but Monroe and others like him knew that bluegrass could not possibly survive by appealing only to its original Southern audience. Many of the "good ole boys" in Durham, Roanoke and Chattanooga who had cheered Flatt and Scruggs in the 1950's were now listening to "ole Waylon" and Merle Haggard and Roy Clark. It was the college kids in Boston and the young professionals in California and Washington, D.C., who were buying the reissues of the old music from the 1940's, and who were listening to the new bands that were developing ideas like those of Keith's.

Washington, D.C., in fact, became a center for the new styles of bluegrass. The group most responsible for this was The Country Gentlemen, formed in 1957 around tenor-mandolin player John Duffey, banjoist Eddie Adcock and singer-guitarist Charlie Waller. Waller was from Louisiana; Duffey was the son of a Metropolitan Opera singer. Both had been exposed to the heady mixture of urban and rural bluegrass that had come to characterize the Washington scene in the 1950's. The Washington-Baltimore area was an ideal melting pot, where young Northern musicians from the folk-

Family harmony: Arnold Watson, Mrs. General Dixon Watson and Doc Watson in concert together in 1966.

revival movement could brush shoulders with the more traditional Southern musicians who were eking out livings playing in the working-class bars of the area. The Country Gentlemen combined the best of these two worlds; they performed superb versions of old bluegrass standards such as "Red Rockin' Chair" and "Poor Ellen Smith," but they would just as often bring out jazz tunes like "Bye-Bye Blues," Harry Belafonte's calypso hit "Banana Boat Song," or Shel Silverstein's parodies. Duffey's trained voice did not have the rural twang of so many bluegrass tenors, and the group's harmony was slick and sophisticated. In Eddie Adcock they found a banjo player who was willing to experiment with a bewildering variety of jazzy styles. It all worked. The Country Gentlemen ap-

Josh Graves and Vassar Clements: dobro and fiddle.

pealed to all kinds of audiences, and in the 1960's they probably played more colleges and coffee-houses than any other bluegrass band. The Gentlemen did a lot to popularize bluegrass—more, probably, than any other band except Flatt and Scruggs.

Other young musicians followed the lead of Duffey, Waller and Adcock into a more progressive, eclectic brand of bluegrass that was soon being called "newgrass," actually an experimental trend that had been set in the early 1970's by one of the founders of traditional bluegrass, Earl Scruggs. When he split from Lester Flatt in 1969, Scruggs formed a band with his two sons and began playing a type of music that was one part bluegrass, one part country and one part rock. Scruggs soon outgrew (some would say turned his back on) his traditional audience, and on a famous television special was seen trading licks with everyone from Bob Dylan to a Moog synthesizer. At about the same time, the Nashville-based Osborne Brothers plugged in their banjo and mandolin and began crafting new three-part vocal harmonies derived from the sound of the main symbol of the Nashville Sound, the pedal steel guitar. But the real axis of the newgrass style was the Washington-Baltimore area; other area musicians like Bill Emerson and Cliff Waldron (who recorded one of the first newgrass standards, "Fox on the Run") flourished, and independent companies like Rebel documented the new sounds. Eddie Adcock soon formed a new band called II Generation, while Duffey formed a new group called The Seldom Scene. Many newgrassers celebrated their new freedom and, like some members of the Outlaw movement, felt a certain scorn toward Nashville. Eddie Adcock said "Nashville can only control their country music. It can't control any other kind of music. Bluegrass is one of these other kinds of music that Nashville can't control."

Newgrass music was characterized, on the surface, by shaggy hair, informal dress (gone were the classic white hats of Monroe's generation), and lots of laid-back jokes about how good the grass was. The music itself included an expansion of the standard bluegrass instrumentation to include, on occasion, drums, chromatic banjo styles, a penchant for long, jazz-like instrumental solos and an eclectic repertory often borrowed from rock. Back in the 1960's, for instance, even Jim and Jesse, Opry regulars, had cut an album of Chuck Berry songs. The 1970's saw groups like the Louisville-based New Grass Revival touring with rock star Leon Russell, and fiddler Vassar Clements appearing with ex-Allman Brothers guitarist Dickey Betts. Adcock's II Generation band recorded newgrass versions of songs popularized originally by groups like The Turtles and Bread, and Duffey's Seldom Scene won a Song

of the Year award in 1974 with their version of "Rider," a piece popularized by The Grateful Dead. (Linda Ronstadt also appeared as a guest on one Seldom Scene album.) Other newgrassers discovered jazz; young fiddlers found themselves listening a lot to Stephane Grappelli and Joe Venuti, swing-era veterans from the 1930's. An album called *Hillbilly Jazz*, produced on an independent label out of Chicago, became a surprise best seller; it featured the likes of David Bromberg and Vassar Clements playing swing-era standards like "C Jam Blues" and "Cherokee." Clements, who had once fiddled for Bill Monroe, became the most popular fiddler of the generation, and his bluesy, angular style influenced thousands. An old-timey band from North Carolina called The Red Clay Ramblers added an

The Country Gentlemen, 1962: Eddie Adcock, John Duffey, Tom Gray, Charlie Waller.

electric piano and a trumpet ("the bluegrass three," as they introduced it) and expanded their repertoire to include everything from "Keep the Home Fires Burning" to Bill Boyd's "Wah Hoo." The David Grisman Quintet and Michael Melford moved even more toward jazz, and soon found that some bluegrass fan magazines wouldn't even review their records. But many of the young musicians echoed the sentiments of John Duffey, who described The Seldom Scene in these words: "We are a somewhat contemporary band who uses the term 'bluegrass' more as a method than a means. We use the instrumentation that is generally associated with bluegrass music, and just play anything we choose to.... This type of music is classified by instrumentation, not especially by song or vocal arrangements." There is much truth in Duffey's statement: A lot of young ca-

Lester Flatt in 1975: loyal to bluegrass as it was in the 40's.

sual listeners applied the term "bluegrass" indiscriminately to any kind of music played with unamplified string instruments, whether it was honest-to-God bluegrass, Western swing, old-time music, folk music or whatever.

This trend was certainly exemplified by the success of guitarist-singer Doc Watson, one of the most influential individual performers of the 1970's. Doc (his real name is Arthel) came from a tiny mountain hamlet called Deep Gap, North Carolina, from a family that was a folklorist's dream: They sang old English ballads, droned archaic fiddle tunes and picked all manner of rags and blues. In fact, folklorists from the Smithsonian Institution first discovered Watson and brought him to all kinds of folk festivals in the 1960's. Yet Watson's music was certainly not "folk" in the narrow sense; before being discovered by the folk audience he had made his living playing all kinds of music, from straight-out

country to rockabilly. He was a consummate stylist and technician; he admitted in 1975, "I'd define my music, or my style, as a conglomeration of a lot of things that I've listened to, plus a few notions of my own." His albums soon began to include original guitar instrumentals as well as traditional pieces and classic Western swing as well as contemporary country. At festivals, acres of fans chanted for him to perform "Black Mountain Rag" or "Brown's Ferry Blues." More than anyone else, Doc Watson made the acoustic guitar the trendy instrument of the late 1970's. Once confined to the role of little more than a rhythm instrument in classic bluegrass, the guitar now emerged as a solo instrument.

Clarence White, a brilliant flat-top stylist who was featured on a classic album called *Appalachian Swing*, inspired a lot of younger musicians in this direction before his untimely death in 1973. One of these younger musicians was Tony Rice, perhaps the hottest soloist in newgrass in 1978, who played with The David Grisman Quintet on the West Coast. Others, and ones who learned more directly from Watson, included Norman Blake, an Alabama guitarist who took his eclectic music seriously, demanded respect and attention from his audience, and on occasion walked out of club dates when the audience got too noisy. A third major young guitarist was Dan Crary from Kansas, who began with The Bluegrass Alliance before leaving for a solo career. All three played what would basically have to be described as traditional music, but they played it with what the old-time jazzmen used to call "hot licks."

Thus the famous split between Flatt and Scruggs became symbolic of an entire generation. Flatt, doggedly sticking to purist modes formed in the 1940's, continued to play to his traditional audiences in the South and steadily sell his three or four thousand copies per record. Scruggs, experimenting with his music, played to college groups and youth markets across the country, his albums becoming fewer but more painstakingly crafted. No longer were the "good ole boys" upset at seeing long, shaggy hair at their bluegrass festivals, and a lot of people doted on how bluegrass music

Lester Flatt with his young talent, 14-year-old Marty Stuart...

brought together the rednecks and the hippies.

By the end of the decade, however, the newgrass movement was affecting even this, and some festivals were pointedly advertised as "newgrass." And, to be sure, not all young groups were experimental; two of the hottest bands of 1977, J. D. Crowe and The New South, and Boone Creek, were basically traditional, and were composed mainly of musicians from the South. To complicate matters still further, the era saw a strong revival of young bands playing deliberately in the archaic, pre-bluegrass style of the 1920's stringbands like The Skillet Lickers. The New Lost City Ramblers, featuring brilliant folklorist/performer Mike Seeger, began to copy arrangements off of old 78's as early as the 1960's. By the middle 1970's bluegrass festivals were full of bands like The Highwoods String Band from upstate New York, who specialized in old twin fiddle numbers; The Hotmud Family from southern Ohio, who were equally at home doing Uncle Dave Macon or Stanley Brothers bluegrass; and The Red Clay Ramblers from North Carolina, who even composed new tunes in old-time molds. Of course, to the typical fan, all these acts were simply "bluegrass," and by 1978, bluegrass, once the most easily defined of musical genres,

was experiencing a perplexing but intriguing identity crisis. It survived just fine, and although the hippie/redneck festival phenomenon lost its cultural force by the end of the 70's, and the festival scene settled down into a long, pleasant haul toward the millennium, the music continued to demonstrate great life and growth.

The "Atlanta Sound" was a heady mixture of black and white music, of rock, gospel, country and soul. Those different musical forms coalesced in Atlanta far more effectively than they did in Nashville, and country artists in Atlanta were generally exposed to a much broader spectrum of music. The city had been the center of country recording in the 1920's and had continued to function as a regional center for major companies up through the 1940's, many of the early recordings being made in temporary studios set up in places like the Kimball House hotel and the old Fox Theater, site of the famous premiere of *Gone with the Wind.*

Some blues had been recorded in Atlanta in the 1920's and 1930's, but Victor's A&R pioneer, Ralph Peer, complained that the blues musicians in Atlanta were not at all of the caliber he expected. However, by the late 1940's the city was devel-

...and Earl with his: three of his sons played in The Earl Scruggs Revue.

oping a healthy rhythm-and-blues culture; Piano Red recorded some of his important boogie woogie there; Little Richard forged a music that was to make him a pioneer in rock, and the 1960's saw the development of important soul groups like the phenomenally successful Gladys Knight and The Pips. Gospel music, black and white, also grew in Atlanta; the city was the scene in 1946 of the first "All-Night Singing," and was home base for major gospel artists like Hovie Lister and The Statesmen and Lee Roy Abernathy. In the 1950's and 60's, meanwhile, Atlanta produced country singers like Brenda Lee and Ray Stevens. In the 70's, though, Atlanta's most prominent contribution to popular music was clearly a gaggle of heavy-duty, country-oriented rock bands: The Allman Brothers, The Marshall Tucker Band, Wet Willie and Lynyrd Skynyrd, the big guys of Southern rock.

The nerve center for much Southern rock wasn't actually Atlanta, but nearby Macon, where, as Sam Phillips' Sun label had done some 20 years earlier, Phil Walden's Capricorn Records had achieved national success by working apart from the established recording centers and experimenting with an unstable fusion of Southern blues, rock and country. Otis Redding had been one of Walden's early discoveries, and it was Walden who, during the late 1960's helped Floridians Duane and Greg Allman form what was to become the first of the Southern Rock bands. The Allman Brothers' new band soon included Dickey Betts as a second lead guitarist, and they experimented with the use of two drummers. Country was only a part of the background and repertoire of the band; equally important was the Allmans' grounding in soul and rhythm-and-blues (Duane had played often behind Aretha Franklin) and Dickey Betts' serious interest in jazz (he was fascinated with Django Reinhardt). But Duane Allman's innovative slide guitar style was attractive to all manner of would-be country fans, and soon the teenaged sons and daughters of old Hank Williams fans were flocking to Allman Brothers Band concerts across the South. In many ways the band was a living symbol of the New South: It was integrated; into drugs, electronics and creating art that was original and yet based on the ingrained traditions of the region's two most dis-

tinctive subgroups, the working-class whites and the blacks. Even when Duane Allman died tragically in 1971, and when other members of the band fought long and painful drug battles, the band continued to produce million-selling records. Though they dissolved in 1976—self-destructed might be a more accurate term—they defined a genre. By the 90's the survivors had reformed and, to some people's surprise, were doing quite well both creatively and commercially.

In 1973 The Allman Brothers Band performed a memorable concert in Nashville that did much to impress the power of the new music on the Nashville community. On that same show was a group from North Carolina, The Marshall Tucker Band. One of the members of the Tucker band later recalled: "Hell, we'd never seen so many people together in one place.... Thought it was a revival or somethin'." Formed around the Caldwell brothers, Toy and Tommy, and George McCorkle (there was no Marshall Tucker in the group; he was a blind piano tuner the boys knew from their youth), the Spartanburg, North Carolina, band found themselves inheriting the mantle of The Allman Brothers Band. As with most Southern rock bands, Marshall Tucker built its career not on media promotion, but on personal appearances: over 300 dates in one year. They managed three Gold records and several hit singles in the mid-70's, but they were more at home in a Southern football stadium concert than in a studio or a television station. Like the Allmans they worked out of the Capricorn studios in Macon when they recorded, and like the Allmans they stressed their own roots—roots that were far more countrified than the Allmans'. All the Tuckers were products of a culture that supported the honky tonk music of the 1950's, Hank Williams music, and it's not surprising that after their records began crossing from the rock onto the country charts, "pure" country singers like Hank Williams Jr. and Waylon Jennings recorded their songs. The group maintained close ties with the Texas "Outlaws" and experimented with what they called "heavy bluegrass," and by 1977 they were attracting a wide enough audience to be asked to play at the Carter inaugural celebrations and tour with Emmylou

The Allman Brothers

Charlie Daniels

Harris. At times the Tucker band seemed more interested in presenting the image of a country band than actually playing like one—a significant step in the evolution of "country" as a public lifestyle choice and point of personal pride.

Even more down-home than the Tuckers was The Charlie Daniels Band: Here there was little difference between image and performing style. Daniels himself came on as a romping, stomping, Mike Fink mountain of a man who loved Southern cooking, Southern drinking, Southern girls and Southern music. One of the most colorful characters in modern country music, Daniels exhibited some of the gusto, boisterousness and sheer love of the music that typified old-time country music pioneers like Uncle Dave Macon. The music his band played was much like Daniels himself. Raw, energetic and undisciplined (concert numbers often stretched out to ten or 15 minutes), it was based on roots even deeper than the Hank Williams/honky tonk tradition that informed Marshall Tucker. Daniels went back to the wild, freewheeling stringbands of the 1920's and 30's and pulled out his fiddle, banjo and slide guitar to modernize such staples as "Orange Blossom Special,"

The Charlie Daniels Band in Holland in 1979.

"Fire On the Mountain," "Foggy Mountain Breakdown" and "Mountain Dew," also writing new songs in those old modes. Although he was closely associated with the Capricorn/Macon crowd, Daniels got his musical education as a Nashville sideman (a 10-year course), and chose to make Tennessee the geographical image in his music. Starting in 1974 he staged a series of annual "Volunteer Jams" (Tennessee is called The Volunteer State) in the Nashville area—marathon concerts that included jamming by most of the notable Southern rock stars as well as Texas breth-

ren like Willie Nelson and Delbert McClinton, Jefferson Airplane/Hot Tuna alumnus Papa John Creech, bluegrass comedienne Roni Stoneman, Nashville types like Tanya Tucker and, eventually, all sorts of musicians Daniels considered to be his musical kin.

At the end of the concerts the assembled musicians often stumbled en masse through "Tennessee Waltz," and not many CDB concerts closed without Daniels singing his less formal anthem, "The South's Gonna Do It Again." Perhaps because of his intense Tennessee orientation, but more likely because his roots in both country and the country music business were considerably deeper than any other Southern rocker, Daniels merged with the country mainstream more successfully than any of his 'billy-rocking brethren of the 70's. He was still very much in evidence on the Nashville scene, if not on the country charts, in the 90's, popular with Opry audiences and grownup Southern rock fans alike.

In the mid-70's, some observers pointed out that in reality there was little stylistic or musical difference between Southern rock and just plain rock, and that the music of The Allmans, Marshall Tucker, The CDB and company was little more than re-imaged basic boogie. Southern rock, however, had some distinctive stylistic elements, such as the use of a twin-guitar lead, an affinity for sets of fast, sharp guitar phrases and glissandos, and lyrics full of references to outlaws, Southern geography and a sort of runty machismo. So if it wasn't *that* different, it was different enough.

The Southern rock and Atlanta Sound bands, and indeed the bands and individual artists who formed both the "newgrass" community and the California country rock movement—all the vari-

Gary Stewart

ous hyphenated-country musicians of the 70's— were influential in one way or another on mainstream Nashville music. Basically, Nashville singers, musicians and producers borrowed what they liked from hyphenated-country just as hyphenated-country had borrowed what they liked from Nashville, and so mainstream country music expanded stylistically— Nashville's 70's and early 80's, in fact, saw greater stylistic growth than any period before or since. Then too, a lot of the people at the center of the various hyphenated or hybrid country movements *became* the Nashville mainstream; Music Row in the 80's and 90's was full of former Southern rock producers, newgrass fiddle players, folk-rock songwriters and so on.

The final word on hyphenated-country, or at least those variants in which blues and rock formed part of the mix, should really be a name: Gary Stewart, the one musician in whom it all seemed to come together. Stewart, a Florida native of Kentucky stock, was a tremendously powerful singer in whom the mountain sound of Hank Williams,

George McCorkle and Toy Caldwell of Marshall Tucker.

the blues-based energy of The Allman Brothers and the rockabilly mania of Jerry Lee Lewis all met and, instead of being diluted in the process of combination, were concentrated into an essence the likes of which has not been heard since. One of the elements Stewart possessed (and the Southern rockers didn't) was a deeply ingrained instinct for the classic hard-core honky tonk country song, and during his brief tenure on the country charts in the mid-70's he came up with some truly great ones: "Out of Hand," "Drinkin' Thing," "Room Above the Street," "She's Acting Single, I'm Drinking Doubles" and more. His *Out of Hand* album was particularly powerful; as critic Jay Orr wrote, it was "a hard stare into the dark-

ness of adultery, jealousy, alcoholism and crime," and "a honky tonk classic." Stewart, however, was, as *The Comprehensive Country Music Encyclopedia* puts it, "chronically beset by personal problems and a dangerous penchant for the wild side of life," and his career dissolved in relatively short order. Although he kept making albums into the 80's, they didn't have the focus of the work he'd done earlier with RCA producer Roy Dea (even though he did rope in Allman Brother Dicky Betts on some sessions), and by the mid-80's he'd retreated to his home in Fort Pierce, Florida, and the Texas club circuit which sustained so many unreconstructed hyphenated-country musicians during and after the Urban Cowboy fad.

Stewart re-emerged onto the recording scene toward the end of the decade, back with Roy Dea, though now on the independent HighTone label out of Berkeley, California. The years and all the abuses he'd stuffed into them had taken a toll on his magnificent country tenor, and his material wasn't quite as exactly on target (it would have been a miracle if it had been), but he still had more spirit, and a stronger connection to the red blood of country music's deepest, darkest souls, than any dozen of the young George Jones wannabes crowding the 90's charts. Naturally, country radio wouldn't play him or even his "oldies." As for the hybrid he and Roy Dea created in their first flush together, it simply vanished from the mainstream. No subsequent country artist even approached the fluid hillbilly rock intensity of *Out of Hand*.

By 1980, the various forms of rock- and blues-based hyphenated-country had quit making waves in the pop mainstream; you couldn't give them away to dedicated followers of fashion with a gun *and* a Calvin Klein bodyshirt. On the other hand, the whole range of non-Nashvillian country-ish music—everything from *Sweetheart of the Rodeo* to "The South's Gonna Do It Again"—had been the formative music of an awful lot of kids who would be in their late 20's, 30's and early 40's in 1990. Nobody in Nashville took much note of it at the time, but that was going to be a *very* important fact of country music life.

In addition to its various "alternative" forms, hyphenated-country music came in distinctly suburban, middle-class colors. The lush new studio sound pioneered by Billy Sherrill in the late 1960's had acclimated listeners to fuller, softer arrangements behind country songs, and thus they became more receptive to pop music recorded in that vein. Thus the early 1970's saw a number of "interlopers" in the country scene, artists who were established pop singers moving—some deliberately, some unwittingly—into the music. Names like Anne Murray, John Denver and Olivia Newton-John began crowding onto the country charts, jostling Tammy Wynette and George Jones, Loretta Lynn and Conway Twitty.

The case of Canadian singer Anne Murray, who in 1970 found her record "Snowbird" topping the country charts, was typical. She had made no effort to promote the song as a country tune, or herself as a country singer. "I had no idea it was a country tune," she recalled later. None of the background of the song was in any real sense connected to the traditional country music establishment. Murray had first heard the song performed by its author, Gene MacLellan, on a Canadian television show, and had recorded it for a small Canadian company.

Murray herself came from a background of classical piano and Italian arias, and was only marginally involved in the Canadian country music scene; she had little interest in country music. "I thought country music was just a bunch of people hangin' onto their noses and singing!" she said. Even when she got a break with a major American record producer, it was with the California-based Capitol Records, and in the 1972 *Country Music Who's Who* she was described as a "Canadian singer." Yet during all this time "Snowbird" was selling over a million copies, both in the United States and Canada, and many of them were being sold as country singles. The record might have been shipped to the stores as a pop product, but it was received as country and was adopted by the country audience now accustomed to the slick sounds of Sherrill and Glen Campbell.

In the early 1970's a number of records were to follow that pattern. Anne Murray herself accepted her new role with grace, and by the time her star was installed in the walkway in front of the Country Music Hall of Fame, she was appearing with Glen Campbell on television and consciously striving for country hits. In 1974, "He Thinks I Still Care" was an even bigger country hit than "Snowbird."

A different sort of crossover pattern was exemplified by another major pop singer of the 1970's, John Denver. Denver got most of his initial national exposure at the tail end of the folk revival of the 1960's. Born in New Mexico, he learned to play both standard and 12-string guitar (a staple of the folk singer) as a teenager, and like others of his generation he listened a lot to early Elvis before he got involved in the folk movement. Peter, Paul, and Mary recorded one of his songs, "Leavin' on a Jet Plane," and it became a Gold record in 1969. He himself became famous after replacing Chad Mitchell in The Mitchell Trio, with whom he performed from 1965 to 1969; The Mitchell Trio was one of the slicker folk acts of the time, an act whose style often verged on pop, and these lessons were not lost on Denver. He went out on his own in 1969 and began producing a couple of albums a year for Victor. These albums were mostly full of original but folk-like melodies, and in 1971 one song, "Take Me Home, Country Roads," broke through in both the pop and the country fields.

From there on, most of his albums reached Gold record status; however, he made no overt attempt to market his product as country music. He didn't work out of Nashville, he seldom recorded in Nashville, and he didn't make even token appearances at the Opry; his television appearances were always on mainstream shows. In spite of this, his records gained airplay on country radio stations, and in 1975 the CMA

Anne Murray

named him Entertainer of the Year and his "Back Home Again" Song of the Year. According to *Billboard*, the song also outsold all other country singles. By 1975, then, the assimilation process was complete: Denver was country.

Actually, the acceptance of Denver as a country artist was not all that painful. Denver, after all, was about the only survivor from the urban folk revival to make a successful transition into country music. The virtues that the folk movement taught him served him well in his new milieu; he at least saw the need to maintain an image of simplicity, even in his well-crafted and carefully planned studio albums. His songs, and the image he presented in concert, came to be built around a new sort of bucolic romanticism. "Thank God I'm a country boy," he preached in one song, while others dealt with the glories of his adopted home state (Colorado), and with the kind of natural "Rocky Mountain High" that appealed to the youth of the 1970's.

In 1975 John Denver was named CMA Entertainer of the Year. With him were Chet Atkins, Billy Walker, Minnie Pearl and Bobby Bare and, below, Jerry Reed.

The tendency to romanticize rural life, of course, had long been present in country music, from the early Vernon Dalhart-Carson Robison paeans of the 1920's, like "My Blue Ridge Mountain Home," but Denver's came at a time when many country performers who had actually lived through such rural backgrounds were trying to *de*-romanticize it; Dolly Parton, who came from an impoverished community in eastern Tennessee, was singing "In the Good Old Days (When Times Were Bad)." However, much of Denver's audience was no longer from the farm or the mountains; they were second- or third-generation urbanites. When they went to a John Denver concert, they saw nothing ironic in his use of one of the most expensive and sophisticated light shows to illustrate his song of simple, basic, homespun pleasures. The fact that this new sort of romanticism could work so successfully not only with the youth audience, but with the country audience as well, showed RCA Victor and every other record company in Nashville that the old notion of the country audience as an identifiable ethnic or geographic entity was finally and completely obsolete.

By 1975, the crossover effect was becoming so common that nobody could treat it as an aberration, an exception to the rule. Country artists were crossing into pop, pop artists were crossing into country, and the editors of trade publications like *Billboard,* who had to attempt to categorize the music and musicians, were puzzling over the impact of the transition. Some members of the Nashville establishment professed that the crossover effect, working either way, was bad, and would destroy the purity of the music, but Billy Sherrill commented that he never knew of a country singer who "kicked in the doors of KHJ [a large Top 40 station in Los Angeles] and said, 'Quit playing my record!'"

The Nashville establishment was having far more trouble in accepting the new pop interlopers into the country field. By 1975 country radio stations were willing to play previously pop artists like John Denver, B.J. Thomas, Linda Ronstadt, Olivia Newton-John, Mac Davis, Elvis, The Eagles, The Ozark Mountain Daredevils, Paul McCartney, Gordon Lightfoot, The Amazing Rhythm Aces and The Pointer Sisters. Out of the Top Ten *Billboard* country music chart-topping albums for 1975, six were by former pop artists.

The extent to which pop had invaded country was matched only by the speed of the invasion. Nashville's Music Row, which prided itself on spotting and anticipating trends, was caught off guard. In 1972, for instance, *Record World* published a massive directory called *Country Music Who's Who,* designed to reflect country's established stars, new stars and behind-the-scenes people. For its time it was a sound, reliable guide to the state of the music, but if you compare it with the Top Ten country albums of 1975, just three years later, you find that six were by artists not even mentioned in the 1972 *Who's Who.* Nashville suddenly found itself playing a new kind of ballgame, with vague and confusing rules.

An instinctive response to that kind of culture shock is to reject the new and to reaffirm the old, and that's what happened: The older Nashville community felt it had to shore up the

Country-pop Olivia Newton-John and bluegrass-only Bill Monroe.

dikes and fight to preserve the well-defined purity of its music. The battle, when it came, centered around a remarkably inoffensive, even benign, figure, Olivia Newton-John, and climaxed in late 1974 and early 1975, a few months before John Denver's CMA triumph. It was a brief but traumatic episode that left its scars on many of the people involved and made a public issue of pop's invasion of country.

Olivia Newton-John was a young Australian singer who, in 1973 and early 1974, began to record pop-oriented material in England. She sang in a strong, clear, young voice, and though she'd had little exposure to country music, her producers often backed her with a steel guitar and dubbed vocal harmonies; the results were records that sounded a lot like the later efforts of folk-pop singer Joan Baez. Furthermore, one of her first successful records was an attractive arrangement of "Banks of the Ohio," a native American ballad that had been recorded dozens of times by all sorts of country singers and been a staple in the urban folk revival of the 1960's.

Perhaps because of the song, as well as the

sound, Olivia's producers found that when they tried to get her records airplay in the United States, more often than not they got it on country stations. When Olivia began touring in the United States in early 1974 she, like Anne Murray, was surprised to find that she was typed as a country singer, and objected, in a mild way, to the label. She told an interviewer: "Since I'm accepted as a country singer, I can do just about anything. So I'm lucky. I think I'm accepted by the country people, but I don't think people think of me strictly as country. Not now, anyway."

The gulf between Newton-John and the traditional country singers soon became apparent to the public. When she was invited to do a guest shot on the Opry, she didn't seem to be suitably impressed with the honor, and she embarrassed everybody by announcing, "I thought the Opry was on Sunday night." A while later Roy Acuff, on a national telecast, referred to her as "Oliver Newton John." Probably no malice was intended in either of these comments—they were honest mistakes that reflected the vast difference

The Amazing Rhythm Aces turned up on country radio.

between the new and the traditional country— but the friction was made more obvious a few months later when Newton-John reportedly said she would refuse to work any more country concerts with artists like Porter Wagoner and Tammy Wynette. Nashville singers saw in this a tacit admission that Olivia had used country radio to establish herself, and was now trying to turn her back on her benefactor.

Things were at that stage in October 1974 when the CMA held its annual awards show, broadcast nationwide from downtown Nashville. At the time, Olivia Newton-John had two albums, *If You Love Me (Let Me Know)* and *Let Me Be There*, on

Billboard's best-seller list; the former was the top country album in October, and the latter had been on the charts for most of the year. *Billboard* had rated her the Number Four country artist (behind Charlie Rich, Conway Twitty and Loretta Lynn) in album sales. Her popularity was undeniable, and partly for this reason the CMA voted her Female Vocalist of the Year over a number of other singers who had been established for years in the country field. By design or by chance, Olivia was not even present for the award, accepting her laurels *in absentia*.

The traditionalists were enraged, and lost no time in expressing their displeasure. A few weeks after the national CMA Awards telecast, a group of about 50 Nashville singers met at the Nashville home of George Jones and Tammy Wynette. Ostensibly, the group banded together to protest the relatively few entertainers on the CMA's board of directors, but in fact they were protesting the increasing acceptance of pop singers into the country community. Bill Anderson, a spokesman for the group, called the Newton-John award "the straw that broke the camel's back." There was, in fact, some support for this idea in the CMA; one board member said, "I don't feel it's right that the country music industry should prostitute itself just for the sake of one hour on national television."

A week later the singers voted to unite into a new organization, the Association of Country Entertainers (ACE); unlike the CMA, which allowed anyone who made his or her living in the music business into its ranks, the ACE was to be restricted to country performers, and the group named a "screening committee" to determine the country credentials of prospective ACE members. The committee was a Who's Who of old Nash-

George Morgan

Jimmy C. Newman

These stars and others like them fought pop's invasion of country in the mid-70's.

Porter Wagoner

Hank Snow

Ernest Tubb, Hank Snow and friends

Roy Acuff

Olivia Newton-John's CMA award was "the straw that broke the camel's back" according to Bill Anderson, shown here with George Morgan and Billy Walker at an Association of Country Entertainers (ACE) press conference.

ville: Dolly Parton, Hank Snow, Johnny Paycheck, George Morgan, Tammy Wynette and Jimmy C. Newman. Even "King of Country Music" Roy Acuff endorsed the group.

Critics, however, pointed out that many of the founders of the ACE were former pop or rock singers who had made a rather complete transition into country, and that earlier country giants like Jimmie Rodgers and Bob Wills had incorporated pop elements into their music. Johnny Paycheck countered that the music content was only part of the issue: "Our chief complaint is that if an artist gets a crossover record that is played on both country and pop stations, that artist has an unfair advantage in the CMA Awards."

Another ACE member, Billy Walker, was more candid about the group's purpose: at a Nashville press conference he explained that many

member were concerned that "outside influences" and the attempts to take country music to a wider audience would dilute country music "until it no longer exists." He continued, "We are mainly people who made country music what it is today, trying to protect our business because we see it flaking off in thousands of directions. We're trying to keep it at home." So finally the confusion and the resentments were out in the open, and country music's identity crisis was front page news across the nation.

ACE had had almost no practical effect—for instance, John Denver's Entertainer of the Year award came after the centrists' revolt, not before—but for better or worse, it drew the battle lines between Nashville factions that had been at cross-purposes for years. On one side were the ACE people. On the other were three groups. First, there were the established Nashville producers who had helped put Nashville on the map and who now wanted to see it move more into pop: people like Buddy Killen of Tree International, Bob Beckham of Combine Music, Don Grant, Bergen White, Allen Reynolds, and of course Billy Sherrill.

Then there were the interlopers, producers attracted to Nashville with the express intent of producing pop records at the city's superb studios; in the 1960's and 70's the list of pop acts recording in Nashville had grown to include Simon and Garfunkel, Johnny and Edgar Winter, Neil Young, Wilson Pickett, Carol Channing, Connie Francis, Grand Funk Railroad, B. B. King, Perry Como, Bob Dylan, Tom Jones—the list goes on. These new producers, such as Buzz Cason, whose Creative Workshop was attracting the best pop acts of the 1970's, complained only that people in New York or Los Angeles were too quick to label any record cut in Nashville as "country." Bob Montgomery, who produced Top 40 hits for Bobby Goldsboro, admitted that on occasion he did not want to publicize the fact that some of his records were done in Nashville "because as soon as I said it, people would say, 'That's a good country record.'" The Nashville pop producers had problems of their own, and in 1976 they talked of forming into a Pop Music Association to parallel the activities of the Country Music Association.

But it was the third group that gave the country traditionalists the most cause for concern: This was the anti-Nashville Sound, anti-Billy Sherrill, anti-John Denver group of long-haired roughnecks known as the Outlaws, a group that did not invade the music from "outside" but grew with the music and effected the 1970's most telling revolution—from the inside.

Waylon Jennings

CHAPTER 12

The Outlaws

Mickey Newbury, the cult-hero writer of "An American Trilogy," "San Francisco Maple Joy," and "She Even Woke Me Up To Say Goodbye," once compared the Nashville artist colony of the late 60's to that of Paris in the 20's—hyperbole perhaps, but nonetheless a measure of the creative energy in that time and place.

And the energy was indeed intense. The talent was there—a new generation in town, a collection of deeply gifted young Southerners drawn to songwriting as their art form—and so was the dynamic, that special combination of competition and collaboration within a relatively small circle which often produces the bursts of creativity we identify and label as artistic movements.

In this case, the label that stuck was "Outlaw." It fit well, as did the terms which often accompanied it, "rebellion" and "revolution," for the new guys' interest in taking country music on an adventure clashed quite violently with the establishment's wish to keep it safe at home, and the upstarts did in fact come to be regarded (with either fear or admiration, depending on the perspective) as heretical, disreputable and quite possibly dangerous.

The establishment attitude was understandable enough. The people running Music Row felt that they had traveled a long, hard road to develop a formula that for the first time was making country music a totally respectable facet of mainstream pop, and they were very reluctant to surrender that newfound security to a bunch of suspiciously well educated, badly groomed, disrespectful young drunks, dopers and misfits—which is putting it more bluntly than anyone in Nashville would have done at the time, Southern circumspection being the rule rather than the exception in those days.

For their part, many of the Outlaws didn't see themselves as revolutionaries of any sort. A much more popular notion was that they were in fact conservatives whose crusade (if indeed they had one, a dubious contention in the first place) was aimed at wresting control of the music from people *they* regarded as heretical, disreputable and possibly dangerous: the marketeers they judged to be ignoring country music's heart, soul and heritage in favor of hard-selling mediocre country-pop to the masses (those being, again, not quite the terms used at the time).

There's no doubt about it, the Outlaws were different. They looked different—they had long hair untouched by Brylcreem or Final Net, and wore black leather and blue jeans in public—and they acted different. As Dave Hickey, the brilliant, often cruelly witty critic who was one of the first journalists to describe the tension between the Outlaws and the establishment, put it, the Outlaws were "just about the only folks in Nashville who will walk into a room where there's a guitar and a *Wall Street Journal,* and pick up the guitar." Hickey, incidentally, was the man who first applied the "Outlaws" label to the artists in question, in a 1973 *Country Music* article. He forgets whether or not he got the idea from "Ladies Love Outlaws," a song Waylon Jennings used as a 1972 album title.

Waylon was one of the three artists regarded as the leading lights of the Outlaw movement; the others were Willie Nelson and Kris Kristofferson. Since each of them made his move to "break out" of Nashville in the three-year period from 1969 to 1972, it's hard to say with any certainty who influenced whom the most, and who made the first move. All three, as well as many other younger writers and singers, were mutual and contemporaneous influences on each other.

Kristofferson came from a background radically different in some ways from that of the typical country singer. He was born in the South, in Brownsville, Texas, but he grew up as an Army brat moving around the country with his family. As a teenager, he found himself listening to the only kind of energized music available to him in the pre-rock early 1950's: the lonesome white blues of Hank Williams. But Kristofferson soon found himself moving into more traditional forms of culture. In college he majored in creative writing, and he won several prizes in a short story competition conducted by the *Atlantic Monthly,* then the country's leading literary magazine. Kristofferson, however, also played a lot of football in college, and he was good enough in Golden Gloves boxing to make *Sports Illustrated.* That combination of good grades, straight arrow character and athletic skills made him a natural candidate for a prestigious Rhodes scholarship, and the early 1960's found him at Oxford University studying the difficult, mystical poetry of William Blake.

Dylan's influential 1969 album, Nashville Skyline.

Before graduating, though, Kristofferson dropped out, began calling himself Kris Carson and began writing country songs. He made *Time* magazine, but that was about it; soon he had joined the Army and was leading a country band of enlisted men around bases in Germany (when, that is, he wasn't training as a combat helicopter pilot). The Army didn't quite know what to make of him—a good ROTC boy gone sour— and finally sent him back to the States with an assignment to teach English at West Point. He made it as far as Nashville and resigned his commission.

This was 1966; Buck Owens and Jack Greene and Glen Campbell were riding high, and country music was still pretty distinct from pop. Kristofferson, who for some years had been responding to the honesty and simplicity of the "pure" music, set out to become a songwriter. He wrote his songs, sang them on demo tapes and made the rounds of the Nashville publishers. He also married, started a family, and held a variety of jobs to keep himself together, everything from bartender to janitor at Johnny Cash's studio. During one particularly bad time, he took a job in the Gulf of Mexico flying helicopters out to oil rigs. Whatever people think of Kristofferson's macho image, he came by it honestly.

His songs were selling, and were being recorded by major Nashville singers. Dave Dudley recorded an early effort called "Vietnam Blues," and Roy Drusky did "Jody and the Kid"; other efforts were recorded by Faron Young, Jerry Lee Lewis, Bobby Bare and Ray Stevens. Many of these early works were just good, typical country songs, distinguished mainly by being well-crafted examples of a well-defined style. Soon, though, Kristofferson was hanging out with some of Music Row's Young Turks, young experimental songwriters who were trying to expand the horizons of the music. These were people like

Kris Kristofferson

Rita Coolidge and Kris Kristofferson at Willie's 4th of July Picnic.

Kristofferson in Pat Garrett and Billy the Kid in the 70's...

And with Barbra Streisand in A Star Is Born in the early 80's. From Army brat to Oxford—and from Nashville to Texas to Hollywood.

Chris Gantry, Mickey Newbury, Tony Joe White, Donnie Fritts—people who were anticipating the ethic of what would become redneck rock, people who did marijuana *and* Lone Star beer, wore long hair *and* cowboy boots. Kristofferson summed up some of the group's contradictions in his well-known song, "The Pilgrim: Chapter 33," with the lines "He's a poet (he's a picker)/He's a prophet (he's a pusher)," and dedicated that song to his Nashville songwriter friends, along with two other notorious free spirits, Jerry Jeff Walker and veteran folk singer Jack Elliot.

An important influence on Kristofferson's scene, if not his writing, was Bob Dylan, whose early 1969 release of *Nashville Skyline*, recorded on Music Row with some of Nashville's best, most traditional sidemen, was a watershed event for Nashvillians and indeed for Dylan's college-educated, baby boomer fans. Many of those people, accustomed as they were to Dylan in a rad-lib, urban folk-rock-druggie-protest mode, were horrified at his apparent turn to country music. Dylan, though, seemed to go out of his way to embrace Nashville. He recorded a whole session of old country standards with Johnny Cash (only a few were released), and even overrode Columbia Records' objections to his use of the word "Nashville" in the title of the new album. Moreover, the songs on *Nashville Skyline* were both personal and conventional, with neither the political sentiments of early 60's Dylan nor his later use of dense, free-allusional imagery anywhere in evidence (they were "country" enough that several Nashville singers covered them), and Dylan took pains to embrace that approach, too. As he told the press at the time, "These are the type of songs that I always felt like writing when I've been alone to do so." His earlier songs, he said, were written in a "New York atmosphere," part of the self-conscious folk movement, but the new Nashville music had "a good spirit."

For many of the young composers in Kristofferson's circle, Dylan's endorsement of Nashville music justified their own faith in the music as a serious medium. And for many of the older Music Row publishers, the success of *Nashville Skyline* (which sold over a million copies and generated a hit single, "Lay Lady Lay") showed them the potential of the "new" country song in the youth market—a market to which traditional country had little appeal. After *Nashville Skyline*, then, the door opened considerably wider for Kristofferson's new songs which, though country in form, reflected the culture of a younger generation. Also, the executives of Music Row began to look with new respect on song-

Mickey Newbury

writers in general. Formerly faceless hacks sitting around a table grinding out songs for the big guys, they now became regarded as poets; sensitive, valuable individuals often as important as the singers themselves.

A few months after *Nashville Skyline*, Kristofferson got "Me and Bobby McGee" recorded by Roger Miller. "Me and Bobby McGee," with its story of countercultural New West rambling, was not exactly a typical country song; it was one of the first of Kristofferson's "new" songs to get wide recognition. Folksinger Gordon Lightfoot picked it up, and then in 1971, Janis Joplin, who had recorded the piece at her last session before she died, made it a big pop success; it was Kristofferson's first "crossover" hit. But even before this, while working as a janitor at Johnny Cash's studios, Kristofferson had interested Cash in some of his songs. By 1970 both Cash's friendship with Dylan, and his carefully nourished "reformed Outlaw" image, had made him a sort of a mentor to the new breed

of young Nashville songwriters. He sang a Kristofferson song on his television show that summer, recorded "Sunday Morning Coming Down," and even wrote a poem to Kris as the liner notes for Kristofferson's first album. All of this helped "Sunday Morning Coming Down" win the 1970 CMA award for Song of the Year. Kristofferson showed up to accept the award wearing shoulder length hair and a scuffed suede suit; he seemed confused, stood with his back to the audience, and finally mumbled a few words of thanks. Master of ceremonies Tennessee Ernie Ford was visibly shaken, and the older Nashville crowd, standing around in their tuxedos and basking in their hard-won respectability, were outraged at this "gesture" on their nationally televised show. They were even more puzzled when they confronted the fact that Kristofferson's winner wasn't a drug or protest song, but just a good old-fashioned beer-drinking lonely song, if perhaps a tad lonelier and more alienated than most. But the next year, Sammi Smith had one of the top country hits with another Kristofferson song,

Outlaws turn Highwaymen: Cash, Jennings, Nelson and Kristofferson on tour in the 80's.

Willie Nelson

"Help Me Make It Through the Night," and Music Row, as always, accepted success. Thus Kristofferson gradually gained a form of acceptance.

The country music fan magazines portrayed the CMA Awards show incident as a major traumatic event in country music's development. Certainly it signaled to the national audience that changes were occurring in Nashville, but it wasn't all that traumatic. Kristofferson's "new" music still had a lot in common with established country tradition. His own albums, produced with crack Nashville session men, used standard instrumentation and arrangements, and his songs were crafted from simple, archetypal country melodies and chord patterns. Kristofferson never failed to acknowledge his respect for Hank Williams, for instance, and his first publisher found his early songs so reminiscent of Williams' that she had to warn Kristofferson about it. Even after the CMA incident Kristofferson continued to have his songs recorded primarily by country artists: Jerry Lee Lewis, Faron Young, Ray Price, Bobby Bare, Ray Stevens. And Kristofferson found himself embracing a large part of the value system of the Nashville scene. He attended a fundamentalist service at the church of the Reverend Jimmy Snow (the son of Hank Snow), got saved and wrote "Why Me," which soon became a staple of modern gospel groups. Even after Kristofferson left Nashville, he still felt his mode was unchanged: "This is country music," he said backstage at one of his late 1974 concerts.

What then was it about the Kristofferson experience that was so revolutionary, so influential? Some people feel the lyrics of his songs,

"Little Willie" in his line-toeing, snappy-dressing days.

though simple and uncomplicated, contained reflections of the new values of the new generation. Kristofferson's protagonists often find themselves alienated not because somebody done them wrong, but simply because of the way life is.

Many country songs talk about freedom in one way or another, but Kristofferson's talked about it in a very open and self-conscious way: "Freedom's just another word for nothing left to lose." On the liner notes to his second album Kristofferson wrote of his songs: "Call these echoes of the goings-up and the coming-downs, walking pneumonia and run-of-the-mill madness, colored with guilt, pride, and a vague sense of despair." His songs also discussed sex in a frank, but easy and open way: "Help Me Make It Through the Night" is direct, but at the same time tender and serious. Some commentators on the music scene, such as historian Bill Malone, feel that if Kristofferson "has really contributed anything new to country music, it is the theme of sexuality openly discussed and endorsed without shame."

Yet all this is to see Kristofferson's influence stemming only from his music, and affecting only other music. His own albums sold fairly well, and his songs recorded by others sold well, but not all that well. Much of the effect Kristofferson had on the music came from the man, from Kristofferson the personality, the performing self. For one thing, a lot of his female admirers were attracted to him simply because of his rugged good looks. A close friend once described Kristofferson as "pretty," an unusual adjective for the world of country music. Country singers have, until fairly recently, hardly been characterized as handsome or pretty or good-looking; Grand Ole Opry faces might be distinctive (such as Porter Wagoner) or rugged (such as Johnny Cash) or intense (such as Hank Williams), but not especially handsome. Kristofferson's rather blatant sex appeal helped establish him as a leading Hollywood actor; by the mid-1970's he was appearing customarily in one or two films a year, and was the only male country singer to grace the pages of *Playboy's* "Sexy Stars of the 1970's."

To other people Kristofferson was influential simply through his lifestyle and individuality. He showed other young Nashville writers that it was possible to function as an *auteur* in Music City, that one could maintain integrity and still have commercial success. In one sense, he raised country songwriting from a vocational skill to a highly self-conscious art—for better or for worse.

One of the Nashville writers who learned from Kristofferson's example was Willie Nelson. In later years, Nelson recalled: "He's got to be recognized as one of the first to really break open both fields [country and pop]

Later Willie in film version of The Red-Headed Stranger.

without following what Nashville put down as the rules of the game. Kris made his own rules, did it his own way. That's why I admire and respect Kris.... It takes a lot of nerve and guts to do what people like Kristofferson have done."

Kristofferson's individuality extended far beyond his long hair and scruffy suits; he was an implausible mix of creativity and domesticity—in his own words, "a walking contradiction." By the mid-1970's he had made films with counterculture figures like Bob Dylan (*Pat Garrett and Billy the Kid*) as well as mavens of the mainstream like Barbra Streisand (*A Star Is Born*); had gotten saved at the Reverend Snow's

revival and done an album called *Jesus Was a Capricorn,* as well as steamy nude scenes with Sarah Miles in *The Sailor Who Fell from Grace with the Sea*. In the 80's he continued working in films, mostly of the non-mainstream kind (starring, for instance, in Michael Cimino's notoriously anti-establishmentarian *Heaven's Gate* and the adventurously futuristic *Trouble in Mind*), and playing the club circuit with his band; he continued to write songs and make the occasional album, but the outspokenly political content of much of his material—most of one of his albums, for example, was devoted to songs about the U.S.-sponsored civil war in El Salvador—kept him far away from radio airplay and popular acceptance. His acting career continued into the 90's, while his most visible role in music was as a member of the Outlaw-all-star band, The Highwaymen, with Johnny Cash, Waylon Jennings and Willie Nelson.

If 1971 was Kristofferson's big year, with both pop and country hits, it was one of Willie Nelson's worst. He hadn't had a decent hit record for a couple of years, he was finding that his membership in the Music Row club was not really satisfying him, and his divorce from his third wife, Shirley, became official. The problems began in late 1970. Shirley had left, he cracked up five automobiles and, to top it off, the year ended with him getting a phone call at a downtown Christmas party: Better get out here, your house is burning down. "When I got there, it was in flames, and there were firemen everywhere," he recalled. "So I ran in and got my stash bag and ran out. I had a pound of good Colombian in there, and I knew I was gonna need it to get high." Willie took his stash, left the burned-out

The crowd

Leon Russell and Willie

Dripping Springs

Tex Ritter and Willie

John Prine at the Picnic

Willie and Sammi Smith

house, and moved to a dude ranch near Bandera, Texas. Though he didn't know it at the time, the fire was to be a major turning point both in his career and in the direction of modern country music.

You can find Willie Nelson's name in the older histories of country music, but you have to look hard. In many ways his story was typical of the Nashville composer-singer who "made it" in the world of the 1960's: He was the composer of a few of the hundreds of songs that made the charts in those years, and the singer of even fewer. Born in 1933 in Abbott, Texas, Nelson learned guitar from his grandfather, and was writing "poems and melodies" by the time he was six. In high school he organized a band (it included his sister Bobbie, who still plays in his outfit today) and grew up in the rough-and-tumble, mixed-up Southwestern musical scene of the late 1940's. From the first Willie accepted Texas music with enthusiasm; when he was only 13 he somehow managed to book Bob Wills and The Texas Playboys into a dance at Whitney, Texas. Like most Texas musicians, Nelson knew Wills, and in 1960,

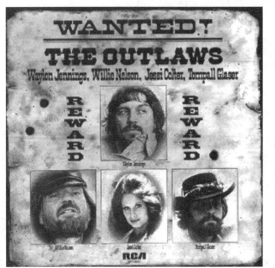

when Nelson started out on his career, the King of Western Swing gave him a ringing endorsement: "I have had the pleasure of being an entertainer for nearly 35 years. During this time I've seen a lot of new talent appear on the music scene, but hardly ever have I seen the likes of Willie Nelson." Wills couldn't have known it at the time, but his testimonial was to become prophecy.

For 10 years Nelson paid his dues. Dropping out of Baylor University in 1952, he began a career as a country disc jockey in Texas and points west like Oregon and Washington; for a time he taught guitar in Houston, and occasionally resorted to trades like door-to-door salesmanship. All this time he was trying to write country songs, and occasionally producing fine ones like "Family

Bible," which he sold for $50. In 1959 he moved to Nashville to write songs for Pamper Music, owned by fellow Texan and honky tonk pioneer Ray Price. Within a couple of years, he found himself with a Number One hit when Patsy Cline recorded "Crazy" in 1961. (The song was revived in 1976 by Linda Ronstadt and became a hit again.) That same year Faron Young hit Number One— for nine weeks—with Nelson's "Hello Walls."

Recording executives thought they saw something promising in Willie's own singing, and Liberty Records gave him a recording contract. His first session was held in Hollywood, not Nashville, and though it contained 13 good Nelson songs and the piano playing of a young Leon Russell, the album broke no sales records. A couple of his singles on Liberty, "Touch Me" and "Willingly" (with Shirley Collins), made the charts, however, and he found himself able to get personal appearances in the West, being especially well liked in Las Vegas. In 1962 Faron Young recorded "Three Days" successfully.

By the mid-1960's Nelson was appearing on the Opry and had landed a contract with Victor, and in 1967-68 he had a string of single hits for that label: "Blackjack County Chain," "The Party's Over," "Johnny One-Time," "One in a Row," "Little Things" and "Bring Me Sunshine." But most of his money and fame still came from the songs he composed for other singers—people like Ray Price, songs like "Night Life." As the country waded through the morass of Vietnam, Willie wrote his well-crafted songs, played golf, toured with Opry regulars and collected his checks from BMI. He built a house on a 400-acre farm in the hills north of Nashville where he had run-ins with neighbor Ray Price's fighting roosters and named two of his pigs Lester and Earl, the Foggy Mountain Hogs.

It was a typical career up until that fiery winter night in 1970, but if you look a little closer,

*Cash as a different
kind of Outlaw.*

Waylon in the 1966 film, Nashville Rebel. Ladies love outlaws.

which he himself did not stand in good stead. As he said of his relationship with the corporate monolith of RCA Victor, "I couldn't get anybody on the executive end of it interested in promoting me as an artist. There was a lack of communication and a lack of knowledge of what the people wanted." His producer, Chet Atkins, was sympathetic, but Willie felt that Chet's own hands were tied. "It was like a huge machine. 'We'll have to talk to New York.'" When he tried to make waves, he got little response. "The people I had been involved with had done things their way for years and years and had been successful. They didn't want to change their way of thinking. And I didn't want to change mine. I had definite ideas, things I wanted to carry out...and according to the regimented bureaucracy, I wasn't doing it right." An unsatisfactory stalemate developed, with neither Willie nor RCA getting what they wanted and both parties growing increasingly frustrated; it went on until Willie's house burned, and he made his decision. He went back to Texas.

you can see a few signs of the events to come. Along with writers like Mel Tillis, Wayne Walker, Merle Kilgore and Justin Tubb, Willie comprised the second generation of writers in the honky tonk tradition, writers who were skillfully using the forms and idioms of that tradition to create hard, tough, almost existential statements of human relationships. When Kristofferson's songs started hitting Nashville, Nelson felt an instinctive relationship: His own records took on a spartan simplicity around this time, with his sharp voice often backed only by bass, drums and steel guitar, a most unusual sound for Nashville in those days. The biggest change coming over Willie, however, was one of lifestyle. He began to hang out with the new writers like Kristofferson, Mickey Newbury, Billy Joe Shaver and Waylon Jennings.

One of the things he saw and liked about them was that they were artists hell-bent on retaining control of their product—an area in

Jessi Colter

Texas music had always been a part of his career. For years he'd been associated with giants of Southwestern music like Bob Wills, Ray Price and Ernest Tubb (in whose band he played for a time). Long before Texas style had become fashionable, Willie had recorded live albums there and had even made an album called *Texas in My Soul*, which included such jingoistic bits as "Remember the Alamo" and the theme song from *Lyndon Johnson's Texas*. Thus it was not surprising that his first "liberated" album, cut in 1973, well after leaving Nashville, was full of Texas songs and Texas musicians. *Shotgun*

Willie, recorded in New York City and produced by Jerry Wexler for Atlantic, featured sidemen like Waylon Jennings, Doug Sahm (fresh from a successful album with Bob Dylan), ex-Wills fiddler Johnny Gimble and ex-Ray Price steel guitarist Jimmy Day; the songs include a couple of Bob Wills standards, as well as newer fare by Nelson and Leon Russell. When Nelson later explained that "what Texas represents to me is where I relax," he was trying to make clear that for him, Texas was not part of any public relations image.

Nor was his break from Nashville and traditional country music all that drastic. In 1972 he began playing concerts in Texas with established country artists like Roy Acuff, Tex Ritter, Roger Miller, Buck Owens and Earl Scruggs. On July 4, 1973, he held his first festival at Dripping Springs—an event that was billed as the largest country music festival ever. Around 60,000 people attended, but this was a lower figure than the promoters had hoped for. The event was more important as a symbol that a new generation of singers and writers had arrived on the scene, for Kristofferson performed, as did Waylon Jennings, Billy Joe Shaver and Tom T. Hall: the cream of the new breed. But there was also Charlie Rich, fresh from his successes with slick Billy Sherrill, and old Nashville too: Acuff and Monroe and Tex Ritter.

That first festival, at least, suggested that Nelson wanted to build bridges between the different, polarized schools of the music; he said of his first concert at Dripping Springs, "It was the first time anyone had seen all types of people together listening to country music. It was actually the first time the hippie and the redneck had gotten together." After the 1973 festival, the Austin

Nashville Sound meets Outlaw movement: Chet Atkins with Waylon and Willie in the 70's.

All-around music man and country soul guru, "Cowboy" Jack Clement.

By 1974, Willie had become the guru to hordes of young Southerners who insisted on wearing T-shirts saying, "Matthew, Mark, Luke, and Willie," and in 1975 he really hit the big time when his Columbia album, *Red Headed Stranger,* became a best seller, breaking over not into mainstream pop but rather the rock charts. The album was produced by Nelson himself with a lean, sparse sound that made Columbia want to overdub it with strings; Nelson insisted on doing it his way, and he won out. A single from the album, "Blue Eyes Crying in the Rain" (an old Fred Rose tune from 1945), sung by Willie with just acoustic guitar backup, became a surprise hit.

paper ran a front page picture of Willie, country-rocker Leon Russell and University of Texas football coach Darrell Royal; it was "the best thing to come out of Dripping Springs.... In my mind it brought it all together."

The Dripping Springs festival became an annual event after 1973, each festival becoming bigger and even more eclectic. By 1976 the likes of Monroe and Acuff had been replaced by The Pointer Sisters, and the festivals were acquiring the reputation of the Newport festival of Outlaw music. They were also becoming mismanaged, brain-frying, counterculture extravaganzas. Disturbed by the turn they were taking, Nelson announced that the 1976 festival would be the last. (The tradition of massive Willie Nelson-sponsored outdoor events was to continue, however. He put the experience he had gained through his picnics into the Farm Aid concerts he began organizing in the 80's, drawing huge crowds to multi-day events whose proceeds went to benefit beleaguered American family farmers and whose performers included regulars like Cash, Kristofferson, Jennings, Dylan, John Cougar Mellencamp, Neil Young and Tom Petty as well as representatives of virtually all streams of American popular music. Farm Aid continued into the 90's.)

However, if any one album was responsible for introducing Willie and his philosophy to the mainstream audience, that album was *Wanted: The Outlaws,* released in 1976 by Victor. The album was conceived as a sort of sampler of "Nashville rebel" music, and included songs by Waylon Jennings, his wife Jessi Colter, and Tompall Glaser in addition to Willie; much of the material had been released earlier, but not in this context. The album contained a number of hit singles, including Willie and Waylon's "Good-Hearted Woman," Waylon's "Honky Tonk Heroes," and Jessi and Waylon's "Suspicious Minds." The style of the music was lean and spare, reminiscent of the tight Texas roadhouse bands. (Tompall even included his version of Jimmie Rodgers' classic "T for Texas.") The album sold amazingly well, and by the end of the year had been certified as a platinum album—a record that didn't sell merely a million dollars' worth (the traditional "Gold" record), but literally a million copies. It was the first strictly country album to be certified as attaining that level of sales, so it was a milestone if for no other reason than that.

As important as the music was the image the album presented of its art-

Tompall Glaser

Disc jockey Captain Midnight and writer-columnist Hazel Smith at Tompall Glaser's "Hillbilly Central" in 1976.

ists: that of the outlaw. The term had been around for a while, both in Waylon's song and, thanks to Dave Hickey, the music industry press, but the new album played it up heavily in its graphics and liner notes. The sleeve was a mockup of an old Western "Wanted" poster, and later the design was to be used often on posters for concerts. In the liner notes, *Rolling Stone* writer Chet Flippo emphasized the split between the Nelson-Jennings crowd and the Nashville scene: "They didn't wear Nudie suits and their music didn't conform to the country norm of songs of

divorce and alcohol and life's other little miseries." The liner notes concluded by asserting that this music was "not country."

Well, it may not have been in the mainstream of 70's Nashville, but it was very certainly in the country tradition and style, and Nelson's next two albums underscored that point: He followed *Wanted: The Outlaws* with a collection of country gospel tunes and a tribute to Lefty Frizzell, a quintessential country singer if ever there was one. But through the *Outlaws* album and its vast success, the image of the Nelson/Jennings-led movement became fixed in the public's mind as a sort of dialectical revolt. Outlaws they were, these guys: proud, independent, Western, rambling men who put individuality before social convention.

The image of the outlaw was nothing new to country music. From the folk ballads about Cole Younger in the 19th century to the popular gunfighter ballads of Marty Robbins, songs sympathetic to men outside the law have always been popular. Even the image of the country entertainer as outlaw is not new: In the 1920's, recorded

Leading Austinite and Western swing revivalist Alvin Crow.

skits portrayed people like Fiddlin' John Carson and the members of The Skillet Lickers as rough-and-tumble moonshiners who were always getting locked up. But as the music sought respectability in the 1930's and 1940's, singers consciously sought to upgrade their image; as we have seen, the singing cowboys were a big step in this direction, and they were always the good guys.

Hank Williams was an Outlaw of sorts—if we count his drinking and the trouble it caused him with the Nashville establishment—and while that might have helped his popularity in some ways with the fans, the management of the Opry saw it only as a threat to their image. By the mid-1960's, however, it became obvious that the outlaw image could become an asset rather than a liability.

Johnny Cash played a significant role in that change. His pill-popping, nights-in-jail period during the 1960's; his musical focus on Native Americans, Western bad men and other anti-authoritarian themes; his championship of prisoners' rights, his quitting the Opry—all these fac-

tors, and his apparent willingness to play up his own checkered past, cast him in the role of a nonconformist, if not an outright rebel.

His TV show, begun in 1969, took some of the edge off his image, as did his marriage to June Carter and his public embrace of Christianity—now he was squarely in the camp of that other Western stereotype, the reformed outlaw—and when younger musicians showed up for recording sessions at his House of Cash studio, they were often a little startled to find that they were forbidden to smoke or drink on the premises, but even so, the Man in Black continued to be recognized as an innovator who had defined a more realistic and humanistic mode for the country musician to work in.

Merle Haggard was less overt in his use of the Outlaw image, but he had after all done time in San Quentin, and in some ways was more of a real-life outlaw than Cash. And although he refused to emulate Cash and record a prison album, he did write and sing about his prison experiences in hit songs like "Mama Tried" and "I Take a Lot of Pride in What I Am," and he never ducked questions about it. His audience of working-class Americans was obviously aware of his background, his "toughness," and by the late 1960's, younger people were also finding him appealing; Arlo Guthrie, of all people, began singing "Okie from Muskogee," and the Grateful Dead incorporated "Mama Tried" into their psychedelic performance extravaganzas. Thanks to Haggard (and Cash), the dictum that country singers need project the pious image of a Roy Acuff or a Bill Anderson was no longer

*Asleep at the Wheel,
1974: Gene Dobkins,
Chris O'Connell, Ray
Benson; front, Floyd
Domino, LeRoy Preston
and Lucky Oceans.*

*Football coach Darrell
Royal, artist Jim Franklin,
Billy Joe Shaver, Waylon
Jennings at Armadillo
World Headquarters.*

universal, or commercial, by the 1970's.

The success of the Outlaw image had other implications as well. Kristofferson, Nelson and Jennings had shown that the personality of the artist was becoming as important as his songs or singing talents or ability to use the Nashville pipeline. The singer could now function as a sort of culture hero. In the old days, all the personality of a singer that could come across to much of his audience was what was on the old 78 record label. There were no fan magazines, no television close-ups, no major festivals; no way for a fan to get to know much about his favorite artist except through his music. But by the 1970's, the country singer had access to all manner of media: colorful album covers, extensive media exposure, films, festivals, magazine and newspaper coverage. Singers who were singers and nothing more were facing a dilemma not unlike the old silent film actors who were suddenly confronted with the change to sound. The spotlight was much, much brighter, and it was on almost all the time. For better or for worse, the public relations agent was finding work in country music.

Since the late 1950's, image had been a part of rock music, and the youth market accepted the concept of the performing self as a natural dimension of the music scene. Furthermore, from the time of Elvis and Chuck Berry up through The Beatles and The Rolling Stones and on into the acid rock of the early 1970's, rock musicians had utilized, in various forms, an Outlaw image with shades of drugs, sex and revolution. Thus by the 1970's, the youth market had found that country music could offer them the same terms as rock: strong personalities willing to buck the system, whether it be Nashville or the Bank of America. If Billy Sherrill had figured out a way to make country hits cross over into mainstream pop, Kristofferson, Nelson and Jennings found a way to get country to cross over into rock. If Sherrill went after the middle-aged housewife in Topeka, the Outlaws went after her teenaged sons, and after the "young adults" in the 18-to-30 age bracket, the bracket whose rapacious buying power makes

sales-oriented demographers drool. And the Outlaws were rewarded in ways traditional Nashville never was: platinum albums, films, national media coverage, 90,000-plus festival attendance.

By the mid 1970's, Outlaw music—"progressive country" is a milder term—had attracted a widely diverse group of practitioners and a broad-based and eclectic audience. Next to Willie Nelson, the most influential member of the group was Waylon Jennings. Born in Texas in 1937, Jennings, like Nelson, grew up listening to the sounds of Texas' most famous musical sons, Bob Wills and Ernest Tubb. Early in life, Waylon saw music as a way to escape from poverty; he recalls, "It's kind of like they say sports is with black

The Armadillo, Austin's answer to Carnegie Hall (plus beer garden).

dudes. It's a way to get up and away from something that's bad. I'll tell you what it is: Either music or pull cotton for the rest of your life...."

Jennings' first musical experience, though, came not with a country band, but with the now-legendary rockabilly band headed by fellow Texan Buddy Holly. After Holly's death, Jennings worked for a few years as a disc jockey in Texas, then played clubs around the Phoenix area. It was the Kennedy era, and the folk music boom was under way. Jennings moved with ease into the "folk" (that is, Northeastern coffeehouse) mode, and among his first records were versions of Dylan's "Don't Think Twice, It's Alright" and Ian and Sylvia's "Four Strong Winds." Even af-

Michael Martin Murphey as cosmic cowboy with Willie and others, and Kinky Friedman and his family backstage at the Armadillo.

tive, "chicken-pickin'" style of electric guitar), songwriter and performer. For RCA/Victor and Chet Atkins he was a good, steady album seller, and he began grinding one out every six months; between 1966 and 1973 he released two dozen albums. But even within the confines of Nashville success, he showed a fondness for the eclectic, the different. Like Kristofferson, his strong personality led him into films; he played the lead and wrote the music for a 1966 American International potboiler called *Nashville Rebel*, a film that enhanced his image as a proto-Outlaw. In 1970 he worked on the music to the Mick Jagger film, *Ned Kelly*, and he recorded duets with The Rolling Stones' leader and with Kristofferson.

Jennings was caught up in the Nashville songwriting renaissance of the late 1960's and was one of the first to record some of the new-style songs of Kristofferson, Mickey Newbury and Shel Silverstein. Soon he was expanding his horizons further into the pop/rock field, recording Jagger's "Honky Tonk Women," Chuck Berry's "Brown Eyed Handsome Man," Simon and Garfunkel's "Bridge Over Troubled Water" and Jimmy Webb's "MacArthur Park" (which won him a Grammy in 1969,

ter he came to Nashville in 1965 and signed an RCA/Victor contract, Jennings continued to attract attention as a folk-styled performer. One of his early RCA albums, released in 1969, was called *Country Folk* (even though it was a rather typical product of the Nashville Sound, replete with The Anita Kerr Singers; the only real "folk" material on the album was old-time minstrel Dick Burnett's "Man of Constant Sorrow"), and for a while the songs he was writing, like "Julie," were long, folkish ballads.

Jennings went on working successfully in Nashville, as a session man (playing his distinc-

and did a lot to help his songs cross over into pop charts). None of the pop action, however, should obscure the fact that prior to 1972, many of Waylon's songs were solidly in the traditional country vein: hits like "Love of the Common People," "I've Got You," "Walk on Out of My Mind" and "Don't Let the Sun Set on You in Tulsa."

Willie and Waylon had been friends from Waylon's Phoenix days: Willie, in fact, had advised Waylon not to follow him to Nashville. During the 1960's both men saw themselves as blood brothers waging a common fight against the formulaic post-Nashville Sound music philosophy of the day, and when Willie broke out in 1972, the lesson wasn't lost on Waylon. After Waylon saw Willie get out of his RCA/Victor contract and gain the right to control the production and marketing of his own records, Waylon followed suit; he went over the heads of the RCA/Victor's Nashville executives to the New York bosses. Pointing to a picture of Willie hanging on the wall of the New York office, Waylon reportedly said, "You've already made a mistake with that man, Hoss. Don't make the same mistake again."

They didn't, and Waylon soon had a new contract that gave him the same kind of freedom Willie had. He also hired a New York manager named Neil Reshen, an aggressive veteran who'd earned the notches on his gun protecting another maverick genius, jazzman Miles Davis, from the big boys of the music business. Reshen's part in making a reality of the Outlaw movement's bottom line—creative control by the artist—was considerable, even if his negotiating style did offend Nashvillians (and most other people) to a degree hitherto unimaginable in a business still ruled by Southern courtesy. As Willie Nelson, who also turned his affairs over to Reshen, once said Waylon had told him, "Having Neil for a manager is like having a mad dog on a leash."

Some of the inspiration for Waylon's shift to an offensive business posture came from the spectacular success of the 1973 Dripping Springs festival. Witnesses reported that Waylon's eyes nearly popped out of his head when he saw the number of people in the audience at the festival, where he had joined Kris Kristofferson, Charlie Rich, Rita Coolidge and others in performing free for their friend Willie Nelson, but although that event convinced him that his music, like Willie's, could attract hippies, rednecks and middle-of-the-roaders, he didn't follow in Willie's footsteps and move to Austin. Instead he chose to stay put in Nashville and fight his battles there, and fight he did: By late 1973 he was in total production control of his own recordings and was working almost exclusively at the studio of Tompall Glaser, himself a leading figure in the Outlaw movement.

Tompall had begun his career in Nashville as

Legendary Lost Gonzo singer-songwriter Jerry Jeff Walker.

leader of The Glaser Brothers, whose harmony singing established them as a very popular Nashville act in the early 60's. Tompall ran into a Nashville rut, however: Trying to push new-style country songs by the likes of John Hartford, he ran up against the conservatism of the 60's generation of music-business leaders. His response was to go out on his own. Using the proceeds from a successful song-publishing business, he built a modern recording studio and presided over it, making the studio available for the kind of extremely expensive, time-consuming approach to recording that could do justice to the Outlaws' musical ambitions. Tompall also had a lot to do with the business end of the Outlaw movement; he was one of the first Nashville artists to face down the recording companies and grab control of his own (and others') product. For many years, in fact, the commonly perceived Waylon/Willie duo was in fact a trio; Tompall stood behind them both with his studio and his savvy. He and Waylon shared office space for three of Waylon's most significant years, then quarreled and went their separate ways—Waylon into a more pop, rock 'n' roll-oriented organization, and Tompall back into his studio with yet another twist on the Nashville scheme of things, a "hillbilly blues band" featuring himself and two stellar ex-members

Accordionist Flaco Jimenez, keyboardist Augie Meyers and singers Doug Sahm and Freddy Fender: The Texas Tornados in the 90's.

of Bobby "Blue" Bland's band, guitarist Mel Brown and drummer Charles Polk.

During his stay at Tompall's, Waylon also connected with another luminary of the Outlaw cadre, "Cowboy" Jack Clement, who produced his *Dreaming My Dreams* album. Clement, who began his career as Sam Phillips' assistant at Sun Records and went on to produce such figures as Jerry Lee Lewis and Johnny Cash, had been in Nashville for 10 years by the time he worked with Waylon. His string of "legitimate" country successes—the discovery and production of Charley Pride, endless other production credits, and a string of hits as a songwriter ("Miller's Cave," "Guess Things Happen That Way," "Ballad of a Teenage Queen" and many others)—compensated for his manner and general approach to

life, which most music business Nashvillians thought to be quite bizarre. Clement would, perhaps, have been more comfortable producing at the Old Vic than in 60's Nashville, but nevertheless he stuck to his guns, building a string of studios and encouraging protégés into his determinedly high quality school of country-record production, among them Allen Reynolds (Crystal Gayle, Garth Brooks) and Garth Fundis (Trisha Yearwood *et al.*). His insistence on a classic combination of melody and beat and his accompanying philosophy of "organic" recording set the trend for the Outlaws, while his protégés carried his lessons into mainstream country music.

During the formation of the Outlaw movement, Clement and Tompall Glaser provided both studio expertise and shelter to the singing stars and other personnel of the Outlaw cadre. In Clement's case, that role continued into the 90's. At his "Cowboy Arms Hotel and Recording Spa," a large house on Belmont Boulevard converted into an office/recording studio/guest quarters, one might on any given day encounter anyone from Johnny Cash and John Prine to Don Everly and Marty Stuart and whomever the visiting English rocker of the week might happen to be, plus all manner of songwriters, journalists, editors and other personnel with what, in the 90's as well as the 70's, could be loosely described as an "alternative" mentality.

With the involvement of Tompall (and, for a while, Clement), Waylon was able to take the time to produce records with the care and effort he felt they deserved, and then turn the finished tapes over to RCA/Victor when he was satisfied with them. Stellar albums like *This Time*, *Ramblin' Man* and *Dreaming My Dreams* resulted from the new arrangement. Waylon was just as willing to use "non-country" instruments on his records as was Billy Sherrill, but for different reasons: Sherrill's motives were rooted in marketing considerations, whereas Waylon was out for aesthetic effect. "If a beat complements a song, then use it," he said. "If a kazoo complements that song, then we got just as much right to use that as anyone else—or horns, or anything.

Doug Sahm and Willie, 1974

But don't use them just to make it where it will get played in certain areas."

During the early years of the Outlaw movement, Nelson and Jennings were often looked on as co-leaders, or as co-conspirators. Both had gone from Texas dirt-farm beginnings to Nashville success; both liked well-crafted country songs in the classic honky tonk mold. Yet the two men were very different characters: Willie was more up front, the organizer, the socializer, the crowd lover who would do four-hour sets when other people would do 30 minutes. Waylon was moody, introverted, hard to know. It was Willie who showed up on televi-

Billy Joe Shaver, the Outlaw songwriter's songwriter.

sion in 1976 when he and Waylon swept the CMA Awards, both losing Entertainer of the Year honors only because votes were split between them. They had, however, great respect for each other's musical abilities, and, more important, each other's integrity. As Jennings told reporters at the height of the Outlaw movement, "We've been called crazy and wild and everything, but if they look at us, they know we're men. We stand up for what we believe in, and I think that's something people respect."

Waylon was also responsible for recording, in 1975, a song that became something of an anthem for the Austin scene: "Bob Wills Is Still the King." Besides being a tribute to Wills, the song made the difference between the Nashville and Austin scenes quite explicit: The Opry in Nashville was still "the home of country music," but "when you cross that old Red River, Hoss, it just don't mean a thing, 'cause once you're down in

Texas, Bob Wills is still the king."

The separateness was emphasized by a strong revival of interest in Wills' music that began in the early 1970's. It wasn't that Wills' music had ever fallen into any serious eclipse with traditional country music fans; in fact, Wills himself was still recording in Nashville until his incapacitating stroke in 1969. But in 1970 a number of things happened to popularize his music, and Western swing in general, with young new audiences who didn't remember him from the dance halls of Texas and Oklahoma, and with people who were not fully into country music. First, Merle Haggard recorded an album in tribute to Wills using some of the old members of his band (*A Tribute to The Best Damn Fiddle Player in the World*), and Haggard's popularity assured that the music would receive a wide hearing. Among the indirect by-products of that album was a well-documented and well-produced set of historic Wills material that made his original great recordings available once again. His final recordings were brought out in 1974 (shortly before his death) in a deluxe boxed set and promoted through the pages of magazines like *Rolling Stone*. A full-length biography of Wills appeared, and the former sidemen who had helped define Western swing were sought out and honored. Johnny Gimble, a former Wills fiddler, was named Instrumentalist of the Year by the CMA in 1976.

Soon a full-fledged Western swing revival was taking its place next to Jennings and Nelson as part of the Austin scene. The first "revival" band to achieve national prominence, and to appeal mainly to a young audience, was Asleep at the Wheel, which surfaced in West Virginia around 1970. Formed around Ray Benson and Reuben "Lucky Oceans" Gosfield, the band came into Texas after a stint in Berkeley, picking up Chris O'Connell and others along the way. They soon attracted a following that wanted to hear "Take Me Back to Tulsa," "Cherokee Boogie" and the band's original songs in the older modes such as "Don't Ask Me Why I'm Going to Texas." Floyd Tillman, one of the old-time honky tonk Western performers who made guest appearances with the band, summed up their style: "They're like the old bands, but with a difference: They play take-off solos. That's more like rock. Still I love 'em or I wouldn't play with 'em. They've moved the music back in the dancehall where it belongs." That last statement is important, for it emphasizes the fact that much of the Austin swing flourished in the same setting that had seen the original: the road-houses, bars, honky tonks, and dance halls of the Texas plains. At a time when the forum for Nashville music was increasingly concert halls of one sort or another, the informal, beer-drinking and pot-smoking atmosphere of the roadhouse seemed quite a cultural contrast. It was far removed from the formality of the brand new Grand Ole Opry House.

Even more faithful to the Western swing tradition than Asleep at the Wheel was Alvin Crow and The Pleasant Valley Boys. Until 1975, Crow had primarily a local reputation, playing with many older Wills veterans like fiddler Jesse Ashlock at funky Austin dance halls such as the Broken

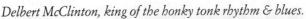

Delbert McClinton, king of the honky tonk rhythm & blues.

Spoke. Crow, a classically trained musician originally from Oklahoma, was one of the most aggressive spokesmen for the new Texas music (as opposed to the Nashville music). "Nashville's not interested in me. I won't fit into their hit machine...I have the same ideas as everybody else in this town. None fit into the Nashville pattern."

Austin soon saw a number of other local bands playing versions of Western swing: Frieda and The Firedogs, Marcia Ball and The Misery Brothers, and a truly freaky country act called Kinky Friedman and His Texas Jewboys, who specialized in numbers like "Asshole from El Paso" and "Get Your Biscuits in the Oven and Your Buns in the Bed." (Friedman was in fact an Austin native, even though by the mid-1970's he was seldom appearing there. He moved to New York in the 80's, becoming a much appreciated denizen of the Lone Star Cafe scene and eventually making a sudden, successful career swerve into mystery writing.)

Other bands were attracted to Austin for the same reason groups were once attracted to Nashville: to energize themselves from the musical excitement there. Some merged Western swing with rock. A California band, Commander Cody and His Lost Planet Airmen, enjoyed modest success as they combined country, swing and 1950's rock; they became extremely popular during their stay at the Armadillo World Headquarters in Austin, a large dance hall (with a beer garden) which, like San Francisco's Fillmore West in the late 60's, had become the center of the countercultural music scene. The Lost Planet Airmen broke up in 1976, but that same year saw the rise of ZZ Top, a three-piece Texas band that pushed Texas music even further in the direction of rock (and blues). Spawned in Texas beer joints, the band made little claim to country-ness, but they never let anyone forget their Lone Star State identity. Their concert stage consisted of a three-dimensional, panoramic map of Texas, and they usually shared the stage with two specially trained vultures, a longhorn steer, a buffalo and four (count 'em) rattlesnakes. In 1976, their concert touring drew more people than any rock band

Yet another Austin creative success: Joe Ely, here in the late 70's.

had ever drawn in a single year.

Other aspects of the Austin scene involved musical styles quite distinct from Western swing, and many of them resist easy categorization. Outlaw ideology was not so much musical as personal, involving, among other things, a healthy sense of tradition, a certain pride in redneck culture and an obsession with individual freedom; and so the scene could include, for instance, artists who got their start in the urban folk revival, or what was left of it in the late 1960's: people like Jerry Jeff Walker and Michael Murphey.

Walker was a New Yorker who wrote a very successful song called "Mr. Bojangles" about an old minstrel; it was widely recorded, and Richard Nixon once said it was his all-time favorite. For the next few years Walker bummed around the country before finally settling in Austin, where he acquired a stature next only to Willie Nelson's as a leader of the young poet-singers clustered in the town. Michael Murphey, for his part, popularized the term "cosmic cowboy," a catchword that soon caught on in attempts to describe the part-hippie, part-redneck values of the Austin crowd. Then there was Doug Sahm, leader of a late 1960's rock group called The Sir Douglas Quintet ("She's About a Mover") who developed his unique style from his serious roots in black, Cajun and Tex-Mex music. By the early 1970's Sahm was singing "Faded Love" with Bob Dylan and moving into progressive country. By the 90's, still digging his roots, he had joined his old friends Flaco Jimenez, Augie Meyers and Freddy Fender, in a new version of The Texas Tornados.

The talent was thick on the ground in Austin, some of it based there, some of it visiting frequently, some of it on sabbatical from Nashville, California, New York, Boston, or any other American musical center. There was Billy Joe Shaver, an old

Kristofferson buddy from Nashville regarded by insiders as anyone's songwriting equal (Waylon certainly thought so; he recorded a whole album of Shaver songs, *Honky Tonk Heroes*). There was Guy Clark, who wrote "Desperados Waiting for a Train" and "L.A. Freeway" among others, and for many years functioned with his wife Susannah, also a writer, as den parents for Nashville's songwriting underground. There was Delbert McClinton, a Ft. Worth native who mixed rhythm-and-blues with honky tonk music to stunning effect, particularly in

Austin scene singer-songwriters Guy Clark and David Allan Coe.

live performance, and Joe Ely, another fiery performer and bandleader who was the hardest rocker to come out of the Austin scene and also perhaps its strongest indigenous songwriter (though honors in that department could easily be shared by his Lubbock high school buddies Butch Hancock and Jimmie Dale Gilmore, with neo-beatnik cult hero Townes Van Zandt also in the running). And of course there was David Allan Coe, perhaps the most self-conscious of the new breed (one of his songs was entitled "Willie, Waylon and Me"), a singer who was so caught up in the Outlaw image that he put himself in the awkward position of insisting that his prison record was worse than his warden said it was. But Coe, like so many others around the Austin scene as residents or visitors, was fully capable of greatness. Some of his songs, like "Delta Dawn" and "Would You Lay with Me (In a Field of Stone)," both recorded by the young Tanya Tucker, are all-time straight country classics.

To go with the new alternative country music, Texas soon developed its own media: local television, radio and films (including one effort entitled *Outlaw Blues*), as well as soon defunct publications like *Pickin' Up the Tempo*, and the nationally distributed *Country Rambler* and one long-term survivor, *Texas Monthly*. Plus, *Rolling Stone*, the rock magazine, often printed material by one of its lead writers on the Austin scene,

Chet Flippo. National magazines made much of the challenge Austin was posing to Nashville, but the very devotion to freethinking nonconformism that had attracted so many of the progressive artists to Austin in the first place prevented the scene from developing a close-knit musical culture like Nashville's.

Texas was by no means the only non-Nashville residence center for the "new" country music. As country gained increasing acceptance by a Northern audience, a number of singers moved to reaffirm their Southern roots, and hyphenated-country hot spots got started in cities all over the nation. Soon it was possible to find little Austins in all sorts of seemingly unlikely places—New York's tony lower Fifth Avenue, for instance, home of the Lone Star Cafe—and there to indulge the kind of catholic musical taste typical of the great Southwest: a veritable kaleidoscope of country, blues, folk, rockabilly, Cajun, Tex-Mex, Western swing, R&B and any combination thereof. The term "roots music" was not yet in vogue at the time, but that's a good descriptor of the musical mix in Austin and its satellites.

Beneath the concrete facts of places to play and musicians to play in them, there were some general undercurrents. Beginning in the late 1960's, after the bitter taste of the civil rights struggle had faded, a sort of redneck chic had been developing in middle-class America. For

Country music goes to the White House: Willie Nelson, President Jimmy Carter and Charley Pride. A long strange trip indeed.

the Northerner, this led to a more open acceptance of country music in general; for the Southerner, it led to a new pride in Southern folk culture and in Southern identity. Jimmy Carter's election to the presidency in 1976 accelerated the trend even more. His inauguration, in fact, could easily have been mistaken for one of The Charlie Daniels Band's Volunteer Jams (or Willie Nelson's brain fries); one of the enduring images of that scene is of Jimmy and Rosalyn Carter, and some 3000 formally dressed political insiders, boogying along as best they could to "Orange Blossom Special" cranked up to megaspeed and rock 'n' roll volume by a stage full of hairy, hard-core hippiebillies including The CDB, elements of The Allman Brothers and Marshall Tucker bands, and whomever else the Secret Service would allow within decibel range of the new boss (no coincidence: just as Bill Clinton was "elected by MTV,"

Jimmy Carter owed a great deal of his popular support and campaign financing to people in the hyphenated-country business). Another classic image from those days is of Willie Nelson, as he admits in his autobiography, smoking marijuana on the White House roof with a person he refuses to identify in print while he and his then wife, Connie, were staying in the Lincoln Bedroom as guests of President and Mrs. Carter. Quoth the bard (speaking of his life, though he could just as well have been commenting on the musical goings-on that had elevated him to such heights): "So I let the weed cover me with a pleasing cloud and reflected on what a long, strange trip it had been..."

Politico-musical partying aside, however, the Southernization of American pop culture was at one of its historic peaks as the 1970's gave way to the 80's. For the first time in a long time, or maybe the first time ever, it was hip to talk with a drawl and boogie with a twang.

Collectively, though, the artists who had wrought that change did not do very well as the decade drew to a close. Although their commercial success continued and even escalated for a while (notably with Willie's *Stardust* album of Tin Pan Alley chestnuts), the creative passions at the heart of the Outlaw movement had dimmed. The songs weren't as moving or original, and the records were compromised by lackluster production and indifferent performances. Moreover, most of the really brilliant supporting players who gave depth to the Outlaw movement, people like Joe Ely and Billy Joe Shaver, hadn't succeeded as commercial recording artists for one reason or another, and so there was a disheartening sense of failure in the ranks. And of course, most of the significant players in the Outlaw drama were tired. They'd had a strenuous decade.

By 1980 there was in effect no Outlaw movement left. There was just Waylon doing his thing, and Willie doing *his* thing, and most of the others trying to figure out how to get by. And although the genie the Outlaws had conjured from their lamp would remain at large in the country music world, it was as if a law of physics were acting on Nashville: For every action, there is an equal and opposite reaction.

Dolly Parton

CHAPTER 13

The Center Holds

In the fall of 1976, Linda Ronstadt and Emmylou Harris were asked to be guests on the new syndicated television show, *Dolly,* starring Dolly Parton. Both responded with enthusiasm, and what resulted was an important and symbolic meeting of minds. The three women—one from the heart of Nashville, two from the center of baby-boomer country rock—swapped songs, listened to each other's tapes, did trio harmonies on "Silver Threads and Golden Needles" and "Bury Me Beneath the Willow," and got along famously. As Linda later recalled admiringly of Dolly, "I've never met anybody so free of neurosis as that person.... She taught me that you don't have to sacrifice your femininity in order to have equal status."

The seed planted on the *Dolly* show wouldn't bear fruit for 11 more years, when the three women finally released their wonderful *Trio* album, but the event did have contemporary significance. Dolly was bridging a certain culture gap by offering artists as "alternative" as Ronstadt and Harris to the prime-time TV audience, and they were covering an even greater distance by endorsing her with their crowd—for, while it was one thing for ex-hippie rockers and college kids to identify with rebels like Waylon Jennings and Willie Nelson, it was quite another for them to buy into the down-home country values celebrated by the outrageous Ms. Parton. That,

though, is what was happening in 1976-77: Dolly's most pristine, pre-Hollywood work was emerging from its Nashville cocoon to circulate in cutting-edge musical consciousness.

She wasn't the only such country singer, either, or indeed the most unlikely. That distinction went to George Jones, whose profoundly retrogressive honky tonk world view was one of 1977's hottest tickets in trendsetter territory. That year saw *Alone Again,* his hardest hard-core country record for a decade, reviewed with enormous enthusiasm by the ultra-urbane *Village Voice* (which also named it one of the Top Ten albums in its year-end critics' poll), and *Rolling Stone,* not to be outdone, named him its Country Artist of the Year.

Jones reacted characteristically to all the hoopla, and it's hard to say whether he helped or hindered his career by failing to show up for the big New York showcase his record company staged at the Bottom Line club. He certainly got the movers and shakers' attention—they had plenty of time to ponder the nature of hard-core hillbilly reality as they sat around waiting for him to appear—and some heavy gossip-column glamour did indeed accrue to the formerly provincial legend of "No Show Jones."

Dolly, on the other hand, was very much present for her Bottom Line benediction, and moreover she generated such excitement that

Dolly Parton and Porter Wagoner with Jo Walker-Meador, executive director of the CMA, and Johnny Rodriguez in 1973.

there's no question she did the right thing. She became a personality for the duration, and the toast of Manhattan for at least 12 hours (especially in the gay bars, where her Mae West-meets-Marilyn Monroe image was interpreted as deliciously high camp). Hollywood was the obvious next stop, and that indeed is where Dolly went, professionally and creatively speaking. Under new management, she launched a high-profile film and television career and began aiming her music at what she and her handlers assumed to be widest possible market, a process involving a radical turn away from the traditionally rooted, intensely personal music with which she'd quite rightly won the awe and admiration of country

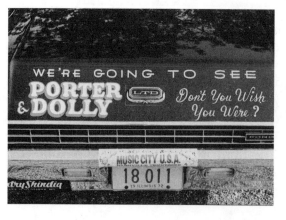

fans up to and including Harris and Ronstadt.

Ironically, the musical identity Dolly began to lose when she took her business from Nashville to Hollywood was something she'd only just found. And the story of her struggle to find that identity forms an important chapter in the story of modern country music. It's a story that brings us back to our original point of departure, Nashville, and the effects of the various musical trends, movements and revolutions of the 70's.

An account of Dolly's early career reads like the archetypal country music success story. She was raised in a rural, dirt-poor family ("My mama had 12 kids when she was 35 years old") in the hills of Sevier County, Tennessee, just a few miles from where English folk-song collectors had found surviving English ballads as late as the 1920's. All the Parton children got a solid grounding in the old-time gospel music sung at the local Church of God; "Great Speckled Bird" was one of the anthems there. By the time she was seven, Dolly had modified an old mandolin with guitar strings and was composing her own songs. Even then she looked to music as her potential deliverance from poverty in the hills, as did many of her contemporaries—the same way their counterparts in the urban ghettos looked to athletics. "Music was a freedom," she has said, and even though "none of our people had ventured out of the mountains with it," she was determined to take that path. And she did. As a teenager she won a spot on Cas Walker's famous Knoxville bluegrass show, and on the day after she left high school in 1964, she took the bus to Nashville. With the help of an uncle, she was able to establish herself as a singer and songwriter. She had a modest success with a song called "Dumb Blonde" (the symbolism of which, unsurprisingly, was to haunt her for years).

Her big break came in 1967, when she was asked to join Porter Wagoner, a very popular straight country singer from Missouri who wore rhinestone wagon wheels on his jackets and hawked a good old Tennessee patent medicine called Cardui. For seven years she was a feature of Wagoner's shows, and his singing partner on innumerable duets. She gained a following during those years, but as she later explained, she knew the fans were attracted as much to her figure as to her original songs or vocal style. By the early 70's, though, she could look at the changes in the country music business and recognize the possibility that there might be an audience willing to accept her on her own terms—the kind of audience Waylon Jennings and Willie Nelson had found, the new demographic in which country music was accepted more as art than as ritual. She couldn't reach that audience as part of

Dolly did just fine in New York, thank you. With Olivia Newton-John and Andy Warhol, and, below, with John Belushi in 1977.

Wagoner's troupe, so in 1974 she broke from Porter and went out on her own. At the time she said that the move would "just mean more people are aware of what I can do—my writing."

She was right, and by 1975 and 1976 she was attracting nationwide attention, winning all kinds of industry awards, and producing some of the most distinctive hit songs of the decade. The CMA voted her Best Female Vocalist for both 1975 and 1976, and her appearance at the 1976 Grammy Awards show drew a riotous ovation. Dozens of singers recorded her songs; she made appearances on *The Tonight Show; The New York Times* reviewed her songs and lauded them as "full of a poetic imagery both true to life and evocatively expressed"; and in late 1975 she became the first female country entertainer to have a nationally syndicated television show—the highest-budgeted show ever to be syndicated from Nashville, and one that soon garnered over 130 markets, many of them in Northern cities.

Dolly didn't change her image, though. Others in the front rank of 70's country/pop might be dressing down in blue jeans and sweatshirts, but she continued to appear in tight, flashy, sequined outfits crowned with a towering blonde wig. She once commented that "Part of the magic of me, I think, is that I look totally one way, an overall artificial look, but I am totally another.... My appearance has become just a gimmick. It goes back to having nothing as a child."

She added a few more intriguing observations in an interview with *Ladies' Home Journal.* "I always think of her, the Dolly image, like a ventriloquist does his dummy. I have fun with it. I think, 'What will I do with her this year to surprise people? What'll she wear, what'll she say?'" And talking about the original source of the image, she explained that "I always liked the look of our hookers back home. Their big hairdos and makeup made them look more. When people say less is more, I say more is more. Less is less. I go for more."

The songs which propelled her to glory were also inspired by "back home." They were full of the images and values of the rural eastern Tennessee hills, and in some cases they even echoed the tune patterns of the old-time music of the 1930's and 40's: her first successful hit as a single artist was a rendering of "Muleskinner Blues," a workhorse going back

With Jane Fonda, Lily Tomlin and Dabney Coleman in the 1980 blockbuster hit film, Nine to Five.

to Jimmie Rodgers days, and her own "Tennessee Mountain Home" could easily have fit into The Carter Family's repertoire. "My Daddy Was an Old-Time Preacher Man" was full of personal references, and "Coat of Many Colors" and "In the Good Old Days (When Times Were Bad)" both grew out of her family's experiences. And while many of her songs made the age-old association of mountain life with innocence and city life with wickedness, her brilliantly original "In the Good Old Days" also captured the ambivalent nostalgia of so many Southern singers who grew up in poverty and find themselves unable to completely romanticize it. Nor did she romanticize love. In songs like "Jolene," "Bargain Store" and "Love is Like a Butterfly," she dealt with the country theme of mating and losing from a distinctly realistic feminine perspective, "Jolene" being an especially intriguing example of the sociology of sexual politics.

Some of Dolly's new audience doubtless responded to her refreshing feminine-but-not-feminist perspective; others continued to respond to her tight pants suits; and still others, introduced to real country music through pop artists in the early 1970's, responded to her strong ties with the music's conventional aspects. But a great many more simply responded to her unique singing style and to her voice. As Dolly has observed, "My voice was real different—not that it's good, because a lot of people just cannot stand to hear me sing. Anybody with a real different voice, a lot of people don't like to hear them sing, but people who do like them usually like them especially well."

It's a voice encompassing radical extremes— "so small and high-pitched, it sounded like a kid" in Dolly's words, but also edged with a haunt-

The makeover

The late 70's and early 80's saw mainstream artists like Mel Tillis hold onto their fans and their share of the charts. The Bellamy Brothers were also hitmakers of the era.

In a way, her ascent to major stardom came in the nick of time, for she'd had a problem with nodes on her vocal cords since 1973, and national-level success meant that she didn't have to risk everything by continuing the standard country singer's grueling schedule of one-nighters. Not that she was long for the strictly country circuit anyway; her ambition was driving her to much bigger places.

Hollywood was the first destination, a non-Nashvillian management and production team the first big move in the new campaign, and "Here You Come Again" the first song in the whole new ball game she'd decided to play. Originally recorded by pop star B.J. Thomas, it was chosen by her new producer, Gary Klein, and endorsed by her new manager, Sandy Gallin, and it was pop all the way—so much so that Dolly, burned by Music Row criticism of her "desertion" to L.A., had serious misgivings when she heard the final mix. As Klein recalled, she pleaded to have a steel guitar added, "so if someone said it isn't country, she could say it is and prove it." Klein had steel man Al Perkins overdub a prominent new part, and "she was so relieved. It was like her life sentence was reprieved."

All was forgiven, at least in public. As well as topping the country charts for five weeks straight, reaching Number Three on the pop charts, driving her album to platinum sales, winning her a Grammy, and securing the California-based Academy of Country Music's Entertainer of

ing timbre reminiscent of stylists like Eartha Kitt and even Billie Holliday. At first Nashville didn't know what to do with it. Nobody thought it was right for straight country. Her first record company made her do rockabilly songs, and initially, RCA Victor's Chet Atkins was hesitant to record her at all. Wisdom prevailed, however, and Dolly was still with RCA when she triumphed at the CMA awards shows in '75 and '76.

the Year award, "Here You Come Again" also got Dolly named Entertainer of the Year by the Nashville-establishment Country Music Association.

Dolly had begun the new phase of her career by explaining, in 1976, "My music is beginning to grow. I, the person, am country, and my music is country, but still, it's got a universal sound. It's just Dolly Parton's music. There is no way to classify it." If that statement makes perfect sense and, simultaneously, no sense at all — you can't say there's no way to classify your music when two sentences ago, you yourself classified it as country—it's understandable. The whole "Is it pop or is it country?" quandary, which consumed so much time and energy in the 70's (and the 60's, 80's and 90's), is such a quagmire that even someone as sharp as Dolly must disappear through the quicksand from time to time. And of course the ambiguity of her statement revealed what was in fact an insoluble dilemma. How on earth did you get yourself a new set of business partners, a new sound, and a whole new audience, without offending any of the people you'd left behind?

Well, you didn't, and so Nashville's late 70's featured a reverse image of the Olivia Newton-John tussle—controversy over one of *us* trying to get out, as opposed to one of *them* trying to get in. The whole flap subsided eventually, but from the viewpoint of a musical historian, not to mention a fan of hard country music and deathless songwriting, it must be said that when Dolly left Nashville and producer Bob Ferguson, she very clearly left her best work behind her. Faced with her big- and small-screen personality and her post-Nashville recordings, in fact, it grew harder and harder to remember that one of the most gifted writers in the music's history was hiding beneath all that high-profile sugar, brass and sass. It was an almost purely inverse equation: As the public personality Dolly had invented for herself won more and more space on the checkout counter gossip racks, the power and

beauty of her music faded away. So while she did sterling service as Nashville's brightest female lure during the late 70's and the 80's—there's no doubt her TV and movie performances drew millions into the country music marketplace—those were also the years of her decline as a creative artist.

You could, if you wanted, view Dolly's move into the show business mainstream as a kind of coming-out party for country music, the point in history at which expansion finally became the main dynamic of the country music business. For Dolly's winning of the prime time heart, following as it did the Outlaws' capture of the baby boomer imagination, was the trigger for a full 15 years (so far) of commercial growth—a progressive saga of more and more new folks singing some

Crystal Gayle, with producer Allen Reynolds: 70's start, 80's success.

sort of country, and more and more new folks listening to it.

Expansion has of course been the big story about country music in recent times, and repetition has made it familiar: between the late 70's and the mid-90's, history progressed straightforwardly in increments of millions (that is, Gold, platinum, double platinum and finally multiplatinum sales figures) from Dolly and the Outlaws to Kenny Rogers, then to Alabama, then to Randy Travis, then to Garth Brooks, Billy Ray Cyrus and beyond. There are, though, other histories, the least told of which is the least surprising: the fact that while media and music business attention in the late 70's (and since) focused almost exclusively on the big "expansion acts," there continued to be a very solid core of more traditional artists doing very well indeed, thank you, with more traditional country music. When you look at the *Billboard* charts from the 70's, then, you see the names of innovators—the Nashville Sound slickers, the Outlaws, the Californian and Southern country rockers, the new pop-country megastars—but you also see the names of many more, less celebrated artists. Their albums didn't go platinum, and they didn't win Grammys or attract *People Magazine* feature writers, but they were still a vital, active force on the charts and on the circuit, and in aggregate they sold considerably more records and tapes than their more fashionable peers.

A whole litany of names fits here: Mel Tillis, Webb Pierce, Ray Price, Sonny James, Freddie Hart, Johnny Duncan, Jean Shepard, Bill Anderson, Margo Smith, Roy Drusky, Jack Greene, Jeanne Pruett, Jerry Reed, Roy Clark, Joe

Gene Watson

Stampley, Moe Bandy. And of course, one level up, there were the biggest stars of the 60's still enjoying varying degrees of commercial and creative success—Johnny Cash, Merle Haggard, Tammy Wynette, Loretta Lynn, Glen Campbell, Marty Robbins, Charley Pride, Conway Twitty—plus a group of new artists who emerged during the 70's and were well established in the mainstream by 1980: Gene Watson, Vern Gosdin, Don Williams, Crystal Gayle, Janie Fricke, John Conlee, The Oak Ridge Boys, The Statler Brothers, The Gatlin Brothers, The Bellamy Brothers, T.G. Sheppard, Mickey Gilley, Eddie Rabbitt, Barbara Mandrell and Ronnie Milsap.

The new artists came into the Nashville production system from all over the map: The Oak Ridge Boys from the gospel circuit, where they'd been a highly controversial, longhaired, rocking and rolling sensation; The Bellamy Brothers from the pop charts, where they'd had a huge hit with "Let Your Love Flow" in 1976, then worked in Europe until they connected with Nashville, their target of choice in the first place; Crystal Gayle via her big sister, Loretta Lynn, and then a connection with two ally/protégés of producer "Cowboy" Jack Clement, arranger Charles Cochran and producer Allen Reynolds; Mickey Gilley not through his cousin, Jerry Lee Lewis, but via his own successful recording scene in Houston; Gene Watson straight from that same Texas honky tonk circuit; Don Williams via a successful folk-pop vocal trio, The Pozo-Seco Singers, and then a connection with Allen Reynolds and another Clement graduate, producer Garth Fundis; Vern Gosdin through an early 60's stint in a California bluegrass band with Chris Hillman

Don Williams with Pete
Townshend, Eric Clapton,
Danny Flowers and
Ronnie Lane.

(later of The Byrds, more recently of The Desert Rose Band), then a Nashville connection via Emmylou Harris in the mid-70's; Janie Fricke via the studio system, where she worked as a background singer until graduating to duettist status on Charlie Rich's "On My Knees"; Eddie Rabbitt via songwriting, notably for Elvis and Ronnie Milsap (not bad for a lad born in Brooklyn and raised in New Jersey); Larry Gatlin via Dottie West, whom he met while singing in Las Vegas, and his brothers via Tammy Wynette, for whom they worked as backup singers; John Conlee via his job as a Nashville disc jockey (far superior, connection-wise, to his previous career as a licensed mortician); T.G. Sheppard via his job as a Memphis record promotion man; Ronnie Milsap also through Memphis, where he was a successful local rock/R&B performer before taking his act to Nashville and signing on to open Charley Pride's shows; The Statler Brothers through Johnny Cash, who took them on as his opening act in the early 60's; and Barbara Mandrell via her father's family band, then almost a decade of relentless hard work as a major

Larry Gatlin

label solo artist until her first Number One single in 1978, which in turn led to her network TV show in 1981.

Stylistically, the centrist artists of the late 70's were more diverse than those in the early 70's, with a range all the way from Don Williams' meticulous slow country-folk waltzes to The Bellamys' salaciously punnish pop (as in "If I Said You Had a Beautiful Body, Would You Hold It Against Me"), with everything from classic Texas honky tonk to barely country-popified R&B in between. Lyrically, though, they stuck to the classic formulae for the most part; unhappiness in love had been the subject of more than half the Number One country songs between 1966 to 1976, and the next decade was no different. A few top hits made more explicit references to physical love, but that was the only sign of any real new direction.

Of course, the perils of the heart—cheating,

betrayal, loneliness—had been subjects central to country music since the 40's (as, to a lesser extent, had happier love), so the continued reign of romance at the end of the 70's shouldn't have been particularly surprising. At the time, however, it was, for it meant that things hadn't changed as much as most critics and music businesspersons had assumed they were going to. Despite the "new morality" of the 70's, neither the Outlaws' poems of introspective individualism nor the Southern rockers' geo-historical anthems were evident at the top of the charts. Despite country's new status with Hollywood and Madison Avenue, most of the industry's real business was still being done through the classic channels of radio airplay and bus touring to one-night stands at state fairs, concerts, and club dates. For many mainstream country singers, in short, both the medium and the message were pretty much the way they'd been before the age of Opryland, Billy Sherrill, Willie Nelson and The Charlie Daniels Band. And that would continue to be true until the 90's, at which point video had rewritten the rules of the business from top to bottom. In a way, then, the story of the country music centrists is a continuum, independent of trend cycles, running from the late 60's to the late 80's, with some players emerging and others fading away at various points along the line, and a very select few maintaining their prominence throughout.

One way to trace that continuum is to look at the charts. Although they reflect only radio airplay (not sales figures), and are notorious for the ease with which they could be manipulated, they do a reasonable job of telling us which artists mainstream country fans, not country-rocking baby boomers or suburban countrypolitans, were listening to at any given point. So it's an interesting exercise to go through a chronology of *Billboard* country chart-topping singles during that time—more specifically, between January 1, 1968 and January 1, 1990.

T.G. Sheppard and Jerry Reed celebrate a joint venture into movie theater ownership in the mid-80's.

Scoring more than a dozen Number One hits during that period were: Reba McEntire with 13 Number Ones between '83 and '90; T.G. Sheppard with 14 from '75 to '86; The Judds with 14 between '84 and '90; Loretta Lynn with 15 from '68 to '78; Sonny James with 16 between '68 and '74; Waylon Jennings with 16 from '74 to '87; The Oak Ridge Boys with 16 between '78 and '89; Eddie Rabbitt with 16 between '76 and '88; Mickey Gilley with 17 between '74 and '83; Don Williams with 17 from '74 to '86; Crystal Gayle with 18 between '76 and '87; Earl Thomas Conley with 18 from '81 to '90; the same number for Tammy Wynette between '68 and '77, and for George Strait from '82 to '90; 19 for Kenny Rogers between 1977 and 1987; 20 for Willie Nelson between '75 and '90; 23 for Dolly Parton from '71 to '90; 26 for Alabama in the 10 years from 1980 to 1990; 29 for Charley Pride between 1969 and 1983; and, way up at the top of the heap, Ronnie Milsap with 35 between '74 and '90, Merle Haggard with 36 from '68 to '88, and none other than Mr. Conway Twitty with no less than 40 between 1968 and 1986.

When you play with those numbers a little further, calculating what you might call an artist's "hit factor" by dividing how many chart-toppers they had by how many years it took them, you see just how important the non-trendy, non-expansionist artists were. For instance, Earl Thomas Conley had an average of two Number One singles per year, or a hit factor of 2.0, compared to 1.1 for Waylon Jennings. T.G. Sheppard outscored Crystal Gayle, and Mickey Gilley. The Oak Ridge Boys and Don Williams all had higher hit factors than Dolly Parton and Willie Nelson. Kenny Rogers and Alabama, the two great expansion acts of the late 70's and early 80's, had hit factors of 1.9 and 2.6 respectively over 10 years, but Merle Haggard ran at 1.8 for 20 years, Charley Pride averaged 2.1 hits per annum over 14, and Conway Twitty cruised through 18 straight

Irlene and Barbara Mandrell

years at a rate of 2.2. And the act with the highest hit factor of all between '68 and '90 wasn't The Judds at 2.333 or even the mighty Alabama at 2.6, but Sonny James, who burned from '68 into '74 at 2.666.

Stylistically, the most significant centrists of '68-'90—Sonny James, Charley Pride, Merle Haggard, Conway Twitty and Ronnie Milsap—were, like those before and after them, a very mixed bunch.

Sonny James' career in the major leagues began in 1957 with his recording of the powerful teenage ballad "Young Love," which did extremely well for him, reaching Number One on the country charts and spending several weeks competing with Tab Hunter's cover of it for the top spot on the pop charts. The teen idol life wasn't for Sonny, though; fate steered him where his own instincts probably would have anyway, and his pop career did a fast fade. He spent the rest of his professional life, a good long run until the mid-80's, on the straight country circuit.

His formula for consistent chart success was simple, and remarkably effective: he chose songs that had been hits for other artists, usually in other fields of popular music, and recorded them his way. That approach had worked for others before him, notably Red Foley, and it's worked since for singers as diverse as Linda Ronstadt and Ricky Van Shelton, but nobody employed it quite as skillfully, or for quite as long, as Sonny James. From pop songs like The Seekers' "A World of Our Own" and Petula Clark's "My Love" to blues originals like Ivory Joe Hunter's "Since I Met You Baby" and even Jimmy Reed's "Bright Lights, Big City," his covers usually featured clean, simple arrangements, smoothly powerful vocals and class; they weren't the bland copies that country versions of rock, blues and R&B songs tend to be, but thoughtfully conceived reinterpretations. As Sonny himself told *Billboard*, "Every song I used to get, I would go over it many times when I was on the road before I'd ever go in the studio, and I'd always have this arrangement in my mind...and it's really crazy how those arrangements come about. You hear a song, and you say 'How can I come up with an arrangement without destroying the song?'"

He came up with a lot of them and destroyed very little, if anything; many of his covers, particularly of pop hits, still sound more convincing than the originals.

James was promoted as "The Southern Gentleman"—producer Ken Nelson's way of balancing the youthful image he'd created by changing "Jimmie Loden" to "Sonny James"—and that was appropriate. Throughout his career, James held fast to the values with which he'd been raised in Hackleburg, Alabama, and which governed The Loden Family act with whom he made his stage debut at the age of four, joining his mother, father and two sisters. He was never a drinker, for one thing—hardly the norm for a country

Babs, a little older but no less winning, on her bus.

singer of his day—and moreover he refused to perform anywhere liquor was served. That kept him out of most of the venues available to his competition, but he didn't care. "I didn't feel that it would be the best influence on fans of mine who otherwise would not go to a place that would serve beverages," he explained to *Country Music*. "I mean, I feel you have a certain responsibility, regardless of what occupation you're in. You're either going to be a good influence or a bad influence on people. So being brought up in a small community like I was, we were taught to try to be—and certainly everybody has faults— we were taught to do the best you can, to the best of your ability, for your fellow man. I think that just came across in my recording career."

And he stuck to his guns. Even in the mid-

70's, with the fires of Outlaw revolution flaring all around him and many of his fellow singers raunching up their songs and images accordingly, he was able to declare that stability was still the key element of his career. "I think once you've got a style, and you don't vary too much from it, you let people know that you're hanging in there with that kind of music," he said. "This is the way I've geared my life, and I've never become a controversial artist." As the interviewer to whom he said those words noted, he said them with pride.

Sonny James had his last Number One in 1974, but he continued to show up on the charts for the next eight years and did some sterling work during that time, notably his bicentennial celebration album, *200 Years of Country Music*, and his early 80's recordings with Ricky Skaggs and The Whites. For an artist whose star had burned with such heat—16 Number One hits in six years is hot by any standard, anytime—his fade into semi-retirement was remarkably graceful: a pleasant confluence of his own stability and his fans' loyalty that might be difficult to duplicate in the country music business today.

Sonny James

Fan loyalty is also a prime ingredient in Charley Pride's tenure as a stalwart of the country mainstream, which began in 1965 and continues to this day, although the last of his Number One singles came in 1983. But other than that, and the fact that Pride has always been a straight country singer in the classic mold, the characteristics he shares with his contemporaries have never been as newsworthy as the element which makes him unique: he is the only black man ever to have topped the country charts, let alone done so 29 times over 14 years.

His accomplishment is all the more remarkable considering the fact that the recording business was only his second career choice. Baseball, not music, was what young Charley Pride wanted to play, and it was with great disappointment that he finally abandoned that dream after going to New York and being turned down flat by the Mets; he was 25 then, and knew that semi-pro was as far as he would go. In a way, though, baseball led him to music: he got his first break when a baseball fan who owned a nightclub saw him singing between innings. He started singing at the man's club, keeping his day job as a smelter at the Anaconda Mining Company, and then Red Foley and Red Sovine caught his act one night and told him he should go try out in Nashville. Thus began one of the odder oft-told tales of Music Row.

Pride's first connection, via Red Sovine, was with Jack Johnson, a journalism school graduate who was then a public relations man with Cedarwood Publishing. Johnson was impressed with Pride's voice and style, which he identified correctly as a direct and legitimate descendant of Hank Williams and Lefty Frizzell (strange but true: Pride's evenings back in Mississippi, where he and his family picked cotton, had been spent listening to the Grand Ole Opry and any other country music his radio would receive). Johnson also saw the materialization of exactly the opportunity he'd been seeking. "I had been looking for a Negro singer to bring into country music for some time," he said a few years later. "I thought the industry was ready for it, and I guess in retrospect, I was right. I used to ask shoeshine boys if they knew any Negroes who liked country music. I got some pretty weird looks."

The echoes of Elvis' fall into Sam Phillips' lap are obvious, though warped by their trip through the looking glass. A white man burning to sing the music of city blacks becomes a black man in love with the music of white country folk; one is greeted by an audience ecstatic in their approval of his person but, initially anyway, an industry wary of his music, while the other's music is welcomed by industry and audience alike, but only because nobody knows who the singer really is. For when Jack Johnson finally found a

Sonny James on
the road again.

Joe Stampley led a minor honky tonk revival with and without duet partner Moe Bandy.

Nashville producer willing to cut records on a black country singer—Jack Clement, who not so incidentally had begun his career working for Sam Phillips in Memphis, recording Elvis and the other Sun rockabillies—and Clement finally persuaded Chet Atkins at RCA to listen, the right approach to marketing Charley Pride seemed obvious to everyone involved: push the records to radio stations without photographs of the artist or any other hint that he might be anything out of the ordinary; wait to see if they did well; and only then, when listener demand had already been created, reveal the singer's race.

The stratagem worked well. Pride's career got off to a smooth start, and it's probable that once his identity became known, his uniqueness was actually an asset. As Jack Johnson noted in the early 70's, when Pride and Clement were well into their 19-album adventure together and Pride had already achieved the ultimate industry accolade, the CMA's Entertainer of the Year award for 1971, "It still amazes me. I've seen big, burly

redneck truck drivers...if you told 'em they were gonna have a black guy as a co-driver, they'd go nuts. But I've seen 'em at shows right before Charley comes on stage. There's this something in the atmosphere, this electricity in the air. You can feel it. When he walks on stage they go crazy. He could be purple, and they'd still love him. It makes me wonder about everything. You know, sometimes I think white people in the South don't really dislike colored people. It's just this incredible competition thing."

All the same, Pride had a hard row to hoe. As he recalls about his early years in the business, "There were just a thousand little innuendoes I had to deal with, a thousand things I had to be able to decipher and react to and just keep movin' on and being Charley Pride, the man, the American. This was something Eddy Arnold never had to face, and something Hank Snow never had to face."

The flak began even earlier, back in his childhood. "My own sister, she'll tell you today, she used to tease me for singing country music. It was 'Why you singin' their music? Why you singin' white folks' music?'"

He was singing it because it just drew him, of course, the way it draws Japanese executives, Pakistani cab drivers, Irish rock 'n' rollers, whomever, and he for one doesn't think that's so strange. Neither does he think he's unique. "You know, Negroes, a lot of 'em love country music," he once said. "It just gets difficult because there's this business of your music and my music."

Obviously, though, he didn't let that difficulty deter him. Why not? "I think it was a little bit of destiny," he has said, "and a little bit a part of determination to be oneself, in spite of." He has also said, in response to one of an eternity of questions about his race and his role, "I'm no color. I'm just Charley Pride, the man, the individual. My ancestry is African, Caucasian and Indian, with maybe a little Chinese on my mother's side...I consider myself not to have skin hangups, by the fact of my success, and because I'm able to walk out and be accepted as Charley Pride, a total individual flailing around in the midst of all the hang-up folks."

As an individual he's gained respect over the years for his talent, intelligence and tenacity, if not for any great charm or humor—but considering all his years of treatment as a cultural oddity rather than a singer (particularly outside the South and in the mainstream media), he might be forgiven for taking himself a touch too seriously at times. If interviewers hadn't kept demanding that he explain himself, after all, he might never have been forced to entertain notions like the one he voiced to a *Country Music* writer at the height of his high years. "At this moment, I am the epitome of American music," he said. "I sound like Elvis, Ernest Tubb, B.B. King, Bob Dylan, Nat King Cole and Frank Sinatra. When you hear me sing, you hear all

of those combined into one. I am the epitome of the whole ball of wax—color, style and music. I believe in three ingredients of American music: country, gospel and the blues. When you hear those three, you hear it all. When you hear me, you hear those three."

Grandiosity notwithstanding, Charley Pride never functioned as anything but a hard core, down home country singer with a legion of loyal fans among the friends and neighbors. He never got slick and he was never judged hip, so he didn't share the expansion audience of the 70's (and neither, it goes almost without saying, did he attract black fans in any significant number). All of which was perhaps inevitable, for even if he'd had his shot at the pop market, with a big crossover hit or two, it's doubtful that any American audience outside the South would have felt able to claim him as their own. For very different reasons, the social philosophies of both urban baby boomers and suburban "countrypolitans" simply could not assimilate the idea of a black country singer as anything but a joke, and a bad one at that.

He isn't a joke, of course—he's dead serious—but if you're looking for ironies, he's your man. And perhaps the most poignant of those ironies

Moe Bandy backstage with a Hank Williams guitar, Charly McClain and Jim Owen.

grows from an analogy he's used throughout his career. "I'm sure that Jackie Robinson would have loved to have been just another baseball player," he said in the early 70's, "but society put him in the position of being the first known Negro in the major leagues. I come along years later. I'm in the same position." But of course that wasn't quite accurate, and still isn't. Jackie Robinson was followed through the door he'd opened by a host of his fellows; for Charley Pride the door opened long enough to let one man through, then closed behind him.

It's possible, then, that he will be remembered more for his lonely road, and the complexities represented by his career, than for his record as

Charley Pride meets and greets at Fan Fair in 1974.

a singer and hit maker. Which is not how it should be. Everything else aside, the one overwhelming, utterly unambiguous fact is that during a 14 year period beginning in 1969, Charley Pride sang no fewer than 29 good straight country songs to the top of the charts.

A man who joined him at RCA, and has to some degree shared his aura of separateness throughout an even more impressive career—35 chart-toppers between 1974 and 1990, and steady success since—is Ronnie Milsap. Blind from an early age, Milsap came to country music via a long and winding road that included a hit in the R&B market (where, in a reversal of Charley Pride's entry to country, he was mistak-

enly assumed to be black); touring with singers like James Brown and Smokey Robinson; and years of session work in Memphis (including some for Elvis). His first approach to Nashville, in fact, didn't occur until he found his own recording career going nowhere in Memphis, and a lifetime of club dates and other people's sessions awaiting him; only then was the impression he'd always had of Nashville, a reflection of too many horror stories he'd heard about how difficult it was to make it in the country music business, outweighed by his fear of staying where he was. And anyway, he says, he'd always loved country. It's what he listened to for his own pleasure, especially during his last few years in Memphis.

For him, making it in Nashville didn't turn out to be that hard. He arrived in town with a job for him and his band already secured—a nightly engagement in the lounge on the top floor of the King of the Road motel, then the hottest spot in town for music business people—and that did it: In very short order he had a manager (Jack Johnson, Charley Pride's connection), a recording contract with RCA and a country hit, "I Hate You," on the radio.

The secret of such quick success was simple: Milsap was a virtuoso singer, musician and showman. Nashville insiders still remember how thoroughly he blew them away at the King of the Road with his wildly soulful mix of country, blues and whatever else felt right. As one of them put it to writer Dave Hickey shortly after Milsap delivered his first tapes to RCA, "Man, they're great...but using Ronnie to sing nothing but country is like crop-dusting with a 747." True enough, Hickey replied, "but it sure is good for the crops."

Milsap's virtuosity is part pure talent, part education, and for the depth of that education he has his blindness to thank. If he hadn't been blind, his parents wouldn't have handed him over to his grandparents at birth, and he wouldn't have been sent away to the Governor Morehead School for the Blind in Raleigh, North Carolina, at the age of six, and he wouldn't have received the daily tuition in classical violin and piano provided by that institution. Milsap recognizes the irony. "The school in Raleigh is really what

Charley Pride

Ronnie Milsap reads his chart position in Braille with Joe Galante, Chet Atkins, an R&R exec and producer Tom Collins.

changed my life," he says. "It's crazy to say it, but in some ways it's a blessing that I was born blind. I was totally taken out of the environment that my father's family...generations before me had been in. Taken totally out of that and forced into something else. If I'd been born sighted in western North Carolina and gone through the public school system there, I certainly wouldn't be doing what I'm doing now. The only problem is, when you're six years old, and you're sent off to school by yourself, it's not entirely easy.... When they told me the Bible story about Joseph being sold into slavery, I thought they were talking about me."

He survived to become a fixture on the North Carolina concert piano recital circuit, and then, during his high school years, to lead and play electric guitar in a dance band he called The Apparitions ("It was four blind guys, and we bumped into a lot of walls together"). Eventually he dropped out of college, where he was taking pre-law courses, to play music full time—and hence to Atlanta and Memphis and a little of everything: dance-oriented country rock at the Playboy Club in Atlanta, pure R&B on the Memphis club circuit, pop piano behind Petula Clark and

Ronnie Milsap

Dionne Warwick in Chips Moman's American Studios, whatever seemed appropriate at the Graceland parties for which Elvis hired the local "white Ray Charles."

As a country star, Milsap began his career quite conservatively, making finely crafted middle-of-the-stream recordings and touring with Charley Pride, his recording label and management mate. Soon, though, he was breaking out all over the musical map, and that's how he continued doing things through the 70's and 80's: nobody knew whether the next Ronnie Milsap release was going to be a lush pop ballad, a flash of retro rock 'n' roll, a soulful blues lament, a dance extravaganza, or a straight-down-the-beam country song such as Lefty Frizzell might have sung. His records kept sounding different, too: gearshifts in the song department were usually accompanied by radical alterations of production style.

Part of the impetus for this erratic path came from Milsap's sense of adventure—he's an inveterate experimenter, technologically as well as musically—but another force was a certain tension between him and his marketers. His own account of his experience with *Images*, the first album he produced himself in his own studio, says it all.

"Man, we were cuttin' some stuff!" he recalled. "I was down there doin' all these crazy sounds, singin' through vocorders, stackin' tracks and havin' the time of my life. Technically, just havin' a ball! And then the record came out.... Immediately some folks started sayin', 'Well, he's not country anymore!' Well, that's bullshit. Most people in this town don't have the country background that I have. And nobody can question my love for country music. Nobody.

"But it was really neat. Country radio was sayin', 'Gawd-a-mighty, what is he doin'?' So we went back in the studio and cut some more stuff. We cut this thing called 'Sassy, Sassy', and man, I

Milsap in concert for In Concert (the show). Ronnie racked up Number One hits faster than any other artist on the scene.

thought it was hot! I was in there singin' octaves and double parts and all, and just havin' a great time. Well, pretty soon, Jerry Bradley [then head of RCA's Nashville Division] came over and heard it. He said, 'Please, I'm beggin' you on my knees, please don't release that record!' So I went back in there and cut 'Just because I ask a fer-riend about herrrrr...' and some other real straight country things, for an album which was called *Milsap Magic*. Which was good, because it kind of put me back on the wagon and patched things up on the country radio level again."

And so it went. Milsap and RCA and country radio spent most of the 70's and 80's doing their lively little tango, and in the process Milsap racked up Number One hits faster than any other artist on the scene. So although he never penetrated the baby boomer audience the way Willie and Waylon did, his effect on the course of country music during and after his time may well have been more profound. His sonic adventurism was,

after all, more important than Willie Nelson's classicism or Waylon's Telecaster twang in the expansion of country radio's stylistic turf in the 80's—and of course where radio went, there went Music Row. Milsap, in effect, was Nashville's *USS Enterprise*, boldly going where no man had gone before. It was he, more than any other Nashville artist, who expanded the known universe of country radio and made it safe for various kinds of colonists lining up in his wake: second-generation rockabillies, dyed-in-the-wool pop singers, white soul men, generic rock 'n' roll bands and whoever else needed a new market and was willing to work within the Nashville system.

Conway Twitty, on the other hand, didn't expand anything and wasn't any kind of fast-moving object. He was more like modern country's Grand Canyon, just staying where he was, drawing the crowds and getting a little deeper every year. Even his fans recognized that aspect of his longevity, calling him, affection-

Conway Twitty

ately, "Ole Cornway."

He had an amazing career. Between 1958, when "It's Only Make Believe" topped the pop, R&B and country charts simultaneously, and his death in 1993, he had 50 Number One country singles. As late as 1988, when singers 20 and even 30 years his junior were the norm, only four country artists sold more CDs and tapes than he. At the time of his sudden death at the age of 59 from a ruptured abdominal aneurysm, there was no reason to think he couldn't have continued for another 10 years.

Duet partners and friends, Loretta and Conway.

His success was the product of a potent combination: business ethics far higher than strictly necessary, and a very special relationship with his women fans, mostly but by no means exclusively ladies of his generation.

As journalist John Pugh once observed, Twitty, "family man, businessman, tee-totaller, unfailingly generous, courteous, and gentlemanly," specialized in songs whose persona was "a lechering type of guy who wouldn't hesitate to take any woman he had half a shot at: a guy who sings of undressing innocent young things who've never been this far before, who lies in bed next to his wife with Linda on his mind, who slips off to a rendezvous with somebody else's wife because the fire's gone out at home" (in "You've Never Been This Far Before," "Linda on My Mind" and "After the Fire Is Gone," every one of them a country chart topper). Moreover, he delivered such songs so convincingly, but performed with such decorous restraint, that he was "able to evoke both a simultaneous rush of unrestrained passion and an almost religious admiration." All of which forced Pugh to a bemused but accurate conclusion: "It is clear that about half the women in the country want to be ravished by the world's oldest Boy Scout."

Twitty was well aware of that, and while he always stopped short of addressing the matter directly, which would have been in poor taste, he did pass along some oblique observations. "What I do is a little like being a doctor," he said in 1990. "You know, people tend to be a little afraid of young doctors, but the longer a doctor has been around, the more comfortable people are around him and the more they'll trust him to deal with things that they wouldn't let anyone else deal with. And it's the same with country music. You're dealing with feelings and emotions that are way down deep inside of people. They have to trust you enough to really let you get into their ear close enough to really whisper, 'Helllooooooo, Darlin'...' And they won't let just anybody do that." He added, somewhat redundantly, that "the older you get, the better you get, the more you know what you're singing about, and the more careful you're going to be about the songs you deal with."

Twitty, of course, wasn't Twitty, but Harold Jenkins, born in Friars Point, Mississippi, in 1933, the son of a riverboat captain. He took his stage name from Conway, Arkansas, and Twitty, Texas—according to one account, towns through which he'd passed one day on the road, and to another the two points on a map where, in an intentionally random search for his new identity, he stuck a pin. Maybe both stories are true; he told them both at different times. Conway said that as a child and teenager, he loved country music (and blues and gospel), but when the time came for him to choose his path as a musician, he was too intimidated by his heroes—Hank Williams, Lefty Frizzell, Webb Pierce, Ernest Tubb, Eddy Arnold—to consider a career in Nashville. But then he heard Elvis on the radio, and "I thought, boy, I believe I can do that. I may not be able to compete with Webb and Lefty, but I can do what this guy does."

Merle Haggard and his thousand-mile stare.

He went to Memphis and auditioned for Sam Phillips at Sun Records, but Sam never gave him a recording contract. A few months later, though, MGM Records did. His first single was "It's Only Make Believe," his own song, released in September 1958, and *ka-boom!* The record was so hot, and the singer such an unknown, that many people thought "Conway Twitty" was Elvis recording under a pseudonym. MGM disabused them of that notion once it was no longer useful, and Conway's career as a teen idol was under way. He did well, but not brilliantly: the highest he climbed in the pop charts after "It's Only Make Believe" was the Number Six spot, with "Lonely Blue Boy" in 1960 (his preceding and succeeding singles, "Danny Boy" and "What Am I Living For," reaching Numbers 10 and 26 respectively), and it's fair to say that his pop career had run its course when he switched to country in 1965.

The change was just fine with Conway; it's what he'd been wanting for years. "Right after 'It's Only Make Believe' was Number One in the country field, I started trying to get Jim Vinneau to let me record some of that country stuff," he recalled in the early 70's. (Vinneau was Conway's producer at MGM.) "And he said, 'Well, maybe later on down the line we'll do some.' You see, at that time country and western was hurting pretty bad. The rock thing had just taken over everything, even the country bands...and everybody liked that new type of music, rock 'n' roll, and it really hurt country music. Back then, a Number One country record would sell maybe 30 thou, and it would stay in the Number One position for months. So they thought it might hurt my career. So I said, 'Let me do it under another name—anything. I just want to do some country music.' And they said they would. But then, after five or six years, I began to realize they weren't really going to." He did finally persuade MGM to let him cut some country tracks, but all for naught: they weren't released until he'd taken his wondrous high end and sensuous little growl

to Decca and established a new, all-country career under the guidance of Owen Bradley. He moved his home to Nashville in 1968 and settled in for the duration.

There's not much else to say about Conway's astounding career. He had his high points, notably the lady-killing "Hello, Darlin'" and his string of wonderful duets with Loretta Lynn ("After the Fire Is Gone" being recognized by more than a few fans as *the* country duet), and he had his (relatively) low times too. The steady pace of his success began faltering in the late 70's—that is, his singles didn't automatically proceed straight to the top of the charts, as some 30 of them had since the late 60's—but even then, he dealt with it. He narrowed the age gap between himself and his competition by adopting a whole new image (a natural Afro-ish hairdo in place of his grease job, turtlenecks and classy casuals instead of Nudie suits); he began talking onstage (his gimmick for 14 years had been total silence); he changed producers, saying a respectful *sayonara* to Owen Bradley in favor of the much younger David Barnes, and added more contemporary songs and a new crew of musicians. It all worked fine; the tempo picked right back up again, and "Ole Cornway" kept on trucking with the best of them, slickers and outlaws and New Traditionalists and hat acts and whoever, for another decade-plus. In the 90's he started shedding his extra-musical businesses—notably Twitty City, the Nashville tourist trap in which all his various ventures, from the Twittyburger restaurant chain to his forays into mobile homes, banks and what-have-you, climaxed to the point of threatening to eat him alive—and the results of his new focus on music were quite evident. His last recordings, released shortly after his unexpected demise, show an artist every bit as vital as the man who ruled the country charts in the 70's.

We'll never know what could have happened if he'd survived. Given the climate in country radio at the time of Conway's death—basically, the market had been transformed into a youth-oriented Hunk of the Month Club—it's doubtful that even MCA Records, the most powerful of the Nashville labels, could have placed a 60-year-old artist in contention for the top of the charts. On the other hand, it's a virtual certainty that Conway could have won back the hearts of the better critics, continued doing very well indeed on the road, and provided the ladies with many more years of expert attention from their very favorite physician of love.

If Conway was the very definition of a Nashville centrist in the 70's and 80's, Merle Haggard continued to embody the role of the outsider during those decades. His position was both literal—he lived in California, preferred to record there, and did very little mixing with Nashville music business insiders—and figurative: loneliness, powerlessness, a longing to escape in one way or another and a sense of dislocation pervaded his work, as did a perception of himself as a voice in the wilderness crying out to kindred souls as the tides of the times swept over him; you had to go a long way in the 70's, probably all the way to punk-rock London and New York, to find a popular recording artist with a vision of contemporary society as bleakly angry as Haggard's. And he struck a powerful chord: the unsettling "If We Make It Through December," for instance—a song described by critic Daniel Cooper as "probably the most depressing Christmas song ever to hit the charts"—connected with a popular sentiment strong enough to establish it at Number One on December 25, 1973.

In the 80's, Haggard was still capable of absolutely riveting new songs and performances ("Big City," the devastating "Out Among the Stars" and several others), but his work as a whole became increasingly uneven, and the distance between him and the Nashville mainstream grew wider. By the 90's, it was hard to hear his voice

George Jones—50's

in the music at all, except in the singing style of dozens of younger men. Country radio wouldn't play him, and it seemed he was on his way to join that other brilliant, still powerfully creative giant of country music, Johnny Cash, in the business' new old-guy ghetto.

Not so George Jones, who in 1994 was by far the favorite old guy in Music City, U.S.A. His was the first name out of every young singer's mouth when the subject of influences arose, and he was basking in the sunlight of universal acclaim and record company attention—a situation unique among his generational peers.

Jones' early career as a Texas honky tonk singer has already been touched on: Suffice it to say that, like Dolly Parton, he came from a rural working class Southern fundamentalist background and that he came by his music honestly. He broke into Nashville in 1955 by singing "Why Baby Why" (a song that's gone on to become a honky tonk standard) and had the first big peak in his career in 1962-63, when he won all sorts of awards from *Billboard*, *Cashbox* and the CMA; "She Thinks I Still Care" was the top country record of 1962. By 1964, though, Buck Owens had replaced him as the leading honky tonk singer, and he went into a sort of holding pattern in which he toured widely (especially on the West Coast), recorded an uneven series of albums, and dropped off and back on the Opry.

By 1969, on the heels of the Dylan-and-Cash-inspired Nashville chic movement among the young, Jones found that some of his hard country records were getting airplay on pop stations and that he was being discovered by college students who found him, in the words of journalist Paul Hemphill, "quaint." It was at this time that he married Tammy Wynette and began working with her producer, Billy Sherrill, on his own records. Sherrill would occasionally saddle him with strings and background choirs, but he couldn't

George Jones—1980

George Jones with his pre-Tammy duet partner, Melba Montgomery, in the late 60's.

the nation's leading authority on country music, has described his voice this way: "Sometimes dropping into a low register, then sweeping into a high wail, often enunciating his words with rounded, open-throated precision, but occasionally moaning them through clenched teeth and with the classic pinched-throat delivery of the Southern rural singer, Jones demonstrates why many people consider him the greatest country singer of all time."

Or, as Patrick Carr put it in the 1977 *Village Voice* review that triggered the second rise of the George Jones star in urban intelligentsia circles, "he sings as if he never unclenches his teeth, like the notes come from somewhere way the hell at the back of his head. His pitch is perfect, his little quirks and tricks and sobs smooth and effortless and totally under his control. As a singer, he is as intelligent as they come and should be considered for a spot in America's all-time Top Ten."

Jones has also always been a staunch defender of hard country music; he was one of the prime movers of ACE, the Nashville organization devoted to maintaining the purity of the music in the face of the pop invasion, and in 1975 he reopened his nightclub in downtown Nashville, Possum Holler, because he felt there was really no place in Nashville (aside from the Opry) where a person could hear real country music. Possum Holler was to be a "place for the ones that love the kind of music I love—pure country music." By this he meant a club that would book the likes of Melba Montgomery, Porter Wagoner, Bobby Bare and even Waylon Jennings—and, of course, George Jones.

take the distinctive eastern Texas twang out of George's voice; even amid slick, cream puff arrangements he sounded like a hard, hungry country singer. Sherrill hit two separate winning streaks with George, the first with him alone, the second with duets between him and Tammy that at least rivaled, and sometimes surpassed, Conway Twitty and Loretta Lynn's work together. George continued to sing some real masterpieces on his own during that streak of duets—"The Grand Tour," "I Just Don't Give a Damn," "Ragged but Right"—but his drinking got the better of him, and in 1975 he and Tammy broke up.

Jones has always been known as a "singer's singer" in country music, and he has been listed as the favorite of such notables as Buck Owens, Charley Pride, Waylon Jennings, Connie Smith, Conway Twitty, Emmylou Harris, Randy Travis and virtually all the Young Country singers of the 90's. He has a fine voice, of course, but it's the depth of his control that really impresses his peers, and the perfection with which he has adapted his technique to the basic country instruments, fiddle and steel guitar. Bill Malone,

Jones has been one of the most versatile and prolific recording artists in the music's history. Nobody knows for sure just how many George Jones albums have been released so far, but estimates range all the way from a hundred to over 200. Jones himself can no longer keep track of them all, but given how many of his albums have been reissued and repackaged and rearranged, the 200 figure may not be too far off. None of his albums have attained the platinum status of *Wanted: The Outlaws* or dozens of 80's and 90's country discs, but their sheer number is a good indicator of their overall impact.

Most of them have been pretty much straight-ahead country: "You're always going to hear a fiddle on a George Jones record," he has said. Fans like to remember certain classic performances: "Don't Stop the Music," "Just One More," "Window Up Above," "She Thinks I Still Care," "White Lightning," "If My Heart Had Windows," "A Girl I Used to Know," "I'll Share My World with You," "Walk Through This World with Me" and the song considered to be his modern masterpiece, "He Stopped Loving Her Today." Jones' influence cannot, however, be measured by a monster hit or two. Like many hard country singers, he makes his impact through his consistency and his ability to maintain a steady, predictable musical identity.

By 1977 Jones seemed on the threshold of yet another peak in his career. His hit album *Alone Again* was cut with the same kind of basic five-piece country band he'd used in the 60's (a change George talked Billy Sherrill into by pointing out the Outlaws' immense success with that style of recording), and it succeeded brilliantly, both as a creative work and a cultural event. It was, in fact, a turning point of sorts—or at least

it was perceived as such, which in pop-cultural terms amounts to the same thing. Patrick Carr stated the theme of that shift in his *Village Voice* review. Asking the reader to imagine him- or herself in Nashville, trying to get in with the in crowd, he wrote, "Now, everyone, including you, is just tickled pink that Willie Nelson can win CMA awards and accept them in his sneakers, that good ol' country music seems to have turned into some bizarre combination of biker flick and counter-culture rerun, but saying you think Willie is the Shakespeare of the Southland isn't going to get you any further than the men's room. People who were looking for Willie with thumbscrews two

Man and wife, George and Tammy, happy together with producer Billy Sherrill.

Sometimes George Jones showed up. Here with Linda Ronstadt and Bonnie Raitt at his New York showcase in 1981.

years ago are now sending proposals of marriage. Forget it. What you do is, you sneak over to the jukebox, find one of those records that features George Jones singing his heart out on some incredibly dumb, corny song, and you play it. Then, at the appropriate lull, you happen to mention that in your considered out-of-town opinion, George Jones is definitely, unequivocally, the best there ever was or will be, period."

Carr suggested further embellishment. "You point at the jukebox and you say, very firmly, 'That's where it's at, man. While not denying that the newly found social acceptability of your cocaine habit is pleasant in a certain scheme of things, and that if you were to write a song about making whoopee with dead armadillos it's entirely possible that Waylon could have a country hit with it within the next five years, I maintain that Waylon & Willie's main significance lies in the fact that their commercial success enabled

George Jones to cut real country records again.' You are now an honorary Southerner, and are invited to people's houses."

Behind the sarcasm, Carr had a point. In 1977 there was indeed a sea change happening in country music. It could be interpreted as weariness with the high-voltage adventurism of the outlaw movement, or as a desire for more familiar ground (classic honky tonk country being, after all, the music on which many of the Outlaws' fans were raised), or it could simply have been the inevitable turning of the trend wheel; whatever goes up in popular culture must come down in a while, and whatever was down must come up. And although the temptation to generalize in these matters should perhaps be resisted, it is nonetheless true that the late 70's in the United States were a time of growing disenchantment with some of the values that underlay the outlaw movement: introspection, tolerance, free thinking and anti-authoritarianism. The age of Reagan and Rambo was dawning, after all. On the other hand, it might just be that country fans, and country musicians, can only go for so long until it's time to get basic again and cry in their beer.

That's one perspective. Another is the perspective from 1977, when the first edition of this book was written. It poses different questions, but not so surprisingly, they're just as relevant. They can end this chapter as fittingly as any contemporary notions.

Writing of George Jones, the first edition noted that "his records were being heard on juke boxes across the country, North and South, rural and urban. Jones had done this without really compromising his music, without slicking it up, without adding new content, and without adding a beat to it. Was he benefiting from the groundwork of the pop-country singers who had introduced a large segment of America to the notion of country? Was he reaching an audience that, like the folk-revival audience of the 1960's, had tired of imitations and was now wanting the real thing? Or had country music itself become so diffuse and complex that even Jones, with his hard-country approach, was now regarded as only a representative of a sub-genre of the music, like bluegrass, honky tonk, Sherrill-style, Southern rock, or whatever? Had the music become nationalized and broadened enough to appeal to a mass audience, or had America become Southernized and willing to embrace a philosophy of grass-roots populist nostalgia that included country music?

"Whatever the answers, it seems oddly significant that by 1977, after almost 10 years of revolutionary change and disruption and reaction, two of the hottest figures in country music were Dolly Parton and George Jones, both charter members of the classic country music establishment."

Mickey Gilley and "the bull."

CHAPTER 14

Urban Cowboys and Roots Revivalists

Country music's 80's didn't really begin at the turn of the decade; they began three years earlier, in 1977, when Kenny Rogers took his first big country hit, "Lucille," to the top of the charts. It was, as they say, the start of something big.

Rogers, who had turned his career toward Nashville when his rock band, The First Edition, went belly-up, sent "Lucille," a brilliantly hooked little story song found for him by Nashville producer Jerry Butler, to the top in October 1977. He never looked back. In short order he was outselling everyone else in the field, drawing even more fans than Dolly Parton towards Nashville's marketing net, and triggering a general stampede into the middle of the country-pop road behind him. For while Waylon and Willie and the boys continued, as Patrick Carr put it, to redefine country music as a "bizarre combination of biker flick and counterculture re-run" with a heady run of Gold and platinum albums through the late 70's, the rapid rise of the sedate, impeccably groomed Mr. Rogers suggested a powerful parallel universe: Perhaps, despite the Outlaw sentiment loose in the land, Billy Sherrill's "housewife washing dishes" was not such an unpromising customer after all. She and her sisters in the heartland might well turn out to be eager consumers of countryish crooning—especially since Elvis, long the King of their marketplace niche,

was no longer available for personal appearances, and Charlie Rich was no longer interested (Presley died in 1977; Rich hung on in a low-key way in Memphis until his death in mid-1995).

Rogers, who was 39 when "Lucille" topped the charts, had already experienced the kind of career straight country singers of his generation could only fantasize. With the pop-folk New Christy Minstrels and then the pop-rock First Edition (formed around himself and three other refugees from The New Christy Minstrels), he had toured the world, starred in his own syndicated TV show, and been a consistent presence on the pop charts for almost three years—The First Edition's hits in 1968-70 included "Reuben James," "Ruby, Don't Take Your Love to Town," and, of course, "Just Dropped In (To See What Condition My Condition Was In)," a number the official Kenny Rogers Career Chronology characterizes rather aptly as "slightly psychedelic."

As far as he was concerned, The First Edition gave Rogers his ticket to permanent security, a highly desirable commodity in a world view formed during his poverty-plagued childhood in Houston. Instead of security, though, he got sudden failure, and a lesson. He told *Playboy* that "I think having my group, The First Edition, crumble beneath me when I was counting on it to take me through my whole life really made me aware of how temporary success is. It can

Kenny Rogers

just go. You're never safe."

By nature a cautious man, he learned the lesson well, developing a philosophy of music and business designed to ensure maximum commerciality and security in an ever-changing competitive environment. Over the years of his enormous success he would base his business on reliability—his own, his investments'—and his music on what he has called "controlled experimentation." As he said in 1983, "There are common denominators I try to maintain, because there are an automatic 750,000 to one million people who buy my albums the moment they're released. I want to keep that audience. Any other people I'd like to buy my records, I have to sell to. So I try different stuff, things unusual for me. If I get lucky with the new material and get a hit, it opens up new areas. If I don't get lucky, it doesn't hurt, because most people tend not to remember songs

Kenny in his "slightly psychedelic" days.

they don't like. You just have to know when to stick your neck out and when to pull it back."

His calculation paid off handsomely at virtually every stage of his expanding career. When he forsook Larry Butler as a producer in favor of R&B singer/writer Lionel Richie, it worked just fine: the result, Richie's song "Lady," was the first Kenny Rogers single to jump from the top of the country charts to the top of the *Billboard* Hot 100 (and what's more, stay there for a full six weeks). When he called in Barry Gibb of The Bee Gees (fresh from the immensely commercial *Saturday Night Fever* soundtrack) to produce his *Eyes That See in the Dark* album in Miami, that worked too: "Islands in the Stream," a duet with Dolly Parton (the latest in a series of successful matings that had included Dottie West, Sheena Easton and Kim Carnes), sold more copies than any single in RCA's history. Another album with yet another star producer, George Martin,

the Englishman who had molded The Beatles' sound, yielded yet another mega-hit, "Morning Desire."

And so on. "The Gambler," parlayed into a television property, became the highest-rated TV movie of 1980 and spawned wildly successful sequels and Western-themed specials that continue to this day. TV Christmas shows with Dolly Parton bored the bearded balladeer yet further into the all-American heart. December 1984 found him accepting two platinum album certifications, his tenth and 11th since 1978—a feat unequaled by any artist before him—and two years later it was startling, but not very surprising, when a poll conducted by *PM Magazine* and *USA Today* found him to be the "favorite singer of all time"—more popular, that is, than Barbra Streisand, Bruce Springsteen, Frank Sinatra and Elvis.

For a time, then, Kenny Rogers was nothing less than the biggest pop star in the world—and in a way, the last of his breed (for a while, anyway, until the wheel of the cycle turned another 360 degrees). As critic James Hunter, noting the "country suburbanite persona" of his subject, observed quite astutely, "Rogers established himself as a mass-market pop star before Michael Jackson forever changed the playing field of American pop, and as such, he is one of the last superstars to make a commercial virtue of his conventionality instead of his creative idiosyncrasies."

Rogers himself has always recognized the importance and value of his regular-guy image, middle-of-the-stream music, and nonthreatening degree of native talent. He has said that "I have nothing specific to offer except professionalism and commerciality"; that he has spent his career "kind of joking my way through, half-singing"; and in 1988 he told *Country Music* that to him, "music is a vehicle to get me to the next golf course." At that time, though, he added a crucial rider to his self-humbling. "I do have one very important talent a lot of people don't: I can pick hit songs."

He might have added another: that since his First Edition days, he'd also had the career guidance of Ken Kragen, a Harvard graduate whose managerial skills were second to none in any area of the entertainment business. Kragen, like

With Ken Kragen, the country-popper's manager of choice...

Dolly Parton's Sandy Gallin, came from the larger New York/Hollywood axis beyond Nashville's reach. As one of the first of a new breed of entrepreneurs, middlemen and executives who would enter the country music market in increasing numbers in the years to come, he could offer what no Nashville insider could: access to the major players in the national/international show business community, and the ability to breeze through barriers (of class, of culture) im-

penetrable and even unseen by the good ole boys back on Music Row.

Even a great salesman needs a solid product, though, and in Kenny Rogers, Kragen had a beauty—a commodity approaching mass-market perfection; an artist of such broad appeal that he really was, as one of his many critics described him, "the Wonder Bread of American pop."

If spice was not an ingredient, then, who cared? Certainly not Kenny. He actually boasted about his blandness. "I'm a pretty boring guy," he said in his *Playboy* interview. "However, I think that to be as boring as I am and to have done what I have is pretty incredible. It gives hope to other boring people, telling them if they bust their ass, it can happen."

That last point is one he's often stated in terms of the American dream—yes, even for a ho-hum dude from a Houston public housing project there is "the possibility in this country of succeeding from nothing"—and that's one of the things he has said he stands for. The other, "the importance of family life," might seem an odd choice for a man with several divorces under his belt, but that's show business.

And anyway, the Kenny Rogers image, not his reality, continued to be the important thing, in terms of both its sales potential and its impact on the direction of country music in the 80's. For the huge success of the Kenny Rogers combination—country identification; a safe, clean-living public persona; and music incorporating popified elements of any style fitting the material, from country to calypso to rock to disco—was to become the blueprint for a new age of Nashville product. Strong characters with hard-edged music were on their way out, and "entertainers" were on their way in.

The ascent of the regular-guy image could, of course, be seen as a reflection of a broader movement, the shift towards conservatism in most areas of social and political life in the early 80's, but however that dynamic worked, it was certainly Kenny Rogers who showed Nashville the way. He never got the credit he deserved from the Country Music Association, which exacted its revenge for his slightly psychedelic past and "outside management" by repeatedly refusing him its Entertainer of the Year award (meanwhile making certain his sales were included in its promotional statistics on country music market growth), but the numbers speak for themselves. When *Kenny Rogers' Greatest Hits* ended up selling more than 12 million copies around the world—*Wanted: The Outlaws* had sold two million—folks on Music Row took notice. The middle of that road looked good indeed.

The factor which really centered Nashville's bandwagon, however, was something of a fluke:

not a musical phenomenon, but a movie. *Urban Cowboy*, starring a mechanical bull and John Travolta and Debra Winger as working singles living a night life of cow-boogie fantasy in Mickey Gilley's cavernous Texas honky tonk, accomplished the neat pop-cultural trick of creating the phenomenon it supposedly reflected. Like its predecessor, *Saturday Night Fever* (also starring dancing John), *Urban Cowboy* began as a nonfiction magazine article depicting a strictly localized subculture—young blue-collar Brooklynites in *Saturday Night Fever,* young blue-collar Houstonians in *Urban Cowboy*—and ended, after movie dramatization and massive doses of hype and hoopla, as an international dance and fashion fad.

The movie's effect was immediate and intense.

...and with fiancée (now second ex-wife) Marianne Gordon at a charity ball game. Alice Cooper is at right.

Urban super-cowboys Mickey Gilley, John Travolta, and, with Cher, Johnny Lee.

the big hit song of the movie; gave a powerful boost to the already well established career of Gilley himself; and greatly enlarged the number of urban/suburban Americans exposed to country music on a regular basis. And that growth was spectacular: Between the years 1979 and 1983, the number of radio stations programming country music full time in the United States rose from just over 1,400 to almost 2,300 and, by some estimates, the year following *Urban Cowboy*'s release saw a full 50 percent rise in actual sales of country records and tapes—in a disco- and soft rock-dominated popular music market which had been experiencing a serious overall decline since 1978.

History has been unkind to *Urban Cowboy*. A decade later (and a lot sooner than that in some circles) the whole experience was remembered by almost everybody in the business, from record executives to *Village Voice* critics, as a kind of communal root canal. For one thing, much of the most successful music was trivial, trashy and cynically conceived—"hack disco in a cowboy hat" as one critic put it—and that had a disheartening effect on Nashville's creative community. For another, the

Reaching a consumer culture in which cowboy style had already been rendered hip by Waylon & Willie and safe by Kenny Rogers, it spread Western clothing stores and mechanical bulls across the nation virtually overnight (no small feat, with mechanical bulls running $8,000 apiece). It also created the brief stardom of Johnny Lee, the Gilley's club singer whose "Lookin' for Love" was

commercial success was short-lived, and when the bubble burst, it left a most unpleasant aftertaste. By mid-1984, country record and tape sales had fallen back below 1979 levels, and there wasn't a media trendsetter in the nation who'd give a Nashville act the time of day.

Those were bad times, for in country music circles there was depression, not just economic recession: the feeling that perhaps, in chasing after the fool's gold of a fickle urban audience, deeper loyalties had been betrayed and resources of more lasting value squandered.

Such feelings were very real, as was the decline in Nashville's financial fortunes in the early mid-80's, but still, *Urban Cowboy* definitely had its bright side. Even if its most audible-visible manifestations do resonate in the memory with a tinge of something close to horror—Johnny Lee's "Pickin' Up Strangers," the sight of Truman Capote and Ethel Kennedy in full Ralph Lauren designer cowboy drag dancing disco to Eddie Rabbitt live at Bloomingdale's—its trickle-down economics did add country to the night life menu in a lot of urban areas and keep a lot of fine country/rockabilly/roots musicians working a lot of good honky tonks all over the U.S.A. Moreover, *Urban Cowboy* money created an expansive mood in the executive offices of Music Row, making it possible for Artists & Repertoire personnel to fund some new music of significant depth and/or originality. Thus, while mainstream interest focused on issues such as just how tightly a pair of Wranglers could be made to adhere to the buttocks while still allowing one to cow-boogie the night

Gilley giving it all at Gilley's, his huge Houston honky tonk.

away (with the staggeringly made-over Dottie West leading the parade), the first three years of the 80's saw the Nashville breakthroughs of Rosanne Cash, Ricky Skaggs, George Strait and John Anderson. Those years also saw the commercial rise of the "new" Hank Williams Jr., the first flush of immense success for Alabama, and the beginning of Reba McEntire's major league career.

In truth, then, Nashville's case of the post-*Urban Cowboy* blues obscured some very healthy new facts of country music life. A knowing eye could roam the field, in fact, and mark each of them: gifted, intelligent young artists inspired and emboldened by the creative energy of the Outlaw movement, and a baby boomer audience the Outlaws (and country rockers from Dylan

Alabama—Mark Herndon, Randy Owen, Teddy Gentry and Jeff Cook—in an early publicity shot for RCA.

to The Eagles) had readied for them; an ever-growing younger audience badly served by rock's fragmentation into a collection of strictly defined, mutually exclusive styles (disco, punk, funk, metal, rap, etc.); an older, middle-of-the-road pop market, softened up by Kenny Rogers and Dolly Parton, now ripe for further exploitation; a societal swerve toward just the kind of "traditional values" the music of white working-class rural America could quite convincingly claim to represent; and, last but by no means least, that huge new net of radio stations filling the airwaves with countryish music from sea to shining sea.

What you had in Nashville in the early 80's, then—before, during, after and despite the *Urban Cowboy* fad—was a big, well-fueled steamroller poised to go wherever it wanted. And for

the next decade, that's exactly what it did, eating up the available turf with never a backward lurch.

A very significant component of the juggernaut was Alabama; the band, that is, not the state. A four-man team comprising three country cousins from DeKalb County in the extreme northeastern tip of Alabama ("The Sock Capital of the World") and a Northern drummer unrelated by blood, they were by far the most commercially successful country act of the early 80's.

They were also the first major country act to be organized and promoted as a band on The Beatles model, a self-contained unit of instrumentalists capable of handling their own vocals and generating their own songs, and that was a major factor in their success, particularly among younger fans. Their audiences, in fact, were noted for large numbers of young teenagers: brand new fans who might never have been drawn towards country had Alabama not presented it to them within the familiar, youth-oriented context of a rock format and rock staging. And these, moreover, were kids: not the old hippies and college crowds drawn to the Outlaws or even the raunchier Southern rock fans, but a new generation. Much younger than the traditional country audience and much more conservative than traditional rockers, they were a potent new force on the scene.

Alabama pleased them greatly, and pleased their parents too, for here was something new: a band with all the energy of rock, but little of its risk or excess. Alabama didn't threaten anyone's eardrums or even their morals. In fact, they followed rules of public decorum straight out of Sunday school: smoking, drinking, drugging and profanity by band and crew were forbidden at their appearances. All the same, guitarist Jeff Cook did wear a Confederate flag cape and play solos with his teeth, and lead singer Randy Owen did stomp around whipping up a storm; they were serious about their showmanship. Before they hit on the idea of naming themselves after their home state, in fact, they called themselves "Wild Country" (as, it seems, did sev-

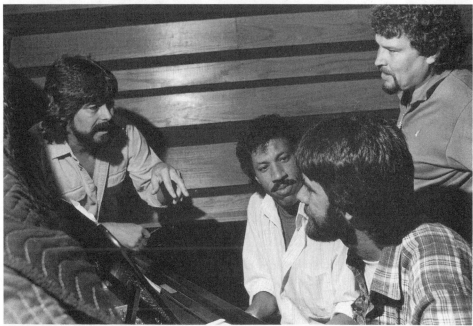

Alabama reels in the youngsters at Fan Fair, above, and records with Lionel Richie.

eral other bands; hence the name change).

They were ideal for mass consumption. Combining powerful church-raised blood harmony singing and an anthematic approach to their subject matter, they fell very naturally on the country ear as well as tapping deeply into strong streams of Southern, rural and working-class feeling. Songs like "My Home's in Alabama," "Tennessee River," "Mountain Music," "Dixieland

Delight," "Roll On (Eighteen Wheeler)" and "Forty Hour Week" were remarkably effective in evoking pride and nostalgia among their target population, and moreover they did so without challenging anything or offending anyone else (save perhaps critics suspicious of the degree of calculation involved in such songs). Combined with their instinct for truly catchy material and their firm command of all the most reliably crowd-pleasing tempos, techniques, chord progressions and clichés available to a workaday American pop musician—earned the hard way, over a decade as a bar band playing everything from The Rolling Stones to Hank Williams—those assets made for an act with broad appeal indeed.

Ironically, the element that gave Alabama their competitive edge in the younger end of the market also created difficulties for them within the Nashville system. Their being a band, as opposed to a solo act or a singing group, was in fact perceived quite negatively. Partly that was because the whole Nashville music-making system was based on the idea of a shifting parade of singers supported by a more or less permanent corps of deeply talented studio musicians who could be relied upon to do a producers' bidding exactly and efficiently. If you were to drop a self-contained band into such a system, who knew what might happen? It might take weeks to get the right sound out of them, at who knows what cost in money, time and temper. Also, as Alabama guitarist Jeff Cook has observed of the Nashville attitude, "It seemed to be the opinion of the major labels back then that if you were a band, you would have a hit record and then have internal problems and break up."

Hank Jr. as a teen

Even after they'd penetrated the national charts, rising to number 16 with "My Home's in Alabama" on MDJ Records, an independent Dallas label, the four members of Alabama weren't accepted as a band. Cook recalls that when they were given a spot on the "New Faces" show at the 1980 Radio Seminar in Nashville, the showcase from which emerged their relationship with producer Harold Shedd and their deal with RCA, "We didn't even get to play our own instruments. Just sing. They used studio pickers, and Mark [Herndon, the band's drummer], who doesn't sing, sat out in the audience. It was real weird. It was one of the few times in my life that I walked on a stage to sing and didn't have something in my hands to play."

Affairs at RCA weren't much different. Alabama went out and performed their own concerts, but studio musicians were responsible for the instrumentation on their records. As bassist Teddy Gentry admitted, it wasn't until 1984's *Roll On* album that he provided the bass tracks: "Before, if we happened to be doing a song that I was familiar with, I'd go ahead and play in the studio. But otherwise, instead of holding the session up, trying to learn a new song, I'd go ahead and let the session musicians do it."

That situation, and the music industry's if not the public's knowledge of it, wasn't comfortable for the band, and relations between them and the Nashville establishment were difficult at times. "That sort of thing, having to do our singing without playing, followed through for a long time," Gentry recalled. "It seemed like forever. Like, we'd go to do TV shows, and nobody would take into consideration that we weren't just a vocal group, like The Oak Ridge Boys or The Statler Broth-

Hank Williams Jr.

More Hanks: Bocephus with his mom and Hank Killian, a singer she was pushing.

Roll On album was the first Nashville album ever to "ship platinum"—to feature an initial distribution of a million or more units). In other ways, though, the band's huge success posed some important questions about the direction the Nashville music industry was taking. Bob Allen alluded to such issues in *Country Music* in 1984.

"While some have applauded the band as the saviors of Dixie-fried country-rock and the heirs apparent to the throne vacated by legendary Southern rockers like The Allman Brothers and Lynyrd Skynyrd, others have dismissed them as bubblegummers with Southern accents," he wrote. "To some, they are the quintessential country stars of 80's; to others, they are merely a flash-in-the-pan novelty, a shallow contrivance of Nashville's relentless media-blitz machinery: country music's answer to The Monkees."

Others were even more scathing. The *Arizona Daily Star* called them "bloodless as a Coke commercial—a Disneyland version of country music." The *Northwest New Jersey Daily Record* characterized their records as "cliché-ridden...country-western Muzak." After a Hollywood show, the *Los Angeles Herald-Examiner* called them "oily pretenders."

Strong words for basically inoffensive music, but understandable, for Alabama was after all turning the mainstream of country mu-

ers. We were a band, not just somebody who grabs a microphone and starts singing with a 40-piece orchestra behind him. We finally had to start getting a little nasty about it, in order to get the point across."

They showed some talent in that area, too. With the press in particular their attitude quite often fell into the range between surly defense and aggressive offense, particularly when asked about their recording sessions or invited to grapple with other issues of originality, creativity and commerciality.

In one way that tension was just a sign of the times; low-intensity conflict between thin-skinned musicians and critical presspersons, a feature of the rock world since the mid-60's, had finally come to Music City (as had rock-level money, a great deal of it flowing toward Alabama. Their

Birthday bash with manager Merle Kilgore.

Dickie Betts, Porter Wagoner, Willie Nelson, Bobby Bare, Waylon Jennings, Jessi Colter, Kris Kristofferson, Jim Varney and George Thorogood all showed up for Hank Jr.'s video, "All My Rowdy Friends Are Coming Over Tonight," in 1984.

sic around—away from its roots in the white man's blues and the adult artistry of writers like Willie Nelson and Merle Haggard, and toward a simplistic kind of country-imaged pop aimed primarily at teenagers and suburbanites. That annoyed a lot of people who had loved country music longer than most of Alabama's fan club members had been alive.

Something else annoyed many of Alabama's fellow country artists. The malleability of Owen, Gentry, Cook and Herndon in the studio, and the bottom-line fact that neither their abilities as instrumentalists nor their gifts as creative artists made such an arrangement particularly unjust, represented a significant reversal of fortunes in the struggle between artists and record companies that had been at the heart of the Outlaw movement. In the end, Willie and Waylon and the boys had wrested creative control of their music away from their record companies only by proving that their way of recording was the money-making way, and had

thereby caused Nashville executives to at least briefly reassess their own infallibility in creative matters. The success of Alabama, an act controlled more tightly by their record company than any Outlaw or even any established straight country singer would have permitted in 1980, helped get things back on track in that area. As one emerging artist of the period put it, anonymously, "Those guys [in Alabama] did whatever they were told, and the record companies got to kind of liking that. They were tired of singers telling them what to do; they liked these new guys, these hungry, respectful guys. So that became an important thing to them, a new artist's attitude—almost as important as how well you could sing, and sometimes more important."

Whatever the storms in their way and their wake, though, Alabama soldiered on, proving that they were more than the country Monkees and much more than a flash in the pan: By 1985 they had no fewer than two quadruple-platinum,

Rosanne Cash

one triple-platinum and two single-platinum albums to their credit, and were still sending their new singles to the top of the country charts; they had four Number One hits that year. They still couldn't get much respect, though, and after 1986 they also had trouble getting spectacular sales. By the end of the decade their run at the top was clearly over, but ironically they made what many critics consider their best album, *Southern Star*, in 1989. Even Bob Allen wrote about its "lively band-style performances and bright vocal harmonies" and conceded his "grudging respect." Maturity was becoming Owen, Gentry, Cook and Herndon.

The book isn't closed on Alabama. They were still going strong in the mid-90's, at which point the three founding cousins could look back on a full quarter century of playing music together for a living—which, as Randy Owen observed in 1990, "sure as hell beats working swing shift at the sock factory." At that point Owen, never previously noted for public humility, was also secure enough to offer what might be the

Then husband and wife, Rodney Crowell and Rosanne Cash.

final word on himself and his band. "I couldn't count how many people are better guitar players or better singers or better songwriters than I am," he said, "and other groups can play our songs probably as good as we can. But we've stuck together."

Alabama's effect was enormous. Obviously, they changed the character of Nashville music by breaking down a door previously closed to bands and making it possible for a succession of successful acts, from Exile and Sawyer Brown to Restless Heart and Shenandoah, to exploit the

opening. Less obviously but far more significantly, they were the catalyst of a major shift in country music's audience (or, if you prefer, Nashville's market). Basically, they brought a new center into the equation. Country's pool of older, pre-Alabama fans remained, but the teen and sub-teen Alabama fans of the early 80's possessed the magic combination: youth and numbers, the Holy Grail of the radio ad salesman's and record executive's quest; many, many young persons more motivated than any other demographic group to spend their money on music, and statistically predestined to do just that for an average of five more years, at which point they would become the second most motivated music consumer group in the demographic universe. The industry would have had to be foolish indeed to do anything but pander as diligently as possible to whatever such an audience demanded in the way of musical entertainment, and of course it wasn't that foolish, and thus began the trend that would have to wait until the mid-90's for a name: Young Country.

Meanwhile, much else was afoot. Hank Williams Jr., for instance. Inhabiting a reality entirely separate from that of his contemporaries in Alabama—he was blood-red steak and moonshine and mayhem to their meat loaf and Miller Lite, real down and dirty Dixie rock raunch to the sanitized echo they were selling—Hank Jr. brought yet another segment of the population toward Nashville's fold. Nashville didn't want anything to do with them, or with him, for more than a

Rodney Crowell

few years, but in the end the kids who entered the 80's as small-town teenage rebels loyal only to sex, drugs and Southern rock 'n' roll would, like Bocephus himself, have mellowed enough to allow a little old-fashioned country grace into their lives. By the early 90's, they too would be prime customers for Nashville product.

Hank Jr., "Bocephus" to his late father, is one of the great characters of country music—a fact not guaranteed by his lineage, but certainly expected of him on that account: The son of Hank and Audrey Williams, blessed and cursed in more or less equal parts by the weight of their legend, would almost have to be a great show, if nothing else.

And that he was. For the first years of his career the boy, then young man, was a fascinating Hank Williams imitator, following as exactly in his daddy's musical footsteps as his mommy and MGM Records could make him. Then, full grown in 1975, he became a great drama as, in rapid succession, he left Nashville for Alabama and his father's music for his own (the wild and wonderful Southern rock/honky tonk *Hank Williams Jr. & Friends* being his emphatic declaration of independence);

Rosanne Cash, working mother, at home.

came close to losing his life, and did lose parts of his face, when he fell 500 feet off a cliff while hunting in Montana; and suffered the death of his mother. He emerged from '75 bent but not broken, though, and went on to build his own little Dixie-rebel empire among the South's hardcore young boogie fans, presiding over the festivities in fine style and flipping Nashville the metaphorical bird as he pursued his various passions—guns, beauty queens, anything else loud,

fast and beautiful enough for ol' Bocephus—with gusto. His music, distinctly rowdy since '75, turned anthematic in ways much more provocative than Alabama's innocuous odes to the Southland ("A Country Boy Can Survive," with its menu of implied and explicit prejudice, paranoia and menace being the peak of his form), and for a while it seemed as if he might give himself over entirely to bombast and braggadocio, spending half his time singing about the legend of Hank Williams Jr. according to Hank Williams Jr., and the other half working through a kind of dirty-laundry list of redneck resentments. He spared us all, however, and adopted a suppler, more humorous touch—a cover of Fats Waller's sly "Ain't Misbehavin'," for instance— while also cooperating in the mending of fences between himself and the Nashville establishment. Which certainly saved face in Nashville; the CMA's practice of handing out its biggest awards to artists nowhere near as popular (or as legitimately country) as the Cullman, Alabama, Southern folk hero and major national recording artist had grown more embarrassing every year since the late 70's.

Hank Jr. wasn't the only best-selling country recording artist ignored by the powers-that-were in Nashville's early 80's. Rosanne Cash spent those years writing and recording some of the most creatively intriguing and commercially successful music in town, but lived and worked un-Awarded in a world almost as separate as Cullman from the CMA mainstream. As in the case of ol' Bocephus, it was a matter of both personal style and audience: Cash wasn't the type to tolerate

Ricky Skaggs and Keith Whitley got their start as teens working with Ralph Stanley.

much Music Row schmoozing, and her music, while just as country-radio-friendly as Hank Jr.'s when the chips were down (she had 11 Number One *Billboard* country hits in the 80's), found a good percentage of its fans among people not considered Nashville's natural constituency: while Bocephus drew Dixie's rebels without a cause, Rosanne drew the urban intelligentsia.

That figured. She herself had been raised in cosmopolitan California and was at first uninterested in her father's field of endeavor. After a period in New York studying acting at the Lee Strasberg Institute and a while in London working for CBS Records, she wound up in Nashville as a student of creative writing at Vanderbilt University, not an aspiring hillbilly singer; her first musical heroes had been The Doors and The Beatles, not Hank and Lefty and Johnny and Elvis, and as to her opinion of Nashville, she told *Country Music* in 1988 that "to me, it was a bunch of people wearing plaid pants who'd never heard of The Beatles...Nashville just seemed so behind."

Destiny called, however: In a reversal of the usual process—one for which most bright young things might seriously consider selling their souls, and cheaply too—CBS Records came looking for her to record an album. Her semi-reluctant brushes with the music business, most significantly a never-released album she'd made for

the German Ariola label, were the catalyst of CBS's interest, but it would be absurd to imagine that her name didn't help, too.

Ms. Cash was and is an unusual country artist. For one thing, her work has been an *auteur* odyssey, a chronicle of songs taken directly from her own life and feelings with very few holds barred, for which there isn't a parallel in modern Nashville, the only (somewhat) similar creative journeys, those of Merle Haggard and Dwight Yoakam, being quite emphatically non-Nashvillian.

Then too, she doesn't go about the business of music the way almost every other country artist does, with steady touring and regularly released albums; she has never toured consistently, and has let years go by between albums (three, for instance, between *Rhythm & Romance* and 1988's *King's Record Shop*). She couldn't have done that, of course, without her non-country following and record sales, an area in which *Rolling Stone* posited that "she might well be the finest female singer in pop music today."

There were arguments in the 80's that Rosanne Cash wasn't a country artist at all, just a person who happened to be working in Nashville and had been routed into her record company's country channels because she was Johnny Cash's daughter. Quite aside from the fact that such arguments approach meaninglessness in the context of Kenny Rogers, Alabama, The Oak Ridge Boys, Lee Greenwood and many other CMA-endorsed middle-of-the-roaders active in the 80's, there is also the point that Ms. Cash and her prominent singer/songwriter/bandleader/producer husband, Rodney Crowell, were at the center of a musical and social community of great importance to the Nashville music industry as a whole, a core of writers and musicians influential out of all proportion to their numbers. These people—among them guitarist Albert Lee, writer/

Ricky Skaggs

"Picky Ricky" records with his idol and fellow-Kentuckian, Mr. Bill Monroe.

cal development which ran concurrent with, but counter to, the Country Lite of Kenny Rogers, Alabama and the like in the early 80's.

The significant year was 1982. It was then that Ricky Skaggs, George Strait, and John Anderson all scored their first chart-topping singles, and set in motion a trend toward the musical philosophy which tied them together despite their very different musical styles: traditionalism.

On the face of things, Skaggs was the least likely new star of the day: a fervent fan of elders such as Bill Monroe

picker Hank DeVito, singer/songwriters like Steve Earle and Kevin Welch, producer/keyboardist Tony Brown, writer Paul Kennerly and the woman he married after her move from California to Nashville in the mid-80's, Emmylou Harris—were the rough 80's equivalent of the Miller/Nelson/Kristofferson/Clement/Glaser axis that pushed the boundaries of country music in the late 60's and early 70's: a core of prolific, highly creative innovators who, unlike the middle-of-the-roaders, were also committed to continuity with the music's past.

In some ways these people were separated from the more traditional country music community by their origins (many of them were college graduates from solidly middle-class families) and by what one must, reluctantly, call their lifestyles: there was a lot of health food and weighty literature around their circles. Also, the kind of causes one might find them championing—perhaps gay rights, certainly environmental awareness—were not, typically, admired by the Nashville majority. But these people were after all Southerners who had come by their music as honestly as anyone else in town, and they did belong.

They were a force for change of a diffuse, intangible sort, a kind of cultural broadening, and they were also important in supporting a musi-

and The Stanley Brothers and a virtuoso musician trained since childhood on the bluegrass circuit, his closest brush with the country mainstream was a stint in Emmylou Harris' Hot Band. But the combination he offered—vintage songs, smooth, high-lonesome vocals and superb bluegrass picking with a touch of rockabilly edge—proved instantly appealing as soon as it was offered by a major label. The first single from his first Epic album, an electrified reprise of Flatt and Scruggs' "Don't Get Above Your Raising," got within hailing distance of *Billboard's* Top Ten, and it wasn't a fluke. The next single did even better, and the third, "Crying My Heart Out Over You," which had been a modest hit for Flatt and Scruggs in 1960, went all the way to Number One. So all of a sudden, slap bang in the middle of *Urban Cowboy's* glitz and most conceivable colorations of Country Lite, here came something completely different.

Nobody like Skaggs had made it on Music Row for a long time. Born in Cordell, Kentucky, a remote little mountain community where, as he noted in 1981, "the post office fell in the creek five years ago," he was a genuine hillbilly. By the age of three he was singing harmony with his mother on all the old mountain songs. At five he began learning to play the miniature mandolin given him by his father, a welder by trade and guitarist by avocation. At seven, after considerable stage experience in the family band with his mother and father at local theaters and churches, he earned his first big money: $52.50 for showing off his skill on Flatt and Scruggs' syndicated television show. He might even have become a Grand Ole Opry performer at that point too, if the Opry management hadn't thought better of it. For one thing, there was the potential for a problem with the musicians' union. For another, Skaggs recalls, "They said, 'He shouldn't be singin' truck-drivin' songs and baby, I'm in love with you. He should be singin' kids' songs.' And my dad just didn't go for that at all."

Skaggs had to wait nine more years, until he was 16, before hitting the big time again. That's when Ralph Stanley himself, the great musical

hero of the Kentucky hills, invited the teenager to join his Clinch Mountain Boys on the road during summer vacation, and to bring his friend Keith Whitley along with him. Skaggs and Whitley, playing in a band with Skaggs' father and Whitley's brother, had worked hard at recreating the harmonies for which Ralph Stanley and his late brother, Carter Stanley, were justly famous, so their presence in The Clinch Mountain Boys was much appreciated by Stanley Brothers fans. The arrangement worked out fine, and the two boys hired on full-time as soon as they graduated high school in 1971.

Money was tight, though, too tight for Skaggs, and he lasted little more than a year before being forced to give up the road for a regular job. Fortunately, the Washington, D.C.-based Coun-

New Traditionalists long before the movement: Skaggs, his future wife Sharon White, her sister Cheryl White and Emmylou Harris.

try Gentlemen rescued him, and he played with them until moving to J.D. Crowe's New South band, then forming his own Boone Creek, and finally landing with Emmylou Harris, who'd been trying to recruit him ever since she first heard his undiluted mountain musicianship in D.C. circles. He was an important contributor to Emmylou's music, both as an instrumentalist/ harmony singer and as an arranger and teacher; Emmylou has said that her gorgeous acoustic-bluegrass-style *Roses in the Snow* album, and most of *Light of the Stable* (recorded during the same set of sessions) would not have been possible without his guidance.

For his part, Skaggs learned how to play country-rock and how to master the mysteries of amplification, produc-tion and music business politics at Emmylou's relatively exalted level, and after two years he was ready to try for the big time as an artist in his own right. He left the Hot Band under ami-cable terms, recorded a couple of independent label albums (notably

Naomi Judd, producer Brent Maher, and Wynonna Judd.

the wonderful *Skaggs & Rice* with Tony Rice on Sugar Hill), and in 1981 he graduated to the big leagues and signed his deal with Epic.

Little was expected of him—Rick Blackburn, Epic's Nashville boss at the time, predicted first-album sales of 50,000 at best—but much was de-livered. As Skaggs put it, "They had a real nice surprise when I got all those hits, but it was a surprise." (It was also very profitable. Epic's first Skaggs albums, featuring as they did an artist who was already a master instrumentalist and a fully competent producer and arranger, absorbed bud-gets of no more than $50,000 apiece—not pea-nuts, but a real bargain for such high-quality work, and nothing like what could be spent on a less focused, less experienced artist).

Skaggs was definitely different. As a performer he was much closer to the bluegrass end of the

spectrum than the *Urban Cowboy* show biz ex-treme, keeping his relations with his audience on a strictly musical basis. As a public personal-ity he was anything but a smoothie, displaying a combination of professional perfectionism and fundamentalist Christian philosophy which could sometimes be abrasive and was frequently in conflict with his environment (virtues such as piety and punctuality being generally unesteemed in music business circles, then even more than now). On top of the central fact of his radically different "new" sound, these characteristics acted to draw considerable attention his way—some of it negative, like the "Picky Ricky" nickname that began circulating within the business, but most of it positive. Partly that was because people promulgating "traditional" values were winning accep-tance and admiration in most areas of American life in the early 80's; a character like Skaggs, polite and soft-spoken yet uncompromising in his conservatism, was just the kind of hero for whom many Americans seemed hungry.

He was clear about his intentions. "I'm try-ing to build my audience, build 'em with rooted American country music like it was originally laid down years ago, but with a commerciality fac-tor of the 80's, present it in a way that's fashion-able and acceptable by 90 percent of the buying public," he told *Country Music*. "I feel I can sing and play, doing traditional music but with an 80's approach."

He was aware, of course, that such an ap-proach set him apart from the crowd, and that that had its advantages. "I'm really in a good position, 'cause I get credited with pioneering this new country thing, paving the way, being the first one to go out there against all the odds, so to speak." On the other hand, as he told the *Louisville Times*, "I really do think I'm going

The Judds

against the grain of, quote, country music. I am kind of batting head to head against them. And I really do think that there are some record companies out to get me. I think there's some mud-slinging going on. It's because they don't have acts on their label that are really doing country music." As he saw things, though, the bottom line was simple: "As long as I can please Ralph Stanley and Bill Monroe, I think I've pleased just about everybody I need to please."

Mama and daughter with Wy's musical heroine, Bonnie Raitt, in the 90's.

He accomplished that. Both gentlemen endorsed him enthusiastically and publicly. So did virtually every music critic in America, often in the manner of those about to die of thirst sensing an oasis, and so did some stellar keepers of the country flame. Merle Haggard, for instance, opined that young Mr. Skaggs was "the brightest thing that has happened to country music, and the brightest star on the horizon."

It was, then, a terrifically auspicious debut, and Skaggs went on to justify the praise and fly the banner for vamped-up traditionalism until mid-decade, scoring what many consider his greatest triumph when, overriding Epic's misgivings, he took Bill Monroe's bluegrass classic, "Uncle Pen," to the top of the charts in October 1984. Then, though, his music moved toward the

Nashville mainstream and lost a lot of its heart as well as its impact; the second half of the 80's were not good years for him either creatively or commercially.

On first impression, it might seem as if Skaggs' souped-up traditionalist initiative went nowhere. No major country star, after all, emerged to take those particular reins in hand when he dropped out of the front-runners. In reality, however, his influence was profound, and remains pervasive, for he is the individual most responsible for bringing the ethos of the virtuoso picker and the traditional sounds of the fiddle, mandolin and flat-top acoustic guitar back into mainstream country music. It's quite legitimate to wonder whether Nashville in the 90's would still offer those items as such a significant element of its menu had Picky Ricky not insisted on doing things his way back in '81.

Wondering whether The Judds could have won their slot in 1984 had it not been for Skaggs' trailblazing, however, is foolish. The Judds were such a solid-gold proposition—a very attractive mother-and-daughter duo with harmonies as tight as The Everly Brothers', and personalities intriguing enough for any gossip writer—that they would have risen to the top even if the trend of the day had been Vegas reggae instead of Kentucky neo-traditionalism. Without Skaggs' efforts, though, Naomi Judd might well have had a hard time getting RCA to let her and her daughter record in an intimate, predominantly acoustic setting with a producer of her own choice. As it was, with Skaggs taking each new self-produced nugget of neo-traditionalism straight to the top of the charts, giving Naomi her head must have seemed only minimally risky. And Naomi had after all chosen a producer, Brent Maher, with some serious commercial credentials: Dottie West, Michael Johnson, Kenny Rogers.

Naomi knew exactly what she wanted. "I was looking for a producer who could develop the unique sound that we had in our hearts and minds, not to mention someone I could leave my daughter alone with in the room," she told Bob Allen. "We were determined to keep control of the situation, as far as maintaining the integrity of our music. We wanted to make sure nobody messed with our sound. We needed somebody who realized that our voices were the main instruments, and that all the rest was just decoration."

Brent Maher, in conjunction with guitarist/arranger Don Potter, obliged, and Naomi was well satisfied. As she said after the second Judds/Maher/Potter album, "I just want to tell everyone in the world about Brent and Don Potter. Those two create such a healthy environment to make music in. There's no threat, no embarrassment, only constructive criticism. We all accept each other totally. We have closed sessions, nobody drops by on us. Just the four of us actually create the entire album ourselves." Daughter Wynonna added that "We do demos with just two voices and guitar. By the time we bring the other musicians in, we have the songs all worked out...as well as the basic attitudes and the basic rhythms to them." Such was not standard operating procedure; more often than not in Nashville, songs, singers, and musicians met for the first time during actual recording sessions, and arrangements were worked out as the studio time clock ticked.

The result of the Judds/Maher/Potter method was, then, a marvel of distinctiveness, standing out from the pack in ways that produced an intense and immediate gush of euphoria from all points of the critical compass. *The Washington Post*, for instance, called The Judds "so refreshing, so imaginative it's hard to believe their music was fashioned in the predictable polyester confines of Nashville's country music industry." The album featured "seamless, flowing

They were everywhere: here at Merle Haggard's 50th birthday party.

harmonies...in a warm tapestry of acoustic instrumentation...the rich liquid vocals of daughter Wynonna are marvelously unaffected, her sultry stylings casually touching on blues, jazz and rock." Altogether, *The Judds* was "lusciously melodic and invisibly pop in the most natural way...."

And on it gushed, a veritable orgy of delight in which Naomi and Wynonna seemed to be almost all things to all people: overtly Christian traditionalists standing firm for the old country values in a heathen business and savvy, hipster-attractive potential pop stars with enough potential to stimulate the most secular (mercenary) passions of Mammon and Music Row; strong, independent, modern women leaving good ole boyism in their dust and sex objects outstanding amid male chauvinists everywhere; an act whose basic appeal was fresh and bright and novel and as old as the hills. So right from the start they hooked the whole spectrum, everyone from Yankee music critics to Hollywood gossip persons, and they seemed destined for durable stardom.

It had been a long road for Naomi (Diana) Judd, if not for young Wynonna (Christina Ciminella). A native of East Kentucky, Naomi had migrated with her husband to Hollywood in the early 70's and worked in various jobs—as a model, a girl Friday for an Oriental millionaire, a secretary for The Fifth Dimension pop-soul

John Anderson, a roots revivalist with substance, awaiting his 90's comeback.

group—before returning to Kentucky and raising her two daughters as a single mother in the tiny town of Morrill, which she characterizes as having had "a population of about 50, and most of them cousins." In Morrill, Naomi says, she and her girls lived a simple life: no TV and no telephone, just an old Maytag washer/wringer (later immortalized in song) and a radio that played the Grand Ole Opry on Saturday nights. "It was a very conscious decision on my part to live that way. I wanted my daughters to be close to our family and our heritage. I wanted them to learn where they came from, and be free to develop their imaginations."

Christina (Wynonna) developed her voice, and Mama noticed. "As the years went by, I'd teach Wynonna the words to songs. Because my voice is a shade lower than hers, I'd naturally go into a harmony instead of singing with her. But the more we sang together, just a home entertainment kind of thing, the more fun we had. And we just kept doing it more and more and getting better and better. We learned songs by The Delmore Brothers...we loved The Everly Brothers' harmonies too, and we also learned a lot of old bluegrass-gospel songs off The Stanley Brothers' albums." The Andrews Sisters, The Boswell Sisters and Appalachian singers Hazel and Alice were other favorites, and Wynonna brought more contemporary flavors to the pot: Joni Mitchell, Delbert McClinton, and her great musical heroine, Bonnie Raitt.

Back in Hollywood, rock-pop-blues had in fact been all Wynonna listened to: "We just weren't involved in country music at all. I think if I had heard Ricky Skaggs back then, I would have said 'Ugghh!!! Spare me! That sounds like *twang* to me!'"

The idea of a career in music didn't occur in Kentucky. That happened in Marin County, California, the next stop along the Judd line, where Naomi earned a nursing degree which got her a job in a hospital after the family's final move, to Franklin, Tennessee, in the spring of 1979. At that point Naomi began actively seeking a recording deal for Wynonna and herself in nearby Nashville. It was her job, incidentally, which led to her first acquaintance with Brent Maher, whose daughter came under her care after an auto accident.

The Judds fulfilled the commercial promise so obvious in their debut with RCA. They were consistently successful for as long as they sang together, honing in tighter and tighter on their winning formula of nostalgia and intense senti-

John Anderson—
early 80's.

mentality, and exploiting the appeal of their family relationship with all their might. Wynonna's voice grew stronger by the year, Naomi's savvy deepened, and their act survived the occasionally very public storms between them until their tearful acceptance speeches became a fixture of virtually every awards show after 1985. Even in 1994, when Naomi had retired from her singing career (due, she said, to a life-threatening case of viral hepatitis) and Wynonna had gone on alone to duke it out with Reba McEntire for the Queen of Country Music crown, Mama was still to be seen at the Academy of Country Music's podium, citing her daughter's Female Vocalist of the Year award and what she described as the full remission of her own disease as "proof that God exists."

By the end of their career together, The Judds' work seemed, and probably was, contrived, even hackneyed, and it was hard to remember just how ear-opening they had sounded in 1984. But back then they were indeed very startling, and the fresh air they blew into the scene did indeed change the sound of mainstream country music quite radically. Coming on top of Ricky Skaggs' powerful bluegrass-rockabilly initiative, it confirmed the more-or-less-traditional, acoustic-organic approach as a strong strain in the commercial country music to come.

John Anderson, on the other hand, seemed to have very little effect on the course of the music. Despite the fact that he was a much stronger singer than Ricky Skaggs in the early 80's (and, after a remarkable comeback from several years of relative obscurity, a much stronger commercial entity in the 90's), his neo-traditionalist angle went hardly anywhere.

Anderson, a central Florida native more smitten with Jimi Hendrix than Hank Williams dur-

ing his first years as a musician, was a character described quite aptly by the title of his first Number One single, "Wild and Blue." Inclined much more toward the Saturday night than the Sunday morning side of country music, and looking much more like a Dixie-rebel rocker than a blown-dry 'billy such as Skaggs, he chose to follow paths blazed by artists none too popular as early 80's role models: hard-core honky tonkers like Hank Williams and Lefty Frizzell, and latter-day Outlaws like Gary Stewart and The Allman Brothers. His music, while doing a fine job of staying within the lyrical boundaries of mainstream country's better traditions (among other assets, he had a great ear for wordplay), tended to push at the edges of the form: the fiddle-and-banjo background to "Wild and Blue" was unusually unrestrained, and the beat behind "Swingin'" quite a bit heavier than anyone else would have chosen. The sources of his songs were also telling: songwriters included Billy Joe Shaver, the funky free spirit who composed Waylon's entire *Honky Tonk Heroes* album in 1973 ("I'm Just an Old Chunk of Coal"); Robert Altman, the director of *Nashville* and many another esteemed and/or reviled movie ("Black Sheep"); and of course Anderson himself, usually in collaboration with Lionel Delmore, the son of Alton Delmore of The Delmore Brothers ("Swingin'" and many others).

It's interesting to wonder what might have resulted from Anderson's initiative had his run at the top of the charts been more sustained than it was (three Number Ones between December 1982 and December 1983, then none until a decade later), for he very plainly had more potential than any other rising star of the early 80's for tapping into country's strongest currents. His singing, for instance, conveyed a sense of con-

Nashville's lower Broadway area, once home to a hell-raising ethos. The industry tried to change that in the 1980's.

siderably greater depth and turbulence than Skaggs'. He didn't have Skaggs' experience in the studio, though, or his savvy in the business end of the music business. If he had, perhaps he could have forced his music through the maze of obstacles that appeared in his way even before "Swingin'" had finished its tenure at the top of the charts. But he didn't, and his career momentum was wasted in one disaster of record company politics after another. Which might or might not have been inevitable; Anderson has sometimes implied that in addition to the negative effects of events attributable to happenstance—say, a key promotion man leaving the company just as the new John Anderson single was released—his early career suffered from what amounted to an ideological clash between his values and the standards beginning to be applied by Nashville's executive corps.

He articulated that thought in a 1993 *Country Music* interview, when Patrick Carr asked for his comment on the proposition that "these days,

in order to get a recording contract and a commitment from a record company, first of all you have to be stone cold sober, and next, you have to kiss their ass."

"You're exactly right on both counts," Anderson replied. "I mean, they about didn't give me a deal for those type of reasons...and this whole change in attitude about the drinking and the drugs and stuff, I think that started when all these new people, all these producers and executives, began coming into Nashville from the West Coast in the early-mid 80's, and saying 'Hey, we're getting tired of dealing with these artists who come in here and get drunk and raise hell. We're getting tired of dealing with this artist who goes out there and smokes pot and blows off his interview.'...Well, I hate to say it, but some of the greatest artists in the world did exactly that. Some of the greatest sons of bitches who ever walked did that. But even at their most screwed up, some of these cats came in and cut some real sincere music, while a lot of the guys that

George Jones and Johnny Paycheck.
Definitely "hard to handle."

got signed because they were straight and sober and somebody in the company liked 'em, they had to have their records fabricated. You know—stay in the studio and work and work on it, and finally fix it to where the ole boy's singing in tune.

"Well, what's happened is they've let a good bit of mediocrity slip into our business, where at one time only veterans and great ones stood. They sign some ole boy that they just kinda like, that maybe can't sing so well, but by God he's a hard worker."

There is of course a difficult question at the heart of this matter: How much license and indulgence can a creative artist demand of his or her producers and marketeers? Anderson's statements, after all, must be placed in context, and the context is Nashville in the 80's, a creative community ravaged, as were other arms of the music and entertainment business at the time, by cocaine. Use of that drug had been so destructive to the creativity, productivity, health and sanity of so many important contributors to the life of Music Row—everyone from songwriters and singers to producers and publicists—that to put it as simply as possible, it had all gone too far, and a purging reaction had begun. So while some artists might well have been denied their shot, as Anderson suggested, because they "smoked pot and blew off interviews," others were passed over because they were destroying their vocal chords and their reason with cocaine.

A case in point is George Jones, whose legendary voice and superb technique were so depleted by alcohol and cocaine in the early 80's that according to his producer, Billy Sherrill, the recording of "He Stopped Loving Her Today" took more than a year of sporadic sessions. Some of them, Sherrill said, produced as much as a whole verse of satisfactory vocal track, while others produced just a phrase and still others rendered nothing at all (talk about "having to have their records fabricated"). At one point, Jones was living in the back of his Cadillac with a cardboard cut-out of Hank Williams and talking in the voice of Donald Duck. He was both a perverse ideal—the live hard, die hard example of

Ole Hank being confirmed as *the* most glamorous way to go (the great George Jones was doing it, after all)—and, simultaneously, a cautionary nightmare: a squalid and sickening waste. But then again—and here the irony comes hard—there's just no denying it: "He Stopped Loving Her Today" was an immensely powerful piece of work, so moving that fans polled by a leading magazine in 1992 chose it as the best country recording of all time.

Just as in Jones' case, complexities and contradictions swirled confusingly within Nashville's neo-conservative sea change in the mid-late 80's. The changes weren't just about drugs, or just about creative control, or just about commerciality: They were a tangle of all those currents and more, and often they combined to make what could only be called a mess. That's certainly what they did in the case of Steve Earle.

Lauded by an impressive cross-section of country music insiders as the most gifted artist to come down the Nashville pike in years, Earle was a Texan songwriter-around-town whose first major label album, *Guitar Town*, was released by MCA in 1986 to enthusiastic and almost universal critical acclaim. Here, according to the general consensus, was a talent on the order of Merle Haggard or Hank Williams: a uniquely gifted songwriter and singer so obviously more talented than his peers that there was simply no question that he deserved every superlative sent his way.

There were, however, some significant problems. First was the difficulty of promoting songs as strong as Earle's to mainstream country radio. Earle kept his music even closer to the hard edges of country and rock than John Anderson did, and lyrically he was in a class by himself. In the course of his semi-underground career as a sort of radical rockabilly beat poet—Woody Guthrie meets Johnny Cash meets Jack Kerouac—he'd developed a writing persona that was part Outlaw, part working stiff, part lyrical intellectual. Sometimes he wrote from his own vantage point; other times he wrote through the eyes of an assumed character he called "Bubba"—the factory hand who "took a left where I generally

Steve Earle

take a right" and headed off toward Mexico one Monday morning in "The Week of Living Dangerously"; the Vietnam veteran tending his marijuana plants and planning nasty surprises for the feds up "Copperhead Road."

The Bubba songs, then, were obviously unfit for country radio consumption. The more personal songs were less obviously so, but still a hard sell. They were certainly poetic enough, and catchy too, but they didn't express conventional sentiments and they weren't romantic; they all touched chords of hard reality that just weren't compatible with suburban drive times.

Even without mainstream radio support or significant other promotion, though, Earle's first album sold very well: more than 300,000 units, at the time a most unusual accomplishment. Obviously, then, he had significant market potential—but he also had a market problem. As one of the first Nashville artists to connect with a split audience of hard rock and hard country fans, but practically nobody in between, he was a square peg in a round hole. Nashville's promotional apparatus, geared exclusively toward intense concentration on a relatively small number of

A late 80's version of country: Steve Earle with Radney Foster, Bill Lloyd and Joe Ely.

key country/pop radio programmers, couldn't help him. So while he was really the least of anyone's worries, marketing-wise (no artist who sells a third of a million first albums via reviews and word of mouth can logically be said to present any kind of marketing problem), he did in fact perplex MCA. Considerable anxiety became attached to his case.

His personal style didn't help. A tattooed, pony-tailed, chain-smoking muscle car aficionado sartorially inclined toward biker jackets and cameo T-shirts, he had four failed marriages behind him by the time he hit his early 30's, and

wasn't in the least apologetic about anything at all. There again, those factors weren't a problem among his natural constituency of urban hipsters and rural rebels, but on neo-conservative Music Row, however folks felt personally—and many industry people liked Steve Earle and loved his music—his image was the kiss of death. And on top of everything else, he had a drug habit of the increasingly obvious sort.

It all ended very badly, with his record sales plummeting after their initial promise, MCA shunting him over to its pop division, and many harsh words spoken, mostly by Earle. By the time it was all over he'd made just four studio albums for MCA along a stylistic path beginning in his own brand of spare, gut-tingling rockabilly, moving through a denser form that came to be known as "power twang" and ending in a kind of wild, woolly fusion of heavy metal, Celtic drone and fiercely felt folk-rock: powerful music, all of it, and deeply influential among some significant core groups of Nashville songwriters, musicians and producers.

The mid-90's found Earle, still in Nashville and recording (but without a major label contract), trying to deal with his addiction in a process

*Tanya Tucker and
Gary Stewart, 1989*

watched by more than a few powerful people with more than passing interest. Perhaps, if he survived, he would return for another shot. Music Row, which by then had broken the neo-conservative mold by dealing in acts built on an image of rebellion and rowdiness (Travis Tritt, for instance), might even figure out how to market the genuine article.

Back in '86 and '87, his sorry saga hadn't inspired anything in the way of new marketing strategies. Quite the contrary, in fact: Mostly what it did was convince the industry at large that there was no point whatsoever in committing company resources to anyone who, in the catch-all euphemisms of the day, was "hard to deal with" or had "personal problems."

And from a businessman's perspective, there really wasn't any point, for the business itself was undergoing profound and sweeping changes that relegated artists of the classic honky tonk-hero type to the trash heap of history. Rednecks, rebels, drunks, dopers and otherwise socially provocative persons simply could not be relied upon to perform the way stars in the new marketplace were expected to—showing up bright-eyed and bushy-tailed at the crack of dawn for *Good Morning America* tapings; pressing the executive flesh at music industry conventions; huddling in strategy sessions with lawyers, accountants and investment counselors; recording in carefully planned time slots bracketed by other commitments of every conceivable sort —telephone chats with entertainment editors in Oslo or Australia, meetings with marketing directors from Sears or Revlon or Taco Bell, show dates strung together unforgivingly across time and distance with almost military precision —it was getting tough. The workload of a front-line country star was growing to the point where only a clear-minded, well-organized, relatively healthy and even-tempered individual willing to

forgo rest and recreation could handle it. A contender almost had to be a workaholic, in fact; certainly he or she needed to possess deep reserves of stamina and stability, because the slack was going out of the game.

Put simply, country was getting big. Its commercial growth through the 70's and 80's had brought it into what was essentially a new world: a place where the various bottom lines of the country music business were no longer matters to be ignored, or contemplated with interest only in terms of tax write-offs, by corporate headquarters in New York and Los Angeles. Serious profits were now at stake, and therefore the trains had to run on time.

One artist who saw the writing on the wall, understood its implications, and acted accordingly was Tanya Tucker. Having spent the late 70's and early 80's in a saga of scandal pyrotechnic enough to qualify her as one of the first country performers to regularly grace the covers of checkout-counter tabloids like the *Star* and *National Enquirer*, and having done poorly as a recording artist during those years, she found herself in mid-1986 with what she understood very clearly to be one final shot at staying in the big time, a new recording contract with Capitol Records. The rules, as she told *Country Music* with her usual candor, were simple: Either she behaved herself professionally, keeping her "partying" discreet and coming through 100 percent on all her work commitments, or she lost her slot. A spirited Tanya Tucker was fine. An undisciplined Tanya Tucker wasn't.

"After all," she said, "nobody's gonna invest in a racehorse that won't run. Nobody wants a horse that just hangs out in the barn and kicks at its stall." She was right. Nashville was through with balky, high-strung, unpredictable types. It wanted its stars sure and steady, and it went and got 'em that way.

Dwight Yoakam

CHAPTER 15

The Great Leap Forward

As the mid-80's became the late 80's, even the most astute observer could have been forgiven for missing the sound of the country music juggernaut locking onto a long, straight track. The scene at the time was, after all, anything but uni-directional, suggesting a frisky night at the circus more than the calming ride with steady-handed cowpokes it very soon became.

Consider the widely varied "hot acts" of the day. As well as those basically bland, separate-but-equal colossi of the Country Lite market, Kenny Rogers (for Mom) and Alabama (for the kids), a veritable rainbow coalition of folks were vying for a share of the friends' and neighbors' discretionary incomes.

From the Las Vegas end of the spectrum (though not the geography) there came The Oak Ridge Boys, who had combined gospel harmony singing, hip couture, and good old-fashioned sex appeal into an act that became the envy of televangelists and Main Room showmen everywhere. Also from Vegas—in his case literally; he'd been a croupier there—came Lee Greenwood, a diminutive smoothie whose trademarks were *Miami Vice*-style facial stubble and a musical persona "sincere" enough, in critic Michael Bane's well-chosen words, to gag a pony. Greenwood quickly ensured himself a lifelong career of personal appearances in patriotic circles with his recording of "God Bless the USA," the hugely crowd-pleasing paean he wrote with Paul Overstreet in 1985.

The Frozen North contributed its share of talent, too. Though no Hank Snow by any means, Canadian folkie singer/songwriter Gordon Lightfoot continued a respectable string of country successes that had begun in the late 70's. His countryperson, lower-case lesbian vegetarian k.d. lang, began kicking in her bizarre brand of cow-punk, initially produced in England by distinguished roots-rocker Dave Edmunds, in 1987, then gravitated towards Nashville for a sumptuous celebration of Patsy Cline-like torch/swing songs produced by none other than Owen Bradley (Cline's producer) before moving on to chic-er pastures, her final split with the country music industry coming in the early 90's when her militant opposition to hunting and meat-eating wore out her welcome. Her tangential, then non-existent relationship with country music and the Nashville industry did not, however, prevent her from winning a Grammy for Best Country Vocal Performance, Female, in 1989 (NARAS, the Grammy voting body, having adopted the practice of bestowing their awards on the most urbane, least "country" country artists available).

Another oddball and Grammy winner (Best Country Vocal Performance, Male, 1989) was Lyle Lovett, the sardonic Texan singer/songwriter

The Oak Ridge Boys and Lee Greenwood in Vegas. Greenwood was a croupier before Nashville stardom.

noted by the public at large for his unique hairstyle and eventual marriage to movie star Julia Roberts, but also appreciated in urbane "alternative" circles for his *avant*-retro musical vocabulary, ironically twisted lyrics and overdeveloped sense of style. In most ways Lovett was a world unto himself, but from a historical perspective he filled much the same niche as 70's blues stylist/character Leon Redbone, though on a more elitist level and scale. Never a major star and therefore never in danger of burnout, he was still going strong in the mid-90's.

The bi-coastal world also contributed to the Nashville melting pot. From Hollywood, via the *Dukes of Hazzard* TV series, came handsome young actor/singer John Schneider with four (count 'em!) Number One singles in the mid-80's, despite what Bob Allen described as his "noncommittal but competent warbling" and a mu-

sical identity suggestive of "Merle Haggard's wimpy, anemic baby cousin." The New York theater world, meanwhile, sent down an appropriately tougher, brasher, more sophisticated contestant in the form of Ms. K.T. Oslin. Texan born and bred, and trained and hardened in the low-paying world of the Manhattan actor (where her best money, as is often the case, came from parts in TV commercials), she didn't strike out for a songwriting career in Nashville until she was in her late 30's, and didn't achieve her breakthrough as a singer until her mid-40's. Then, after the huge success of her song, "80's Ladies"—one of those records which, like Jeannie C. Riley's "Harper Valley P.T.A." and Loretta Lynn's "The Pill," perfectly defined a certain stage in the lives and times of American women of a certain age—she continued to upset odds and confound stereotypes. Her style trod a fine, intriguing line between real high-fashion glamour and intentionally tacky parody thereof, hardly an area in which Nashville offered much expertise (as journalist Bob Millard put it, the "Annie Oakley-in-Spandex look" was the Music Row *mode de rigueur* at the time), and she was frank, funny and unapologetically assertive.

Those qualities did not endear her to many Nashvillians—as she observed in 1989, "when I show up someplace, an awful lot of the guys are thinking, 'Oh, God, here comes that loud-mouthed bitch from New York'"—but others welcomed the wake-up call she offered. As one of the first women in mainstream country to write and record successful music without having to give away the lion's share of control or financial reward to a male patron, she demonstrated that despite the odds, a "girl singer" *could* take charge on Music Row. She had a short career at the top, though. The demands of her new trade, chiefly the need to write first-class new songs in double time despite constant touring and endless other schedule commitments, were not for her, and she was in and out of the charts in three short years.

Unlikely entries into the country field continued. Michael Johnson, a soft-rock type who'd had a big 70's pop hit with "Bluer Than Blue," began recording in Nashville, reached the top of the country charts twice in early 1987, and was regaled as *Billboard*'s Top Country Singles Artist of the Year before finding himself in market never-never land. T. Graham Brown, who dressed as a hip lounge lizard and specialized in barely countrified Memphis rhythm &

blues, came up from the Georgia bar band scene and spread good cheer out of all proportion to the number of his chart toppers (three) before he too faded back into the middle distance. At that point, Sylvia Allen, known to her public by her first name only, was already just a memory on Music Row. Her journey from record producer's secretary to Scavullo-posed, soft-focus country-pop sex symbol (and role model; her fans were mostly young teenage girls) peaked with her perkily breathless recording of "Nobody" in 1982, then descended gradually until her disappearance from the charts in 1986 and her conversion into a writer and singer of songs for children.

And so the parade continued; the changes in the country music business, all of which could be reduced to one word—expansion—were obvious in the sheer number of performers competing for a spot in the Music Row lineup.

Judy Rodman, who'd apprenticed as a singer of commercials, jingles and radio station I.D.s in Memphis (where for a while she roomed with

The Oak Ridge Boys' lineup changed in 1987 to include Steve Sanders.

Janie Fricke), came on strong indeed with a Number One hit in 1986, but her career was stalled by the failure of her record company, Mary Tyler Moore's MTM Records. Holly Dunn was caught in that shuffle, too, but she had the advantage of a couple of years in the charts behind her when MTM folded; she continued recording with Warner Bros., scoring her first Number One single in 1989, and she was still active in the mid-90's. Deborah Allen, a sensuously voiced singer/songwriter who first attracted attention in 1979 with the duets she overdubbed onto old Jim Reeves songs, kept writing and singing through the 80's (with a hit in '84) and was still a contender in the 90's.

Eddy Raven finally—finally!—got into the charts in 1983, only to continue adhering to country-pop formulae when, as critic Daniel Cooper put it, he could have given "your Steve Winwoods and Van Morrisons an understated run

for their money.... Someone send this guy to Muscle Shoals with a five-piece pickup band."

Kathy Mattea, a folkie/new traditionalist/middle-of-the-roader whose music tended to inspire the question "Who *is* that?" too often for her chances of true celebrity, began her long, eventually successful trek to the top in 1984; the similarly successful but somehow non-distinctive Steve Wariner began *his* journey in 1985. Baillie and The Boys, a frothily attractive country-pop trio led by singer Kathy Baillie, first hit the charts in '87, and Earl Thomas Conley, who had scored his first Number One country hit in 1981 after arriving on the charts in '75, continued to do just that throughout the decade. In fact, he sent 16 consecutive singles to the Number One spot, which in terms of radio success qualified him as a superstar, and then some (in the 80's, only Alabama topped his string of hits). But Conley, who was enormously influential in an area about which

Sweethearts of the Rodeo, Randy Travis, K.T. Oslin, Michael Johnson, k.d. lang and Lyle Lovett tour in London, 1988.

Sawyer Brown in a typical pose. The lady is their video "Betty Boop." The bald guy is TV weatherman Willard Scott.

nobody could ever get very excited, the creation of generic-sounding mid-tempo ballads ideally suited for radio programming designed to attract the widest possible demographic, labored in almost uncanny obscurity.

Cued by the success of Alabama, bands began to proliferate. There was the cartoonish Sawyer Brown, who got their start on Ed McMahon's *Star Search* TV talent show and went on to do very well for themselves with a relentlessly cute, crowd pleasing approach to whatever flavor of country-pop was selling at any given point in time. Then there was the much less startling, more tasteful Exile, who found their fortunes in the country market after the pop well ran dry for them, and went on to score no fewer than ten Number One hits during the 80's and watch their sound, described by Bob Allen as "consistently competent, determinedly mainstream, and uniformly faceless," become a key ingredient in the mellow new middle-ground sound of country radio. Restless Heart, who re-

leased their debut album one year after Exile's, brought an even higher level of competence to their music, impressing fans of hot picking and endearing themselves to the radio audience with well-organized, soulfully sung accounts of the struggles of the heart, and they too did very well commercially.

So did Highway 101, but they were a band of a whole different color. Or rather, a different sex. Paulette Carlson, their lead singer, was a performer and songwriter of such singular strength that her perspective dominated the group completely. A Minnesotan who had been kicking around Nashville for almost ten years before manager Chuck Morris built Highway 101 around her, Carlson wrote some of the best country songs of the 80's—material as tough as it was insightful, and as original as it was commercial—and she did just as much as K.T. Oslin to advance the cause of female singer/songwriters before she and her band parted company in 1990. Her replacement, young Nikki Nelson, wasn't half

K.T. Oslin

Steve Wariner

Flashes in the late 80's country pan. Some lasted, some didn't.

Jo-El Sonnier and Eddy Raven

Nanci Griffith

Dan Seals

Janie Fricke with Mark Gray and The Forester Sisters.

Earl Thomas Conley and Pointer Sister Anita

The O'Kanes

Tanya Tucker and
T. Graham Brown

Lyle Lovett

Foster & Lloyd

Highway 101

k.d. lang

Kathy Mattea

bad, either, but no woman in Nashville could truly fill Carlson's boots. Carlson herself couldn't, for that matter. Her post-Highway 101 work, as one of the artists controlled by producer/executive Jimmy Bowen, wasn't significantly different from a dozen other women's.

Highway 101 were more than just another development of the Alabama prototype. They were the first 80's country band to combine real rock with real country (as opposed to diluted solutions thereof), the result being a highly energized hybrid critics began calling "power twang" (and applying to other mavericks like Steve Earle and Dwight Yoakam). Then too, Carlson's songs were far more original, spirited and intelligent than those written or chosen by the other bands. And finally, Highway 101 had style. Along with the edge in their music came a visual edge, a kind of revved-up, high-heeled Outlaw look, verging on glitter and funk, which pointed straight at country's emerging relationship with a new, tuned-in young audience.

Juice Newton, Reba McEntire and Emmylou Harris.

Other hybrids drew their own audiences in the mid- and late 80's. Dan Seals, formerly "England Dan" in the soft rock duo of England Dan and John Ford Coley, moved to Nashville and shot straight at the country market (his aim, aided by producer Kyle Lehning, being true; nine Number One country singles in the 80's for Mr. Seals, including one with Marie Osmond, a mildly successful refugee from her own pop past, as his duet partner). Country-rock-popper Juice Newton stayed in California, but also did well in the straight country field. "The Sweetest Thing (I've Ever Known)," a song written by her partner, Otha Young, and recorded by her in 1981, had reversed the trend of her hits up to that point by rising higher on the country charts than the pop charts. By '83 she'd vanished from the pop charts, but in '86 and '87 she had a very healthy

series of country hits, beginning with "Hurt," a pop song that had already succeeded for Timi Yuro (1961), Connie Cato (1975) and Elvis (1976). Like Linda Ronstadt before her, Newton made the revival of former hits a profitable habit, and also like Linda Ronstadt, she disappeared from the country recording scene quite abruptly, in her case in 1990.

Michael Martin Murphey was another first-generation California scenemaker who succeeded in the pop field (with "Wildfire" in 1975) before achieving Nashvillization in 1982 with "What's Forever For," between times operating as a cosmic-cowboy-around-Austin, then Colorado. After connecting with the country mainstream he rode that soft current as if born to the job until ambling off into the cowboy music revival of the early 90's.

The Nitty Gritty Dirt Band and New Grass Revival also came in from aging-hippieland as the second half of the 80's caught up with them. The Dirt Band did reasonably well in the country radio game and drew considerable attention to themselves with a reprise of their 1972 lightweight-hippies-meet-heavyweight-pickers recording/publicity stunt, *Will the Circle Be Unbroken*. New Grass Revival didn't fare so well, though. The spirit behind the band, which had begun its journey playing ballistic bluegrass-style interpretations of rock-pop-folk songs in the funkiest settings they could find—opening for The Grateful Dead, for instance—didn't thrive in the radio-oriented country market, and the group disbanded in 1989, leaving behind a significant history of innovation and inspiration. Its virtuoso members followed their various muses, mandolinist Sam Bush and banjoist Bela Fleck in particular remaining on the country scene as much-sought-after session musicians.

Yet another old hippie who courted country radio in the late 80's—quite successfully—was

Chris Hillman, formerly Gram Parsons' band mate in The Byrds and The Flying Burrito Brothers and one of the prime movers of the country-rock style throughout its history. For his first concerted effort to reach mainstream country fans (who of course weren't the kind of folks they'd been in 1968, when Hillman and the other Byrds traveled to Nashville to record *Sweetheart of the Rodeo*), he assembled a corps of elite West Coast hip-country musicians, including John Jorgensen, Herb Pedersen and steel player Jay Dee Maness, called them The Desert Rose Band, and set out to make tight, twangy, eminently singable love songs while looking sharp in the newly reviv-

The Dirt Band's 1972 album, Will the Circle Be Unbroken, included Doc Watson.

ing Nudie the Tailor mode. The image was very effective—slightly grizzled but very fashionable guys with hot licks and big histories—and so were the songs; Hillman and company laid down a string of enviably crisp, rhythmic little radio hits that livened up the "countrypolitan" airwaves considerably and almost rivaled Highway 101's work. Not quite, though—Hillman's vocals weren't in Paulette Carlson's league—and the string was a short one. Hillman began indulging his taste for socially conscious lyrics, and the band lost its focus. Then it lost Jay Dee Maness, then John Jorgensen and then its recording contract.

The Desert Rose Band's crowd, featuring a fair proportion of college-educated, middle-class people (many of them, like Hillman, former

hippies), was also the natural audience for some other acts that plugged into the Nashville recording and marketing system during the late 80's.

For instance, songwriters (Radney) Foster & (Bill) Lloyd came up with a combination of smart lyrics and a modernized Buddy Holly/Everly Brothers sound that might have earned them a long career on the roots-music circuit, and perhaps even a few country radio hits, if they'd sustained their creative energy. As it was, they faded fast and went their separate ways in 1990. Nanci Griffith, the fragile-voiced Texas folkie who'd built a devoted audience in college/coffeehouse circles all over the world, was another relatively short-lived item on Music Row. She was recruited from the minor-label league by MCA in 1987 and, initially, the move lit a creative fire under her. Soon, though, she ran into the problem that had sunk New Grass Revival: country radio programmers didn't bite on her singles, and her music lost its spirit in the subsequent confusion, reviving only when she left MCA for the more folkie-focused structure of Elektra.

Something like the same thing happened to Cajun traditionalist/rockabilly/honky tonker/rhythm-&-bluesman Jo-El Sonnier. After a career which had included recordings in French on Louisiana labels in the 60's and a stint as a straight country artist on Mercury in the 70's, Sonnier appeared on RCA in 1987 with a brilliant album, *Come On Joe*, that danced all over the roots-musical map in very high style indeed; what it accomplished in the interface between zydeco, rock, blues and country has never been equaled. But that wonderful synthesis wasn't what country radio wanted, so it disappeared. Sonnier moved to Liberty Records in 1991, coming under the mainstreaming influence of producer Jimmy Bowen and recording thereafter with little creative or commercial success.

As Sonnier's case and several others reveal, unsuccessful mainstreaming was quite a prominent theme in the second half of the 80's. The problem lay in the awkward interface between the natural development of the music by artists like Sonnier, New Grass Revival, Steve Earle and others, and the programming policies of country radio.

Basically, radio was becoming increasingly centralized and ever more cautious—fewer and fewer people were making decisions on the content of tighter and tighter playlists designed to please (and avoid offending) larger and larger numbers of increasingly middle-of-the-road listeners—and that was happening just when the more creatively ambitious members of the generation of musicians following Waylon and Willie and the boys (and girls) were beginning to really cut loose. In other words, there wasn't a natural fit between the most exciting musicians on the country scene and the audience Music Row was geared to reach.

In practice, the repeated failure of attempts to hammer square pegs like Sonnier into radio's round hole resulted in a simple new fact of life on Music Row: henceforth, the most adventurous new artists would no longer be candidates for big recording and promotion budgets. And for many people in all areas of the business, particularly those who'd been drawn toward Nashville by the innovative music of the 70's, that was very frustrating.

Agonies along those lines were of course ameliorated by the fact that thanks to the ever-gathering strength of the radio mainstream, the money was getting better all the time. Still, it's an ironic sidelight to the dazzle of Nashville's rising star that in the late 80's and early 90's, many of the insiders who'd laid the foundations for the boom found themselves increasingly less moved by the music. And musicians of extraordinary vision started arriv-

ing at an all too clear fork in the career road: either they mainstreamed their music, or they sought out a niche in an alternative market. Usually that meant recording on a low budget, getting their names around via print reviews and airplay on college and community radio, and working the club and festival circuit.

There were of course exceptions, though not many.

Dwight Yoakam, for instance, took a route to major stardom which in retrospect could be characterized as a very effective end run. Coming up through the Los Angeles club scene that produced a variety of punk/cow-punk/roots-rock bands like X, The Blasters, Los Lobos, Rank & File and Lone Justice in the early and mid-80's, he began a major-label career in which sales to an urban audience and airplay on rock and alternative radio stations were as important as, if not more important than, mainstream country activity.

Yoakam, in fact, didn't achieve his first Number One country single ("Streets of Bakersfield," a duet with Buck Owens from his third Warner Bros. album) until 1988, at which point he'd been outselling most other contemporary country singers for three years. Like Hank Williams Jr. and

Roy Acuff was on board for both versions: here with The Dirt Band for Round Two.

Rosanne Cash, then, he was a monster in Nashville's closet: a legitimate major country star, creatively important and commercially more successful than 95 percent of the field, who didn't officially exist—not at all as far as the Country Music Association and its awards were concerned, and hardly at all on country radio.

Yoakam didn't make it easy for Nashville to like or accept him. For one thing, he was quite blunt about his opinion of mainstream country music's direction in general, and certain issues in particular, for instance CBS' dumping of Johnny

New Grass Revival: Sam Bush, Bela Fleck, Pat Flynn and John Cowan, pre-'89.

Cash in 1987. Neither did he avoid talking about how he'd first tried to make it in Nashville and been rejected as "too country." That didn't go down well on Music Row, especially since the marketplace had quite convincingly demonstrated whose commercial judgment, his or that of Nashville's major label executives, was more sound (in a market where chart-topping country albums routinely sold less than 100,000 copies, his first album topped 850,000). Relations between country headquarters and Yoakam's Hollywood outpost became so sour that when Steve Earle scrawled "Dwight Yoakam eats sushi" on a wall in the MCA Records building, most Nashvillians applauded enthusiastically.

The point at issue behind Earle's ire—whether worthwhile country music could still be made in Nashville, with Yoakam, who'd never made it there, saying it couldn't, and Earle, who had, saying it could—gets confusing quickly, and should perhaps have been restated in terms of whether worthwhile country music could still be *promoted* in Nashville. The insult itself, though, was on the money. Dwight Yoakam did indeed eat sushi.

And he hung out with movie people. And he'd been to college, and he quoted Rimbaud and Nietzsche. And his jeans were so tight, there wasn't room between skin and denim for an undersized flea, a grain of sand or even an agent's heart. Naturally, then, people wondered where he was coming from and what he was up to.

Country Music captured the spirit of that suspicion in its first Dwight Yoakam cover story in 1988. Dwelling on the Yoakam image and characterizing his publicity pictures as "those calculated studies in quintessential cowpunk chic," the article noted that "they're so perfectly late-80's *Vogue*-Western hip, affairs of such moody, hollow-cheeked, cooler-than-thou trendiness, that unless you're one of the MTV-fixated bimbos at whom they seem to be aimed, you just want to puke all over the stuck-up little fashion plate's custom-kneeholed Levi's."

Even Yoakam's music, which harkened back to the golden age of Johnny Cash and Lefty Frizzell and contained not a shred of contemporary "countrypolitanism" (and was therefore much admired by most critics, including *Country Music*'s), was questioned: "Don't you wonder why that's the music he's chosen? Could it not be that one day a few years ago in Tinseltown, young Dwight was sitting around in his Hollywood hills apartment, wondering how to break out of his poverty rut, and all of a sudden it hit him with all the force of a macrobiotic vegetables *al dente* high: Hip retro country! *That's* the ticket!

"Might he not have realized...that he could sell this stuff not only to the hipsters of the young urban leisure class, but also to a potentially much bigger market of hicks and squares, all those frustrated real-country record buyers strangling out there in the hinterlands on a force-fed diet of schmaltz and pseudo-rock?"

Was he, in other words, a carpetbagger?

No, he wasn't. The article, having indulged in devil's advocacy, went on to spell out the reality of Yoakam's case: that he was simply a smart dude who knew the value of an image and loved country music. His parents, displaced Kentuckians, had been fans of the country/rockabilly greats of the 50's, and he'd grown up in Ohio loving those guys too. And still did.

"Why do I make the kind of music I do?" he said. "It's from remembering when Mom finally got wall-to-wall carpeting. It's from listening to all those Johnny Cash and Johnny Horton and Buck Owens records my Dad played. Stonewall Jackson, too, like when Dad bought 'Don't Be Angry' for Mom—you know, like, *Here you go, darlin', listen to this, here's the way I feel.* I mean, I wrote 'Readin', Writin', Route 23' because I remember standing outside the house on a Friday night, watching all those Ohio and Michigan license plates heading for their old homes in Kentucky, then watching them all head back North to the factories again on Sunday night. I know what it was like for all those families who went North to find work after World War II, left their whole world behind them. We used to joke that people like us, who ended up in Columbus, were the ones who ran out of gas before they got to Detroit. Hillbillies, man, out there struggling to get their kids a better life..."

Yoakam's credentials were in order, then. Still, he was one of the more unusual pillars of the honky tonk faith. It is inconceivable, for instance, that any country singer

Chris Hillman, pre-Desert Rose.

but him would talk about his or her work the way he introduced 1993's *This Time.*

"I think, you see, that we're in a waiting room," he reflected, "and we're in the waiting room for a purpose. But the purpose is not always revealed to us. So there's no point wondering why there's no kitchen, or no hot and cold running everything. But there's perfection to be achieved in an imperfect universe. The only perfection is imperfection, and the assimilative nature of it, the assimilative functional quality—and that's what has brought me, musically and stylistically, to this album."

None of that, whatever it meant, had any effect on the bottom line: that *This Time* was a great modern honky tonk album and another step for Yoakam down the line of legitimate descent from Owens, Haggard and Parsons. As *Country Music's*

Desert Rose Band: elite West Coast hip-country, headed by Chris Hillman. The original lineup also included Bill Bryson, Jay Dee Maness, John Jorgenson, Herb Pederson and Steve Duncan.

Buck Owens with Dwight Yoakam, who coaxed him out of retirement, making their "Streets of Bakersfield" video in 1988.

review noted, "Dwight's methods...have produced a combination of most uncommon delights: a body of work at once supremely adventurous and utterly classic, and an almost uniquely natural progression from album to album. Only Emmylou Harris...can match Dwight as an innovator-preserver of the country form; only Rosanne Cash's *auteur* odyssey has progressed with such undistracted momentum; and there's nobody at all who has combined their talent, vision, stamina and business support into such an unbroken string of wonderful records."

One of Yoakam's "methods" was to keep himself separate from the social and political whirl of the country music business, which isn't hard if you live and record in Los Angeles, but which must nonetheless have required a certain singleness of purpose. Another was to put most of his effort into recording rather than touring—again, not so difficult when you can sell hundreds of thousands of discs and tapes through radio and print exposure alone, but demanding in terms of saying "no" to substantial financial incentives.

Both these factors helped maintain the clarity of his work and its uniqueness: his records sounded startlingly different from any others when he first appeared in 1986, and they were still sounding unique in the mid-90's.

Part of the credit for that belongs with Pete Anderson, the producer and guitarist who began working with him as his prospects turned from grim to hopeful in the L.A. clubs catering to the roots-rock and cowpunk bands of the mid-80's. It was on that scene, after his rejection by Nashville and his failed attempts to find an audience for his music on L.A.'s blue-collar country bar circuit, that Yoakam finally began to gain recognition—just in time; he'd almost given up and "gone off and taught school or something." Anderson functioned as his bandleader and creative partner during the cowpunk days, and was still with him in the mid-90's, his contributions significant enough that Yoakam used the term "we," not "I," when he talked about making records.

Anderson was also the man behind the *A Town*

South of Bakersfield records, which corralled the various visions of country circulating in "alternative" L.A. onto vinyl. Some of the stars of those anthologies remained on the country recording scene, and were even roped a little closer into the mainstream—Jim Lauderdale, Lucinda Williams and Rosie Flores being the best known, along with Yoakam himself—but others of real worth existed as little more than a blip on the major labels' radar screens, if that: Crazy Hearts, Re Winkler and the fondly remembered Lonesome Strangers (who lasted quite a while, comparatively; long enough, anyway, to make a whole album for the Oakland-based HighTone label in 1989).

The music on the anthologies, and of course on the L.A. scene, was refreshing, to say the least. Most of the musicians were young, hip and intelligent, and possessed an appealing combination of humor and dedication to the traditions of the music. Many of their songs had a comforting familiarity—strong echoes of Hank Williams, Johnny Cash, Ernest Tubb *et al.*—which was set off nicely by odd, off-center, often highly original lyrics. These were talented musicians enjoying themselves, and any way you looked at it, their music was at least as interesting as the California country rock of the 70's.

Nowhere near as commercially successful, however. As Mark Humphrey wrote in the Country Music Foundation's excellent *Country on Compact Disc*, the alternative country bands were "struggling for a toehold in a marketplace niche that just doesn't exist" while "Nashville viewed what was happening in L.A. as an anomaly it wasn't sure it could sell to the Corn Belt and needn't try, what with polite young men like Randy Travis arriving from small Southern towns daily."

Basically, then, the 80's ended with Dwight Yoakam all alone as L.A.'s representative on the

Yoakam with producer-bandleader-guitarist Pete Anderson, top, and Grateful Dead rhythm guitarist Bob Weir.

Manuel

country charts. He wasn't the only thing happening, by any means, for the L.A. scene simply wouldn't quit producing fine new country music (of which more anon), but he *was* all a consumer would encounter in the average American music store.

In mainstream-musical terms, then, Yoakam was something of a dead end. He didn't influence Nashville, and Nashville didn't influence him, and that seemed to be the way everyone wanted it. As he told *Country Music* from his home high in the Hollywood hills in 1993, "Yes, I suppose it *is* a splendid kind of isolation I have here. I mean, living in L.A. these past 15 years has given me a very solitary perspective on myself, and on my music. It's helped me maintain, hopefully, a unique perspective."

Reba McEntire

In other ways, though, his influence was profound. For one thing, he was a teen-and-hipster-magnet of the first order, attracting new country music consumers who were a fair bit more urbane than the young folks drawn by Alabama *et al.* Also, his presence on the scene comforted a lot of people who'd been country fans for more than a year or two; at least, it was felt, there was *somebody* successful still out there doing the progressive country thing, pushing at the boundaries while staying true to the past. Then too, he was one of the first exponents of video in the country market, and he remains one of the only country artists to use that medium adventurously.

Lastly (and leastly), he changed the way country music looked. He brought the highly tailored, rhinestone-studded creations of Manuel, protégé of the late Nudie the Tailor, back to the forefront of country chic; banished for the foreseeable future any notion of sitting room in jeans worn by male country stars, and upped the ante in the game of competitive hatsmanship spreading rapidly through country music. He had by far the biggest cowboy hat on any album cover anywhere until Ricky Van Shelton, another singer getting a little thin on top, appeared under *his* mega-brim in '87 (Garth Brooks, of course, was out-hatting and out-balding both of them, and everyone else, in 1989).

Yoakam was still going strong in the mid-90's—strong indeed, for his music was getting deeper and darker by the album (some trick in a boot-scoot-dominated market), and his commercial prospects were, if anything, brighter than they'd ever been. And he remained a man and an artist of intriguing contradictions: the only conservative macrobiotic New Age gun nut, hard-rocking bluegrass fan, lifetime-teetotaling honky tonker and enthusiastic depressive ever to moan the white man's blues.

By late 1993 he was even beginning to sound as if the most appropriate mantle—the Merle Haggard mantle, the role of the bleak-eyed outsider singing sadly from the West—was settling around his shoulders. He said, for instance, that when he first struck the melancholy opening chords of "Lonesome Road," *This Time*'s clos-

ing song, that "I had a sense of loss, of self-loss; a feeling of turning at the end of a journey and seeing no visible reason for it, realizing that there seems to be no validity to what you've done." But two minutes later he was raving about a Stanley Brothers song with such pure glee that he could have been a big old kid in a musical candy store.

While Yoakam was mining his solitary mountain out in Hollywood, others were digging toward various kinds of roots elsewhere.

One of the most significant among them was Reba McEntire, whose long campaign to record her own kind of country music her own way finally began to succeed in 1984—eight full years after her first appearance on the country charts with "I Don't Want to Be a One Night Stand" in

Reba and her first Number One in hometown Stringtown.

1976. Producer Harold Shedd was the catalyst that enabled her to make *My Kind of Country*, the album of which she later said, "nobody was doing that kind of thing, and it really did feel like country music was slipping away."

McEntire did seem like something of a throwback, an old-fashioned hard-core country singer with a thick Oklahoma twang and the air of a genuine cowgirl about her—not surprisingly, since her father was a world champion steer roper and she herself had competed on the rodeo circuit as a barrel rider while also working in the family act, The Singing McEntires, with her sister Susie and brother Pake. Here was one performer who could pull off "back to the ba-

A very 90's Reba overlooks Sunset Boulevard. Bye bye, hard country. Hello, show biz.

sics" country with no problem at all.

She did that, superbly. Her next album, *Have I Got a Deal for You*, produced by Jimmy Bowen, was another gem of classic form and skillful, energized singing, and it confirmed Miz McEntire as the new Queen of mainstream country. It also elevated her to the status of a single-name country star in the tradition of Loretta, Merle, Tammy and Waylon: Now she was simply "Reba." In 1986 the CMA gave her its top award, Entertainer of the Year.

She began branching out from the straight country mold early in her career at the top, beginning with "Whoever's in New England" and the album of the same name, and continuing (first with Bowen, later with Tony Brown) into experiments with any style she fancied, and by the early 90's she'd developed from an Oklahoma cowgirl into an all-American, no-holds-barred pop singer. Unlike some others who'd traveled that road before her, though, she didn't lose the af-

fection and respect of her straight country fans, and neither did she lose their business. Her music was so consistently strong, and her identification as a country character so firm, that she was able to take them along with her. And of course her manner—frank, funny, spunky and fiercely independent—was hugely appealing to virtually any kind of crowd. It wasn't at all surprising that the mid-90's saw her still leading the pack of female country singers by a safe margin, looking back on some fine movie performances (notably her hilarious turn as half of a survivalist couple in *Tremors*) and controlling an impressive group of business ventures.

Another strong performer whose career got rolling in the mid-80's was guitarist/mandolinist Marty Stuart; 1986 was the year when he emerged from a supporting position in Johnny Cash's band to launch a solo career with a CBS mini-album.

Stuart was a true virtuoso (he'd started playing mandolin with Lester Flatt's band when he was just 13) and, like Yoakam, a deeply dedicated and knowledgeable country music fan (and collector: he played Hank Williams' Martin D-45 and toured in Ernest Tubb's old bus). But also like Yoakam, he'd grown up in the rock 'n' roll generation (in his case in Mississippi) and added its values and energy to his musical vocabulary. By the time he was ready to try for his own career as a singer, he'd run the gamut from touring with a true grassroots gospel group, The Sullivan Family, to working with Bob Dylan as a member of the legendary Rolling Thunder Revue—the very highest high point, say those who saw it, of the folk-rock movement. He'd also apprenticed with "Cowboy" Jack Clement (his "executive lifetime producer") at the whimsically named Cowboy Arms Hotel and Recording Spa, the location of almost everything funny but deep in Nashville during the late 70's and early 80's, and played on the records of Neil Young, Billy Joel, Emmylou Harris, Waylon Jennings and Willie Nelson, among others.

If Yoakam was the loner in the West, Stuart was the exact opposite. A born enthusiast and a gifted diplomat, he functioned almost from the beginning of his musical career as a catalyst of ideas and a connection-maker between people—often people from different sides of all kinds of fences. It was he, for instance, who brought the song "The Highwayman" to the joint venture of Cash, Nelson, Jennings and Kristofferson which became an album and a touring act under that name, and he who persuaded Manuel the tailor to move to Nashville, thus accelerating the re-glitterbilly-fication of modern country which he saw, correctly, as both a modern glamour ploy and a pointed salute to the heroes of his past; and so on with many little acts that promoted soulful progress and the communal good. Stuart performed the catalyst/connector function so well and so naturally, in fact, that in 1993 the Greater Nashville Chamber of Commerce made him its official Ambassador of Tourism.

Musically he trod much the same path as Yoakam, blending homage to the masters and commitment to new frontiers with skill and passion. As *Country Music* said of him in 1991, "Cer-

tainly, there are a few picker/singers with Marty's raw talent, but there's nobody with his depth in the most demanding areas of popular music—bluegrass at its highest level, first-class Nashville session work, major league rock 'n' roll—and even more to the point, there's nobody with his vision. Nobody else would have stood in the heart of modern Nashville and taken quite such an unfashionable position—country as music meant to blow you away—and then held it against all odds until it began to seem, well, almost profitable." Of his *Tempted* album, released that same year, the magazine said, "it's the first contemporary Nashville album to do a superb job of playing to the marketplace—it delivers five to six killer mainstream radio hits—while also seizing the neglected reins of country's historically strongest stalking horses and making that buggy run. The bloodlines of all the great movers are in this record: E.T. and his Texas Troubadours

Trio: Dolly Parton, Linda Ronstadt and Emmylou Harris.

from the 1940's, Carl Perkins and Johnny Cash and his Tennessee Three from the 50's, Buck Owens and his Buckaroos from the 60's, Waylon and his Waylors from the 70's...it's strong stuff: virtuosos working the edge with power, taste, finesse and feeling." Which seemed to be the general consensus among sensible critics and others who knew which way was up. As Karen Schoemer wrote in *Country on Compact Disc,* "Stuart understands the heart of country music— its glitz and its grime, its roots and its living traditions—and he conveys its truths masterfully."

Stuart got off to a rocky start in '86, with CBS releasing his first mini-album as part of a "Young Country" promotion, then canceling his full-length follow-up, *Let There Be Country,* and dropping him from its roster. He was picked up by MCA in 1989, though, and with the help of producers Tony Brown and Richard Bennett (the man who played that killer Duane Eddy guitar on Steve Earle's *Guitar Town,* thus putting the "twang" in "power twang"), he embarked on a series of ever more accomplished and heartfelt albums, somehow managing to keep his footing and expand his audience without so much as a glance toward the middle of the road. In the mid-90's he looked like being a source of very high-voltage energy for a long time to come, and, as *Country Music* concluded, "the most effective link between the music's past and future for which we fans could pray."

The New Traditionalist trend which had prompted CBS to sign Stuart in the mid-80's produced a flurry of other artists who fit a back-to-basics profile in substance or image.

The Whites, a family band which featured Ricky Skaggs' wife, Sharon White, and virtuoso Jerry Douglas on dobro, emerged from the gospel/blue-

Marty Stuart with his then father-in-law and boss, Johnny Cash, in 1981. Marty has made some good connections.

grass circuit for a brief major label career, turning their acoustic, close-harmony sound to a pleasant blend of swing, gospel, grass, and pop. Sweethearts of the Rodeo, comprising sisters Kristine Arnold and Janis Gill (Vince Gill's wife), took their name from The Byrds' groundbreaking album of 1968, dressed as movie cowgirls, and turned *their* fluid blood harmonies and virtuoso pickers (Mark O'Connor on fiddle, Augie Meyers on accordion) to light, rhapsodic odes to love and country life which deepened the farther they progressed down their ultimately frustrating major label career path. The Forester Sisters, four church-trained siblings from Lookout Mountain, Georgia, did better in the mainstream. Remarkable for the quality of their harmonies and their ability to dart out of left field now and again with an arresting song like the amusingly acerbic "Men" and then turn around and make a truly heartfelt gospel album, they proceeded down *their* family road (featuring four Number One hits between 1987 and 1989) with wit, strength and surety of purpose, almost but not quite giving The Judds a run for their money.

Last among the commercially successful, acoustically oriented harmony acts of the mid-80's (not counting The Judds, whose success had ignited the major labels' shopping spree for such properties) were The O'Kanes. Although unrelated by blood or even geography (Jamie O'Hara was from Ohio, Kieran Kane from New York), these formerly semi-anonymous songwriters came up with a blend of old-time-country sound and contemporary-cosmopolitan consciousness which scored some mid-level country hits and provoked gushes of praise from the kind of critics who wouldn't have been caught dead with a Tammy Wynette album. O'Hara and Kane went their separate ways in 1990.

Marty Stuart and "The Killer," Jerry Lee Lewis, during the Class of '55 recording sessions in 1985.

Keith Whitley

History must also record the one-time-only existence of a harmony-singing trio to beat the band, the collaboration between Emmylou Harris, Dolly Parton and Linda Ronstadt released in 1987 under the title *Trio*. Eleven years from idea to action, this acoustically-oriented joint venture between the three great country divas of their generation had to struggle through all kinds of obstacles before entering the recording studio in early 1986 under the guidance of producer George Massenburg. Running a glorious gamut of material from Jimmie Rodgers' "Hobo's Meditation" to Kate McGarrigle's "I've Had Enough" and Phil Spector's "To Know Him Is to Love Him," it was a beautifully sung, exquisitely crafted and significant album, pulling the themes and values of the New Traditionalist movement together into one sublime work and transcending that movement in the doing. It had its dark side, though. As one critic reflected a few years later, "*Trio* was a bittersweet delight. By demonstrating that Parton and Ronstadt could still outshine every other female on the planet when it came to pure country singing, it showed us exactly what their own relentlessly wrong-headed recording careers had been denying us for a decade or more." That it did—but it was still one of the best country albums ever made, and it was very clearly the high point of the New Traditionalist movement.

Just below it (and not by far) was another blink-and-you-missed-it proposition, the debut album by a trio of sisters, The McCarters, from Dolly Parton's home town of Sevierville, Tennessee. Entitled *The Gift*, it too was beautifully sung and framed in a perfect New Traditionalist production. Moreover, The McCarters sounded rather like Ronstadt, Harris and Parton might have if they'd gotten together when they were young and strong, then rehearsed for years instead of days; The McCarters, in other words, demonstrated talent and accomplishment plus potential with a capital "P." But *The Gift* sank with hardly a ripple in 1988's marketplace, and by the mid-90's The McCarters could boast of only one other major-label album, a 1990 release that steered doggedly down the center of the country-pop mainstream and also submerged quickly and quietly.

The New Traditionalist current was strong, though, and it pulled in some solo artists of very high quality. Keith Whitley, for instance, moved from bluegrass to the mainstream and released his first RCA album in 1984. Once Ricky Skaggs' partner in Ralph Stanley's Clinch Mountain Boys during the early 70's, and his close friend before and after, Whitley released two albums on RCA and scored three Number One country hits before dying of acute alcohol poisoning in May 1989—an event foreshadowed by some of his last lyrics and a long history of out-of-control drinking which at one point had prompted RCA chief Joe Galante to deliver a sober-up-or-leave ultimatum. By all accounts, including those of

Keith Whitley and Lorrie Morgan's wedding day, 1986.

his widow, singer Lorrie Morgan, Whitley made a serious attempt at a sober life before embarking on the drinking binge that killed him.

At the time of his death, his music had just hit its mainstream stride. It was something to be proud of, too: The work he did with producer Garth Fundis (recorded but not yet released when he died) achieved depths of classic, love-tortured honky tonk intensity unique in his generation. So he could have been a contender. As it is, he's more often remembered as "the Jimi Hendrix of country music"—not for any musical similarity, of course, but because of the orgy of publicity, promotion and musical repackaging which followed his death, a good deal of it a good deal longer on sleaze than on substance.

Vern Gosdin was an older and much steadier hand, *his* kinship with the George Joneses of

"The Voice," Vern Gosdin: the most accomplished but least credited hard core country singer of the modern era.

this world existing only on the level of hard-country vocal genius, not hard-drinking self-destructiveness (which in Jones' case took a turn for the better when he sobered up in the early 80's). Gosdin—"The Voice"—had been on the country scene for a long time when the New Traditionalist trend caught up with him. He and his brother, Rex, were in a California bluegrass group, The Golden State Boys (which became The Hillmen when Chris Hillman took them over), and in 1967 he made an album with Rex and former Byrd Gene Clark before quitting the music business and going home to Alabama. The Muse called, though, and in 1976 he had two country hits on Elektra with Emmylou Harris singing harmony vocals. That was all the glass and mirror business was to see of Mr. Gosdin; he resumed his career as a full-time musician and proceeded with a career on three consecutive labels (A.M.I., Compleat and Columbia) which took him into the early 90's.

It was a career of superb hard country moments;

to many ears, Gosdin was at least George Jones' equal when it came to singing pure brokenhearted barroom laments of the utterly classic sort—"Today My World Slipped Away," "Set 'Em Up Joe," "I'm Only Going Crazy" and lots more. Jones had more charisma, of course, not to mention the advantage of a hellishly glamorous legend, but when the definitive beer-weeping-country time capsule is assembled and sealed, The Voice has to be in there with The Possum.

A singer at the opposite extreme of most things except a Nashville career boosted by the New Traditionalist trend, Ms. Suzy Bogguss enlivened 1989 with a fine, free-spirited album, *Somewhere Between*, that delivered some great things—a mixture of drop-dead singing (as Chet Atkins said of her flawless contralto, "she is always in the tone center"); deftly original, organic production (by singer/songwriter Wendy Waldman, virtually the only woman to produce another artist's record on Music Row); and inspired song choices (Merle Haggard's riveting title track, Patsy Montana's swingingly playful "I Want to Be a Cowboy's Sweetheart," her own and Gary Scruggs' cleverly punnish "Take It Like a Man")—and it was generally such an accomplished and refreshing piece of work that it seemed to promise the world. But Bogguss' next release, created under the supervision of Jimmy Bowen, then newly enthroned as head of Liberty Records, was a whole different story. Like Paulette Carlson, Jo-El Sonnier and many before and since, she got mainstreamed—though in her case the conversion was commercially successful. She went on to become one of the mainstays of 90's country, making finely crafted but never surprising recordings of intelligently chosen songs in the one-from-Carole-King-and-James-Taylor contemporary Nashville mode.

Patty Loveless' track was very different. A coal miner's daughter and Loretta Lynn's cousin, born Patricia Ramey in Pikeville, Kentucky, she connected with the Nashville mainstream after several years as a Top 40 bar-band singer preceded by a spell in Nashville as a backup singer and songwriter for The Wilburn Brothers. Right from the start of her recording career she displayed a keen understanding of how to mix classicism and modernism and come out ahead in both fields, and her clear, supple, Kentucky-accented vocals forged a fine string of albums that gave no ground at all to popification. She was in fact the most consistent (and consistently improving) woman country artist of her time; by the mid-90's her singing, having survived surgery for polyps on her vocal chords, was approaching a kind of country ultimate in power, expressiveness and nuanced control. Moreover, her public persona, in which level-headed strength seemed to lie beneath a degree of modesty or even shyness

most unusual in an entertainer, had a good old-fashioned country appeal which earned her high marks among fans and business people alike.

By the mid-90's Loveless too was a mainstay of the country scene, on approximately the same substantial but not superstar level as Suzy Bogguss, but on a very different musical track.

Part of the difference came, of course, from the two women's unique creative perspectives, but the influence of their producers was also a factor. Both producers were men, and both were figures of very great importance to the development of Nashville music in the 80's and 90's—importance equal in its way to the influence of Owen Bradley, Chet Atkins and Billy Sherrill on the country music of previous decades.

Tony Brown, who produced Patty Loveless' MCA records (sometimes with Emory Gordy Jr.), moved into production work only after a long career as a musician. Born in Greensboro, North Carolina, he began as a gospel piano player, working with the pre-mainstream Oak Ridge Boys and The Sweet Inspirations before taking over keyboards for Elvis, and then for Emmylou Harris and her Hot Band when the King died in 1977.

Suzy Bogguss with one of the ladies who inspired her finest music, Patsy Montana.

His career as an executive began in 1978 when he took a job as head of Artists & Repertoire for an RCA-backed pop label in Los Angeles. That venture folded, and he accepted RCA's offer of a job in Nashville. A short tenure ensued, during which he signed Alabama, among others, but soon he eschewed the pleasures of executive office and went back to being a full-time musician, playing keyboards for Rosanne Cash and Rodney Crowell, his former Hot Band mate, in their Cherry Bombs band. In 1983, though, he returned to RCA (signing Vince Gill, another Hot Band alumnus), then accepted an offer from MCA. At that point he'd acquired a strong interest in the art of record production, and the MCA job promised a lot of hands-on work within an in-house production system.

It delivered. He was still with MCA in the mid-90's, having produced a long string of extremely successful albums by George Strait, Reba McEntire, Wynonna Judd and many others, and risen to the position of president of MCA/Nashville. He was named *Billboard*'s top country producer in 1990, 1991, 1992 and 1993, and that publication also rated MCA its number one country label for three of those years.

Producer, exec, musician: Tony Brown.

Given Brown's choices as a musician, it was no surprise that he turned out to be a producer unusually well attuned to the artists he helped through the studio process, and unusually interested in artists on the cutting edge. It was he, for instance, who signed Steve Earle to MCA (and produced Earle's three greatest albums); he also signed Joe Ely, Marty Stuart, Marty Brown, Rodney Crowell, Kelly Willis, The Mavericks and Patty Loveless, among others—a virtual Who's Who of the cream of the progressive country crop.

In the broadening of country music that accelerated through the late 80's into the 90's, Brown was responsible for much of the process by which American roots music of all sorts made its way into the Nashville mainstream—in his hands an enriching process, not the dilution it could have been (several other producers took care of the dilution job quite well, ensuring the reduction of country's once distinctive character to a few stylistic touches on a pop framework that had already absorbed and genericized other folk styles). Brown tried to mix the full range of styles at his disposal onto tape at full power, and often he succeeded brilliantly. It was very unusual for artists, even the hard-edged ones, to emerge from his production process less exciting than when they entered it.

All in all, Brown was such a powerful live wire amid so many dim bulbs during the late 80's and early 90's that if Nashville's worthier singers, pickers, and songwriters didn't go to bed each night praying he'd still be there in the morning, they should have. It was even a little frightening, thinking how much hung on him. Not that there was much cause for real concern. The possibility of ill health or accident always existed, of course, and by the mid-90's there were some indications that he might be losing some of his own more edgy creativity for whatever reason—overwork, a surfeit of corporate responsibility—but his touch with superstars like George Strait, Reba Entire, Wynonna Judd and Vince Gill was proving so golden (or rather, multi-platinum) that his throne seemed as safe as he wanted it to be.

When Brown went to work for MCA in 1984, his boss was Jimmy Bowen, the other producer/executive most significant to the course of modern country music. Those two were a very successful couple, taking MCA from sixth to first in the *Billboard* rankings of Nashville labels, but in some ways they were an odd couple, too. It's possible to see them as perfect foils—Brown the gospel-rooted supporter of funk and soul, Bowen the master of pop—but then, too, they're just as easily cast as ideological adversaries. Either

Patty Loveless

way (or both), it's plain that historically speaking, you couldn't have one without the other. There was great demand for both their styles.

Bowen arrived in Nashville in 1978, leaving behind what could only be described as a successful career as a pop producer for artists as diverse as Frank Sinatra, Kenny Rogers (in his First Edition incarnation), Kim Carnes, Glen Campbell and Dean Martin (yes, that was Jimmy Bowen behind the console on Sinatra's "Strangers in the Night"—*and* "That's Life," *and* Dino's "Everybody Loves Somebody"). In the mid-70's, though, the call of new pastures beckoned, and perhaps Bowen also saw some writing on a wall; his official bio says that "his reputation was not helping him at a time when rock 'n' roll was pushing adult acts off the charts. The acts he was being offered in Los Angeles were increasingly reclamation projects, and he decided to relocate."

Jimmy Bowen made country sound "as good as" pop.

Once in Nashville his path zigzagged confusingly. He was with MCA in 1978, then Elektra/Asylum, which merged into Warner Bros. in 1983, after which he went back to MCA (in 1984) and stayed there for four years until launching his own MCA-distributed label, Universal. That operation lasted a year before he took over as president of Capitol-Nashville and, after changing that operation's name to Liberty Records in 1992, found himself facing the mid-90's with full independent control of a national/international operation with its own business and legal department in Nashville—which, as he put it, "means that you can finally have lunch in Nashville and make a record deal." Pre-Bowen, you could lunch in Nashville all you liked, but you'd still have to fly to New York or L.A. to do the serious business.

Quite apart from his reputation as a maker of hits and player of record company politics, Bowen is generally recognized as the individual most re-

sponsible for upgrading the technology and methodology of Nashville recording during the 80's. That might not seem like such a big deal (what, after all, is one set of meters and switches as opposed to another?), but in reality it was very significant indeed.

There was, for instance, the very essential matter of his motive. As he said in 1989, "When I came here, they were spending $12,000 to $15,000 on albums when the competition in other types of music were spending $100,000 to $150,000. If you want Reba McEntire to get a bigger share of the consumer market in this country, she's got to sound as good as Whitney Houston. It's illogical to think otherwise."

Whether or not it really *is* illogical to think otherwise, the implications of Bowen's vision were profound indeed. For if country music was to "sound as good" as pop music, it had better sell as well as pop music, or the money spent getting it to "sound as good" would turn black ink into red all over Nashville. Under Bowen's hand, then—as he led the country recording industry into a brave new world of all-digital technology and pop-style, studio time-consuming recording methods—the stakes of the game escalated dramatically. By 1990 it was virtually impossible to make an album in a front-line Nashville studio, with front-line session musicians, for less than a (very) bare minimum of $50,000. Established stars with virtually guaranteed sales potential spent a great deal more.

That introduced a whole new bottom line to the business. Basically, a $50,000 album would have to sell 50,000 units for the record company to break even, and *that* meant changes. It meant that any artist unlikely to achieve 50,000 sales was not going into the studio. It meant goodbye to the recording careers of country singers past their commercial prime, and goodbye to opportunities for country singers likely to appeal to only a small segment of the market, and goodbye to new artists with big potential who were slow in realizing it. In the cause of economic survival, the focus *had* to be on music with at least a strong chance of selling quickly to an expansion audience. Bread-and-butter success in 70's terms—$15,000 spent, 20,000 units sold, everybody happy—didn't exist any more.

Bowen came in for his share of abuse. Although he had done some brilliant production work in Nashville, his first album with George Strait being perhaps the peak of his form ("a masterpiece...that blended modern roots-country with classic pre-rock American pop," wrote journalist James Hunter), many critics and musicians did not enjoy his development of what his bio calls "a highly organized production system that not only makes the most efficient use of his talents as a producer, but yields consistently high-quality recordings."

That system, in which his artists and assistants did most of the actual album-making while he monitored them all closely and called all the important shots, tended to result in music that sounded, and was, formulaic. There was a "countrypolitan" sameness to most of it—a sameness of tempo, arrangement and lyrical reach—which was perhaps appreciated by radio programmers looking to keep large demographic cross-sections of humanity pleasantly mellow during evening drive time, but which drove many fans of more original music, and many people who had once been excited by the artists Bowen mainstreamed, to distraction. *Country Music*'s review of Suzy Bogguss' first album with Bowen, for instance, opined that "the arrangements are so utterly predictable, so stone cold dead between the ears, that you wonder how real live musicians could stand to play them." It concluded that all that remained of Bogguss'

brilliant potential was "the sound of Bowen's machine, and a great singer going to waste."

Most published comments weren't nearly as unflattering, of course, especially in the music trade press, where Bowen's upping of the marketplace ante was viewed with great approval. Privately, though, many people in the country music business disliked the whole idea of having to change in order to compete with pop on pop's turf. They liked country music because it *didn't* sound and operate like pop. (The more things change...)

But what a picture Bowen painted! Miz Reba McEntire, Nashville's own little rodeo firebrand, slugging it out with the poster girl of third-generation urban soul at the top of the *Billboard* Hot 100! George Strait zapping Michael Jackson and Paula Abdul! Now, *that* was worth a million-dollar digital mixing board and a not-so-fond farewell from the funky old pickers, prophets and road warriors of yore. Even if it wasn't, the top studios needed the new technology anyway, to compete with Bowen. So they got it, and the race was on.

One way to view country's massive late 80's/early 90's expansion, then, is to see it in terms of necessity as well as opportunity. The potential fans were out there, for sure, and so were the performers who could reach them—that was the opportunity—but the economics of scale also drove the boom. In the recording industry, investments in new equipment and personnel had to be paid off and costly new recording methods and promotional devices (videos) funded. Likewise, in the radio industry, the very high prices for which stations were changing hands had to be recouped. In a symbiotic process, these factors worked toward one unavoidable conclusion: more ears.

More ears, that is, with more disposable income. Whitney Houston fans. Young adults. Michael Jackson fans. Teenagers.

George Strait

CHAPTER 16

Hat Acts and High Times

It's early 1994 and Tracy Lawrence, the latest hunky tonking young hat to mosey down off the high plains into our warm little electronic town hall, is hosting the night's entertainment, cable channel VH-1's *Country Countdown*: this week's favorite country videos, ranked by viewer response.

Tracy isn't doing brilliantly with the lines he's being fed—like many of the day's hottest country acts, he's so new that TelePrompters are still a novelty to him—but he's not doing badly, either. His intros to the clips sound as if he at least knows what he's saying, whether or not he can relate to it. But when he sees a line that really means something to him march across his TelePrompter, you can tell. He gives it that extra boost.

Like this line: "And now, at Number Four this week, the man who started it all"—a big, wide grin here, and a pause for dramatic emphasis—"Mr. Randy Travis!"

That seems to make sense for a moment, since by 1994 Randy Travis does have a kind of progenitorial air about him, but when you think about it, you have to wonder: What exactly *did* Randy Travis start?

He didn't start the style in which he sang, for sure; that was George Jones, and before him Lefty Frizzell and other classic country singers. He didn't start the hat parade, either; that was George Strait

or Dwight Yoakam, depending on your point of view (and anyway, Travis doesn't even wear a hat). Neither did he start the greater parade, country's long succession of handsome, clean-cut young guys singing good old-fashioned honky tonk music for audiences composed largely of teenage girls and 20-something women; that was George Strait, too. He didn't even start country's double/triple/quadruple-platinum sales boom; Alabama did that. So again, what *did* he start?

He started a perception, that's what. When he hit the country scene in 1986 with his first album, *Storms of Life*, he possessed a combination of characteristics which at that particular time in those particular conditions made a magical kind of impression, particularly on people whose job it was to promote and publicize new blood on the show business scene.

You could put it that way, or you could put it more simply: Randy Travis had the looks and the image—the air, the attitude, whatever—to send the nation's entertainment media persons scurrying *en masse* for their cameras, microphones and word processors. He had "STAR!" written all over him the way neither Alabama nor George Strait (nor Kenny Rogers, nor the Outlaws) did or could have. Moreover, his star power was such that the media, and their general public consumers, experienced a sudden, dramatic shift of perception. Riding on the calm,

George Strait with his Ace in the Hole Band, one of the best in the business. Western swing and honky tonk redux.

crooked grin of Randy Travis, country finally became cool.

No wonder, then, that young Tracy Lawrence found himself speaking those lines in 1994. In the mind of the star-driven scriptwriter who put the words in his mouth, Randy Travis probably did Start It All. But of course he didn't, and George Strait did.

Strait was a cowboy, a real one. He grew up working weekends on his father's ranch in Pearsall, Texas, and when MCA signed him in 1981, he was managing a ranch near San Marcos, Texas. Between times he'd served a hitch in the Army, earned a degree in agriculture from Southwest Texas State University, and worked a lot of ranch jobs, dancehalls and honky tonks, acquiring along the way a thorough knowledge of the music of his masters.

One was the King of Western Swing. "Bob Wills and The Texas Playboys are simply the best band there ever was," Strait said in 1984. "Merle Haggard's tribute album to Wills [*The Best Damn Fiddle Player in the World*] is what really got me

turned on to Wills. After that, I really just fell in love with his music."

Merle Haggard was the second member of his holy trinity, and George Jones was the third. "There was a period of time when I listened to nothing but Merle Haggard and George Jones," he said. "But then, there was a period of time when Haggard and Jones were the only two keeping pure country music alive."

Philosophically, then, Strait was a direct descendant of the honky tonk royalty, and his experience in the clubs and dancehalls of southwest Texas only strengthened the link: "When you're just a local act, and you're doing Merle Haggard and George Jones songs, people want you to sound like the records, so that's what you do: you sing like Merle or George. And pretty soon, that's just the way you sing. That's your style."

It was indeed, and he and his crackerjack Ace in the Hole Band, whom he'd recruited during his last year in college, stuck to it. "We always did the good old songs; we were never a Top 40 band. That was one of the things we wouldn't do, and it cost us a few jobs. A lot of the stuff that was out at that time [the mid-late 70's], we didn't consider it to be the kind of stuff that we thought of as real country music. I just don't like to go into a country dancehall expecting to hear a country band, and they're onstage playing 'Taking Care of Business' or stuff like that."

Strait's insistence on the hard country verities struck a deep, resounding chord, particularly among longtime fans, a reaction reflected quite accurately, if somewhat jestingly, by a *Country Music* cover story in 1986: "Once upon a time, not too long ago, there came riding from the

Strait and his audience: appreciation all 'round.

Great Southwest a man. He was a good and comely man, young and strong, clean of limb and pleasant of face and pure of heart and vocal chord, and by these signs and his tall white hat we knew him: He was the Awaited One. Amid the din of false prophets and deluded disciples and down-

right infidels whose noise had caused us to lose our way, it was he and his good clear voice that would light our path; he would Keep It Country and Never Go Pop; his voice would sing us back home. Here in the Church of Honky Tonkal Holiness we thanked the Lord High Merle for sending him among us, and we praised his perfect name: George (as in Jones) Strait (as in arrow)."

A change in the wind was most definitely implied. The enthusiasm with which Strait was received on the concert circuit (where, unlike in radio, real fans have to shell out real money to hear the music they really want) signaled quite clearly that rockers, folkies, smoothies, disco-maniacs and lounge lizards aside, there was great demand for this new kind of man. The good old-fashioned good guy was back in style.

It helped, of course, that Strait was dark, cleancut and handsome. Previous flare-ups of honky tonk revivalism, notably those centered around Gary Stewart, Moe Bandy and George Jones himself, had lacked that particular element, just as they hadn't been distinguished by any great emphasis on healthy living. So here in fact was something new and different indeed, a phenomenon not seen before in the annals of country music: a singer of cheatin', drinkin', bad-luck-and-trouble songs who looked as fit as a cowboy aerobics instructor and appeared to lead a life of (married, settled) middle-class decorum.

Strait ain't fakin' it. He's run ranches, and he has an agriculture degree.

It sure was novel, but it sure did work. In fact, it ushered in a whole new class of country performer, one who appealed to both the traditional hard core audience and a brand new market. As one writer put it, Strait's concerts were "a cross between Saturday night at the Grand Ole Opry and The Beatles at Shea Stadium." As John Morthland wrote in greater detail in 1984, "It is a maxim that country music stars simply are not sex symbols to teenage girls, but teenage girls seem to have this thing for Strait anyhow. He is young (31) and, as the cliché goes, ruggedly handsome. That tells part of the story, but only part; the rest defies explanation. I have no theories as to how a 16-year-old girl can identify so strongly with an adult song like 'If You're Looking for a Stranger,' but I saw dozens of them who had finessed their way to the lip of the stage, swooning at him as he sang that song."

Perhaps the explanation, if one is really needed, has to do with a teenage girl's alternatives to country stars like George Strait and Alabama in the early 80's. That period did after all feature rock's descent into a forum for impenetrably intellectual-elitist art school graduates and snarling, chicken-chested lugs whose lives seemed to revolve around male bonding, misogynism and their makeup: the one a set in which teenage girls weren't even recognized as existing, the other a crowd who had more respect for their used guitar picks.

But whatever the root of Strait's mass sex-symboldom, the effect was startling. The man himself, however, seemed to take it in his stride. A seemingly modest individual disinclined toward public emotionalism, he never had much to say about the phenomenal tide of female adulation that swept him up every time he walked on stage, his only comments coming from the perspective of the working musician. "That was a great thing that happened," he told Bob Allen in 1988. "It's something I don't guess you ever really get used to, but it sure makes it a lot easier to come on

stage when the crowd's reacting like that. I feed off of it, the whole band feeds off of it. You really get pumped up and get into it."

The teenage/traditionalist fan alliance, which Strait had taken a long full step farther than Alabama by playing classically styled swing and honky tonk music of very high quality—the songs, his band and his singing were all top-notch—gained the momentum of a right and natural force. Here was music in which adults, kids and people in between could all be included, and included they were. Strait, then, was the man who quite literally pulled it all together, keeping the various potentially warring camps of country music from spinning off in opposite directions, and loosing the Nashville juggernaut to start its long, linear roll.

As an artist of overwhelming importance to the course of modern country music, he received what had become the CMA's standard response to extraordinary achievement and massive popularity with the fans as opposed to the businesspersons—inadequate recognition belatedly conferred—and indeed, he is not often fully credited by the second generation of hunky tonkers who occupied the country charts and video screens of the mid-90's. Typically, those performers cited his heroes, Haggard and Jones (particularly Jones, who by '94 had become the very model of the well-behaved living-legend-around-town), or the younger Randy Travis. But the fact remains that George Strait set country music's modern direction more firmly than any other artist of his time.

He stayed at the top, too. With a long string of clever, classically conceived ballads, most of them about love gone wrong and many of them written by Dean Dillon, a singer/songwriter who had definitely been to honky tonk heaven and hell on earth, he kept hitting the radio mark time after time, and backed it up with concerts that satisfied country aficionados just as thoroughly as the girls and ladies of his constituency; a typi-

Randy Travis

Lib Hatcher leads the way for husband and client Randy Travis. Clint Black's there too.

cal Strait show would include covers of hits by Bob Wills, Hank Thompson, Webb Pierce, Hank Williams and other country legends performed to the hilt by Strait and his band (whom many critics compared favorably to Merle Haggard's mighty Strangers).

It all went very well for Strait, and in June 1994 he celebrated his 25th Number One country single and a record of remarkable consistency: 18 Number Ones in the 80's, seven in the 90's. A measure of both his supremacy and the changes he had wrought was that at 41, he was the oldest singer on the upper end of the country charts.

The man to whom his achievements are so often attributed, Randy Travis, came upon the big-time recording scene five years later than he did, and although Travis appeared to be even straighter than Strait and was lauded by the media as such, he was anything but. Back behind the placid exterior of Travis, born and raised Randy Traywick in Marshville, North Carolina, stretched a more than recreationally misspent youth.

"I got into drugs and alcohol at a real young age, about 12," he said in 1990. "I started smoking pot, then got into speed and acid and stuff. I did MDA. I did psilocybin mushrooms.... I was doing so many drugs. I mean, a lot of drugs. By the age of 15 there wasn't a day that went by when

I wasn't using drugs or alcohol or both. Even at work, cleaning out turkey houses and spreading the manure on the fields, I was stoned. And then I was running with the wrong people, too. I wanted to run with the big boys and be tough, so that's what I did, and we got into all sorts of trouble like that: fighting, breaking and entering, all kinds of things.

"I don't know why I didn't get killed. I totaled four vehicles. One time when I was 14, I took my brother's car, a 396 Chevelle that was real quick, and went drinking and driving. The police started chasing me, so I ran, and it went on till there was five or six of them on me. There was no way they could catch me in that car, but I wrecked it running about 130: hit the grass and lost it, ran backwards through a hedge, spun it around a few times into a field, tore everything up, bent the A-frame, totaled it. But it never turned over. That's the only reason I'm alive today. And there were a bunch of times like that."

That wasn't all, either. Travis' route to freedom from a life of crime and chronic intoxication was Mary Elizabeth (Lib) Hatcher, a nightclub owner in her 30's who stood up for the 16-year-old in court when he was facing five years' jail time for grand theft auto, got him off with probation, and gave him a job and a home, the latter her own. The next decade saw the departure of her husband, a move to Nashville and a tireless campaign to bring young Randy to the attention of the major record companies. Eventually, after he'd been rejected at least once by every record company in town, Martha Sharp of Warner Brothers signed him in 1985 and put him together with producer Kyle Lehning. *Storms of Life* resulted, and the rest is history: several years of major stardom and intense speculation on the nature of Travis' love life, followed by the marriage of Travis and Hatcher in 1991 (which was followed by even more speculation).

In Randy Travis, then, the country music industry had quite an item on its hands: a truly inspiring success story (his second album sold five million copies at an unprecedented rate and stayed at the top of the country album charts for 43 weeks, exceeding all previous records by far); a comedy of errors (all those record company rejections); and a soap-operatic mystery to titillate even the most jaded Music Row gossips.

Musically, Travis was all throwback. His heroes, he said, were "Well, George Jones, of course, and Hag, and Lefty. Most of all, though, I guess Hank [Williams]. He was the first I really liked. Me and my brother Ricky had this lady guitar teacher when I was eight, and she taught us some of his songs. What a writer, man. And a singer, too. A real poet, you know." And although Randy and Ricky Traywick played Creedence Clearwater Revival songs and the like when they had their first band, Randy's interest in such material was minimal. He had no interest in singing anything but pure country, he said, "and anyway, now I probably couldn't. I learned all my phrasing from Hag and Lefty and them, you see, so probably my voice just wouldn't fit rock or pop. I'll probably never do anything but country." And by the mid-90's, true to his word, he hadn't. The best of his recordings continued to reach for what critic Michael Hedges called "this timeless quality, new country that tasted vintage," and the best of his performances put across the sense of "a young guy with an old soul."

Sometimes it seemed almost miraculous, the authority with which he sang his songs of loss, despair and regret. So there was another mystery: a voice from a psyche wrecked on the road of life, but no tread marks. Travis, in fact, was an exemplar of physical flawlessness and robust good health, toned by well-informed nutrition and daily workouts in the gym, and he seemed as carefully

tuned emotionally as he was physically. Not even the closest examination of his calm, contented, perfect-gentlemanly public self revealed the middle-aged man inside the voice, or for that matter the hell-bent young Randy Traywick.

Travis, it's true, really changed the country music game, taking it national/international as it hadn't been taken since the heyday of Johnny Cash and establishing a rock-solid foothold in places where it was truly a novelty: network television "magazine" shows; the most prominent sections of mass-

Cowpokes on the range for a TNN special: Roy Rogers, Randy Travis, Holly Dunn and Michael Martin Murphey in Montana in 1991.

circulation celebrity fanzines; and the world of media aimed exclusively at women and girls, a huge battlefield on which Travis was the first country singer to present a serious challenge to the hegemony of young male television, movie and pop music stars. And his concerts in the most major of major-metropolitan markets—Los Angeles, New York and London—were sold out and reviewed in terms ranging from admiring to ecstatic.

Travis dominated the country scene so completely that according to the old logic of the business, there was little point in trying to launch a competitor. The old logic wasn't relevant any more, though, because the kids brought into the market by Travis and his precursors operated at a much higher cyclic rate than the old-style country fans: though intense, their enthusiasm for an idol (or a dance, or a sound, or a style of dress) burned out relatively quickly, to be replaced by an equally intense enthusiasm for something new. After Travis, then, there was a kind of weird pause during which you could almost hear Nashville's production line shifting gears, searching for the right ratio.

Ricky Van Shelton of Grit, Virginia, formerly a pipe fitter, was the first new product off the line. In a way he was an almost perfect hybrid for the teenage/traditionalist market: a singer who specialized in melodramatic revivals of songs that had been hits for country singers of his father's generation, but was presented as a kind of sultry trailer-park Adonis—as critic Ken Tucker put it, "a sullen bruiser whose trademark is a big white cowboy hat offset by a teeny white T-shirt." Actually, it was more of an undershirt, the better to show off those big soft-focus biceps.

As a fashion statement, swoon-inducer and maker of almost

Ricky Van Shelton, the man from Grit, as was.

surefire radio hits, Shelton did well. Ultimately, though, his shortcomings, which were those of a transitional model, showed through. For one thing, he wasn't quite as young as he needed to be, his glamour shots having created only the illusion of trailer park perfection. Then too, he tended to be lacking in charm and he drank too much (as he later admitted); not a good combination, especially in the new Nashville. In the 90's he found himself sobering up, but reaping what he had sown as he watched younger, prettier, even more scantily clad and pectorally

perfect contenders swarm past him up the scream-meter.

Clint Black, on the other hand, was a stayer. A highly intelligent, generally good-humored Texan whose Sicilian great-grandfather had been a professional violinist, he had a lot of charm and a more than adequate dose of savvy. In the beginning he also had substantial muscle behind him in the person of Bill Ham, long the manager of Texan crunch-blues-boogie band ZZ Top and the biggest wig on the Houston music business scene. Black and Ham, who had found what they wanted in each other— Black a fast-track entree to a major recording label (RCA) and a big-money career launch, Ham a client who could be a major contender in the country market— parted company acrimoniously down the line, but initially things couldn't have gone better. Black hit the ground running with his first album, *Killin' Time*, and immediately became the hottest act Nashville had to offer. Incidentally, he departed from what was coming to be the standard hat act profile: He was single, not securely married, and instead of making one particular style of large white cowboy hat his own, he was a switch-hatter, varying shapes and colors and even going with the black more often than not.

Black was significant on a purely musical level because he was the first major star to marry straight, George Jones-style hard core country with music whose stylistic roots were in the 70's soft rock of Loggins and Messina, Jim Croce, Jimmy Buffett, The Doobie Brothers and even Bob Seger in his quieter moments. That union,

Ricky Van Shelton, as marketed. This was the publicity shot that triggered Nashville's beefcake wars.

which had been getting closer to reality in Nashville music for several years, was effected by Black and his songwriting partner/guitarist/bandleader, Hayden Nicholas, in high style; these were gifted artists, every bit as clever as the writers whose styles inspired them, and they came up with some real gems—sometimes songs that actually managed to contain the best of both worlds, sometimes finely turned examples of a single type like "A Better Man" and "Put Yourself in My Shoes," both classically framed, very convincing lost-love country tearjerkers, the latter nicely enlivened with

a streak of good old Texas swing.

Black and Nicholas also managed the difficult trick of continuing to write successful popular songs that were genuinely personal-autobiographical as they and their band, crew and business retinue hurtled to and fro across the landscape of the new country stardom, an environment whose rapidly rising pressures were becoming ever more dangerous to a performer's creative health—particularly since many of the new country stars of the late 80's and 90's, unlike most of their predecessors, didn't have the advantage of long, hard

Clint Black

years on the regional or national club circuit behind them. Many of them had no idea what the job entailed until they were actually doing it. Living night and day on a bus; being unable to eat healthily or exercise; having their time monopolized by an endless succession of colleagues and supplicants; never being alone: These were often unwelcome surprises cruelly unrelated to the popular land-of-milk-and-honey conception of a star's life.

Black, though, was ready for the stresses of the big time. "I didn't have any misconceptions," he said in 1991. "I knew it was gonna be tough. I didn't know what it entailed and what it would be, and what kind of luxuries I'd be afforded, but I had it set in my mind for so many years that my bags were packed, and whatever it took, I was gonna do it."

Clint Black concerts were very much like George Strait, Randy Travis and Ricky Van Shelton concerts, affairs described by Patrick Carr as "the usual hunky tonk arrangement, a handsome clean-cut cowboy down there in the lights singing songs about love while up in the seats the old-guard fans try to concentrate on the music, not the youngish women going giddy all around them...you can lose your bearings pretty easily: It sounds as if someone had spliced a 1989 George Michael audience track onto a 1962 George Jones concert." Carr, like Morthland before him, was bemused by the clash between the content of the songs—bleak stuff—and the audience's excitement. "Truly impressive new heights of hormonally activated obliviousness being achieved here," he noted.

Clint with songwriting collaborator Hayden Nicholas.

The year of Black's launch, 1989, was also the debut year of the two other hats who would dominate country music into the mid-90's. The first was Alan Jackson, a tall, shy, thoughtful Georgian who looked like an idealized cross between Hank Williams and George Armstrong Custer and, as if that by itself weren't enough to win most country hearts and minds, sang and wrote very consciously in the tradition of Hank, Lefty, Merle and George (no James Taylor, etc.). He was to be a consistent concert crowd pleaser and a favorite within the industry for several years before his commercial success eclipsed that of Clint Black; by 1995 he was at the top of the business, drawing as many fans as the redoubtable Miz Reba McEntire, with only the third hat of '89 above them both: Garth "Bazillion" Brooks.

Well. Garth Brooks. Just the thought of him sends shivers through the wallet. His impact on the country music business was so immense that simply stating the fact of the matter, that as critic Rob Tannenbaum wrote, he "sold more than 30 million records in his first four years, obliterating Nashville's standards of success," doesn't cut it. Saying that he doubled the numbers might convey a sense of what he meant to the industry—that after Garth, the top dollar a person could earn in the country music business was at least a hundred percent more than before Garth. Then there's a simple little illustration of the new wealth's scale, Brooks' surprise gift of matching Jaguar sedans to his two managers.

It's hard to describe the thrill that little act sent through Nashville. People in the country music

Alan Jackson

business had been operating for so long under the weight of their prideful inferiority complex, and had been working so hard to establish equality with the outside world, that to see one of their own make such a wonderful Elvis-like gesture— and to know that it wasn't vainglorious or unjustified, that Garth Brooks really was the most popular musician on the planet, more popular than Whitney Houston and Michael Jackson combined—well, it felt like victory. Never in the field of musical competition had so many in such a small community fought so hard for so long, through so many years of risk, faith, compromise and CMA lobbying, to prevail so grandly in the end.

The triumphant atmosphere was described by Michael McCall in an early 1992 *Country Music* cover story set around Brooks' first concert in Nashville since his third album, *Ropin' the Wind*, had entered the pop charts at Number One.

"The spectacle he unleashed that cool November night awed even those who thought they'd seen it all," wrote McCall. "It was almost as entertaining to watch industry veterans react to the euphoric atmosphere as it was to watch the crowd itself."

McCall went on to describe what had become the standard Garth Brooks concert experience—the audience on their feet for the entire show, mouthing the words to all the songs as Brooks swung on ropes, danced through pyrotechnics, sprinted around the stage, fell to his knees, and otherwise drove the hysteria level as high as he could—and then he reflected on its context. "The hysterical reaction Brooks draws has long been a part of American culture. It's happened to Frank Sinatra, to The Beatles, to Bruce Springsteen, to Michael Jackson, even to New Kids on the Block. But when has it happened to an artist who proudly says he plays country music?

"There are stories about the tens of thousands who lined up for Hank Williams' funeral, and veterans like Minnie Pearl and Chet Atkins say Roy

Acuff's popularity was so massive during World War II that hundreds of fans would line the streets of Southern towns waiting for his concert caravan to roll by. Since the coming of the rock 'n' roll era, though, it hasn't happened to a country artist." McCall noted that tickets for the Nashville concert, 10,000 of them, had sold out in 21 minutes, breaking all records set by entertainers in any field: a feat matched or exceeded at virtually every venue Brooks played from mid-'91 on.

So whence came Garthmania?

It began quietly, with the success of Brooks' first album (which rendered three country Number Ones) being out-flashed by the money and

Jackson in his "Chattahoochie" video: Boyhood memories made a hit song.

muscle behind Clint Black; while Black was delivered onto the country scene from above, as it were, by Bill Ham's powerful rock-pop machine, Brooks came in through the street entrance with management that couldn't even pretend to be big time.

It was his second attempt at Nashville, his first, in 1985, having lasted less than a day and taught him, in his own words, that "yeah, there's nothing like an idiot with confidence. I was sitting in Merlin Littlefield's office at ASCAP when someone he called 'one of the best songwriters in Nashville' came in, and he needed help paying back a $500 loan. At that time I was making $600 a week playing in a club in Stillwater, Oklahoma. That's when reality hit me right between the eyes."

By 1988 he'd learned a thing or two, and when he returned from Oklahoma, he was prepared for a long, hard haul. He soon found management in the persons of publicist Pam Lewis and lawyer Bob Doyle, then quickly connected with Jimmy Bowen's Capitol-Nashville and producer Allen Reynolds, the experienced hand who had guided the recordings of Crystal Gayle, Don Williams and others. So at that point he had one of the best sets of ears in Nashville on his team, and the country music business' most aggressive and ambitious marketer.

Hats in good company: Alan Jackson with wife Denise, Hank Jr. with wife Mary Jane.

Right from the start, it was clear that Brooks had a truly unique quality about him. Wherever it came from—perhaps his mother, Colleen Carroll, briefly a Capitol recording artist in the 50's—there was an intensity inside and around him that was the exact opposite of the Strait/Black/usual-cowpoke calm. This boy put on a show. The quavering passion of his vocals, the flash-bang energy of his stage persona, the heart-on-his-sleeve, foot-in-his-mouth dramas of his personal life: this was great stuff, more than adequately colorful for celebrity far beyond the borders of the country world. He could be "the Elton John of Oklahoma" (as one writer suggested) and then some.

Elton John isn't such an unlikely comparison.

The renowned English pop-rocker had, after all, the same theatrical flair and egomaniacal vulnerability, and he was also just as unlikely a sex object, being a somewhat pudgy, balding figure among competitors far more physically impressive. Then too, there were more similarities than differences between the music Brooks was calling country in the 90's and the music John had called glitter-rock in the 70's. Brooks' musical mentors, as well as the Hank/Merle/George holy trinity every country newcomer after 1985 had to name whether they meant it or not (Brooks seemed to mean it), were, after all, Elton John's peers. As Rob Tannenbaum observed very accurately, a careful listening to Brooks' records revealed "a textbook of 70's pop: the confessional lyrics of [Dan] Fogelberg and James Taylor, the mellow Colorado ease of Poco and Firefall, the fluid melodicism of Fleetwood Mac and Bread, and the thick guitar pomp of Kansas and Boston." If you watched his shows, of course, you saw the pyrotechnic staging with which Kiss had blown his mind as a teenager.

Not surprisingly, Brooks was a controversial star. Many of his peers and a significant number of critics found fault with various aspects of his celebrity, his act, and his music. TNN and CMT both banned one of his videos, "The Thunder Rolls," because it depicted marital violence and implied child abuse, and others were displeased by the plea for racial and sexual liberation in "We Shall Be Free," not to mention Brooks' revelation that his sister, who played bass in his band, was a lesbian. Sometimes it seemed, in fact, as if the man had made it his personal mission to topple country music taboos (and maybe he had). His songs were full of sex out on the edges, the kind of violence that didn't come clean, and sociopolitical sentiments far indeed from country's long-standing conservative bias. Likewise, his confessions to journalists about cheating on his wife trampled all over Nashville's line between public and private life.

There were other gripes. Some people didn't think it was okay to call yourself country when, as Brooks did with Billy Joel's "Shameless," you got yourself a hit simply by sliding a steel solo into a used pop song and singing it, even more theatrically than the original, in a cowboy hat. And a lot of country stars started getting serious headaches when their managers started telling them just how much it was going to cost, hiring those consultants and buying those new tractor-trailers full of up-to-the-minute staging technology, just so they could follow Garth. Keeping up with him was of course out of the question.

Then again, upping the ante had become the rule in Nashville, not the exception, and Garth poured so much new money into the business that nobody was very seriously upset by anything he did. For the most part, they were too busy coping with the new, breakneck, big-time pace his planetary success had imposed on the country workplace. After Garth, Nashville just wasn't the same old laid-back scene.

One of the reasons for that was a sudden new fact of overall music business life, which also happened to be one of the major factors in Garthmania's extraordinary growth. It was what one might call "The Great Bar Code Coincidence": a changeover in the gathering of data for the weekly *Billboard* charts from a system in which store clerks were responsible for reporting sales figures, to

More hats: Buck Owens, Clint Black, Dwight Yoakam, Garth Brooks, Ricky Van Shelton, Clint (again) and Tracy Lawrence—with Pam Tillis and Sammy Kershaw.

Garth Brooks

a computerized system in which data came directly from sales registers.

Once the new system was up and running, it revealed what people in the country music business had known for a long, long time: that country music retail sales had been very severely under-reported in the old system. Now the truth was out, and all of a sudden, the music business bosses in New York and Los Angeles, and the entertainment media, were faced with the fact that in many cases, country artists were outselling supposedly much "bigger" pop stars. Reba McEntire was indeed the equal of Paula Abdul, and Garth Brooks, whose *Ropin' the Wind* album was impacting the retail marketplace with full force just as the system changeover went into effect, found himself at Number One on the pop charts. Which was, of course, a major news story, and was treated as such—but without the explanation of events just recounted. According to popular media coverage at the time, Garth Brooks and country music in general had simply exploded. One day, ho-hum; the next, a sensation!

The truth of the matter— that country's commercial growth had been long and steady, not inexplicably sudden; that major country artists had been outselling their pop competition for some time; and that Brooks, though a hugely popular, dynamic star, wasn't that far ahead of the Nashville pack—disappeared into media never-never land, and the breathless ballyhoo over the new guy in the hat at the top of the pop charts sent his sales even higher into the heavens. Which, when all is said and done, left at least one question: How would the history of country music after 1992 have been different had Clint Black or Reba McEntire, not Garth Brooks, been the hottest-selling artist in country music during the week of the Great Bar Code Coincidence? We'll never know. We do know that once the "new" charts had been released, Jimmy Bowen

hosted an industry event at the CMA in which, just to be crystal clear about it all, he pointed out not just his own brilliant success story (Garth) on a large blow-up of the week's pop charts, but every other record company's, too. It was a victory speech: Bowen's great vision had actually become reality.

Garth was a major instigator of change in the processes at the heart of the country music business, but he was also a product thereof. Most significantly, he benefited from the process in which video, the new marketing aid, and radio, the traditional tool, had worked together to turn the old rules of the game upside down.

Between the mid-80's and early 90's, country radio had undergone an almost complete transformation. One factor was the centralization of ownership and programming. More and more, individual stations were components in multi-station groups, and more and more, individual stations were told what music to play (and not play) by specialist programmers—independent consultants or corporate programming directors—who might be located thousands of miles away, controlling any number of stations. Often, the only functions of local on-air personalities were to read local news and commercials, run contests and promotions, and conduct interviews with the stars when and if they came to town. Neither the jocks nor anyone else at the station had any control of the songs going out over "their" air.

Among other things, that meant an end to significant regional variation in country radio; the songs playing in Waco, Texas, were often the same ones, often in the same sequence and rotation, playing in Binghamton, New York. It also meant the end of regional entry—a regional singer could no longer get his or her record played on a powerful local or regional station without the endorsement of a major national record label—and the

Garth's spectacular stage show included fire, smoke and smashed guitars. Some fans resented the waste of a perfectly good guitar. Others were awed.

final sayonara to any hopes still lingering around the offices of independent labels that their music might one day ride the big-time airwaves. In the new, long-time-coming order, there was only one road to radio airplay: through the major national labels to the group programmers.

And there, there was a terrific traffic jam, for the centralization of control had combined with radio's audience-growth imperative to cut playlists down to the fewest, most popular songs possible.

That was the new fact of life which meant the most, and what it meant was a change from what insiders called "artist-driven" to "song-driven" programming. As the matter was stated in 1991 by *Radio & Records* editor Lon Helton, "Seven years ago, a programmer would have preferred to play a mediocre record by an established artist than a great record by a new artist. It used to be that established artists could put out any piece of junk, and it would go Top Five. Now, with established artists and even with the new, young, hot people, if they don't have an excellent song, it's not going to go."

That meant a revolution. To a record company, it meant that brand new talent, young men and women they'd signed just months ago, were now equal-opportunity competitors in the country marketplace. It really didn't matter anymore whether a performer had paid his or her dues, or had years or even decades' worth of fans out there among the friends and neighbors. If they didn't get their hands on that hot song and record it that hot way so that it fit with the "sound" of the new country radio, they weren't going on the air.

The more experienced performers were even at a disadvantage, for in the new scheme of things, singers weren't going to be taken seriously by radio if they didn't have a hot video to add oomph to the record, and their record companies weren't going to front the money for a video if they didn't look hot in the first place—if they didn't look at least warm, anyway, or at the very least young(ish). The big new youthful, pop-trained, more affluent, less rural audience didn't want to watch middle-aged hillbilly ladies and creased-up ex-cons they'd only heard of in a Randy Travis interview clip.

By the early 90's, then, the country mainstream had finally come to where pop had always been. If you weren't a hot young(ish) thing, you either didn't get on the bus in the first place, or you got kicked off and sent down to the minors. That was the bad news. The good news was that thanks to the massive growth spurred by country's youthification, the minors were a whole lot bigger than they had been. They were, after all, what used to be the majors, for the old fans hadn't gone anywhere, and they still wanted their favorites.

Mainstream country had begun to "go video" in 1983, when the CMTV all-video network began operating from a facility in Hendersonville, a small town just outside Nashville, with literally a handful of videos (some of which they generated by providing a crew to produce clips on artists who otherwise wouldn't have used the new tool). At the same time, The Nashville Network, owned by the Grand Ole Opry's parent company, began broadcasting a menu of everything from game shows to bass fishing.

CMTV remained a pure video network, akin to the early MTV, even after it was bought by The Nashville Network's owners, Gaylord Entertainment Company (formerly WSM, Inc.) in 1991. By

1994, rechristened CMT, it was reaching 25 million households in the U.S., two million in Canada and, as a separate network called CMT Europe, more than eight million in Britain. In the words of its press release, it had "grown into a major 24-hour cable network with a reputation for introducing cutting-edge music videos," was providing "a fresh selection of music videos tailored for an audience of young adults," and had become "a powerhouse for breaking new country artists like Billy Ray Cyrus and creating trends like the 'Young Country' programming format which many radio stations are adopting."

Garth Brooks, Jimmy Bowen and the star's mother, Colleen Carroll, also a singer.

That wasn't all hype and hoopla, either; CMT, which under its new ownership featured "reformatted...music, imaging and cross-promotion with radio" and "enhanced day-to-day dialogue with major record labels" was a very powerful, much-used marketing tool. The Nashville Network, whose audience tended to be older but whose reach was far greater—60 million U.S. homes in 1994—backed it up with its own video programming and talk/music shows.

The combination of centralized, song-driven "Young Country" radio and wide-reaching video networks was immensely effective when it came to launching new stars. Together, the two media provided market penetration of unprecedented speed and depth—radio doing its traditional job of introducing new music, only much faster and more thoroughly than it ever had, while video served to put across the identity of the singer with brand new force.

Clint Black was given a lesson in the power of video early in his career, when he was playing a string of dates in the West just before his "Killin' Time" single had been released to radio. The video of the song, however, was already in heavy rotation on CMTV. "I couldn't believe it," Black recalled in 1991. "We went and sold out—packed out—a place in Phoenix, and another ballroom in Tucson, and a club in Palm Springs, and the response was tremendous. I mean, for never having been there before and not having

Clint Black makes a video: Mid-90's videos cost about $80,000, half the budget for a whole digital album. They were a powerful marketing tool.

a single out, it was amazing."

Joanne Gardner, Nashville's leading video producer/director at the time, had some comments on Clint and his clips. "Clint Black is absolutely a video star," she said. "He came out of nowhere, and he's got those dimples. He looks very cute in those jeans, and they take care to show you exactly how cute he does look, every time, every video. And that just plain works." She added that "Some of these crooners today sort of remind you of the music of an earlier day. But those crooners back then didn't wear incredibly tight blue jeans—or if they did, we weren't able to see lingering closeups of them."

Having cogently described one of video's jobs, she identified another. "I don't really know sometimes, when I hear those voices on the radio, which hat is singing. But those videos come on, and wham! I know what Clint looks like, and I know what Alan looks like, and I know what Garth looks like, and I know what Randy looks like. I think video is imperative in keeping the players straight."

It really was, too, especially since there were getting to be so many new players, and they really did sound very much alike (for if they hadn't, they wouldn't have been on the radio). The 1990-91 season, for instance, produced Aaron Tippin, Billy Dean, Joe Diffie, Doug Stone, Mark Chesnutt, Mark Collie, Rob Crosby, Travis Tritt, Mike Reid, Collin Raye, McBride and The Ride, Brooks & Dunn, Tracy Lawrence, Sammy Kershaw, Jeff Chance, Lee Roy Parnell and Billy Ray Cyrus, among others: nothing short of a deluge, unthinkable ten or even five years previously. They came at the fans so thick and fast that, as one writer put it, "without video, folks would have had to quit their jobs and ignore their kids, just to put a name to a voice."

Even Garth Brooks, back in '89, had been somewhat anonymous—just another fresh-faced, sensitive young guy in a humongous cowboy hat—but video sure fixed *that.*

A weightlifter even before stardom, Aaron Tippin shows Ralph Emery his palmetto tattoo on TNN television.

It was the hugely effective film collage accompanying "The Dance," from his first album, that really opened the floodgates behind Brooks' career, making it obvious to everyone that here was more than just another cowpoke. With its sea-to-shining-sea sweep of heart-tugging all-American images—everything from JFK with his kids to the doomed Challenger crew—"The Dance" showed just how broad Brooks' vision was, and just how grand his ambition. Beneath those ten-plus gallons of Western imaging there raged the spirit of a New Age mass-pop samurai, fully in control of his beast (musically, anyway) and hair-trigger ready, as the saying of the day went, to "Go for it!" Here was a guy who'd do just about anything, mix and match whatever he could get his hands on, to stir the emotions of Everyman.

Brooks himself knew how important "The Dance" was. He personally took the production of the video far past deadline and over budget in his quest for just the right feel, and was ecstatic when it won the CMA's Video of the Year award

in 1990. Although he also won the Horizon Award recognizing supremacy among newcomers that year (to his surprise), he said that "I had really gone there for the video award. Once I got that, I said, 'Just relax.'"

The effect of the clip was immediate and immense: Album sales, which had been climbing steadily through the release of three singles, skyrocketed. As Brooks told it later, "Capitol said they didn't put any singles out on 'The Dance,' so all the sales on that were albums. You know, for a song to come out and your album isn't even Gold yet [500,000 units wholesaled], then suddenly you go to platinum [a million units wholesaled], it's amazing. I thought that only happened in rock." Up to that point, of course, it *had* only happened in rock.

Something else that had only happened in rock, and not for almost 30 years, was a brand new dude with a brand new dance. And just as Chubby Checker had come from nowhere to set the world a-Twist via Saturday morning TV in the early 60's,

Billy Ray Cyrus

Billy Ray Cyrus emerged from the gloom of door-knocking Nashville obscurity to drive the nation nuts via videotape in the 90's.

What can you say about Billy Ray? A decent, humble, handsome fellow possessed of modest but reliable talent and a body he'd sweated into truly stellar shape, he had the luck (and the perseverance) to connect with not just The Song ("Achy Breaky Heart," of course) but The Magic, in the form of Nashville choreographer/ex-Vegas dancer Melanie Greenwood (one of Lee Greenwood's former wives), and The Moment: The world, it seemed, was ready, ready, ready to do the cow-cow-boogie one more time. Greenwood's dance, the Achy Breaky, to be followed by the Tush Push, the Reggae Cowboy, the Boot Scootin' Boogie, and so on ad infinitum, swept the dance floors of honky tonks everywhere (and opened up a few thousand new ones), and Billy Ray Cyrus became a mighty sex symbol. While he posed his musculature in auditoriums vibrating with the screaming ardor of everyone from tots to grannies, his album, *Some Gave All*, climbed to the top of the *Billboard* pop charts faster, and stayed there longer, than any previous debut by anyone, anytime.

Big of bicep, and of heart: Cyrus the gentleman.

In Nashville, though, they weren't exactly dancing in the streets. Garth Brooks was one thing—at the very worst a carried-away charismatic folkie-popper who'd chosen, God bless him, to wear a cowboy hat—but Billy Ray's act crossed too many lines for comfort; in comparison, Brooks' rope-swinging antics looked positively down home. So while nobody could fault the Cyrus boy personally (for he really was a gentlemanly young fellow), a great many performers and industry people agreed when Travis Tritt complained about him "turning country music into an ass-wiggling contest." (Tritt, meanwhile, was turning it into a blues-boogie jam, not to mention breaking its "speak no evil" rule.) There was a frigidity toward Cyrus, most notable when he appeared on the Academy of Country Music Awards show, that reminded some veterans of the way Elvis, the original pelvis shaker, had been cold-shouldered by the Opry.

Those same veterans, however, could also have echoed what Senator Lloyd Bentsen had just said about Vice President Dan Quayle's election campaign claims to the JFK legacy: "We knew Elvis Presley, Mr. Cyrus. Elvis Presley was a friend of ours. You are no Elvis Presley." And he certainly wasn't. Still, he was a very decent young man (it bears repeating), and he took his lumps well, and when it came time for his second album, defiantly and/or defensively titled *It Won't Be the Last*, most of his critics gave him the break he'd earned. It was even said that given the chance, he might develop into a reasonably good country singer.

Billy Ray Cyrus was the icing on the Garth Brooks cake, a huge extra bonus injected into a music-making community already awash in cash. As a substantial new-generation country star, though, he wasn't alone. The field of freshman contenders had cleared somewhat just before, during, and after his ascent, and by the time his career had settled down a little, there were some distinct leaders among the new names pushing at radio and video.

Mary Chapin Carpenter, formerly a dyed-in-the-unbleached-wool folkie on the Washington, D.C., circuit, rose to the fore as a kind of humorous, high-spirited modern country boogie queen. Tanya Tucker continued her long, wickedly classy run at the top, Suzy Bogguss came into her own

Jimmie Dale Gilmore and Marty Brown

Alison Krauss

The country scene in the mid-90's had become many things to many people.

Mary-Chapin Carpenter,
Lucinda Williams and
Patty Loveless

Kevin Welch, Carlene
Carter and Marty Stuart

Iris DeMent

Faith Hill

Raul Malo & The Mavericks

Suzy Bogguss

Lorrie Morgan and Sammy Kershaw

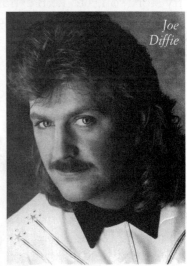

Joe Diffie

Brother Phelps and John Michael Montgomery

Trisha Yearwood

commercially, and Trisha Yearwood came out of nowhere, thanks to Garth Brooks, who chose her to open his shows. A banker's daughter and the first person with a music business degree to reach the top of the country charts, Yearwood sounded a lot like a tougher Linda Ronstadt and vied for critical acclaim and commercial supremacy with Wynonna Judd, who without Mama along for the ride was sounding much more like Bonnie Raitt thinking about Eartha Kitt than any country precursor. At the very peak of country womanhood, of course, Reba McEntire maintained her fiery, down-home-queenly dominance. By that time her mastery of virtually any idiom she chose, from dramatized Cole Porter-like ballads to classic country story songs to R&B extravaganzas, was virtually a foregone conclusion. Patty Loveless continued to do well commercially and creatively, balancing modernity and country classicism just superbly.

The leading new men, on the whole, were less interesting. Vince Gill, the tender-voiced tenor who'd served a long stint in the country-rock band Pure Prairie League before going to work in Emmylou Harris' Hot Band (with Rodney Crowell and Tony Brown), finally got the respect and the sales he'd been seeking as a solo artist for several years. Travis Tritt, a young Georgian who said his musical heroes were the leading lights of the Southern rock and Outlaw movements, took on country's vacant bad-boy job and did very well with a combination of Ken Kragen's ultra-powerful management, some widely

publicized uppity remarks, an image best described as Son of Bocephus, and concerts Lynyrd Skynyrd would have been satisfied to call their own. Kix Brooks and Ronnie Dunn, meanwhile, stomped all over the charts with a more mainstream brand of high-energy boogie music—they were the boot-scoot kings of the scene in '93—and Alan Jackson did the opposite, rising gracefully to the top of the business without recourse to on-stage pyrotechnics either mechanical or personal, and with straight-down-the-line honky tonk music (one of his favorite co-writers was Randy Travis, one of his favorite companions George Jones). Jackson was for sure one calm and modest cowpoke. So was the original model, George Strait, who just kept defying the age-keyed glass ceiling of New Country and hitting that mark of his time after time. He had some company out there on the outer fringes of senility and the true blue depths of honky tonk soul; John Anderson had come

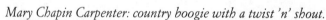
Mary Chapin Carpenter: country boogie with a twist 'n' shout.

back from obscurity into the charts, not quite decrepit even if he was pushing 40, and those grizzled old Bellamy Brothers kept on kicking, too. Semi-old guy Marty Stuart, getting up there in his mid-30's, just got better and better creatively and stronger and stronger commercially.

Those artists, and all the many others competing with them, were operating in an environment of very rapid growth and change—a place offering great opportunity, but also disorientation. It was often more than passingly difficult in the new country marketplace to perceive

Wynonna solo after Naomi Judd's retirement. Her commitment to blues came more to the fore once Mama was gone.

the most basic essential: which way was up.

Some of the new trends, though major, were relatively straightforward, for instance the emergence of Branson. In one of the major Sunday-feature stories of the decade, that formerly small, sleepy Ozarks town had been transformed from a speck on the map of Missouri into a kind of family-style Las Vegas focused on country music. It was, in its way, a brilliant success—not just in terms of visitor appeal and cash flow (both of which were enormous), but also as a superb solution to the problem of how perfectly viable country stars with large numbers of fans among what was once the mainstream country audience could continue to have profitable careers in the new Young Country age. In Branson, a star like Roy Clark, one of the pioneers of the scene, could build himself a classy little theater, with Moe Bandy's place just down the street and Mel Tillis' up the hill and Barbara Mandrell's next door, and settle into doing two or three shows a day, six or seven days a week, for as long as customers kept coming. He wouldn't have to live the road life during the Branson months—he could sleep in his own bed in his own house in beautiful country—and, just as importantly, he could keep the lion's share of the money the friends and neighbors handed over at the door: the promoters, agents and other middlemen in the standard touring arrangement were out of the deal entirely.

In a way, then, Branson represented a real revolution, a seizure of power by the artists. Basically, formerly chart-topping performers with theaters in the new mecca of old-style mainstream country could, if so inclined, tell the people who had once controlled their careers, including the Nashville record company executives who had abandoned them for a shifting beauty contest of twentysomething upstarts, to go jump in the lake. And Mom, Pop and the kids could spend a wonderful star-studded week in a pleasant, non-urban setting. As a tourist destination, then, Branson offered considerable advantages over Nashville if one's orientation was country music, relaxation, country music, more relaxation, and more country music.

Another trend, a little older than the Branson initiative, was a major shift in the way country music's most essential ingredient, the song, was created. Beginning in the early 80's, the traditional way of writing songs, which featured one man or woman alone with his or her muse in whatever circumstance, from a publishing company office at two in the afternoon to some lonely creek bank at dawn after an all-night drinking session, gave way to something else again: col-

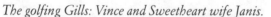
The golfing Gills: Vince and Sweetheart wife Janis.

laboration. Increasingly, hit songs were created by two, three, or even four or five people who had gathered for precisely that purpose, sometimes at someone's house, often in "writing rooms" at one or another of the song publishing operations scattered around the Music Row area. Cynicism would be easy in this context—the notion of country songs being created between the hours of ten and six by teams of ambitious, BMW-driving young college graduates is, after all, quite appalling in a certain scheme of things—but in reality there was nothing inherently anti-creative in the process of collaboration, or co-writing as it came to be called. Most of the time, more polished songs could be produced from an original idea more quickly than might have been the case with one writer working alone, and, in industry terms anyway, that was good. Demand for consistently first-rate new material (if not works of singular genius) grew so rapidly during the 80's and 90's that reliability and rate of output from Music Row's "song factories" became factors absolutely crucial to the continued health of the business—a situation made all the more central by the fact that the proportion of new performers who were not also writers was on the rise.

Co-writing, once it became familiar, was an idea whose time had most certainly come, and by the late 1980's there were just as many multiple- as single-author new songs. In the 90's the trend moved toward two-person teams. A very effective, increasingly popular combination seemed to be that of a singing star/writer—Marty Stuart or Alan Jackson, for instance—matched with a major league home run hitter like Harlan Howard or Kostas,

Master producer Tony Brown and master musician Vince Gill at work in the studio: platinum all the way.

the songwriting giants of their day. And of course the proliferation of writers was accelerating along with every other aspect of Music Row life.

The growth process had been going on since the early 80's, of course, but in the 90's it was particularly noticeable. There were many more singers, songwriters, pickers, publishers, promoters, managers and middlepersons of every conceivable stripe working the Music Row area, and they were coming from everywhere: from California, New York and even Europe as much as from the South and the Midwest. Music Row itself was growing, too; almost all the major record companies had raised or were raising large, luxurious new office buildings above the Nashville skyline, and virtually every other music business operation in town was expanding and upgrading on a significant scale.

Reba McEntire

Greater Nashville itself was also booming: growing in population and importance as a regional business center, throwing up smart new hotels and office buildings all over downtown and turning run-down older properties, most notably in the area between the Ryman Auditorium and the Cumberland River, into chic little eateries, night-clubs, specialty shops and the like. By the mid-90's, in fact, you could dine out more or less however you pleased in Nashville, on anything from sashimi to nouvelle cuisine, and do it well— not so unusual in a largish Southern city at the time, but not universal, either.

You could also go to the Ryman Auditorium, the Grand Ole Opry's longtime home replaced by the Opryland facility in 1975, and once again hear first-class live country music. The building, which had been renovated and refurbished into a fully equipped, air-conditioned concert

Princess, prince, queen: Trisha Yearwood, Vince Gill and Reba.

hall (at a cost, they said, of $40 million), opened for business in the summer of 1994. That year was also the first in which Nashville's mayor's office joined with music business leaders in attracting media and travel people to the city for an impressive array of activities and celebrations scheduled around Fan Fair week, an event once viewed by the city fathers as just another low-rent eyesore run by the trash from Music Row. Country's new bazillions were of course crucial to that change in attitude, but so was the sound of tourist herds thundering thataway toward Branson, and the consequent rumbling of motel and tour bus operator dissatisfaction.

Altogether, both the city of Nashville and the country music business centered there had come a long way up in the world. For all the musicians and music executives dropping in from London or L.A. through American Airlines' new hub,

then, a sojourn in the Buckle of the Bible Belt was not quite the adventure it once had been. In breaks between recording sessions on Music Row, you could watch the session jocks, many of them true internationalists at that point, nibbling on mesquite-grilled swordfish-endive salads and raspberry torte served by Manhattan-trained caterers, or chatting casually with their stockbrokers on cellular phones. A whole week could pass without sight or even scent of grits, ribs or hush puppies, and sometimes not a single person in a whole roomful of country music professionals was talking Southern.

It was disorienting, but stepping back from the scene, a central logic revealed itself. Basically, country's growth dynamic could be seen in terms of a process wherein Nashville was attracting more and more of the American musical pie; not just dollars and fans, but music makers both primary (musicians) and secondary (business people). The city and the country music business was a long way into a process in which the industry's desire to expand had met and matched a confluence of other circumstances. Those were many and varied, but together they added up to a single result: A hole had grown in the center of American popular music, and Nashville had filled it.

You could hear the hole opening up on the radio through the 80's as the music business reacted to ever-growing separatism in the generations coming of consumer age after the mid-late 70's: yawning social and cultural chasms between punks and mainstream rockers, who despised disco fans, who wouldn't mix with rappers, who warred with metalheads, who were looked down upon by "alternative" types, who went beyond separatism into factionalism with sub-group loy-

Travis Tritt and Marty Stuart

alties to thrash, industrial and other mutually exclusive genres...the many factions, and the music by which they defined themselves, grew more exclusive by the year, to the point where a young person unwilling to commit him- or herself to such tightly structured peer groups and narrowly defined listening protocols had nowhere to go—but country.

Almost unbelievably, country was also the only place left for somewhat older people, folks anywhere from their late 20's to their early 50's in the mid-90's, who were not satisfied with radio stations playing endless reprises of the music they'd grown up with. They wanted new music, and they weren't getting it—except on country stations.

Boot-scootin', tush-pushin', cowboy-beatin' Brooks & Dunn.

Association, which has always had a deeply vested interest in making the country music market look as big as possible but which gets most of its vital statistics from less partisan sources, showed that: Revenue from sales of country albums more than doubled between 1990 and 1993; country's share of the popular music market was 16.5 percent in 1992, up from 8.8 percent in 1990 and 6.8 in 1988; over 2,600 radio stations programmed country music in 1993 (up from just over 1,000 in 1980 and just over 500 in 1971), making country the leading format in the U.S.; between 1992 and 1993, the highest rate of growth (that is, new listeners to country) was

Through the 80's into the 90's, then, Nashville acted as a kind of refugee center for American music and musicians. The 60's and 70's versions of rock, pop, folk and even rhythm-and-blues found a home in the studios of Music Row, and singers, writers and pickers who had never for a moment considered themselves "country" found themselves contemplating, then making, a move to Tennessee. The scene offered, after all, a decent livelihood and a decent life. Nashville was a fine place to raise kids, and it was possible for a good musician to live in comfort there, supporting a family and, with all the studio work available, avoiding the thrills and spills of the road unless he or she really wanted them.

The statistics, such as they were, supported the obvious large-scale migration to country that began in the late 80's and accelerated in the early 90's. Some 1993 figures from the Country Music

among the 18-to-24 age bracket, a 34 percent climb; and between those same years the number of country music listeners in households making more than $50,000 a year increased by six million, or 21 percent, while the percentage for households making more than $60,000 a year rose by even more—39 percent, or 4.1 million. And there was a whopping rise from '92 to '93 in the number of people listening to country music in the Northeastern states: an increase of 48 percent (compared to 19 percent in the West, 18 percent in the Midwest, and seven percent in the South). Finally, Recording Industry Association of America figures released in 1994 showed percentages of people listening to country music at least once a week: 44 percent of all white Americans, and 20 percent of all African and Asian Americans.

So country's great broadening, its Great Leap Forward, was real. Its youthification, its cultural

Branson, Missouri, 1994

and geographic diffusion, its penetration of the middle class and even the world of the rich: all these phenomena were quantifiable. You could put numbers on them. Folks in Nashville loved that.

Some of them fretted, though. Singer/songwriter Kevin Welch, for instance, reflected a feeling within Nashville's creative community that just as in Urban Cowboy days, the boom of the early 90's might well be followed by depression and its consequences. "A lot of us here are worried," he said. "The record companies have gotten into cloning—you know, one more hot young boot 'n' scoot guy after another until you don't even know who you're listening to—and that can't last. The consumers are going to get bored, then they're going to get pissed off and reject the product. And when that happens, the business people will be standing there saying the same thing they did the last time: 'What happened? Where did all the money go?' Then they'll start cost cutting, dropping artists like me."

Randy Travis also worried. "Five years ago…I could listen to the radio and hear a song, and even if I'd never heard that song before, the first time it was played, I knew who was singing it. Now, I hear songs two or three times, and I'm still sitting there going 'Who in the heck is that?' And I think we're getting into a little bit of dangerous territory, because there's a lot of things coming out, and these people sound just alike…. Music, everything, goes through cycles, and maybe we're seeing that happen. We talk about the business being great, but the reality is that record sales have dropped off some in the last couple of years."

Others were more sanguine, believing that even if a depression was just around the corner in the mid-90's—and if history is any teacher, it probably was, since the immutable law of fashion is that what gets pumped up must surely get torn down—the path of country music was not one that could be obliterated. And almost inevitably, any tearing down that might occur in the popu-

lar music marketplace would in due time be followed by another cycle of pumping up.

There remains the question of just what country music had become in the mid-90's. The answer to that, more than at any time in its history, had to be an old standby: many things to many people. If you took a quick survey of the more popular entertainers calling themselves country, you found yourself looking at a pretty broad main stream: a kind of musical Mississippi in whose powerful, sometimes muddily confusing currents all manner of sediments from the continental complex of cultures were moving.

Supersongwriters Harlan Howard and Kostas with Patty Loveless.

By the time it encountered the mixing boards of Music Row studios on its way to the bottleneck of country radio, however, that river tended more toward tameness than turbulence. Among the hitmakers of '95 who were not Garth Brooks—Vince Gill, Alan Jackson, Reba McEntire, Travis Tritt, Wynonna Judd, Clint Black, Trisha Yearwood, Mary Chapin Carpenter, Aaron Tippin, Kathy Mattea, Doug Stone, Joe Diffie, Tanya Tucker, John Anderson, Lorrie Morgan, Brooks & Dunn, Suzy Bogguss, Tracy Lawrence, Sammy Kershaw, Tracy Byrd, and many others including newcomers like John Michael Montgomery, Faith Hill, Martina McBride, Brother Phelps and Tim McGraw—there was a tendancy to put one's mildest-mannered side forward, to avoid the subject of real pain, and, if possible, to provide a beat folks could dance to, fast or slow. The more a ballad resembled a track that could have ruled the suburbs 20 years earlier, the better; country's mid-90's were alive with the echoes of James Taylor, Carole King, The Eagles, and all the other sensitive superstars of 70's soft pop. Upbeat, up-tempo love songs had become very popular, too, and so had musical admirations of the dancin', datin', Lite beer-drinkin' cowboy-beat lifestyle. Much of the scene resembled a grown-up, twanged-up version of *American Bandstand* a good deal more than the adult, hard-truths-and-troubles matrix of Roy Acuff, Hank Williams and George Jones.

That did not go unremarked by the keepers of country's flame. In 1995, just as he had two de-

Sleepy LaBeef

cades earlier when he and his colleagues fought the "countrification" of pop stars like John Denver and Olivia Newton-John, George Jones himself expressed the feelings of many longtime fans.

"Most of the stuff that's out today, up-tempo, is strictly in the rock vein," he told *Country Music*, "and most of the people who are successful at all with ballads are pop... They've changed country music by doing it that way, and now, what you're hearing is, the soul and the heart is gone. All you got is framing. This new so-called country is nothing but rock stuff for kids to dance by and to get through to the kids, and to hell with the older people that helped country music get established to start with! They've throwed them to the wolves!"

He had a point, at least as far as the radio mainstream was concerned. In the mid-90's, commercial radio wasn't at all a promising source for the deepest gifts country music had always offered, the time-perfected elegance of its old song forms and instrumental combinations and the almost magical way in which those formulae could transform pain, drama, tragedy, and hardship into beauty. The Appalachian settlers who'd brought their music with them from the British Isles, and even the country recording stars of the 30's and 40's, might well have failed to find any meaningful continuity between the music they called their own and the two or three dozen thoroughly market-researched songs heavy-rotating coast to coast on 2,600-plus country stations in 1995.

That, however, meant very little to the true progress of the

Billy Joe Shaver, his guitar-genius son Eddie and bassist Keith Christopher in 1994.

Out of step, or a step ahead? Junior Brown: quite an item with mid-90's hipsters, teens and 'billies too.

music, because off the most heavily beaten track, up the many tributaries to country's main stream, a great deal of truly inspired and inspiring music was being made. Never, in fact, had there been such strength and vitality evident almost everywhere on the scene.

In California, on-from-cowpunk individualists like Rosie Flores, Heather Myles, Chris Gaffney, Stanley Wycoff, Bob Woodruff, Jim Lauderdale, former Blasters leader Dave Alvin, and the wonderful Jann Browne kept pushing at the boundaries where true country met other reality-based American roots music in typical Western pioneering spirit. And of course Dwight Yoakam forged ahead on his lonely quest.

In Austin, Townes Van Zandt, Butch Hancock, Jimmy Dale Gilmore, Kelly Willis, Steve Young, Tish Hinojosa, Delbert McClinton and the mighty Joe Ely were producing folk/rock/country/blues/ Cajun/Tex-Mex fusions as strong and soulful as any music ever played in that energized town. Evangeline, an all-woman band from Louisiana,

was doing likewise. In Massachusetts, Sleepy LaBeef, one of the original rockabillies, finally made an album as great as he was. In Miami, of all places, The Mavericks, led by Cuban-American Raul Malo, made a wonderfully passionate, eccentric rockabilly-honky tonk first album before moving to Nashville to make somewhat more mainstream music of great style and substance.

On the acoustic/folkie fringes of the country scene, meanwhile, brilliantly moving work was being done by Iris DeMent, Maura O'Connell, John Prine, Peter Rowan, Lucinda Williams, Laurie Lewis, Alison Krauss, Tony Rice and all manner of others, particularly on the progressive bluegrass scene.

Closer to the mainstream, and sometimes even in it, there were also some truly exciting performers and writers at work. Tanya Tucker, who'd been a sensational hard country singer as a teenager in the 70's, was exhibiting the benefits of long experience (and undiminished talent) in the 90's; her singles, still made with producer Jerry Crutchfield, who'd replaced Billy Sherrill after her

Emmylou Harris

first hits, could usually be relied on to hold the center with style, an unfailing honesty to both herself and her audience, and often a much appreciated extra touch of soul, spin or wicked humor. John Anderson, meanwhile, seemed to be using his revived prime time to become her male equivalent, a reliable shot of smart, energized integrity dead on target in the commercial center. And Emmylou Harris continued to deliver *her* speciality. She'd pulled off a feat which paralleled her assembly of the Hot Band in the 70's, an all-acoustic, all-star unity called The Nash Ramblers with whom she toured and recorded a live album at the Ryman Auditorium in 1991, and with whom she was moving ever further into the heart of traditional country music she'd been exploring in 1980 with *Roses in the Snow*. She was also acting as Chairman of the Board of the Country Music Foundation in the mid-90's, lending her harmonies to the recordings of all kinds of other artists, and serving as patron saint to many a Nashville aspirant. Virtually every young woman to break into the business from the late 80's on named her as a primary influence and role model.

Stalwarts like Tucker, Anderson, and Harris were by no means alone. Carlene Carter had come back from England to make the best of her great talents in country. Billy Joe Shaver, whose songs had given Waylon Jennings his deepest material in the 70's, made the most moving album of his career in 1994. Kevin Welch, in Nashville for more than a decade, was writing and making music that went far beyond his "Western Beat" handle, and had teamed with other radio-excluded musicians (including Kieran Kane, formerly of The O'Kanes) in a fully independent, artist-owned record company that pointed one way toward a future for non-mainstream Nashville music. Country's two offbeat-revivalist Brown's, Marty and Junior, still had recording contracts despite possessing the seemingly deadly combination of low sales and critical acclaim, and Shelby Lynne, potentially the most powerful country-blues-swing singer on the

scene, was also still connected. Lari White, Joy Lynn White (no relation) and Bobbie Cryner all made debut albums of knock-'em-dead quality in 1993 and 1994. Pam Tillis, with considerably greater experience and success under her belt, charted a consistently gracious course through both the center and the fringes of the Nashville music scene.

By mid-to-late 1994 there were even signs that the country music industry's soul-destroying insistence on youth as a prerequisite for employment (or at least serious promotion) might be starting to crumble, and therefore some of the best country singers of the day might not, after all, be forced to choose between no career at all and their very own theater in Branson.

George Jones and John Anderson in their 90's incarnations. Both reborn.

In 1994, Johnny Cash made a more powerful, honest, ambitious album than he'd made in 20 years (though only by going completely outside the Nashville system) and was splashed all over *Time, Newsweek* and *Rolling Stone*. Willie Nelson had accomplished more or less the same thing in 1993 (though only by hiring pop/rock superproducer Don Was). Loretta Lynn, Tammy Wynette and Dolly Parton made a classically hardcore country album, *Honky Tonk Angels*, in 1994, and Tammy Wynette also reactivated her professional union with George Jones, an event for which fans of both parties, and the classic hard country duet, had been waiting almost two decades. Among the somewhat younger crowd,

Johnny Cash

Linda Ronstadt returned to the country-ish fold in 1995, and found herself featured in a novel forum. The weekly *Gavin Report*'s new "Americana" chart, which took its data from a mixture of small-market country, Adult Alternative and public and listener-supported radio stations, placed her in Top Ten contention with the likes of Steve Earle, Heather Myles, John Prine, Alison Krauss, and The Highwaymen. The new chart, like the Branson initiative, was quite plainly a reaction against the trends in mainstream country radio. And that's where things stood as it came time to bring this book to a close.

Full circle: Jeanne Pruett, Porter Wagoner, Marty Stuart and Little Jimmy Dickens re-open the renovated Ryman Auditorium, 1994, with Opryland exec Bud Wendell, left.

Looking back on the course of country music between the late 70's, when the first edition of this *Illustrated History* was written, and today (mid-1995), the most significant phenomenon is clear: growth. Planned or accidental, staggering or predictable, fortunate or disastrous, it was indisputably vigorous: In pure numbers with no values but those of the cash register attached, the country music industry grew incredibly in those 19 years (from 1988 to 1993 alone, Nashville music industry sales figures more than doubled). And inevitably, that changed the nature of the music itself, for better or worse (or both), forever.

Ultimately, then, we're left to contemplate the same essential question with which we chose to end the first edition of this book:

Where will the creative power of the music rest—with the artist or with his or her merchandiser? The settlers who brought their music across the ocean and into the hills had no merchandisers, nothing at all to come between musician and audience. Yet country music would have remained at the level of the local courthouse steps or county fair had it not been commercialized. Commercialization, after all, is the one quality that separates country music from folk music, and gives it its unique blend of nobility and hucksterism. This is why the history of the music has been a history of the singers and pickers, and a history of the shuckers and gunners. The music will change and will grow, just as it always has, and it will continue to move a great many people who have rather little in common except the universal emotions of pity and fear, love and hate, and the strength to endure.

...They've all moved away said the voice of a stranger
To a beautiful land by the bright crystal sea
Some beautiful day I'll meet them in heaven
Where none will be a rank stranger to me.

Billy Joe Shaver in the Texas hills.

This story will never be finished. It was not finished in 1979 when this book was first published, and it is not finished now. Like a river continuously flowing, the music played and sung by the men and women in this country who live in the country—and those descended from them—flows on. Like the roots and branches of a huge and mighty oak crowned by myriads of leaves, there is a symmetry between the music's past and its present—an ever-flowering that is part of a mighty whole. Familiar faces appear and disappear, ultimately forever, except in memory or in pictures. Others, perhaps ultimately just as dear, take their place.

Through the pages of this book march a vast array of artists and performers, each of whom, in his or her day, however long or short, won hearts. Many more are mentioned and never shown. The audience itself, vaster than the Pilgrim band—and also pilgrims—rarely appears at all, but it is felt. To them, the listeners, are dedicated the following pages—a gallery of those gone, those still here—all, like others before them and those who will come after—unforgettable.

Will the circle / Be unbroken / By and by Lord / By and by

Yes. Unbroken.

THE END

Johnny Cash and Waylon Jennings

Loretta Lynn and Conway Twitty. His life wa cut short while he was still in his 50's

Minnie Pearl and Roy Acuff: They were friends for many years. He went before her.

*The West Coast's Gene Autry
and Cliffie Stone*

orter Wagoner

*Dolly Parton and
Roy Acuff*

nk Snow

*Bill Monroe—
called The Father
of Bluegrass*

Cowboy Jack Clement with Johnny Cash, June Carter Cash, Carlene Carter, Helen and Anita Carter, and Waylon Jennings and Jessi Colter.

Willie Nelson

Mother Maybelle, taken by son-in-law Johnny Cash

Janette Carter, daughter of Sara and A.P., runs old-time music evenings near Clinch Mountain in Virginia.

Waylon Jennings

Jerry Reed and Chet Atkins

George Jones

Kitty Wells and Johnny Wright—husband and wife

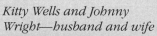

One called "King," the other called "Possum"—Roy Acuff and George Jones

Roy Rogers and Dale Evans with Barbara Mandrell

Eddy Arnold

706 Union Avenue, Sun Records' home, where rockabilly was born.

Rose Maddox

Carl Perkins, Johnny Cash and Jerry Lee Lewis—The Million Dollar Quartet minus one who is gone— taken by Marty Stuart.

Roy Rogers

Ernest Tubb—E.T.,
The Texas Troubadour

*Ralph and Carter
Stanley, just before
Carter died.*

Ralph Stanley

The Ryman in the rain

*Marty Robbins,
Mr. Versatility*

Cain's Ball

Johnny Cash with
Loretta Lynn and Loretta's
husband, Mooney.

llie Nelson and
erle Haggard

Bill Monroe and
Emmylou Harris

ob Wills

Willie Nelso[n]

*The Statlers
with Barbara
Mandrell—
Harold Reid,
Phil Balsley,
Don Reid
and Jimmy
Fortune*

*George Jo[nes]
and Tam[my]
Wynette*

Merle Haggard

*Randy Travis and
Ralph Emery
with a fan*

E.T.

About the Authors

Patrick Carr has been with *Country Music Magazine*, once as its Editor and now as a columnist and Editor-At-Large, since its first issue in 1972. He has also been a book editor, a syndicated radio reporter, and a music columnist for *The Village Voice*, and his writing on music and other subjects has appeared in *Rolling Stone, The New York Times, The Los Angeles Times, Melody Maker, Playboy, Us,* and many other periodicals. He is the author of *Backstage Passes: Life on the Wild Side with David Bowie* (1993), *Sunshine States* (1990), and *Gun People* (1985). He has been acknowledged by *People Magazine* as "the Dean of country music journalism."

Douglas B. Green is a one-time author, editor (at the Country Music Foundation Press) and contributor to *Country Music Magazine, Billboard, Bluegrass Unlimited* and other music magazines. In the early 80's he left journalism and the halls of academe for life as a performer, as leader of the retro-roots cowboy trio, Riders in the Sky. You'll know him as Ranger Doug.

William Ivey is a noted scholar, researcher and executive in the field of American popular and folk music. The Director of the Country Music Foundation in Nashville, Tennessee, since 1971, he has authored several major TV scripts (documentary) on country music and has served as National President of NARAS, chaired its Board of Trustees, and chaired a committee of the National Endowment for the Arts. In 1994 he became a member of the President's Committee on the Arts and Humanities.

Bob Pinson, for many years head of the Acquisitions Department for the Country Music Foundation in Nashville, is best known for his extensive discographies, including the comprehensive Bob Wills discography in the Wills biography, *San Antonio Rose.* A pioneering scholar in Western swing, Pinson is also involved in research on Hank Williams.

Nick Tosches, a writer and music critic, is the author of the controversial book, *Country! Living Legends and Dying Metaphors in America's Biggest Music.* A contributor to *Country Music Magazine, Rolling Stone, Penthouse, Esquire, Playboy, Vanity Fair* and *The New York Times,* he has also written *Hellfire: The Jerry Lee Lewis Story* and a study of Dean Martin titled *Dino: Living High in the Dirty Business of Dreams.*

Roger Williams is the author of the critically acclaimed biography of Hank Williams Sr., *Sing a Sad Song,* originally published in 1970, revised in 1981 (with a discography by Bob Pinson).

Charles K. Wolfe is a distinguished researcher and author of some 14 books and numerous articles on folk and country music, including *The Grand Ole Opry: The Early Years, 1925-35* (now out of print) and biographies of Grandpa Jones, Lefty Frizzell, Bill Monroe, Mahalia Jackson and others. He has annotated over 150 albums, winning Grammy nominations three times, to date, for his liner notes. His latest book, *The Life and Legend of Leadbelly* (co-authored with Kip Lornell), won the ASCAP-Deems Taylor award for music writing in 1993. He writes and teaches from his base in the English Department of Middle Tennessee State University in Murfreesboro, Tennessee, where he is close to the action of Uncle Dave Macon Days and other old-timey events. His writings and photographs from his collection have appeared in *The Journal of the American Academy for the Preservation of Old-Time Country Music,* and he is a Contributing Editor of that publication.

J. R. Young has been a regular contributor to numerous magazines, including *Rolling Stone* and *Country Music Magazine,* and is presently a Hollywood screenwriter.

Subject Index

Index of Illustrations

Photo Credits

All photos not listed below are from the archives of Country Music Magazine.

Elvis Allen Collection: *Bluebird record, 115; Dalhart record, 119; Wills record, 125; Reeves record, 141; Presley record, 252; Cline record, 276.*
Nelson Allen: *Billy Joe Shaver, 528.*
American Federation of Musicians Collection: *Harry Truman & James C. Petrillo, 191.*
Eddy Arnold Collection: *Pee Wee King & Eddy Arnold, 206; Eddy Arnold, Minnie Pearl, Tex Ritter & Roy Acuff, 212; Hank Garland, 275.*
Atlanta Historical Society: *Atlanta's Peachtree Street, 38.*
Austin City Limits (TV): *Austin sign, 149.*
Mae Axton Collection: *Johnny Cash, Mae Axton & George Jones, 144; Mae Axton & Elvis Presley, 251.*
Russell D. Barnard: *Johnny Cash & Loretta Lynn, 537.*
Gene Bear Archives: *Massey sheet music, 79; Prairie Ramblers & Patsy Montana, 79; WLS artists, 82; Buck Nation songbook, 83; "Cool Water" sheet music, 97; Ernest Tubb, 110; Moon Mullican, 114; Ken Maynard, 117; Stuart Hamblen, 118; O'Daniel sheet music, 122; Hank Thompson & Brazos Valley Boys, 132; Leon McAuliffe, 133; Lefty Frizzell & recording band, 137; Rex Allen, Jack Jones & Jimmy Dean, 143; William S. Hart, 153; Tom Mix, 154; John Wayne, 155; Gene & Ina Mae Autry, 156; Autry sheet music, 157; Gene Autry & others, 158; Roy Rogers, 161; Dale Evans, 163; Gene Autry & Melody Ranch cast, 164; Wakely Trio & Gene Autry, 165; Johnny Bond, 166; Johnny Bond, Ray Whitley & Cass County Boys, 167; Jimmy Wakely & others, 168; Jimmy Wakely, 169; Spade Cooley, 170; Spade Cooley, Tex Williams & Smokey Rogers, 171; Cliffie Stone, Merle Travis & others, 176; Sons of the Pioneers & Bing Crosby, 177; Rex Allen, Nudie, Gene Autry, Eddie Dean, Roy Rogers & Smokey Rogers, 180; Rex Allen & Nudie, 181; Wesley Tuttle, Tennessee Ernie Ford & Eddie Kirk, 188; Foy Willing & The Andrews Sisters, 189; Wesley Tuttle, Jimmie Dean & Merle Travis, 193; Autry songsheet, 194; George Wilhelm & Elton Britt, 197; Tennessee Ernie Ford, Jimmy Wakely & Cindy Walker, 198; Tillman songbook, 198; Hank Snow & Nudie, 207; Hank Williams & The Drifting Cowboys 218; Hank Thompson & The Brazos Valley Boys, 227; Johnnie & Jack, Ernest Tubb & Kitty Wells, 230; Hank Snow, Ernest Tubb & Carrie Rodgers, 233; Merle Haggard, 301; Johnny Cash, 302; Oak Ridge Quartet songbook, 459.*
Barry Bond: *Garth Brooks, 504.*
Harold Bradley Collection: *Ernest Tubb & early band, 127.*
Paul J. Broome Collection: *Owen Bradley, Anita Kerr & The Anita Kerr Singers, 272.*
Patrick Carr Collection: *Nelson Picnic program, xiii; Grateful Dead album, 327; Byrds album, 327; Flying Burrito Brothers album, 327.*
Clair Dezan/Wilf Carter Collection: *Wilf Carter, 92.*
Johnny Cash: *Maybelle Carter, 532.*
CBS Records Collection: *Marty Robbins, 238; Johnny Cash, 265; Tammy Wynette, 284; Johnny Cash at Folsom Prison, 303.*
Center for American History, University of Texas: *Bill Boyd & Art Davis, 118.*
Stephanie Chernikowski: *Floyd Tillman, 135; Willie Nelson, 364; Delbert McClinton, 383.*
Chuck Wagon Gang Collection: *Chuck Wagon Gang, 112.*
Cincinnati Historical Society: *WLW marquee, 93.*
Buell Cobb Collection: *Sacred Harp school, 8.*
Country Music Foundation: *Bradley Kincaid, iv; Clayton McMichen, 23; Ralph Peer, 36; Columbia Records catalog, 51; Gene Autry, 80; Zeke Manners, 84; Cowboy Slim Rinehart, 99; Red River Dave McEnery, 100; Gene Autry, 150; Webb Pierce & others, 211; Pee Wee King & Redd Stewart, 214; Webb Pierce & The Wondering Boys, 224; Ray Price & Darrell McCall, 226; Don Gibson, 226; Lefty Frizzell, 235; Don Gibson, 280; George Jones, 414.*
Dallas Morning News/David Woo: *Garth Brooks, 504.*
Wayne Daniel Collection: *Gid Tanner, 46.*
Bob Dees Collection: *Waylon Jennings & Buddy Holly, 260; Buddy Holly, 261.*
Dennis Devine Collection: *Johnny Cash & Elvis Presley, 250.*
Frank Driggs Collection: *Woody Guthrie, 102; Buddy Holly, 147; Molly O'Day, 222; Faron Young, 224; Wynonie Harris, 244; Fats Domino, 244; Alan Freed, 246; Freed placard, 246; Bill Haley, 247; Elvis Presley, 248; Elvis Presley, Steve Sholes & The Jordanaires, 250; Elvis Presley, 253; Carl Perkins, 255; Jerry Lee Lewis, 256; Jerry Lee Lewis, 257; Everly Brothers, 262; Bob Dylan, 324; Lovin' Spoonful, 325; The Band, 326; Allman Brothers, 345; Waylon Jennings, 370.*
Epic Records Collection: *Tammy Wynette, 287.*
Marshall Falwell Jr.: *Bobby Bare, 316; Connie Smith, 316; Jeanne Pruett, 319; Marty Robbins, 319; Richard Nixon & Roy Acuff, 320; Charlie McCoy, 329; Pete Drake, 329; Bluegrass festival, 338; George Morgan, 355; Porter Wagoner, 355; Ernest Tubb, Hank Snow & others, 355; Hank Snow, 355; Roy Acuff, 355; Billy Joe Shaver, 382; Dolly Parton, Porter Wagoner, Johnny Rodriguez & Jo Walker-Meador, 390; Larry Gatlin, 398.*
D.P. Farrell: *Ralph Stanley, 535.*
M. Geddings Collection: *Billy Walker, 139.*
Georgia State University Archives: *Skillet Lickers, 45; Riley Puckett, 49; Hometown Boys, 50; Atlanta's Biltmore Hotel, 58.*
Douglas B. Green Collection: *Bob Nolan, 97; Riders in the Sky, 182.*
Ken Griffis Collection: *Sons of the Pioneers, 96.*
J. Allen Hansley: *Garth Brooks, 504.*
Jim Herrington: *Bill Monroe's mandolin, cover photos; Vince Gill & Tony Brown, 515.*
Curtis W. Hilbun: *Ryman re-opening, 527.*
Len Holsclaw Collection: *Country Gentlemen, 341.*
Donna Jackson Collection: *Bob Wills, 124; Bob Wills & Texas Playboys, 126; Hank Thompson, 130; Hank Thompson songbook, 131; Al Dexter, 134; Carl Smith, 224; Marty Robbins, 239; Wynn Stewart, 298.*
Ramona Jones Collection: *Merle Travis, Hank Penny & Joe Maphis, 179.*
Leonard Kamsler: *Loretta Lynn & Sissy Spacek, 309; Ryman Auditorium, 318.*
Joe Knight Collection: *Don Law & Lefty Frizzell, 234; Don Law & Marty Robbins, 273.*
Harry Langdon: *George Jones & Tammy Wynette, 538.*
Les Leverett: *Carl Smith & others, 225; Hank Locklin, 229; Moon Mullican, 245; The Jordanaires, 266; Jim Reeves & Chet Atkins, 268; Chet Atkins, 269; Chet Atkins & Jim Reeves, 270; Owen Bradley & Conway Twitty, 273; Patsy Cline, Jim Reeves & Grandpa Jones, 279; Hank Locklin & The Jordanaires, 281; Conway Twitty, Loretta Lynn, Jan Howard, Doyle Wilburn, Bill Anderson, & others, 290; Opryland, 320; Sonny James, 404.*
Les Leverett Collection: *Uncle Dave Macon, 70; Roy Acuff,*